STEINBECK
A LIFE IN LETTERS

Edited by
ELAINE STEINBECK
and
ROBERT WALLSTEN

A Life

STEINBECK
STEINBECK
STEINBECK
in # LETTERS

THE VIKING PRESS NEW YORK

Frontispiece photograph by Toni Frissell

Maps by Libra Graphics, Inc.

First published in 1975 by The Viking Press, Inc.
625 Madison Avenue, New York, N.Y. 10022
Published simultaneously in Canada by
The Macmillan Company of Canada Limited

LIBRARY OF CONGRESS CATALOGING IN PUBLICATION DATA
Steinbeck, John, 1902–1968.
  Steinbeck: a life in letters.
  Includes index.
  1. Steinbeck, John, 1902–1968—Correspondence.
PS3537.T3234Z53 1975   813'.5'2   75-15756
ISBN 0–670–66962–8—Limited edition
ISBN 0–670–66961–x—Regular edition

Printed in U.S.A.

Preface

"In sixty years I've left a lot of tracks," John Steinbeck wrote in 1962. This is a record of some of those tracks: books written and read, journeys made, places visited, people met and loved and hated, as well as some projects never realized, works begun and abandoned, ideas conceived in multitudes and dying as they were born. It is the record of a questing, weighing, synthesizing, creating mind that never rested—that resented rest, except the kind of rest he found in work. But chiefly and always, it is the record of a man learning his craft.

In his youth the Depression lay heavy on him and his friends, writers, mostly, like himself—unrecognized as yet, too poor to drive far or take a train to see each other. There was only this one way to keep in touch. Actually, he preferred this way because he was diffident in ordinary face-to-face contact. "I write as usual because I have never been able to trust speech as communication of anything except love and desire or hustling."

"It is a form of talking." But talking on the telephone appalled him. "I write instead of telephoning because I have never been able to communicate over the telephone." For that inability we can be grateful because it forced him to write more letters.

vii

And the letter-writing habit, ingrained over the years, became at last inseparable from the work itself. It was his way of warming up: mornings, before he started work, he got the juices flowing by writing letters.

He wrote them on and with anything available—his father's business paper, pages torn from a ledger, hotel stationery purloined on trips—but the most typical was the legal pad and the soft pencil. This became almost a trademark. When a friend opened an envelope and saw the familiar crabbed and nearly indecipherable hand on ruled yellow paper, he knew he had a letter from Steinbeck.

The pencil was his instrument. He was passionate about pencils, about the way they felt between his fingers, about their weight and pressure. He boasted of calluses from holding them. "I sharpen all the pencils in the morning and it takes one more sharpening for a day's work. That's twenty-four sharp points. I can make a newly sharpened pencil last almost a page."

From time to time, however, he switched to pens, pens of all kinds, each carrying its own mystique. Once in Somerset he fashioned his own pens from the quills of "a grandfather goose."

His handwriting varied. Typically, it was minuscule. He once congratulated himself on having squeezed more than five hundred words on a postcard. Partly this was Depression-born to save paper, but it soon became a habit—one that from time to time he decided to break. "Trying to write this manuscript big. It's just silly, this tiny writing." To this end he scrawled or printed, but looking at the whole body of his correspondence, the impression is of a tiny scribble that often needs a magnifying glass to be easily read.

But he lived in the mechanical age, and he could not ignore a machine so fascinating as the typewriter. He wrote enthusiastically whenever a secondhand or new typewriter came into his life and assumed that everyone he told shared his fascination with the touch, the type faces, and the symbols it was capable of.

In the preparation of this book several thousand letters were collected, often six or seven written on the same day, so that it seems a kind of miracle that in addition Steinbeck found time and energy for the twenty-nine titles he published. He kept copies of few of his letters and none of his more personal ones. Our compilation was built around the large collections which we knew existed and which form the backbone of this book: the more than six hundred letters covering a span of forty-odd years to Elizabeth Otis, his friend and literary agent; those that started in the twenties and went through his life to his college roommate, Carlton A. Sheffield; and those to his editor, Pascal Covici. These were the nucleus. The next step was to locate and lure back other letters or photocopies of them. We had two major sources: a list of people who had congratulated Steinbeck when he received the Nobel Prize and another of those who had sent condolences when he died. We wrote them all. We asked for all kinds of letters—serious letters, funny letters, business letters, love letters, good-humored and ill-tempered letters—reflections of the many moods of a moody man.

Nearly everybody responded. Some letters were still in the possession of the original addressees, some had been disposed of to collectors or university libraries. A surprising number had been kept from the time when Steinbeck's name was unknown. People heard of the project and volunteered material or suggested further sources. Letters poured in.

Of course there were disappointments: a few flat refusals, correspondents unable to find letters they were sure they had kept, letters lost when recipients had died. A few dealers refused because, they said, publication would lower the market value of the originals. And some close members of Steinbeck's family felt that their privacy would be violated by seeing their letters in print.

But we had many more than we could use in a volume designed for the general public with no pretensions to inclusiveness. All letters were read aloud, some several times over as they survived elimination. We began by reading collections of correspondence to a single recipient, but it soon became clear that if we were to trace Steinbeck's development as man and writer, his letters must be evaluated and presented chronologically. This involved the tricky business of assigning dates where he had not done so and where envelopes with postmarks were lost. Ordinarily the year meant nothing to him. The month usually had to be learned from the contents. He frequently headed a page with something as uninformative as "Tuesday—I think."

The tests of internal evidence were several: where was he

living? Though in the early years he moved about so much, often using letterheads from previous addresses, that uncertainty was compounded. What flowers did he say were blooming? What pets were ill? What holidays was he celebrating? But because manuscripts are the milestones of a writer's life, the basic problem was to place these milestones in time: what was being published, and what was he working on? Here again we encountered difficulties because he started so many works he did not finish, or even name, and because he rewrote some of them so many times.

He himself had told a friend, "There is a difference between writing letters and answering them." Those that were mere answers we discarded. Inevitably in such a huge output there were trivial, tedious, repetitious, or "duty" letters, and these, too, were eliminated, as were some whose impact had been dulled by the passage of time. But we still had too many and were forced to conclude that we must sacrifice almost all material that had ever been published before.

Among the letters we retained, we have abbreviated a good number. Steinbeck was an austere self-editor of works intended for publication, but by his own confession he frequently over-wrote, and he did so especially in letters to people he knew well. He neither reconsidered nor made corrections, any more than he would have in conversation. He often rambled, repeated, or mentioned matters that readers might find obscure. These passages we have cut.

There has been only one criterion throughout: is it interesting? In no case have we omitted a letter or a passage from a letter to alter or modify either meaning or intention.

In a way he left us instructions. He advised a friend who was planning to give his collection of Steinbeck letters to a library, "If you would look through these and ink out references that might hurt feelings of some living person, it might be good." On the other hand, when he was considering the publication of a diary that was later issued posthumously as *Journal of a Novel,* he spoke of retaining "the personal things," and added, "They do give it a bite." We have tried to follow both precepts.

More than two years passed as our work progressed. Material piled up, gaps in time were filled, chronology sorted itself out. And it was not till we reread a nearly completed first draft that, with some astonishment, we saw the real nature of the book. It was not an anthology to be merely sampled. It was a narrative. In a way that even Steinbeck could not have foreseen as he was creating the individual jigsaw pieces of this puzzle whose final picture would be visible only at a distance and in its entirety, he had, in these letters that deal with the "many tracks" he left, written the story of his life.

E.S.
R.W.

New York City, 1975

Note

Early in his career John Steinbeck stated a position about the technical side of his manuscripts from which he never deviated. He was writing to a friend, another writer.

"I want to speak particularly of your theory of clean manuscript and spelling as correct as a collegiate stenographer and every nasty little comma in its place and preening of itself. I have the instincts of a minstrel rather than those of a scrivener. When my sounds are all in place, I can send them to a stenographer who knows *his* trade and he can slip the commas about until they sit comfortably and he can spell the words so that school teachers will not raise their eyebrows when they read them. Why should I bother?"

If this was his attitude about manuscripts, his disdain for spelling and punctuation in letters may be imagined.

We have assumed the role of the collegiate stenographer only up to a point. In order to retain a characteristic wayward color, we have corrected only the most outrageous misspellings, and added punctuation only for purposes of readability.

For similar purposes of readability, we have not used ellipses or other devices to indicate internal cuts. Nor have we used footnotes. Necessary information has been placed in narrative bridges or sometimes within letters. Dates or points of origin supplied by us appear in brackets, as do certain identifications or editorial comments within the text of the letters themselves. An appendix contains facts about letters quoted—the present location of the originals and where, when, and to whom they were written. References in this appendix are by page number except in those cases where ambiguity results from there being more than one letter on a page. Such references are additionally identified by a few words from the first line of the letter.

A book like this confronts its designer with extraordinary and complicated problems. We are fortunate that it was Barbara D. Knowles of The Viking Press who solved them. We are grateful to Professor Jackson J. Benson of San Diego State College for his zeal in providing us with photocopies and microfilm transcriptions of many letters, and to the scores of Steinbeck correspondents, librarians, and curators who were kind enough to share their letters with us. They are individually listed in the appendix. Most particularly, we are grateful to Elizabeth Otis, to whom John Steinbeck bequeathed all rights in the letters written to her and who has most generously turned them over to us.

Our special thanks go to Gertrude Chase who joined us in this project at the beginning and who soon proved herself far more than a secretary. Her efficiency, enthusiasm, perseverance, and good humor made a complex task considerably lighter.

Contents

CALIFORNIA

Lake Tahoe

Sacramento●

●Stockton
●Manteca

San
Francisco○   ●San Jose
            ●Santa Cruz
            ●Salinas
            Monterey
                ●King City

Pasadena●●Montrose
                ●Van Nuys
Los Angeles●●Eagle Rock
                ●Laguna Beach

Sacramento

● Stockton

● Manteca

San
Francisco

Palo Alto
●
Stanford
●
●San Jose

Los Gatos
●

Santa Cruz
●
Watsonville
●

Del Monte ●   ● Salinas
Pacific Grove ● CORRAL
              DE TIERRA
Pebble Beach ●   Monterey
Carmel ●

● Big Sur

1923 1928
1924 1929
1925 1930
1926 1931
1927 1932

*...thinking
ponderously
and seeking...*

1902 John Ernst Steinbeck born February 27 in Salinas, California. His father was manager of a flour mill and treasurer of Monterey County; his mother had been a schoolteacher. He was the third of four children and the only son.

1919 Graduated from high school. Began intermittent attendance at Stanford University.

1924 First publication, two stories in the Stanford *Spectator*.

1925 Left Stanford. Went to New York City. Wrote short stories but could find no publisher.

1926 Returned to California and continued to write, supporting himself with a variety of jobs.

1929 First novel published, *Cup of Gold*.

1930 Married Carol Henning and moved to the family cottage in Pacific Grove.

1931 Began permanent association with McIntosh and Otis, his literary agents.

When John Steinbeck was twenty-four and broke, he found a way to support himself while working at what mattered most to him—becoming a writer.

"I had a job as caretaker on a large estate at Lake Tahoe [in his native California]," he wrote later. "It required that I be snowed in for eight months every year. My nearest neighbor was four miles away."

Here he wrote, and several times rewrote, his first novel, *Cup of Gold;* and it was from here that he wrote to Monterey to Webster F. Street ("Toby"), who had been a collegemate at Stanford University.

𝒯o Webster F. Street

Lake Tahoe
Winter 1926
Monday

Dear Toby:

Do you know, one of the things that made me come here, was, as you guessed, that I am frightfully afraid of being alone. The fear of the dark is only part of it. I wanted to break that fear in the middle, because I am afraid much of my existence is going to be more or less alone, and I might as well go into training for it. It comes on me at night mostly, in little waves of panic, that constrict something in my stomach. But don't you think it is good to fight these things? Last night, some quite large animal came and sniffed under the door. I presume it was a coyote, though I do not know. The

3

moon had not come up, and when I ran outside there was nothing to be seen. But the main thing was that I was frightened, even though I knew it could be nothing but a coyote. Don't tell any one I am afraid. I do not like to be suspected of being afraid.

As soon as you can, get to work on the Little Lady [*A Green Lady,* a play Street was writing]. Keep your eye on cost of production, small and inexpensive scenes, few in the cast and lots of wise cracks, as racy as you think the populace will stand. Always crowd the limit. And also if you have time, try your hand on a melo drahmar, something wild, and mysterious and unexpected with characters turning out to be other people and some of them turning out to be nobody at all.

And if you can find a small but complete dictionary lying about anywhere send it to me. I have none, and apparently the Brighams [his employers] are so perfect in their mother tongue that they do not need one.

I shall send you some mss pretty soon if you wish. I have been working slowly but deliciously on one thing. There is something so nice about being able to put down a sentence and then look it over and then change it, sometimes taking half an hour over two lines. And it is possible here because there seems to be no reason for rush.

If, on going through Salinas, you have the time, you might look in on my folks and tell them there is little possibility of my either starving or freezing. Be as honest as you can, but picture me in a land flowing with ham and eggs, and one wherein woolen underdrawers grow on the fir trees. Tell them that I am living on the inside of a fiery furnace, or something.

It's time for me to go to the post office now, I will cease without the usual candle-like spluttering. Write to me when and as often as you get a chance. I shall depend on the mail quite a lot.

love
John

Depending on the mail had already become a habit. Midway in his life, in a letter, he recalled his youth in Salinas:

"We were poor people with a hell of a lot of land which made us think we were rich people, even when we couldn't buy food and were patched. Caballeros—lords of the land, you know, and really low church mice but proud."

After graduation from Salinas High School, he entered the freshman class at Stanford University in 1919 when he was seventeen.

He had many of the usual preoccupations of young men of his age. As he wrote one girl:

"We have been dancing twice a week in the pavilion. There is a stern and rockbound row of old ladies who have constituted themselves chaperones."

And to another girl:

"I cannot step out much, Florence, because I have lots of ambitions and very little money so my fun from now on must be very prosaic."

"I am poor, dreadfully poor. I have to feed someone else before I can eat myself. I must live in an atmosphere of dirty dishes and waitresses with soiled ears, if I wish to know about things like psychology and logic." [He was working in the City Café, Palo Alto.]

He held many jobs to finance his education. Sometimes he dropped out of college for whole quarters at a time to earn tuition for the next quarter. "Now I will work and go to school and work again."

He clerked in a department store and in a haberdashery shop, he worked as a surveyor in the Big Sur, and as a ranch hand near King City, which later became the setting for *Of Mice and Men*. And of another job, he wrote years later:

"When I was in college I was a real poor kid. I got a job breaking army remounts for officers' gentle behinds. I got $30 a remount or fifty with basic polo. You know—haunch stops and spins and stick work around head and ears and pastern. I didn't walk without a limp for months. They must have got some of those remounts out of the chutes on the rodeo circuit. But I needed the dough bad and I figured it was better to limp and eat than to be whole and hungry."

Several times through this period he worked for the Spreckels Sugar Company—"Always on the night shift," a friend recalls, "apparently as somebody to keep the laboratory open, though he sometimes said he was 'Night Chemist'; or at the company plant in Manteca, near Stockton, 'loading and stacking sacks of sugar, twelve hours a day, seven days a week.'"

Already it was clear that the most important thing in his life, the driving force, was literature—reading whatever he could, struggling to master language, testing and straining at high-flown imagery and dramatic attitudinizing—what he himself called "distinguished writing."

To Carl Wilhelmson, a classmate and another would-be writer:

"At times I feel that I am playing around the edges of things, getting nowhere. An extreme and callow youth playing with philosophy must be a pitiable thing from your point of view. Today was a long day, the hours went by so slowly that I thought of many things and finally went into a mental sleep. I sat on a pipe and watched, and spoke in monosyllables to those who were about me, and I knew so many things which they did not know, there were so many worlds open to me whose existence was beyond their powers of comprehension, and I such a young lad."

To Carl Wilhelmson

Palo Alto
April 7, 1924

Dear Carl:

Here, on this paper, there are only you and me, and the things that each of us tries so hard to understand, clambering up through long, long researches into the past, and think-

6

ing ponderously and seeking, and finding that for which we looked a glorified question mark.

It would be desirable to be flung, unfettered by consciousness, into the void, to sail unhindered through eternity. Please do not think that I am riding along on baseless words, covering threadbare thoughts with garrulous tapestries. I am not. It is the words which are inadequate.

You know so much and I can tell you nothing, and I don't think I can even make you feel anything you have not felt more poignantly than I, who am a mummer in a brocaded boudoir.

I wrote of miners' faces around a fire. Their bodies did not show in the light so that the yellow faces seemed dangling masks against the night. And I wrote of little voices in the glens which were the spirits of passions and desires and dreams of dead men's minds. And Mrs. Russell [an instructor] said they were not real, that such things could not be, and she was not going to stand me bullying her into such claptrap nonsense. Those were not her words but her meaning, and then she smiled out of the corner of her mouth as nurses do when an idiot child makes blunders. And I could not stand that, Carl, so I swore at her because I had been out all night in the making of my pictures. And now she is very cold, and she means to flunk me in my course, thinking that she can hurt me thus. I wish that she could know that I do not in the least care.

And I wish you were back, because you could understand the things I try to say, and help me to say them better, and I know you would, for you did once.

John Steinbeck

Later that spring, again to Carl Wilhelmson:

"There have been six short stories this quarter. [Two of these appeared in the Stanford *Spectator*.] I wonder if you remember the one about the machinist who made engines and felt a little omnipotent until his own machine pulled his arm from him. Then he cursed God and suffered retribution at the hands of God or thought he did. That has finally been done to

7

my half satisfaction. Of the others, one was perfectly rotten, two were fair, three were quite good. About the only thing that can be said for them is that they do not resemble anything which has ever been written.

"Miss Mirrielees [his instructor in creative writing] is very kind, she hates to hurt feelings. She says that she thinks my stuff ought to be published but she doesn't know where. Don't get the idea that I am swimming against an incoming tide of approbation, I'm not. For every bit of favorable criticism, I get four knocks in the head. Oh! well, who cares?"

Recalling this period later, he wrote his collegemate, Robert Cathcart:

"I first read Caesar and Cleopatra about seven or eight years ago, and was so impressed that I immediately wrote a sequel to it concerning the coming of Marc and his battle with the few and carefully misunderstood principles Caesar had left with Cleopatra. It was a failure. I was about seventeen at the time. And as I shall never write another play, I bequeath the idea to you."

"You asked me what I had been reading," he wrote Mrs. Edith Wagner, mother of two boyhood friends from Salinas. "Here is the last list which we brought from the library, The Book of the Dead from existing papyri, Les Femmes Savantes of Molière, which I had never read in French before and a low detective tale labeled L'Homme du Dent d'Or by a man of whom I never heard, and who in the French fashion manages to get his murder accomplished in a bedroom; La Barraca of Ibañez, which is shorter and I think more effective than his others; some short stories by Katherine Fullerton Gerould, and she certainly is the master of her kind of short stories. I have just finished the autobiography of Casanova and The Judge by Rebecca West which is a wonderful piece of writing. If you haven't read it you must for it is one of the best things I have read in many a day. In a maniacal period this summer I went through Pushkin and Turgenev."

He left Stanford for good without a degree in June 1925, and managed to get a berth to New York as a "workaway" on a freighter through the Panama Canal. For the next year he lived unhappily in Brooklyn and later in a room overlooking Gramercy Park.

"I guess I hate New York," he was to write in 1935, "because I had a thin, lonely, hungry time of it there. And I remember too well the cockroaches under my wash basin and the impossibility of getting a job. I was scared thoroughly. And I can't forget the scare."

He did eventually get work as a laborer on the construction of Madison Square Garden, on 50th Street and Eighth Avenue. Then his mother's brother, Joseph Hamilton, got him a job on the New York *American*, about which he later wrote:

"Worked on N. Y. American and from what the city editor said when he fired me, I don't think the American remembers it with any more pleasure than I do."

And even later he recalled:

"I worked for the American and was assigned to Federal Court in the old Park Row post office where I perfected my bridge game and did some lousy reporting. I did however perfect a certain literary versatility. This was during Prohibition, and Federal judges as well as others in power were generous with confiscated whiskey to the press room. Therefore it became my duty sometimes, as cadet reporter, to send the same story to Graphic, American, Times, Tribune and Brooklyn Eagle each in its own vernacular when some of my peers were unable to catch the typewriter as it went by. Then I was fired. I learned that external reality had no jurisdiction in the Hearst press and that what happened must in no case interfere with what WR wanted to happen."

Out of funds and discouraged by his inability to sell any of the stories he had been writing, he returned to the West Coast in the summer of 1926, working his way once again on a freighter. For the next two years, when he was twenty-four and twenty-five, he supported himself and his writing by odd jobs in the Lake Tahoe area, like the snowbound one as a caretaker mentioned earlier. He also worked at the local fish hatcheries and as driver of the mail-coach at Fallen Leaf Lodge, which belonged to Toby Street's in-laws.

Following is the first of a number of introspective letters written on his birthday. It was written, like many similar ones, to his college roommate, Carlton A. Sheffield, variously called "Duke," "Dook," "Juk,"

9

or even "Jook." Probably Steinbeck's closest male friend, Duke Sheffield is his only correspondent who appears throughout this book, from first chapter to last. He was less than a year older than Steinbeck and had entered Stanford the same semester. "Knew Steinbeck," Sheffield writes, "but only as a class-mate with whom I occasionally boxed, always losing." Later they roomed together, and sometimes their odd jobs coincided, as when they worked together at the Spreckels factory in Manteca, though Sheffield most often worked as a newspaperman or as a teacher.

To Carlton A. Sheffield

Lake Tahoe
February 25, 1928

Dear Duke:

It is a long time since I have begun a letter such as I mean this to be: an unhurried dissertation in which there is no sense of duty. Perhaps I have lost the power to write such a letter. Of late it has been my habit to write one page of short, tacit observation, which might have given you the idea that I am become nervous and short. And you, of late, have been determinedly cynical. Thus our letters.

My failure to work for the last three weeks is not far to find. I finished my novel and let it stand for a while, then read it over. And it was no good. The disappointment of that was bound to have some devastating, though probably momentary effect. You see, I thought it was going to be good. Even to the last page, I thought it was going to be good. And it is not.

Why are you telling me about the things you go to? Are you ashamed or proud? Do you want me to know you attend such gatherings? I think you think I look down on Rosalind [Rosalind Shepard, a girl friend of Sheffield's], and you want to justify her. You make fun of these things and yet they must impress you to some extent. I know they would impress me. I have always been a little afraid of a woman who wore a dress that cost more than a hundred dollars.

I have a new novel preparing but preparing very slowly. I am not quick about such things. They must roll about in my mind for an age before they can be written. I think it will take me two years to write a full length novel, counting the periods when I walk the streets and try to comb up courage enough to blow out my brains.

Isn't it a shame, Duke, that a thing which has as many indubitably fine things in it as my Cup of Gold, should be, as a whole, utterly worthless? It is a sorrowful matter to me.

As usual I have made a mess of this letter. I didn't finish it the other night. Now it is late the night before the [mail] boat, and I shall get very little written on it. Do you realize that I am twenty-six now? I don't. I don't feel twenty-six and I don't look that old, and I have done nothing to justify my years. Yet I don't regret the years. I have enjoyed them after a fashion. My sufferings have not been great nor have my pleasures been violent. I wish we might resurrect a summer out of the heap of years, but that is not possible at this time. Some other summer we will try.

Am I to be allowed to meet Rosalind, or are you afraid of me now? I should really like to. I feel none of the old antagonism toward her at any rate. I have been cutting wood violently to keep from being lonely. And I am lonely just the same. I wish you would write more often. I am on the point of joining a correspondence club if you don't.

A triumph. I am learning to chew tobacco, not the lowly Star but the lordly Boot Jack, a bit under the tongue you know and swallow the spit. I find I like it. It is snowing again. Confound it, will the winter never be over? I crave to have the solid ground under my feet. You cannot understand that craving if you have never lived in a country where every step was unstable. It is very tiresome and tiring to walk and have the ground give way under you at every step.

I am finishing the Henry ms out of duty [*Cup of Gold*, a fictionalized biography of Henry Morgan, the pirate], but I have no hope of it any more. I shall probably pack it in Limbo balls and place it among the lost hopes in the chest of the years. Good bye, Henry. I thought you were heroic but you are only, as was said of you, a babbler of words and rather clumsy about it.

I shall make an elegy to Henry Morgan, who is a monument to my own lack of ability. I shall go ahead, but I wonder if that sharp agony of words will occur to me again. I wonder if I shall ever be drunken with rhythms any more. Duke has his Rosalind, but I have no Rosalind nor any Phryne. I am twenty-six and I am not young any more. I shall write good novels but hereafter I ride Pegasus with a saddle and martingale, for I am afraid Pegasus will rear and kick, and I am not the sure steady horseman I once was. I do not take joy in the unmanageable horse any more. I want a hackney of tried steadiness.

It is sad when the snow is falling.

> love
> jawn

When he suggests meeting Rosalind, and asks, "Or are you afraid of me now?" he is probably referring to the following letter which he had written two years before, to the girl Sheffield had then just married, and who had since died. It is a letter that, among other things, explains and illuminates Steinbeck's friendship with Sheffield. Based on the conviction that Sheffield had been misled into matrimony, it is an early example of that passionate excess, of both loyalty and vindictiveness, which would characterize Steinbeck's behavior about people and issues throughout his life.

To Ruth Carpenter Sheffield

> 38 Gramercy Park
> New York
> June 1926

Dear Ruth:

I received notice of your marriage to my friend. I resolved to write you a letter containing a threat, an appeal and an explanation. On your reception of these three I must base my esteem of you. I agree that my esteem may seem of little consequence.

I love this person so much that I would cut your charming throat should you interfere seriously with his happiness or his manifest future. You have in your hands the seeds of a very great genius, be careful how you nourish them. If Duke loves you, then you have qualities which are impeccable, and to which I must bow. But you cannot tear in a day the cloth which was long and careful in the making. Thus I appeal to you, since you were given the honor of being the victim, to sacrifice yourself, not to this person's person, but to the children of his brain. If you are big enough you will have understood this before now, if not, all of my telling will only make you angry.

I have promised some explanation of my position. Neither this person nor myself had a brother. Because of these things, we went through our very young years lonely and seeking. We had no intimates, practically no friends. We made enemies readily because we were far above our immediate associates. In college we met, and at every point the one seemed to supplement and strengthen the other. We are not alike, rather we are opposites, but also we are equals. The combination was put to severe tests. We took the same girl to dances and things, and the friendship grew. We fought bloodily and the matter was strengthened. We worked in a vicious heat and emerged to find a wonderful comradeship. The outcome was a structure of glorious dream. Are you understanding me at all? He was the cathode and I the anode. We laughed, quarreled, drank, were sad, considered life, ethics, philosophies. We did not always agree. More often we openly disagreed. But always in the back of the mind of each there was the thought that the one was not complete without the other and never could be. It would have been easy, from our constant attendance one on the other, to draw obscene conclusions, but our fists quite precluded any such feeling. We were constantly together. Do you wish to interfere in this so that you may have him more surely to yourself, or would you rather attempt to come into the circle? Perhaps you can. I do not know you. Undoubtedly each of us supplies a great need in him, take care that you do not overstep your need and your usefulness.

Meanwhile I congratulate you as one who has found a very

13

precious thing. I give you my utmost respect and allegiance as long as you are worthy of it. I shall regard any attempt at alienation as an act harmful to him, because I know that I am necessary to him as he is necessary to me.

May I not hear your attitude?

Sincerely
John Steinbeck

The following summer he met the girl who was to be his own wife. Carol Henning and her sister, tourists on holiday, visited the Tahoe City Hatchery while he was working there.

Later in 1928 he moved to San Francisco, where Carol had a job. He shared an apartment with Carl Wilhelmson and started a new project. Webster F. Street, unable to complete his play, *The Green Lady,* to his satisfaction, had turned it over to Steinbeck to do what he would with it. The material went through many mutations in the next several years. After numerous rewrites and title changes, it eventually emerged as Steinbeck's second published novel, *To A God Unknown.*

While in New York Steinbeck had looked up a Stanford friend, Amasa Miller ("Ted"), who was starting a career in the law. Because no professional literary agent had yet shown any interest in Steinbeck's manuscripts, Miller had offered to try to place them. Not until late January 1929—almost four years later —was he able to wire Steinbeck from New York that at last he had an acceptance: Robert M. McBride and Company would publish *Cup of Gold.* A notation on the telegram Steinbeck sent back indicates that the novel had been read and rejected by seven other publishers.

In the fall, he learned that another classmate and fellow writer, A. Grove Day, was living in New Jersey.

To A. Grove Day

Jackson Street
San Francisco
[November] 1929

Dear Grove:

At present Carl Wilhelmson and I live in the upper storey of an old house here in S. F. It is a good life and very cheap. Like a squad of fleas, ferocious and very serious, we still make forays and dignified campaigns against the body of art. It is funny and a little sad (for the onlooker) and lots of fun (for us). We take our efforts to write with great seriousness, hammering away for two years on a novel and such things. I suppose in this respect we have changed less than any one you knew in Stanford. It is funny too. We have taken the ordinary number of beatings and I don't think there is much strength in either of us, and still we go on butting our heads against the English Novel and nursing our bruises as though they were the wounds of honorable war. I don't know one bit more about spelling and punctuation than I ever did, but I think I am learning a little bit about writing. The Morgan atrocity [*Cup of Gold*] pays enough for me to live quietly and with a good deal of comfort. In that far it was worth selling. I have a novel about finished [one of the versions of *To a God Unknown*] and Carl has finished two and is about a third through his third. It is an awful lot of work to write a novel. You know that because you have done it. I have been working on the present one nearly a year and have not completed it. The final draft will not be done before April I'm afraid. We don't do much else nor think much else.

That's us. I know no news. Every once in a while I hear a bit of news about somebody I know but when I try to repeat it I find that I have either forgotten it or have mixed it up with something I have heard about some one else. I thought I would be getting to New York this winter, but that seems impossible. I won't have enough money and in the second place I do not want to move before I have finished this piece of work. There was every excuse for the first being bad, be-

15

cause it was the first I ever did but I lack that excuse now.

That seems to be all there is about me. It is such a simple life to tell about. Most of our tragedies we have to make up and pretend.

But do write and tell me about the things which have happened to you.

Sincerely,
John

To Amasa Miller

[San Francisco]
[November 1929]

Dear Ted:

Your little note came the other day. It came, in fact the day of the big game. Such a game it was. The first half was enough to induce a sort of racial apoplexy in the stands. I think it was the most exciting football game I ever saw.

Ted, I swear to God that if I ever finish this novel I shall take to writing the tritest kind of plot stories or even true confessions. This is so damned hard. I have never worked so hard in my life and I don't seem to be getting ahead much. I don't know when this will be finished. There are about three hundred and twenty-five pages done and about seventy-five to do, and I want to let it rest for a while when I get it finished so that I can stand off and get some perspective on it.

You said in a former letter that I had some money coming on the first of November and here it is nearly the first of December and none has shown. I am ashamed to go home.

Carol and I get on as well as always and are together much of the time. Fillmore Street has put red and green and yellow lights on the arches across the street and is very festive. There are mechanical toys in all the store windows. No rain, it is to be another dry year. I can never remember when we did not have a threat of a dry year. The natives cannot remember that this is not a wet country and so about Christmas every year they begin to moan about the dryness of the year and the possible damage to the crops. And the crops never seem to suffer very much, taking, as they do, most of their irrigation from the sea air. It is absurd. Everything is absurd. I wish I weren't, but I think I am absurder than any of the rest.

I learn from obscure sources that I have paresis, that I am a woman, a Jew, that I, in the Morgan, have written a book aimed at the Catholics, that I have given up writing and am frantically looking for a job so that I can get married. Many are the stories I hear about myself. I have mistresses I have never met. When I hear that I am a sodomist and a zoophalist then I shall know that I have reached the high point of fame, but I suppose I can hardly expect such exaltation for many years.

And that's all. Write to me soon.

jawn

To A. Grove Day

San Francisco
[December 5] 1929

Dear Grove:

It is a very long time since I have started a letter with any anticipation of enjoying the writing of it.

Long ago I determined that any one who appraised The Cup of Gold for what it was should be entitled to a big kiss. The book was an immature experiment written for the purpose of getting all the wise cracks (known by sophomores as epigrams) and all the autobiographical material (which hounds us until we get it said) out of my system. And I really did not intend to publish it. The book accomplished its purgative purpose. I am no more concerned with myself very much. I can write about other people. I have not the slightest desire to step into Donn Byrne's shoes. I may not have his ability with the vernacular but I have twice his head. I think I have swept all the Cabellyo-Byrneish preciousness out for good. The new book is a straightforward and simple attempt

17

to set down some characters in a situation and nothing else. If there is any beauty in it, it is a beauty of idea. I seem to have outgrown Cabell. The new method is far the more difficult of the two. It reduces a single idea to a single sentence and does not allow one to write a whole chapter with it as Cabell does. I think I shall write some very good books indeed. The next one won't be good nor the next one, but about the fifth, I think will be above the average.

I don't care any more what people think of me. I'll tell you how it happened. You will remember at Stanford that I went about being different characters. I even developed a theory that one had no personality in essence, that one was a reflection of a mood plus the moods of other persons present. I wasn't pretending to be something I wasn't. For the moment I was truly the person I thought I was.

Well, I went into the mountains and stayed two years. I was snowed in eight months of the year and saw no one except my two Airedales. There were millions of fir trees and the snow was deep and it was very quiet. And there was no one to pose for any more. You can't have a show with no audience. Gradually all the poses slipped off and when I came out of the hills I didn't have any poses any more. It was rather sad, but it was far less trouble. I am happier than I have ever been in my life.

My sister [Mary] is married to Bill Dekker and has two very beautiful children. They are the only children whom I have ever liked at all. They live in Los Angeles and enjoy themselves.

I don't think I write very interesting letters any more. I have this pelican of a novel hanging about my neck and it is decomposing and bothering me about every hour of the day. I dream about it. I can't enjoy a party because it is not done. I write two pages and destroy three. It is over-ambitious I think.

I am engaged to a girl of whom I will say nothing at all because you will eventually meet her and I think you will like her because she has a mind as sharp and penetrating as your own.

I think that is all. I hope you will not let a great time pass before answering, though I realize that there is nothing to answer.

Sincerely,
John

To A. Grove Day

2441 Fillmore Street
San Francisco
[December] 1929

I am answering your letter immediately.

I want to speak particularly of your theory of clean manuscripts, and spelling as correct as a collegiate stenographer,
and every nasty little comma in its place and preening of
itself. "Manners," you say it is, and knowing the "trade" and
the "Printed Word." But I have no interest in the printed
word. I would continue to write if there were no writing and
no print. I put my words down for a matter of memory. They
are more made to be spoken than to be read. I have the
instincts of a minstrel rather than those of a scrivener. There
you have it. We are not of the same trade at all and so how
can your rules fit me? When my sounds are all in place, I can
send them to a stenographer who knows *his* trade and he can
slip the commas about until they sit comfortably and he can
spell the words so that school teachers will not raise their
eyebrows when they read them. Why should I bother? There
are millions of people who are good stenographers but there
aren't so many thousands who can make as nice sounds as I
can.

I must have misinformed you about my new book. I never
never read Hemingway with the exception of The Killers. I
have not lost the love for sound nor for pictures. Only I have
tried to throw out the words that do not say anything. I don't
read much when I am working because novels have a way
of going right on whether you are writing or not. You'll be
having dreams about it that wake you up in the night, and
maybe you'll be kissing some girl the way she expects it, and
all the time your mind will be saying, "I'll do the thing this
way, and I'll transpose these scenes." A novel doesn't stop at
all when your pen is away.

Next week maybe I'll be moving to Los Angeles with Carol
and we'll have some kind of a little house on the outskirts and

you can come to see us. We haven't much money but it's very cheap to live out here. Maybe you'd like to settle near to us. I don't like Stanford and never did. Prigs they are there and pretenders. Maybe you could get a part time job in the south and we could sit in front of a fire and talk, or lie on the beach and talk, or walk in the hills and talk. I'd like you to know Carol. She doesn't write or dance or play the piano and she has very little of any soul at all. But horses like her and dogs and little boys and bootblacks and laborers. But people with souls don't like her very much.

Let me hear from you as soon as you can.

                                                          john

Later he was to write:

"Remember the days when we were all living in Eagle Rock? As starved and happy a group as ever robbed an orange grove. I can still remember the dinners of hamburger and stolen avocados."

To Amasa Miller

2741 El Roble Drive
Eagle Rock, California
[Early 1930]

Dear Ted:

I have been doing so many things that there has been no time to write. I moved down here with many furnitures and then Carol and I got hitched which required some messing about and then there was a great deal to be done on this little house, painting and gardening and fixing of toilets which is always necessary in a tumbled down house. Anyway, merry Christmas and so forth.

By dint of a great deal of labor we have made quite a nice place of this. We pay only fifteen dollars a month for a thirty foot living room with a big stone fireplace, a bed room, a bathroom, kitchen and sleeping porch. It was a wreck when we found it, but it is the envy of all of our friends now.

I have been working quite successfully. Find the need of a new title and am wild about it. I have been trying to get one and it is the hardest thing on earth.

The sun is so warm down here it makes me feel very good. We live on a hill in a very sparsely inhabited place which is heavily wooded. The neighbors are good with the exception of one virago. We have a Belgian shepherd puppy, pure black, which is going to be a monster. And all of the time I am getting work done which makes me more happy than any of the other things.

I hope to hear from you very soon and when I get this draft finished in triplicate I shall send one copy east for the usual criticism. I have already decided to make very definite changes so the criticism will not all be valid.

> sincerely
> john

To Carl Wilhelmson

> Eagle Rock
> [Early 1930]

Dear Carl:

I do not know how long it is since I have written to you. Everything has been in a haze pretty much for the past three weeks. I have been working to finish this ms. and the thing took hold of me so completely that I lost track of nearly everything else. Now the thing is done. I started rewriting this week and am not going to let it rest. Also I have a title which gives me the greatest of pleasure. For my title I have taken one of the Vedic Hymns, the name of the hymn—

21

You surely remember the hymn with its refrain at the end of each invocation "Who is the god to whom we shall offer sacrifice?" Don't you think that is a good title? I am quite enthusiastic about it.

Carol is a good influence on my work. I am putting five hours every day on the rewriting of this one and in the evenings I have started another [*Dissonant Symphony*]. I have the time and the energy and it gives me pleasure to work, and now I do not seem to have to fight as much reluctance to work as I used to have. The start comes much easier. The new book is just a series of short stories or sketches loosely and foolishly tied together. There are a number of little things I have wanted to write for a long time, some of them ridiculous and some of them more serious, and so I am putting them in a ridiculous fabric. It is not the series in Salinas at all. I shall not do that yet. I am too vindictive and harsh on my own people. In a few years I may have outgrown that.

The dog is growing like a weed. He is three times as big as he was when we got him. You can see him grow from day to day. It has been quite cold here for the last few days with a good deal of rain and wind. But we have a big fire place in the house and the hill side behind us is covered with dead wood so we do not suffer. Indeed we enjoy it. You know, we really do not live in a city at all. We are out on a wooded and very sparsely-settled hill side. In three minutes you can climb to the top of the hill and be above everything and away from everything. It is much better than living in a city.

Are you working, and if so on what? It must be wet as hell up there now. You have told me things about the rainy season up there and it seems to be mostly floods. Carol and I thought of taking a run up to Salinas but we got a plumbing bill for about thirty dollars and a stop was put to that.

Duke is well and Maryon [Sheffield's second wife] has been slightly unwell but has recovered.

Let me know how you are and what you are working on.

Sincerely
John

To Amasa Miller

Eagle Rock
[1930]

Dear Ted:

Herewith enclosed is the ms. [*To An Unknown God*] which has been taking up so much time in the last year and a half. I know that it will not seem worth the effort. I shall insure it heavily. Please let me hear from you immediately you receive it for I shall be anxious. There is a carbon but it is on inferior paper and is only held for a safeguard in case this is lost.

If McBride should decide to take this tell them that I want a short foreword in which some mention of Toby Street should be made. I shall write that later. He has decided that he didn't do as much on this as he at first thought he did. But such a foreword is really necessary. On the other book I asked for a dedication and they paid no attention. If the foreword is refused they can go to hell.

Sincerely
john

To Amasa Miller

Eagle Rock
May 28, 1930

Dear Ted:

Your letter was received this morning. I was very glad to hear of the advance in your legal prestige, for it must be very definitely that. It should raise your standing in the firm too if what you told me when you were out here is still true.

Your news of McBrides came as a final touch to a week of disaster, a series of small and tragic incidents leading up to

23

the death of our dog Bruga who died in convulsions which seemed to be the result of poison. The rejection was nothing as compared to that. I wish you had been a bit more full about it though. What reason did they give for rejection if any? Really the rejection is a relief. I think McBride handled the last one as badly as it could well have been handled. A timid half-hearted advertising campaign which aimed at the wrong people by misdescribing the book, slowness, bad taste in jacket and blurb. Reviewers, after reading that it was an adventure story said, quite truly, that it was a hell of a bad adventure story. It was worse than that. It wasn't an adventure story at all. Am I still held by that clause in the contract, to submit a third ms. to McBride, because I think I should attempt to break it if I were. I am not discouraged at all. Rather am I heartened. The Unknown God remains a pretty fair book and a very interesting book.

Aren't you rather sick of handling this stuff? You can turn it over to an agent any time you wish. When Day rejects it, I should like it to be submitted to Farrar and Rinehart. Miss Mirrielees of Stanford is a friend of Farrar and she recommended the firm to me very highly. Also Carl Wilhelmson who is here with us now, advises me to give them a try.

I don't think that John Day will accept this book. That firm has had such a tough time with beginners lately that they will probably be touchy. However this book has merits and should go fairly well in the right circles.

Carol is well but very much broken up about Bruga. She never had a dog of her own before and she had become horribly fond of the little wretch.

I solicit your attention.

sincerely,
John

To Amasa Miller

Eagle Rock
[1930]

Dear Ted:

I have just happened to think, if this God thing is ever published it will be in imitation of somebody or other. My chief reading has been pretty immaculate. I have re-read Xenophon and Herodotus and Plutarch and Marcus Aurelius and that is about all except Fielding, and yet I suppose I shall be imitating Hemingway whom I have never read. Both of us use the English language which is enough to draw down the wrath. And he started using it first too and I merely copied him.

You ask about the new work. I have been gloating and sorrowing in my freedom. It seemed good to be without the curse of a literary foetus and at the same time I have had a feeling of lostness, much, I imagine, like that felt by an old soldier when he has been discharged from the army and has no one to tell him what time to brush his teeth. Bad as novels are, they do regulate our lives and give us a responsibility. While this book was being written I felt that I was responsible for someone. If I stopped, the characters died. But now it is finished and the words of it are being put down in nice black letters on nice white paper, and the words are spelled correctly and the punctuation is sitting about in proper places, and most of the foolishness has been left on other sheets with blue marks through it.

There is something I have wanted to ask you. Did McBride's sell enough of the Cup to pay for its publication? I know that during the holidays every store sold out completely and I wonder whether that had any effect. I hope they at least made a decent interest on their outlay.

I'm twenty-eight years old now and I must have at least one book a year from now on if I can manage it. The next one will be short as can be and shouldn't take as long as the last. This one [*Dissonant Symphony*] offered too many problems, not only psychological but anthropological, to be done quickly. I

25

hope the thing doesn't read like a case history in an insane asylum. My father was very funny about it or did I tell you this? He was terribly interested from the first but quite disgusted at the end. After my careful work in filling the book with hidden symptoms of paranoia and showing that the disease had such a hold as to be incurable, my father expected Andy to recover and live happily ever after.

Carl Wilhelmson's Wizard's Farm is being published by Rinehart and Farrar this summer. I am very anxious to see it. It is a very good book. I think you saw parts of it when you were out here. I am over at the Sheffields' house using their typewriter because Carol is plugging away on mine.

jawn

To Amasa Miller

[Eagle Rock]
August 6 [1930]

Dear Ted:

I have received Farrar's rejection of my manuscript. It is terse and to the point. The man makes no bones about his rejection and I like that. But now that I have it, I do not know what to do next. I know nothing whatever about the market.

Aren't you getting sick of trundling this white elephant around? It is discouraging, isn't it? Nobody seems to want my work. That doesn't injure me but it must be having a definite effect on you that you are handling a dud. Let me know what you think about it.

Our house here has been sold over our heads and we are going back north to the Grove. In many ways we are glad to leave the south although we are very fond of this house. It is pretty hot down here now and my mind seems more sluggish than it usually is.

affectionately
john

According to Carlton Sheffield John and Carol Steinbeck had done "such a beautiful job of rebuilding the Eagle Rock shack that the owner evicted them and gave it to his daughter as a wedding present."

They moved north to live rent free in the family three-room summer cottage in Pacific Grove on the Monterey Peninsula. This was the "home" to which Steinbeck kept returning throughout his life. His father gave them a monthly allowance of twenty-five dollars and Carol contributed her earnings from various jobs.

To Amasa Miller

[147–11th Street]
[Pacific Grove]
[Summer 1930]

Dear Ted:

Your letter and Harper's rejection came this morning. From what you say, I hope the book can get a berth with Little Brown, but I have very small hope of its ever finding a home. On the other hand, the very fear publishers have of it might make it go. Sometimes something of that nature happens.

I started to write to you yesterday and then went to the county fair instead to see the polo ponies and jumpers. That is one advantage to Pacific Grove and Monterey and Del Monte that should pull at you. Carol is secretary to the Secretary of the Chamber of Commerce of Monterey so I will ask her to send you bushels of literature on the peninsula. As a matter of fact I think it is a grand place. But in the way of business, the place is growing all the time. There are thirteen fish canneries here, and within a couple of years the new breakwater is going in which will bring a greatly increased population because it will become a deep water port and hundreds of big ships will stop here. Look over the literature and tell your wife that it is the most wonderful place in the world. This sounds like a prospectus. As a matter of fact,

I am very much emotionally tied up with the whole place. It has a soul which is lacking in the east.

As you know, or do you, I finished a ms. labelled Dissonant Symphony. I sent it to this here now Scribner's contest and have received not the slightest word from it. If I had a name, some firm might bring it out as a little book because it is a nice piece of work. It won't get by Scribner because this contest will doubtless attract the best technicians in the country among which I am by no means numbered.

I'm working on another novel [untitled—later destroyed] which will get some spleen out of my system. Bile that has been sickening me for years.

Now I'm going out to the county fair again to see a polo game. Gawd, I wish you could be here to go with me. The horses are perfectly lovely. The insides of my legs itch for the saddle. I have not ridden for two years.

Affectionately
john

Shortly afterwards, he added about Carol:

"She grows visibly in understanding, in culture, in kindness and in erudition. She understands many things more quickly and more thoroughly than I do. And the old defiance, which came from young wounds and disappointments, is wearing off. She is grand. I would have great difficulty in living without her now."

To Carl Wilhelmson

[Pacific Grove]
[Late 1930]

Dear Carl:

And I had about thought you dead from the great silence. I was very glad to get your letter this morning. I have neither seen Midsummer Night nor seen it mentioned but I don't get papers. Someone told me it was being extremely well received by critics. My God still goes without a master. I got a letter from Little Brown saying it wouldn't sell but that they wanted to print it anyway and couldn't this year. That is probably the usual bull.

You are to remember that we can always put you up. I don't imagine you want to live here but it is a good place. I have uncovered an unbelievable store of energy in myself. The raps of the last couple of years, i.e. the failure of the Cup, and the failure of my other things to make any impression, seem to have no effect on my spirit whatever. For that reason, I have high hopes for myself. Of course, the hundred page ms. flopped heavily. Just now I am busy on another one. Eventually I shall be so good that I cannot be ignored. These years are disciplinary for me.

Financially we are in a mess, but "spiritually" we ride the clouds. Nothing matters.

Write soon and say what your plans are.

Affectionately,
John

To Carl Wilhelmson

[Pacific Grove]
[Late 1930]

Dear Carl:

It is a gloomy day; low gray fog and a wet wind contribute to my own gloominess. Whether the fog has escaped from my soul like ectoplasm to envelope the peninsula, or whether it has seeped in through my nose and eyes to create the gloom, I don't know. Last night I read over the first forty pages of my new novel and destroyed them—the most unrelieved rot imaginable. It is very sad.

We went to a party at John Calvin's in Carmel last week. These writers of juveniles are the Jews of literature. They seem to wring the English language, to squeeze pennies out of it. They don't even pretend that there is any dignity in craftsmanship. A conversation with them sounds like an afternoon spent with a pawnbroker. Says John Calvin, "I long ago ceased to take anything I write seriously." I retorted, "I take *everything* I write seriously; unless one does take his work seriously there is very little chance of its ever being good work." And the whole company was a little ashamed of me as though I had three legs or was an albino.

I am very anxious to see a copy of Midsummer Night. When I can afford to, I will buy it. It was different with my own first novel. I outgrew that before I finished writing it. I very definitely didn't want you to have it just as I didn't want to have it myself. I shall be glad to arrive at an age where I don't outgrow a piece of work as children outgrow shoes.

This letter would seem to indicate that I am unhappy. Such is not the case. As long as I can work I shall be happy (except during moments of reflection) regardless of the quality of the work. That is a curious thing but true.

There was a great fire last night. The Del Monte bath house burned to the ground. We got up and went to it and stood in the light and heat and gloried in the destruction. When Cato was shouting in the Roman Senate "Carthago delenda est," I wondered whether in his mind there was not a vision of the glorious fire it would make. Precious things make beautiful flames. The pyre that Savonarola made of all lovely and profound, wise and beautiful things of northern Italy must have been the finest fire the world has seen. I believe there is an account which says that when Caesar burned the great library at Alexandria, the populace laughed and groaned in exquisite despair.

You say you are striving for tenseness in your ms. I feel increasingly that you and I are the only ones of our entire acquaintance who have retained any literary responsibility and integrity. That is worth while regardless of the badness of my work.

Modern sanity and religion are a curious delusion. Yesterday I went out in a fishing boat—out in the ocean. By looking over the side into the blue water, I could quite easily see the shell of the turtle who supports the world. I am getting more prone to madness. What a ridiculous letter this is; full of vaguenesses and unrealities. I for one and you to some extent have a great many of the basic impulses of an African witch doctor.

You know the big pine tree beside this house? I planted it when it and I were very little; I've watched it grow. It has always been known as "John's tree." Years ago, in mental playfulness I used to think of it as my brother and then later, still playfully, I thought of it as something rather closer, a kind of repository of my destiny. This was all an amusing fancy, mind you. Now the lower limbs should be cut off because they endanger the house. I must cut them soon, and I have a very powerful reluctance to do it, such a reluctance as I would have toward cutting live flesh. Furthermore if the tree should die, I am pretty sure I should be ill. This feeling I have planted in myself and quite deliberately I guess, but it is none the less strong for all that.

I shall stop before you consider me quite mad.

Sincerely,
John

To Amasa Miller

Pacific Grove
[December 1930]

Dear Ted:

I think the manuscript ["Murder at Full Moon"] enclosed in this package is self explanatory. For some time now, I have been unhappy. The reason is that I have a debt and it is making me miserable.

It is quite obvious that people do not want to buy the things I have been writing. Therefore, to make the money I need, I must write the things they want to read. In other words, I must sacrifice artistic integrity for a little while to personal integrity. Remember that when this manuscript makes you sick. And remember that it makes me a great deal sicker than it does you.

Conrad said that only two things sold, the very best and the very worst. From my recent efforts, it has been borne to me that I am not capable of writing the very best yet. I have no doubt that I shall be able to in the future, but at present, I cannot. It remains to be seen whether I can write the very worst.

I will tell you a little bit about the enclosed ms. It was written complete in nine days. It is about sixty two or three thousand words long. It took two weeks to type. In it I have included all the cheap rackets I know of, and have tried to make it stand up by giving it a slightly burlesque tone. No one but my wife and my folks know that I have written it, and no one except you will know. I see no reason why a nom de plume should not be respected and maintained. The nom de plume I have chosen is Peter Pym.

The story holds water better than most, and I think it has a fairish amount of mystery. The burlesqued bits, which were put in mostly to keep my stomach from turning every time I sat down at the typewriter, may come out.

Don't let it make you too sick. It only took nine days to write and it didn't have any effect on me whatever. I feel very badly about it, but I won't be very happy anyway unless this debt is paid. It isn't a large debt but it is worrying me.

Carol and another girl, both of wide experience, are opening a small publicity and advertising agency on the peninsula. Come west soon and be their attorney.

Let me hear from you when you can. And if you don't get either card or present from me this Christmas, you will know that I am broke. I so warn you in advance. And I hope you have a good drunken Christmas.

affectionately
John

While living in Eagle Rock, the Steinbecks had met another young writer, George Albee, with whom they exchanged frequent letters when they moved north.

To George Albee

Pacific Grove
January 1931

Dear George:

I don't remember whether or not I have written since Christmas. It doesn't matter. We got your note. Thank you! Cards we did not send. Christmas broke us as it was, so that we must live nine days on two dollars and five cents. I think we can do it although the last few of those nine may find us living on rice. That doesn't matter either. It's rather amusing. The holidays were pretty exciting. We bought things and arranged them for all of my little nieces and nephews. Then Christmas eve we watched the workings of the god-given attitude, greed. It must be god-given because no other creature except man possesses it. It is our instinct stronger than the sexual and developing only slightly less early than the

33

instinct to eat. The children grabbed things, tore off the papers, and grabbed other things. They squalled if they were not all served at once. And they are not bad as greedy children. They are very normal.

A letter from Maryon [Sheffield] this morning described a New Year's party which must have been a counterpart of the one last year. What are you doing? I don't feel like writing. I've been writing all day.

John

To George Albee

Pacific Grove
1931

Dear George:

Your letter this morning aroused a degree of argumentativeness in me—a good sign that the great depression is about over. It strikes me that the world is not nearly as hostile as you are. You fight it so, George. I think it angers you because it pays so little attention to you.

Fine artistic things seem always to be done in the face of difficulties, and the rocky soil, which seems to give the finest flower, is contempt. Don't fool yourself, George, appreciation doesn't make artists. It ruins them. A man's best work is done when he is fighting to make himself heard, not when swooning audiences wait for his paragraphs. An elevated train two doors away can have far more to do with a fine book than advance royalties or "an eager printer's boy waiting in the hall." If you don't want to fight them you shouldn't be writing. One can force attention by making one's work superb. Only practice can do that.

Things like this hurt. My sister is staying over night. I say —"I have a new story. I wish you'd listen to it." She says, "I'd love to." The story is three weeks of thinking and working. I am proud of it. It makes me laugh because it is so funny. I can hardly read the end because it is so sad. Its characters

34

are my own children. And after supper, my sister walks up town and buys a Saturday Evening Post. I do not read her this story. It is silly. But why should I be angry when she would rather read a story whose value is $3,000 rather than one from my ragged notebook—in first draft and unsaleable. How can I blame her when I wouldn't like to read my own first drafts if I hadn't written them? It takes a great expert to judge a story in manuscript. You must remember that before you let your feelings be hurt.

I think Carolyn would be a good wife. You don't want your wife to think you a genius. No wife ever could and it would be terrible if she did. I had a mistress once who thought I was. I was young enough to think I was too. I had to leave her in sheer boredom and disgust. It's too onerous to be a genius.

John

To George Albee

Pacific Grove
February 27, 1931

Excuse this kind of writing. It is the only kind I am capable of just now. A visit to the dentist this morning has battered my outlook. I meant to answer your last letter before this. In my last letter I had no intention of giving you advice. Advice is not my nature anyway. I blunder terribly, George. I go through life a grazing elephant, knocking down trees I am too stupid to consider formidable. My blindness and unawareness terrify me in the few moments of light. I'm twenty-nine today, and I haven't thought enough things or done enough things to be that old. This afternoon my parents will drive over to get us and take us to dinner. Dinner at Highland or Del Monte. The check will be not less than thirty dollars, and I can't pay a dentist bill. There's something silly about it. I don't just know where it is, but it's crazy some way.

In a rougher age I would have been eliminated I guess. A saber tooth would have grabbed me while I looked stupidly at pond lilies.

When I was sixteen or seventeen I spent a goodly time looking in mirrors bemoaning my ugliness, turning my head to see whether some position or other wouldn't soften the coarseness of my features. None of them did. The people I admired and envied! If I could only have looked forward I wouldn't have minded so much. The beauty of the school, at thirty-two,—baldness and astigmatism and the gin which society forced him to drink, have made him look like a slender pig. The lovely girl I didn't dare speak to because my lips were thick and my nose resembled a wen, is sagging under the chin and her eyes have the worried look of half-successful people who only buy at the best markets and who will mortgage the house rather than keep a car two years.

Then after a while I stopped looking in mirrors. It was safer. I didn't see myself for a number of years, and when I finally did look again, it was a stranger I saw, and I didn't care one way or another what he looked like.

This was begun some days ago. It probably doesn't mean anything. I am having trouble with my manuscript. Most of my troubles arise in something like that. Also I have a toothache, two huge fever blisters, and the itch of departing novocaine. These are enough to disrupt any philosophy. In addition—this paper which was guaranteed to take ink, didn't very well. I feel peeled of my skin and the nerve ends quivering in the air.

I'm having a devil of a time with my new book. It just won't seem to come right. Largeness of character is difficult. Never deal with an Olympian character. I think better times will come to me pretty soon. March is a curious month for my family. Every disaster of every kind—death, sickness, financial stress, during the last two generations of my family, has occurred in March. My mother goes through the month with her teeth set, fully believing it is an evil month for us. If a March passes without evil she celebrates.

Aren't you ever coming up again? This is the grand time of the year, and you didn't even see the coast country. It is the most fantastic place. We have no car now, but I drive my folks places. They are enjoying it so much.

[unsigned]

36

To George Albee

Dear George:

I have been filled with a curious cloying despair. I haven't heard a word from any of my manuscripts for over three months. It is nerve wracking. I would welcome rejections far more than this appalling silence.

My new novel slumbers. I doubt myself. This is a very critical time.

Carol's business is growing nicely. She gets prettier all the time. I'm more in love with her than I ever was. Sometimes I waken in the night with the horrible feeling that she is gone. I shouldn't want to live if she were.

I wish you would come up. There are so many things I want to talk to you about.

We are just as broke as ever. More so, if that is possible. Money would probably kill me as too rich air would.

I shan't send this today. I haven't a stamp and probably I shall want to write some more tomorrow.

John

To Amasa Miller

[Pacific Grove]
[June 1931]
Dear Ted:

I had your letter this morning. Your house in the country at the place the name of which I could not read, sounds charming indeed. This country is becoming a desert. The ten dry years are on again and if they continue very much longer we will be conserving water. The usual dejection is falling

37

over the country people and they are making plans to move. The farmer is the most chicken-headed of humans. Let one man succeed in a crop and the whole Valley puts in that crop and floods the market while there is a shortage of the thing they have cut out.

Things are the same with me. I am working on two novels, not simultaneously but a few months on each. I don't know how long I can hold out now. Universal rejections are bound to induce a kind of a mental state, but that I can overcome if only I can keep away from the successful paper pulp boys. Financially I should have been dead long ago, but I'm not. Things go on and I am not in jail. I live on twenty-five dollars a month now. Carol of course, supports herself and puts twenty-five in the pot every month so we have fifty for expenses. And we manage. I thought in writing the murder rot that I was doing a fairly sure thing, but obviously I was not. I think your plan to turn it over to an agent rather a good one. It would keep your hands clean anyway. I have completely lost hope in the other two things. I think they might as well be yanked out of circulation. Apparently they make no impression at all and they are wasting both your time and that of the publishers to whom they are submitted. Curiously enough their failure does not make much difference to the present work. The God must have been to ten publishers by now and has only received a decent note from one. That is pretty fair indication of its appeal. I don't know much what to do. Mostly I don't think about it if I can help it.

Have you completely given up your plan of coming west? You have not mentioned it for a long time.

Please don't let such a long time elapse before your next letter. It is more disheartening by far than the rejections. If I weren't so damned pig-headed I'd quit this bosh and go to work with a shovel.

affectionately.
[unsigned]

To Amasa Miller

[Pacific Grove]
[1931]

Dear Ted:

I remembered some things I wanted to ask you. First—does McBride still hold the copyright on the Cup and what arrangement did they make for the disposal of the extra copies and what is the chance of acquiring that copyright without buying it?

Second—by now you must know or have some strong conviction about the Unknown God. Do you honestly think it has the least chance in the world? Do you think it worth while to resubmit to John Day as they suggested or was that bull on their part? Wouldn't it be a load off your shoulders if you put the whole caboodle with an agent? I wouldn't mind. It must be rather disheartening to you to collect my rejection slips. Carl Wilhelmson recommends Mavis McIntosh of McIntosh & Otis at 18 East 41st Street, if you want to unload the stuff. His name should be used.

Third—on what grounds was the murder story rejected? Was it the sloppiness of it or just that it wasn't a good enough story? Do you think there is the least chance of selling it? Are you discouraged about the whole business? Have these rejections carried any editorial interest at all?

I know it is hard to write when you don't know what I want to know. Rejection follows rejection. Haven't there ever been encouraging letters? Perhaps an agent with a thorough knowledge of markets would see that the mss. were not marketable at all and would return them on that ground. You see the haunting thought comes that perhaps I have been kidding myself all these years, myself and other people—that I have nothing to say or no art in saying nothing. It is two years since I have received the slightest encouragement and that was short lived.

I shall finish at least one novel this year. It will probably be better than the others. I am leaving the long fine book for a while to do a shorter one. The big book should take a num-

39

ber of years. It is a fairly original plan (the new book) and quite a vital story or really series of stories [*The Pastures of Heaven*].

I guess that's all. Will you please write and answer the questions though? You must understand how anxious I am.

Affectionately,
John

Ted Miller followed the suggestion and delivered the unsold manuscripts to the literary agency of Mavis McIntosh and Elizabeth Otis. Steinbeck's relationship with this firm was to last for the rest of his life—almost forty years—and is documented by more than six hundred letters.

To George Albee

Pacific Grove
May 1931

Dear George:

Last night we went berserk and bought a quarter of a pound of wonderful jasmine tea. It is the grandest stuff I have ever tasted, and I have fully made up my mind to give up liquor in all forms in its favor. The strawberries are beginning to ripen and great excitement reigns in this household.

This week I had a letter from Mavis McIntosh, and, if I had not known her method of doing business, I should be very suspicious of her boundless enthusiasm for my mss. However I am fond of anyone who can raise my spirits as she has raised mine. And the personal interest evinced makes me think that she will actually try to find a publisher for me.

Also I will not be cut off from communication any more for she will let me know whether anything has happened. Have you sent mss. to her, too? I hope you have. Carl Wilhelmson recommended me and Carl is one of her especial pets. [Albee took his advice and sent samples of his work to McIntosh and Otis. He too became a client.] I am rewriting one more short story to send out and then I shall go back to The Pastures of Heaven. Truly I was beginning to get quite dejected. You can talk about my having seen print, but you forget that I am five years older than you are and that nearly three years have gone by since I have had the least encouraging word. When she sees your work she will drop me like a hot coal. Anyway, it's very nice, isn't it?

Tillie is well and nearly handsome again. Sometime after she has had puppies for me to watch, I shall write some stories about Tillie.

Twice a year my father [Monterey County treasurer] has to take money to the State Treasury and he has to do it in person. It amounts to something over a million dollars this time. Of course it is only a certified check so we won't need an armoured car. A couple of weeks ago he drove over, and when I went out to see him, he had a deputy sheriff with a shotgun and a sub-machine gun with him and the back seat of the car was full of bonds. It was terribly exciting. It is the first time he has done that and I think he was scared. I would have been. He won't ever do it again. A hundred thousand dollars in unregistered bonds is quite a temptation to a young highwayman.

That's all. Let me know when you hear from Miss McIntosh.

Affectionately,
(Carol is wildly excited)
John

To Mavis McIntosh

Pacific Grove
May 8, 1931

Dear Miss McIntosh:

Thank you for your letter. I am sorry I must answer it from memory; Tillie Eulenspiegel, the Airedale, has puppies, as sinful a crew as ever ruined rugs. Four of them found your letter and ate all of it but the address. I should imagine they were awed by the address if I had not learned that they hold nothing in reverence. At present they are out eating each other, and I must try to remember the things I should answer.

I have no readable carbon of Murder at Full Moon. If you think it advisable, I shall have one made. The quicker I can forget the damned thing, the happier I shall be.

To An Unknown God should have been a play. It was conceived as a play and thought of and talked of as such for several years. But I have no knowledge of the theater nor any knowledge of dramatic technique. Does one find a collaborator in such a case? I didn't know the novel dragged, and I thought I was fairly aware of its faults. It is out of proportion because it was thought of as two books. The story changes tempo and style because it changes speed and spirit. I tried to fit the style to the subject, that is all. I should like to write it again.

In a few days I'll send you some short stories. They are amusing, but I'm afraid unsaleable. I wrote them to amuse myself. Perhaps it would only waste your time to send them.

The present work [*The Pastures of Heaven*] interests me and perhaps falls in the "aspects" theme you mention. There is, about twelve miles from Monterey, a valley in the hills called Corral de Tierra. Because I am using its people I have named it Las Pasturas del Cielo. The valley was for years known as the happy valley because of the unique harmony which existed among its twenty families. About ten years ago a new family moved in on one of the ranches. They were ordinary people, ill-educated but honest and as kindly as any. In fact, in their whole history I cannot find that they have

42

committed a really malicious act nor an act which was not dictated by honorable expediency or out-and-out altruism. But about the Morans there was a flavor of evil. Everyone they came in contact with was injured. Every place they went dissension sprang up. There have been two murders, a suicide, many quarrels and a great deal of unhappiness in the Pastures of Heaven, and all of these things can be traced directly to the influence of the Morans. So much is true.

I am using the following method. The manuscript is made up of stories, each one complete in itself, having its rise, climax and ending. Each story deals with a family or an individual. They are tied together only by the common locality and by the contact with the Morans. Some of the stories are very short and some as long as fifteen thousand words. I thought of combining them with that thirty-thousand word ms. called Dissonant Symphony to make one volume. I wonder whether you think this is a good plan. I think the plan at least falls very definitely in the aspects of American life category. I have finished several and am working on others steadily. They should be done by this fall.

That is all I can think of. If there was more to be answered it is in the stomachs of those khaki-colored devils in the garden. They are eating the fence now. The appetite of a puppy ranks with Grand Canyon for pure stupendousness.

I am very grateful to you for your interest and to Carl Wilhelmson for his recommendation. He, by the way, is so abjectly melancholy that I imagine he is either in love or very happy about something.

Sincerely,
John Steinbeck

To Amasa Miller

Pacific Grove
1931

Dear Ted:

I don't like to be so completely cut off from you as I have been during the last few months. If you are commuting from the country I know why you haven't written, but I should have written oftener.

Life goes on here. I continue writing even more than usual. At my death, my estate will consist of many bales of paper, most of it written only on one side. It should be worth a pretty sum.

My adventures with McIntosh and Otis have been amusing. Said house pursues a policy of flattery. At the request of Miss Otis I have dispatched a number of the short stories. They have been hailed, appreciated and sent back post paid. Have not heard from Miss McIntosh for some time, but I guess my novels are saddening her. Apparently she can't even sell my detective story. I don't quite understand their policy, but obviously they try to sell the things. Whatever became of the ms. unfortunately named Dissonant Symphony? I am getting along pretty well with the companion piece—really some very good stories in it, and interesting to do.

Tillie has had distemper but we are pulling her out of it nicely. The medicines and shots in the neck ruined us though. Having lost Bruga partly through carelessness, we weren't going to take any chances with Tillie.

I am daily expecting to receive both of my novels back. That will be a blow but I don't see how I can escape it. My work is improving, I think—and eventually I shall be able to dispose of all of it, but this is rather a long period of waiting, don't you think? Joe Hamilton [his uncle] writes that some of his friends who were making ten thousand a year can't sell a fifty-dollar story. What chance have I then? Luckily such considerations do not often assail me.

We have had hot weather here if you can imagine it. But

today the fog has come in and we are back to normal. My garden is so lovely that I shall hate ever to leave it. I have turtles in the pond now and water grasses. You would love the yard. We have a vine house in back with ferns and tuberous begonias. We have a large cineraria bed in bloom and the whole yard is alive with nasturtiums.

I feel very sad. It is the feeling of impending doom when one is comfortable and in health. I guess it is an apprehension of the jealous gods. One can't be as happy as I have been for very long. There's a law against it. I have worked hard and enjoyed my work and it is the punishment of man to hate his work. Sooner or later I will have work that I hate.

That's all. Drop me a line from the train if you haven't any other time. I'm jealous of your isolation.

Affectionately,
John

To Mavis McIntosh

Pacific Grove
August 18, 1931

Dear Miss McIntosh:

I think I told you in an earlier letter that the imperfections of the Unknown God had bothered me ever since I first submitted the book for publication. In consequence of this uneasiness, your announcement of the book's failure to find a publisher is neither unwelcome nor unpleasant to me. If I were sure of the book, I should put it aside and wait for some other story to gain it an entrance. But I know its faults. I know, though, that the story is good. I shall rewrite it immediately. Whether my idea of excellence coincides with editors' ideas remains to be seen. Certainly I shall make no effort to "popularize" the story.

I have a carbon of the Unknown God. It will not be necessary to return the original.

Mr. Miller will hand you a manuscript of about thirty thousand words [*Dissonant Symphony*]. It is an impossible length

45

for marketing. I had thought perhaps it could be included under one cover with the ten stories which will make up The Pastures of Heaven. The name is bad, but that can be readily changed. Will you let me know your opinion of this plan?

The Pastures stories proceed rapidly, perhaps too rapidly. They should be ready to submit by Christmas.

Thank you for your help. I am an unprofitable client.

Sincerely,
John Steinbeck

To George Albee

[Pacific Grove]
[1931]

Dear George:

The Sheffields left last Friday or Saturday I guess it was. We had an awfully good time and I enjoyed having them. Now I wonder when you will be coming up. Have been expecting to hear every day.

As to the shoes—people in our circumstances can't be giving each other presents. It would be ridiculous. Too much food could be bought with the money and we must hold out in the matter of food. If we don't go low on it we may manage to do the thing we want to. It's a kind of endurance contest at best. So forget the shoes, but thank you for the thought.

I learn that all of my manuscripts have been rejected three or four times since I last heard. It is a nice thing to know that so many people are reading my books. That is one way of getting an audience.

Hurry and come up or at least let me know when you are coming. We are anxious to see you. I pulled all Tillie's whiskers out to strengthen their growth. She looks like hell now. We are ashamed to be seen with her.

Write soon.

John

46

To George Albee

Pacific Grove
[1931]

Dear George:
This is the day between—one ms. finished yesterday and the next one not quite hatched. It will be by tomorrow though. [He is referring to the separate stories in *The Pastures of Heaven.*] This is a good day to write letters.

I'm pretty happy over these stories. That is because they aren't finished, I guess.

It isn't unusual that you worry about my financial future. Everyone I have ever known very well has been concerned that I would eventually starve. Probably I shall. It isn't important enough to me to be an obsession. I have starved and it isn't nearly as bad as is generally supposed. Four days and a half was my longest stretch. Maybe there are pains that come later. Personally I think terror is the painful part of starvation.

Thirty years later he had not forgotten.

"Tonight I am going to cook my old Pacific Grove Starvation Special," he wrote his wife Elaine in Texas. "I hope it is as good as I remember it but I must remember that I was awful hungry when it tasted good. I won't even tell you what it is made of. You have enough problems without nausea."

You are sanguine about my inheritance. There will be nothing, you know. I'll be lucky if I have this house. No—money is not for us. Other people get Phelan Awards [an award of money given in California for writing]. Probably because they want them badly. My one long chance was to have married money and I didn't do that. I have come to be a complete fatalist about money. Even the law of averages doesn't hold with me. Any attempt to get me any kind of an award is pre-doomed to failure. Furthermore I seriously doubt that my brand of literature will ever feed me. And I

47

haven't sense enough to worry about it. If eventually I have to go to work digging ditches, I shall have had my chance.

I read only a page or so of Look Homeward, Angel. The pages I read seemed to be a hodgepodge of quotations. I shall read all of it sometime since you recommend it so highly. I was somewhat deterred from reading it by the overwhelming praise of Sinclair Lewis.

It is a gray day with little dusty spurts of rain. A good day for inwardness. Only I doubt that I have many guts of my own to look inward at. That is one of the great troubles with objective writing. A constant practice of it leaves one no material for introspection. If my characters are sad or happy I reflect their emotions. I have no personal nor definitive emotions of my own. Indeed, when there is no writing in progress, I feel like an uninhabited body. I think I am only truly miserable at such times.

Carol is probably going to work next week. [Her advertising agency had closed.] She looks forward to it. It is not good for her to be housed here with me all day. I am too impatient of movements or noise in the house. And it is such a small house.

You see, my letters are bound to be tiresome because I can talk of nothing but the work I am doing. Monomania!

This probably sounds like a doleful letter and it shouldn't be because I don't feel at all doleful.

John

To George Albee

[Pacific Grove]
[1931]
Monday

Dear George:

Exciting things—yesterday we bought two mallard ducks for the garden. The drake has an irridescent green head. They are beautiful. They swim in the pond and eat the bugs in the garden. We are pretty excited. They cost our amusement quota for this month but are worth it. Named Aqua and Vita. Carol hated to go to work this morning and leave them because they are so interesting. They do not ever step on the plants—just edge between on their big clumsy feet. They very promptly caught and ate the goldfish but we don't care. It's nice to have things like ducks. We won't ever have to feed them for there are bugs enough in the garden to keep them going. You never saw anything so beautiful in all the greenness of our garden as these luxurious ducks.

I have had a couple of fallow days—absolute disgust and lack of faith in my own work and inability to go on. This nearly always happens when a book is nearly done. I shall force it this morning. And the story I am working on charms me more than any of the others. I wish to heaven you could read these things. I need a little encouragement I guess. The other day I asked a young friend to read one and he felt that he should criticise because that was what one did to a ms. So he tore a pretty nice story to pieces and showed me how to do it. It was funny because he hit all the places which are simply matters of opinion and tore up some of the nicest writing I have ever done. Such things reassure one in the matter of believing critics.

I wish you could see Aqua and Vita. They are very very charming. Read 25 by Beverly Nichols last night and am still a little sick.

Sincerely
John

To George Albee

Pacific Grove
[1931]

Dear George:

It has rained a great deal. Now it is Monday morning, and, after a Sunday of dissipation I am faced with work. It's a gray morning. There is only the key story to do. Here is a nice and appropriate thing. The ducks were mallard—green irrides-

49

cent heads, russet of breast—pale blue wings and orange feet, beautiful birds. But they muddied the pond and pulled up lobelias. Also I was flat broke and had no way of finishing my ms. So I sold the ducks to buy paper for the stories. I wish the stories were as beautiful as the ducks.

Yesterday we indulged in the only luxury in months. We bought and charged a chess board and pieces. Two dollars. It will eat up the winter evenings.

One thing I am sorry for. These stories will go out without any expert reading. I wanted Miss McIntosh to read them, but I can't get to Palo Alto and she can't come here yet and I can't wait. I have too many stories to write. Queer about this rush—isn't it? It's as though I knew my days are limited.

There—it's raining again. Our garden is most charming in the rain. To get back to ms. Sometimes I think these stories are very fine. There's material for ten novels in these stories. That was the method, you remember. In the last story of thirty pages I covered three generations. You can see how packed they must be. I should send them to you and to Duke if I had time. I'm fairly convinced that I can't get a publisher for them. They make too much use of the reader and readers don't like to be used.

I guess I'll go back to the Unknown God. That title will have to be changed. Because the story will be cut to pieces and the pieces refitted and changed. It won't be much the same story.

There is no companionship of any kind here. Carol and I are marooned. This is probably a good thing. I throw myself into work. How are monies? Our poverty is tiresome, but I can see no change in it. Only work. I must cut down two trees for fire wood and that will take some time.

Sincerely
John

To Amasa Miller

[Pacific Grove]
[December 1931]

Dear Ted:

   After the silence of ages, I have three letters from you all on the same day: To you I say Merry Christmas and Happy 1932. I found several things in your letters which were very amusing. The first is the complete belief of M. and O. that I conceal masterpieces. I have written to them denying this. In the south I have a friend who harbors an immense admiration for my work in spite of the fact that he has seen very little of it [George Albee]. He wrote to them telling them about my bales of mss. and they demanded it. I sent them all I had which they, with great dispatch, sent back to me. I am concealing nothing except a few little things too dirty to print and some stories written for Toby Street's kids. You see I took two years to write the Cup, a year and a half to write the Unknown God. In the last year and a half I have written the Dissonant Symphony, the detective story, six short stories, part of a novel that is too huge for me just now and The Pastures of Heaven. About a hundred and seventy-five thousand finished words since the end of the Unknown God. Where then are the masterpieces? Before the Cup, the stories are so feeble and childish that I destroyed them all as a matter of course. If you should see them again please tell them that the things they are seeing are really the best I can do. If there's nothing in them then there's nothing in me and they'd better give me up as a "writer".

   The Pastures of Heaven I sent off last Saturday. It should be there by the time you receive this. If the reader will take them for what they are, and will not be governed by what a short story should be (for they are not short stories at all, but tiny novels) then they should be charming, but if they are judged by the formal short story, they are lost before they ever start. I am extremely anxious to hear the judgment because of anything I have ever tried, I am fondest of these and more closely tied to them. There is no grand writing nor any

51

grand theme, but I love the stories very much.

Carl Wilhelmson is married. I had his announcement this morning. Is your divorce desirable? I mean will it make a demand of alimony on you? I hope you get it without scars.

I've been working like a dog on this last ms. Now I shall take a little time off before starting the next. There are a number of silly little stories that have been bothering my dreams for some time. I'll get them off my chest without injuring my rest at all.

We're going to S. J. [San José] for Christmas. Toby and Grove Day are coming down next weekend to celebrate. Toby with his guitar. The whole bunch of us will probably get horned like owls. Toby gets to singing so loudly that the police interfere. Were you at the beach with us the night he nearly drowned in his soup? I heard a gurgling noise beside me and there was Toby with his nose submerged in his soup snoring it in and gradually drowning. I have a feeling you were there.

Anyway don't please keep aloof so long next time.

affectionately,
John

To Mavis McIntosh

Pacific Grove
January 25, 1932

Dear Miss McIntosh:

This letter may be pertinent if Miss Phillips [Vice-President of William Morrow and Company] is reading the novel To an Unknown God. I have no intention of trying to patch it up. It would surely show such surgery especially since it was finished nearly two years ago. I shall cut it in two at the break and work only at the first half, reserving the last half for some future novel. With the material in the first half I shall make a new story, one suggested by recent, and, to me, tremendous events.

52

Do you remember the drought in Jolon that came every thirty-five years? We have been going through one identical with the one of 1880. Gradually during the last ten years the country has been dying of lack of moisture. This dryness has peculiar effects. Diseases increase, people are subject to colds, to fevers and to curious nervous disorders. Crimes of violence increase. The whole people are touchy and nervous. I am writing at such length to try to show you the thing that has just happened. This winter started as usual—no rain. Then in December the thing broke. There were two weeks of downpour. The rivers overflowed and took away houses and cattle and land. I've seen decorous people dancing in the mud. They have laughed with a kind of crazy joy when their land was washing away. The disease is gone and the first delirium has settled to a steady jubilance. There will be no ten people a week taken to asylums from this county as there were last year. Anyway, there is the background. The new novel will be closely knit and I can use much of the material from the Unknown God, but the result will be no rewritten version.

Perhaps it will be as well to let Miss Phillips see this plan. It will give her a better idea of what to expect.

Your letter was encouraging. Thank you.

Sincerely,
John Steinbeck

To Amasa Miller

[Pacific Grove]
February 16 [1932]

Dear Ted:

Thank you for doing all that work. It was a lot of trouble. Miss Mc. dismissed the ms. [*The Pastures of Heaven*] by saying the form doesn't interest her, but it may interest someone else. The Pastures has begun its snaggy way. Morrow won't publish as a first novel, but will if a more closely integrated

53

work can precede it. Publishers are afraid of short stories unless the writer of them has a tremendous name. And so I presume that the Pastures will go the way of all the others. Miss Mc. was non-committal about it. Meanwhile I work at the Unknown God. I have changed the place, characters, time, theme, and thesis and name so maybe it won't be much like the first book. It's good fun though.

I wonder you don't lose faith in my future. Everyone else does. For myself, I haven't brains enough to quit. Maybe you haven't brains enough to get out from under the wreck. Thirty years hence I'll still be working. I am very happy when I'm working.

Have McBride's relaxed their grip on that copyright?

I'm pretty damn sick of my consistent failure. Everyone says nice things and no one buys my books. Wurra—wurra. M. and O. have been kind and have expended lots of stamps on me. I wonder how soon they'll get sick of it.

Please write more often.

> Affectionately,
> John

Eleven days later, on his thirtieth birthday, big news came.

"M. and O. wired today," he wrote Ted Miller. "They have palmed off the Pastures on somebody. I don't know any more about it because I have only the telegram."

A few days later he had more details.

To George Albee

Pacific Grove
[March] 1932

Dear George:

The Pastures has been curiously fortunate. Cape and Smith accepted it with some enthusiasm within three days of its submission to them. According to M. & O. they showed a nice enthusiasm and intend to feature it on their fall list. I am very glad, more for my folks' sake than for my own. They love it so much. Dad's shoulders are straighter for it and mother beams. I am no longer a white elephant, you see. I am justified in the eyes of their neighbors. It is very good. I received the telegram on my birthday. It was nice of Miss O. [Elizabeth Otis] to wire. If this firm will only allow me a dedication to my parents, they will be extremely happy.

I was going rapidly and well on the new book, but this little encouragement is bound to have a stimulating effect. In addition Carol has a job—$50.00 a month. She is deliriously happy. She's wanted a job so badly.

Sincerely,
John

1932 1935
1933 1936
1934

Steinbeck (signature)

"...scared
and boastful
and humble..."

1932 *The Pastures of Heaven* published.

1933 *To a God Unknown* and the first two parts of *The Red Pony* published.

1934 His mother, Olive Hamilton Steinbeck, died. A short story, "The Murder," won O. Henry prize.

1935 His father, John Ernst Steinbeck, died. *Tortilla Flat* published, his first success.

1936 *In Dubious Battle* published.

Carol Steinbeck's job was in the laboratory of a friend who was already exerting a vital influence on Steinbeck's life and thinking: the marine biologist, philosopher, and ecologist, Edward F. Ricketts. Steinbeck had met him in 1930 and had passed many hours on Cannery Row in Monterey at his Pacific Biological Laboratory which collected and distributed West Coast biological specimens to institutions and individuals throughout the country. This laboratory was to become the background for several of Steinbeck's stories and novels, and Ricketts himself, under varying aliases, would appear as a character in them. He and Steinbeck collaborated on *Sea of Cortez* and maintained a close friendship till Ricketts's death in 1948.

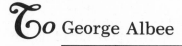

To George Albee

Pacific Grove
[March] 1932

Dear George:

Thank you for sending the letter, you see I have nothing but the telegram and I have been afraid the thing had fallen through. The letter reassured me of its acceptance but was also slightly redolent of horse shit. If you believe all the nice things then you ought to believe all the nasty things that will be said later, and then they cancel each other out.

Carol is working now and loves it. She has two rattlesnakes and about 200 white rats to love. She introduced Tillie to the rats and they ignored each other.

59

I don't know why the publication of a book should impress you. I've met a number of people who publish books and judging from most of them, the fact of publication seems to make a horse's ass of a man. So forget about it. I've never heard of a book that made any money and I have no desire to speak before women's clubs. Waiting for these contracts has stopped my work a little, that's all. And you must remember that the moment Mr. Ballou buys a book it's his property and he has to think it wonderful or he can't sell it. That's the first principle of salesmanship: believe in your product no matter how rotten it is.

That's all

Affectionately
John

Robert O. Ballou, former literary editor of the Chicago *Daily News,* had joined the publishing firm of Cape and Smith a few years before. It had a distinguished roster of writers who were also published by the parent firm of Jonathan Cape in England. In 1932 company reorganization caused the firm to be rebaptized Jonathan Cape and Robert Ballou, Inc. It was at this point that contracts with Steinbeck for *The Pastures of Heaven* and two subsequent novels were signed.

To Amasa Miller .

[Pacific Grove]
March 14, 1932

Dear Ted:

Your letter came this morning for which I thank you. I have read and signed these new contracts. Naturally they seem good to me. A crust would have seemed good. Ballou's letter was friendly. He seemed over-impressed with the book but that is probably his method of dealing with clients. From all I can learn (which is little) the house is a good, conservative old one. I should have gone on working for twenty years, but I must admit a little encouragement is a lifting thing for the spirit. I am about a third finished with the first draft of the new version of the Unknown God. I think I like it pretty well this time.

Darn it, I thought I had finished and mailed this. I just found it in a book. I'm sorry. My sister is up from Los Angeles and yesterday she presented me with a nice pair of riding breeches so I can ride with her. We are going out tomorrow. I'll probably be awfully sore but it will be good to cinch a beastie again. It must be over two years since I have had my feet in stirrups. A few months ago, after slight indulgence, I rode a colt bareback and unbridled, me in tweeds. If I'd been sober I'd have been tossed on my can but being pickled, I did a first rate rodeo and only came off when we went under a bush. The colt was trying to crawl into a gopher hole.

Affectionately,
John

To George Albee

Pacific Grove
[March] 1932

Dear George:

You'll be anxious to hear about these contracts. They seem to me a little crazy. There are three contracts, one for The Pastures of Heaven and one each for two later mss which are simply named by their succession. The publisher binds himself to publish the things sight unseen. If McIntosh hadn't assured me that he was a good business man I should think he was an angel trying to put some money on art. McIntosh says I will be allowed a drawing account against even the unwritten books. I don't imagine I shall take advantage of it.

61

She also says that, since Jonathan Cape is an English firm, I am practically guaranteed English publication. Now doesn't the thing seem a little bit crazy?

All of this sounds impossible to me of course. Nothing so nice has ever happened to me. I still think the man is insane to buy books without seeing them. That's about all I can think of, I knew you'd want to know.

Affectionately,
John

Soon afterwards, Ted Miller sent the assignment of McBride's copyright.

"For myself I would hate to see the Cup reissued," Steinbeck wrote him. "I've outgrown it and it embarrasses me. But my father talked continually about the copyright, which he thinks is valuable. Now that he has it in the safe, he is happier."

In June Steinbeck replied to his publisher's request for publicity and biographical material.

To Robert O. Ballou

Pacific Grove
June 10, 1932

Dear Mr. Ballou:

Your telegram puts a burden of embarrassment on me. I have no reluctance toward writing an "unreticent story of my life." Immediately there arises a problem of emphasis. Things of the greatest emphasis to me would be more or less meaningless to anyone else. Such a biography would consist of such things as—the way the sparrows hopped about on the mud street early in the morning when I was little—how the noon bell sounded when we were writing dirty words on the sidewalk with red fuchsia berries—how Teddy got run over by a fire engine, and the desolation of loss—the most tremendous morning in the world when my pony had a cold.

What you undoubtedly want is about two paragraphs of facts. I've forgotten so many of the facts. I don't remember what is true and what might have been true. It hasn't been a story to write about, you see. Nothing much has ever happened.

As for the picture—I hate cameras. They are so much more sure than I am about everything. I am sending you a photograph of a large drawing which I like. I hope it will do.

I can't say how much I wish this kind of thing weren't necessary. I feel like a man who has been to a horse race, and who is asked, "What were you doing while the race was on? What were you doing with your hands? How did your face look?" He wouldn't know, and I don't know.

There are some things I can prove. If I put them down, will you write this thing? And if you don't like any of it, you can make one up that you do like. It doesn't matter to me.

Sincerely,
John Steinbeck

Through this period Steinbeck had been working on another and final rewrite of *The Unknown God.* He customarily used a ledger for his writing. Sometimes this contained the manuscript itself and other times notes which preceded the day's work, and which he called his "daybook" or his "workbook." At one time he wrote in used ledgers from his father's office, on the backs of pages already covered on one side with accounts. He actually bought the ledger in which *The Unknown God* was written, and it is more than likely that poverty at least partly dictated his choice of a bound book of pages instead of separate sheets of manuscript paper. Certainly it was poverty that caused his choice of ink. As he wrote Duke Sheffield:

63

"A year ago Holman's department store had an ink sale—ink that had been so long in stock that it was as ripe and rich as Napoleon brandy, cobwebs on the bottles. Two bottles for five cents. I bought two and used them. On page 167 the green was exhausted and I went back, but the sale was over and I bought one bottle of blue for ten cents."

This ledger of *The Unknown God* also marks the first time he directed the entire concept and approach of his work, not to a faceless and generalized audience, but to a single person. It would be his practice for the rest of his life.

To Carlton A. Sheffield

[Pacific Grove]
[1932

To Dook—[fragments from a ledger]

When I bought this book, and began to fill it with words, it occurred to me that you might like to have it when it was full. You have that instinct so highly developed in magpies, packrats and collectors. I should like you to have this book and my reasons are all sentimental and therefore, of course, unmentionable. I love you very much. I have never been able to give you a present that cost any money. It occurs to me that you might accept a present that cost me a hell of a lot of work. For I do not write easily. Three hours of writing require twenty hours of preparation. Luckily I have learned to dream about the work, which saves me some working time.

Now as always—humility and terror. Fear that the working of my pen cannot capture the grinding of my brain. It is so easy to understand why the ancients prayed for the help of a Muse. And the Muse came and stood beside them, and we, heaven help us, do not believe in Muses. We have nothing to fall back on but our craftsmanship and it, as modern literature attests, is inadequate.

64

May I be honest; may I be decent; may I be unaffected by the technique of hucksters. If invocation is required, let this be my invocation—may I be strong and yet gentle, tender and yet wise, wise and yet tolerant. May I for a little while, only for a little while, see with the inflamed eyes of a God.

I wonder if you know why I address this manuscript to you. You are the only person in the world who believes I can do what I set out to do. Not even I believe that all the time. And so, in a kind of gratitude, I address all my writing to you, whether or not you know it.

Now this book is finished, Dook. You will have to work on it; to help straighten out the roughness, to say where it falls short. I wish I valued it more so that it would be a better gift. It isn't nearly all I hoped it would be. I remember when I finished the earlier book of the same title. I took it to you and you said, "It is very good." And I knew you knew it was terrible, and you knew I knew you knew it. And if this one is as bad I hope you will tell me. I've worked too hard on it. I can't tell much about it.

Anyway—this is your book now. I hope you'll like to have it.

love,
John

To George Albee

Pacific Grove
September 27, 1932

On the 27 of September 1932 I borrowed from George Albee one hundred dollars on the slightly questionable collateral of a contract held by me from Brewer, Warren and Putnam. I promise to repay this one hundred dollars when contractual obligations are satisfied which is within two weeks of the twenty-first of October, 1932.

Signed.

John Steinbeck

Brewer, Warren, and Putnam was the publishing house to which Robert Ballou had moved after the bankruptcy of his former firm. He took Steinbeck's contracts with him, but the only novel of Steinbeck's that the new firm would remain solvent long enough to publish in this Depression year would be *The Pastures of Heaven*.

During a stay of several months in Southern California, Steinbeck continued to work on the final rewrite of *To An Unknown God*.

To Robert O. Ballou

2527 Hermosa Avenue
Montrose, California
January 3, 1933

Dear Ballou,

Your letter came this morning together with one from Mc & O containing the belated check. It was a relief. Tillie, properly Tylie Eulenspiegel [who had recently died], was an Airedale terrier and a very beautiful one. She was beautifully trained—could point quail, retrieve ducks, bring in hares or clear a road of sheep. More important than these though, she had the most poignant capacity for interest and enjoyment in the world. It was much more important to us that she be alive than that people like Hearst and Cornelius Vanderbilt foul up the planet. *She* was house broken.

This book draws to a close. It will (if nothing happens) be

66

ready to send before the end of February. I shall be very glad to have it done. I hope to God you'll like it. I have grave doubts. The title will be To A God Unknown. The transposition in words is necessary to a change in meaning. The unknown in this case meaning "Unexplored."

This is taken from the Vedic hymns. I want no confusion with the unknown God of St. Paul.

That's all. Thanks again for routing out the check.

John Steinbeck

To Mavis McIntosh

Montrose
January 1933

Dear Miss McIntosh:

We live in the hills back of Los Angeles now and there are few people around. One of our neighbors loaned me three hundred detective magazines, and I have read a large part of them out of pure boredom. They are so utterly lousy that I wonder whether you have tried to peddle that thing I dashed off to any of them ["The Murder"]. It might mean a few dollars. Could be very much cut to fit, you know. Will you think about it? It would be better than letting it lie around, don't you think?

I think that, when this is sent off (this new novel) I shall do some more short stories. I always think I will and they invariably grow into novels, but I'll try anyway. There are some fine little things that happened in a big sugar mill where I was assistant chief chemist and majordomo of about sixty Mexicans and Yuakis taken from the jails of northern Mexico. There was the Guttierez family that spent its accumulated money for a Ford and started from Mexico never thinking they might need gasoline. There was the ex-corporal of Mexican cavalry, whose wife had been stolen by a captain and who was training his baby to be a general so he could get even better women. There was the Lazarus who

67

drank factory acid and sat down to die. The lime in his mouth neutralized the acid but he could never go back to his old life because he had been spiritually dead for a moment. His will to live never came back. There was the Indian who, after a terrific struggle to learn to tell time by a clock, invented a clock of his own that he *could* understand. There is the saga of the Carriaga family. Son hanged himself for love of a chippy and was cut down and married the girl. His father aged sixty-five fell in love with a fourteen-year-old girl and tried the same thing, but a door with a spring lock fell shut and he didn't get cut down. There is Ida Laguna who fell violently in love with the image of St. Joseph and stole it from the church and slept with it and they both went to hell. These are a few as they really happened. I could make some little stories of them I think.

I notice that a number of reviewers (what lice they are) complain that I deal particularly in the subnormal and the psychopathic. If said critics would inspect their neighbors within one block, they would find that I deal with the normal and the ordinary.

The manuscript called Dissonant Symphony I wish you would withdraw. I looked at it not long ago and I don't want it out. I may rewrite it sometime, but I certainly do not want that mess published under any circumstances, revised or not.

Sincerely,
John Steinbeck

To Robert O. Ballou

[Montrose]
February 11, 1933

Dear Ballou:

Please don't mind the pencil. I don't own a fountain pen. I am lying in the sun, drinking coffee. Of course I could use the typewriter. For the first time in one solid month it is idle. This is a good day. I shipped mss. to Miss O. this morning.

You should get it before very long. I hope you will like it. The book was hellish hard to write. I had been making notes for it for about five years. It will probably be a hard book to sell. Its characters are not "home folks." They make no more attempt at being sincerely human than the people in the Iliad. Boileau (much like your name) insisted that only gods, kings and heroes were worth writing about. I firmly believe that. The detailed accounts of the lives of clerks don't interest me much, unless, of course, the clerk breaks into heroism. But I have no intention of trying to explain my book. It has to do that for itself. I would be sure of its effect if it could be stipulated that the readers read to an obbligato of Bach.

There are several things in your letter that I must answer. The Hymn to a God Unknown was, of course, written about three thousand years ago. It must have been chanted, but I know of no music. The disadvantage of setting Sanskrit characters in the end papers is that it would give an Eastern look to the book.

Your letter sounds a bit disconsolate. The working of publishing houses must be nerve wracking, but I should think it would be heartening. More and more competitions going out. And the need for books is leaping, not dropping. I know a French boy who started a haberdashery just before the crash. On all sides of him stores went under but he continued merrily. I went to see him the other day and asked him how he did it. He said, "I come from French peasant stock. We waste nothing. I have very little overhead. Such things as 'service' and luxury are killing my competition. If I make a dollar it is my dollar." If you can hold out for a year without falling into the mess the others have, you will be the "Publisher." Your method is sane. Knopf says that only 1 percent of the books are sold because of advertising. And advertising is the most expensive item, isn't it? I can't tell you how pleased I am to be associated with you.

The Murder I thought might be sold to a pulp if it were cut down. Even a little money would be better than a bunch of grapes. [It was sold to *North American Review* and was included among the *O. Henry Prize Stories* the following year.]

We are very happy. I need a dog pretty badly. I dreamed of dogs last night. They sat in a circle and looked at me and I wanted all of them. Apparently we are heading for the rocks. The light company is going to turn off the power in a few days, but we don't care much. The rent is up pretty soon and then we shall move. I don't know where. It doesn't matter. My wife says she would much rather go out and meet disaster, than to have it sneak up on her. The attacking force has the advantage. I feel the same way. We'll get in the car and drive until we can't buy gasoline any more. Have two more books almost ready to start but a month of messing around won't hurt. But I do need a dog. Tillie haunts the house terribly.

Please let me hear as soon as you can, what you think of this new book. It was an important piece of work to me. I wanted to make a beautiful and true book.

Sincerely,
John Steinbeck

His mother's sudden serious illness would now force John and Carol Steinbeck to divide their time between the family home in Salinas and the little house in Pacific Grove.

To George Albee

Box 6
Salinas, California
[1933]
Wednesday

Dear George:

This is a very sad time. Mother seems to be slipping badly. Every other day she seems to be a little better and then the next she slips back a little weaker. My father doesn't know how sick she is and we aren't telling him. He has enough worries as it is. Don't tell anyone down there what I just said. I am sometimes astounded at the way things get about, unbelievable. Anyway we are expecting the worst and hoping it may not be the very worst, that is a paralysis.

I am taking up the harmonica in my usual thorough way. I decided that there was no future in the peedle pipe, no chords. Besides my new peedle pipe is in B and the accordeen is in D and while we do a fairly good peanut vendor, and the combination hits hearts and flowers as it should be hit, for serious music you just can't put B and D together and make anything sweet of it. So I got a D harmonica and we are getting hot.

I have the pony story about half written. [*The Red Pony*] I like it pretty well. It is more being written for discipline than for any other reason. I mean if I can write any kind of a story at a time like this, then I can write stories. I don't need publication so why should I send it to Story which pays nothing. If I can't hit a paying magazine I'll put it away for the future collection that everybody dreams about. It is a very simple story about a boy who gets a colt pony and the pony gets distemper. There is a good deal in it, first about the training of horses and second about the treatment of distemper. This may not seem like a good basis for a story but that entirely depends upon the treatment. The whole thing is as simply told as though it came out of the boy's mind although there is no going into the boy's mind. It is an attempt to make the reader create the boy's mind for himself. An interesting experiment you see if nothing else. I'll send you a carbon of it when I get it done. It will take about three more days. Maybe four. I have to go to the hospital this afternoon while they draw some blood from mother. It

[unfinished letter]

To Robert O. Ballou

Salinas
June 1, 1933

Dear Ballou:

We came to my home because my mother was ill. She has grown steadily worse and five days ago suffered a stroke of paralysis which put her left side out completely and permanently. And there it stays. She has improved now and may live on in this state for a year or even more. Needless to say I shall not be in New York this summer or any other time for a long time in the future. I am badly needed here and I have no regrets about that except that my work seems to be at a standstill. I spend about eight hours a day in the hospital. Thought I would take my little pad and work there, but the tiny scratching of the pen is irritating to the patient. I have been very ill myself and I know how such a sound can be utterly maddening. If this continues, she will be brought home and then I shall continue in another room just out of her ear shot. I have been trying to go on at night but find it very slow. It is difficult to concentrate. I guess we are all pretty tired. But it is good discipline. Perhaps you can see now, why I was insistent on the dedication last year. I have sisters who might help out but they all have children who get something every time anything happens. Besides I have no inclination to go away. That is a curious thing. I've always thought I would want to run away but I don't. That is the end of a paragraph of woe.

We have a new dog. I will send you his picture when I take it. He is an Irish terrier pup, a beauty. His owner died and we bought him from the dog hating wife. A great bargain. He is not nervous nor noisy the way so many terriers are. I will surely photograph him when I get the direction to do anything.

I wish you would tell me whether you are going to publish this book and when. In weaker moments I imagine a conspiracy of silence.

Please let me hear from you before too long.

Sincerely,
John Steinbeck

To George Albee

[Salinas]

[1933]

Dear George:

I have forgotten how long ago I wrote to you and what I told you. Did I write very frequently? I can't remember. I have your letter this morning. I don't know whether I told you that mother is now paralysed and will linger perhaps a year. It has been a bad time. The pony story, you can understand has been put off for a while. But now I spend about seven hours a day in the hospital and I am trying to go on with it, but with not a great deal of success, because partly I have to fight an atmosphere of blue fog so thick and so endless that I can see no opening in it. However, if I can do it, it will be good. Anyone can write when the situation is propitious. I'd like to prove to myself that I can write in any circumstance.

I hate to think what a year here will do to us. Perhaps nothing. I am pretty rubber. Carol is the one who will suffer. She takes things harder than I do, but she has been wonderful about the whole thing.

Went to the hospital and got a few pages of the pony story done although I suspect it is pretty rotten. But between bed pans and calling relatives I got some done. I shall hate to spoil it because it is really a fine story. Carol is going bicycling this afternoon. She had her bicycle fixed up and skids about the streets on it. Poor kid, she needs some kind of relaxation. She hasn't had any fun in a long time. And I don't see much chance that she will have any for some time to come. I would send her away for a while if she would go. I imagine that the English edition of The Pastures is out because I have begun to get letters from clipping bureaus.

I think I would like to write the story of this whole valley, of all the little towns and all the farms and the ranches in the wilder hills. I can see how I would like to do it so that it would be the valley of the world. But that will have to be sometime

73

in the future. I would take so very long. There doesn't seem
to be anything more to say.

bye
jon

It was while observing the course of his mother's
illness that notes which Steinbeck had been making
at random for many years suddenly came into focus
—with the collaboration of Ed Ricketts—and a turning point in his creative life was reached. Even at
the time it seemed so important to him that, contrary to his custom, he dated in full the letter in
which he first wrote about it.

To Carlton A. Sheffield

Pacific Grove
June 21, 1933

This is not a letter to read unless you have so much time
that you just don't care. I just want to talk and there is no one
to talk to. Out of the all encircling good came a theme finally.
I knew it would. Until you can put your theme in one sentence, you haven't it in hand well enough to write a novel.
The process is this (I am writing this at the risk of being
boring. One can refuse to read a letter and the writer of it will
never know.) The process is this—one puts down endless
observations, questions and remarks. The number grows and
grows. Eventually they all seem headed in one direction and
then they whirl like sparks out of a bonfire. And then one day
they seem to mean something.

When they do, it is the most exciting time in the world. I
have three years of them and only just now have they taken

a direction. Suddenly they are all of one piece. Then the problem begins of trying to find a fictional symbolism which will act as a vehicle.

Let me quote a few of the notes. The coral insect working with hundreds of billions of others, eventually creates a strange and beautiful plant-like formation. In the course of time numberless plants create the atoll. Architecturally the atoll is very beautiful and good. Certain groups in Europe at one time created the Gothic spire. They seem to have worked under a stimulus as mysterious, as powerful and as general as that which caused the coral insects to build.

Note—in nineteen seventeen this unit was in a physical and psychic condition which made it susceptible to the inroads of the influenza germ. This germ at other times was not deadly, and, when encountered now, causes discomfort but not ordinarily death. It has been shown that at the time mentioned the germ had not changed but the receptivity of the race had.

Note—in Mendocino county a whole community turned against one man and destroyed him although they had taken no harm from him. This will sound meaningless to you unless you could see the hundreds of notes that make them meaningful to me. It is quite easy for the group, acting under stimuli to viciousness, to eliminate the kindly natures of its units. When acting as a group, men do not partake of their ordinary natures at all. The group can change its nature. It can alter the birth rate, diminish the number of its units, control states of mind, alter appearance, physically and spiritually. All of the notations I have made begin to point to an end—That the group is an individual as boundaried, as diagnosable, as dependent on its units and as independent of its units' individual natures, as the human unit, or man, is dependent on his cells and yet is independent of them.

Does this begin to make sense to you? The greatest group unit, that is the whole race, has qualities which the individual lacks entirely. It remembers a time when the moon was close, when the tides were terrific. It remembers a time when the weight of the individual doubled itself every twenty-eight days, and strangely enough, it remembers every step of its climb from the single cell to the human. The human unit has none of these memories.

The nature of the groups, I said, were changeable. Usually they are formed by topographical peculiarities. Sometimes a

75

terrible natural stimulus will create a group over night. They are of all sizes, from the camp meeting where the units pool their souls to make one yearning cry, to the whole world which fought the war. Russia is giving us a nice example of human units who are trying with a curious nostalgia to get away from their individuality and reestablish the group unit the race remembers and wishes. I am not drawing conclusions. Merely trying to see where the stream of all my notes is going.

One could easily say that man, during his hunting period, had to give up the group since all the game hunters must; and now that his food is not to be taken by stealth and precision, is going back to the group which takes its food by concerted action. That if one lives by the food of the lion he must hunt singly, if by the food of the ruminants he may live in herds and protect himself by his numbers.

It can be placed somewhat like this for the moment—as individual humans we are far superior in our functions to anything the world has born—in our groups we are not only not superior but in fact are remarkably like those most perfect groups, the ants and bees. I haven't begun to tell you this thing. I am not ready to.

Half of the cell units of my mother's body have rebelled. Neither has died, but the revolution has changed her functions. That is cruel to say. The first line on this thing came from it though. She, as a human unit, is deterred from functioning as she ordinarily did by a schism of a number of her cells.

And, when the parts of this thesis have found their places, I'll start trying to put them into the symbolism of fiction.

The fascinating thing to me is the way the group has a soul, a drive, an intent, an end, a method, a reaction and a set of tropisms which in no way resembles the same things possessed by the men who make up the group. These groups have always been considered as individuals multiplied. And they are not so. They are beings in themselves, entities. Just as a bar of iron has none of the properties of the revolving, circling, active atoms which make it up, so these huge creatures, the groups, do not resemble the human atoms which compose them.

This is muddled, Dook. I wouldn't send it to anyone else in this form. But you and I have talked so much together that we can fill in the gaps we leave.

We were awfully glad to get both your letters. Write often, this is a deadly time for us. And you might put your mind on the problem I have stated. If you could help me put it into form, I probably would have less trouble finding my symbols for reproducing it. You will find the first beginning conception of it among the anthropologists, but none of them has dared to think about it yet. The subject is too huge and too terrifying. Since it splashed on me, I have been able to think of nothing else.

It is an explanation of so many mysterious things, the reasons for migrations, the desertion of localities, the sudden diseases which wiped races out, the sudden running amok of groups. It would explain how Genghis Khan and Attila and the Goths suddenly stopped being individual herdsmen and hunters and became, almost without transition, a destroying creature obeying a single impulse. It would explain the sudden tipping over of Prohibition, and that ten years ago the constitution of the US was a thing of God and now it is abrogated with impunity. Oh! it is a gorgeous thing. Don't you think so?

I am ignorant enough to promulgate it. If I had more knowledge I wouldn't have the courage to think it out. It isn't thought out yet, but I have a start. Think of the lemmings, little gophers who live in holes and who suddenly in their millions become a unit with a single impulse to suicide. Think of the impulse which has suddenly made Germany overlook the natures of its individuals and become what it has. Hitler didn't do it. He merely speaks about it.

I'll stop before I drive you as crazy as I have become since all my wonderings have taken a stream like force. All the things I've wondered about and pondered about are seeming to make sense at last. Why the individual is incapable of understanding the nature of the group. That is why publishing is unsure, why elections are the crazy things they are. We only feel the emotions of the group beast in times of religious exaltation, in being moved by some piece of art which intoxicates us while we do not know what it is that does it. Are you as nuts as I am now?

love
john

To Carlton A. Sheffield

Dear Dook:

I had your letter in answer to my hectic one. And I was sorry that you went off into consideration of the technique of the novel which will result. I can see how it will be done all right, but I am in more interest just now to get the foundation straight and the physical integrity of it completed.

My sister Beth is coming over for a few days. Perhaps we might get up to Sausalito while she is here to relieve us. Can't tell, though. Everything gets out of hand this year. There's probably something wrong meteorologically.

Nothing is changed here. This is going to be a very long siege. The doctor says it may last for years. There's a sentence for you, for we can't leave while it lasts. There is no way out. I finished one story and it is ready to be typed, about ten thousand words, I guess [*The Red Pony*]. There was no consecutive effort put on it. If it has any continuity it is marvelous. I can't think of any possible medium which would include it. It was good training in self control and that's about all the good it is. Now I have my new theme to think about there will be few loopholes in my days. I can think about it while helping with a bed pan. I can make notes at any time of the day or night, and I think I shall delay the writing of it until I have the ability for sustained concentration. However, if the time is too long I can't even wait for that. I'll have to go to work on it. The pieces of it are fast massing and getting ready to drop into their places.

I think this is all of this letter.

love
john

Now he began using the word "phalanx" for the "group" or "group unit" he had been describing.

To George Albee

[Salinas]

[1933]

Dear George:

I have your letter of this morning. Mary just went home. We liked having her, but she brought her children which took all her time from helping, and the noise they made was out of place in this house of gloom and melancholy. They made us nervous. I like them. They are the best children. But this is no place for any child. We are taking care of a dead person. We work as hard as we can to keep from thinking of it. We try all we can to keep out of her mind.

I can answer all of your questions now. But I hesitate because of the work it entails. I shall try though, because you need help and this will help you, not because it is something I have discovered. I haven't discovered it. The discovery has come as all great ones have, by a little discovery by each of a great number of men, and finally by one man who takes all the little discoveries and correlates them and gives the whole thing a name. The thesis takes in all life, and for that part, all matter. But you are only interested in life and so am I.

We know that with certain arrangements of atoms we might have what we would call a bar of iron. Certain other arrangements of atoms plus a mysterious principle make a living cell. Now the living cell is very sensitive to outside stimuli or tropisms. A further arrangement of cells and a very complex one may make a unit which we call a man. That has been our final unit. But there have been mysterious things which could not be explained if man is the final unit. He also arranges himself into larger units, which I have called the phalanx. The phalanx has its own memory— memory of the great tides when the moon was close, memory of starvations when the food of the world was exhausted.

79

Memory of methods when numbers of his units had to be destroyed for the good of the whole, memory of the history of itself. And the phalanx has emotions of which the unit man is incapable. Emotions of destruction, of war, of migration, of hatred, of fear. These things have been touched on often.

Religion is a phalanx emotion and this was so clearly understood by the church fathers that they said the holy ghost would come when *two or three were gathered together*. You have heard about the trickiness of the MOB. Mob is simply a phalanx, but if you try to judge a mob nature by the nature of its men units, you will fail as surely as if you tried to understand a man by studying one of his cells. You will say you know all this. Of course you do. It has to be written in primer language. All tremendous things do.

During the war we had probably the greatest phalanx in the history of the world. If we could devote our study to the greater unit, we would be capable of judging the possible actions of the phalanx, of prophesying its variability, and the direction it might take. We can find no man unit reason for the sudden invasion of Europe by a race of Hun shepherds, who were transformed overnight into a destroying force, a true phalanx, and in another generation had become shepherds again, so weak that an invasion of Tartars overwhelmed them. We can find no man unit reason for the sudden migration of the Mayas. We say Attila did it or Ghenghis Khan, but they couldn't. They were simply the spokesmen of the movement. Hitler did not create the present phalanx in Germany, he merely interprets it.

Now in the unconscious of the man unit there is a keying mechanism. Jung calls it the third person. It is the plug which when inserted into the cap of the phalanx, makes man lose his unit identity in the phalanx. The artist is one in whom the phalanx comes closest to the conscious. Art then is the property of the phalanx, not of the individual. Art is the phalanx knowledge of the nature of matter and of life.

Dr. [Walter K.] Fischer at Hopkins [Marine Station, Pacific Grove] said one day that you could find any scientific discovery in the poetry of the preceding generation. Democritus promulgated an accurate atomic theory four hundred years before Christ. The artist is simply the spokesman of the pha-

80

lanx. When a man hears great music, sees great pictures, reads great poetry, he loses his identity in that of the phalanx. I do not need to describe the emotion caused by these things, but it is invariably a feeling of oneness with one's phalanx. For man is lonely when he is cut off. He dies. From the phalanx he takes a fluid necessary to his life. In the mountains I saw men psychologically emaciated from being alone. You can't find a reason for doing certain things. You couldn't possibly find a reason. You are dealing with a creature whose nature you cannot know intellectually, of whose emotions you are ignorant. Whose reasons, directions, means, urges, pleasures, drives, satieties, ecstasies, hungers and tropisms are not yours as an individual.

I can't give you this thing completely in a letter, George. I am going to write a whole novel with it as a theme, so how can I get it in a letter? Ed Ricketts has dug up all the scientific material and more than I need to establish the physical integrity of the thing. I have written this theme over and over and did not know what I was writing. I found at least four statements of it in the God. Old phalanxes break up in a fine imitation of death of the man unit, new phalanxes are born under proper physical and spiritual conditions. They may be of any size from the passionate three who are necessary to receive the holy spirit, to the race which overnight develops a soul for conquest, to the phalanx which commits suicide through vice or war or disease. When your phalanx needs you it will use you, if you are the material to be used. You will know when the time comes, and when it does come, nothing you can do will let you escape.

There is no change with mother nor can there be for a long time to come. I hope this letter will give you something to chew on. Don't quibble about it with small exceptions until the whole thing has taken hold. Once it has, the exceptions will prove unimportant. Of course I am interested in it as tremendous and terrible poetry. I am neither scientist nor profound investigator. But I am experiencing an emotional vastness in working this out. The difficulty of writing the poetry is so great that I am not even contemplating it until I have absorbed and made a part of my body the thesis as a whole.

I corrected and sent back the proofs of the God this week. It reads pretty well. Ballou is rushing it so it may be out

81

among the earliest of the Fall books. And that is all for this
time.

Love to you and Anne and I do wish I could talk to you.

john

"The fictional symbol which will act as a vehicle"
for the phalanx theory appeared in several guises
after this period, among them in *The Leader of the
People* with its description of the "westering" migration; in *In Dubious Battle;* and, notably, in *The
Grapes of Wrath*. Professor Richard Astro of Oregon
State University mentions the famous turtle in
Chapter Three of that novel, "symbolically repre-
senting the Joads' weary trek westward," and points
out that an ancient Roman phalanx in close-order
advance with shields locked overhead was called a
testudo or tortoise. Was Steinbeck aware of this?
There is no way of knowing.

Meanwhile, earlier and throughout that summer of
1933, he had been writing frequently to Albee.

To George Albee

[Salinas]
[June 1933]

Dear George:

Nothing is changed here. Mother gets a little stronger but
not less helpless. There are terrible washings every day. 9–12
sheets. I wash them and Carol irons them. I try to sneak in
a little work, but Mother wants to tell me something about
every fifteen minutes. Her mind wanders badly. This story
which in ordinary times I could do in four days is taking over
a month to write and isn't any good anyway. Carol is working

like a dog. She stays cheerful and makes things easier for all of us. It's hard to cook for nurses. If I can have two good days, I'll finish this darn story. It really isn't a story at all.

One of my sisters came last week and took charge, letting us go to the Grove for two days. The weather was fine and the garden beautiful. I got my importance in the picture straightened out. It's hard to break through now I am back. One's ego grows under this pressure until one's feelings are more important than they deserve to be. It's hard to keep scaled down.

A letter from Ballou says he thinks he can get the money for fall publication. He says the other houses are as badly off as he is and M. & O. agree. I really want to stay with him if he can make it.

John

To George Albee

Salinas

[1933]

Dear George:

I presume, since I have an impulse to write to you, you must either be writing to me or contemplating it or have just finished it. Nothing is changed here. I am typing the second draft of the pony story. A few pages a day. This morning is a good example. One paragraph—help lift patient on bed pan. Back, a little ill, three paragraphs, help turn patient so sheets can be changed. Back—three lines, nausea, hold pans, help hang bedding, back—two paragraphs, patient wants to tell me that her brother George is subject to colds, and the house must be kept warm. Brother George is not here but a letter came from him this morning. That is a morning. One page and a half typed. You can see that concentration thrives under difficulties since I have a fear and hatred of illness and incapacity which amounts to a mania. But I'll get the story typed all right sooner or later and then I'll correct it and then Carol will try to find time to finish it and how she is going to do that I haven't any idea.

I have my new theme out of all this [the phalanx theory]. I am scared to death. It is as much huger than the last book as the last book was larger than The Pastures. In fact it has covered my horizon completely enough so there doesn't seem to be anything else to think about, for no possible human thought nor action gets outside its range.

I presume you are swimming every day and basking and generally enjoying yourself. In a way I envy you and in another I don't. I wouldn't miss the ferocious pleasure of this thing of mine for any compensation. The illness (which by the way is the cause of the beginning conception) is worth it —everything is worth it.

I have heard no more from the east. Mc & O are probably mad at me for turning down the comparatively sure ready money from Simon and Schuster. But I can't help that. I feel much safer with Ballou than I would with Simon and Schuster.

I have a great many little blisters on my hands and on my forehead. Ed says it looks like an allergy. It may be a subconscious attempt to escape sick room duty. If it is, I will have to overcome it with some powerful magic of the consciousness—exorcism of some sort or other. I can't have the submerged part playing tricks and getting away with them.

That's all for today. I'll expect a letter in the next mail.

john

To George Albee

[Salinas]
[1933]

Dear George:

One piece of advice I can offer, and that is that you should never let any one suggest anything about your story to you. If you don't know more about your character and situation than anyone else could, then you aren't ready to write your story anyway. It is primarily a lonely craft and must be accepted as such. If you eliminate that loneliness of approach, you automatically eliminate some of the power of the effect. I don't know why that is.

I can't tell which of the endings you should use. The second sounds very Dostoievsky, and after all you never saw a prisoner flayed. You may argue that your reader never did either and so how can he tell. I don't know, but he can. You might be able to make your second ending ring true, but you would be almost unique in letters if you could. I have somehow the feeling that you will abandon this book. Not because it isn't good but because publishers are in a peculiar condition now. That you are heartily sick of the book is apparent. One thing you will have to do about your genius, though. You will have to give him some dignity and depth. You are writing about Howard Edminster, and while Howard may write superb poetry, his life and acts are those of a horse's ass and a charlatan. Meanwhile your age does not justify that you waste tears over one book. You are growing out from under it and so you can never catch it again. Put it away and, at some time when publishing changes, you will find an out for it. That isn't my advice, you know. I can't tell you how to work and how to think. My method is probably wrong for you. Certainly my outlook and vision of life is completely different from yours.

The pony story is finally finished and the second draft done. I don't know when Carol will find time to type it, but when she does, I'll send you the second draft and then you won't have to bother to send it back. It is an unpretentious story. I think the philosophic content is so buried that it will not bother anybody. Carol likes it, but I am afraid our minds are somewhat grown together so that we see with the same eyes and feel with the same emotions. You can see whether you like it at all. There never was more than a half hour of uninterrupted work put on it, and the nausea between paragraphs had to be covered up. I don't see how it can have much continuity, but Carol says it has some.

I guess that's all. There is no change here. Mother's mind gets farther and farther from its base. She is pretty much surrounded by dead relatives now.

bye
john

To Carl Wilhelmson

Salinas
[1933]

Dear Carl:

This has been a very bad year all around for us. Sometimes I get so shot that I feel like running out on the situation, a thing impossible of course. There are barriers psychological as well as physical. I have never run into so many barriers. It is really the first time I have been unable to run out of danger. I can't get much of any work done, and the few words I do put down are written in the midst of constant interruptions.

In general I guess we are all right. Carol is about ready for a breakdown maybe. You know one publisher after another went broke from under us. My new book [*To A God Unknown*] was held up for a long time and then I got four offers for it, and left it with Ballou because I like him and trust him, and I neither like nor trust the others. And so it will be out in the Fall. I sent the proofs back the day before yesterday. The last one [*The Pastures of Heaven*] seems to be getting a better break in England than it did in this country, but I can't tell much about that for some time.

I wish I could get to see you, but I don't see how I can. I have to help in the office. Isn't it funny, my two pet horrors, incapacity and ledgers and they both hit at once. I write columns of figures in big ledgers and after about three hours of it I am so stupefied that I can't get down to my own work. I can see very readily how office workers get the way they are. There is something soddenly hypnotic about the columns of figures. Once this is over, I shall starve before I'll ever open another ledger. Sometimes we get away over a week end but Palo Alto is quite a long trip away or is it Berkeley where you are living.

I shouldn't be writing to anybody. It is impossible to keep the melancholy out of the tone of the words. I'll put this letter away and if I hear from you I'll add a line or two and send it.

[unsigned]

To Carl Wilhelmson

Salinas
August 9, 1933

Dear Carl:

This loss of contact has been curious. I hope that now it is over. Enclosed is a letter I wrote to you a long time ago [the preceding letter] and never had your address to send it.

This condition goes on, one of slow disintegration. It will not last a great time more, I think. For a long time I could not work, but now I have developed calluses and have gone back to work. It seems heartless when I think of it at all. You are much more complex than I am. I work because I know it gives me pleasure to work. It is as simple as that and I don't require any other reasons. I am losing a sense of self to a marked degree and that is a pleasant thing. A couple of years ago I realized that I was not the material of which great artists are made and that I was rather glad I wasn't. And since then I have been happier simply to do the work and to take the reward at the end of every day that is given for a day of honest work. I grow less complicated all the time and that is a joy to me. The forces that used to tug in various directions have all started to pull in one. I have a book to write. I think about it for a while and then I write it. There is nothing more. When it is done I have little interest in it. By the time one comes out I am usually tied up in another.

I don't think you will like my late work. It leaves realism farther and farther behind. I never had much ability for nor faith nor belief in realism. It is just a form of fantasy as nearly as I could figure. Boileau was a wiser man than Mencken. The festered characters of Faulkner are not very interesting to me unless their festers are heroic. This may be silly but it is what I am. There are streams in man more profound and dark and strong than the libido of Freud. Jung's libido is closer but still inadequate. I take pleasure in my structures but I don't think them very important except in the doing.

Tillie died you know and now we have another dog named

Joddi. An Irish terrier and beauty. We like him. He is one of the toughest dogs I have ever seen although only a little over six months old.

Your preoccupation with old age would be shocked out of you by seeing what I see every half hour all day, true age, true decay that is age. A human body that was all dead except for a tiny flickering light that comes on and then seems to go out and then flickers on again. Our life has been uprooted of course, but that doesn't matter if I can find my escape in work.

I have a book coming out in a couple of months. I don't think I would read it if I were you. It might shock you to see the direction I have taken. Always prone to the metaphysical I have headed more and more in that direction.

I have to go to the office now and write a few figures in a ledger. Then I will come home and to my afternoon's work. I'll write again in a little while. And let me hear from you again you old man.

affectionately,
john

To Robert Ballou at this time he was writing:

"My father collapsed a week ago under the six months' strain and very nearly landed in the same position as my mother. It was very close. Paradoxically, I have started another volume [*Tortilla Flat*], and it is going like wildfire. It is light and I think amusing but true, although no one who doesn't know paisanos would ever believe it. I don't care much whether it amounts to anything. I am enjoying it and I need something to help me over this last ditch. Our house is crumbling very rapidly and when it is gone there will be nothing left."

And on November 20:

"He is like an engine that isn't moored tightly and that just shakes itself to pieces. His nerves are gone and that has brought on numbness and loss of eyesight and he worries his condition all the time. Let

88

it go. We're going on the rocks rapidly now. If mother lives six months more she will survive him. If she dies soon, he might recover but every week makes it less likely. Death I can stand but not this slow torture wherein a good and a strong man tears off little shreds of himself and throws them away."

To Edith Wagner

Pacific Grove
[November 23, 1933]

Dear Mrs. Wagner:

I am dreadfully sorry you are ill. I hope the treatments work out quickly. Illness doesn't shock me the way it did. There's a saturation point and I seem to have reached it. You'll be well again soon. The pain is another thing. I don't like pain. I hope you will be well soon.

I have been in Salinas. My father is so completely worn out that I sent him over here with Carol and I went to Salinas. Now he is back there while Mary is up, but I'll bring him back next Saturday. He is eating himself with nerves. The Grove seems to quiet him. And mother remains the same— no change at all.

I'm glad you like the book [*To a God Unknown*]. The overthrow of personal individual character and the use of the Homeric generalized symbolic character seems to bother critics although a little study of the Bible or any of the writers of antiquity would show that it is not very revolutionary. The cult of so called realism is a recent one, and anyone who doesn't conform is looked on with suspicion. On the moral side—our moral system came in about two hundred years ago and will be quite gone in 25 more.

When we came over here a month ago, I got to work finally and did three fourths of a book. I thought I was going to slip it through, but dad's decline beat me. This is indeed writing under difficulty. The house in Salinas is pretty haunted now. I see things walking at night that it is not good to see. This last book is a very jolly one about Monterey paisanos. Its tone,

I guess, is direct rebellion against all the sorrow of our house. Dad doesn't like characters to swear. But if I had taken all the writing instructions I've been given, I would be insane. I try to write what seems to me true. If it isn't true for other people, then it isn't good art. But I've only my own eyes to see with. I won't use the eyes of other people. And as long as we can eat and write more books, that's really all I require.

We bought a second-hand radio to hear the Fall symphonies and it is a menace, for when dad is over here, he listens to all of the loudest speeches and that kills work. You know I should be writing a cheerful letter if you aren't feeling well. Instead I write a list of complaints.

Don't think there is any courage in my work. If you demand little from life you limit its ability to strike at you and you can say what you wish about it.

I do hope you feel better now.

love
John

To George Albee

[Pacific Grove]
February 25, 1934

Dear George:

You remember that when you were up here we asked for a sign and the [ouija] board said that it would come to me on the day of my mother's funeral. There was no sign except this one, if you can call it a sign. I asked you to pick a day for an attempted communication and without any knowledge you picked the day of my mother's funeral. I tried to get through to you. I tried to tell you that she had died and that she had been buried that day and that I had been forced to be a pall bearer. I did it by making the words in yellow on a black background. In the middle of the crying, I stopped and wondered whether it was getting through and instantly the black ground was full of yes's of all sizes. I wondered whether anything did get through. I was pretty much stunned by the terrors of the day and probably didn't have much force left but I tried with what I did have. Also I tried to tell Miss Otis that I had just sent her a new story that Carol likes immensely.

I think you got out of the murder story about what I wanted you to. You got no character. I didn't want any there. You got color and a dream like movement. I was writing it more as a dream than as anything else, so if you got this vague and curiously moving feeling out of it that is all I ask. I shall be interested to know what you think of the story, The Chrysanthemums. [This and "The Murder" became part of *The Long Valley.*] It is entirely different and is designed to strike without the reader's knowledge. I mean he reads it casually and after it is finished feels that something profound has happened to him although he does not know what nor how. It has had that effect on several people here. Carol thinks it is the best of all my stories. I'll have some more before long.

Just now my father is with us. Every nerve I have is demanding that I be alone for a little while even for a day to make adjustments, but that has been impossible so far. Maybe later in the week it can be done. I have to figure some things out. I don't even know what they are yet. I do think I'll go on with short stories for a little while though until I get my adjustments made. I wish Carol could go off for a little rest. She has taken it on the chin throughout. I can't use my freedom yet because I can't conceive it yet. The other has grown to be a habit.

We are going to Laguna with Ed Ricketts next month. He has to get some live octopuses and send by plane to New York, and we are going to make Laguna our base for catching the things. It will be a nice change. We won't be there much over a week I guess. We have enough money to live two more months so I will have to get busy and make some more I guess. I have thirty pounds coming from England if I ever get it. That will allow some more months but the money to go any place has not showed up nor will it unless I should be lucky enough to sell some short stories. I have kind of yearnings for Alaska but I don't know. Trying to stave off reaction until maybe there won't be any. Carol's book of poems is getting popular and she is swamped with demands for copies. Ballou asked to see them, she sent him a copy as a Christmas present and never heard a word from him even that he had got them. Which was thoughtless of him because it is work to get one of the copies out. She will make a copy for Anne pretty soon. I think they are swell. I guess that is all. It's all I can think of anyway.

love
john

Jesus I wish you two were out here and we could go camping. That's what I need. The grass is green and all the flowers are out and I'll just have to get out in the country for a little.

bye.

To George Albee
WHO HAD MOVED TO NEW YORK

[Pacific Grove]
[1934]

Dear George:

I think I am in a kind of mood to write you a letter. I got yours a little while ago. I have been writing on my new ms. which I will tell you about later, for a good many hours and I think a change will do me good.

You ask what I want? You know pretty well that I don't think of myself as an individual who wants very much. That is why I am not a good nor consecutive seducer. I have the energy and when I think of it, the desires, but I can't reduce myself to a unit from which the necessary formula emanates. I'm going to try to put this down once for all. I like good food and good clothes but faced with getting them, I can't round myself into a procuring unit. Overalls and carrots do not make me unhappy. But the thing which probably more than anything else makes me what I am is an imperviousness to ridicule. This may be simply dullness and stupidity. I notice in lots of other people that ridicule or a threat of it is a driving force which maps their line of life. And I haven't that stimulus. In fact as an organism I am so simple that I want to be comfortable and comfort consists in—a place to sleep, dry and fairly soft, lack of hunger, almost any kind of food, occasional loss of semen in intercourse when it becomes troublesome, and a good deal of work. These constitute my ends. You see it is a description of a stupid slothful animal. I am afraid that is what I am. I don't want to possess anything, nor to be anything. I have no ambition because on inspection the ends of ambition achieved seem tiresome.

Two things I really want and I can't have either of them and they are both negative. I want to forget my mother lying for a year with a frightful question in her eyes and I want to forget and lose the pain in my heart that is my father. In one year he has become a fumbling, repetitious, senile old man, unhappy almost to the point of tears. But these wants are the desire to restore the lack of ego. They are the only two things which make me conscious of myself as a unit. Except for them I spread out over landscape and people like an enormous jelly fish, having neither personality nor boundaries. That is as I wish it, complete destruction of any thing which can be called a me. The work is necessary since from it springs all the other things. A lack of work for a while and the gases concentrate and become solids and out of the solids a me comes into being and I am uncomfortable when there is a me. Having no great wants, I have neither great love nor great hate, neither sense of justice nor of cruelty. It gives me a certain displeasure to hurt or kill things. But that is all. I have no morals. You have thought I had but it was because immorality seemed foolish and often bad economy. If I objected to accounts of sexual exploits it wasn't because of the exploits but because of the cause of the accounts.

The reason we want to go away is primarily so that the two things I want may have a chance to be removed. That may be impossible. But forced and common visits to a grave yard are not conductive of such forgetfulness.

You are right when you think I am not unhappy in this new arrangement. I never come up to the surface. I just work all the time. In the matter of money, my conception doesn't extend beyond two or three hundred dollars. I love Carol but she is far more real to me than I am to myself. If I think of myself I often find it is Carol I am thinking of. If I think what I want I often have to ask her what it is. Sometimes I wish I had sharply defined desires for material things, because the struggle to get them might be very satisfying. If one should want to think of me as a person, I am under the belief that

93

he would have to think of Carol.

I am writing many stories now. Because I should like to sell some of them, I am making my characters as nearly as I can in the likeness of men. The stream underneath and the meanings I am interested in can be ignored.

Between ourselves I don't know what Miss McIntosh means by organization of myself. If she would inspect my work with care, she would see an organization that would frighten her, the slow development of thought pattern, revolutionary to the present one. I am afraid that no advice will change me much because my drive is not one I can get at. When they get tired of my consistent financial failures, they will just have to kick me out. I'm a bum, you see, and according to my sister, a fake, and my family is ashamed of me, and it doesn't seem to make any difference at all. If I had the drive of ridicule I might make something of myself.

This is probably a terrible sounding letter. It isn't meant so. I am working so hard and so constantly that I am really quite happy. I don't take life as hard as you do. Some very bitter thing dried up in me last year.

And now I want to do one more page today before I sit down and look at the fire. The trouble is that I look at the fire and then get up and go to work again. I get around that by taking down the table and putting my manuscript book under the lower shelf of the book case where I must get a stick to get it out. Usually I am too lazy to get the stick.

I hope this letter does not depress you. It is common that anything which is not optimistic is pessimistic. I am pegged as a pessimistic writer because I do not see the millenium coming.

that's all
[unsigned]

In February, he had written Mrs. Wagner:

"I have been doing some short stories about the people of the county. Some of them I think you yourself told me."

94

Mrs. Wagner became the source of another story, a personal reminiscence about a meeting she had once had with Robert Louis Stevenson. Steinbeck wrote it under the title "How Edith McGillicuddy Met Robert Louis Stevenson."

To Edith Wagner

POSTCARD

[Pacific Grove]
June 4, 1934

Dear Mrs. Wagner:

Your letter came this morning. I didn't know you had done a version of the story and I sent mine off with a lot of other stuff. I will do whatever you wish about the affair, divide in case of publication or recall the manuscript. Please let me know.

Carol is in Salinas working for my father and I am over here trying to write myself out of a hole.

I'm terribly sorry if I have filched one of your stories. I'm a shameless magpie anyway, picking up anything shiny that comes my way—incident, situation or personality. But if I had had any idea, I shouldn't have taken it. I'll do anything you like about it.

Thank you for your letter. I get so few. I write so few.

John

To Edith Wagner

[Pacific Grove]
June 13 [1934]

Dear Mrs. Wagner:

I am writing to my agents today, asking them to hold up the story. It is awkward for this reason—they've had the story for at least two weeks and since they are very active, it has undoubtedly gone out. However, it can be stopped. I hope you will let me know how yours comes out, as soon as you hear. If it should happen to have been bought by the time my letter reaches New York, it can be held up. Mine, I mean.

Pacific Grove summer has set in, fog most of the day. The people who come over from the Valley love it, but I wish the sun would shine.

Well, I hope nothing untoward happens about this story. In sending it away I enclosed a note saying it had been told me by you. Plagiarism is not one of my sins. I'll write you when I hear any outcome.

Affectionately,
John

To Mavis McIntosh

Pacific Grove
1934

Dear Miss McIntosh:

I want to write something about Tortilla Flat and about some ideas I have about it. The book has a very definite theme. I thought it was clear enough. I have expected that the plan of the Arthurian cycle would be recognized, that my Gawaine and my Launcelot, my Arthur and Galahad would be recognized. Even the incident of the Sangreal in the search of the forest is not clear enough I guess. The form is that of the Malory version, the coming of Arthur and the mystic quality of owning a house, the forming of the round table, the adventure of the knights and finally, the mystic translation of Danny.

The Arthurian legend had fascinated Steinbeck since childhood. As he wrote later:

"When I first read it, I must have been already enamoured of words because the old and obsolete words delighted me."

However, I seem not to have made any of this clear. The main issue was to present a little known and, to me, delightful people. Is not this cycle story or theme enough? Perhaps it is not enough because I have not made it clear enough. What do you think of putting in an interlocutor, who between each incident interprets the incident, morally, esthetically, historically, but in the manner of the paisanos themselves? This would give the book much of the appeal of the Gesta Romanorum, those outrageous tales with monkish morals appended, or of the Song of Solomon in the King James version, with the delightful chapter headings which go to prove that the Shulamite is in reality Christ's Church.

It would not be as sharp as this of course. But the little dialogue, if it came between the incidents would at least make clear the form of the book, its tragi-comic theme. It would also make clear and sharp the strong but different philosophic-moral system of these people. I don't intend to make the parallel of the round table more clear, but simply to show that a cycle is there. You will remember that the association forms, flowers and dies. Far from having a hard theme running through the book, one of the intents is to show that rarely does any theme in the lives of these people survive the night.

I shall be anxious to know your reaction to the Communist idea [which was to become *In Dubious Battle*].

Thank you for your letter.

Sincerely,
John Steinbeck

The problem of the theme of *Tortilla Flat* was solved by chapter headings that clarified the moral points, and by one sentence in the Preface:

"For Danny's house was not unlike the Round Table, and Danny's friends were not unlike the knights of it."

To George Albee

[Pacific Grove]
January 15 [1935]

Dear George:

This is the first time I have felt that I could take the time to write and also that I have had anything to say to anything except my manuscript book. You remember I had an idea that I was going to write the autobiography of a Communist. Then Miss McIntosh suggested that I reduce it to fiction. There lay the trouble. I had planned to write a journalistic account of a strike. But as I thought of it as fiction the thing got bigger and bigger. It couldn't be that. I've been living with this thing for some time now. I don't know how much I have got over, but I have used a small strike in an orchard valley as the symbol of man's eternal, bitter warfare with himself.

I'm not interested in strike as means of raising men's wages, and I'm not interested in ranting about justice and oppression, mere outcroppings which indicate the condition. But man hates something in himself. He has been able to defeat every natural obstacle but himself he cannot win over unless he kills every individual. And this self-hate which goes so closely in hand with self-love is what I wrote about. The book is brutal. I wanted to be merely a recording consciousness, judging nothing, simply putting down the thing. I think it has the thrust, almost crazy, that mobs have. It is written in disorder.

In the God I strove for a serene movement like the movement of the year and the turn of the seasons, in this I wanted to get over unrest and irritation and slow sullen movement breaking out now and then in fierce eruptions. And so I have used a jerky method. I ended the book in the middle of a sentence. There is a cycle in the life of a man but there is no ending in the life of Man. I tried to indicate this by stopping on a high point, leaving out any conclusion.

The book is disorder, but if it should ever come to you to read, listen to your own thoughts when you finish it and see if you don't find in it a terrible order, a frightful kind of movement. The talk, and the book is about eighty percent dialogue, is what is usually called vulgar. I have worked along with working stiffs and I have rarely heard a sentence that had not some bit of profanity in it. And in books I am sick of the noble working man talking very like a junior college professor. I don't know what will become of this book. It may be too harsh for anyone to buy. It is not controversial enough to draw the support of either the labor or the capital side although either may draw controversial conclusions from it, I suppose. It will take about a month to whip it into shape for sending. If you see Miss McIntosh will you tell her? I should have it off by the fifteenth of February.

It is called Dubious Battle from the lines in the first part of the argument of Paradise Lost:

Innumerable force of Spirits armed,
That durst dislike his reign, and, me preferring,
His utmost power with adverse power opposed
In Dubious Battle on the plains of Heaven,
And shook His throne. What though the field be lost?
All is not lost—the unconquerable will,
And study of revenge, immortal hate,
And courage never to submit or yield:
And what is else not to be overcome?

I was very near collapse when I finished this afternoon. But I've been thinking and dreaming it for some months now. Only the mechanical revision is needed. It won't take much polish. It isn't that kind of a book.

I suppose in a few days I'll get out of this lost feeling. Just now I feel that I have come up out of a deep delirium. I must put in the beginning of this book a guarantee that all persons places and events are fictional because it all has happened and I don't want anybody hurt because of my retelling. Lord, I hope it has in it one tenth of the stuff I tried to put in it. Can't tell. Can't ever tell. People who are easily revolted shouldn't read it. Oh! what the hell. I'm just talking on. And I'm too tired to be writing a letter. I've written thirty thousand words in the last eight days. I'll finish this letter later. I'm going for a walk down by the water.

It is the next day. I am luxuriating in laziness, with a fine sense of sin, too, but shall get back to work tomorrow. I got rid of most of the tiredness last night and with the help of a little glass of very nice chartreuse, which beverage I love. The first part of this letter is rather frantic.

Carol's mother sent her an insurance policy to bury Carol in case of her death. It has brightened our whole day. Had been intended as a Christmas present but got delayed. It would have made a nice Christmas present, don't you think?

The sun is shining so nice. One of Ed's collectors got very drunk in the lab the night before last and tipped over a museum jar, left his pants and shoes and disappeared. Ed was angry. The next morning the collector Gabe came in in a long overcoat and a pair of rubber boots. Ed said, "I should think you could at least keep sober on the job." And Gabe who was very friendly put his arms around Ed and said, "Eddie, I know I have a bawling out coming and I forgive you." "Forgive, hell!" yells Ed. "Now Eddie, don't think you can embarrass me," Gabe says. He turns around and spreads the tails of the overcoat, showing that he had on a pair of blue jeans in which there is no seat and exposed is a large pink tocus. Gabe says, "Eddie, I've been visiting people like this. If I can do that, you couldn't possibly embarrass me and I forgive you for trying." Ed got down from his chair and everybody had a drink. Ed says, "What can you do with a man like that?"

Ed is fine. And he is feeling pretty fine now too. He was over yesterday afternoon. This is a long letter, I guess. All about me. I haven't had such a going over for some time. I like this typewriter. It is very fast. I see a cat. You see two cats. Who are the cats. That will be all, sir. You can just take this letter out and put it in an envelope if that's the way you feel. No tricks, sir. We have our standards and by God sir, no wart hog like you is going to lower them.

I beg your pardon
     for being,
          sincerely yours

                    Rabbit Steinbeck

The next letter marks Steinbeck's first mention of Pascal Covici, then publisher and editor of the firm of Covici-Friede. He would be friend and editor till his death. Originally, Ben Abramson, a bookdealer in Chicago, had called his attention to the young writer and to the two novels he had already published.

To George Albee

[Pacific Grove]
[1935]

Dear George:

The book came this morning two days after your letter [an advance copy of Albee's novel *Not in a Day*, published by Knopf]. It found us in a mad manuscript period. Carol batting out finished copy like mad [of *In Dubious Battle*]. But I'm letting her read the book first. She takes little rests and plunges into it and lets out bellows of laughter. I envy both her and you. She reads very fast and I read very slowly. She'll be through with it tonight. So I shall only start this letter and finish it when I have read Not in a Day. I don't like the dust jacket. Saving the back flap, I burned it. But I think the binding and boards and set up and printing is superb. Knopf does that sort of thing so darned well.

Yesterday I went collecting with Ed. The first time I had been out in a long time. It is fine spring now and I enjoyed it a lot. Went over to Santa Cruz. Carol wouldn't go because she was typing and wouldn't take the time off. It would have done her good. But we're broke now and one hamburger was all we could afford. I had been working longer than she had so I took the day off. Today back at revising and proofreading. I'm making dumplings for dinner. I hope they're good. It's a dirty shame Carol has to work so hard. She's putting in nine hours a day at it. I wish I could do it but my typing is so very lousy.

I had a letter from Covici which sounded far from over-enthusiastic. I liked it. It gave me some confidence in the man. I like restraint. Covici says, "I am interested in your work and would like to arrive at an agreement with Miss McIntosh." My estimation of him went up immediately. It is nice to know that he is more enthusiastic than that, of course. This morning I got applications on the Phelan Award sent at your request. I shall probably fill out the blank and send it in. I don't know whom to get to sponsor me but maybe I'll think of some one. That's all for now.

Now it's Monday morning. Carol has gone to work for the S.E.R.A. [State Emergency Relief Administration.] Poor kid has to put in six hours there and then come home and type ms. She has nearly two hundred pages yet to do. What a job. She is taking it awfully well as usual.

I read Not in a Day last night. Finished it about three this morning. I don't know whether it is high or low comedy but I do know it's awfully funny. My own work seems stodgy and heavy by comparison. I hope you will read Tortilla Flat some time. That is neither heavy nor stodgy. Anyway I'm glad you wrote this book and I am convinced that it will release you from the necessities for working on fan magazines. I hope it sells a million copies. Congratulations.

I have a great deal of proof reading and correction to do and besides that I am doing the house and the cooking and bedmaking. So I'll sign off. But I am pleased with Not in a Day. Don't let it make a slave of you. I mean, if it sells well, people will want another just like it, and don't let them have it. For right at that point of capitulation is the decision whether the public is going to rule you or you your public.

I simply have to go to work. Goodbye. You have complimented me greatly by sending the book.

jon

The sponsor he chose for the Phelan Award was Ann Hadden, then librarian of the Palo Alto Public Library. She had known him since his boyhood in Salinas.

It has been pointed out that Steinbeck had a unique and personal way with official correspondence, of which he was to write a great deal in the time to come. This is the earliest sample.

To Ann Hadden

Dear Miss Hadden:

Thank you very much for your offer to help. I shall explain the situation. The James Phelan Award for Literature is coming due, and a friend sent me an application. It is only open to natives of the state. Now there is one space on the application after the following demand: Give names of three persons competent in your field and acquainted with you personally to whom the Trustees may apply for confidential information about your qualifications for the fellowship.

What confidential material they could wish I don't know. Possibly about my habits. I'm afraid you don't know much about those. I will tell you.

I have all the vices in a very mild way except that of narcotics, unless coffee and tobacco are classed as narcotics. I have been in jail once for a night a long time ago, a result of a combination of circumstance, exuberance and a reasonable opinion that I could lick a policeman. The last turned out to be undemonstrable. I don't think the trustees would be interested, but they might. I am married and quarrel violently with my wife and we both enjoy it very much. And last, I am capable of a tremendous amount of work. I have just finished a novel of a hundred and twenty thousand words, three drafts in a little over four months.

I am embarrassed for having to ask any one to vouch for me. It seems to me it would be better if I could simply submit a book and be judged upon the strength of it.

I have a long and very different novel nearly ready to write but I have thought I would have to put it off until I had laid aside enough money to allow for no interruption. This award is for one thousand dollars. It runs for one year but since we ordinarily live on four hundred a year, the money would let me do what I really want to and what the thesis of the novel really deserves, that is take two full years to the work.

I hope this will not cause you to go to any great trouble. I have little hope of being awarded this fellowship. But since it is rather easy to do, I think I shall, if you are willing to help me.

Sincerely,
John Steinbeck

His letter succeeded in eliciting her sponsorship. In writing to the administration of the Phelan Award, she said:

"After he left home for college I saw very little of him, but kept in touch through his parents and friends.

"The library of which I was in charge helped him through correspondence with research one winter for his *Cup of Gold* which he was writing while snowed in at Lake Tahoe.

"In my opinion John Steinbeck has decided creative literary ability; his development being quite marked from his first novel *Cup of Gold* through *Pastures of Heaven* to his recent book *To A God Unknown.* I believe he has the qualification in personality and character to justify an investment in his future education."

He did not win the award.

To Mavis McIntosh

Pacific Grove
February 4, 1935

Dear Miss McIntosh:

Herewith the signed contracts [for *Tortilla Flat*]. They seem fine to me. Thank you. You have been very good to me.

We'll get the new book off to you about the fifteenth. Title has been slightly changed to include one more word, In Dubious Battle. Much better sound and also gives a kind of an active mood to the thing. I guess it is a brutal book, more brutal because there is no author's moral point of view. The speech of working men may seem a little bit racy to ladies' clubs, but, since ladies' clubs won't believe that such things go on anyway, it doesn't matter. I know this speech and I'm sick of working men being gelded of their natural expression until they talk with a fine Oxonian flavor.

There are curious things about the language of working men. I do not mean the local idioms, but the speech which is universal in this country among traveling workers. Nearly every man uses it individually, but it has universal rules. It is not grammatical error but a highly developed speech form. The use of the final g in ing is tricky, too. The g is put on for emphasis and often to finish a short hard sentence. It is sometimes used for purpose of elision but not always. Certain words like "something" rarely lose the final g or if they do, the word becomes "somepin" or "somepm." A man who says thinkin' will say morning if it comes on the end of a sentence. I tell you these things so you will understand why, in one sentence having two present participles, one g will be there and the other left off. This is a pretty carefully done ms. If you will read such a sentence over, aloud, you will see that it naturally falls that way.

I hardly expect you to like the book. I don't like it. It is terrible. But I hope when you finish it, in the disorder you will feel a terrible kind of order. Stories begin and wander out of the picture; faces look in and disappear and the book ends with no finish. A story of the life of a man ends with his death, but where can you end a story of man-movement that has no end? No matter where you stop there is always more to come. I have tried to indicate this by stopping on a high point but it is by no means an ending.

I hope Mr. Covici will be interested in this book. I am very tired. This has been completed quickly.

Sincerely,
John Steinbeck

To Wilbur Needham
STAFF BOOK CRITIC FOR THE LOS ANGELES *TIMES*

Pacific Grove
[Early 1935]

Dear Mr. Needham:

I am grateful to you for your active interest. It is only a few weeks ago that we heard that Covici-Friede had conceived a rather frantic regard for my work to the extent that he [Covici] has contracted for all of it and is going to reissue some of the old ones. He is bringing out one in May called Tortilla Flat and possibly this one we are now on earlier. It is called In Dubious Battle.

I am very much pleased of course. We have been very close to the end these last couple of years. Thank you for your trouble. You see, it is not needed now, I mean of course, the finding of a publisher. Ballou is a fine man and a sensitive man but I do not think he is fitted to fight the battle of New York. He is a gentleman. He can't bring himself to do the things required for success.

I should like to discuss with you a plan of work so difficult that it will take several years to do and so uncharted that I will have to remake the novel as it is now understood to make it a vehicle. I want to go to Mexico to do it and it may be that we shall be able to go this summer. I hope so, for I am anxious to get at it before very long.

I hope you will come up to see us when you can.

Sincerely,
John Steinbeck

When he sent the manuscript of *In Dubious Battle* to McIntosh and Otis, he reminded Miss McIntosh that if Covici refused the book in the contracted time, he had had other offers, and besides:

". . . you will find a well-aroused interest in my work both at Houghton, Mifflin and at Random House."

To Mavis McIntosh

Pacific Grove
[April] 1935

Dear Miss McIntosh:

I confess that I am deeply shocked at the attitude of Covici, not from pique but because it is a perfect example of the attitude which makes the situation in I. D. B. what it is. Does no one in the world want to see and judge this thing coldly? Answering the complaint that the ideology is incorrect, this is the silliest of criticism. There are as many communist systems as there are communists. It should be obvious from the book that not only is this true, but that the ideologies change to fit a situation. In this book I was making nothing up. In any statement by one of the protagonists I have simply used statements I have heard used. Answering the second criticism that the book would be attacked by both sides, I thoroughly anticipated such attack in trying to do an unbiased book. And if attack has ever hurt the sale of a book I have yet to hear of it.

That is the trouble with the damned people of both sides. They postulate either an ideal communist or a thoroughly damnable communist and neither side is willing to suspect that the communist is a human, subject to the weaknesses of humans and to the greatnesses of humans. I am not angry in the least. But the blank wall of stupid refusal even to look at the thing without colored glasses of some kind gives me a feeling of overwhelming weariness and a desire to run away and let them tear their stupid selves to pieces. If the fools would only change the name from Communist to, say, American Liberty Party, their principles would probably be embraced overnight.

I guess this is slopping over enough. I am sorry that the book cannot go through. I would do it just the same again. I suppose in the event of an English sale, the censor would clean up my carefully built American language.

As for submitting another book to Covici—you will do as you think best about that. I am so tired. I have worked for so long against opposition, first of my parents who wanted me to be a lawyer and then of publishers who want me to be anything but a writer, that I work well under opposition. If ever I had things my own way I would probably go dry. This will knock out all plans of going to Mexico I guess. I had hoped to be able to start off the big book which would take a long time and would be a very grave attempt to do a first-rate piece of work. However, Covici should know saleability, and obviously I don't. Oh, the devil. We've managed to live thus far and write what we want to write. We can probably go on doing it.

Right today I am discouraged. I won't be tomorrow.

Sincerely,
John Steinbeck

Now the correspondence, excepting a few letters to other members of the agency, begins to focus on

Elizabeth Otis. She became, as will be evident, far more than a literary representative. He was soon, and always, to trust her as mentor, guide, friend, and confidante.

To Elizabeth Otis

Pacific Grove
May 13, 1935

Dear Miss Otis:

I have your letter this morning, also two from C-F [Covici-Friede].

Mr. Latham of Macmillan's came to see me. Asked if I were tied to C-F. I said they had just rejected a book. He said he wanted to see it and I told him to apply to you.

Let me say at the beginning of this paragraph that I would rather stay with Covici-Friede than anyone I know. I like the way they have worked on Tortilla and I like their makeup and everything about them. This letter this morning from them offers to publish I. D. B. if I wish it. Of course I wish it. It is a good book. I believe in it, and damn it, we're living on relief. Why wouldn't I want to publish it?

> Shortly before he had written to Miss Otis:
>
> "In any re-revision of I. D. B. I hope that you will tell Mr. Covici that neither theme nor point of view will be changed. It might also be well to remind them that an advance is due upon acceptance, an advance which would do much to make my life a merrier affair."

Let's get to this rejection now. I had a letter, unfortunately destroyed, in which they said they didn't want to print the book and they gave three pages of reasons for not wanting to print it. Between you and me I suspect a strong communist bias in that office, since the reasons given against the book are all those I have heard from communists of the intellectual bent and of the Jewish race. Do you think I am right? My information for this book came mostly from Irish and Italian communists whose training was in the field, not in the drawing room. They don't believe in ideologies and ideal tactics. They do what they can under the circumstances.

I'm a bit twisted. My father went into his fatal illness two days ago. We don't know whether it will be a week, or as it was with my mother, ten or eleven months. It is the same thing. Cerebral leakage. I have been running back and forth to Watsonville [where Esther Steinbeck Rodgers, Steinbeck's sister, lived] so often that I am bewildered and possibly not coherent. Anyway, I hope this is a satisfactory letter in some respects.

Sincerely,
John Steinbeck

To Elizabeth Bailey

POSTCARD TO STEINBECK'S GODMOTHER

[Pacific Grove]
May [1935]

Dear Miss Bailey:

It was a lovely letter.

At first I thought I should send the ten dollars back to you but I won't. I have no place to work. When I do work which is most of the time—Carol has to creep around. For a long time I've wanted to build a little work room in the back yard, using second hand lumber. Ten dollars will do it. Thank you.

I should have preferred no service at all for Dad. I can think of nothing for him so eloquent as silence. Poor silent man all his life. I feel very badly, not about his death, but about his life, for he told me only a few months ago that he had never done anything he wanted to do. Worst of all he hadn't done the work he wanted to do.

Come some time and see the new work room.

love
John

To Elizabeth Otis

Pacific Grove
June 13, 1935

Dear Miss Otis:

If you have anything of mine the New Yorker could use, fine. The only things I can think of are the short things like the Vigilante or possibly St. Katy which I would like to make someone print. I'm not being cocky but I have never written "for" a magazine and shan't start now.

One very funny thing. Hotel clerks here are being instructed to tell guests that there is no Tortilla Flat. The Chamber of Commerce does not like my poor efforts, I guess. But there is one all right, they know it.

My father's death doesn't change any plans but does give us freedom of movement for the first time in three years. I can't get used to having no illness in the family.

While I think of it—I am very much opposed to drawing money from any publisher for work that has not been done. I'd much rather have less and have it without any obligation. The idea of a salary doesn't appeal to me at all. I intend to write what I want to.

The publicity on TF [*Tortilla Flat*] is rather terrible out here and we may have to run ahead of it. Please ask CF [Covici-Friede] not to give my address to anyone. Curious that this second-rate book, written for relaxation, should cause this fuss. People are actually taking it seriously.

I had an awfully nice letter from Bob Ballou. Wish I could have stayed with him but I'm so awfully sick of not being able to have shoes half-soled.

In your dealings you need make no compromise at all for financial considerations as far as we are concerned. Too many people are trapped into promises by gaudy offers. And my father's estate, while small, will keep us for a number of years if necessary. And we've gone through too damned much trying to keep the work honest and in a state of improvement to let it slip now in consideration of a little miserable popularity. I'm scared to death of popularity. It has

III

ruined everyone I know. That's one of the reasons I would like In Dubious Battle printed next. Myths form quickly and I want no tag of humorist on me, nor any other kind. Besides, IDB would reduce popularity to nothing but I do think it would sell.

I suppose it is bad tactics but I am refusing the usual things —the radio talks, the autograph racket, the author's afternoons and the rest of the clutter—politely, I hope, but firmly.

Will Heinemann buy TF? [This is the British publishing house which would publish all Steinbeck's work.] I suppose To A God Unknown failed miserably in England as it did here.

By the way, the rainy season is on in Mexico now. We can't go until August I guess, if then. I'll leave this open in case anything else occurs to me.

That's all,
John Steinbeck

In the *O. Henry Prize Stories of 1934* in which "The Murder" had appeared, Steinbeck, reading over the competition, had come on a story by Louis Paul, and had written George Albee:

"Look out for a young man named Louis Paul, who wrote a story in the O. Henry collection, magnificent. That boy is going to do things."

To Louis Paul

POSTCARD

Pacific Grove
[Late summer 1935]

Dear Louis Paul:

It was good of you to write. I like that. The odd thing is that since I read Jedworth I've had a strong impulse to write to you. That was one of the finest stories I ever read. Publishers are all right. They are the natural enemies, though. The wildcats to us quail.

I'm a couple of books ahead—not because I write so quickly but because I'm published so slowly. We're planning to drive to Mexico soon.

I wish you lived closer. I'd like to talk to you. God willing I'll never go east again. Don't worry about my making money. I haven't the gift.

Anyway, it was swell of you to write. I wish you would again.

John Steinbeck

To Mavis McIntosh

Pacific Grove
July 30, 1935

Dear Miss McIntosh:

Your letter and enclosed contracts came today. It is rather sad that now I am being deluged with offers of a lot of nice people who want to be my business representatives, who assure me that they can make more money for me than you are making. And finally who completely fail to understand that I am extremely happy where I am. I don't want to make much money and I like this contract. Please assure Mr.

113

Covici that I am awfully pleased to stay under his imprint. I enclose both copies of the contract.

Rather an amusing episode. There is a little magazine here run in conjunction with a stable. I gave them a story which Miss Otis had sent back as "outrageous" in return for six months use of a beautiful big bay hunter anytime I want him, day or night. I send you the title page of the story and guarantee you ten percent of six months riding but you will have to come here to get it. I should like that very much indeed. I haven't had a horse in years and am utterly delighted at this trade.

> The "little magazine" was the *Monterey Beacon,* and the story, which would become one of Steinbeck's most famous, was "The Snake." After the success of *In Dubious Battle* and *Of Mice and Men, Esquire* published it in 1938, and in the same year it appeared in the short story collection, *The Long Valley.*

I have no idea how Tortilla Flat is selling. It has made a lot of noise out here, but whether it was just noise or not I have no idea. I wonder whether you can give me an idea of its sale so I can see whether royalties on that book will cover the Mexican journey.

There were some shorts with you. I have had several letters from editors wanting them. I have referred them to you. I like some of those stories.

I'll be very glad to see Mr. Covici when he comes out here. If he is alone we shall be happy to have him stay here.

Sincerely,
John Steinbeck

To Louis Paul

[Pacific Grove]
[September 1935]

Dear Louis Paul:

Thanks awfully for the copy of Jedwick. Did I call him Jedworth?

You ask why I don't take Hollywood's filthy money. Nobody's asked me, sir. I like to think I wouldn't take it but I probably would. I've been around there quite a bit and I dislike it so much that I wouldn't want to. On the other hand we've been so filthy broke for so long that I would probably go nuts if anyone waved a ten dollar bill. Aren't these nice straight lines? There's a lined sheet underneath.

All is fuss in this house. We're starting for Mexico next week and there's the packing of thousands of doll rags. Our Ford is a wreck but under the hood is an overhauled engine and the tires are new. Yesterday by the use of oratory I didn't know I could use, I persuaded a bank to declare me solvent. And I had the local federal judge swear that I had no Syrian, Armenian, Asiatic or negro blood. As our local Mexican consul says, "Sumteems dose pipples doon't kips the law."

I heard the other day that Covici is reissuing my two earlier books that failed so miserably. They were better books than this last one too but no one would read them—wurra wurra.

We have a small sail boat here and hate to leave it but we must and it will keep for us.

I wish I could send you a copy of T. F. but I haven't any. Couldn't you steal one? If you buy one you will be the first genuine purchaser I know.

I don't know how long we'll be away. Maybe six months, maybe two years.

I'm very grateful for the copy of Jedworth.

Sincerely,
John Steinbeck

In September Miss McIntosh wired Steinbeck in Mexico that the firm had sold the picture rights to *Tortilla Flat*.

"It is rather amusing what the Mexican operator must have thought of your wire," Steinbeck replied. " '4000 dollars for Tortilla.' Probably thought it was either a code word or a race horse."

To Elizabeth Otis

Manchester 8
Mexico D. F.
November 3 [1935]

Dear Miss Otis:

I really should have wired an appreciation of your wire but wires are expensive. Your letter came this morning. Maybe with this security I can write a better book. Maybe not. Certainly though I can take a little longer and write a more careful one. And it will be possible to contemplate an illness without panic. I do not see what even Hollywood can make of Tortilla with its episodic treatment, but let them try and I won't go to their picture so that is all right. On an average I go to about one picture a year.

Our plans are fairly jelled by now. I think we will start for home about the seventh of January. I don't get any work done here. It would be possible to place a blame but it would be more an excuse, I guess. Anyway I can work at home and that's where we will go. Bad news the other day. Our boat broke its moorings and drifted and was salvaged and the salvage award was so much that we will have to sell the boat to pay it and come out clear. I don't care much. It was our first experience in owning anything and a lesson. We will not own anything except the cottage and the necessary and small automobile again. We knew we shouldn't anyway. Maybe a dog.

It is funny that the Irish Free State has me on the censored list. If they knew that my parentage was pure Ulster, they would all the more. The dirty rednecks. Let them be reading their beads and their stomachs full of whiskey, and let them parade under the sun with the chests of them stuck out and their knives between the two shoulders of good men and the dark come. What did they but run off the stern tip of Ireland like the rats they are and Orange after them. Free State indeed, and ask any one of the itching devils are they free of the gray crawlers under their shirts?

I don't know what it means to be on the bottom of a best seller list. Is it two thousand copies or five or ten? In writing to Mr. Covici I asked him, but have had no answer. Thank you again for your letter and its news.

Sincerely,
John Steinbeck

To George Albee

[Mexico]
[1935]

Dear George:

I am not proud of this sale of Tortilla to pictures but we'll slap it into government bonds which are cashable and forget about it. It won't be much when we get it what with splits with Covici and agents' fees but it will be a nest egg. The old standard of living stays right where it has always been.

The air down here has a feel, you can feel its texture on your finger tips and on your lips. It is like water.

Carol is having a marvelous time. The people like her and she them. Wherever she goes, howls of laughter follow. Yesterday in Tolucca market, she wanted to fill out her collection of pottery animals. She went to a puesta and said I want a bull (quiero un toro). That means I want a stud, colloquially. The whole market roared. Most of her pottery animals have flowers painted on them. The rat, instead of being embarrassed pointed to me and said, Segura, tengo un toro pero el no tiene flores en el estomago (sure I have a bull but he has no flowers on his stomach). Then the market just fell to pieces. You could hear the roars of laughter go down the street as each person was told the story. Half an hour later they were still laughing. And when Carol bargains, a crowd collects. Indians from the country stand with their mouths open. The thing goes from gentle to fury to sorrow to despair. And everyone loves it. The seller as much as any one.

My own bargaining yesterday was triumphant. The ordinary method is to run the product down, to be horrified at the badness of the work or the coarseness of the weave or the muddiness of the colors. But I reversed it. One serape priced at fifteen pesos I said was too beautiful. That it was impossible to give it a value in money because it was beyond any offer at all—by that time the duenno was nearly in tears. However I was a poor man and if ten pesos might be accepted, not as payment for the beautiful thing but as a token of esteem, I would take the thing and love it all my life. The method aroused so much enthusiasm not only with the duenno but with the collected market crowd, that I got it for ten without even a squeak. That will be a story in the market too. I like what one market woman said to Carol. Carol said, I would like to buy this but I am not rich. And the market woman—you have shoes and a hat, of course you are rich.

Oh this is enough of a letter and I want to go to the roof.

love to annie
john

To Joseph Henry Jackson
BOOK REVIEWER FOR THE SAN FRANCISCO *CHRONICLE*

Pacific Grove
[1935]

Dear Joe:

I feel very bad about this Commonwealth Club award [for *Tortilla Flat*]. I don't know who offered the book in competition. I assure you that the refusal to go isn't the small mean thing it seems. I would like you to know exactly why I can't go.

Nothing like this has ever happened to me before. The most I have had to dodge has been a literary tea or an invitation from a book shop to lecture and autograph. This is the first and God willing the last prize I shall ever win.

The whole early part of my life was poisoned with egotism, a reverse egotism, of course, beginning with self-consciousness. And then gradually I began to lose it.

In the last few books I have felt a curious richness as though my life had been multiplied through having become identified in a most real way with people who were not me. I have loved that. And I am afraid, terribly afraid, that if the bars ever go down, if I become a trade mark, I shall lose the ability to do that. When I do I shall stop working because it won't be fun any more. The work has been the means of making me feel that I am living richly, diversely, and, in a few cases and for a few moments, even heroically. All of these things are not me, for I am none of these things. But sometimes in my own mind at least I can create something which is larger and richer than I am. In this aspect I suppose my satisfaction is much like that of a father who sees his son succeed where he has failed. Not being brave I am glad when I can make a brave person whom I believe in.

I am very glad that the book got the prize, but I want it to be the book, not me. Those people in that book were very dear to me, but I feel that if I should accept a reward which in this case belongs to Danny and Pilon and the rest, I should not only be cheating them, but cheating them should cut myself off from their society forever.

This is not clear, concise, objective thinking, but I have never been noted for any of these things. If I were a larger person I would be able to do this and come out of it untouched. But I am not.

And will you help me out of it? Will you please present the committee as much or as little explanation as you think wise or necessary? I don't know. I have no social gifts and practically no social experience.

Mean while, don't think too harshly of me for this bolt. I hate to run away but I feel that the whole future working life is tied up in this distinction between work and person. And while this whole argument may seem specious, I assure you it is heartfelt.

Regards
John

While awaiting public and press reaction to *In Dubious Battle*, Steinbeck began preliminary work on the novel that was to become *Of Mice and Men*.

To Louis Paul

[Pacific Grove]
[February 1936]

Dear Louis Paul:

I don't like communists either, I mean I dislike them as people. I rather imagine the apostles had the same waspish qualities and the New Testament is proof that they had equally bad manners. But this dislike is personal. I never knew D. H. Lawrence either. The whole idea of the man turns my stomach. But he was a good writer, and some of these communist field workers are strong, pure, inhumanly virtuous men. Maybe that's another reason I personally dislike them and that does not redound to my credit. However, that's not important.

I haven't an idea what the press will do, nor do I much care. I have enough money now to live and write for three years if we are careful and I can get a hell of a lot of words down in three years.

You ask why you never see my stuff in Esquire. I guess they were never interested. I have a good many stories in New York but no one wants them. I wrote 9 short stories at one sitting recently. I thought some of them were pretty good, too, but that's as far as it got. The North American Review used to print some at 30 dollars a crack.

I have to start [writing] and am scared to death as usual— miserable sick feeling of inadequacy. I'll love it once I get down to work. Hope you'll be out before too long.

Sincerely,
John Steinbeck

To Louis Paul

[Pacific Grove]
[March 1936]

Dear Louis Paul:

I've started to answer a letter from you for quite a long time. This morning your enclosures came. I had not seen Mary Ann McCarthy's review in the Nation [of *In Dubious Battle*]. I'm sorry to see that, like her famous namesake, she didn't get a goddam clam. The pain occasioned by this review is to some extent mitigated by the obvious fact that she understood Caesar's Commentaries as little as my poor screed, that she doesn't know her Plato very well, and that she hasn't the least idea of what a Greek drama is. Seriously what happened is this—Mary Ann reviewed Tortilla Flat, saying that I had overlooked the fact that these paisanos were proletariats. Joseph Henry Jackson, critic on the S. F. Chronicle took her review and played horse with it. So Mary Ann lay in ambush for me to give me my come-uppance. And boy, did she give it to me. Wurra! Wurra!

I'm looking forward to seeing you this spring. And since I'm stuck here until I finish this job that really isn't begun, I hope you'll be able to come through our way. It's desperately beautiful now and will be more so in another month.

Did you know that Herman Shumlin is to produce In Dubious Battle as a play in the fall? That's what I hear anyway. Mary Ann will be glad.

What will you be doing—working in Hollywood? It's time I got back to work. Thanks for the review. It shall be my inspiration.

John Steinbeck

The Nation review of *Tortilla Flat* had said, among other things:

"The subject matter of *Tortilla Flat* is surely grim enough, but Mr. Steinbeck's approach to it is wholly in the light-hearted, fantastic tradition; it suggests such novels as *Vile Bodies* and *South Wind* . . .

"Mr. Steinbeck's attempt to impose a mood of urbane and charming gaiety upon a subject which is perpetually at variance with it is graceful enough, but the odds are against him . . .

"The situations are rife with possibilities which, despite the amount of indifference to them manifested by Mr. Steinbeck and his characters, it is not always easy to ignore."

Joseph Henry Jackson, "playing horse" with this review in the San Francisco *Chronicle*, referred to "a patronizing sneer from a reviewer afflicted with the class itch." It was Steinbeck's error to believe that this was Mary McCarthy, who had indeed written the review preceeding that of *Tortilla Flat*, and whose name appeared at the end of her review but ahead of the *Tortilla Flat* review, which, in fact, was written by one Helen Neville. Nevertheless, it was to mark the beginning of a feud that was to last the rest of Steinbeck's life.

Mary McCarthy, still in her early twenties and a recent graduate of Vassar, did review *In Dubious Battle* in *The Nation* under the title "Minority Report." She called the work: "academic, wooden, inert . . . The dramatic events take place for the most part off-stage and are reported, as in the Greek drama, by a breathless observer. Mr. Steinbeck for all his long and frequently pompous exchanges offers only a few rather childish, often reiterated generalizations . . . He may be a natural story-teller; but he is certainly no philosopher, sociologist, or strike technician."

Whether this was the result of "lying in ambush to give me my come-uppance" is conjectural. But Steinbeck believed it was.

As for Herman Shumlin's projected production of *In Dubious Battle*, he contracted with John O'Hara to do the dramatization. In a letter to Elizabeth Otis, Steinbeck reported:

"Now for the dramatic thing. John O'Hara stopped on his way to San Francisco. I do not know his work but I liked him and his attitude. I think we could get along well. I do not believe in collaboration. If he will maintain the intention and theme of the book (and I am convinced that he will) I shall not interfere at all. He said he would come up in a month with some script to go over. I am pleased with him as the man to do the job."

Years later, O'Hara reminded Steinbeck of this meeting in characteristic style:

"It is a warm and good friendship that began that warm afternoon in Pacific Grove, A.D. 1936, with some Mexican dish cooking on the stove, an English saddle hanging on a peg, your high school diploma on the wall, and you trying to explain about phalanx man."

But Steinbeck's optimism about the *In Dubious Battle* dramatization proved unjustified. As he wrote Elizabeth Otis later:

"O'Hara has not answered my letter. Anyway, I started blocking I. D. B. several days ago, and today and yesterday finished the first scene. And it is lousy. It sounds just what it is—a re-hashed novel. No life —just dead. Maybe someone else can do it. This story was conceived in its present form. It is so real to me that when I compress, leave out incidents and characters and scenes, I'm just lying about something that really happened."

To Louis Paul

POSTCARD

Pacific Grove
[1936]

Dear Louis Paul:

I'm answering your letter in haste. After two months of fooling around my new work [*Of Mice and Men*] is really going and that makes me very happy—kind of an excitement like that you get near a dynamo from breathing pure oxygen and I'm not going Saroyan. Anyway this work is going quickly and should get done quickly. I'm using a new set of techniques as far as I know but I am so illy read that it may have been done. Not that that matters at all, except that the unexplored in method makes the job at once more difficult because I can't tell what it will get over and more pleasant because it requires more care. I'm not interested in method as such but I am interested in having a vehicle exactly adequate to the theme. Enough of this, when the work is rolling it's almost impossible not to be a bore.

It is raining hard. The roof of my little house is roaring.

I hope you do manage to come west. I'll get back to work.

John Steinbeck

To Elizabeth Otis

Pacific Grove
May 27, 1936

Dear Miss Otis:

The check for $94 arrived. Thank you very much. I am enclosing the statement for your records. English criticism always amazes me, mostly because they consider us so foreign. I never think of the English as so strange. There is a Mexican word—Americanado. It means literally Americaned but by connotation queer, unusual, unpalatable, incomprehensible, crazy. That is the way the English think of us too.

Minor tragedy stalked. I don't know whether I told you. My setter pup, left alone one night, made confetti of about half of my ms. book [*Of Mice and Men*]. Two months work to do over again. It sets me back. There was no other draft. I was pretty mad but the poor little fellow may have been acting critically. I didn't want to ruin a good dog for a ms. I'm not sure is good at all. He only got an ordinary spanking with his punishment flyswatter. But there's the work to do over from the start.

We're putting up a little shack near Los Gatos to escape the nasty fogs that hang around here all summer. My wife is building it while I stay here and work. It will be ready in about a month and then I will go up there. I'll send you the change of address when I know what it is.

I should imagine the new little manuscript will be ready in about two months. I hope you won't be angry at it. I think it has some thing, but can't tell much yet.

I'll get this off. I hear the postman.

John Steinbeck

1936 1938
1937 1939

Steinbeck

"Such excitement will never come again."

1936 Moved to Los Gatos, California.

1937 *Of Mice and Men* (novel) published; chosen by Book-of-the-Month Club. *The Red Pony,* in three parts, published. *Of Mice and Men* (play, which won Drama Critics' Circle award) produced.

1938 *The Long Valley* and the fourth part of *The Red Pony* published.

1939 *The Grapes of Wrath* published. Elected to National Institute of Arts and Letters.

Steinbeck's involvement with the lives of the migrant workers, which had already provided the subject matter of *In Dubious Battle,* became even
keener in his mid-thirties. During the summer of
1936, he was visiting the Gridley Migrant Camp,
north of Sacramento, when he replied to a letter
from Lawrence Clark Powell, librarian emeritus of
U.C.L.A:

"I have to write this sitting in a ditch. I'll be home
in two or three weeks. I'm not working—may go
south to pick a little cotton. All this, needless to say,
is *not* for publication—migrants are going south
now and I'll probably go along. I enjoy it a lot."

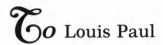

To Louis Paul

POSTCARD

[Pacific Grove]
[1936]

Dear Louis Paul:

Awfully glad to get your letter. I'm very busy now. Doing
a Nation article and a series for the S. F. News on migrant
labor. I've been in the field for the last week. Finished my
new little book [*Of Mice and Men*] and sent it off a week and
a half ago and of course have heard nothing from it. I don't
know whether it is any good or not.

Down the country I discovered a book like nothing in the
world. So I'll be busy as a lamp bug for some months. I like
to be busy. I've been gestating for too long.

I have to write 3,000 words a day for the next five days

["The Harvest Gypsies" for the San Francisco *News*]. So here goes. I'll write you a letter as soon as the series is off.

John

The book he had "discovered" dealt with vigilantes.

To Louis Paul

POSTCARD

Pacific Grove
[1936]

Dear Louis Paul:

I'm delighted that you're coming out. You'll see the new house then. It is just being built now. It's a very beautiful place.

Let me know about when you will arrive so you won't go looking over the whole state for me.

You say you are afraid of symbols. But you see in this country the deep symbol of security is rain—water. And the symbol of evil is drought. There isn't any twisting of symbols there. It's a very real thing. My father lost nearly all his cattle in the year I was writing about. It's a pretty awful thing to have your herd die of thirst and starvation. I was simply trying to reduce that pattern to utterance.

I'm tied up in the new thing. It's a most difficult thing.

I'll be awfully glad to see you.

John Steinbeck

By midsummer the Steinbecks had moved to their new house in Los Gatos.

They had seen Ted Miller in New York in the fall of 1935 when they had stopped there on their way home from Mexico to sign contracts with Paramount Pictures for the film of *Tortilla Flat.* Later, Miller sent an accumulation of letters from the time when he had acted as Steinbeck's ex-officio agent.

To Amasa Miller

Los Gatos, California
[1936]

Dear Ted:

Thanks for the rejections. They still give me the shivers and always will. Each one was a little doom. Had a personal fight with each one. And it's such a short time ago and it may be again.

I'm awfully sorry in a way that I didn't see you more when I was East. And in other ways I am glad. Lord how miserable and rushed and embarrassed I was. I don't like it there. I liked it better before and God knows I hated it then. I'd much rather see you out here where I have leisure and quiet. We live two miles out of town on a hill and few people come here. They have to want to see us if they come because of the distance. There are no casuals.

This isn't a farm we're on. Only two acres. We thought we'd get a farm but that takes attention and I have work to do and I don't like to hire anyone if I can help it. I always feel too humble with hired people and it ends with me doing all the work.

My God, what a nightmare this publicity is. I don't mind being a horse's ass at all. Enjoy it in fact, but I do like to be my own kind—not that it's a better kind but it's more comfortable and I know it better.

131

Don't you ever come West? It will be a long time before I'm East again.

bye and thanks again.

John

To George Albee

[Los Gatos]
[1936]

Dear George:

I seem to have a terrible time writing letters these days. I don't know whether you know what a bomb California is right now or not. I can only assure you that it is highly explosive. I want to see it all and hear it all.

I finished a little book sometime ago [*Of Mice and Men*]. As usual it is disliked by some and liked by some. It is always that way. Covici likes it anyway. It is a tricky little thing designed to teach me to write for the theatre. Now I'm working hard on another book which isn't mine at all. I'm only editing it but it is a fine thing. A complete social study made of the weekly reports from a migrant camp.

Then I did an article for the Nation and a series of articles for the News on migrant labor but the labor situation is so tense just now that the News is scared and won't print the series. Any reference to labor except as dirty dogs is not printed by the big press out here. There are riots in Salinas and killings in the streets of that dear little town where I was born. I shouldn't wonder if the thing had begun. I don't mean any general revolt but an active beginning aimed toward it, the smouldering.

I don't know what you mean by taking to the woods. The woods aren't going to save anyone. And if you want to run you had better start now because you aren't going to have until the end of 1937. You have six months or at most a year. I am not speaking of revolution again, but war. Every news report verifies the speed with which it is coming.

But enough of that sort of thing for the present. This

isn't a new typewriter but we turned in all our old ones and got one that is rebuilt and it is a joy. All the type rightside up and the ribbon reverse works and everything. I have a little tiny room to work in. Just big enough for a bed and a desk and a gun rack and a little book case. I like to sleep in the room I work in. Just at present there is hammering going on. We are building on a guest room. We had none and really need one. It will have big glass doors and screens so that it will really be an outside porch when we want to open the doors. Dr. McDoughal of Carnegie was up the other day and told us we have six varieties of oaks on the place besides manzanita, madrone and toyon. We're in a forest you know.

I have to go to work.

John

The reaction of certain groups who found Steinbeck's literary activities controversial caused Albee, now in New York, to write in concern for his friend's physical safety.

To Mr. and Mrs. George Albee

Los Gatos
January 11 [1937]
Sunday

Dear George and Anne:

Your letter concerning my danger came this morning. The whole thing is changed now. I am not doing any more articles. And they do forget. So there is practically no danger until I commit another overt act. Right now I think my safety lies in the fact that I am not important enough to kill and I'm too able to get publicity to risk the usual beating. Our house is covered by insurance against riots and commotions.

I guess we'll have to pull in our horns financially. I don't expect the little book Of Mice and Men to make any money. It's such a simple little thing.

It is raining hard here now and very dark. I have an electric lantern in my little work room and the rain is pounding on the roof. Very pleasant.

bye
John

And then word came that *Of Mice and Men* had been chosen by the Book-of-the-Month Club.

To Elizabeth Otis

Los Gatos
January 27, 1937

Dear Miss Otis:

Of course this selection is gratifying but also it is frightening. I shall never learn to conceive of money in larger quantities than two dollars. More than that has no conceptual meaning to me. But a part of the money will be used for a long trip this spring. Both of us are such provincial rabbits and we want to move about a little before the rheumatism gets us. And so we plan quite an extended tripping. However, we've planned so many that didn't come off that our fingers are growing together crossed.

The new book has struck a bad snag. Heaven knows how long it will take to write. The subject is so huge that it scares me to death. And I'm not going to rush it. It must be worked out with great care. That's one fine thing this selection will do. It will let me work without a starvation scare going on all the time. This may or may not be a good thing.

It has been colder here than I've ever known it to be. Whole system of weather seems to be changing. In addition there is an epidemic of pneumonia and influenza out here so we go to town rarely and never to the theater. It is remarkable how cataclysmic human change and natural change work together. Wish I could find a corollary. The point of departure is somewhere and it isn't as simple as weather. Maybe the old gods are waking up or maybe a new litter of gods is hatching out.

About the Mice book—already, before publication, there has been a lot of nonsense written about it. I'm not sure that I like adulation. I could defend myself against attack. I wish I were as sure I could defend myself against flattery.

This is a rambling letter.

> Sincerely,
> John Steinbeck

To Pascal Covici

Los Gatos
February 28 [1937]

Dear Mr. Covici:

You do such nice things. The [Diego] Rivera book came and I am very grateful for it. It is a valuable thing and a beautiful job. Thank you.

You know, we've been married seven years or going on seven and one of the dreams of our marriage was that the moment we could, we would do some traveling. Well we're going to do it. My wife has never been on a ship. We're taking booking on a freighter sailing for New York about the first of April. We plan to go on to Europe from there. I'll give you the ship's name before we start. We haven't closed the booking yet. The boat is very slow, 31 days to N. Y.

Joe Jackson told me that you had sold 117,000 copies of Mice. That's a hell of a lot of books.

Anyway I'll hope to see you before very long. You couldn't arrange to sail with us, could you, train here and freighter back. That would be fine.

Anyway thank you again for everything.

John Steinbeck

A number of playwrights saw dramatic possibilities in *Of Mice and Men,* but Annie Laurie Williams, the play agent associated with the McIntosh and Otis office, showed the novel to Beatrice Kaufman, Eastern representative of Samuel Goldwyn Pictures and —more to the point—the wife of the well-known playwright and director, George S. Kaufman. He shared his wife's enthusiasm and enlisting Sam H. Harris as producer, arranged for a fall production of the work, which, as he wrote Steinbeck "drops almost naturally into play form and no one knows that better than you."

"It is only the second act that seems to me to need fresh invention," he continued. "You have the two natural scenes for it—bunkhouse and the negro's room, but I think the girl should come into both these scenes, and that the fight between Lennie and Curley, which will climax Act 2, must be over the girl. I think the girl should have a scene with Lennie *before* the scene in which he kills her. The girl, I think, should be drawn more fully: she is the motivating force of the whole thing and should loom larger."

He made a couple of other specific, small suggestions and asked Steinbeck to send any further ideas he might have. Then Kaufman added:

"Preserve the marvelous tenderness of the book. *And*—if you could feel it in your heart to include a *little* more humor, it would be extremely valuable, both for its lightening effect and the heightening of the subsequent tragedy by comparison."

In considering actors, he wrote that he was undecided as to whether to have "names" or not.

136

"I have just had a tough experience with Margaret Sullavan—we have had to close her play because of an impending baby. Not that Victor McLaglen could have a baby but he could do something else just as bad. Once you have delivered your play into the hands of a star you are helpless when that star misbehaves. On the other hand, without a decent name we will open to four people when we go out of town."

To Elizabeth Otis and
Annie Laurie Williams

Los Gatos
March 19, 1937

Dear Miss Otis and Annie Laurie Williams:

I have several letters from you this morning. This is the last letter you will get from me so I'd better make it complete. I'll go over all the questions.

Your check for $1,902 arrived and thank you very much. Please do not divulge the middle name on the check [Ernst]. I only use it at the bank as a safety measure.

I had George Kaufman's letter and have replied. I hope to have a draft incorporating his suggestions by the time we reach New York.

I hate literary parties and won't go to any if I can possibly get out of it.

Sailing on the Sagebrush, March 23, due in N.Y. about the 15th of April. Please do not tell *anyone* the name of the ship or its arrival. Covici knows and a few people out here. This ballyhoo is driving me nuts.

Regarding the College Humor matter—If a story of mine is as well done as I am able to do it, I wouldn't give a hoot if it were printed in Captain Billy's Whiz Bang. Make the price the limit they will pay and if it doesn't seem enough to you—don't let them. I really don't like the idea that my work can only be printed in certain magazines. I've broken every literary rule when I wanted to. I'm not conforming to some literary model now.

137

I'm down to Woollcott. [Alexander Woollcott whose "Town Crier" was a popular radio program.] I think you know my hatred of personal matters. On the other hand, I should like to have him talk about all work. I simply cannot write books if a consciousness of self is thrust on me. Must have some anonymity. I got Mr. Covici to start killing the pictures. I was recognized in S. F. the other day and it made me sick to my stomach. Unless I can stand in a crowd without any self-consciousness and watch things from an uneditorialized point of view, I'm going to have a hell of a hard time. I'm sure Mr. Woollcott will understand this.

Factual material is this. Born Salinas, California, 1902. Died— ?

If I said Pasadena, I lied, but I lie easily. Educated Salinas and Stanford and not too pleased with the job of either. Reared in Salinas and Monterey and in and on ranches in vicinity. Live near Los Gatos and no mention of where near Los Gatos.

If Mr. Woollcott will soft-pedal the personal matter I'll love him to pieces as Mr. Geezil says. If he insists give him the structure I've told you of Mice. The experiment of making a play that can be read or a novel that can be played. Trying to make a new form that will take some of the techniques of both. Maybe he can build a story on that and will be able to leave me to my "pack of lumbering dogs." Did you see that press release? Toby had become a *pack*. Toby by the way is going to stay with a friend until we get back. Maybe you would do well to show Mr. Woollcott this page. I'm sure that of his own experience he will know that the pressures exerted by publicity are unendurable.

In case of terrible need, you can radio me on the Sagebrush. By the way, if there's any mess please let me know. A letter would reach me c/o the ship in Philadelphia. If there is a fuss we could get off there and go in on a train. I want to get in and settled quietly.

See you all soon.

John S.

After a visit of several months in the Soviet Union and Scandinavia, John and Carol Steinbeck returned to New York, where preparations for the stage production of *Of Mice and Men* were going forward. Kaufman invited Steinbeck to his Bucks County home to make final changes in the script before rehearsals began.

Meanwhile, the "gift" edition of *The Red Pony*—a pet project of Pascal Covici's—had been published.

To Lawrence Clark Powell

Someplace in
Pennsylvania
[Bucks County]
August 23 [1937]

Dear Larry:

Just got in from Sweden a few days ago, hence the delay in answering your letter. Doing some play work down here and in a couple of weeks we'll start home. I'm thoroughly tired of moving around. It's out of my system for some time, I hope. I was expecting a howl about the price of The Red Pony. I wouldn't pay ten dollars for a Gutenberg Bible. In this case, I look at it this way. Covici loves beautiful books. These are old stories reprinted and they don't amount to much anyway so if he wants to make a pretty book, why not? The funny thing is that they're over-subscribed, about five hundred. I didn't know there were that many damn fools in the world —with 10 bucks, I mean. I don't let Covici dictate one word about how I write and I try never to make a suggestion about publishing to him.

Your bibliography is very flattering. I can't think my work deserves it nor can I believe there would be enough general interest to justify any investment in it. However, I don't think there would be any objection on Covici's part. I couldn't very well do a preface. It would be too much like singing at my own funeral. I mean it would be such an egotistical thing to do and I'm not feeling egotistical.

As for the foreign reprints—maybe McIntosh and Otis could tell you. I don't know. And campus publications—I can't remember either. This material is bound to be lousy. There was very little anyway. I wasn't well liked in college and with reason as I remember it.

I hope I'll see you before too long. Let me hear from you.

John S.

While in Sweden, the Steinbecks had become friends of the painter Bo Beskow, four years Steinbeck's junior. They had met in the corridor of the Covici-Friede offices in New York the previous winter: Beskow was there in connection with his mother Elsa Beskow's widely known children's books.

"Bumped into each other in the corridor," Beskow recalls in a recent letter. "The publisher said, 'Mr. Steinbeck has written a book, just out, would you like a copy?' John mumbled something and the publisher translated: 'Mr. and Mrs. Steinbeck are going to Russia and will pass Stockholm.' I gave him my address and went home and read the book in bed to put me to sleep. But it kept me awake to the last word and long after that. I was excited, having *Of Mice and Men* thrown at me without ever having heard of John Steinbeck. They came to Stockholm that summer and we struck a friendship—what warmth and light and fun, those weeks."

Beskow, at this time, had just won first prize in a nationwide mural competition. Later he was to achieve an international reputation for, among other works, his two murals and his portrait of Dag Hammarskjöld in the United Nations Building, New York, and his stained glass windows in Swedish cathedrals. In the summer of 1937 he did the first of three portraits of Steinbeck.

140

To Mr. and Mrs. Bo Beskow

Los Gatos
[1937]

Dear Muggins and Bo:

We have missed you very much. We wish you had come with us and were here. Before I left New York I sent three books. Will you let me know when you receive them? I mean with customs and all, I'd like to know they got there. We drove across the country. Our darling dog is well and happy and now we are settled. Muggins' letter came today and made us happy and sad too. Do write to us. People here marvel at Bo's portrait. Pat Covici wanted you to try to have it photographed in color at his expense. He said he would write you about it.

The little Wilhelmson boat was a joy. We played poker with the master and the steward all the way to New York. It is hot in N. Y. We went to Pennsylvania and finished up the play—back to N. Y. for casting and then we bought a Chevrolet and drove home. That's our history. Now I must get to work.

> Donald Oenslager, who designed the sets and lighting for *Of Mice and Men,* remembered that
>
> "Prior to rehearsals, there was a meeting of the director, George S. Kaufman, John Steinbeck, myself and the producer, Sam H. Harris in Harris' cubicle office on the second floor of the Music Box Theatre. There were both general and detailed discussions on the production. At the conclusion of the meeting, John Steinbeck rose and said that he felt all was in good hands and that his presence was no longer necessary; whereupon he departed for California."
>
> This departure, and the fact that he never returned were to have repercussions later. Steinbeck continues to Bo Beskow:

We have a blood hound supposedly on its way here from Chicago by express and it hasn't come and we can't go out

141

because it might come in our absence and so we wait here for it.

Autumn came yesterday with little winds and today it is really here and the oaks are beginning to lose their leaves. We are going to do some building, among other things a little swimming pool so you must come soon to jump into it.

I have a lot of work to do, must read proof on the last acting version of Mice which then goes to the printer. And I have written no letters since we got home. This is the first. The war cloud is very heavy now. The Japanese affair is close to us but I don't think it would be easy to get this people to fight. We aren't like Europe. The Government can't start a war and just have the people fall in line.

bye and write soon and keep us posted.

I'm sure that our meeting was not one of those things that happens and ends. We are positive of that now. So keep in touch until the time that you will be here.

> love to both of you
> jon

The play, *Of Mice and Men,* with Wallace Ford as George, Broderick Crawford as Lennie, and Claire Luce in the nameless but pivotal role of Curley's Wife, opened at the Music Box Theatre in New York on November 23, 1937. It was an immediate success and ran for 207 performances. Steinbeck later recalled that Elizabeth Otis had given a party after the opening for members of the agency staff and other friends, and that they made a telephone call to Los Gatos to report the evening's triumph. Each, he remembered, said, "Well, we're all here and we've all seen the show."

To Elizabeth Otis,
Annie Laurie Williams,
and Mavis McIntosh

Los Gatos
[November 24, 1937]
Thursday night

Dear Elizabeth and Annie Laurie and Mavis:

You don't know how good it was to hear your voices and how sweet it was of you to take the trouble to phone. It was a pretty exciting night even for us, what with Pat sending wires after every act. I didn't feel it at all until about six that evening and then my stomach began turning loops of stage-fright. I was very glad when it was over and the audience hadn't stoned the cast and mailed poisoned candy to me. A wire from Kaufman says it seems pretty good but he can't tell yet how good. I mean a good first night reaction doesn't mean that it won't close pretty soon, does it? That's a kind of a picked audience and the tough ones are the trippers from Ogden who keep Broadway running. I report with pleasure that on the basis of that first night I am going to get a new typewriter. We've never had one that wasn't pretty decrepit. Anyway, I'm glad it had a good opening and I'll be very anxious to hear the little sidelights that you people can tell. We were all so hysterical over the phone that there wasn't time for much but squeaks of joy. Do write about it, please.

Joe Jackson wired from the Chronicle for consensus of opinion of critics and it came through and they will run it Sunday. So darned nice of him to do it and the critics didn't take pot shots at it as I thoroughly expected them to. I think Carol would really have liked to be there but I couldn't get her to go.

I have a lot of letters to write so I'll get down to Elizabeth's letter which was waiting for me when I got back tonight. I'm glad about the stories. I hope that Esquire knows that this story ["The Snake"] was printed in the little Monterey magazine traded for the use of a horse. You know that. I don't want any kickback. Please make it clear to them. The Murder reprint is swell. Such a lot of money. Now I know I will get a new typewriter. I'll send pictures of the new dog just as soon as I have some of them developed. It is very quiet here after a very very hectic day. I'm bringing you a new client. Louis Paul. He's a swell egg and you will like him. And he's well enough known so that it may not be hard to sell his stories. I like him immensely. Again thank you millions for everything you have all done. I appreciate it and lay out my heart for you to walk on.

John

To George S. Kaufman

Los Gatos
[November 1937]

Dear George:

As the reviews come in it becomes more and more apparent that you have done a great job. I knew you would of course but there is a curious gap between the thing in your hand and the thing set down and you've jumped that gap. It's a strange kind of humbling luck we have. Carol and I have talked of it a number of times. That we—obscure people out of a place no one ever heard of—should have our first play directed and produced by the greatest director of our time—will not bear too close inspection for fear we may catch the gods of fortune at work and catching them, anger them so they hate us. Already I have made propitiation—thrown my dear ring in the sea and I hope no big fish brings it back to me.

To say thank you is ridiculous for you can't thank a man for good work any more than you can thank him for being himself. But one can be very glad he is himself and that is what we are—very glad you are George Kaufman.

It doesn't matter a damn whether this show runs a long time. It came to life for one night anyway, and really to life, and that's more than anyone has any right to hope.

Sometimes in working, the people in my head become

much realler than I am. I have had letters. It seems that for two hours you made your play far more real than its audience and only the play existed. I wish I could transport into some mathematical equation, my feeling, so that it might be a communication unmistakable and unchanging.

And that's all.
John

To the McIntosh and Otis staff

Los Gatos
[November 1937]

Dear All:

It is getting to be almost a daily habit to write to you in answer to nice letters. A friend of mine, hearing that the play has run a week without closing, has christened it Abie's Irish Mice. I like that very much.

If you get any request for stories for Hollywood remember there is still that old Cup which is the only thing I have ever done that would make a good picture. Also, I like the idea of breaking up the Pastures and selling it, but this idea is punitive. It would please me to have them buy little by little what they refused to take as a whole, and when they could have had it very cheaply.

You may notice that I have a new typewriter. We have never had a good one in our lives. Always something of about nineteen twelve. But after we saw this play was going to run a week at least, we went out and got a new one, well—a nearly new one. And look what it has—! ñ ´. A tilda, an exclamation and a grave accent. Or rather an acute. I don't know where to use a grave and nobody knows where to use a circumflex so we didn't get them. But isn't it beautiful? I hadn't realized that science had done so much while I worked on the 1912 model. This is so wonderful that I just write the first letter and the machine spells the rest of the word out. It is going to be a great boon to my spelling. You will notice too that this letter is longer than usual. That is because I can push down these keys with one hand instead of standing up and using both hands.

I'm suspicious of all these nice criticisms. They are out of character. Even Nathan [George Jean Nathan, drama critic]. I was looking for something better from him. I thought he would maintain his aloofness anyway. But even he won't disagree.

That's all I think. And thank you for writing so often.

Love to you all,
John

Jack Kirkland, adapter of Erskine Caldwell's phenomenally successful *Tobacco Road*, had taken an option on *Tortilla Flat*. When he finished his dramatization, he sent it to Los Gatos for Steinbeck's reaction.

To Jack Kirkland

Los Gatos
November 31, 1937
Tuesday

Dear Jack:

Your manuscript came this morning and we, Carol and I, got right to it and spent the day in howls of laughter. It is a gorgeously funny thing and I am very much pleased with it. It should keep an audience in hysterics and I imagine it will get you some attention from the police but you have done it in purity of heart and that is what I was anxious about. It doesn't in the least matter what a man does, it is his manner in doing it. In the criticism I am about to make, some is

146

technical and some, the last scene criticism, is put in because such a thing couldn't happen, it is out of character and completely socially impossible.

The early technical criticisms are two. First the Spanish. A number of times you have used "A donde vas?" as a greeting and such it could be outside but never in the house for it means "where are you going?" You might say it to a man going by the house. Next, you have referred to Sweets as Senora when she is unmarried. Now she might be called Senora in ridicule but from the attitude of the friends I think they and Mrs. Morales would call her Senorita and do it with emphasis.

Next, check all the Mexican phrases with a Mexican. I can't go over all of it unless I can talk with you and the nuance of value in every Spanish phrase is tremendous. In Act one you have Sweets call the others "You paisanos." It wouldn't be done. Paisano is not a term of opprobrium but a declaration of relationship. You say, "You are my paisano." Or, to show you have lived here a great while, "I am paisano." In the first case it means you are my countryman and in the second I am a native to this place.

Next. You have the term "get into bed with" used openly and before two women. I don't think that would happen. I think some circumlocution would be used probably with gestures to clarify it.

Next—in the first act you have made a half gallon of wine go a hell of a long way. Two gallons would hardly suffice. I could drink the half myself.

Now let me get to the last act and the quarrel between Pilon and the priest which I object to. This could not happen. It is unthinkable that Pilon should be unmannerly toward a priest no matter how much he might hate him and he doesn't hate him, and it is even more unthinkable for a priest to be curt with a parishioner. The discipline is too great. Third, unless a man has been excommunicated it is not in the power of a priest to refuse him last unction or any sacrament.

I am sending you another version of the scene. Please understand that I am not muscling in and that this is only a suggestion. Use it if you wish or don't use it.

Don't think me obstreperous in this matter. I don't want to be. I think your play is gorgeous. If you can get the proper actors you will roll them in the aisles.

I wish to goodness you could come west and could talk

about it. I could lead you to hear the real speech spoken so you could get the tone of it in your head.

We'll have a telephone in a few days and then we won't be quite so much out of touch as we have been.

Good bye.

John

To Elizabeth Otis and Annie Laurie Williams

[Los Gatos]
December [1937]

Dear Elizabeth and Annie Laurie:

The dogs of Hollywood are loose. A week ago some one from a Hollywood agency called up and I had to go to town to answer a long distance call and it was a Mr. Marcus of the Myron Selznick office who wanted to come up here to discuss my Hollywood affairs. I told him I had no Hollywood affairs and told him to get in touch with you as my sole agents. I thought that would stop things. But last night there was another long distance call and I had to go to town again to get it and it was Zeppo Marx with a very attractive offer. I didn't ask what it was. I said no and he said it would please me and I said no again and he said he would write me because Hollywood wasn't the same as it used to be and my friends like G. Kaufman had changed their attitude and why shouldn't I? This was funny for George held forth to me for an hour on how he hated Hollywood. Anyway he said he would write and I said you were sole agents and he said he would write anyway. When his letter comes I will send it to you and you can kill that once for all. I don't intend to go to Hollywood at any price whatever and this is not a hold out.

Our telephone will be in by this week end and then at least I won't have to make a five mile run into town to say no.

I have never before come in contact with anyone to whom the word no had no meaning whatever but these seem to be people like that. Let them buy stories that were not written for them, except IDB [*In Dubious Battle*] but I won't work for them.

This is a mad letter. It was raining when I had to go to town last night and Marx had put in the call and then had gone to dinner so I had to wait for him and I'm still mad.

john

To Annie Laurie Williams

TELEGRAM

SAN JOSE [LOS GATOS]
DECEMBER 8, 1937

PLEASE QUERY KIRKLAND REGARDING POSSIBILITY OF COMING WEST TO DISCUSS TORTILLA STOP WILL HELP HIM TWO WEEKS IN REWRITING BETWEEN US PLAY SEEMS LOUSIER EVERY READING DIALOGUE IS OFF TONE VULGARITY CREEPS IN PLAY CHANGES TEMPO AND IN MANY CASES IS DULL BE DISCREETLY PRESSING AND PLEASE WIRE HIS ANSWER

JOHN

To Annie Laurie Williams

Los Gatos
[December 9, 1937]

Dear Annie Laurie:

I suppose I shouldn't have sent that wire. What happened was that we read the thing out loud and it sounded so bad that I got to feeling low and I thought that if only Jack Kirkland would come out we might fix the thing up. You see it doesn't maintain its tone and there is a terrible matter of talk

149

that doesn't lead to anything. It is just a series of black-outs now. I would work with him if he would come out.

There are so many little undertones that he has got wrong. I don't want to maintain my book but I would like to maintain the people as I know them. Let me give you an example. Jack makes them want wine and need wine and suffer for wine whereas they want the thing wine does. They are not drunkards at all. They like the love and fights that come with wine, rather than the wine itself. Many of his scenes are swell. I hope you didn't hurt his feelings and I know you didn't. The whole last scene seems like coming back to someplace where you never were. You are told that Danny is a hell of a guy but on the stage he never proves it and the audience is going to wonder what all the shooting is about. I think Danny should be built up. I think the differences between the others should be shown. His casting of the play is excellent. I mean into scenes. It is only in the details, in the dialogue and in the tempo that it seems to me to need working on. Some of it is very very funny and some of it now on the third reading seems tiresome.

But then let it go. I'll ok the script all except the priest scene just as it stands if he wants me to. But he is going to find that a Mexican with an accent is not going to be able to say many of his speeches.

These are little things but I have a feeling that unless they are taken care of, the play is not going to have any sound of authenticity. You can argue that it doesn't matter because no one in the east ever heard of these people, anyway. Just remember some of the phony dialect in pictures and you will see that it does matter. No one believes that, in fact scorns it. I wish now I had not acted so precipitately about the wire. But I had hit bottom. I don't feel quite so badly about it now but I do think it would be better with some more work.

I think that is all and please don't give Kirkland the idea that I am riding him.

John

In addition to buying several stories that *Esquire* had previously rejected, Arnold Gingrich, its editor, sent Steinbeck a gift of a watch.

To Arnold Gingrich

Los Gatos
January 5, 1938

Dear Mr. G:

In writing to thank you for the beautiful little watch, I am quite swathed in a kind of wonder and in a little fear. I am quite sure you could not have known that in me you had probably the most profound, double-barrelled, synchro-mesh, watch tragedy the world has ever known. I have not spoken of this before. It was too sharp.

Watches from the beginning filled me not only with long-ing but with sorrow and nostalgia and a little despair. But so vital is hope that when I came near to graduating from grammar school, when Elgin and Waltham were explaining in full pages the remoteness of success to a watchless person, I must admit that a little hope flickered. And so I graduated —and I got a signet ring.

All through my two years of first year Latin and my year and a half of second year Latin my time sense was so utterly undeveloped that I rarely got to school on time and some-times left long before it was dismissed. It was only in the last six months that the little worm of spirit moved. With a surge I finished the last month of second year Latin in six weeks. I think I hoped to bribe some kinds of gods with this sacrifice. And so I graduated. I got a Waterman's pen and pencil set.

I think you can understand that my interest in higher edu-cation was nonexistent. My parents persuaded and cursed and appealed to my pride. I weakened and went to college almost frantically unenthusiastic. I had become so antisocial that I am the only person in the world who was ever black-balled from a journalistic fraternity and at a time when they needed the initiation fee. I dragged through three years not bravely but dully. I thought pain could no longer strike. And then came the time—and I couldn't take it. I didn't graduate.

The succeeding years have not been happy but I have been busy. And my sense of time, stunted from the beginning, grew so weak and thin that not only did I not know what time it was nor what day it was but once or twice have been three years out on a check stub.

I am trying to reorganize myself. Am I too old? My bones are brittle. I have sometimes to get up in the night. I feel that my fecundity is not eternal. Oh, I can feel the years a little particularly just before a rain. And now—I get a watch. I wonder if such things always come too late. I wonder if I can go back. I wonder for that matter if I can tell time!

> Sincerely,
> John Steinbeck

Carol Steinbeck went to New York for the opening of the Jack Kirkland adaptation of *Tortilla Flat* on January 12, 1938.

To Mr. and Mrs. Joseph Henry Jackson
IN SAN FRANCISCO

[Pacific Grove]
[January 1938]

Dear Joe and Charlotte:

It would seem that things are piling up which will keep me from going up this week end.

It is pouring rain today. By now you probably know what happened to Tortilla Flat. It was, says Carol, the worst thing she ever saw. The lines were bad but the directing and casting were even worse. The thing closed after four performances, thank God. We are really pretty happy about the whole thing because we think this may be so discouraging to Paramount that they will not try to make a picture at all now.

I get sadder and sadder. The requests and demands for money pour in. It is perfectly awful. WPA worker in pencil from Illinois—"you have got luck and I got no luck. My boy needs a hundderd dollar operation. Please send a hundderd dollars. I will pay it back." That sort of thing. Getting worse every day. Maybe Cuernavaca isn't so far off at that if this doesn't die down. "Liberal negro school going to close if money isn't forthcoming. Can you stand by and see this school close after fifteen years?" Someone told a Salinas ladies' club that I had made three hundred thousand dollars this year. It is driving me crazy. "If you will just send me a railroad ticket to Boise I can come to California and get rid of my rheumatism." They're nightmarish. Some may be phonys but so damned many of them aren't. Nearly every one is a desperate catching at a million-to-one chance. The damned things haunt me. There's no way of getting over the truth and that we have very little money. It's nibbling me to death.

I think Carol is having a marvelous time. She is so rushed that she can hardly breathe but in spite of that she gets off a letter nearly every day. I think she is taking New York and picking its bones. She is seeing everything and doing everything. We will be poor little provincials to her from now on. I'm really glad she went alone because I am prone to say oh to hell with it and not go the places I've wanted to go (my grammar will give you a mild idea of my mental condition).

> bye and
> thanks for asking me.
> john

It was probably unprecedented in the history of the theatre that an actress, midway in the run of a successful play, should begin to have misgivings about her interpretation of her role. But Annie Laurie Williams reported that this was what was happening to Claire Luce in *Of Mice and Men* and asked Steinbeck to write the actress about the character of Curley's Wife.

To Claire Luce

Los Gatos
[1938]

Dear Miss Luce:

Annie Laurie says you are worried about your playing of the part of Curley's wife although from the reviews it appears that you are playing it marvelously. I am deeply grateful to you and to the others in the cast for your feeling about the play. You have surely made it much more than it was by such a feeling.

About the girl—I don't know of course what you think about her, but perhaps if I should tell you a little about her as I know her, it might clear your feeling about her.

She grew up in an atmosphere of fighting and suspicion. Quite early she learned that she must never trust any one but she was never able to carry out what she learned. A natural trustfulness broke through constantly and every time it did, she got hurt. Her moral training was most rigid. She was told over and over that she must remain a virgin because that was the only way she could get a husband. This was harped on so often that it became a fixation. It would have been impossible to seduce her. She had only that one thing to sell and she knew it.

Now, she was trained by threat not only at home but by other kids. And any show of fear or weakness brought an instant persecution. She learned she had to be hard to cover her fright. And automatically she became hardest when she was most frightened. She is a nice, kind girl and not a floozy. No man has ever considered her as anything except a girl to try to make. She has never talked to a man except in the sexual fencing conversation. She is not highly sexed particularly but knows instinctively that if she is to be noticed at all,

154

it will be because some one finds her sexually desirable.

As to her actual sexual life—she has had none except with Curley and there has probably been no consummation there since Curley would not consider her gratification and would probably be suspicious if she had any. Consequently she is a little starved. She knows utterly nothing about sex except the mass of misinformation girls tell one another. If anyone—a man or a woman—ever gave her a break—treated her like a person—she would be a slave to that person. Her craving for contact is immense but she, with her background, is incapable of conceiving any contact without some sexual context. With all this—if you knew her, if you could ever break down the thousand little defenses she has built up, you would find a nice person, an honest person, and you would end up by loving her. But such a thing can never happen.

I hope you won't think I'm preaching. I've known this girl and I'm just trying to tell you what she is like. She is afraid of everyone in the world. You've known girls like that, haven't you? You can see them in Central Park on a hot night. They travel in groups for protection. They pretend to be wise and hard and voluptuous.

I have a feeling that you know all this and that you are doing all this. Please forgive me if I seem to intrude on your job. I don't intend to and I am only writing this because Annie Laurie said you wondered about the girl. It's a devil of a hard part. I am very happy that you have it.

Sincerely,
John Steinbeck

Annie Laurie Williams reported that *Of Mice and Men* continued to play to full houses on Broadway; that the management planned a road tour for the fall; that she had sold English rights, then Scandinavian; and that Warner Brothers was showing interest for a film because one of its stars, James Cagney, was eager to play George. But success had another face. As Steinbeck had already written to Elizabeth Otis:

"My mail has, with the exception of your letters, become a thing of horror. Swarms of people— money, speeches, orders and this autograph business. I didn't know it was such a mania. Well, I'm through. I'm signing no books for anyone except friends. It's getting worse all the time."

But these were not the bitterest fruits of success. A young woman, whom Steinbeck had known as a child, claimed to be pregnant by him. The charge proved deeply upsetting. At the same time, a breach with his old friend, George Albee, took place. "You may be sure," writes his brother Richard Albee, who survives, "that the basic cause was artistic jealousy, and of course it was on the part of George, not John."

To George Albee

Los Gatos
[1938]

Dear George:

The reason for your suspicion is well founded. This has been a difficult and unpleasant time. There has been nothing good about it. In this time my friends have rallied around, all except you. Every time there has been a possibility of putting a bad construction on anything I have done, you have put such a construction.

Some kind friend has told me about it every time you have stabbed me in the back and that whether I wanted to know it or not. I didn't want to know it really. If such things had been reported as coming from more than one person it would be easy to discount the whole thing but there has been only one source. Now I know that such things grow out of an unhappiness in you and for a long time I was able to reason so and to keep on terms of some kind of amicability. But gradually I found I didn't trust you at all, and when I knew that then I couldn't be around you any more. It became obvious that anything I said or did in your presence or wrote to you would be warped viciously and repeated and then the repetition was repeated to me and the thing was just too damned painful. I tried to sidestep, just to fade out of your picture. But that doesn't work either.

I'd like to be friends with you, George, but I can't if I have to wear a mail shirt the whole time. I wish to God your unhappiness could find some other outlet. But I can't consider you a friend when out of every contact there comes some intentionally wounding thing. This has been the most difficult time in my life.

I've needed help and trust and the benefit of the doubt, because I've tried to beat the system which destroys every writer, and from you have come only wounds and kicks in the face. And that is the reason and I think you always knew it was the reason.

john

And now if you want to quarrel, it will at least be an honest quarrel and not boudoir pin pricking.

To Elizabeth Otis

Los Gatos
February 1938

Dear Elizabeth:

Came yesterday morning the check for royalties. Thank you. It has been raining for one solid week and we are thoroughly sick of it. Of course that will make a rich year but it is the longest and wettest rain I remember and it has sealed us in the house. Carol has a sore throat but seems finally to be licking it. The dogs are nuts for exercise.

Carol had such a good time. It comes out little by little. She couldn't remember much when she first got home but every day she remembers something. I don't think it is very real to her now. Just something she dreamed. You were all very wonderful to her. I think it has done something permanent to her ego which never was properly developed.

Unpleasant thing. I finally broke open the thing with

George. At least now if he wants to quarrel it won't be lady quarreling. I feel better about that, but I don't like such things at all.

I'm so darned glad to have Carol back. She can answer the phone and I am permanently out of town. The crowd of speaking engagements continues. I don't know why this insistence on speaking. I am not going to do it, but Carol can say no in much nicer ways than I can.

I imagine the _____ thing will die now [the paternity charge]. It would have been so easy for them if I had kept it from Carol or if I had something to lose so that I would pay rather than fight. Maybe the attorney figured something like that. But even if there had been relations between this girl and me, Carol would have known about it and that would have fallen down in any case. I think Carol's method in a pinch is good. I have several marks on my body, one at least of them disfiguring, and apparent enough so that a wife or a mistress would be sure to have noticed them. Failure to know them would of course prove something. The worst one, a huge empyema scar, though, could be seen in a bathing suit. But I don't think _____ [the girl] would remember that. But I did teach all the kids to swim and she might, but there are others. I hope it never gets that far.

I must go over into the interior valleys. There are about five thousand families starving to death over there, not just hungry but actually starving. The government is trying to feed them and get medical attention to them with the fascist group of utilities and banks and huge growers sabotaging the thing all along the line and yelling for a balanced budget. In one tent there are twenty people quarantined for smallpox and two of the women are to have babies in that tent this week. I've tied into the thing from the first and I must get down there and see it and see if I can't do something to help knock these murderers on the heads. Do you know what they're afraid of? They think that if these people are allowed to live in camps with proper sanitary facilities, they will organize and that is the bugbear of the large landowner and the corporation farmer. The states and counties will give them nothing because they are outsiders. But the crops of any part of this state could not be harvested without these outsiders. I'm pretty mad about it. No word of this outside because when I have finished my job the jolly old associated farmers will be after my scalp again.

158

I guess that is all. Funny how mean and little books become in the face of such tragedies.

John

To Elizabeth Otis

Los Gatos
February 14, 1938
Monday

Dear Elizabeth:

Your letter this morning with check and lots of information. Thank you very much. I'm glad the paternity suit matter is nearly over. And I'm desperately sorry for the break with George but I think it is healthier in the open.

I don't know whether I'll go south or not but I must go to Visalia. Four thousand families, drowned out of their tents are really starving to death. The resettlement administration of the government asked me to write some news stories. The newspapers won't touch the stuff but they will under my byline. The locals are fighting the government bringing in food and medicine. I'm going to try to break the story hard enough so that food and drugs can get moving. Shame and a hatred of publicity will do the job to the miserable local bankers. I'll let you know more about this when I get back from the area. Talk about Spanish children. The death of children by starvation in our valleys is simply staggering. I've got to do it. If I can sell the articles I'll use the proceeds for serum and such. Codliver oil would give the live kids a better chance. Of course no individual effort will help. Ten thousand people are affected in one area. Anyway, I'll do what I can.

The whole state is flooded you know. This is the 19th day of rain.

I guess this is all. I'll let you know what happens.

Bye,
John

To Elizabeth Bailey

[Los Gatos]
[Spring 1938]

Dear Godmother:

I am so sorry you are ill. This continued rain makes for illness. I have a cold but I can't take it very seriously. I've just come from the area where people are not only ill but hungry too. Get well quickly.

Always I hope that sometime I'm not going to be too busy —that sometime I will be able to write a long letter without the feeling that I am playing hookey from work.

Right now with the grass coming up thickly and the mustard beginning to bloom, I am filled with a thousand little memory nostalgias. I'd like to think about them—about how the black birds build nests on the mustard stalks and how Glen Grave's father was angry with us for tramping down his grain to get to the nests. And how six of us on a sunny morning solemnly burned our names on a fence picket with a burning glass—and said—"In fifty years we'll come back and look at it." But you know I did go back (it wasn't fifty years though) and the picket was gone.

Such nonsense. I hope you are better now. It will be a good spring, I think.

love
John

To Elizabeth Otis

Los Gatos
March 7, 1938

Dear Elizabeth:

Dear Elizabeth:

I shouldn't have repeated that for the sake of the letter but it was true enough in intention and quite unconscious. I guess unconscious is very correct as an evaluation of my condition. Just got back from another week in the field. The floods have aggravated the starvation and sickness. I went down for Life this time. Fortune wanted me to do an article for them but I won't. I don't like the audience. Then Life sent me down with a photographer from its staff and we took a lot of pictures of the people. They guarantee not to use it if they change it and will send me the proofs. They paid my expenses and will put up money for the help of some of these people.

I'm sorry but I simply can't make money on these people. That applies to your query about an article for a national magazine. The suffering is too great for me to cash in on it. I hope this doesn't sound either quixotic or martyrish to you. A short trip into the fields where the water is a foot deep in the tents and the children are up on the beds and there is no food and no fire, and the county has taken off all the nurses because "the problem is so great that we can't do anything about it." So they do nothing. And we found a boy in jail for a felony because he stole two old radiators because his mother was starving to death and in stealing them he broke a little padlock on a shed. We'll either spring him or the district attorney will do the rest of his life explaining.

But you see what I mean. It is the most heartbreaking thing in the world. If Life does use the stuff there will be lots of pictures and swell ones. It will give you an idea of the kind of people they are and the kind of faces. I break myself every time I go out because the argument that one person's effort can't really do anything doesn't seem to apply when you come on a bunch of starving children and you have a little

161

money. I can't rationalize it for myself anyway. So don't get me a job for a slick. I want to put a tag of shame on the greedy bastards who are responsible for this but I can best do it through newspapers.

I'm going to see the Secretary of Agriculture in a little while and try to find out for my own satisfaction anyway just how much of the government's attitude is political and how much humanitarian. Then I'll know what course to take.

I'm in a mess trying to catch up with things that have piled up in the week I was gone. And of course I was in the mud for three days and nights and I have a nice cold to beat, but I haven't time right now for a cold so I won't get a very bad one.

Sorry for the hectic quality of this letter. I am hectic and angry.

Thank you for everything.

Bye,
John

Life did not actually publish anything about the migrants' camps till more than a year later, after *The Grapes of Wrath* had made its impact. In its issue of June 5, 1939, it ran a picture story with captions by Steinbeck, some of which were quotations from the novel.

"I've been writing on the novel [about vigilantes] but I've had to destroy it several times," he wrote Elizabeth Otis shortly afterwards. "I don't seem to know any more about writing a novel than I did ten years ago. You'd think I would learn. I suppose I could dash it off but I want this one to be a pretty good one. There's another difficulty too. I'm trying to write history while it is happening and I don't want to be wrong."

To Elizabeth Otis

Los Gatos
May 2, 1938

Dear Elizabeth:

Your letters both to Carol and to me came this morning and were very welcome.

This is the first really free letter I have written for a long time. Yesterday or rather the day before yesterday I finished the first draft of this book. Now just the rewriting, but a lot of it because it is pretty badly done. It is short, just a few thousand over sixty thousand words. We'll finish it and send it on and if you think it is no good we'll burn it up and forget it.

It is a mean, nasty book and if I could make it nastier I would.

This morning I got the swellest letter of my life. From a man named Lemuel Gadberry, believe it or not, and he says he bought m and m [*Of Mice and Men*] and feels that he not only has been degraded in reading it but that he was cheated out of two dollars. I have just written him a long letter praising his high soul and offering to return his two dollars with six percent interest on receipt of the book, that or a copy of When Knighthood Was In Flower.

I have a very good working streak on and, when I finish this rewriting, I think perhaps I will do a few short stories. It is a long time since I have done any. I want to do a few essays too but not necessarily for publication. Feeling very literary these days with words crowding up to come tumbling out and the time between putting them down crowding with them like the forming eggs in a chicken or the spare fangs of a rattlesnake. But I like it even if the words are no good. It is still good fun to write them.

Bye, and
love to you all,
John

Word came that *Of Mice and Men,* the play, had been given the Critics' Circle award. Steinbeck responded to the news with a telegram.

To the Critics' Circle

TELEGRAM

LOS GATOS
APRIL 23, 1938

CRITICS CIRCLE, CARE ANNIE LAURIE WILLIAMS 18 EAST 41 ST NYC

GENTLEMEN: I HAVE ALWAYS CONSIDERED CRITICS AS AUTHORS NATURAL ENEMIES NOW I FEEL VERY MILLENIAL BUT A LITTLE TIMID TO BE LYING DOWN WITH THE LION THIS DISTURBANCE OF THE NATURAL BALANCE MIGHT CAUSE A PLAGUE OF PLAYWRIGHTS I AM HIGHLY HONORED BY YOUR GOOD OPINION BUT MY EGOTISTICAL GRATIFICATION IS RUINED BY A SNEAKING SUSPICION THAT GEORGE KAUFMAN AND THE CAST DESERVE THEM MORE THAN I. I DO HOWEVER TAKE THE RESPONSIBILITY OF THANKING YOU.

JOHN STEINBECK

To Elizabeth Otis

Los Gatos
May 1938

Dear Elizabeth:

There seem to be so many places for me to put my foot even when I try not to walk about very much. What was the matter with that telegram I sent to the Critics' Circle? Annie Laurie seemed ashamed of it. I thought it was all right. Carol thought it was all right. Maybe it got mixed up in the sending. It wasn't abject but I didn't think a group of men as

164

eminent as that would care for an abject one. I guess I just haven't any social sense. So many things can happen. I have never submitted a novel to the Commonwealth Club here which gives a medal every year but Pat has. This year he forgot to or something and I understand that it is being spread that I think I am too good to compete in local things now. Just little things like that all the time. And this not going to New York to see this play which is being used everywhere now (it has got to the fourth-rate movie columnists by now). I'd like to have seen the play but I wouldn't go six thousand miles to see the opening of the second coming of Christ. Why is it so damned important?

> George Kaufman was offended. Coolness between the two men lasted for many years.

I have the letter from George Jean Nathan [President of the Critics' Circle] but will not answer until the plaque comes. Now what in the world will I do with a plaque? Melt it down perhaps and buy a pair of shoes for someone.

I am sending you one of the sets of articles which were just printed from my articles on migrants. The proceeds go to help these people.

Thanks for the checks. What a terrible lot of money. But there's some use for it all the time.

Bye,
John

To George Jean Nathan

[Los Gatos]
May 23 [1938]

Dear Mr. Nathan:

After some delay, the Critics' Circle plaque arrived today. It is a very handsome thing. I thank the Circle again. I like to think there is a perfect line of conduct for every situation.

I've never met any situation like this before. But I do remember a speech of appreciation made by a rider at a dinner where he had received a pair of silver spurs for a championship in ear notching and castrating calves. Cheered to his feet, the winner stood up blushing violently and made the following speech—"Aw shit, boys—Jesus Christ—why—goddam it—oh! the hell with it," and sat down to tremendous applause. You will find that this brief speech has in it every element of greatness in composition—beginning, middle, end, self-deprecation, a soaring quality in the middle and it ends not on a cynical or defeatist note but rather in a realization that nothing he could say could adequately convey his feeling.

It is a beautiful plaque, and I am very proud to have it.

Sincerely,
John Steinbeck

The vigilante novel was abandoned about this time and destroyed without ever being sent to McIntosh and Otis.

Still using the material he had gathered in the migrant camps, he now embarked on a new work, which, though it would remain for several months untitled, would become *The Grapes of Wrath*.

To Elizabeth Otis

Los Gatos
June 1, 1938

Dear Elizabeth:

Your letter and $475 check arrived. I think this is the windup [of the New York run of *Of Mice and Men*] but Carol thinks there is one more [check]. However it is, we've had much more than we deserve. And with care it will keep us for a long, long time.

This is a very happy time. The new book is going well. Too fast. I'm having to hold it down. I don't want it to go so fast for fear the tempo will be fast and this is a plodding, crawling book. So I'm holding it down to approximately six pages a day. That doesn't mean anything about finishing time since perhaps fifty percent will be cut out. Anyway, it is a nice thing to be working and believing in my work again. I hope I can keep the drive all fall. I like it. I only feel whole and well when it is this way. I don't yet understand what happened or why the bad book should have cleared the air so completely for this one. I am simply glad that it is so.

Norwegian rights pay more than British. Maybe the income tax is less.

John.

To Annie Laurie Williams

[Los Gatos]
[July 1938]

Dear Annie Laurie:

Your good letter came this morning. I am very much pleased that the cast will remain intact or nearly [for the road tour of *Of Mice and Men*]. I'm afraid George K. is angry

167

with me for what he must think is a lack of interest. It isn't, but I had this new book on my soul. When it is done I'll be free to do a lot of things.

I am quite sure no picture company would want this new book whole and it is not for sale any other way. It pulls no punches at all and may get us all into trouble but if so—so. That's the way it is. Think I'll print a foreword warning sensitive people to let it alone. I took three days off over the fourth. Getting back to work today. I've just scratched the surface so far. Carol thinks it is pretty good.

Can you get M & M licensed in England? I doubt it for general showing.

Please tell George K. he can make the changes he wishes in script.

> He was referring to the playing version for the cross-country tour. It was feared that sensibilities might prove too delicate for some of the play's language, considered at the time dangerously strong for all but urban areas.

I hope Pat doesn't lose money on the short stories. Competing with Hemingway isn't my idea of good business. [Ernest Hemingway's *The Fifth Column and The First Forty-Nine Stories* came out this year.]

I'll bet it is hot there now. Thank goodness I'm not there. But once this work is done I might do anything. It's the culmination of three years of work.

Have fun. I'm sick of holding a pen. I've done 2,200 words today. So long. Write often.

John

> It began to be apparent that Pascal Covici's firm, Covici-Friede, was having financial difficulties.

To Elizabeth Otis

Dear Elizabeth:

Your letter came this morning. I hope to God that Pat survives.

Eight more days and if nothing happens I should have half of my first draft of this novel done. Again that is not to be told. I'm glad about it though. With crossed fingers, I should have the whole first draft done in about two months and a half. But I've been lucky this far.

In the event the worst happens to Pat I think it would be just as well to be ready. Please use your own judgment entirely in picking a new publisher. I have no choice. I have one or two dislikes but I don't even know that they are fair. Get a Bradstreet report on whoever you pick. All things else being equal, pick the one who makes the highest offer. We'll have to pick up a year of royalties if Pat goes bankrupt. I think that hereafter, if I can get it, it might be a good idea to get all the advance possible. Why shouldn't we be getting the interest as well as the publisher? I'm not being grabby but printers practically always get paid. Writers are an afterthought.

Frankly this hasn't worried me a bit. We have enough to eat on for a long time to come. It does stop negotiations we were making for a little ranch in the hills. Have to stop that until the thing clears or doesn't. This place is getting built up and we have to move. Houses all around us now and so we will get back farther in the country. But next time we'll be in the middle of fifty acres, not two. I can hear the neighbors' stomachs rumbling. I hope to God Pat can do it and I will do anything to help him but hereafter I think the publisher will be the natural enemy. Pat is different.

Don't worry about it. We love you too and trust you and your judgment completely.

Bye. I'm sorry this is being a bother to you.

John

Covici-Friede went bankrupt and Pascal Covici, taking John Steinbeck with him, joined The Viking Press as a senior editor. Both men would remain with this publishing house for the rest of their lives.

Now the Steinbecks bought the ranch near Los Gatos that they had been negotiating for earlier. They lived in the existing ranch structure while they built a new house.

To Mr. and Mrs. Louis Paul

POSTCARD

[Los Gatos]
[September 1938]

Dear Louis and Mary:

We have a title at last. See how you like it. The Grapes of Wrath from Battle Hymn of the Republic. I think it is swell. Do you? Now both of us are working. Carol started typing from handwritten ms. She hopes to catch up before I am done. And at the rate she goes she surely will. Then we'll have a clear copy to work on. I'm even working today—Sat. Hope my energy holds out. Another 6 weeks should do it.

Love
John

To Elizabeth Otis

Los Gatos
September 10, 1938

Dear Elizabeth:

Your letter came this morning—Monday. I don't much understand the meaning of this new contract arrangement but with you there, thank heaven I don't have to. About the title —Pat wired that he liked it. And I too am glad because I like it better all the time. I think it is Carol's best title so far. I like it because it is a march and this book is a kind of march— because it is in our own revolutionary tradition and because in reference to this book it has a large meaning. And I like it because people know the Battle Hymn who don't know the Star Spangled Banner.

You are quite right, we are nearly nuts. The foundations of the new house are going in. Carol is typing mss (2nd draft) and I'm working on first. I can't tell when I will be done but Carol will have second done almost at the same time I have first. And—this is a secret—the 2nd draft is so clear and good that it, carefully and clearly corrected, will be what I submit. Carol's time is too valuable to do purely stenographic work. It will be very easy to read and what more can they want? And still I can't tell how much longer it will be nor how much time and I don't intend to think about it but I am fairly sure that another sixty days will see it done. I hope so. I've been sitting down so long I'm getting office spread. And I'm desperately tired but I want to finish. And meanwhile I feel as though shrapnel were bursting about my head. I only hope the book is some good. Can't tell yet at all. And I can't tell whether it is balanced. It is a slow, plodding book but I don't think it is dull.

I haven't left this desk since March, what with the other book and this one. When I'm done I'll probably go nuts like a spring lamb. Never have worked so hard and so long in my life. Probably good for me but I'm soft now physically and must get in some hard digging work when I finish. To harden up.

171

Elizabeth, I wish you would come out here to help us celebrate its finish. Couldn't you and Larry [Lawrence Kiser, Elizabeth Otis's husband] come out for Thanksgiving? We would have fun. Probably have to camp more or less but it would be a fine thing. You got very little rest this summer.

Love to all,
John

To Pascal Covici

Los Gatos
[October 1938]
Monday

Dear Pat:

We were in S. F. for a few days. Just got back today and found your letter waiting. We've been camping in the old kitchen. Carol hasn't been able to type because of the mess. Today, however, our rooms are done and she began work. I don't know how long it will take her. There have been delays about the house. I note your suggestion that I send pieces of the ms. Really I'd rather not. I want it all together and will send it all just as soon as I can. If you aren't planning to publish before April, there'll be plenty of time. But I'd rather not split it up.

Of course I would like to believe your enthusiasm justified. I'm still tired and it seems pretty bad. And I am sure it will not be a popular book. I feel very sure of that. I think to the large numbers of readers it will be an outrageous book. I only hope it is better than it seems to me now. I'm rested enough now to start revisions. We'll get it done just as soon as possible.

Love to Dorothy and Paco [Covici's wife and his son, Pascal, Jr.] and to you

John

So convinced was Steinbeck that *The Grapes of Wrath* would have no success that he wrote Elizabeth Otis:

"Look, Elizabeth, Pat talked in terms of very large first editions of this next book. I want to go on record as advising against it. This will not be a popular book. And it will be a loss to do anything except to print a small edition and watch and print more if there are more orders. Pat is darling and of course his statements are flattering but he is just a bit full of cheese."

To Elizabeth Otis

[Los Gatos]
[1938]

Dear Elizabeth:

This afternoon by express we are sending you the manuscript of The Grapes of Wrath. We hope to God you like it. Will you let us know first that you received it and second what you think of it. I forgot to put the enclosed in [the words and music of the "Battle Hymn of the Republic"]. I should like the whole thing to go in as a page at the beginning. All the verses and the music. This is one of the great songs of the world, and as you read the book you will realize that the words have a special meaning in this book. And I should like the music to be put there in case anyone, any one forgets. The title, Battle Hymn of the Republic, in itself has a special meaning in the light of this book.

Anyway there it is, and we will be hanging on your opinions because we know so well they will be honest and untouched by publicity.

Love to all of you,
John

Elizabeth Otis wrote in November that she and her husband would come out to California to visit the Steinbecks.

"We are crazy with joy," he wrote her. They arrived in December.

To Pascal Covici

Los Gatos
January 1, 1939

Dear Pat:

I'm laid low for the first time in twenty years. Have to stay in bed for two weeks. Metabolic rate shockingly low. I think I worked myself past the danger point on that book. Broke out in a neuritis and only a basal metabolism test showed the reason. Anyway I'm in bed and can get some letters written for the first time in ages.

We met Elizabeth and Larry in L.A. and brought them up. Enjoyed having them so much. E. and I went over some parts of the book and made a few minor changes. I've never heard whether you like the book so well now that it is finished. I think it is a pretty good job technically. At least I'm not as down-hearted about it as I usually am after finishing.

I hope our wire made sense. The point is this—The fascist crowd will try to sabotage this book because it is revolutionary. They try to give it the communist angle. However, The Battle Hymn is American and intensely so. Further, every American child learns it and then forgets the words. So if both words and music are there the book is keyed into the American scene from the beginning. Besides it is one of the finest hymns I know.

By the way—are there any cheap editions of In Dubious Battle? It has been made required reading in a number of English courses of the University of California and one of the Professors asked and I didn't know. I seem to remember that Blue Ribbon was going to do it. Did they?

It is beautiful here. I can look out the window at the valley

174

below. But I want to get out and plant things.

Write when you have time. It's so long since I've been able to write a letter that I'm rusty at it.

love to all
John

Later, in February, as he returned the proofs, he was to insist once again:

"I meant, Pat, to print *all all all* the verses of the Battle Hymn. They're all pertinent and they're all exciting. And the music if you can."

To Pascal Covici

Los Gatos
January [3] 1939

Dear Pat:

Your wire came this morning and I was going to answer it but it is hard to say anything in a wire and besides the clerks have been getting things pretty garbled lately. Elizabeth and I went over the mss and made some changes. I made what I could. There are some I cannot make. When the tone or overtone of normal speech requires a word, it is going in no matter what the audience thinks. This book wasn't written for delicate ladies. If they read it at all they're messing in something not their business. I've never changed a word to fit the prejudices of a group and I never will. The words I changed were those which Carol and Elizabeth said stopped the reader's mind. I've never wanted to be a popular writer—you know that. And those readers who are insulted by normal events or language mean nothing to me. Look over the changes and I think they will be the ones you made. The epithet shit-heads used on the people in the hamburger stand, I will not change. There is no term like it. And if it stops the reader the hell with him. It means something precise and I won't trade preciseness even if it's colloquial preciseness.

> Elizabeth Otis recalls that one of the purposes of her visit was to see if he would compromise on some of the strong language. The publishers had urged her to, and she asked him if it would be all right if she found a way to remove offending words while retaining the tone of the characters' speech. He said she could try. She sat at a desk going over the colloquial obscenities while Steinbeck lay on a couch, in great pain from sciatica. Eventually she produced a version that satisfied him. She had promised to telegraph these modifications to New York so that the book could go to the printer. Dictating the long telegram over the telephone, Miss Otis had to specify the four-letter words for which she was sending substitutes. But the Western Union operator balked. She couldn't possibly send such language in a telegram, she said. Miss Otis no longer remembers what arguments she used, but she was very firm and finally successful. The proofs were corrected.

Steinbeck continues to Covici:

Now—about all the other books being practice. It isn't true. I've been working three years on this book. In a sense, everything one does is practice for something else. But Pat, let this book ride or fall on its own story. I think the subject is large enough to get by. Actually if there has been one rigid rule in my books, it is that I as me had no right in them. And if that is so of the text, let it be so of the publicity. You really don't need me in it. If you do—then the book is a failure.

I'm getting along pretty well. Should be let up in a week or so. It was a surprise to me when I went down. Haven't been sick since I was sixteen.

I think I wrote everything else in the other letter.

love to you and
Dorothy and Paco
John

On January 9, 1939, Pascal Covici wrote Steinbeck that he, Harold Guinzburg, President of The Viking Press, and Marshall Best, Managing Editor, had been "emotionally exhausted after reading *The Grapes of Wrath.*" Harold Guinzburg had said, "I would not change a single comma in the whole book," and Marshall Best had called it "the most important piece of fiction on our list" as he announced that the initial advertising appropriation would be $10,000. "It seemed like a kind of sacrilege to suggest revisions in so grand a book," Covici went on, but:

"We felt that we would not be good publishers if we failed to point out to you any weaknesses or faults that struck us. One of these is the ending.

"Your idea is to end the book on a great symbolic note, that life must go on and will go on with a greater love and sympathy and understanding for our fellowmen. Nobody could fail to be moved by the incident of Rose of Sharon giving her breast to the starving man, yet, taken as the finale of such a book with all its vastness and surge, it struck us on reflection as being all too abrupt. It seems to us that the last few pages need building up. The incident needs leading up to, so that the meeting with the starving man is not so much an accident or chance encounter, but more an integral part of the saga."

In a postscript, he added:

"Marshall has just called my attention to the fact that de Maupassant in one of his short stories 'Mid-Summer Idyll' has a woman give her breast to a starving man in a railway train. Is it important?"

To Pascal Covici

Los Gatos
January 16, 1939

Dear Pat:

I have your letter today. And I am sorry but I cannot change
that ending. It is casual—there is no fruity climax, it is not
more important than any other part of the book—if there is
a symbol, it is a survival symbol not a love symbol, it must
be an accident, it must be a stranger, and it must be quick.
To build this stranger into the structure of the book would be
to warp the whole meaning of the book. The fact that the
Joads don't know him, don't care about him, have no ties to
him—that is the emphasis. The giving of the breast has no
more sentiment than the giving of a piece of bread. I'm sorry
if that doesn't get over. It will maybe. I've been on this design
and balance for a long time and I think I know how I want
it. And if I'm wrong, I'm alone in my wrongness. As for the
Maupassant story, I've never read it but I can't see that it
makes much difference. There are no new stories and I
wouldn't like them if there were. The incident of the earth
mother feeding by the breast is older than literature. You
know that I have never been touchy about changes, but I
have too many thousands of hours on this book, every incident has been too carefully chosen and its weight judged and
fitted. The balance is there. One other thing—I am not writing a satisfying story. I've done my damndest to rip a reader's
nerves to rags, I don't want him satisfied.

And still one more thing—I tried to write this book the way
lives are being lived not the way books are written.

This letter sounds angry. I don't mean it to be. I know
that books lead to a strong deep climax. This one doesn't
except by implication and the reader must bring the implication to it. If he doesn't, it wasn't a book for him to
read. Throughout I've tried to make the reader participate
in the actuality, what he takes from it will be scaled entirely on his own depth or hollowness. There are five lay-
ers in this book, a reader will find as many as he can and

178

he won't find more than he has in himself.

I seem to be getting well slowly. The pain is going away. Nerves still pretty tattered but rest will stop that before too long. I fret pretty much at having to stay in bed. Guess I was pretty close to a collapse when I finally went to bed. I feel the result of it now.

Love to you all,
John

To the McIntosh and Otis staff

[Los Gatos]
January [20] 1939

Dear All:

Actually I've been in bed two weeks and the pain getting worse instead of better. This afternoon I went to an osteopath. I have always thought them little better than witch doctors. He said a vertebra was out, flipped it, and the pain went away instantly. I'm holding my breath but that's six hours ago and it isn't back yet. I'll go to him again tomorrow. Pray for me. That pain was getting me nuts.

Mavis's letter came today with check [royalty from *Of Mice and Men* on tour]. I was surprised to hear the show was in Philadelphia. Wonder if they are ever coming out here. After the fair opens there will be thousands of stray visitors in S.F. And the coast would welcome that play I'm pretty sure. The check was lots larger this week too.

I feel so good tonight I could yell. It's the first time without pain in six weeks and I'll have the first good sleep in that time tonight.

Carol is planting things and I, big slug, just look on. We put 27 goldfish in the new pool today.

Guess that's all. I wonder if you could get any kind of itinerary from the Sam Harris office. Maybe they haven't one.

Love to you all,
John

179

To The National Institute
of Arts and Letters

Los Gatos
January 31, 1939

Dear Mrs. Vanamee:

I am grateful for the honor of having been elected to membership in the National Institute of Arts and Letters. Please convey my thanks to the committee.

Sincerely
John Steinbeck

In February, Pascal Covici asked Steinbeck for the original manuscript of *The Grapes of Wrath.*

To Pascal Covici

[Los Gatos]
[Received
February 23, 1939]

Dear Pat:

I keep having to say no all the time and I hate it. It's about the manuscript this time. You see I feel that this is Carol's book so I gave her the manuscript. For myself I don't like anything personal to intrude on this or any other book but this one in particular. I think a book should be itself, complete and in print. What went into the writing of it is no business of the reader. I disapprove of having my crabbed hand exposed. The fact that my writing is small may be a marvel but it is also completely unimportant to the book. No, I want this book to be itself with no history and no writer.

Carol has other reasons for not wanting it ever known that the ms exists. Those people who beg things for Spain are after us a good deal. And Carol doesn't want to give this ms away and she knows the campaign will start if any attention is drawn to the script. And of course it is hers.

I'm sorry Pat, but do you really think we've lost a single reader by refusing to do the usual things? By not speaking at luncheons do you think I've lost sales? I don't. And if it were true I'd rather lose that kind of readers. Let's just keep the whole personal emphasis out. It can be done. I haven't been to a tea or a dinner in my life and I'm quite sure no one minds, people forget. Let's have no personality at all. I think the book has enough of its own to carry it. I hope you don't mind too much.

> love to Dorothy and to Paco
> John

In a later letter to Elizabeth Otis he again refers to the use of the "Battle Hymn" in the make-up of the book:

"This song business is very funny. I don't know what is the matter with Pat. But it makes me wonder whether he got the dedication of this book straight. Will you please see that he did. It is supposed to read:
> to Carol
> who willed this book
> to Tom
> who lived it."

Tom was Tom Collins, a psychologist who managed a government camp for migrants near Weedpatch in the Bakersfield area.

To Pascal Covici

[Los Gatos]
[Received March 31, 1939]

Dear Pat:

The books came today [advance copies of *The Grapes of Wrath*] and I am immensely pleased with them. It is a good job. But what with family and relatives I'll have to have about five more copies. Will you send them please and bill me? I really need them to prevent hurt feelings.

I think the way you laid in the Hymn on the end papers is swell. The pageage is less than you contemplated, isn't it? And I'm glad. 850 pages is a frightening length. You know I would like to see the New York reviews. Would you please save them for me? I understand Joe Jackson is going to do it for the Herald Tribune. I'm glad of that. I guess that is all. I just wanted to tell you how much I like the book.

John

Royalty checks continued to surprise him. "What an awful lot of money," he wrote Elizabeth Otis on April 17.

"I don't think I ever saw so much in one piece before. Well, Carol will squirrel it away for the lean times that are surely coming."

He had been reading reviews:

"Do you notice that nearly every reviewer hates the general chapters? They hate to be told anything outright. It should be concealed in the text. Fortunately I'm not writing for reviewers. And other people seem to like the generals. It's inter-

182

esting. I think probably it is the usual revolt against something they aren't used to."

And next day:

"Thanks for the check. I don't expect these things and they are always surprises. The telegrams and telephones—all day long—speak . . . speak . . . speak, like hungry birds. Why the hell do people insist on speaking? The telephone is a thing of horror. And the demands for money—scholarships, memorial prizes. One man wants 47,000 dollars to buy a newspaper which will be liberal—this is supposed to run with a checkbook. Carol turned down the most absurd offer of all yesterday, to write a script in Hollywood. Carol—over the telephone: 'What the hell would we do with $5,000 a week? Don't bother us!' "

To Carl Wilhelmson

Los Gatos
[June 7, 1939]

Dear Carl:

Of course I'd like to see you. The ranch is wonderful now and I resent any time spent away from it. Cherries are just getting ripe and the vegetable garden is finally supplying food and we make our own butter and cheese and have lots of milk to drink. I bought a cow and a neighbor takes care of it delivering to us three quarts a day which gives us all the cream and butter we can use. It's really pretty fine. And the cow just eats pasturage that would go to waste if she weren't there.

I did a silly thing yesterday, coughed hard and wrenched my back. Down in Salinas there was a man who sneezed and broke his right arm. Everyone laughed to beat hell but his arm was broken just the same. And I get no sympathy about this back either.

I'm glad you like this last book. It was a terrible amount of work. Never worked so hard in my life nor so long before.

And I found something I didn't know about and that is exhaustion. I never thought I could get that way. But I found I could.

Our Toby Dog got to thinking too much and one day he just walked away and never came back. The Thoreau of the dog world, I guess. Now we have another dog. A big Dobermann who doesn't think much at all and is much happier for it. Also, having short hair, he doesn't get ticks and burrs.

Yes, please do come down but remember about calling because I would hate to miss you.

affectionately,
john

To Dick Pearce
OF THE PRESS CLUB, SAN FRANCISCO

Los Gatos
[June 1939]

Dear Mr. Pearce:

I'm awfully glad of your letter and I wish I could accept your invitation. But I'm working at a job that doesn't let me stay still long enough to accept anything. Thanks just the same. One of the reasons I would like to accept is that I would like to be in the Press Club and not be thrown out. The only time I ever was there I was thrown out. Happened this way. Dick Oliver and I were in shiny evening clothes and no money and no parties and he said he was a member of the Press Club and we could go sit there until our bus left. It was 2:30 A.M. then. And I thanked him and it was raining. So we went in and it was nice and a fire was burning as I remember. But the attendant didn't remember Dick and couldn't find his name on the list of members. He insisted that we go out again and meant it. So we went out. And as you probably know if you've ever been put out of a place, you feel a kind of unpleasant feeling about it and I'd like some time to sit by your fire with that fine feeling that no one was going to toss me out. All this was years ago but Jesus, it was a wet night.

Again thanks for your invitation. I wish I could go.

Sincerely,
John Steinbeck

By this time film rights to *Of Mice and Men* and *The Grapes of Wrath* had been sold, and work on the screenplays of both was going forward.

To Elizabeth Otis

Los Gatos
June 22, 1939

Dear Elizabeth:

This whole thing is getting me down and I don't know what to do about it. The telephone never stops ringing, telegrams all the time, fifty to seventy-five letters a day all wanting something. People who won't take no for an answer sending books to be signed. I don't know what to do. Would you mind phoning Viking and telling them not to forward any more letters but to send them to your office? I'll willingly pay for the work to be done but even to handle a part of the letters now would take a full time secretary and I will not get one if it is the last thing I do. Something has to be worked out or I am finished writing. I went south to work and I came back to find Carol just about hysterical. She had just been pushed beyond endurance. There is one possibility and that is that I go out of the country. I thought this thing would die down but it is only getting worse day by day.

I hope to be home for about five weeks now but I doubt it. I brought [Eugene] Solow and [Lewis] Milestone [author of screenplay and director of film of *Of Mice and Men*] home with me and we are working on a final script of *Mice* and it sounds very good to me.

About the Digest thing, I really would be happier if it weren't done [an abridgement of *The Grapes of Wrath*]. I don't like digests. If I could have written it shorter I would have, and even a chunk wouldn't be good particularly since Pat refused to give material to anybody else but S.R.L. [*Saturday Review of Literature*] and thereby made a hell of a lot of people mad at me.

I saw Johnson in Hollywood [Nunnally Johnson, who was writing the film script of *The Grapes of Wrath*] and he is going well and apparently they intend to make the picture straight, at least so far, and they sent a producer into the field with Tom Collins and he got sick at what he saw and they offered Tom a job as technical assistant which is swell because he'll howl his head off if they get out of hand.

See you all soon, I hope.

Love,
John

To Carlton A. Sheffield

Los Gatos
June 23, 1939

Dear Juk:

I got home three days ago for a little while and found about five hundred letters that had to be answered. So I have been answering them as quickly as possible and have saved yours until last so that I could give some leisure to it, and leisure is a thing I have almost lost track of. Funny darned thing because I have such a fine flair for laziness. The heat is on me now and really going strong. Remember when I used to like to get mail so much that I even tried to get on sucker lists? Well, I wish them days was back.

Carl Wilhelmson phoned that he wanted to come down Sunday. I'll be glad to see him. He is very changed. Quite gay and looks fine and has filled out. Marriage has been good for him. Haven't seen anybody else. Toby Street had a fortieth birthday party and I went to it and saw Bob Cathcart there.

Yes, the Associated Farmers have tried to make me retract things by very sly methods. Unfortunately for them the things are thoroughly documented and the materials turned over to the La Follette Committee and when it was killed by pressure groups all evidence went to the Attorney General. So when they write and ask for proof, I simply ask them to ask the Senate to hold open hearings of the Civil Liberty Committee and they will get immediate documentary proof of my statements although some of them may go to jail as a result of it. And you have no idea how quickly that stops the argument. They can't shoot me now because it would be too obvious and because I have placed certain informations in the hands of J. Edgar Hoover in case I take a nose dive. So I think I am personally safe enough except for automobile accidents etc. and rape and stuff like that so I am a little careful not to go anywhere alone nor to do anything without witnesses. Seems silly but I have been carefully instructed by people who know the ropes.

Many years later he wrote to his friend Chase Horton:

"Let me tell you a story. When The Grapes of Wrath got loose, a lot of people were pretty mad at me. The undersheriff of Santa Clara County was a friend of mine and he told me as follows—'Don't you go into any hotel room alone. Keep records of every minute and when you are off the ranch travel with one or two friends but particularly, don't stay in a hotel alone.' 'Why?' I asked. He said, 'Maybe I'm sticking my neck out but the boys got a rape case set up for you. You get alone in a hotel and a dame will come in, tear off her clothes, scratch her face and scream and you try to talk yourself out of that one. They won't touch your book but there's easier ways.' "

So they have gone to the whispering campain (how in hell do you spell that) but unfortunately that method only sells more books. I'm due to topple within the next two years but I have

187

that little time left to me. And in many ways I'll be glad when the turn of the thing comes. As it must inevitably.

Hope it isn't too hot up there.

love
jon

To Elizabeth Otis

Los Gatos
July 20, 1939
Thursday

Dear Elizabeth:

Will you tell Pat please, that if I ever refer anything to him by a second person I want him to refuse it. If I want it I'll ask him myself.

The vilification of me out here from the large landowners and bankers is pretty bad. The latest is a rumor started by them that the Okies hate me and have threatened to kill me for lying about them. This made all the papers. Tom Collins says that when his Okies read this smear they were so mad they wanted to burn something down.

I'm frightened at the rolling might of this damned thing. It is completely out of hand—I mean a kind of hysteria about the book is growing that is not healthy.

About the pictures—I don't know. [Nunnally] Johnson wrote that he was nearly finished with script. The Hays office will be the tough nut since it is owned outright in N. Y. But the forces that want the picture made are rallying and they are both numerous and voluble. Meanwhile the Associated Farmers keep up a steady stream of accusation that I am first a liar and second a communist. Their vilification has a quality of hysteria too.

I shudder for you in the heat. I detest the New York heat. Love to you all,

John

To Elizabeth Otis

Dear Elizabeth:

It's a beautiful morning and I am just sitting in it and enjoying it. Everything is ripe now, apples, pears, grapes, walnuts. Carol has made pickles and chutney, canned tomatoes. Prunes and raisins are on the drying trays. The cellar smells of apples and wine. The berries are ripe and every bird in the country is here—slightly tipsy and very noisy. The frogs are singing about a rain coming but they can be wrong. It's nice.

Pat is in S.F. We'll go up and get him on Friday and bring him down here. Will also see the Jacksons—first time in months.

Carol is well and rested. And Grapes dropped from the head of the list to second place out here and about time too. It is far too far when Jack Benny mentions it in his program. Altogether may be some kind of new existence is opening up. I don't know. The last year has been a nightmare all in all. But now I'm ordering a lot of books to begin study. And I'll work in the laboratory.

I should go out and shoot some bluejays. They are driving the birds badly. Mean things they are who just raise hell apparently with nothing but mischief in their minds. But I'll wait until Carol wakes up before I start shooting.

One nice thing to think of is the speed of obscurity. Grapes is not first now. In a month it will be off the list and in six months I'll be forgotten.

Love,
John

1939 1942
1940 1943
1941

Steinbeck

"...*something terrible is about to happen*..."

1939 Film of *Of Mice and Men* released.

1940 Film of *The Grapes of Wrath* released. Awarded Pulitzer Prize for the novel.

1941 *The Forgotten Village* and *Sea of Cortez* published. Separated from Carol Steinbeck and moved to New York.

1942 *The Moon Is Down,* novel published, play produced. *Bombs Away* published. Divorced from Carol Steinbeck.

1943 Married Gwyndolyn Conger.

To Carlton A. Sheffield

Los Gatos
November 13, 1939

Dear Dook:

It's pretty early in the morning. I got up to milk the cow.

I'm finishing off a complete revolution. It's amazing how every one piled in to regiment me, to make a symbol of me, to regulate my life and work. I've just tossed the whole thing overboard. I never let anyone interfere before and I can't see why I should now. This ultimate freedom receded. I'm keeping more of it than I need or even want, like a reservoir. The two most important [things], I suppose—at least they seem so to me—are freedom from respectability and most important —freedom from the necessity of being consistent. Lack of those two can really tie you down. Of course all this publicity has been bad if I tried to move about but here on the ranch it has no emphasis. People up here—the few we see—don't read much and don't remember what they read, and my projected work is not likely to create any hysteria.

It's funny, Dook. I know what in a vague way this work is about. I mean I know its tone and texture and to an extent its field and I find that I have no education. I have to go back to school in a way. I'm completely without mathematics and I have to learn something about abstract mathematics. I have some biology but must have much more and the twins biophysics and bio-chemistry are closed to me. So I have to go back and start over. I bought half the stock in Ed's lab which gives me equipment, a teacher, a library to work in.

I'm going on about myself but in a sense it's more than me —it's you and everyone else. The world is sick now. There are things in the tide pools easier to understand than Stalinist,

193

Hitlerite, Democrat, capitalist confusion, and voodoo. So I'm going to those things which are relatively more lasting to find a new basic picture. I have too a conviction that a new world is growing under the old, the way a new finger nail grows under a bruised one. I think all the economists and sociologists will be surprised some day to find that they did not forsee nor understand it. Just as the politicos of Rome could not have forseen that the social-political-ethical world for two thousand years would grow out of the metaphysical gropings of a few quiet poets. I think the same thing is hap-penening now. Communist, Fascist, Democrat may find that the real origin of the future lies on the microscope plates of obscure young men, who, puzzled with order and disorder in quantum and neutron, build gradually a picture which will seep down until it is the fibre of the future.

The point of all this is that I must make a new start. I've worked the novel—I know it as far as I can take it. I never did think much of it—a clumsy vehicle at best. And I don't know the form of the new but I know there is a new which will be adequate and shaped by the new thinking. Anyway, there is a picture of my confusion. How is yours?

There is so much confusion now—emotional hysteria which passes for thought and blind faith which passes for analysis.

I suspect you are ready for a change. How would you escape the general picture? We're catching the waves of nerves from Europe and making a few of our own.

Write when you can.

John

To Elizabeth Otis

[Los Gatos]
December 15, 1939
Thursday

Dear Elizabeth:

I have so much to tell you that it will take some time. I'll go about it slowly. Your letter first. Many thanks for the $13,000. But remember the excitement when the N. American Review actually paid $90 (on The Red Pony)? Such excitement will never come again.

There is no question of a cut version of Grapes in paper covers. I should never consent to it. So that is out. C. [Covici] can get as stubborn as he wants about it.

Pictures—We went down in the afternoon and that evening saw Grapes at Twentieth-Century. Zanuck has more than kept his word. He has a hard, straight picture in which the actors are submerged so completely that it looks and feels like a documentary film and certainly it has a hard, truthful ring. No punches were pulled—in fact, with descriptive matter removed, it is a harsher thing than the book, by far. It seems unbelievable but it is true. The next afternoon we went to see Mice and it is a beautiful job. Here Milestone has done a curious lyrical thing. It hangs together and is underplayed. You will like it. It opens the 22nd of December in Hollywood. As for Grapes, it opens sometime in January. There is so much hell being raised in this state that Zanuck will not release simultaneously. He'll open in N.Y. and move gradually west, letting the publicity precede it. He even, to find out, issued a statement that it would never be shown in California and got a ton of mail, literally, in protest the next day. He has hired attorneys to fight any local censorship and is trying to get Thomas Benton for the posters. All this is far beyond our hopes.

Now I come to a very curious thing. [Victor] Fleming the director [*Gone With The Wind*] and Spence Tracy have wanted to make The Red Pony. They are nuts to make it. They talked to me about it and I slept over it but didn't sleep at all. It seemed to me that these men are expensive and good men. I don't know whether anything will come out of it, but here is what I suggested. They were to make the film—no salaries. If necessary, money to make it should be collected by subscriptions. I would not only give the story for nothing but would work on the script. When finished, it would be distributed to any town or city which would guarantee to use the proceeds to endow one or more children's beds in the *local* hospitals. Tremendous prices would be asked for seats. They were very enthusiastic. Said they thought they could get not only the best people but equipment and film for nothing. Maybe this is nuts but no film has ever been made for a definite purpose. Tracy is particularly moved because his own little son had infantile paralysis which crippled it. Fleming says that such a film would not make less than $2,000,000 and that's a lot of endowed beds.

> He was also planning with Ed Ricketts to study the coastal waters north of San Francisco for a collectors' handbook, and to make a more elaborate expedition to Baja California, which would result in *Sea of Cortez: A Leisurely Journal of Travel and Research,* to be published in 1941.

Now—the collecting. I got a truck and we are equipping it. We don't go to Mexico until March, but we have the handbook to do first and we'll go north in about a week I guess for the solstice tides. It will be a tough job and I'm not at all sure we can get it done by March. And I have a terrific job of reading to do. Ricketts is all right but I am a *popular* writer and I have to build some trust in the minds of biologists. This handbook will help to do that. The Mexican book will be interesting to a much larger audience, and there is no question that Viking can have it.

Yesterday we went to Berkeley with a design for our traveling refrigeration plant and it is being built. Also ordered a Bausch and Lomb skw microscope. This is a beauty with a side bar and drum nose piece. Primarily a dissecting microscope. My dream for some time in the future is a research scope with an oil immersion lens, but that costs about 600 dollars and I'm not getting it right now. The SKW will be fine for the trip. But that research model, Oh boy! Oh boy! Sometime I'll have one. It may interest you to know that business at the lab is picking up. I can't tell you what all this means to me, in happiness and energy. I was washed up and now I'm alive again, with work to be done and worth doing.

I guess that's all.

Love,
John

To Carlton A. Sheffield

Los Gatos
January 16, 1940

Dear Dook:

I'm home this week cleaning up some copy so I got your letter early. I've been spending the weeks in the Grove and coming home week ends. I've been studying harder than I ever did in school and doing some independent research also.

Reason for this work is pretty obvious, I guess. Apart from the interest I have in it, I like the discipline. I've grown more and more dissatisfied with my work and this will help it, I hope. Besides, it will drop me out of this damnable popularity, for, while it will be a good book, there won't be a hell of a lot of people who will want it. I'm very sick of this prominence business.

Carol gave me Sandburg, Lincoln for Xmas. I already had The Prairie Years. Beautiful job.

After dinner now, and a very nice dinner with curry. Carol made chutney this year with fruit from the orchard and it is wonderful. Tremendous rains almost washed our road out but it held waiting for the next rain. We're so far up that roads are quite a problem.

I have so much to learn and all the time I find holes in knowledge—this isn't known, that has not been investigated. I'm doing (to me) fascinating work trying to relax anemones before killing them. They are terribly retractile and must be thoroughly anaesthetized before the formalin is introduced. Cocaine will do it but that is expensive. Now I have something I think will work but it will have to be carefully worked and quantitatively. It is—heavy mixture of oxygen in the water which gets them very drunk, then a weak solution of aspirin (believe it or not). When they are deeply inert—a shot of epsom salts, fairly strong solution and, after six hours a formalin wick. I foozled it last week with too much aspirin, but I think it will work when I get the amounts worked out and that takes many tries. Sound silly?

John

The "damnable popularity" became almost an obsession.

"You say you are afraid of me," he wrote Sheffield shortly afterward. "I'm afraid of myself. I mean the creature that has been built up. Luckily we don't take a paper so I don't see the things you do. Last night one of my pictures opened in L.A. Fox publicity didn't say it but just insinuated that I had sneaked down for it. Today ten calls have come from L.A. asking if I was there. It's silly but it's crazy silly. I've kind of depended on its dying soon, and it will. Some one else will be on the griddle. Meanwhile, here at the ranch it isn't bad. The phone ordinarily doesn't ring once a day and there are no papers. So you see, you are probably more in contact with this person you are afraid of than I am. I get more cut off all the time because people are, like you, afraid of this thing that has been built up, and I don't see them often. Knowing I am watched, I don't go any place. Knowing I'll be quoted, I don't say anything."

To Elizabeth Otis

Dear Elizabeth:

I haven't written for a long time. But I have had a beastly case of intestinal flu, a painful and knockout full dose and am just coming out of it now. Don't know where I picked it up but it was a lovely flower.

There is really a lot to answer and I hope I don't leave anything out. First the enormous check came yesterday and Carol has gone down now to get our income tax out of the way. It will be something like forty thousand dollars with state and federal. But don't think we are crabbing. We're delighted to pay it. It's a terrific amount of money we're making. Carol is putting it away carefully, well knowing that probably we'll have to live on it the rest of our lives.

I'll give you some little idea of how the Mexican trip goes. Our plans have changed. The country we want to get to is so difficult that we now want to take a purse seiner from Monterey and go all the way by boat. Said boat is 76 feet long. Three in the crew and Carol and Ed and I would be the whole personnel. Carol would have to sleep in the wheelhouse and the rest of us in the forecastle. Each of us would have to stand a watch and the other work to be divided.

There is one other thing I would like you to consider for future reference. This boat charter is expensive and as I said we like the thing to pay its own way. If we do go, do you think you could sell the log as a series of articles? It would be just a day-to-day account of what happens, together with description of one of the least known areas in the world. Not fantastic adventure or anything like that but a clear description of such a boat trip. Just think about it and later we can talk it over.

I guess that really is all.

Love to everybody,
John

On February 28, 1940, four days after his preceding letter, he announced to Elizabeth Otis:

"We'll be off to Mexico within a week. I'm terribly excited as I guess my handwriting shows."

To Elizabeth Otis

[Aboard *Western Flyer*]
March 26, 1940

Dear Elizabeth:

Heaven knows when you will get this. We're putting in to Loreto tomorrow and I will mail it. But I don't know how often mail goes out of Loreto. It is a tiny place, the first town of the lot. Its church was built in 1535. We've been working hard, collecting, preserving and making notes. No log. There hasn't been time. It takes about eight hours to preserve and label the things taken at the tide. We have thousands of specimens. And it will probably be several years before they are all identified. So far the trip has been wonderful. Last night we went high into the mountains on muleback to hunt bighorn sheep. Went with a rancher on a little hidden ranch. No sheep and I was glad of that. And yesterday we were collecting in a tiny bay when a huge manta ray came in. He was about 60 feet across so we got out of the water fast.

Good Friday we were in La Paz and went to mass. And they sang for the stations of the cross an ancient Spanish chant like a madrigal. The priest had a beautiful voice, true and clear, and the music had still the hint of North Africa and went to quarter tones. We're over two weeks out now and must be back at the end of six weeks. So one third is gone. I only hope the rest of the trip is as good as the first has been. We'll be in Guaymas in about a week and our mail will be waiting for us there. I'm tired and deep burned with the sun. So I'll let this ride as it is. I hope everything goes well with you.

We haven't heard any news of Europe since we left and

200

don't much want to. And the people we meet on the shore have never heard of Europe and they seem to be the better for it. This whole trip is doing what we had hoped it might, given us a world picture not dominated by Hitler and Moscow but something more vital and surviving than either. From the simple good Indians on the shore to the invertebrates there is a truer thing than ideologies.

Good-bye. I'll write from Guaymas.

Love to you all,
John

To the McIntosh and Otis staff

[Aboard *Western Flyer*]
Guaymas [Mexico]
April 6, 1940

Dear All:

We got in here yesterday. Your letter was waiting for us at the consulate. And it was awfully good to hear from you. Monday we'll leave here and move down the coast and then run for home. We'll be home two weeks from Monday or the 22nd. Getting a little homesick too. Last night we drank some very old brandy and our crew went on the town. The engineer never did come back. He's probably in jail. I'll go in and look in a little while. There were fights and explosions. The captain got very drunk and isn't up yet. The two seamen are also in their bunks. I just got happy and had fun and so did Carol. Toward the end Carol and an Indian girl were mingling tears at the incredible beauty and terror of life. The Indian girl subsequently passed out and was sent ashore in a rowboat. We sent in for a guitar player and made the whole gulf horrible with song. Well, anyway, it was a party. But we'd been fourteen days at sea and it will do the whole crew good if they are alive at all.

Carol is beginning to be homesick for her garden. But she

has been marvelous on this trip. I don't know any other woman who could have done it.

Have to go ashore now.

Love to you all,
John

In early April, Mrs. Franklin D. Roosevelt made an inspection tour of California migrant camps. According to *The New York Times* of April 3, 1940, when a reporter questioned her, she replied, "I never have thought *The Grapes of Wrath* was exaggerated." This report probably prompted the following letter.

To Mrs. Franklin D. Roosevelt

Los Gatos
April 24, 1940

Dear Mrs. Roosevelt:

I am very sorry I was out of the country when you were last on the coast, for I have looked forward to meeting you with great pleasure. Perhaps on your next swing, I shall be here.

Meanwhile—may I thank you for your words. I have been called a liar so constantly that sometimes I wonder whether I may not have dreamed the things I saw and heard in the period of my research.

Again thank you and I hope I may not miss you again.

Sincerely yours,
John Steinbeck

On May 2, 1940, Steinbeck received a letter from the Reverend L. M. Birkhead, National Director of the Friends of Democracy, an organization which he described as engaged in "combatting the pro-Nazi and anti-Semitic propaganda so widespread throughout the country."

"I hope you will not think I am impertinent," he wrote, "but our organization has had put to it the problem of your nationality. There is very widespread propaganda, particularly among extreme reactionary religionists that you are Jewish and that *Grapes of Wrath* is Jewish propaganda."

To Reverend L. M. Birkhead

Los Gatos
May 7, 1940

Dear Mr. Birkhead:

I am answering your letter with a good deal of sadness. I am sad for a time when one must know a man's race before his work can be approved or disapproved. It does not seem important to me whether I am Jewish or not, and I know that a statement of mine is useless if an *interested* critic wishes to ride a preconceived thesis. I cannot see how The Grapes of Wrath can be Jewish propaganda but then I have heard it called Communist propaganda also.

It happens that I am not Jewish and have no Jewish blood but it only happens that way. I find that I do not experience any pride that it is so.

If you wish—here is my racial map although you know what an intelligent anthropologist thinks of racial theories. As you will see, I am the typical American Airedale.

My grandfather on my father's side was German, the son of a farming family which lived and still lives on a fairly large farm near Düsseldorf. My grandfather came to America in the late fifties in time to be in the Civil War. There has been little communication with the German branch since then except for a visit to Germany about four years ago by a

203

second cousin of mine. He reports that the family still lives on the same farm and that they appear to be good citizens, intensely blond and quite able to prove the nonsensical thing the Nazis insist on. Their name and ours by the way was Grosssteinbeck but the three s's in a row were an outrage to America so my grandfather dropped the first syllable in the interest of spelling.

My German grandfather married a New England woman whose family name was Dickson who came from Leominster, Massachusetts, where her family had lived since the middle seventeenth century.

On my mother's side my blood is all north Irish, my grandfather whose name was Hamilton having come from Mulkeraugh near Londonderry and his wife whose name was Feaghan from nearby.

Anyway there it is. Use it or don't use it, print it or not. Those who wish for one reason or another to believe me Jewish will go on believing it while men of good will and good intelligence won't care one way or another.

I can prove these things of course—but when I shall have to—the American democracy will have disappeared.

Yours is only one of many letters I have received on the same subject. It is the first I have answered and I think it is the last. I fully recognize your position and do not in the least blame you for it. I am only miserable for the time and its prejudice that prompts it.

Sincerely,
John Steinbeck

P. S. On both sides and for many generations we are blond and blue-eyed to a degree to arouse the admiration and perhaps envy of the dark-complexioned Hitler.

In the spring of 1940 the Pulitzer Prizes were announced. Steinbeck won the fiction award for *The Grapes of Wrath,* Carl Sandburg the history award for *Abraham Lincoln: The War Years,* and William Saroyan the drama prize for *The Time of Your Life*

—an honor he refused. Steinbeck commented to Joseph Henry Jackson:

"Bill knows what he wants to do and I don't see that it is anybody's business. His motives and his impulses are his own private property. Do you want to take a quote from me? I suppose I must say something. If you want to print it, fine. Might go something like this:

" 'While in the past I have sometimes been dubious about Pulitzer choices I am pleased and flattered to be chosen in a year when Sandburg and Saroyan were chosen. It is good company.' That's the end of the quote. And it is one of the few times when tact and truth seem to be side by side."

Soon afterwards, the Steinbecks returned to Mexico, this time to Mexico City, where a corporation of which he was a director planned to produce "a little moving picture about the life of an Indian village" on a budget of $35,000: *The Forgotten Village*. Steinbeck was to write the screenplay.

"But the life of an Indian village is tied up with the life of the Republic," he reported to his uncle Joseph Hamilton, working for the WPA in Washington. "The Germans have absolutely outclassed the Allies in propaganda. If it continues, they will completely win Central and South America away from the United States."

News of the fall of France seemed to add urgency to the situation. Steinbeck decided to convey his alarm to the highest authority in the country.

To Franklin D. Roosevelt

2017 Hillyer Place, N.W.
Washington, D. C.
June 24, 1940

The President
The White House

My dear Mr. Roosevelt:

For some time I have been making a little moving picture in Mexico. In this line I have covered a great deal of country and had conversations with many people of many factions.

In the light of this experience and against a background of the international situation, I am forced to the conclusion that a crisis in the Western Hemisphere is imminent, and is to be met only by an immediate, controlled, considered, and directed method and policy.

It is probable that you have considered this situation in all its facets. However, if my observation can be of any use to you, I shall be very glad to speak with you for I am sure that this problem is one of the most important to be faced by the nation.

Respectfully yours,
John Steinbeck

This letter was accompanied to the President's desk by a memorandum of the same date, signed James Rowe, Jr.:

"You may be interested in this letter from John Steinbeck who has just come to Washington from Mexico where he has been making a movie. He seems quite disturbed. He probably has no better information than any other sensitive and intelligent layman who has spent time in Mexico."

A handwritten addendum:

"Archie MacLeish says he thinks you would be interested in talking with him. He is the author of *Grapes of Wrath.*"

MacLeish, the poet, was Chief Librarian, Library of Congress. The next day, the following memorandum reached General Marvin ("Pa") Watson, Secretary to the President:

"Pa: I want to see John Steinbeck the author of *Grapes of Wrath* tomorrow for 20 minutes. F. D. R."

Steinbeck had outlined his ideas in his letter to his uncle:

"I propose that a propaganda office be set up which, through radio and motion pictures, attempts to get this side of the world together. Its method would be to make for understanding rather than friction. I have a smoothly functioning movie crew and could gather several more quickly. I could also work with some Hollywood people, such as [Walter] Wanger, who would do a good job. I think a decent and honorable job could be done, but I doubt if it can be done by the people who are directing it now."

Apparently the President took no action on the proposal, but it was Steinbeck's first venture into the world of international statesmanship, which he would find increasingly fascinating.

To Carlton A. Sheffield

Los Gatos
July 9, 1940

Dear Dook:

It was good to get your long letter. I've been too raddled and confused to write letters for a long time. But with the decline of the pressures on me I'm feeling better and if it weren't for the coming war, I could look forward to a good quiet life for a few years anyway. You know my nature and my old prospects so you must know what a terrible experience this last two years has been.

You ask about the ranch and whether it is an estate. If we were going to sell it, the description would surely sound like an estate. But I'll try to give you some idea of it. At the Greenwood Road place we were finally surrounded with little houses and right under my work room window a house was built by a lady who was studying singing—the mi-mi-mi kind, so we finally went nuts. Carol's father found this little ranch far up the mountain. It is forty-seven acres and has a big spring. It has forest and orchard and pasture and big trees. It is very old—was first taken up in 1847. The old ranch house was built in 1858 I think. So we came up, built a four room house for ourselves, much like the Greenwood road house. There had been an oil well on the place and we used the big timbers and boards for our house. Then we refinished the inside of the old ranch house for two guest rooms and a big winter playroom where one can have parties. So far in our ad we have "two houses—four bedrooms."

Then since Carol loves to swim I asked about swimming pools and I discovered a curious thing. The cost of swimming pools isn't the pool but the machinery for filtering the water over and over since water is expensive. Using city water it costs fifty to sixty dollars to fill a pool once. But we had a four inch head of spring water. Now we built a long narrow swimming pool and turned our spring into it. If it were a city pool with the big pumps and filters, it would have cost between eight and ten thousand dollars. But a concrete tank with a spring running in cost $1,500. So we have a swimming pool to add to our ad.

Then we have a Japanese boy who cooks, gardens, and looks after the place when we are away. And in the summer I have an Okie boy by the day to work around mainly because he needs the money so dreadfully. So there's a staff of servants. You see it really is an estate. But it is one of the most beautiful places I've ever seen. And I hope you'll see it soon now that we have something of a normal life again. The telephone number by the way is not listed. I wish you would write it down. It is Los Gatos 293R1. The operators will not give it out. We had too much trouble with such.

Sheffield had reported that he had tried, without success, to get a job on the San Francisco *Chronicle*.

208

I'm sorry about the Chronicle deal. Wish I had been there because I know the managing editor quite well. And I don't think one gets jobs from below. My weight is decreasing daily and it will continue to do so. If you can think of any way to use what I have left, please tell me. Trouble is that I've refused all favors to papers but maybe I could help a little.

Have you saved any money? I know you have. You always do. Your mystical luck will work and you'll get another job. I would help as much as I could. And of course, you know that in the matter of money, I'm always available while I have any.

I wish you would come down to the ranch. We could stand some talking now. It's time for it. And I'll work with you at anything you want to do.

love
John

To Carlton A. Sheffield

Los Gatos
August 12, 1940

Dear Carlton (if you wish):

I'm taking flying lessons up at the Palo Alto Airport and I love it. There's something so god damned remote and beautiful and detached about being way to hell and gone up on a little yellow leaf. It isn't like the big transports at all because this little thing floats and bobs and yet is very steady and— there's no sense of power at all but rather a sense of being alone in the best sense of the word, not loneliness at all but just an escape into something delightful. I think you used to get it after you had had a lot of guests and they all went home and the house was finally cleaned up and you could turn on the radio and cook your own kind of stew and read and look up and know god damned well that you were alone. And there's something about seeing a cumulus cloud way off and going over there to see what it is like.

My first reason for getting a license was that here I am only about a year and a half from forty and I wanted to learn to handle the controls while my reflexes were still malleable. I saw my father try to learn to drive a car when he was sixty five and he never could do it unconsciously. He had to think every time for the gear shift and he had to think about how to get out of a mess. Well, I wanted to get the controls into my unconscious before I got too old. And the moment I began going up I found something much more than that. Some very delicious thing with no name for it yet anyway, but it does seem to be some extension of aesthetics.

There were callers just then so I had to leave this and come back to it. Yesterday afternoon a car came up and I went out to see who it was. When I got out to the porch there was a group, an elderly man, his wife beside him and three boys arranged on either side. They stood very stiffly and I began to get a little nervous and then suddenly the man bellowed, "Do you know Jesus?" and launched into a sermon. It was five minutes before I could stop him. Gestures and all, and me standing in the door in nothing but a pair of swimming trunks. It was awful. I finally told them I did know Jesus and got them out, but they were prepared to save me even if it killed me.

So long. I'll hope to see you soon.

Love
jon

To Franklin D. Roosevelt

Los Gatos.
August 13, 1940

Dear Mr. Roosevelt:

I assure you that if there were any alternative, I should not bother you with this letter. When you were kind enough to receive me I said I did not want a job. But after listening to the growing defeatism in the country, especially among business men, I find I have a job whether I want one or not.

210

When I spoke to you I said that the Germans were winning in propaganda matters through boldness and the use of new techniques. This has also been largely true in their military activities. At the time I had been thinking that our weapons and tactics would have to come not only from the military minds but from the laboratories.

Perhaps you have heard of Dr. Melvyn Knisely, who has the chair of Anatomy at the University of Chicago. He is a remarkable scientist and an old friend of mine. Discussing with him the problem of the growing Nazi power and possibilities for defense against it, he put forth an analysis and a psychological weapon which seem to me so simple and so effective, that I think it should be considered and very soon. I would take it to some one less busy than you if I knew one with imagination and resiliency enough to see its possibilities.

What I wish to ask of you is this—Will you see Dr. Knisely and me in a week or ten days—see us privately and listen to this plan? Within half an hour you will know that we have an easily available weapon more devastating than many battleships or you will not like it at all. Afterwards—if you agree —we will discuss it with any one you may designate on the National Defense Council.

Please forgive this informality, but frankly, I don't know anyone else in authority whom I can address informally.

May I have a yes-no reaction to this letter at your convenience?

Sincerely yours,
John Steinbeck

In the margin, the last two sentences are bracketed and a longhand note says, "Very nice!" Yet James Rowe, Jr., on August 20 sent an information copy to Marvin Watson, with the message:

"I have sent the original to the President, because my guess is that he will have Steinbeck see someone else."

The President, on September 3, in a memorandum for General Watson:

"Will you arrange for Steinbeck and Dr. Knisely to come and see me on September 12th?"

According to Mrs. Knisely:

"The idea was to scatter good counterfeit German paper money over the land, in big amounts. The then Secretary of the Treasury vetoed the idea."

Steinbeck's own comment on the reaction to the suggestion may be found in a later letter to Archibald MacLeish:

"A friend and I took a deadly little plan to Washington and the President liked it but the money men didn't. That is, Lothian and Morgenthau. It would have worked, too, and would work most particularly in Italy."

To Carlton A. Sheffield

Los Gatos
October 15, 1940

Dear Dook:

After a furious exchange of telegrams with Mexico City I guess I am going down on Friday as scheduled.

I'm very glad that you like the ranch. It is so beautiful that often I am embarrassed to be living here. I think it would be a better thing to visit than to own. But I haven't any sense of ownership about it anyway. If I think of owning, I consider it Carol's ranch and feel that I really am just visiting it.

The loneliness and discouragement are by no means a thing that has passed. In fact they seem to crowd in more than ever. Only now I can't talk to anyone much about them or even admit having them because I now possess the things that the great majority of people think are the death of loneliness and discouragement. Only they aren't. The last time I saw Chaplin (this don't repeat please but it is a part of the same thing) it was the night when the little lady [Paulette Goddard] was leaving him for good. And he said, "When I get this picture opened and all the formal things done, can I please go up to your ranch and kick all the servants out and just talk a little bit quietly about how lonely and sad I am? It will be self indulgence but I'd like to do it." He is a good little man. And he knows so much better than I do the horrors of being a celebrity.

It is so strange—remember how we used to think of Mexico as the golden something and we never really thought we would get there for all our talk. Certainly I never thought I would be going again and again and not particularly wanting to. It's like all the beautiful ladies. I remember wishing so much I could just associate with them. And now they bore me so completely, because they aren't really beautiful at all. I know one or two who make me feel full and warm and excited and happy and they aren't the really beautiful ones at all, I mean the accepted beautiful ones.

Carol has a new hobby which she likes. She takes two big buckets and goes up into the pastures and fills them with dry cow manure and then she brings them down and puts them on the garden and then she makes another trip. It satisfies some profound anthropomorphic economy in her, and besides, she thinks it is a little funny.

I have to go now. The carpenter who built this house fell off a roof a couple of days ago and broke his leg and he is down in a hospital and I want to go down to see him.

See you when I get back.

love
john

Steinbeck's life was now about to take a new course. It happened through his two boyhood friends, the sons of Edith Wagner, Jack and Max. Jack had gone from Salinas to Hollywood in the early days of films as a gag man for Mack Sennett and had then stayed on in the developing industry as a scriptwriter. Max Wagner was an actor. Through them Steinbeck had recently met a pretty girl, a professional singer named Gwendolyn Conger.

To Max Wagner
IN HOLLYWOOD

Mexico
[November 1, 1940]

Dear Max:

I wish you and Gwen were down here. It's all work and not much else. Out at daylight and back after dark. But we're getting a picture on film—one of the first times a Mexican pueblito has been photographed. I hope it is good. I know it is true—so true that in direction we don't say "Do this!" but "Do as you always do." And what natural actors they are. When the film gets to Hollywood I'll show it to both of you right away.

I got a big ring for you. I hope big enough. And something else I won't tell you about. Don't exactly know when I'll be through but sometime between the fifteenth and twentieth. I'll wire you when I am arriving and maybe you and Gwen will meet me because I have little presents for her too.

The days of the dead are here and our village is drunk to a man and a woman. They have been gradually picking up their binges for three days and they have two days to run. They mix pulque and aguardiente and it flops them beautifully. Our problem is mainly light. Herb [Kline, the director] cannot learn that a Mexican answers what you want to hear. He asked if the October sky was clear and of course they said yes. I could have told him that there is rarely a cloudless afternoon in October. You see, this is not like a studio picture. We have to wait for light and catch it as we can.

I'm a little bored because too much picture and not much else. I'd like to play a little, but it's dull having no one to play with. Once in a while I go out with Delgado, our second camera man. He's a good scout but he has only one thing on his mind and he doesn't play at it. It is life work with him.

Besides, he is sleeping with a deputado's wife and is a little jumpy. Any sudden noise and a forty-five appears in his hand. I don't know how it gets there. Anyway, it is not restful. When I go out with him I find myself taking a chair which is at right angles to a line drawn from the entrance through Delgado. It's just an instinct to be out of the line of fire. Deputados are nervous men and the laws don't apply to them.

I think that's about all. Look after Gwen a little, will you? And there's something I want you to do for me when I get back. But I'll tell you about that when I see you.

Love to your family.

Chocolo Chamaco!
John

Steinbeck had hoped to arrange for Max Wagner to speak the narration of *The Forgotten Village,* and had mentioned this hope to Wagner himself.

To Max Wagner

[Los Gatos]
[November 23, 1940]

Dear Max:

I have subjected you to a test no friend has any right to expect any friend to survive. I have wondered if you know I knew the stringency of the test. I did not do it to test you. You knew that. But the test was there. You know that I love you as a friend and trust you beyond ordinary understanding of trust. I have not said it, thinking, in fact, knowing that you knew it.

This last thing was an humiliation to you. Shall I recall it? I said, "Max, I want you to do this thing because it is a thing you could do through love." And I said, "The backers want

[Spencer] Tracy. He has technique and a name that can be counted in money." I did not think his studio would let him do it. He has a great heart. I knew he would want to do it. And then they let him. Do you feel that I have let you down? Understand, that if I wanted to fight I could force the issue. I could make it so that you could do it.

Let me tell you something—perhaps another cowardice, perhaps a wisdom. I don't know. Recently I was at Del Monte and there came to my table people, our dear friends from Salinas. We drank and they said—"When you're in Hollywood do you ever see Wagner?" And I said, "Always." And then there was a word, only one—and I felt my hair rise. You have never fought me so you don't know. And I stood up and in the middle of it—I sat down again because of a grey sadness. I knew then they could not know you and my beating them to death would not let them know. And I sat down. Because I think that only I and Gwen maybe know who and what Max is, how beautiful, how valuable. And in the middle of anger it seemed to me that I would dirty your goodness by fighting and so I killed it by saying—"Max is my friend." And they—the curs, who hate me and are afraid of me, were afraid to violate my friend in my presence. But they would violate both of us if neither of us were there.

And the same thing with this picture. I could force it but that might be bad. I think you with your love could do a better thing than the other with his technique.

You have given me a great deal, Max. I want to repay and I won't know how, because you are beyond the reach of ordinary presents. You have given me loyalty I have almost given up hoping for in all the world. And you have given me friendship when everyone else was using me in some way.

You could have been a great actor if you had wanted to— the feeling was there and from the feeling would have come ability. But you didn't want to. I think you didn't have the mean little ambition. You are proud of me now. I hope you know that I have no pride—that I know the series of accidents which gave me this silly name.

I value you as I value very few people in the world. Know this, Max. When I called you hermano, I meant it in the most tremendous sense I know.

Adios, Max a dios—los dos—espero.

John—qui es y
sera tu hermano.

Please tell Gwen that I am making a song for her and I have never made a song for anyone before. I love you both. And protect her a little, please. For she is dear to me.

A week later he wrote Max again, worried because:

"Gwen writes that you had another heart flurry. I hope you will take it easy a little while. I know you have a very deep and basic unhappiness and I suspect that even you don't know what causes it. Meanwhile I go on arguing for myself—for the three, in fact. Slow up a bit for us if not for yourself."

He hoped Max would come north to visit him.

"I'd like to talk to you. Besides it would be good for you to see your own country. We'll go to the Corral de Tierra and maybe to Fremont's Peak and to the hole in the river. And of course the third who somehow has become an integral part even if she does seem to sneer at Monterey County."

To Webster F. Street

Los Gatos
[December 12, 1940]
Thursday

Dear Toby:

Why is it, do you suppose, that we don't get together any more? Of course, I know you are carrying some big secret in you that is bigger than you and that you've turned inward on your secret. And I suppose I've turned inward on something too. And I don't think there's any suspicion between us—maybe it's all just the grown-up conviction that there isn't any possible communication so what's the use

217

of trying any more? Maybe it's that. Maybe the whole first part of living is frantic attempts to communicate and then all of a sudden you stop trying and that's what makes the eyes change and the manner change. I talked to a girl recently whom I had known in Stanford and she told me she had been very much afraid of me because—she said, "I was afraid if I stopped listening to you for a moment, you'd flare into rage and knock me down." I guess that's the same thing.

But we've become such strangers and no seeming way out of it. You're surrounded with things and I am too. And sometimes I get so dreadfully homesick I can't stand it and then realize that it's not for any home I ever had. And the passionate youthful desire to communicate was the same kind of homesickness. It's curious and it doesn't get any better, only one learns not to talk about it. And if everyone is that way, I wonder why they all learn not to talk about it. Their eyes get dull with disgust or pain or tiredness. I haven't crossed the hump I guess or I wouldn't be writing this letter.

But I sit upon this beautiful ranch in this comfortable chair with a perfect servant and a beautiful dog and I think I'm more homesick than ever.

John

On returning home after a holiday visit to Hollywood with Carol:

To Max Wagner and Gwendolyn Conger

[Los Gatos]
December 26, 1940
Thursday

Dear Max and Gwen:

I'm sending this to Max because Gwen will be moving. I thought I was just nervous the last day I saw you—Sunday. Carol was pretty sick—a hangover, she thought. Sunday night the phone rang and rang until I got hysterical and cut it off. Monday morning we both felt terrible but started out in the rain. God knows how we got here. I was half out of my head when we got here. Joe went for a doctor. I had 104° and Carol 103°. We were deep in the flu. So he sent a nurse up. I'd been off my nut for two days. Just out now and must stay in bed for several days. I don't yet know how I drove that far in that condition. The doctor says it couldn't be done. Whole thing seems like a nightmare. We had no Christmas of any kind and will have no New Year's either. Jesus, I'm weak. But you've had it. You know what it's like—just saps you.

Wire from Herb [Herbert Kline, the film director] says he'll be up with the film about the tenth, so I'll see you about then. This is just a note. I'm all wrung out.

John

Three days later he wrote Max again, this time feeling that subterfuge was necessary: Gwendolyn Conger is referred to as "the secretary" and their rendezvous as "club meetings."

To Max Wagner

[Los Gatos]
[December 29, 1940]

Dear Max:

Since the secretary is moving and the mail is uncertain, I'll make this report through you. It seems that I had more than the flu. I had pneumonia. They piled me full of one of the sulphanilamide compounds and licked it in two days. That's wonderful stuff. Now I am sitting up and am pretty weak but feeling good.

Will you tell the secretary that there will be a meeting under the old rules between the fifth and the tenth. I'll wire you when I am flying down. And I won't stay at the Garden of Allah. Too many people can find me there. I'll take a small apartment somewhere.

Will you also tell the secretary that the heat is on the mail a little bit and some other arrangements will have to be worked out. Fix that at the next meeting of the club.

The film will be up soon now.

And I think that's all. I'll let you know when I'm coming down.

John

To Pascal Covici

Los Gatos
January 1 [1941]

Dear Pat:

I'm very glad you are all recovered again and I hope no recurrences. Had you any idea what was wrong with you? Happy New Year anyway.

We are still house ridden from the flu but should be able

to get out a little tomorrow if the sun shines.

Next week I'll go to Hollywood to do my final work on the Mexican film and then I'll move to Pacific Grove to work on the Gulf book. I'll come up here weekends but must be near the lab for the routine work.

And speaking of the happy new year, I wonder if any year ever had less chance of being happy. It's as though the whole race were indulging in a kind of species introversion—as though we looked inward on our neuroses. And the thing we see isn't very pretty. Before the year is over, I think I will be looking back longingly on the Gulf of Lower California—that sea of mirages and timelessness. It is a very magical place.

It is cold and clear here now—the leaves all fallen from the trees and only the frogs are very happy. Great cheering sections of frogs singing all the time. The earth is moist and water is seeping out of the ground everywhere. So we go into this happy new year, knowing that our species has learned nothing, can, as a race, learn nothing—that the experience of ten thousand years has made no impression on the instincts of the million years that preceeded. Maybe you can find some vague theology that will give you hope. Not that I have lost any hope. All the goodness and the heroisms will rise up again, then be cut down again and rise up. It isn't that the evil thing wins—it never will—but that it doesn't die. I don't know why we should expect it to. It seems fairly obvious that two sides of a mirror are required before one has a mirror, that two forces are necessary in man before he is man. I asked Paul de Kruif once if he would like to cure all disease and he said yes. Then I suggested that the man he loved and wanted to cure was a product of all his filth and disease and meanness, his hunger and cruelty. Cure those and you would have not man but an entirely new species you wouldn't recognize and probably wouldn't like.

There it is—It is interesting to watch the German efficiency, which, from the logic of the machine is efficient but which (I suspect) from the mechanics of the human species is suicidal. Certainly man thrives best (or has at least) in a state of semi-anarchy. Then he has been strong, inventive, reliant, moving. But cage him with rules, feed him and make him healthy and I think he will die as surely as a caged wolf dies. I should not be surprised to see a cared for, thought for, planned for nation disintegrate, while a ragged, hungry, lustful nation survived. Surely no great all-encompassing plan has ever succeeded. And so I'll look to see this German plan collapse because they do not know enough to plan for everything.

I hope you will be well now and that before long you will be coming out our way. Heaven knows when I will get east again. There's no reason to go.

Love to Dorothy and to Paco and again my questionable happy new year.

John

The mood persisted, with the rain, and with "a strange relapse of Carol's flu that keeps her weak and sick," as he wrote Elizabeth Otis toward the end of January.

"Wish she'd go to the desert for a couple of weeks but she doesn't seem to want to. And this time I can't take her. I simply have to get down to my book.

"What a time of waiting this is! Everyone poised between two breaths. I seem to have a lot of writing energy now but it is so bound up in sadness and solar plexus longings that I don't trust it. Sometime I'll tell you—maybe. Greenness going out of life, I guess. Happens to everyone. But no relaxation of the restlessness. That continues—always has and I suppose always will. Seem to have been pacing back and forth always. And it doesn't get any less."

To Louis Paul

[Eardley Street]
Pacific Grove
[1941]
Monday

Dear Louis:

I hadn't been to the ranch for some time and consequently the book you sent me was up there. I am very grateful for it and will get to it immediately. I read snatches of dialogue here and there and liked it very well. I'll write you as soon as I finish it and meanwhile thank you very much.

Am living down here now. Bought a little house to live in and I think I am going to sell the ranch. Inevitabilities caught up with me and I don't much want to discuss them now nor until some time has given some perspective. Anyway I am working very hard on the gulf book and I think it might be something rather good. Work is about the most thing I do now. There's a fine safety in it.

I hope you are doing well. My agents say that book sales are terrible now. I have the little Mexican book of pictures [*The Forgotten Village*]. It is a tour de force and was Pat's idea not mine. But he has sold it to the Book League and so far the critics don't seem to know it is a phoney. It is only a phoney because it isn't a book at all but a trailer for a moving picture and the trailer costs two fifty which is enough for a real book and too much for a trailer. But if Pat is able to sell it I guess that makes it a book to every body but me. I still think it is a trailer.

This house down here has a big garden and is very simple and pretty and about the right size for me. I was kidding myself thinking I was a gentleman farmer. I'm not. I'm half bum and half voluptuary and half workman and that makes me one and a half of something and that isn't enough. Nerves pretty bad but otherwise all right except for the horrors all the time. Funny how easy it seems for other people.

I'd like to see you if you ever get down this way.

affectionately,
John

223

To Max Wagner

Los Gatos
[February 2, 1941]
Saturday Night

Dear Max:

There are several things to report to the club. One—I got a very guarded phone call from Spence [Spencer Tracy] asking me to come down for the narrative. He, I think, is a little afraid of Herb's direction. And I promised him I would. That's for next weekend. I don't know how I'll come down, drive or fly. I'll phone the secretary Monday from Monterey.

When I drove up from Monterey yesterday Carol looked so low and bad and so weak from all this rain that I made arrangements to send her to Honolulu for six weeks. The sun will jack her up. Anyway, she sails next Thursday at noon. I'll either fly south then or drive south. I don't know which, yet. So I'll be seeing you next weekend anyway and maybe a little bitty meeting might be held.

How are you feeling now? I hope the B$_1$ holds and builds some nerves. If you should get this letter Monday morning, would you tell the secretary I'll phone about noon and will just leave a person to person in until the call is completed. I'll call from the lab.

I guess that's all.

John

To Elizabeth Otis

Dear Elizabeth:

Well, I am back from Hollywood and I hope for the last time. Put Carol on the boat and then word that Herb was in the hospital and that Tracy wasn't to be let to do the commentary [for *The Forgotten Village*]. They wanted me down there, so I went. Got Burgess Meredith to do the commentary and he will do a good job too.

I have a good deal of anger left, that's all. The picture is good and should be sold. We got taken by M-G-M and I feel vengeful about it. Here's the story as I finally traced it down. Tracy wanted to do this commentary very much. M-G-M wanted him to do a new version of Jekyll and Hyde which he didn't want to do. So they promised him he could do the narration for me if he would do Jekyll. So he started it. Then they cut him off the narrative knowing he wouldn't stop a picture already in production. I would like to teach them not to tread on me. Mannix [Edward Mannix of M-G-M] is the man I'm after. I intend to blast their production of Tortilla Flat with everything I have. Life has asked me to do a story on the true Tortilla Flat and I may take it just to slap M-G-M. Perhaps you do not think revenge is good but I would like to teach these bastards they can't double-cross me with impunity.

To this end I wish you would read The Yearling again. Just a little boy named Jody has affection for a deer. Now I know there is no plagiarism on The Red Pony. But we are going to make The Red Pony, and two stories about a little boy in relation to animals is too much, particularly if in both cases the little boy's name is Jody. Will you see if we can't stop them from using the name and as much of the story as seems possible? If we don't want money we might easily get a court order. And I want to plague them as much as I can. I have a dozen ways, these are just two. I'd like advice on the second.

The next is funny. Donald Friede wanted to meet me and

Pat arranged it. He worked for two days on me to go into the Selznick agency—only for pictures, you understand—greatest respect for M & O but this has nothing to do with them. His offers were fantastic. He even told a girl I know he would see that she did all right if she would persuade me. I wouldn't mention this to anyone else but I do think it is funny. And of course it got exactly nowhere. The only thing I want in the world not he nor anyone else can give me but I didn't tell him that.

I have one more request to make of you. Do you remember a long time ago I wrote a story called How Edith McGillicuddy Met R.L.S.?

This was the story that Steinbeck had written based on an experience of Max and Jack Wagner's mother.

Well, she has finally released it or rather got back her rights and it was never published. Remember I had to withdraw it? Well, she is very old and crippled now and quite poor. I am sending you the story. Do you think you can sell it? It's my story and under my name. If you can sell it, maybe to a national magazine, get as much as you can for it and I will turn the money over to her. It must not be mentioned in print that she needs the money but you can tell any editor it is a true story. It would make her feel good and would ease the little time she has left if you could do this.

Had a letter from Carol but in Los Angeles. No word from her in the Islands yet but she was having a wonderful time on the boat, already just about owned it. She will have a marvelous time of it.

Good luck and all. And love to you,

John

Steinbeck's story ("How Edith McGillicuddy Met R.L.S.") was published in *Harper's Magazine.* As he wrote Max Wagner:

226

"Look, Max—today I am sending your mother a check for $225. It was all I could get for the little story. The national magazines wouldn't have anything to do with it. God knows it isn't much but she could maybe get some pretties with it."

The story was later reprinted in *The Portable Steinbeck* (revised edition, 1946).

Carol stayed in Honolulu while he worked on the "Log" from *Sea of Cortez*. At the end of March, he reported:

"Carol is getting back next Wednesday. She says she feels fine and healthy. I hope so. She hasn't had an easy time of it in health as you know."

To Mavis McIntosh

Pacific Grove
April 16 [1941]

Dear Mavis:

This has been a hell of a time and I'm pretty shaky but at least I'll try to give you a small idea of what happened. My nerves cracked to pieces and I told Carol the whole thing, told her how deeply involved I was and how little was left. She said she wanted what was left and was going to fight. So there we are. All in the open, all above board. I'm staying with Carol as I must. I don't know what Gwen will do nor does she. Just as badly tied there as ever—worse if anything. Carol acting magnificently. I don't know why in hell anybody would want to bother with me. Anyway, Carol won the outside and G the inside and I don't seem able to get put back together again.

We're selling the ranch. I bought a small house and garden in Pacific Grove but you'd better write me c/o the Lab for a while. Can't even remember the name of the street. Probably will before I finish this. Guess I was pretty close to a complete crack up but probably have passed it now. We're camping down here really now. And I'm trying to pull myself together but pretty bruised as everyone is. Funny thing. All looks hopeless now but I suppose time will fix things. And at least no more whispering is necessary.

This house is at 425 Eardley. I just went and looked. Sorry to have been all this trouble to you. Seem to have got about as low as one can go. Anyway that is our address now. I think things will be all right. Tell Elizabeth any of this you wish but don't trouble her with it. The work is badly shot but I'm fighting with that too. Fun huh?

> Love to you all
> John

Six years later Steinbeck wrote Bo Beskow in Sweden about this period:

"When I wrote the text of the Sea of Cortez, Gwen and I were hiding in the pine woods in a cabin and she would sleep late and I would get up and build a big fire and work until noon when she woke up and that would be the end of work for the day and we would go walking in the sand dunes and eat thousands of doughnuts and coffee. I worked very hard."

To Elizabeth Otis

> [Pacific Grove]
> May 19, 1941
> Monday

Dear Elizabeth:

I had your letter with the check in it a few days ago. Many thanks. I've been very raddled and torn out by the roots. Nightmared, etc. In many ways I have more of a sense of peace than I have ever had and am working hard but I get the horrors pretty often. It's an awful thing to me to be cruel. I don't do it well. Meanwhile, as you know, I am having my assets gone over very carefully and will give Carol half and her interest in my contracts will probably make it more. Terrific income tax this year and heavier next will cut it down of course.

I'm putting an awful burden on you. Came very close to cracking up and I guess did but not finally. Getting stronger now though. The work saves me a lot. If only Carol can be happy and whole, it will work. I don't know. I had arrived at your advice independently, not to try to think but to let the work go on and time get in some licks. Seems to be the only thing. I don't know that it is true but from her letters Carol seems more perturbed about people finding out about the separation than about the separation itself. Her terrific pride, I guess. But she is being very fine. I hope she is finding some content.

We got off a lot of ms. to you which you probably have by now. It is more than Pat asked for. A brutally peremptory letter from him to Ed this morning demanded it.

Don't expect any sense from me for a while or maybe never. If I can get a little in work that's all I can expect.

Meanwhile my love to all of you and don't think too badly of me—or do if it is necessary.

John

It was no doubt in reference to this period that, much later, in "About Ed Ricketts" (prefatory section in *Log from the Sea of Cortez*) he wrote:

"Once, when I had suffered an overwhelming emotional upset, I went to the laboratory to stay with him. I was dull and speechless with shock and pain. He used music on me like medicine. Late in the night when he should have been asleep, he played music for me on his great phonograph—even when I was asleep he played it, knowing that its soothing would get into my dark confusion."

229

To Pascal Covici

Pacific Grove
June 19, 1941

Dear Pat:

Good letter from you this morning which I will answer at once. I'm glad you like that subtitle [*A Leisurely Journal of Travel and Research*]. It seems with every word to define some part of the book.

I'm pretty sure the book will be good but that doesn't mean it won't flop completely. But I do think if it gets a slow start, it will gradually pick up because there is much more than just collection in it. Gradually it will be discovered that it is a whole new approach to thinking and only very gradually will the philosophic basis emerge. Scientific men, the good ones, will know what we are talking about. In fact some of them out here already do. It will only outrage the second-rate scientists who are ready to yell mysticism the moment anything gets dangerously near to careful thinking and a little bit out of their range.

As for myself, and you say you are worrying about me—I would give up worrying. I am working as hard and as well as I can and I don't dare do anything else. I've been pretty near to a number of edges and am not away from them yet by any means but I find safety in work and that is the only safety I do find. There is no ego in my work and consequently there is no danger for me in it. All of it is extension. If it once became introverted I wouldn't last twenty-four hours. But I know that and thus I am able to take care of myself. When this work is done I will have finished a cycle of work that has been biting me for many years. Some one has to sit out these crises in the world and try to see them in perspective. Perhaps this book does that and perhaps it doesn't. But it does say by implication that the world will go on and that this isn't the first time.

My personal life is a curious thing which I won't permit myself to think about yet. I don't want it to get important until I have finished this work. And don't worry about my cracking up. I won't. You'll get the book and you won't be ashamed of it, I don't think, although you will probably be pretty much scorned and excoriated for having printed it. Because it does attack some very sacred things, but not at all viciously. Rather with good humour which may be much more devastating.

You say that you hope all will be well with me. That is a nice thing to hope although you know it won't and can't be. I haven't a hell of a lot more time but I have some. I make messes every where but I guess everyone does only with some people they don't show. So don't worry about me. I can see myself pretty objectively and the picture is a little silly.

love to you all
John

Among the reports on work and questions about business in letters of this period, there is always a paragraph that reflects his personal crisis. On June 24, to Elizabeth Otis, he wrote:

"Letters from Carol full of goodness and sweetness and they help a lot. I suspect that I am in such turmoil that I won't have anything to do with myself for a good long time. I don't have to as long as there is work to do. And after that there will be more work to do."

And on July 4, to Pascal Covici, "still shaky" from having finished a first draft of *Sea of Cortez*:

"Thanks for the thoughts. Certainly there is fulfillment here but the haunting is here too and I don't know when I will lose that. Maybe never. There are great changes in me, some for the better and some, socially at least, for the worse. Word comes to me from Hollywood that I am drinking myself to death and indulging in all kinds of vices. As a matter of fact, I am drinking very very little and if that other is a vice then I'm vicious. And I'm doing more work than I ever did. I love the things people say. See if the manuscript sounds like drinking.

231

"This book is very carefully planned and designed, Pat, but I don't think its plan will be immediately apparent. And again there are four levels of statement in it and I think very few will follow it down to the fourth. I even think it is a new kind of writing. I told you once that I found a great paltry in scientific thinking. Perhaps I haven't done it but I've tried and it is there to be done."

To Elizabeth Otis

[Pacific Grove]
July 18, 1941

Dear Elizabeth:

We are working like beavers and should finish second draft about next Wednesday, that is of my part. Pat says he wants carefully corrected second draft rather than waiting three weeks for perfect third draft so we will send it to you as soon as it is corrected. I think it reads pretty well.

I am of course holding my breath about C. [Carol] I wish I could get over the horrors about her. It comes back and back in a blind blackness that is awfully sharp. There is only one possibility for me, only one in all of them, and that is that she should meet someone whom she could fall in love with, someone who is good and strong and good to her. If that doesn't happen the haunt is not going to be laid over. I know how much she needs help. God knows I'm no bargain. Probably as difficult to live with as anyone in the world. But I haven't been lately.

Throughout all of this people say and think that if I had just done so and so and if Carol had just done so and so it would have been all right. But there was no trick that would make it whole. It was a basic disagreement that went even into our cells. You can't get peace and unconscious understanding out of some trick of behavior. Well, enough of this. I'll try to work it out. I wonder why you think September is a critical month. I am making no plans except work plans because I think hell will pop and that before very long. But

I'm sure I can take it now whatever happens. And that is a good thing to know. I wish I could lose the pictures of abject horror though. I wish you could come out.

The ranch is a worry. It just lies there and I can't bring myself yet to go back to it. Haven't had time of course but soon I must do it.

I hope you have a good vacation.

Love to you all.

John

The worries continued, obtruding themselves into all other preoccupations. At the end of September, he wrote Elizabeth Otis and Mavis McIntosh, apparently in response to a suggestion of the latter's:

"I really can't see any reason for my staying and 'taking it,' because I've taken it many times and no good comes of it. So we had more or less planned to go East and then it was taken out of my hands. I had a request which amounts to a command to go to Washington for a conference. I had made certain suggestions. Then we will go on to New York. I may write my play there. [This is the first mention of the play that became *The Moon Is Down*.] I suppose it is cowardly to run away but if anything could be accomplished I would stay. I shall write Carol the truth—that I intended to go so that she would not be embarrassed and then that I had to go too. Galleys on the *Sea* started coming today and we'll whip them out. What will hurt more than anything else is that all our friends like Gwen. My sisters and all the acquaintances. And I guess that's all. I hope Carol can find some peace somewhere. She couldn't with me."

Steinbeck and Gwendolyn Conger moved East at about this time, and his old friend and now his attorney, Webster Street, became for a while his most intimate correspondent.

233

To Webster F. Street
IN MONTEREY

[c/o Burgess Meredith]
[Suffern, New York]
[October 18, 1941]

Dear Toby:

I should have written you before but I have been terribly rushed. I've been working on script and doing some work to try to get The Forgotten Village released and now at last I am up at Meredith's place and I'm working on a play. It is very beautiful up here and I am working and resting at the same time.

Thank you, Toby, for everything. I know I'm socially wrong —the wife deserter and cad—but I suddenly gave up. I tried for thirteen years, did everything I could and failed. Maybe a better man than I could succeed. I wasn't good enough. But maybe I'm good enough for someone else whose standards aren't quite so strict and who thinks in terms of giving as well as receiving. I don't want her feeling hurt about any of this.

Let her think anything of me she wants. She will want to think me bad or she can't think herself good and that doesn't matter to me. I'm neither bad nor good but some of both. I know how hard this is to handle, Toby. As to a divorce, that will have to come from her since she has committed no crime against the marriage and I have. That must be her decision since she is the wronged one. Let her take anything out of the house that she wants.

Love to you and
many thanks
John

To Mrs. Franklin D. Roosevelt

c/o Burgess Meredith
Suffern, New York
[Late October 1941]

Dear Mrs. Roosevelt:

I want to thank you for your interest and help in the matter of the censorship of The Forgotten Village. I spoke with Miguel Covarrubias a day or so ago and he told me something of your help. I detest the application of the words "inhuman" and "indecent" to this film. It seemed to me that it was undertaken and carried out with considerable purity of motive.

Anyway, I am exceedingly grateful for your advocacy.

Very sincerely yours,
John Steinbeck

To Webster F. Street

[Bedford Hotel]
[New York]
November 17, 1941

Dear Toby:

Your letters to Gwen and me came last night and we were very glad to get them. I had been away all day working. This funny small hotel and the little kitchenette have become a haven for us. Very few people know we are here. It is mostly thought that we live in the country and we do often enough to keep up the illusion. It's rather a pleasant room.

I finished my play and heard it read and the last act is very sour and has to be done over. I started and suddenly got one of those gray barriers that come from overwork. So I took two days off. I went to the meeting of the Board of Regents and

235

heard the arguments about The Forgotten Village and I think they will uphold the censorship, not because of the picture but because the censor board is an authoritative committee and to interfere with its findings would be to weaken its prestige.

I have seen [Herman] Shumlin one day and [Oscar] Serlin another day and I'm seeing another producer this afternoon. None of them have read the play yet. No one may want it. And I really don't care very much. There's no imminence. I have now four irons in the fire. The Play—which has no name yet, The Forgotten Village, The Red Pony, The Sea of Cortez, and one new one. All of them may crash for all I know. But I feel singularly free and a little wild. I don't know why. Something in the air, something crazy. I might even go and buy a suit and a red dress for Gwen.

Monday

It was a little wild. I got two dresses for Gwen and ordered three suits. My clothes were falling off me and I needed them. Gwen wrote you Saturday. Did she tell you the Regents reversed the censor board and The Forgotten Village can now open?

Very low today. Went out in the country yesterday but I didn't drink much. One of my periodic lownesses. I don't have them terribly often any more. And this one will go. Sense of frightful complication and confusion and fun. Well, I'll finish my play this week anyway and it may be absolutely no good. But at least I am a little rested from it.

Guess that's all right now. I have a sense that something terrible is about to happen but that is not very unusual for me.

Love,
John

At this point, Gwendolyn Conger changed the spelling of her name to Gwyndolyn, and is henceforth referred to as Gwyn.

To Webster F. Street

Dear Toby:

Two good letters from you and made us feel good to get them. We spent our Thanksgiving in a hotel room, Gwyn with a cold. At last the cold weather is here so the colds can go. I don't know why that is so but it is. I deplore your dogless-ness in beach walking. You should have your own personal dog marked private or clipped private.

The play? It's about a little town invaded. It has no generalities, no ideals, no speeches, it's just about the way the people of a little town would feel if it were invaded. It isn't any country and there is no dialect and it's about how the invaders feel about it too. It's one of the first sensible things to be written about these things and I don't know whether it is any good or not.

> He was writing broadcasts for what was to become the Office of War Information.

I have to go to Washington to do some work in about a week. May have to move there which is terrible because of the housing shortage; but the work is to be done and I have to do it. So there's no lack of work. In fact I have a wonderful idea for a book I'd like to work on. It's wonderful how much work I can do. I'll see that you get a copy of the book, the Sea I mean when it comes out. They haven't even got manufac-tured books yet.

[unsigned]

To Webster F. Street

[New York]
December 8, 1941

Dear Toby:

Last afternoon was the attack on Honolulu. Wasn't that a quick one? We'll take some pretty brutal losses for a while I'm afraid, but I think the attack, whatever it may have gained from a tactical point of view, was a failure in that it solidified the country. But we'll lose lots of ships for a while. I'm going to work very soon now. Got an extension for purposes of this play. Its new title is The Moon Is Down and it should go into some kind of production this week. I just finished the play script last night.

The reviews of The Sea of Cortez are extremely good and lively. Tomorrow I'll send you one. I wonder whether I should send one to Carol? I sent her a carbon and she never mentioned it to me and she told Pat it wasn't any good. What do you think? What would hurt her least—to get it or not to get?

I wonder whether they picked up my [Japanese] gardener. I guess they will before very long. I suppose if they do you might just as well lock up the house. I wish you would sell the truck. There isn't any reason to keep it that I can think of. I'm taking a job which will probably be for the duration and there is no need to hang on to that truck. I'll keep my car though. I'll try to put things in pretty good shape before I get into the work. I may have a day or a week or a month. But I'll let you know and where I can be reached. Things move fast.

Love,
John

To Webster F. Street

Dear Toby:

I'm up a little earlier than usual so maybe I'll be able to write you a letter without being interrupted. I've been working on my play, testing lines and words and scenes and Lee Strasberg the director has been here every day. The trouble with Shumlin was very simple. He didn't want the kind of play I had written and he did want another kind of play. Serlin does want this kind of play. Maybe it's no good but it is this way. And I'm very tired of it. I should get it all done this week.

I'm feeling low this morning. I'd like to be west and God knows when that will be—maybe not until the war is over. I guess Carol hates me very much and I don't like to be hated. I'd like to go to that little house and settle for a while. No soap. I guess you'd better have the telephone cut off.

Gwyn is well. This suitcase life is not very satisfactory to her. She wants some place to light but there is none in sight. She doesn't complain at all though. And when I do get called I don't know where it will be—maybe Washington, maybe not. The new little book [*The Moon Is Down,* novel] will be out the end of Feb or early in March. Viking Press thinks it will sell a lot of them. The Sea is moving very slowly and it will never make any money. I'm awfully glad we did it and that way.

It's nice in New York now—a light snow on the tops of buildings and the air is crisp and wonderful to walk in. I've had too much on my mind to let go and just walk in it. Maybe I should.

Anyway the physical clearness of my own personal life should come out in or within two weeks. Then I'll let you know. Meanwhile Gwynnie sits on a bag of dynamite, but she is good about it. I think she wants security more than anyone I ever knew. Carol thought she did and didn't. But Gwyn who has never had any has really a gift for it—an inner security which could make an outer one if given half a chance. And so far she hasn't had that chance. If we could even take a house or an apartment in Washington that's all she wants. She wants to cook. She doesn't talk about any of these things. Do you know that the little time in the Grove is the only time since she was a little girl that she ever had a home? And oddly enough it is the only time I ever had one either.

You know it's a funny thing—I've written myself out of my lowness in this letter. I feel better and clearer. I can see this director today without dreading it. The sun has come out on the snowy roofs and there's a barrel organ playing in the street. Maybe there's some gaiety in the world. That need have nothing to do with comfort. But I'm more patient than when I started writing this letter.

After the war is done, if I can, I know what I want if my domestic difficulties and my finances will permit it. I want about ten acres near the ocean and near Monterey and I want a shabby comfortable house and room for animals, maybe a horse, and some dogs and I want some babies. Maybe I can't ever get that but it's what I want. And I'm pretty sure it's what Gwyn wants too. Then maybe I want a small boat. I suppose there isn't a chance in the world of having these. Something will come up but I'm going to try and get them just as soon as the war is over. And I may not even wait for that to start getting the babies. I know now that Gwyn can run a hospitable house where I am welcome. That's the astonishing thing. I've never been welcome. That's why our houses were so doleful. There was no hospitality in them. It is curious that I sit here and plan what is probably an impossible future. My earning years in terms of money are nearly over. Not that I won't work and probably do good work. But the years of a writer financially are very few. And there will be no chance of picking up another reserve. But that is all right too. We'll get along. There's love in the house even here.

I guess that's all. I've run off at the mouth a good deal. A kind of babbling. But seems to have been necessary.

Love
John

Webster Street was Steinbeck's only correspondent through the winter of 1942. Because of problems of his own, he had moved into Steinbeck's house.

"I can't tell you how glad I am that you are in the house with fires going and somebody enjoying it," Steinbeck wrote him. "It is a pleasant little house and we miss it, but we miss the people out there even more, among whom you are paramount. You'll find you get a lot of thinking done in that house."

In almost every letter he writes something about the house.

"You will look after the rabbits, won't you? Gwynnie worries that they will be hurt or hungry."

And:

"I don't imagine we will get out there to see the nice garden before it is all weed grown again. Would you get my guns out of the study and oil them a little if they are getting rusty? I wish we could be out there with you sitting beside the fire."

He reverts to the immediate past—the horrors, as he calls them.

"I still get them all the time. Kind of something that goes on in the back of my mind—what could I have done to save it? I think I still have the desire to be good. And hurting people isn't good and I've hurt C. —consequently I'm not good. This apart from the fact that we were destroying each other."

He champs with impatience at the delays of bureaucracy.

"Washington is still letting me dangle here and I'm getting pretty disgusted about it. They won't let me go away. I'm going to the country tomorrow because I am so fed up with the city I am nearly nuts. I know if I get fifty miles away I'll be called back."

And:

"I'm finding curious things about gov't. My outfit does not assign me and will not release me for other work. Some very pleasant jobs are offered me and I can't take them. I'm getting angry about it. This has been a year in which I've been held in suspension, but I've got a lot of work done in spite of it."

He reports with satisfaction and awe about the success of *The Moon Is Down* in book form.

"The new book is doing frighteningly well. Prepublication it is outselling Grapes two to one. In trade edition there will be a pre-publication sale of 85,000 and Book of the Month Club is ordering 200,000. It is kind of crazy. The hysteria of the bookshops in ordering is very wild. The play is being cast now and should go into rehearsal about the 15th of February and will open about a month later."

And through it all, he is happy.

"My emotional life has been good. Gwyn works at a relationship and this is a new and lovely thing to me. She likes being a woman and likes being in love. This is a new experience to me."

"I seem to take energy from a good relationship with Gwyn that makes me want to work all the time."

Years later, Steinbeck's old friend, the novelist John O'Hara, said of Gwyn to Elaine Steinbeck: "She had the most beautiful skin I ever saw on a woman."

To Webster F. Street

[Bedford Hotel]
[New York]
February 14, 1942

Dear Toby:

I don't want to chisel in any way from Carol. I want to give her everything I can. I don't think she will be single long. She will have a lump of money and she is very pretty. I hope to goodness she is happy. Ed writes that she seems to be having a very good time with the Army set. I hope so. The complaint is just. I was cruel to her physically and mentally and she was cruel to me the same way and neither of us could help it.

I am sad at the passage of a good big slice of my life. It could have been ecstatic. That was the age for it. But I still have energy and I am still capable of loving a woman very much. So it isn't really too late for either of us.

It's the first divorce our family ever had and it makes me sad.

[unsigned]

They took a house across the river from New York City at Sneden's Landing.

To Webster F. Street

Palisades, Rockland County
New York
[April 8, 1942]
Tuesday

Dear Toby:

The show opens tonight in New York and there is a very scared cast. They were cocky in Baltimore and they took a beating and now they are properly humble and I think will be much better for it. Gwyn and I are not going. I can't seem to get very excited but a curious kind of wave of excitement is going through theatrical New York. I never saw anything like it. I think the publicity has been so great that the critics will crack down on the play.

So far my work for the government is working out nicely. I go on every night and in the daytime.

Not I, of course. I send the stuff in. I had my voice tested the other day and it was just as I knew it would be. My

243

enunciation is so bad and the boom in my voice is so bad that I can't be understood. I am glad too because now they will never ask me again.

Gwyn has gone down the river to get a fresh shad with roe for dinner. Almost my favorite fish in the world and baked it is perfectly wonderful. Gwyn is not going to catch this fish but to buy it fresh caught at the river side.

It is a fine warm day today and the doors are all open and certain baby flies are wandering around helplessly with wet wings and I am so friendly feeling that I do not even club them down and I really should do. I'll let their wings get dry and then I will miss them.

We are going to sit and have stingers tonight and when the show is over they will call from New York and tell us how it went and then at three o'clock the first reviews will come out and they said they would phone those and I'm not at all sure I want to hear anything at three o'clock. But I can't hurt feelings. And I will answer the phone which fortunately is beside the bed. But I bet there is not much listen about me.

Well, I'll finish this later.

Dear Toby:

And now it is two days later. I'm sending you the reviews and as you will see they are almost uniformly bad. Furthermore, they are almost uniformly right. They don't really know what bothered them about the play, but I do. It was dull. For some reason, probably because of my writing, it didn't come over the footlights. In spite of that it will probably run for several months. It is too bad it isn't better. I don't know why the words don't come through. The controversy that has started as to whether we should not hate blindly is all to the good and is doing no harm. What does the harm is that it is not a dramatically interesting play.

Write soon.

John

Toward the end of the month he wrote to Street:

"Oddly, the play goes on to crowded houses in spite of the critics. The critics have all stopped being critics and have turned propagandists. They are judging what should be told the people, what is good for the people to know. And the people are doing a better job than the critics. They're taking the war fine and working like hell to get it over. They don't seem to need hatred. It's a mechanical war and this is a pretty good mechanical people. I've seen some of the plants now and the men are doing a hell of a job."

Then, turning to his and Toby's similar personal problems:

"I know how you feel and what you go through. Because I'm not done with it by any means. The pain comes from breaking the pattern and from nothing else. You are missing the place you hated to go to but it was a place to go to. Don't let your mind trick you too much. Recapture the memory of the thing that drove you out. That disappears quicker than the other and makes for the unbalance."

In "About Ed Ricketts," Steinbeck reported receiving at the laboratory various surveys written by Japanese scientists before Pearl Harbor.

"Here under our hands were detailed studies of the physical make-up of one of the least-known areas of the world and one which was in the hands of our enemy. Here was all the information needed if we were to make beach landings. We drafted a letter to the Navy Department in Washington. Six weeks later we received a form letter thanking us for our patriotism. I seem to remember that the letter was mimeographed. Ed was philosophical about it, but I got mad. I wrote to the Secretary of the Navy."

To The Honorable Frank Knox
SECRETARY OF THE NAVY

Palisades
May 5, 1942

Dear Mr. Secretary:

I believe that the best way to get information to its proper place is to send it to the chief. I hope you will give the following to the officer of naval intelligence most able to understand and make use of it.

It is not generally known that the most complete topographical as well as faunal information about any given area is found in the zoological and ecological reports of scientists investigating the region.

For a number of years, my partner Edward F. Ricketts and I have been charting the marine animals of the coast of North America and through this work have looked into the publications from other parts of the world, including the Japanese Mandated Islands.

No Occidentals have been allowed to land in the Mandated Islands since they were taken under Japanese control.

The only publications or information to come from these Islands have been the reports of Japanese biologists, who are fine research men and truly pure members of the international scientific fraternity.

The reports are found to contain maps, soundings, reefs, harbors, buoys, lights and photographs of these areas. The information, if not already in the possession of Naval Intelligence, could be very valuable.

Yours truly,
John Steinbeck

"Nothing happened for two months," Steinbeck recalled in "About Ed Ricketts." "I was away when it did happen. One afternoon a tight-lipped man in civilian clothes came into the laboratory and identified himself as a lieutenant commander of Naval Intelligence."

The officer asked if Ricketts or Steinbeck spoke Japanese.

'No—why do you ask?'
'Then what is this information you claim to have about the Pacific Islands?'
"Only then did Ed understand him. 'But they're in English—the papers are all in English! The Japanese zoologists wrote them in English—sometimes quaint English but English.'
"That word tore it. The lieutenant commander looked grim. 'Quaint!' he said. 'You will hear from us.' But we never did. And I have always wondered whether they had the information or got it. I wondered whether some of the soldiers whose landing craft grounded a quarter of a mile from the beach and who had to wade ashore under fire had the feeling that bottom and tidal range either were not known or ignored."

To Webster F. Street

Palisades
July 23, 1942

Dear Toby:

My military status is this. I am appointed Special Consultant to the Secretary of War and assigned to Headquarters of the Army Air Force. The commanding general of the Air Force is writing the Draft Board requesting that I do not be called. I have said that if I were called I would not take a deferment. When this work is done in about three months I will be inducted in the army in the G3 section of the Air Force. I am also a foreign news editor of the Office of War Information. In the early fall probably in September I have to go west to write and oversee a moving picture for the Air Force in Hollywood and after that I take up the G3 work I mentioned. Maybe I am wrong about the number, maybe I mean G2. Intelligence section is the one I mean. I can't keep track of numbers. I am to have a new subsection that has just been authorized.

This coast is completely changed by the gasoline rationing and the dimout. I was in Times Square last night and it is kind of ghostly. Now there are no big signs and the crowds of people seem to be quiet and shadowlike. The streets are very dimly lighted and the traffic signals are blacked out except for thin slits very hard to see. You don't go very fast. You are only allowed to turn on your traffic or rather your parking lights. I don't go into town very often.

I think that is all now.

Love,
John

John Steinbeck and Gwyndolyn Conger went to California in September, as scheduled.

The picture for the Air Force, published in book form the same year, was *Bombs Away: The Story of a Bomber Team.* The picture idea about the Japanese invasion was rejected by O.W.I. as not in the public interest. To Elizabeth Otis and Annie Laurie Williams ten days later:

"We have a very nice house, rented for three months. Gwyn is well. She says we have been living this way for over a year and we can take it some more. She is a very wonderful girl, doing what grousing she has to over little tiny things and then when something important comes up, doing none at all."

248

To Annie Laurie Williams

[Van Nuys, California]
January 8 [1943]

Dear Annie Laurie:

Today Kenneth MacGowan of 20th Century asked me to come out and talk to him. It seems that the Maritime Commission has asked Hitchcock to do a picture about the men of the merchant marine and he wants me to write the story. [This led to *Lifeboat.*] I told them I would like to try it on these terms—that I work a week on it and if I didn't like what I was doing and it didn't seem right for me I would destroy what I had and they could if they wanted pay me for a week's work. If on the other hand I liked what I did and they liked it, then I would finish it and they could deal with you about what they would pay for the story, always understanding that it would be plenty. They accepted that very gladly. I have a number of ideas for such a story. If it should seem to be good then maybe Hitchcock will go east with me and we will talk to some of the seamen who have been torpedoed. I shall write it as a novelette which I will be free to publish if I want to. Of course if the thing on starting doesn't move in my mind and hands I'll simply toss the whole thing out and forget it and Twentieth Century understands that perfectly. They also understand that I may be called to service at any time. Anyway it is exciting and I will enjoy the trying. They are very nice people to deal with as you know.

Love to you all and we'll see you soon.

john

Carol Steinbeck's divorce was about to be granted.

249

To Webster F. Street

Dear Toby:

We are going to New Orleans to be married. Gwyn is going next week and I'll go down about the 27th if I can get a plane.

The next is confidential. I'm so tired of government that I'm going to try something else. Am making passes at being accredited a correspondent from the Herald-Tribune or Colliers or A.P. or something and if it works I will go overseas soon after the 1st of April. I know what I want to do and see and I'll get somebody to send me. It may not work but neither does the army nor the gov't. I run up against nothing but jealousies, ambitions and red tape in Washington. I want a job with a big reactionary paper like the Herald-Tribune because I think I could get places that way I couldn't otherwise.

From what I have seen so far, if I go into the army I would prefer to be a private. The rest is very like the fraternity system at Stanford. I have not been notified of rejection by the way.

I think a big push is starting soon and I would like to see it. That is why I am trying to go as war correspondent. But maybe no one will want me. I only started on this line a day ago.

Love,
John

Four days later Toby informed Steinbeck that the divorce had been granted.

"I can't say there was any joy in that final decree," Steinbeck wrote him. "In fact, it snapped me back into all the bad times of the last years. The final failure of an association. But the association had no chance of succeeding from the very first. I can see that now and can recall step by step how two people hurt each other for eleven years. That's done.

"My corresponding moves along and I should be able to work it out early next week. I think I'd rather go over in a troop ship than fly over. According to the Swedish radio, Moon, which opened two nights ago in Stockholm, is a smash hit. Willie [the dog] is going up to the country around Nyack for the week we will be away. He is looking forward to it."

And, finally, the marriage on March 29, in the courtyard of Lyle Saxon's house in the French Quarter of New Orleans.

"We had a good wedding and a good time and everybody was kind to us and now we are a little bit tired out. It was quite a party."

To Nunnally Johnson about the same time:

"It was a good and noisy wedding. I wish you could have been there. It would have wakened all of your latent romance. People cried and laughed and shouted and got drunk. Oh! It was a fine wedding."

To Webster F. Street

TELEGRAM

NEW YORK
APRIL 5 [1943]

WAR CORRESPONDENT HERALD TRIBUNE ACCREDITED WAR DEPARTMENT EUROPEAN THEATER DEPARTURE MIDDLE APRIL

JOHN

1943 1946
1944 1947
1945 1948

Steinbeck (signature)

"...I half way
believe that I
dreamed you."

1943 War correspondent in European Theater for the New York *Herald Tribune.* First edition of *The Portable Steinbeck* published.

1944 *Lifeboat* (film) released. Birth of son Thom. Moved back to California.

1945 *Cannery Row* published. *The Red Pony* published in four parts. *A Medal for Benny* (film) released. Returned to New York.

1946 Son John born. Awarded the King Haakon Liberty Cross (Norway) for *The Moon Is Down.*

1947 *The Wayward Bus* published; Book-of-the-Month Club selection. *The Pearl,* story published, film released. Correspondent in Russia with photographer Robert Capa for the New York *Herald Tribune.*

1948 *A Russian Journal* published. Separated from Gwyndolyn Steinbeck. Went back to California.

To Webster F. Street

Dear Toby:

I guess I am not going to be allowed to do anything the easy way. Your wire last night indicates that board 119 is doing its usual shit.

If I seem a little bitter it is because I have never had any trouble with generals, with secretaries of departments, but a year and a half has been made horrible by little men with temporary authority who, armed with envy, have pushed me around, lieutenants and such who could put in secret reports they thought I would never see and so forth. I just get a little frantic at the mess. At my age, my only chance of getting near combat area is in the capacity I am working on, and now if I am cut off by these sons of bitches, shit. I get so god damned disgusted with stupidity.

John

By June, the situation was resolved. Leaving Gwyndolyn Steinbeck in the apartment they had taken in New York, he arrived in London as a war correspondent. As he wrote Toby:

"I'm putting about all the stuff I see into the daily work and consequently do not try to write it in letters."

255

To Gwyn, he wrote:

"I have stopped writing to anyone at all except you. I write to you nearly every day and I wonder whether you get my letters."

These letters form a sort of journal, and excerpts are presented here.

To Gwyndolyn Steinbeck

London
July 4 [1943]

My darling:

This is Sunday the Fourth and the streets are full of American homesickness. I have it too. I walked for hours last night and talked to so many of the soldiers. They are angry about the messes in Washington and they are homesick. The reason I have put the date at the top is that I finally have got a calendar. Bob Vining of the navy gave it to me and it is tacked to the wall and I can find out any time I want what the date is, provided of course that I know the day of the week.

I've really got a low time now. Liquor is so expensive and so bad that I do not fall back on it. I guess I've just got what the troops have. It is quite a hot day and hasn't rained in two weeks or more. Already the grass is getting brown. But it looks as though there might be some rain soon. It is getting muggy. This isn't a day to work but I must. I think I'll do a piece today about homesickness in London. That's what is happening here.

I love you and I am homesick too.

[July 1943]

Darling, you want to know what I want of you. Many things of course but chiefly these. I want you to keep this thing we have inviolate and waiting—the person who is neither I nor

256

you but us. It's a hard thing this separation but it is one of the millions of separations at home and many more millions here. It is one hunger in a great starvation but because it is ours it overshadows all the rest, if we let it. But keep waiting and don't let it be hurt by anything because it is the one really precious thing we have. Later we may have others but so far it is a single unit—and you have the keeping of it for a little while. You say I am busy, as though that wiped out my end, but it doesn't. You can be just as homesick and lost when you are busy. I love you beyond words, beyond containing. Remember that always when the distance seems so great and the time so long. It will not be so long, my dear.

July 8 [1943]

Dear Gwyndolyn:

The mails are terrible. Who knows, maybe a lot of letters will come over today.

It is a kind of a grey day with big clouds and the city against them is very beautiful. I have become such an assiduous worker that you wouldn't know me. The hulk that sat in the green chair day in and day out is replaced with a medium young executive, well dressed, courteous, clean, on his toes—business as usual and the chin up and nose on the grind stone. This transformation is happily not permanent. This discipline is good but I can't think what for. It is nothing I am sure that the home double bed won't cure.

The grey day is turned to rain now, a very pleasant and necessary rain.

love to baby
john

July 12 [1943]

My darling.

I wish I could go with this letter. To see you and to hold you would be so good. I know it will seem a very short time when it is over but now it seems interminable like an illness. I have small magic that I practice. When I go to bed, I build up what you look like and how you speak and some times I can almost feel you curling around my back and your breath on my neck. And sometimes it is so real that I am shocked that it isn't so.

257

It is raining today and coming on to the time when it will rain nearly all the time. And this morning which is Monday it fills me with gloom. I'm writing the gloom out on you and am loving it. This letter seems much closer than the others.

I love you very deeply and completely—that goes through everything and in everything. Every day I hope I will hear from you and at night I haven't. Maybe today. Some of the mail must come through. Perhaps they have held it up, needing the space. I don't know.

Good bye my darling wife. Keep writing.

I love you.

Somewhere in North Africa
August 13 [1943]

Darling:

I haven't written for several days because I've been on the move. It seems silly to head this one "Somewhere in Africa," like saying just somewhere. Anyway this is a large city on the Mediterranean which I can't even spell [probably Algiers]. I've felt guilty about you taking all the hot weather this year but now you have your revenge. It was 140° when I landed— terrible searing heat. Up here on the sea it is only about 115° and the nights are bearable. The call came suddenly and surprised even me for I had been refused before. So I hopped it while I could. Right now I have the G. I. skitters which come to everyone and is painful but it will be gone tomorrow. Coming from cool England the heat can bowl you over.

Here I made my first error. Instead of applying for a billet from the army and getting, after hours, a cot with sixteen other men, I went up to the desk and in some of the sourest high school French asked for a room and got it. The army doesn't know how it happened. No one ever thought to try that method. I have a bath and a toilette and I am not even a general. The room itself is torn up quite a bit. Blast from bombing has loosened the wall paper. No windows nor mirrors of course. The big window is walled up with only two small holes, left open at the top. There are two small beds covered, believe it or not, with Mexican serapes.

I'm lying down to write this. It is the only way to keep from dripping on it. I shan't be here very long before I move on. Just please keep writing to London and I'll be back there probably in three weeks. This is a very crucial time. But the

258

nearer you get to a battle front, the less news you hear. You probably know much more than I do. I'm not even going out to dinner tonight. I'll sit here and write to you and rest my stomach. Hadn't had any fruit since I left New York and of course here it is wonderful.

It's coming on to get dark and it will cool off then some. Down in the desert it was full moon and Arabs howl at the moon—a high howl that goes on for hours and sounds a little like coyotes. If you can imagine sitting in a garden and hearing American swing played on a phonograph over the background of howling Arabs, you have something.

Damned if those senators didn't arrive here about the same time as I. By now they are fighting among themselves and they are reducing American prestige to an all time low which is very, very low. We must be inspired to have made so many mistakes. Some of the reporters over here are viciously resentful of me and some are very kind. But every once in a while one of them goes out of his way to tell me how much my stuff stinks. I think they are probably right. I get very tired of it.

August 19 [1943]

My darling:

It is almost impossible to keep clean here. The water is cold and dribbles and the soap doesn't seem to take hold. I think I am getting dirtier and dirtier but it isn't quite so noticeable since my complexion is getting darker and darker every day.

I have with me a camera man and an enlisted man and we have been jogging about the country seeing a great deal and taking some pictures. Yesterday I traveled through country that looked just like that stretch between Moss Landing and Monterey, with sand dunes and then the sea. The sea was the same blue as in Monterey and it made me very terribly homesick. And I wondered what has happened to the little house and how every one is.

I am still looking for Bill Dekker [Steinbeck's brother-in-law, married to his younger sister Mary] and still haven't found him. But I will in time.

I wonder what this being apart has done for us. To you, for instance, has it made you think our thing was good or do you suspect it? It has made me think it is exceptionally good and desirable. You said in one letter that you would probably

259

have changed your whole way of life. I hope not so radically that we cannot get back to the good thing it seemed to me. The good nights with the fire going. This winter I must have the little fairy stove connected so that when we go to bed the coals can be glowing. I wonder whether you found a maid at all. I think you will agree with me from now on that we need one. I hate to wash dishes and always will. I did too damned much of it when I was a kid. And I don't like to sweep and all stuff like that. But we will try to get someone who comes in for the day rather than an in-sleeper, that is of course as long as we have an apartment.

Goodbye my darling. I would give something very large to be able to hear from you, but I don't know any way to accomplish it.

Keep good and patient for just a little while now.

August 24 [1943]

Darling:

I hope you will answer my cable because I am pretty worried about you. Six weeks it is now since I have heard.

My dear, I am very tired of being without you, very tired indeed. We shan't do this again but it was necessary this once. I get sudden fits of jealousy too that are baseless and useless but seem to come on without warning.

I think the heat is making me a little dingy. It seems to me that I cannot remember much of anything. The series of bad dreams continues. But I think everyone is having them, at least dreams that go on and on. I'm getting to the point where I half way believe that I dreamed you.

August 25 [1943]

Dear:

Last night I went with the naval officers to a monastery in the country and in a huge dark church, the brothers were at evening prayer singing Gregorian music with only two little candles burning in the great place. I stood in the choir loft and looked down on this thing and it was very wonderful, the sound bellied up with great fullness. Afterwards we talked to the brothers and they are all nationalities. One was from Massachusetts and another a German and a third a Hollander and some French. And they were very quiet. Staying

260

in the monastery were a few officers who have worked too hard or been under too great a nerve strain and they are there in that very quiet place just getting rest that can't be got any place else. They listen to the music and sleep and it does them a great deal of good.

It really isn't so very bad. The great trouble is the one you know, the loneliness. That I can't dissemble or disassociate. I remember best the coffee in the morning and the music at night and the dictionary sessions and the painting of chairs and where shall we eat tonight. Let's have a whale of a big Christmas and not only string popcorn but also string cranberries and also whatever tinsel we can find. Let's have a really Christmas. There won't be very much to buy for presents but we'll get some things and we'll have a goose if you can find one, a great fine goose that falls apart if you speak above a whisper. I've thought and thought and it does seem that the corner in front of the lower bathroom door is the best place for the tree. It is very funny in this heat to think of a fine cannel coal fire but I do think of it. And maybe it will be snowing. You get to dwelling on these things.

There is a theme that is beating in on me and it is the theme of Africa. It is a very strange place. It looks so like California and it is a place that has never been a nation and only a kind of a piece of loot for four thousand years and probably more. All of the time I am conscious of the many kinds of soldiers who have tramped over these roads but always to raid and to loot. You rarely find a man who says I am Algierian. He is French or Arab or German but never African. And yet the place has such charm and such beauty in some ways that people come back again and again to it. I know I would like to bring you here when there is peace again.

August 28 [1943]

Darling:

Your cable of worry about Mary was just forwarded to me from London. Bill was reported missing on July 17. I just got the flash and the report must have gone to Mary. Poor dear. I don't know what to do. I have asked for any supplementary information and have been unable to get any. You see it is forbidden to send a personal cable and a letter will take so long to reach her that it will be lost news. The report is simply missing in action and nothing more.

I would feel much better about everything if I knew you were all right and well and steadfast. I have been turned toward you like a compass the whole time. And I will get another letter off to you as soon as I can.

love to you my dear

I had only finished that when I had another report on Bill. About a week after the invasion of Sicily, he went out with troops and did not return and that is all that is known. He had just been promoted to the rank of Lieutenant Colonel and was decorated in absentia. His commanding officer will write to Mary and give her all the information available. There is no evidence that he was killed. He simply did not come back. And that is absolutely all anyone knows so far. I would like you to use your own judgement about telephoning Mary. Perhaps she would like to come now to stay with you. I wish I were nearer to help her if there were anything in the world I could do. There have been many amazing returns from impossible situations.

Mary will do what she has to do. I am sure that she has been prepared for this shock for many months. Help her all you can, dear. I wish I could. She knows at least that Bill wanted it this way. He was not a very happy man and he had not found what he wanted and he was looking for it. Maybe this was it. Maybe this was it all along.

You may tell Mary for me I believe Bill very much alive. I do not believe Bill is dead.

[After the Salerno landing]
September 20 [1943]

Gwyn darling:

Well we're clear of it—at least nearly.

I'm gay today—maybe because I'm still alive but more I think because I've been as far away from you as I am going and now I'm starting back—slowly, perhaps, but always in that direction. And it makes me very happy. Because I've done the things I had to do and I don't think any inner compulsion will make me do them again.

You should see my costume—ragged dirty khaki shirt and trousers, canvas rope soled shoes bought in an Italian town —no hat or cap, nothing but a helmet. As soon as I get to a base I'm going to throw it all away and start fresh.

September 22 [1943]

Darling:

That last was written on a ship and now I am back at a base —still a little deaf but extremely happy

Because

There was a packet of letters from you all through July and one in August and the V mail one from Sept. 1. I got in touch with Bill's general and he is going to get me a full report and if it is anything good I'll cable. I cabled the office today to call you and tell you I was out of it and safe.

I can't tell you how much the letters meant. I lined them up and went to bed—the first bed I'd been in in three weeks and I spent an evening with them. They were two months old but that didn't matter, they were you. And now from having nothing to talk about, I have lots.

I've had a charmed life these last three weeks or someone had me in prayers or something. There was one tough night when you were with me all the time. I wonder if you knew it. It was the 14th and really a rough time. But I haven't a scratch and my ears are coming back so I can hear quite well again.

I don't let myself think about time. I would go wacky. This marriage is something strong in me beyond belief. I'm burned black and my hair is cropped—quarter of an inch long for very good reasons and generally I'm a flea bitten, mosquito bitten, scratched up mess. The only white part of me is under my ring. I've never had it off not once since I left home—not even to wash my hands.

[London]
[Fall 1943]

My darling—

I got you a present today and I hope it goes with this letter. Open the box very carefully because it is glass. They are 18th century English glasses—between 1760–70. Called cotton white twist glass. They are very rare fine specimens and the art of making them has been lost. They shine like diamonds and look wonderful with silver on a dark table. Candle light makes them wonderful. Nearly all of them are collector's pieces but we will drink wine out of them.

263

You say you feel cut off and not part of me. I surely feel you are part of me all the time.

Darling I miss you so badly.

I see all these thousands of lonely soldiers here and they are going through the same thing. There's a kind of walk they have in London, an apathetic shuffle. They're looking for something. They'll say it's a girl—any girl, but it isn't that at all.

The whores line the streets in the black out. They have umbrellas for when it is wet. Many of them are refugees. Some have little flashlights and as you pass they turn it on their own faces, on and off, quickly. When there is no light the soldier lights a cigarette and in that way gets a quick look at his love. Then they go into the park or in a door way. It's the saddest damned thing. And venereal disease is way up—terribly up. But there's something about these poor drab little things soliciting in the rain. Well, anyway, that's what these soldiers think they are looking for.

I have two bets that the German war will be over in December. This is based on no knowledge at all and I am laughed at loudly. With my record of intuition I suppose I couldn't find a better way of prolonging the war.

love to you.
J.

The "journal" is finished. Steinbeck returned to New York.

Many years later, writing to his friend Joseph Bryan III, he said:

"I have a book coming out in the fall—the war pieces I did for the H.-Tribune. I hadn't seen them since the war. There are many things in them I didn't know I was writing—among others a hatred for war. Hell, I thought I was building the war up."

In the introduction to this book, which was entitled *Once There Was A War,* he wrote:

"This war that I speak of came after the plate armor and longbows of Crécy and Agincourt and just before the little spitting experimental atom bombs of Hiroshima and Nagasaki. [These accounts] are period pieces, the attitudes archaic, the impulses romantic, and, in the light of everything that has happened since, perhaps the whole body of work untrue and warped and one-sided. The pieces in this volume were written under pressure and in tension. They are as real as the wicked witch and the good fairy, as true and tested and edited as any other myth."

To Webster F. Street

[New York]
December 13, 1943

Dear Toby:

It has suddenly turned quite cold here but no snow yet. We've both had colds but not bad ones and the flu has become epidemic. Also I have a symptom or two that you will probably recognize. Sudden blank brain—not knowing who or where I am. They only last a few seconds, and are followed by a blinding headache which lasts a few seconds and then all right.

We're going to leave here on the 11th of Jan. but will be back in a couple of months or sooner. I'm going to try to get some perspective on the war by going away from it. I don't understand it now.

Had a letter from Ed [Ricketts]—who seems to be doing well. Heaven knows when we'll get out there but probably next fall. Probably everything will be changed by then. There is a curious sense of change going on. Kind of a rumble. No one seems to notice it but it has an ominous sound to me and I think hell is stirring.

It's nice sitting in here by the fire and cold as hell outside. I'm working on a funny little book that is fun and it is pretty nice [possibly *Cannery Row*]. I don't even go to movies. The crowds are so great everywhere and you get pushed around so much that I don't bother to try any more.

Well—we'll be back before too long.

'Bye,
John

To Twentieth Century-Fox Film Corporation

New York
January 10, 1944

Dear Sirs:

I have just seen the film Lifeboat, directed by Alfred Hitchcock and billed as written by me. While in many ways the film is excellent there are one or two complaints I would like to make. While it is certainly true that I wrote a script for Lifeboat, it is not true that in that script as in the film there were any slurs against organized labor nor was there a stock comedy Negro. On the contrary there was an intelligent and thoughtful seaman who knew realistically what he was about. And instead of the usual colored travesty of the half comic and half pathetic Negro there was a Negro of dignity, purpose and personality. Since this film occurs over my name, it is painful to me that these strange, sly obliquities should be ascribed to me.

John Steinbeck

To Annie Laurie Williams

TELEGRAM

MEXICO CITY
FEBRUARY 19, 1944

PLEASE CONVEY THE FOLLOWING TO 20TH CENTURY FOX IN VIEW OF
THE FACT THAT MY SCRIPT FOR THE PICTURE LIFE BOAT WAS DIS-
TORTED IN PRODUCTION SO THAT ITS LINE AND INTENTION HAS BEEN
CHANGED AND BECAUSE THE PICTURE SEEMS TO ME TO BE DANGER-
OUS TO THE AMERICAN WAR EFFORT I REQUEST MY NAME BE
REMOVED FROM ANY CONNECTION WITH ANY SHOWING OF THIS FILM

JOHN STEINBECK

"We are leading a very quiet life, just resting like
mad," he wrote Annie Laurie Williams on February
21 from Mexico. "I find I needed it more than I knew.
Gwyn is fine and so is the other that you know
about." [She was pregnant.]

With regard to the telegram Steinbeck had sent
about *Lifeboat,* he wrote in the same letter:

"It does not seem right that knowing the effect of
the picture on many people, the studio still lets it
go. As for Hitchcock, I think his reasons were very
simple. 1. He has been doing stories of international spies and master minds for so long that it
has become a habit. And second, he is one of those
incredible English middle class snobs who really
and truly despise working people. As you know,
there were other things that bothered me—technical things. I know that one man can't row a boat of
that size and in my story, no one touched an oar
except to steer."

Steinbeck's charge of distortion is supported by Robert E. Morsberger, Chairman of the Department of

267

English at California State Polytechnic University, who has made a study of the subject. He quotes Hitchcock's statement that after engaging a second novelist and then a professional screenwriter, he himself did some rewriting on the screenplay, so that Steinbeck's original narrative—realistic, thoughtful, grim, and politically aware—was considerably altered. Steinbeck's request to have his name removed from the credits was not granted.

To Carlton A. Sheffield

330 East 51st Street
New York
April 12 [1944]

Dear Dook:

It has been a very long time of not writing and not hearing. During my fuss in California I rather purposely cut myself off because I didn't see any reason for putting a very unhappy thing on other people and then the war came along and I got mixed up in it. You will laugh to think that for a year and a half I tried to get into the army but was blackballed from this largest club in the world. I am very glad of it now but at the time I was very sad about it. Had I succeeded I would either have been guarding a bridge in Santa Fé or writing squibs for the Santa Ana Air Force Monitor. As it is I've had a look at the war, too much of a look I guess.

Having some strange symptoms which continued, I went to a doctor last week and found that both ear drums had been burst and that there are probably little vesicles burst all over my body, in the head and under the skin and in the stomach. He says that in some cases where post mortems have been performed the vesicles even in the marrow of the bones were found to be burst. Anyway it will take from a year to two years for the little clots to absorb and it just has to be weathered. I can hear quite well now so the drums are healing or are healed but the others, the nervousness, dreams, sleeplessness etc. have to take their own time. I took a very bad

268

pasting in Italy but oddly enough was not hit at all. It occurs to me that there are about fifty thousand men who are having the same trouble. There is going to be a frightening amount of it after the war.

We are living in an apartment at the above address and Gwyn is going to have a baby in July which makes me very glad. Then I am going to make a picture in Mexico [*The Pearl*] next winter and after that we hope to get back to California. I am very homesick for it. The kid will be old enough to travel by next winter so we will take a house and work out of it. The film is to be made in Lower California with an all-Mexican cast and director and money. It should be a lot of fun. We just got back from a couple of months down there. I hadn't realized how tired I was until I went into a partial collapse and just sat and watched things for two solid months. Had intended to do some writing but had no heart for it.

Now I am back at work and working every day on a silly book that is fun anyway. We have here the lower part of an old brownstone with a yard and we have a sheep dog who is as crazy as all my dogs are. If in New York at all this is a pleasant place to live. It doesn't at all look like a New York apartment and it does have a yard. And like most people who live here a while, we rarely go out of our neighborhood. This is the most insular town. Little islands of people who never go out of their districts. It is very different in the west although you always stuck very close to home.

I wish that you would let me hear the things that have happened to you and what you are doing.

Ours is a comfortable relaxed house and we like each other very much and that is a good thing. I didn't know it was possible. And this might be a very good baby because of that easiness and relaxation. I am looking forward to it with great pleasure.

The war news is good but I know how it is warped by the papers. When we were winning great victories in Italy and marching triumphantly on the Germans, we were actually getting the shit shot out of us. And I remember one report how we had broken through the German lines. Actually what happened was that Jerry retreated during the night and we couldn't find him, and that's how we broke through his lines. But there were some strange and wonderful things that happened too, things to be told later. But to tackle the cosmic foolishness of war is beyond me and I just get tired thinking about it.

Do write and let me know all the things that have happened in the great blank. I'd like so much to hear.

as always
jon

To Webster F. Street

[New York]
July 4, 1944

Dear Toby:

I have been working madly at a book [*Cannery Row*] and Gwyn has been working calmly at a baby [Thom Steinbeck] and it looks as though it might be a photo finish. That should be a good omen if you like omens.

It has been a very cool summer so far, thank God. We'll catch it later but it would be bad for Gwyn now. She will be about ready in another week. And still she isn't puffy. In fact she is prettier than ever and she is very calm and nice. It has been a very good pregnancy.

Working at home today. I have been working over at the Viking office.

Ed writes that he had a vacation and spent it in the library at Berkeley. He seemed in good shape and in good spirits. It has been hard to do a book because I've had to work for the treasury and the army too and it is kind of sneaking a book out. But it is a kind of fun book that never mentions the war and it is a relief to work on.

It is a long time since I have heard from you. Do things go all right? I haven't been drinking anything because of work and because Gwyn lost her taste for it and it is no fun alone. Maybe we'll pick it up when the baby arrives.

The war goes well, doesn't it—the fighting part of it anyway. The Russians will win it pretty soon perhaps.

Well anyway let me hear from you.

John

To Jack and Max Wagner

TELEGRAM

NEW YORK
AUGUST 2, 1944

BOY NAMED THOM SIX POUNDS TEN OUNCES BOTH DOING SPLENDIDLY

JOHN

To Webster F. Street

[New York]
August 25, 1944

Dear Toby:

This has been a busy and an exciting time. Thom seems to be a baby-shaped baby and I like him very much. There isn't much to like about him yet. He just eats and sleeps and shits but I can think of worse kids. Gwyn is still a little peaked but is on the mend now. We're planning to go out there about the 1st of October. Our lease is up here and we won't renew. Probably rent a house until we find the place we want. Have lots of energy and a good desire to get to work. I think getting back will be good for me.

We may settle up the valley or on the coast but we'll take a long time looking first. And I don't want a place so big or so complicated that I can't leave it some months out of the year either. This has been a good flat. The nicest and most comfortable I have seen in New York, but I surely don't want to live here.

I have a good feeling about going back. Hope nothing overturns it. And I do want to sit on the rocks and fish and not catch anything.

Thom is a good healthy kid with red hair and blue eyes and

271

he can't see yet but there's nothing to look at anyway.

We'll be seeing you before too long.

'Bye,
John

To Carlton A. Sheffield

New York
September 27, 1944

Dear Dook:

The apartment is all torn up now. We are getting out—going back to Monterey. I've rented two small houses down the coast—one to live in and one to work in. I've had a wonderful sense of going home but just lately I'm a little scared. Probably the same thing as your saying you aren't at ease with me. There must have been a change in me and in everyone else. I'd like to settle there if I can. Gwyn and baby are flying out and I am driving a second hand Buick station wagon with household goods. I'll make it in six to eight days with luck.

Apparently in response to a remark of Sheffield's about child-raising and self-expression, he continued:

There's so much horse shit about babies; schools change every ten years. Mary raised a couple of nice ones by forcing them to be considerate or leave the room so I think it can be done. And this fatherhood is interesting but also surrounded by horse shit. I think people act the way they're expected to act. I see nothing remarkable in this child at all. He's going to be reasonably pleasant looking and he has all his members and is healthy. And because he is healthy he doesn't cry unless he is hungry. If I can I'm going to build a cell for him because that's where they belong for several years. They are mean little animals. And that is that. Neither of us are gaga

272

but we're very glad to have him and we'll have some more.

I finished the book called Cannery Row. It will be out in January. If Pat Covici sends me an extra proof I'll send you one. I don't know whether it is effective or not. It's written on four levels and people can take what they can receive out of it. One thing—it never mentions the war—not once. I would be anxious to know what you think of it. You'll find a lot of old things in it. I find I go back to extensions of things we talked about years ago. Maybe we were sounder then. Certainly we were thinking more universally. The crap I wrote over seas had a profoundly nauseating effect on me. Among other unpleasant things modern war is the most dishonest thing imaginable.

Anyway, from October 15 until Xmas I am going to try to do a script for a picture to be made in Mexico [*The Pearl*], all Mexican direction and acting and even Mexican money. Then in January, I'll go down and watch them make it. It is a chance to do an honest picture and I am going to try it. I have complete control of the picture and very good people are involved in it.

Within a year or so I want to get to work on a very large book I've been thinking about for at least two years and a half. Everything else is kind of marking time. Work is still fun and still work. It hasn't ever got any easier.

After all these years I'm learning to use a pencil and to write big. One of those incredible things happened the other day. When I was off the coast of Italy I went with British torpedo boats for a while—raiding the shipping at Gaeta and Genoa and over between Corsica and Sardinia before they were taken. I had a little school note book and one night we were off Genoa and I was below making some notes and an alert sounded so I went on deck and it was pitch black. Then all of a sudden a flak ship started firing on us and I hit the deck because tracers scare hell out of you and the boat started running and twisting. Well that was the last I saw of my note book. Recently it arrived in the mail from England. Sent by the Ministry of Information. I suppose it got stuck in the slats some place and the skipper sent it in. Now I remember that skipper. He was 26 and his name was Greene-Kelly. He was killed eight months ago when he attacked two E boats. He sunk one and crippled the other and then two more came down on him and sunk him. But my note book got back.

You can reach me through the lab. I'll write you the other

273

address when I know it. It will be a rural box number. Meanwhile, I'll hope to see you soon.

bye
John

The legend on which the film of *The Pearl* was based had been told in a few sentences in *Sea of Cortez,* which had been a collaboration by Steinbeck and Ed Ricketts.

To Pascal Covici

[Monterey]
October 24 [1944]

Dear Pat:

No word from you so I don't know whether you got back or not. Anyway, we bought a house in Monterey. You may think this precipitate but it is a house I have wanted since I was a little kid. It is one of the oldest and nicest adobes in town—with a huge garden—two blocks from the main street and yet unpaved and no traffic. Four blocks from the piers. It was built in the late 1830's before the gold rush and is in perfect shape. We are very happy to get it. And we'll move in about the 10th. I'll send you some pictures of it. I hope to live in it for a long time. It is something you can close up and not worry.

All colds are over now. The weather is brilliant as usual this time of year. Gwyn is here deep in plans for decorating the new house. It was built by the Soto family and is called simply Soto House. Its garden is eight city lots and no new neighbors and the whole surrounded by adobe wall. You'll like it. And it is a laughing house.

that's all
John

In a later letter to Covici Steinbeck described the garden, and plans for work:

"Plenty of room for trees, both walnuts and almonds. There are two pear trees already over a hundred years old. I think I may get an office to work in. I would probably work better if I just went into an office and sat four hours a day. As at Viking. Four doleful walls and a ground glass door are about my speed, particularly if the door says 'Accountant.' "

It worked out differently.

To Pascal Covici

[Soto House]
[Monterey]
[November 1944]

Dear Pat:

I seem to be flooding you with letters, but here is a story I think you will like. You remember I told you I was going to get an office to work in. In Monterey there is only one office building, owned by a man named Parsons. I tried to reach him for three days and this morning got him by phone. I said, "I want to rent an office for a couple of months." "Very well," he said, "we have some vacancies. What is your name?" "Steinbeck," I said. "And what is your business?" "I'm a writer," I said. There was a long pause and then—"Do you have a business license?" "No," I said, "none is required in my business."—Another long pause, then "I'm sorry—we don't want people like that. We want professional people like doctors and dentists and insurance."

Isn't that wonderful? So I cleaned out the wood shed and set up a table and I'll work there. I just thought you'd like to know that I can't get an office in my own home town and that the building owner never heard of me. Sic transit or perhaps it never existed.

So long
John

275

At the end of November, reporting progress on *The Pearl,* he wrote Covici again.

"Long distance phone call last night. Man from Christian Science Monitor. Wants to come down Sunday to discuss Cannery Row. Seems they have heard that I said half the whores were Christian Scientists. On the phone I said, "Would you be upset if it were so? There were only two chief woman characters in the life of Jesus and one was Magdalene." "No," he said, but he wanted to discuss it. So he's coming over on Sunday and the discussion should be fun. Maybe if I work it right we can get banned not only by Boston but by the Christian Scientists as well. The ideal is to be banned by everybody—then everybody would have to read it.""

The garden occupied him as usual.

"I have been planting cypress trees to fill in some of the old ones that have died. They seem to belong here. The Monterey cypress is unique in the world except for one part of China, and the myth is that the Chinese explorers long centuries before Columbus planted them here. It is known that the Chinese planted trees instead of flags as a token of discovery."

To Mildred Lyman
OF THE MCINTOSH AND OTIS STAFF

[Monterey]
December 2, 1944

Dear Mildred:

Beautiful cold morning. Friday night Gwyn pinned one on me. One of those fine natural binges that is not planned and is easy and natural. So last night I went to bed early and now I'm waiting for the Christian Science man.

Pat writes that advance sales on Cannery Row are beyond his expectations—60% beyond, he says. But you know Pat. Perhaps his enthusiasm exceeds his figures. Gosh, it's a beautiful day. Brilliantly sunny and clear. Some night next week Gwyn and I are going out with the sardine fleet. She has never been and it will fascinate her. It is a very spectacular thing and very exciting when they come on the fish.

I can look out at the garden from here where a little Spanish man is trimming the overgrown bushes and trees and doing a fine job of it. Sunday morning is a good time here. It's the Sundayest morning you can imagine. It lacks only chickens talking. When I was little I imagined that chickens made a very special kind of gobble talk on Sunday morning.

Well, the Xtian Science man came and he seems very nice and cagey and clever. He wondered if people wouldn't get the wrong impression. I said that some people always got the wrong impression. There wasn't much he could say without giving the impression of snobbishness. When he left, he said, "I just leave this thought with you. If they practiced prostitution *and* Christian Science, they were not good Christian Scientists." And I said, "Well, that's all right, because they weren't very good prostitutes either." So he laughed and we parted on a friendly basis. He said they would have to make a statement and I said I would be upset if they didn't.

Nurse's day off. Gwyn is making formula. And we're going to have baked beans tonight—Boston style.

Love to all,
John

It was a happy Christmas.

"Gwyn gave me some beautiful old American glass," he wrote Elizabeth Otis. "And, since her eyes have tested OK by the State, I got her a little convertible Ford to learn to drive. We had a large noisy tree decorating party with a Mexican orchestra. Gwyn got a bad cold out of it.

"Pat did the most beautiful thing for Gwyn. He bound original, typescript, corrected galleys all separately, and then had a case made like a big book and included page proofs and finished book."

277

And to Covici:

"Gwyn will write you but she has to stay in bed a couple of days now. She has a bad cold brought on by exhaustion. My sister gave me an olive wood box my father had left for me full of papers I didn't even know about. My grandfather's Civil War papers. His marriage license, his citizenship papers—last night we went over some of them. Passes for my grandmother to go through the Union lines signed by guerrilla officers. Deeds to property in Palestine and in Florida. A bill for a headstone for my grandfather's brother 'murdered by the Bedowin' in Jaffa in 1853."

As for the new book:

"The better people in this town don't know whether they like Cannery Row or not. They are waiting to see what other people think. This attitude is always true of better people. The critics say at once that it is not true to nature and that it is in bad taste. In nature two things do not occur—the wheel and good taste. So what do they want? Robert Nathan always writes in good taste—so does Kathleen Norris."

And, finally:

"There is a time in every writer's career when the critics are gunning for him to whittle him down. This is my stage for that. It has been since The Grapes of Wrath."

To Jack and Max Wagner

Monterey
[January 23, 1945]

Dear Jack and Max:

Things are lightening up a little here. The nurse was sick and poor Gwyn has been taking care of both the baby and the nurse. I thought Gwyn would end up in the hospital but she is all right and is getting some sleep finally.

278

Thom is fine and gay. Getting to be a kind of personable child. He has been very happy ever since his last tooth came through.

And I'm in the last stretch of the Pearl. I should finish this draft in about a week. Fernandez [Emilio Fernandez, who would be the director] is supposed to come up some time around the first to the 15th of Feb. to work on shooting script. I won't go to Mexico until I know the cameras are rolling. I know how the delays are.

Cannery Row took a frightful pounding by the critics and they went too far. Annie Laurie phoned to say that her telephone rang all the time from studios wanting to buy it and what should she do. So I told her she was on her own—to sell or not sell—whenever she was ready. She has a magnificent sense of timing for such things. And she knows what we want. A lot of money, control of the script. And this time I am going to ride herd on it. I'll act as consultant—for a consideration. I thought the adverse criticism would hurt the book but she says quite the opposite. The sales are tremendous and that's what interests the studios—not the critics.

There has been frost every day for a week. I've never known Monterey to be like that.

I guess that's about all. I've got to go to work. The Pearl is really in its last stages. It's a brutal story but with flashes of beauty I think.

Let me hear from you.

John

Steinbeck and Jack Wagner, who was assisting him on the script of *The Pearl*, left for Mexico at the beginning of April 1945, with Gwyn and the baby following. But before his departure, Steinbeck confided to Pascal Covici something that was troubling him deeply. He had first mentioned it late in December of the year before:

"What saddens me is the active hatred of the writers and pseudo-writers around here. It will not be terribly long before we will be associating only with fishermen. There is a deep and active jealousy out

279

here that makes me very sad. I haven't mentioned
it before."

By spring, it was a deep conviction.

To Pascal Covici

[Monterey]
[Spring 1945]
Dear Pat:

This is a private letter really. We're going back to Mexico
in a few days. And I'm glad to go. You remember how happy
I was to come back here. It really was a home coming. Well
there is no home coming nor any welcome. What there is is
jealousy and hatred and the knife in the back. I'm beginning
to think I made a mistake. I don't mind that but I'm not going
to let a mistake ride me on through. This is no new thing. I've
tried to conceal it and explain it and analyze it and make a
joke of it and to ignore it. It's much more than a feeling.

Our old friends won't have us back—always except Ed.
Mostly with them it is what they consider success that gets
in between. And the town and the region—that is the people
of it—just pure poison. I laughed about being refused an
office. But the local gas board cut off my gas in spite of the
fact that I had a job with the War Food Administration. Ours
is the first request to repair a house that has been rejected.
60 homes are being built for rent but we can't get a plank to
replace a rotten board in the kitchen. These are just two of
many things. I hate a feeling of persecution but I am just not
welcome here.

But I'm not going to jump any guns. We're going to be in
Mexico four or five months and then we'll give it another try
and if it doesn't work we'll clear out.

Maybe you can figure something, but this I can tell you, I
was happier in New York. Living is people, not places. I have
no peers here—in notoriety and so called success—and the
people who are coming up are ferocious. There's no one to

280

talk to except Ed. You see, Pat—I would and can forget all the publicity etc. but these people can't and won't.

This isn't my country anymore. And it won't be until I am dead. It makes me very sad.

John

In Cuernavaca he worked hard on the script of *The Pearl.* Gwyn's knowledge of music proved helpful in transcribing regional themes for the film.

To Elizabeth Otis

Cuernavaca, Mexico
May 3, 1945

Dear Elizabeth:

Just got your letter yesterday. Naturally I am very glad and frankly relieved that you like The Pearl. It was so full of experiments and I had no idea whether they would come off at all. Gwyn made some recordings of the basic music—the Family and Pearl themes. The Evil music is not finished. Gwyn is going to try to have a pressing sent to you. These themes are ancient Indian music long preceding the Conquest. And I think they are beautiful. Anyway, I'm terribly pleased that you like the story and that Pat does. I hope that you and he will consider very carefully whether another little book is a good idea. I can't imagine how Colliers could print it because of its length but I wish they would. They are getting such a good reputation.

No, it didn't seem far away when the President died. The only violence I heard of was Alice Leone Moats' father who came out on the hotel porch and said, "Well, I hear Rosenberg is dead," and a Spanish girl slapped him across the mouth and walked away.

Interesting. Scripps-Howard wired me asking me to write about Ernie Pyle. I did and wired asking how to send it. They replied by wire that it was too late. This was ten days after his death and he was no longer news to Scripps-Howard whom he had been practically supporting. *Sic* etc.

I guess the Germans will fold in a couple of days. It seems so unreal. When they go down they're much better than up. Hitler and Goebbels yesterday. Berlin. Hoped for for years and you can't really believe it when it happens.

Will be seeing you in the fall. Love to all,

John

To Annie Laurie Williams

Cuernavaca
June 26 [1945]

Dear Annie Laurie:

There is a thing I want to discuss with you. I was approached the other day by an outfit that calls itself Pan-American Films with the proposition that I do a film on the life of Emiliano Zapata. Now there is no other story I would rather do. But there are certain things in the way.

I have, as you know, work ahead for a long time to come. I would not even be ready to make a start until a year from this fall.

The difficulty of making it straight would be very great. There are still men living and in power who helped to trick and murder Zapata. I would only make it straight. I would require gov't assurance that it could be made straight historically. This will have to be an iron bound agreement because Zapata could be one of the great films of all time as by a twist or a concession it could be a complete double cross of the things Zapata lived and died for.

We're still plugging away at the shooting script. In the States I wouldn't do it but here I want to give them a tight story for the first time. It's a battle with energy because the dysentery still persists and that doesn't leave much strength.

282

We celebrated St. John's day with 10 dozen skyrockets and we named big ones for you and Maurice.

> Love to you both,
> John

The effects of the dysentery lingered. Almost three weeks later he wrote Elizabeth Otis:

"We thought we had picked up amoebae and were having a feces examination. The chemist wrung his hands. 'What a small world,' he said. 'I had just put down Cannery Row and I had no idea I was examining the stool of the author. Que mundo pequeñito!' "

To Pascal Covici

> Cuernavaca
> July 12 [1945]

Dear Pat:

I am heartily sick of this picture now and there are stirrings in me for new work. This is like beating a down dog. I've never liked rehashing—but I'll do it this time and it is once for all. There's too much new work to do—to go over one's old.

Two days earlier he had written Covici:

"I'm even writing this shooting script and it is the last one I shall do. It amounts to reducing your story to the most literal terms possible so that a camera can take it. And since most of my work depends on suggestion rather than literalness this is a little tiresome to me."

His letter continues:

The people down here are very kind to us. And I hope
out of this stay to write a book that may be something for
them to have. For the Wayward Bus could be something
like the Don Quixote of Mexico. The more I think of it the
better I like it and the better I like it the longer its plan
and the wider its scope until it seems to contain the whole
world. From the funny little story it is growing to the most
ambitious thing I have ever attempted. Not that it still
won't be funny but funny as Tom Jones and Tristram
Shandy and Don Quixote are funny. And it isn't going to
take a little time to write but a long time and I don't care,
for my bus is something large in my mind. It is a cosmic
bus holding sparks and back firing into the Milky Way
and turning the corner of Betelgeuse without a hand signal. And Juan Chicoy the driver is all the god the fathers
you ever saw driving a six cylinder broken down, battered
world through time and space. If I can do it well The
Wayward Bus will be a pleasant thing.
So long—we'll have fun.

John

In 1956, writing to Charles Brackett, who was preparing to produce the film of *The Wayward Bus,*
Steinbeck recalled the novel's beginnings:

"I don't think I ever told you the origin of this story.
It was first projected in Mexico, and its first synop-
sis was written in Spanish for Mexico. At that time
it had a wonderful title, I think. It was called El
Camion Vacilador. The word vacilador, or the verb
vacilar, is not translatable unfortunately, and it's a
word we really need in English because to be 'vaci-
lando' means that you're aiming at some place, but
you don't care much whether you get there. We
don't have such a word in English. Wayward has
an overtone of illicitness or illegality, based of
course on medieval lore where wayward men were
vagabonds. But vacilador is not a vagabond at all.

Wayward was the nearest English word that I could find."

To Pascal Covici

Cuernavaca
[1945]

Dear Pat—

Last night a very strange thing happened. Anciently it would have had a very definite effect on a person. The moon came up red and sullen through a black haze. We sat on the porch watching it because of its very threatening color. These black clouds like mares' tails moved up from the horizon, big black streaks. Jack Wagner yelled suddenly— "Look!" It was a very strange thing. The clouds spelled in huge black letters JOHN right across the moon. It was very definite and lasted five minutes before it drifted away. We called Gwyn to look at it. I have seen letters in clouds before but never four definite letters. In an age of portents it would be effective. Such a thing might have caused the Magna Carta not to be signed.

so long,
John

"My feelings about Monterey don't seem to change," Steinbeck wrote Pascal Covici on July 10, 1945. "The old nostalgia was knocked right out of me the last time. And I'm afraid for good. I thought it might be a momentary pique or anger. But it isn't. It isn't as hot as it was but my distaste for going back increases rather than softens."

Late in 1945 the Steinbecks sold their Monterey house. Gwyn Steinbeck went ahead to New York

285

with Thom, and her husband followed in the car from Mexico City with the houseman.

To Jack Wagner

156 East 37th Street
New York
December 15, 1945

Dear Jack:

Well we got here. Dreadful trip. Car broke down 100 kms out of Mexico City. My expensive overhaul was a snare. They charged me but didn't do any work. What cheap shits of thieves they are. I would like really to kick that garage to pieces. Just chicken shit thieves. We pushed the car 1,800 miles before we could get a repair job. The whole country is frozen and we nearly froze to death. No sleep for three days. They didn't like Victor to go in restaurants in Texas. Altogether a nightmare of a trip.

Gwyn had found this apartment. Not gaudy but warm and to have found one at all is quite a trick and I was so tired it looked like heaven to me.

Thom is fine and very charming.

The city is covered with snow and very lovely. I'm crazy about winter.

Merry Xmas and will see you soon.

John

He wrote to Max Wagner early in 1946:

"We bought a house here and are fixing it up. It should be ready to move into early in March. It is going to be a wonderful house."

286

Actually, it was two adjoining houses with a common garden on East 78th Street.

"Gwyn," he continued to Max, "is not very well. This pregnancy has hit her hard and she has been a miserable kid but Lord, is she beautiful. We went to the theatre last night and she really looked so wonderful. I hope she feels better soon."

His impression of the city had undergone a dramatic change:

"New York is a wonderful city," he wrote Jack Wagner. "I'm glad to be putting down some kind of roots here. It is going to be the capital of the world. It isn't like the rest of the country—it's like a nation itself —more tolerant than the rest in a curious way. Littleness gets swallowed up here. All the viciousness that makes other cities vicious is sucked up and absorbed in New York. It is truly the great city of the world—an organism in itself—neither good nor bad but unique."

To Webster F. Street

175 East 78th Street
New York
March 17, 1946

Dear Toby:

Quite a long time without hearing from you.

Our house is nearly finished. I moved into the basement to work a couple of weeks ago and we should be in the house in about two weeks more. That is going to be such a relief. Just the process of spreading out is going to be a joy. Imagine being able to get away from the family and getting to the toilet without an elaborate plan and a time schedule.

The working cellar is fine—gray concrete walls and cement floor and pipes overhead. A comfortable chair and desk and filing cabinet in which I hope to file bills so I can find them. All fine—no window, no ability to look out and watch the postman and the garbage wagon. I'll go on with my book now [*The Wayward Bus*]. Gwyn only has a couple more months of this condition and she is very glad of that but says that it is longer than all the rest and I can see how that would be too.

Today is St. Patrick's Day and a beautiful day. Mostly it rains and gets all those Irish wet but that doesn't prevent them from wearing purple robes and dripping purple rain all over Fifth Avenue. Hearst has got himself in a hassle. He has been printing nothing but accounts of Cardinal Spellman. As Artie Deutsch said, Spellman got more publicity than any Cardinal since Dizzy Dean.

I have been feeling lousy in my mind but today there seems to be some break in the clouds and maybe the darkness will go away. It has been a period of blue despair such as I haven't had in quite a long time. I don't know what it was based on and maybe it isn't over but I do feel better today. Such things are very mysterious. I finally found my pipes in the stuff that was sent out and they taste unbelievably delicious. They taste like work.

I hear from Mexico that the picture looks very good. We are kind of pulling in our horns a little this year. When these two houses [on 78th Street] are all fixed up then we can let ourselves out a little. But the way Gwyn feels now she doesn't want to let out any more.

So long,
jn

To Carl Wilhelmson

New York
[Spring 1946]

Dear Carl:

I haven't heard from Dook Sheffield for a long time. He seemed so touchy that I gave up. He obviously didn't want any more to do with me and I don't even want to investigate why. I think a dislikeness of experience is largely responsible with all of these things.

I have been doing a great deal of work, most of it no good and most of it thrown away. It seems like a great waste of time but that seems to be my pattern. It gets harder to do all the time, I guess, as I learn more about the pure technical difficulties. I'm working on a thing now that is giving me hell —a long novel. I want to take a long time with it. It seems to me that I have been rushing for five or six years, rushing as though I were trying to beat something. But if I had a fatal idea that I am easy to kill I should have lost it. Everything missed me in Europe. Also I should be done with fear but I guess I'm not.

I hope you do get to work. The getting to work is a purely mechanical thing as you well know—a conscious and self-imposed schoolroom. After that, other things happen, but the beginning is straight pushing.

We have a young son nearly two years old and another baby coming in June. I like the one very much. He is gay and fine. There is nothing instructive in single parenthood but association is first interesting and then a kind of affection grows up the way it does with a puppy. Only a human puppy knows so much more that he is more interesting.

The pure difficulty of learning to talk fascinates me. Nearly every waking hour is spent trying to learn that complex process. I don't seem to have many of the traditional parent's reactions or maybe no one has. I suspect that many of the attitudes of parents are literary and picked up in the slick magazines and written by childless people. Or perhaps I am subnormal. I have, for instance, no sense of possession about this child. I am quite sure that any baby I associated with would have the same effect on me.

That's all. Write when you feel like it.

John

To Jack Wagner

Dear Jack:

During the last few months I have been worried about you because the stories that you were drinking again were persistent. If you were there was nothing to do about it but it seemed such a sadness that all the effort had gone for nothing. I knew in Cuernavaca that you were kidding yourself about the beer. Beer is just the same as anything else. And I suppose you shouldn't use it either for refreshment, which it isn't, or for sexual insecurity. All that was and is your business. But I have little patience with it as you well know—less and less in fact. We've been having the runaround from a very dear and famous person who is on it. Dear as she is—and clever—it isn't worth it as I told her recently. She is using other people's emotions too deeply. Fuck her and you too if you are back on it.

I know it must have got pretty hectic toward the end down there. Everyone hating everyone. It will really be amazing if a good thing comes out of it [*The Pearl*]. But everyone who has seen it, and that is nearly everyone in Mexico, says it is quite impressive.

For two months I've been fighting the Bus and only now have I got a start which seems good. I've thrown away thousands of words. But I think it is good now. And at least it is moving.

We still haven't a phone but the new house is very pleasant otherwise. Gwyn only has about a month yet to go and she is pretty uncomfortable and uncomplaining. But she feels lousy and this last month is longer than all the others put together. She and I will be very glad when it is over.

Let me hear how everything is. You probably won't. But try to anyway.

So long,
John

To Webster F. Street

[New York]
June 14, 1946

Dear Toby:

Well, it got born the day before yesterday and it is a boy. Gwyn is pretty well considering and the baby is fine. I think it is our family. It is enough. I'm pretty tired. A couple of nights sleep will fix me up though. That and a drink or so.

Now it is later and I have had both sleep and the drink and I still feel confused. Maybe that's the way I will always be. Gwyn had a bad night last night but that is usual the third day after. She is much better this morning. It is still fine and cool here. I don't know how long this can last. Next week I'll have to get back down to work. I don't want to interrupt this book too much. It is going too smoothly. At least it was and I think will again.

Thom is a very fine boy. He has just discovered a shrill shriek that is very piercing. He is experimenting in tones of awfulness. When it gets too bad I whistle on my fingers which is so much more awful than any scream he can give that he gives it all up in pure admiration.

Love,
John

On the same day he announced the news to Jack Wagner, adding:

"The new baby will be named John and is already called Juanito. Even Thom calls him that although he has never seen him. Thom is completely bilingual so far and prefers Spanish."

Late in the summer the Steinbecks heard from Ed Ricketts that his mother had died.

291

To Edward F. Ricketts

New York
[August 1946]
Monday

Dear Ed:

I had your letters this morning, two of them, and I am writing immediately. The matter of death is very personal—almost like an idea—and it has to be discovered and accepted over and over again no matter what the age or the condition of the dying. And there is nothing for the outsider to do except to stand by and maybe to indicate that the person involved is not so alone as the death always makes him think he is. And that is why I am writing this letter.

The enclosed is for anything you want or need it for. It does occur to both Gwyn and me that in all of this there is some necessity of saving yourself, and I don't mean physically, and it is a thing that would occur last to you. We thought that you might like to use it to come on to see us for a couple of weeks. We thought further that a complete change of background and people for a little while might have restorative effects beyond almost anything. Perhaps we are wrong, but believe please that we would be very happy if you would do that. Think it over anyway.

I spoke to Pat about the Guggenheim thing this morning and he suggests that you give Viking Press as one of your sponsors. He says that the interest of a publisher sometimes has some weight. So please remember that, will you?

The book sails on and I must admit that I am fascinated with it. It may be no good at all. I don't know but it holds my interest which is the most important thing.

That good Gwyn is making a lemon pie or two this afternoon than which nothing is lemoner nor nicer nor that I like more. The children are well and getting along nicely.

love to you
from both of us.

jn

292

There is no record of Ricketts having accepted their invitation.

In the fall, John and Gwyn Steinbeck sailed for Denmark, whose proportionately large book-buying public had long been Steinbeck enthusiasts. Otto Lindhardt, his former Danish publisher, recalls that Steinbeck once observed that Denmark was the only country in the world to keep all his books in print.

To the McIntosh and Otis staff

Copenhagen
October 30, 1946

Dear Elizabeth and Mildred and Annie Laurie and all:

We are ensconced in the Hotel and Gwyn has a sore throat and we have been considerably pushed about. Coming in there were about thirty cameramen with flashlights and it was dreadful. The phone started calling while we were still at sea and the only way I saved myself from complete hell was by seeing all the reporters yesterday morning. I didn't know anyone treated writers like this. It is the sort of thing that would greet Lana Turner if it became known that she was going to come into Grand Central Station without any clothes on. And it is all so kind and well meant but it is very embarrassing. Every morning there is a mound of books to be autographed, and presents. Went to a night club last night and the orchestra leader played Stephen Foster in my honor. We've seen old friends and new ones, have had millions of toasts and the trip over was a dream.

Today we went to the legation to lunch. There was a Danish baroness or countess there [Baroness Blixen] with her attorney. It seems that during the war in desperation she turned to writing and in English. She used pseudonyms [Isak Dinesen] and had little idea of publication. She wrote Seven Gothic Tales which caused quite a stir and Random House published it. Now she has another which is Book of the Month selection for January. She has no representative in

293

America and now the picture companies are after her and she came to ask me what to do. Her attorney says he is out of his depth. Naturally I told her about you. She is an incredible little woman. I do recommend her to you. Her work needs the management you can give it. You can reject her if you wish but I think she might be a profitable and pleasant client.

We are really having a good time but we will only know later whether it has been a vacation or not.

We went to see castles yesterday and Gwyn loved them. I got an idea for a wonderful story from it.

Copenhagen has not been physically hit badly. The air raid shelters are everywhere, but they planted grass on them. That is like the Danes. It is a lovely country. And now that they have stopped photographing us we can relax.

> Love to you all,
> John

They went on to Sweden, where Steinbeck had a reunion with his old friend, the artist and writer, Bo Beskow. It was during this visit that Steinbeck sat for his second Beskow portrait.

To Bo Beskow

> New York
> December 16 [1946]

Dear Bo:

The photographs of the portrait arrived and I took one of them over to Viking Press. It has caused a great deal of enthusiasm and makes me all the more anxious to have the original as soon as possible.

Have not been feeling well. I don't know why. I am taking some vitamins to see whether it could be a food deficiency.

The depression has lasted too long this time and I don't like it at all.

I have not gone back to work and that bothers me. I shouldn't take these long rests. They aren't good for my soul or whatever it is that makes you sick. I make myself think that I will go back to work right after Christmas and maybe I will. I think Gwyn and the children will go to California for a month or six weeks about the first of February to let the children see their relatives. But I will just stay here and get back to work. Marital vacations are sometimes good things. Not that we need them very much. But just as the trip to Europe made us love our house so we get to liking each other with a little time spent apart.

Relationships are very funny things. I've wondered what I would think if this one were over and I think I would only be glad that it had happened at all. I don't think I would rail at fortune, but then it is impossible to know what you would do in any given situation unless you have experienced it. It was and would be silly of me to make any sort of judgement about your difficulty because I do not know all the factors. But you'll never get out clear no matter which way you go. A man going on living gets frayed and he drags little tatters and rags of things behind him all the rest of his life and his suit is never new after he has worn it a little. I've had such a bad time the last three or four weeks. The complete and meaningless despair that happens without warning and without reason that I can figure unless there happens to be some glandular disarrangement. So I am trying to do what I can about that and to see whether the feeling will go away.

Next Sunday we have our tree decorating party. It will be a fairly large party with at least forty people but they are all nice people. In fact about the best in the city for interest. Gwyn is going to have a midnight supper and I will make a monster bowl of punch and there we will be. The idea is to decorate our Christmas tree in the course of the evening. All sorts of arguments usually develop, aesthetic ones.

It should be a very fine Christmas.

Good luck and come out from under,

The letter is unsigned. Instead it is stamped with a drawing of "Pigasus," the flying pig which Steinbeck used throughout his life as a symbol of himself, earth-bound but aspiring. Sometimes the pun is spelled with Greek letters, and often it is accompanied by the motto *"Ad Astra Per Alia Porci"* ("To the stars on the wings of a pig"): "a lumbering soul but trying to fly," he once explained it and another time, "not enough wingspread but plenty of intention."

In February 1947, *The Wayward Bus* was published. An advance copy had gone to Jack Wagner in January:

"I hope you will like it although 'like' is not the word to use. You nor anyone can't *like* it. But at least I think it is effective. It is interesting to me—the following—This book depends on mood, on detail and on all the little factors of writing for its effectiveness. It has practically no story. Yet the picture companies seriously read synopses of it and think that is the book. The Bus, incidentally, has 600,000 Book of the Month and 150,000 trade first edition before publication. And with all that I had to borrow money to pay my income tax."

About the same time, he wrote Bo Beskow in Sweden:

"The advance sales of the Bus are stupendous. Something near to a million copies and it is still two weeks to publication date. This is completely fantastic. The people who are going to attack it are buying it like mad."

And to Wagner again, on February 16:

"The reviews of the Bus out today. I should never read reviews, good or bad. They just confuse me because they cancel each other out and end up by meaning nothing. I should let them alone. The book is getting good notices mostly here, although a couple of my congenital enemies are sniping. That is good for a book. The more arguments the better."

Even a year later in a letter to Covici he shows some residual irritation at the reception of *The Wayward Bus:*

"I hope some time some people will know what the *Bus* was about. Even with the lead, they didn't discover."

The "lead" is undoubtedly the quotation from *Everyman* facing the title page:

> I pray you all gyve audyence,
> And here this mater with reverence,
> Byfygure a morall playe;
> The somonynge of Everyman called it is.
> That of our lyves and endynge shewes
> How transytory we be all daye.

The New York *Herald Tribune* now hired Steinbeck to visit the Soviet Union with Robert Capa, the photographer. Steinbeck's dispatches would later be the basis of his book, *A Russian Journal,* published in 1948. But the trip took place in spite of an accident. In the spring of 1947, the Steinbecks had had a piano moved into their house. It was lifted from the street to the second-story window, from which a hip-high protective railing had been removed. This railing was replaced faultily, so that some time later when Steinbeck leaned on it, it gave way. He fell forward into the areaway, injuring his knee and foot seriously enough to be hospitalized for a period.

He wrote the Wagner brothers:

"I'm very tired of the hospital. I was lucky not to have broken my back. Little John is all well now and Thom is fine but will probably have mumps in a week. He has been exposed. And I've never had them. That can be bad."

His apprehension was not borne out. A little later he wrote:

"I'm pulling out for Paris tomorrow. Gwyn follows Tuesday. She'll be back in 4 weeks but I'm going on to Russia for the Herald Tribune and won't be back until the 1st of October. Should be quite a trip and it will be good to get back to straight reporting. My knee is getting better all the time but I will be a number of months with a cane."

297

To Pascal Covici

Kiev, Ukraine, U.S.S.R.
August 11 [1947]

Dear Pat:

A short note anyway. We've been down here for a week and will stay until next Friday. It is beautiful country and a beautiful city but it was brutally, insanely destroyed by the Germans. The rebuilding goes on everywhere but under the great difficulty of no machinery yet. My note book is getting very full and Capa is taking very many pictures, many of them fine I think. These Ukrainians are hospitable people with a beautiful sense of humor. I am setting down whole conversations with farmers and working people for fear I might forget them. We are lucky to be able to come here. We have seen so many things.

August 13

Just came from a farm. Very good time and lots of information. We are the first foreigners who have been in the country here in many years. The children look at us in wonder for they have only heard of Americans and sometimes not too favorably. The farmers and working people are a pleasure to talk to and even the necessity of talking through interpreters does not eliminate the salt of their speech.

Thank you so much for meeting Gwyn. She was really dead tired. Those flights are exhausting. I've only had one letter but there will probably be others waiting in Moscow. I try to cable now and then to relieve her mind. I have no news of America, and it is rather nice. I couldn't change anything and it is good to be away from the turmoil for a little. Why don't you drop me a note and let me know how things are going. Address c/o Joe Newman, Hotel Metropol, Moscow.

Evening is coming now. We are going to a symphony concert in the park on the cliff above the Dnieper. Playing Brahms and Prokofiev. I have a dreadful time with the spelling of Russian names and my language is limited to about 10 words, most of which have to do with drinking.

Please call Gwyn when you get this. I like her to hear from me as often as possible.

The time won't be very long until we will get home, only about six weeks. I'll be glad of a few days in Prague. I have always wanted to see that city which I have heard is very beautiful.

That's all Pat. Do drop me a line.

love
John

Joe Newman, mentioned above and in the following letter, was chief of the *Herald Tribune* bureau in Moscow. Steinbeck, with his taste for somewhat complicated nicknames, would shortly begin referring to him as "Sweet Joe" Newman. He derived this from the Russian name Svetlana, soon metamorphosed to "Sweet—lana," then to "Sweet—" anyone else.

To Gwyndolyn Steinbeck

Stalingrad, U.S.S.R.
August 20 [1947]

Dearest Doxie:

We are at it again. Got in at two and had to get up at three.

This town really destroyed, not by bombing but by shell fire and the houses pitted and carved by machine gun fire. Every single building is hit. Factories in ruins. This must have been the greatest fight of all time. The hotel is rebuilt and quite comfortable. This is the melon growing section.

It seems to me that I'm going to be very tired of moving around by the time I get home. It will have been 3 months and a half living out of a suitcase. I'll be ready to sit and work or maybe just sit for a little. There will be a lot of impressions to get settled too.

All hell has broken loose. I admit our Russian is limited, but we can say hello, come in, you are beautiful, oh no you don't, and one which charms us but seems to have an application rarely needed: "The thumb is second cousin to the left foot." We don't use that one much. So in our pride we ordered for breakfast, an omelet, toast and coffee and what has just arrived is a tomato salad with onions, a dish of pickles, a big slice of water melon and two bottles of cream soda. Something has slipped badly. Also an argument. Our room is full of flies—vicious nervous flies. The attendant called our attention sternly to the fact that the window was open and we retaliated with equal sternness that there is no glass in the window and to keep it closed has only theoretical value in keeping out flies. English is not spoken here. On arriving a young woman in the hotel said "good morning" with a beautiful accent which would have reassured us more if it had not been four o'clock in the afternoon. We have just ordered the vodka in place of the cream soda. If we get a cutlet we are not surprised. God! we got tea.

Capa suggests that the reason there aren't more flies is that they aren't mass produced yet. At the end of the five year plan they will have many more.

Love to you all and most to you my doxie

John

The next letter mentions what would appear five years later as *East of Eden*. Its original or working title was *Salinas Valley*.

300

To Webster F. Street

Dear Toby:

I have a great deal of work to do this year and I would like to get it all done by this summer because then I would like to stop everything to do a long novel that I have been working on the notes of for a long time. It seems to me that for the last few years I have been working on bits and pieces of things without much continuity and I want to get back to a long slow piece of work. I need to go out there for a lot of research so I may be out in California this summer. I'd be glad if I could for a little while. I'm living too hectic a life but then so are you and so is everyone.

Amazing that you should be a grandfather although I don't know why it should be amazing. I could easily be if I had got to work earlier. My kids are thriving and are becoming very interesting to me now. The oldest one is beginning to reason and is lots of fun and the youngest who is a clown by nature is very gay. He may not have much brains but he is going to have a hell of a wonderful life if he keeps the disposition he has now. That's about what it takes, a good disposition. I never had one and that is the reason for the kind of life I lead, I guess, although my disposition is better now than it ever was.

I don't think there is anything too difficult to understand about P———. She is just a natural virgin who can't grow up and never will. Such girls may be wonderful in the hay because they put on an act but not every night and not for long, because the act gets tiresome to them. That is why natural spinsters make much better mistresses than wives. They don't have to do it very often that way and so their interest is kept up not only by the rarity of the stuff but by the self-drama of the situation.

I had a wonderful time in Paris. I had never been there you know, and I wish I had been there years ago. Gwyn didn't like it terribly much but I did and I'm pretty sure I have not seen

301

the last of it. There is something there, there is really something there.

Winter is coming and that is the season I love in New York. I feel wonderful when it is cold. I guess I was never more healthy in my life than the winters I spent at Tahoe. I am just a cold weather kid and I am miserable in heat.

Well anyway I may be coming out to see you before too long. I would like to. I would like to just sit with you for a few days without any rush. I don't know what the hell I'm rushing about. There is some terrible kind of urgency on me and that is a bunch of nonsense. Maybe I'll get over it when I get this deadline piece out of my system. I hate to write to deadline but I have to on this. My typing never gets any better. I guess it is never going to get any better. That is one of the comforting things about the middle age I am in. Always before I could promise to reform and now I know I'm just never going to do it so I don't bother. The only thing I can really do is work and I might as well face it. I don't have any other gifts but I can work and if it doesn't amount to a damn it was still hard work.

Anyway I am going to plan within the next year to sit with you a while if you still want to. It wouldn't be bad to take some kind of inventory—not that it will change anything because you aren't ever going to change either and the joke is that if we had only known it, we never were from the very beginning. Maybe the self-kidding is part of the process. Maybe I couldn't have stood myself as I am when I was younger and so had to make all the plans about changing.

I guess that will be all now. I've got to get back to work. I have a hundred pages to get out before Thanksgiving. Christ, I remember when an eighteen-page story threw me for weeks. Maybe they were better then but I don't even care about that. The hell with it. I'm doing the best I can with what I've got.

So long and write more often.

jn

To Paul Caswell
EDITOR OF THE *SALINAS-CALIFORNIAN*

New York
January 2, 1948

Dear Mr. Caswell:

I am gathering material for a novel, the setting of which is to be the region between San Luis Obispo and Santa Cruz, particularly the Salinas valley; the time, between 1900 and the present.

An exceedingly important part of the research necessary will involve the files of the Salinas papers; will it be possible for me to consult these files? Do you know what has happened to the files of the Index-Journal and would it be possible for you to arrange my access to them?

I expect to be in Monterey soon after January 20th; could you let me know as soon as possible (by collect wire if necessary) if these files can be thrown open to me.

I will very much appreciate your help in this project.

Very truly yours
John Steinbeck

A week later, Caswell replied by telegram:

"YOU ARE WELCOME TO SALINAS NEWSPAPER FILES."

To Pascal Covici

Dear Pat:

Arrangements have finally been made for the photographing of the Salinas papers which will give me as fine a reference library on the daily history of a community as it is
possible to have. The oblique information in these old papers
is enormous in addition to the direct information. I have now
checked the stories of old timers against the reports of the
papers of the time, and I find that old timers are almost
invariably wrong not only in their information but in their
attitudes. Time is the most violent changer of people.

I've been into the river beds now and on the mountains and
I've walked through the fields and picked the little plants. In
other words I have done just exactly what I came out here to
do. What will come out of it I don't know but I do know that
it will be long. There is so much, so very much. I've got to
make it good, hell, I've got to make it unique. I'm afraid I will
have to build a whole new kind of expression for it. And
maybe go nuts doing it—and pay the price for doing it and
climb on it and tromp on it and get my nose rubbed in it. I
hope I have the energy to do it and without accidents I think
I have. The yellow pads will catch hell for the next few years
and nobody better try to rush me because I will not rush this
one. I'll make a living at something else while I am doing it.
But it's the whole nasty bloody lovely history of the world,
that's what it is with no boundaries except my own inabilities. So there.

The country is drying up as badly as the time I wrote about
it in To A God Unknown. It is the same kind of drought that
used to keep us broke all the time when I was growing up.

I guess that is all. I just wanted to send you a report.

John

About this time, he wrote Annie Laurie Williams:

"Have been going around the country getting reacquainted with trees and bushes. On a low tide I went collecting in the early morning.

"Well, it is time for me to get out in the wind and look at the grass which is coming up on the hill. That's what I am out here for."

To Pascal Covici, he wrote:

"All goes well here. I am getting a superb rest. The rain is over and the hills are turning green. I sleep about twelve hours every night and then go out and look at bushes.

"I have been seeing people I haven't seen for years. Things do not change so much. People erode and there are some new buildings, but on the whole there is not much of a change. And the hills don't change. This is sea monster time. One has been reported in the Bay again. I would like to see him myself some time. Lots of people have seen him."

A letter to Paul Caswell shows the kind of details he was interested in from the files:

". . . the front pages and a selection from the rest of the paper: for instance, the editorials on subjects of either momentary or permanent interest, advertising of foods, clothing, at intervals of, say, every six months. Personals and back page country news."

To Bo Beskow

[Monterey]
February 12 [1948]

Dear Bo:

You haven't heard from me because I have been resting. I had got pretty badly knotted up with the tiredness but that seems to be dropping away. I have a room in a cottage court

305

and I like it very well. I'm seeing old friends and drinking an occasional toast and going into the hills and looking at bushes and trees and things like that.

We had a very large Christmas and the kids got too many toys, most of which were put away for a little slower issue. There were so many things given them that they were only confused. I don't like this lushness. I am looking forward to the time when Thom can travel with me, and that won't be so very long.

The Russian pieces in the papers were very successful here. I don't know what the book will do. The Russians have been doing such bad things lately with their art stultifications and their silly attacks on musicians and the decree about no Russian being allowed to speak to foreigners that it makes me feel sad. It looks as though we were the last ones in for a very long time. Under the new decree we could not have spoken to any of the people we did. They have already destroyed all good or even interesting painting. There isn't much of any good writing and now they knock over music. The stupid sons of bitches. I wonder whether there is any secret writing or painting being done. It would surprise me if a few creative individuals weren't practising in cellars. And the small Russian people are such nice people.

It is barely possible that I may be in England for a little while this summer but not absolutely sure. I would like to sit still for a while but I'm restless you know and sitting still is only an ideal like celibacy and complete cleanliness.

I'm back with my own kind of people here now, the bums and drinkers and no goods and it is a fine thing.

I'm glad you had Christmas with your kids. I miss mine quite a lot. They are funny little bugs. And there's something terribly sad about them to me. They are such determined little humans with their chins down, living like the devil as hard as they can.

A few of my nieces now in college came down for a vacation from the university. They are very pretty girls and they seem to have so much more sense than girls did when I was that age. I enjoyed them no end and they liked me because I don't try any of the elder statesman stuff on them. It is a strange but genuine friendship.

I think through fatigue and other things I have been down near to the insanity level lately and it is odd how I can feel the tensions roll away from me. I sleep about twelve hours every night and every night it is better, the sleep better and more restful. It is truly a good medicine, something I guess like your trips to the south. One of the best things is being alone.

Give my unrequited love to the beautiful blonde girls in the Swedish Airlines offices, such lovely sweet-smelling girls.

ñiyaɡus

To Gwyndolyn Steinbeck

[Monterey]
February 17 [1948]

Dear Honey:

Tuesday already. Again last night to bed at ten. Now quite early morning. Cloudy and likely to rain. This is the driest year anybody ever remembers. Yesterday was like a spring day. I went to Salinas and worked at the paper and then drove out toward the hills and found the old stage road which I haven't been over since I was about ten years old and we went to Hollister that way in the surrey. Went over it to San Juan and do you know there were hundreds of places that I remembered. Kids do retain all right. Stopped in San Juan a while and then drove back over the old San Juan Grade which in the memory of most people is the only one. They have completely forgotten that which was once called the Royal Road and it is now just a country dirt road, which is what it always was, of course. Also working about getting the film made of the paper for later study. This is going to be fairly expensive but it is clearly deductible so it doesn't matter.

No word from you so I guess you are all right.

The enclosed is a letter Ed and I wrote to Stanford Press the other night. This new edition of Between Pacific Tides has been dawdling for two years. Thought you might enjoy the letter.

307

This is the letter to Stanford University Press, written on Pacific Biological Laboratories stationery:

"Gentlemen:
May we withdraw certain selected parts of Between Pacific Tides which with the passing years badly need revision? Science advances but Stanford Press does not.

There is the problem also of the impending New Ice Age.

Sometime in the near future we should like to place our order for one (1) copy of the forthcoming (1948, no doubt) publication, The Internal Combustion Engine, Will it Work?

Sincerely,
John Steinbeck
Ed Ricketts

P. S. Good luck with A Brief Anatomy of the Turtle."

I am getting quite homesick. I miss you very much. But more and more I see that this book is the book and it has to be done by me. It may be my swan song but it certainly will be the largest and most important work I have or maybe will do. That's why I don't want to slip up on it in any way. I want all my material to be right and correct. Fortunately for me the owner of the Salinas paper is a foreigner, a good newspaper man from New York State and a man who knows what I am trying to do. I am told that a little quiver of terror has crept through old Salinas at the project. I am on no punitive expedition. I just want it straight.

I have a whole life and adventures in Salinas all of which are new to me. It would be fun to collect them sometime. They are old timers' stories by now. There is one by a grocer about how I engineered the complete cleaning out of his store. Actually I was a very law abiding little boy.

Also I find that the adventures of Max [Wagner] and John Murphy have all been moved over to me, even the throwing of the roast of beef through the glass door at City Hall. They worked so hard and I get all the credit. I have become a giant kind of half criminal, half ape over there. It works all over. Jack [Wagner] told me that it is told as truth in Cuernavaca by the waiters at the Marik that I was taken to jail there after a fight, but that it took fourteen policemen to do it and the blood flowed in the streets. What chance has any true history if this is the way people remember things?

Well that is about all. Let me know whether the valentine ever got there.

love
john

To Edward F. Ricketts

[New York]
[April 1948]

Dear Ed:

I am practicing for the novel very hard and I think I am getting some place. I do not want to start it until I am pretty sure that I have what I want in style and method but I am gradually getting through to the light. It is going to be bitterly resented by critics and the reader starting it may have some kind of hard going until he gets used to it but I do think that once he does, most other things might seem a little pale and bloodless. Anyway I am excited by the experiment.

It will be a hell of a long experiment though, nearly half a million words and by far the most ambitious book I have ever attempted. God help us all, we go on trying to climb that miserable mountain and it is always higher than the last rise we scrabbled onto. It seems to me that I have more than I can do and it frightens me sometimes until I think how it would be if I had less than I can do.

The circus in Madison Square Garden is sold out for the whole season. I want to take Thom. It will be the first circus when he is old enough and he is at the time now when it can be pure dream material. But there are no tickets. I am moving heaven and earth to try to get them for Saturday.

Next Tuesday I shall go into the hospital and have the varicosities in my legs removed. I will have to be in the hospital for a week because it is a large job and they don't want any of the ties to break loose. I should have had it done years ago but now finally I will complete it. The legs are not at all painful but I am told that the burst places are a lovely play ground for potential embolisms.

so long now

jn

To Bo Beskow

Bedford Hotel
New York
April 29, 1948

Dear Bo:

I am just sprung from the hospital yesterday. And I am very weak. Didn't realize how weak I was nor how doped I had been in the hospital. I guess it is a very great shock to the system to have all those veins removed. It took the surgeon four hours to dc it and I was very tired before he was through. But it is all over now and although the stitches are still in my legs I shall be all right in a couple of weeks. But I can't do much of any walking before then. I have to sleep in my office now because I can't climb stairs yet. My office is a hotel room at this above address but it has an elevator so I stay the nights here until we are all in order. I have a tank of tropical fish here which amuse me very much and rest me too. Their movement is very fine.

You are right. I am on my marathon book, which is called Salinas Valley. It is what I have been practicing to write all of my life. Everything else has been training. I feel that I am about ready to write it. It will take maybe three years to write and it is going to be the best that I have learned and a lot that I have never even indicated. It is rather like your [stained glass] windows. I wouldn't care if it took all of the rest of my life if I got it done. It is going to take enormous energy.

I am doing something which is secret but I will tell you about it. I am trying to buy or lease the old home ranch about which the Red Pony and many of my stories were written. My family sold it long ago to a man who is very old now and who is very rich. So I wrote to him. I haven't told Gwyn anything about this. I don't know whether she would approve or not. She loves New York and she says she will never leave it but I have to have something too. And the boys should have a chance to find out what they would like. Also the things they can get from the country now they will never be able to get again. So that is my secret.

I wouldn't fix the old house up at all, not even put in electricity. It would just be a place to go to and to get refreshed. I know it is necessary to me because before I went into this health thing I was very close to a crack-up. I was warned that I was by a very good neurosurgeon here and it wasn't just an opinion. That danger is over now, I am pretty sure, but I would love to have the old place to go to for a few months of the year and let the boys find out about animals and horses and grass and smells besides carbon monoxide.

I do not want to run it as a ranch. Just to go to live in the old house and to walk in the night and hear the coyotes howl and the roosters and to see the rabbits sitting along the brush line in the morning sun. I don't know whether it will work out but that is what I am trying. And if you ever mention it in a letter you had better send that letter to this address. I get most of my mail here anyway. Of course it is very possible that the old man will have no part of it. I would like to write parts of my book out there if I could, though it doesn't matter at all where I write it. Down in a manhole if necessary.

I guess that is all for now. I will write more often I think now. So long.

John

May 11, 1948, marked the first of two blows that would end a period of Steinbeck's life and change its course. On that date, at dusk, not far from the Pacific Biological Laboratories that had been both a kind of refuge and a house of learning for Steinbeck, his good friend Ed Ricketts, driving across the Southern Pacific tracks, was struck by the evening train from San Francisco. Steinbeck rushed to California. Ricketts lingered for three days and died. Ten days later,

311

Steinbeck had returned to New York. As he wrote Paul Caswell on May 20:

"Things have changed since I was out there and this death of Ed Ricketts changes them even more. For the next few months I will be unable to do anything about anything."

To Bo Beskow

Hotel Bedford
New York
May 22, 1948

Dear Bo:

I got back from Monterey to find your letter. You see, Ed Ricketts' car was hit by a train and after fighting for his life for three days he died, and there died the greatest man I have known and the best teacher. It is going to take a long time to reorganize my thinking and my planning without him. It is good that he was killed during the very best time of his life with his work at its peak and with the best girl he ever had. I am extremely glad for that. He had just finished a plankton paper that was masterly. I will over the next few years, if I am able, edit his journals for the last fifteen years which contain his observations in every field. It is very important thinking to my mind.

Naturally this changes all of my plans about the summer and about nearly everything except my big book. You are right in your intuitions about the office and the ranch. There is nothing to do but to sit it out and that I will do, but meanwhile, if I possibly can, I will get the ranch to fall back into. As to the immediate future, I don't know. I may do a picture of the life of Emiliano Zapata if I can find someone to do it honestly. The great danger of Zanuck is that he writes and he can't but he thinks he can. I don't mean Zanuck, of course, I mean Selznick. They all sound alike. But Zanuck did a good picture for me in the Grapes of Wrath and Milestone did a good one in both the Mice and Men and the Red Pony. The

312

last has not been released. The Pearl is a pretty good picture but I could not protect its pace. It is a little slow. I will send you a copy of the book in the next day or so. It has line drawings by Orozco. Many people do not like them but I do and it is the only book he has ever consented to illustrate and that to me is a very great compliment.

I thought for a day or so that I would run to Sweden to lick my wound and that might be a good thing too but that wouldn't be good for you and in the second place I have too much to do. There are certain responsibilities here that I can't shake off.

I haven't asked about your girl because I thought you did not want to talk about her. I have thought that men and women should never come together except in bed. There is the only place where their natural hatred of each other is not so apparent. Many animals from deer to dogs have no association between the male and the female except in the rutting season or the heat of the female. In this way they may be very biologically wise because the warfare between the unaroused male and female is constant and ferocious. Each blames the other for his loss of soul.

One pays for everything, the trick is not to pay too much of anything for anything. That was Ed Ricketts' discovery and he practiced it. He did not pay too much for a clean floor or for family or for luxuries which did not give him a really luxurious feeling. Many people disapproved of this and envied him at the same time. I among them because I am paying much too much for everything. You remember the people who bought real gold watches at country fairs and found that they were not only not gold but had no works either. This is quite a common thing in all directions.

Letters from me turn into long things. The book will be written. I have to get over a number of shocks but it will be written all right and good or bad at that. I have had the death feeling very strongly for some time now as you know but maybe this was it. I am capable sometimes of horrifying clairvoyances. They come out of the air. My mother had the second sight and so has one of my sisters, and I seem to have it a little. But I don't have the death feeling now. I know that my book has to be written, and for many reasons.

Well, I will be writing to you often now. There are times of verbosity and times of silence. And I may try to fill up one lack with you and you must not mind that. Whenever I thought of a good thought or picture—I wondered what Ed would think of it and how would he criticize it? The need is there. Maybe you who have taken part of that will have to take all of it now, at least for a while.

Let me ask you to answer to the address on this paper. Because my intellectual life is here now.

So long for now.

Jn

To Webster F. Street

New York
May 25, 1948

Dear Toby:

You are not the most episcotory thing in the world these days but I hope you will be able to bring me from time to time some kind of progress report of what happens out there. As you know Ed was very close to me and meant very much to me. I liked him and I would have done anything in the world for him and when ever it was possible I did what I could. The laboratory without Ed is just a run down piece of real estate and any attempt to maintain it or hold it together is either a piece of morbid wishful thinking or an attempt to use the place simply as a place to live.

Now, there is something else that I want you to look into. I loaned Ed a thousand dollars very recently. I have his correspondence on it and he was to have signed a note for it as he indicates in his letters. This thousand was to be his share of the expenses for the book we were going to do together. That I will have to get back some how. He may have spent it on other things. I know he was pretty strapped and that his beer bill alone was more than he was making.

In spite of what people generally consider, I do not have any money. I have no savings at all and the last couple of years I have joined the great majority and gone into debt at tax time. I spend on trips and things like that only such things as are clearly and legally deductible in the carrying out of my writing. What I am getting down to is that the money must be returned because I haven't got it and I will have to borrow it next year to pay my taxes and pay interest on it. This is what I wanted to tell you.

I think you know that I put a high value on friendship. I have been kicked in the behind quite a bit on this account and that is perfectly all right and I would do it again but there are a number of reasons why I have to toughen up. I have a long book to write, a three year job. There are other situations arising which I will not go into now but that is the one firm and unalterable thing I have. That god damned book is going to get written. I'm forty-six now and if I am going to be a writer I'd better god damned well get to it. I've piddled away a great deal of my time and I haven't an awfully lot left. I don't think you can find anybody in my acquaintance to whom I have not loaned money and that is all right but now I need help in the way of indulgence and support and I am asking for the kind of support I have given to everyone else. Jim Brady used to say that it was fun to pay off if you could afford it, and so it is but I can't afford it any more. I've got trouble coming and bad trouble and I have the book to write and I am going to have to have at least the spiritual support of my friends if I have any.

affectionately
John

Steinbeck was later to write, in "About Ed Ricketts":

"We worked and thought together very closely for a number of years so that I grew to depend on his knowledge and on his patience in research. And then I went away to another part of the country but it didn't make any difference. Once a week or once a month would come a fine long letter so much in the style of his speech that I could hear his voice over the neat page full of small elite type.

"Knowing Ed Ricketts was instant. After the first moment I knew him, and for the next eighteen years I knew him better than I knew anyone, and perhaps

I did not know him at all. Maybe it was that way with all his friends. He was different from anyone and yet so like that everyone found himself in Ed, and that might be one of the reasons his death had such an impact. It wasn't Ed who had died but a large and important part of oneself."

Something of this feeling permeates the letter he wrote Ritchie and Tal Lovejoy, friends from the days of his first marriage. Tal [Natalya] was Russian and had been born in Sitka; Ritchie was a journalist.

To Ritchie and Natalya Lovejoy

New York
May 27, 1948

Dear Ritch and Tal:

There's been a lot of thinking to do. By some intelligence greater than our own, we were able to stay drunk enough or withdrawn enough during the immediate thing. But that comes to an end and I have been sitting alone in my hotel room for some days now. Impact is not sharp now—all dulled out. It would be interesting if we all flew apart now like an alarm clock when you pry off the mainspring with a screw driver. Wouldn't it be interesting if Ed *was* us and that now there wasn't any such thing or that he created out of his own mind something that went away with him. I've wondered a lot about that. How much was Ed and how much was me and which was which.

And another strange thing, I have a great feeling of life again. It's not the same but it is vital and violent. Almost as though I were growing new tissue. Do you feel that at all? There were times of cold terror about doing it alone but now the prop is out and I have a feeling that I can. It won't be the same but it will be done. Do you feel that at all? You know how sometimes in candle light, the room darkens and then lights up again and seems to be brighter. It's kind of like that. I haven't yet got used to the unreality of this new reality but I am sure now it is going to be all right. I remember Ed's words for it even—"This species has experienced channels for all pain and all sorrow and all happiness possible. They are ready when they are needed."

Then there's another thing. The rock has dropped in the water and the rings are going out and God knows where they will go or for how long or what patterns they will change obliquely. I have to tell this to someone and I guess you are the ones to tell. Nothing about me is the same. It is all changed. Tightening up now but in a different way. Almost a relief to be alone. As though some kind of conscience were removed and a fierceness I haven't had for many years restored. I'm going to work now as I have never worked before, because for the time anyway, that's all there is.

I've been going back over everything. Surprising how many tiny things you can remember—gestures, attitudes, words, expressions and a million incidents. I have wanted to do them once and then put them away for good. And let go.

Don't tear yourselves to pieces so. That's not good nor useful to anyone.

Summer is coming. There's heat in the air today. And I haven't really anything to say, I know.

So long
John

To Bo Beskow

Bedford Hotel
New York
June 19, 1948

Dear Bo:

I had your cable and your good letter but they arrived while I was in Mexico. I am going to write a moving picture while I get on my feet. It is about one of the greatest men who ever lived. His name was Emiliano Zapata. It will be unbearably hard work and that will be a good thing. I have to do that. Gwyn is taking the children to California tonight to stay with her mother for a couple of months. I will stay here and

317

work. It would have been nice to go for a rest but I don't think I could have stood it. After a while I will rest or maybe never. It doesn't much matter. A certain amount of energy must be poured out from one fire or another and then it is done. This Zapata job is worth doing. It can be very fine. I sent you the Pearl recently. I hope it arrives.

I am out of sadness and into fierceness now. That is natural to the organism that feels under attack I guess.

I'm getting this off to you now but in a little while I will write you a long and detailed letter.

So long and I wish I could have rested.

John

To Bo Beskow

New York
June 24, 1948

Dear Bo:

I got back from Mexico last week. Went there to set up research on the life of Zapata which I want to do as a film. This will be very hard work and that is what I need. I should have it done by Christmas and it is a very large job.

I haven't really the slightest idea what is going to happen, Bo. I just have to wait and see. It is a highly complicated thing—as complicated as yours, only different in some ways and there are no exits. I guess you know how that might be. You will simply have to use intuition. There is no second person. In that respect it is unlike yours. The last 10 days I have been drinking too much—not drunk but drinking. That is about over now. It was kind of "between two things" drinking. This is not a sad letter and I don't want it to sound that way. I may be a little vague, however—but I don't think even that. Blood is flowing in my veins again instead of buttermilk.

I wish I could have gone to Sweden but it was not in the cards. Resting I could not do. I need violent work, and violent play, and I am going to have both.

Very strange thing—I had a kind of crack-up over the

318

weekend. It seems to be all over now but it was a little frightening. Got too tired I guess with too many things. Most things are going smoothly. Research is moving and the story line smoothing out. I have a way to beat the fatigue now which is to go into a closed room and shut the door for 24 hours. That seems to work.

> Affectionately,
> John

And now in mid-August he finally spoke of the second blow of 1948. He had been on the verge of identifying it, he had referred to it obliquely, he had put it off, avoided it, hinted at it since May.

To Bo Beskow

> 58 West 58th Street
> New York
> August 16, 1948

Dear Bo:

After over four years of bitter unhappiness Gwyn has decided that she wants a divorce, so that is that. It is an old story of female frustration. She wants something I can't give her so she must go on looking. And maybe she will never find out that no one can give it to her. But that is her business now. She has cut me off completely. She feels much relieved now that she has done it and may even be a good friend to me. She will take the children, at least for the time being. And I will go back to Monterey to try to get rested and to get the smell of my own country again. She did one kind thing. She killed my love of her with little cruelties so there is not much shock in all of this. And I will come back. I'm pretty sure I have some material left. But I have to rest like an old dog fox

319

panting beside a stream. I have great sadness but no anger. In Pacific Grove I have the little cottage my father built and I will live and work in it for a while. Maybe I'll come to see you next winter and we'll "sing sad stories of the death of kings"—with herring.

I suppose Gwyn will quarrel over property settlement but she will have to quarrel with lawyers. It is very strange. She did it, wanted it, is upset by it. She will have to have a lot of money until she remarries or makes some other arrangement. It doesn't matter. I really need very little. It is amazing how little I do need.

I don't know whether I ever told you about my little house in Pacific Grove. My father built it before I was born. It has only three rooms and a little garden. But it's a pleasant little house with big trees and I think I will go back to it. Carol and I lived in it for years. I don't for a moment think I will be unrestless there but I'll be restless and lonely anywhere. But at least it will be a place for the transition time and a place to work and I can always leave it. I'll try to get to Sweden maybe next spring or maybe for Christmas. That will be a bad time for me this year and maybe we could raise a little hell to cover up. You see I really do not have any plans. It's all mixed up.

I'll close now and write again when I am a little more settled. I'm pretty much bruised now.

Affectionately,
John

To Webster F. Street

[New York]
[August 17, 1948]

Dear Toby:

This letter is privileged material—all of it. After four years of bitter unhappiness, Gwyn has decided that she wants a divorce. I am inhibiting her and she can't stand me. Now that she has decided, she seems much relieved. There need be no trouble and I can try to build back some of the things that have been torn out of me. This will be a clean one, I think. She will take the children, at least for a while. All of this, however, will be arranged.

I have a little life yet to lead. I'm pretty banged up. In fact I have been for quite a long time as you know. I've got to build back and at the same time I have a lot of work to do. I think I will go back to Monterey to do it—not out of nostalgia but simply because I think I can get rested there. I would like to have my cottage back.

I'm not rushing but sometime soon after the first I will probably be out to see you.

I have a feeling I can get some rest and simplicity in that house. And maybe just fixing the garden up will be good for me.

Please let me hear from you as soon as you can at the address on this envelope. We'll have some good times yet.

Affectionately,
John

Please don't mention any of this. Maybe we can keep this clean. Gwyn wants to also.

To Bo Beskow

New York
August 1948

Dear Bo:

Since I wrote a day or so ago I have been thinking and thinking in circles, and it comes out the same. I'll go home for a while and then to Mexico for the picture, and then I would like to spend Christmas with you. And then it should be time for me to start on my long book and maybe a little ease may have set in. Only one thing—by my settlement I am going to be very broke for a very long time and that may limit my movements to some extent.

I'm trying to shake the first gloom. There's no good in being sad. I must be careful about not going out with any women until after the settlement is signed. Have been singularly unguilty in this and I don't want to spoil it now. You probably know about our crazy divorce laws. They don't make any sense.

Now it is the next day and this is a dawdling letter. Today my son Thom visited me and in the afternoon we went toy shopping and it was fine. I shall miss him very much because now he is becoming good company. Am more cheerful today. Went to look at rehearsals of a new musical comedy. Did some work and went out to dinner with a very pretty girl. And found I could be interested—which is fine. I'm fairly definitely decided on California now. I think it will be good. Life Magazine has a large coverage in pictures of Sweden in mid-summer and it reminded me so of the summer—long ago—when Carol and I were there.

And then I remembered that Carol was always angry at me too. I think now I will try to have no more wives. I'm not good for them and they are not good for me. If I marry again I will be really asking for trouble. The difficulty of course is that I like women. It is only wives I am in trouble with. We'll yet have some fun with our lives. I'm just now beginning to believe that for the first time in many months—even years. It's like a little tingle up the spine. I think I didn't know how heavy the weight was. And the possibility of its being lifted is just now apparent.

There's the end of a long dull letter.

Affectionately,
John

To Webster F. Street

Dear Toby:

No answer from you yet and there is no reason for writing this except that for the first time in years I have time for writing letters and for thinking and for reading. It is rather remarkable. I had almost forgotten. My plans haven't changed. I'll call you when I get in.

I am more relaxed than I have been in a very long time. I've been fighting off this separation for a long time, holding it back with all my strength. And now that I have lost—I have the first sense of rest for a very long time. Even some energy and some fierceness coming back. That is all to the good I think. Maybe a new start. I must admit I am a little along into middle age for new starts but I don't feel so. It will be good to be absolutely alone for a while. I'll get things sorted out and back to sources again.

Maybe you and I will have some good times again. There's no reason why not. This city has never been good for me. I have been doing a routine that is foreign to me. That doesn't mean I won't come back and enjoy it but I won't be living here. I think I won't live anywhere—really. You know six months has usually been the limit before I get restless. And now there is no reason why I shouldn't move when I get restless. And I darn well will.

I imagine the separation agreement will be signed next week. Gwyn will get most everything of course. And I will be pretty broke for a while but in a few years I imagine I can build up some kind of reserve again. And I really do not need much money. It has only done bad things for me. My tastes have not become more complicated than they were. Transportation, food, shelter and sex. And all of them can be very simple.

Of course you know I am just writing to see the ink run out. Except for work I am going to live from day to day if I can.

And I think I can. There isn't any other way for me.
I'll be seeing you.

John

"She will go to Nevada," he continued to Toby Street a few days later, "and I will not appear unless she should violate the settlement, in which case I would fight the divorce. It is to be an incompatibility charge or I won't play. I haven't been guilty of anything.

"It is complicated and I don't know all of it. Gwyn was being robbed of something. I think she has enough talent to make her nervous and not enough energy to do anything about it."

To Webster F. Street

[New York]
[August 27, 1948]

Dear Toby:

Yesterday we signed the separation agreement and as usual my wife gets about everything I have. My nerves are pretty good. In the thick of this they got pretty bad. We will think quite a bit about this Fallen Leaf [at Lake Tahoe] business. It sounds mighty good. Can very possibly do it.

Neale, my fine man, is driving my car out. He will get there about the 11th. He is a good man and will keep me fed and washed and clean. I've had him quite a long time. Ex-navy C.P.O., colored and very intelligent, excellent driver, cook, valet and damn good friend. He will stay with me as long as he wants to.

There is only one thing that makes Gwyn unhappy. She

has nothing to blame me for so she can feel superior. If I were any kind of gentleman I would give her some public thing to hate so she could feel justified in doing what she has done. I'm son of a bitch enough not to do it.

I am very anxious to get to the cool coast. This god damned climate drives me crazy. The utter insanity of living in a place like this doesn't occur to the 9,000,000 people who inhabit New York. Except for visits I think I shall not be here any more as a resident. But one should do everything I guess. And I've done nearly everything except contentment. I'm really looking forward to quiet and some peace. I want to walk some, particularly at night.

So long. See you soon.

John

**1948
1949**

[signature: Steinbeck]

"If one finds it —
there is no need
for words."

1948 Elected to American Academy of Arts and Letters. Divorced from Gwyndolyn Steinbeck.

1949 Film of *The Red Pony* released. Returned to the East Coast.

In 1959, looking back on this period of his return to California in September, John Steinbeck wrote:

"The little Pacific Grove house is many things to me but its last patina is of the wild and violent heart-broken time after Gwyn, which stays with me like the memory of a nightmare. I don't think I will ever get over that."

To Pascal Covici

Dear Pat—

The thing makes a full circle with 20 years inside of it. Amazing, isn't it? And what wonderful years and sad ending ones. I am back in the little house. It hasn't changed and I wonder how much I have. For two days I have been cutting the lower limbs off the pine trees to let some light into the garden so that I can raise some flowers. Lots of red geraniums and fuchsias. The fireplace still burns. I will be painting the house for a long time I guess. And all of it seems good.

There are moments of panic but those are natural I suppose. And then sometimes it seems to me that nothing whatever has happened. As though it was the time even before Carol. Tonight the damp fog is down and you can feel it on your face. I can hear the bell buoy off the point. The only proof of course will be whether I can work—whether there is any life in me. I think there is but that doesn't mean anything until it gets rolling. Women I will have to have of course, only I wonder if I have learned to keep them in their place. They have a way of sprawling all over and that I can't have any more. I haven't enough time and I couldn't take another sequence like the last two.

Anyway this is just a note to tell you I'm in a new shell or an old one, like a hermit crab and the ink is now out of two of my pens and this is the last one. I have no more ink in the house tonight. I'll keep you posted.

Affectionately
(and write to me)
John

To Pascal Covici

Pacific Grove
September 12 [1948]

Dear Pat:

It is night and the low fog is down and the buoy is bellowing off the reef and it is very fine. I have a good fire going and no one is likely to come over tonight. I'm getting rested and working hard outside too. This whole place is a mess but in two weeks you won't know it. Garden will be cleaned and replanted and the house will be painted inside and out. And during that time I do not intend to touch a pen to manuscript. My hands are getting calluses already. I don't know many people here any more and that is a good thing. It will be more time for working and reading. Oddly enough I do not feel lonely at all yet. I know I will soon enough. I know it will come like little fingers of ice but not so far except once or twice a kind of blind panic. However, that is perfectly natural and would happen to anyone.

This house is also almost completely without furniture. Various non-rent paying tenants have seen to that. I don't need very much but some I guess I must have. I have a bed (new) my old work chairs and a card table to write on and

330

that is all I actually need. It will cost something to paint this house but that will be all right too. I have to buy everything for it—even pots and pans and knives and forks but Woolworth still lives, thank God. I remember how Carol used to be afraid I would get loose in Woolworth's with five hot dollars in my pocket. It was a nightmare thought to her. She never got used to it.

This garden needs peat moss and fertilizer and needs it badly and it is going to get it too. It is going to be a very pretty garden if I can make it so. It is getting late now. I've kind of nodded away the evening. And I have to get up early tomorrow because then the work starts. But I wanted to get a note off to you.

bye
John

To Bo Beskow

Pacific Grove
September 19, 1948

Dear Bo:

I am sorry I have not answered your two letters before. This is the little town I came out of and it is very good to be back in it. The ocean is only two hundred yards away and it is very fine. Even though the house is torn up with repairs and paint I have a sense of peace here and the horrors of the last few years seem (for the moment at least) remote. How long it will last I do not know, but it is like a strong curative medicine now. I have trimmed the trees and replanted the garden and the house is to be repainted inside and out and a new matting laid down. Very good. I think maybe like your place in the south of Sweden. I know I have to go back to Mexico in a little over a month but it will be here that I will return.

One of the best things is being alone. I had almost forgotten how nice that can be. And there is a thing of fixing over a house, not for someone else but for myself. I haven't done that since before I married Carol. There is almost an aching selfishness about that. I even have a small sense of sin about it. The picture placed is the one I want. The colors are the ones I want, the chairs are for me to be comfortable. I eat at any time of day or night and never chicken which I detest and learned to eat because both of my wives liked it. When my pants are hot, I go out and get a girl *when* I want her and if that one is not available another one is. This may seem sad to you that I discover such things as though they were new in the world but so they seem to me.

There will be only one test of this and that is whether any good work comes out of it. I am not going to touch paper for several weeks yet. I want this damp sea fog to get deeply into me and the fine wind over the kelp on the rocks. It is only now after a rest that I see how I have been used but it is all right now that it is over. I don't care if I never have any money again. It didn't ever give me any peace or satisfaction. And I need very little here.

But it will all boil down to work. If I can write again then I can be happy again. I know I will put off doing it for fear it has all been drained out of me, although I don't for a moment believe that. Indeed, I feel the stirring of some power.

This is going to be my home from now on. I do not mean I will not go away from it because I know my restlessness, but there has to be a seed-center, an anlage from which other things grow. It is a little shingled house of three rooms with a little rock garden. It has very little money value and that is the way I want to keep it.

Gwyn has gone to Reno to get a divorce (her freedom she calls it). She gets everything because I don't want anything. I can have the children in the summers and I do want them. And I think I will get them. She will have worked out a perfect justification. She will never be to blame for anything in her life. I think I knew this all along but I would not let myself know it. Only now do I permit it to be seen. This is a long letter, completely taken up with myself. I will write another soon which will not be so egocentric. But I am a little amazed at myself and I am trying to set it down. I will write soon and do you also.

I would love to see your new windows. And I will before too long.

Affectionately,
John

This theme of his own refusal to be aware of what had happened around him is echoed in a letter to Covici:

"I'm afraid I built a person who wasn't there. I'll tell you about that some day. Not wanting to know, I didn't know."

His day-to-day confidant through this period continued to be Pascal Covici.

To Pascal Covici

[Pacific Grove]
[September 19, 1948]

Dear Pat:

You are right—I do get the horrors every now and then. Comes on like a cold wind. There it is, just a matter of weathering it. Alcohol doesn't help that a bit. I usually go into the garden and work hard.

At that moment Ritch and Tal Lovejoy came in for a cup of coffee and then I watered the garden and here it is dusk. A very quiet Sunday and I've enjoyed it. My hands are literally tired from moving rocks. And it is a fine feeling.

It has been one of the dark days that I like very well—overcast and almost cold except that flowers like it and seem to be on fire in such a light. I think flowers' colors are brighter here than any place on earth and I don't know whether it is the light that makes them seem

333

so or whether they really are.

I debated strongly about whether to dress and go out to dinner or whether to cook something and stay home in quiet and determined on the latter.

So I'll close and I will send you more reports.

October 18

Dear Pat:

I got to reading Auden's introduction to the Greek portable and it is very fine. He is such a good writer. Have you read Lady Godiva and Master Tom by Raoul Faure? A really blistering study of a woman.

I shall be going to Los Angeles with Kazan about the first of November and to Mexico soon after. Probably be gone for about a month.

> Elia Kazan, the theatre and film director, was to be closely involved in the creation of *Viva Zapata!*

I have not worked on The Salinas Valley. I don't want to now until everything is clear because I think I am about ready for it and I'm letting it stew. It would be bad if the whole conception turned out no good. But I'll do it anyway. I am really looking forward to the doing of it, good or bad.

I miss Ed and I don't all at the same time. It is a thing that is closed—that might possibly have been closing anyway. Who can tell? Great changes everywhere and every which way. I still get the panic aloneness but I can work that out by thinking of what it is. And it is simply the breaking of a habit which was painful in itself but we hold onto habits even when we don't like them. A very senseless species. There is no future in us I'm afraid. I can hear the music beginning to turn in my head. And by the time the spring comes I hope I will be turning with it like a slow and sluggish dervish or some mushroom Simon Stylites, a fungus on a stone pillar.

Friday

Dear Pat:

The week I've put in planting—things I'll probably never see flower—either because I won't be here or I won't be look-

334

ing. I have no sense of permanence. This is a way stopping-place, I think, as every other place is. I've made my tries at "places" and they don't work. But this is a good way stopping-place and a good one to come back to—often.

I awakened the other night with a great sense of change happening somewhere. Could not sleep any more and all night the sense of change, neither pleasant nor unpleasant but happening. It hung on for several days. Gradually my energy is coming back a little at a time. It is so strange that I could lose it so completely. One never knows what he will do ever.

Just now the rain started, very gentle and good. I hope it rains a long time. There has not been enough.

I'm sorry I was so closed in, in New York. But I realized more than any time in my whole life that there is nothing anyone can do. It's something that has to be done alone. Even with women, and that's good, there is largely no companion-ship except for a very little while.

This has been a long bleak day.

Saturday

Curious sleepless night after a long time of over-sleeping. There was a great thunder and lightning storm in the night and rain fell. Maybe the changing pressure kept me awake. I know I'm very sensitive to changing pressures.

Beth [his sister] is supposed to come down today. I hope she does. It is a long time since I have seen her. We have a lot to talk over. And she is usually so surrounded that there is no chance to see her alone.

Monday

This is turning into a diary. Beth did come down and I got to see her alone for the first time in a long time. She is well but of course is working too hard as always.

This time I am going to send this

love
John

The tone—but not the content—changes with other correspondents.

To Nunnally Johnson

POSTCARD

Pacific Grove
[1948]

Dear Nunnally—:

Your forwarded letter has arrived and I thank you for your spiritual succour spelled any way I wish. Your firm position behind husbands could mean a sense of guilt also but who cares.

It is possible that I shall leave my cave and bear skin here for the gilded haunts of beauty namely H'wood, natcherly. I have no longer your telephone number and so I cannot call you. But I will try to sneak up on you some how.

I find myself in a curiously original position, namely with a spanked bottom and in a state of original desuetude. Dames and me don't get along and they always win.

love (phooey)
John Steinbeck

To Mr. and Mrs. Joseph Henry Jackson

Pacific Grove
October 26, 1948

Dear Joe and Charlotte:

I have been meaning to write for a long time but house fixing has interfered. Strange thing, Joe—tonight I couldn't sleep and I wrote a little story that was so evil, so completely evil that when I finished it I burned it. It was effective, horribly effective. It would have made anyone who read it completely miserable. I don't mind evil if anything else is accomplished but this was unqualifiedly murderous and terrible. I wonder where it came from. It just seemed to creep in from under the door. I suppose the best thing was to write it and the next was to burn it.

It's getting cold so early. There is a nasty light of tomorrow coming through the blinds.

The wind is ashore tonight and I can hear the sea lions and the surf and the whistling buoy and the bell buoy at Point Joe and China Point respectively. China Point is now called Cabrillo Point. Phooey—any fool knows it was China Point until certain foreigners became enamored of our almost non-existent history. Cabrillo may or may not have first sighted this point, but them Chinks raised hell on it for fifty years, yes, and even buried their people there until the meat fell off and they could ship them cheaper to China. Mary and I used to watch them dig up the skeletons and we stole the punks and paper flowers off the new graves too. I used to like that graveyard. It was so rocky that some of the bodies had to be slipped in almost horizontally under the big rocks. And it has just occurred to me that I'm a talkative bastard. So I'll clip off the qualifying adjectives and relax in the *now*.

love to you both
John

I've lost your home address.

As the divorce became final the "diary" to Pascal Covici resumed.

To Pascal Covici

[Pacific Grove]
November 1 [1948]

Dear Pat:

Well that is over. Thanks for your letters. They helped. I'm leaving for Hollywood tomorrow and for Mexico on Friday. I'm pretty much relaxed, I think, things have been about as disgusting and nasty as they can get and they didn't kill me. I wish I could thoroughly believe that this is to be a new leaf. I wish I could be sure I have learned something. I am not sure of either. But I can try. At least if I try it again there will be a shudder of apprehension.

Gwyn once told me she could do anything and I would come crawling back. At the time I was very much in love with her but even then I told her not to depend on it. A woman holds dreadful power over a man who is in love with her but she should realize that the quality and force of his love is the index of his potential contempt and hatred. And nearly no women or men realize that. We will not mention this again in a post-mortem sense. Only if it becomes active will it be necessary. I think I am getting strength back— perhaps more than I have had in 17 years and perhaps more than I ever had. I want the hot words to come out again and hiss on the paper and I think they may. My needs are filled.

I hope you will write to me. I thank you for the fine bale of yellow pads. I shall make good use of them, I hope. And on your next trip out here I will get you drunk on red wine and music and the old ghosts we have neglected will walk again and wail on the wet rocks. This is a time of change and maybe of destruction, but the waves and the tide will not change, no matter how much we blast or are blasted. The black roots of the little species may put out new leaves. It is about time. There has been nothing erected for a long time. Matter is creative, that we have known and studied, but we have forgotten that the grey lobes in the head are creative too —the only and unique creative thing in the whole world of our seeing and hearing and touching.

338

A lot of high flown language but let it flow. Never again does it have to stoop to critics, or friends or lovers. It can be as good or as silly as it can be, not wise and smart and little.

And that's all for now. I will write to you from Mexico. I'm working on the life of a very great man but primarily a man. It would be good to study him closely. His life had a rare series—beginning, middle and end, and most lives dribble away like piss in the dust.

I'll be talking to you soon.

Mildred Lyman, of the McIntosh and Otis office, visited Steinbeck just before he left for Mexico, and wrote a worried letter to Annie Laurie Williams:

"He is deeply disturbed and frightened about his work. If it doesn't go well in Mexico I honestly don't know what will happen. The fact that so much time has elapsed without his accomplishing anything to speak of worries him a great deal. He has a defense mechanism which is constantly in action and it is hard to get behind that. What John needs more than anything right now is discipline. I'm afraid that he wanted to get to Mexico for reasons other than writing. I heard quite a bit while I was with him about the gal, and I don't think that bodes any good. She's a tramp. He writes tons and tons of letters late at night. He is in a strange mood and has very peculiar ideas of women these days. He eats at odd hours and not properly, stays up late and sleeps late and tries so hard to convince himself that he likes it. He talks about not liking to eat lunch or dinner until he feels like it but I noticed that whenever we went out for either meal he ate like a farmhand and enjoyed it. I presume he will come out of it but my only hope is that it will not be too late as far as his work is concerned."

November [14, 1948]

Dear Pat:

I came back. Mexico was not right, not good, now. I have to learn in unintelligent ways. I'm breaking certain chains. Maybe they will come right back. I don't know. But I'm home again—at least until restlessness gets me again. No plans except work—I'm so far behind, Pat. The sickness has been worse than I have been able to admit even to myself. Must be getting better because now I am beginning to be able to see

339

that it was there at all. At my advanced age I have to go back to some kind of childhood and learn all over again. This is ridiculous. Telling doesn't make it intelligible, I guess.

Monday

Dear Pat:

Just a note tonight. I'm going to work pretty soon. Working at night is good here. It is very quiet and it keeps me from going out and it leaves me a good part of the day to work in the garden—enough exercise to keep my bowels turning over.

Very brilliant and cold weather—the sun like metal and a fine chill in the air at night. We will have a very wet year later I think. I hope.

You must not worry about me. I am all right. This is the worst season and I am still all right and it will get less bad. That anyone can depend on. That's the law.

My house is now completed but there are the usual million things to be done in the garden. That always is there to work in. I'm going to trim my trees even more tomorrow to let more light in toward the ground so my flowers will be very early. And I have built a little potting shed with plastic on wire over it so I can force the little plants to start particularly early. There has been very much done here and now I can take it more slowly. I have no desire to rush anything.

Affectionately,
John

To Bo Beskow

Dear Bo:

Your long letter came a couple of days ago and I have waited until tonight to answer it. I wanted not to be interrupted once I started with it. My little house is now done and I am very glad to be in it.

I shall have my boys in the summer and I want to arrange my work so that I can devote all of my time to them. I shall rent a boat and we will look at the little animals on the shore and I will let them look through microscopes, and we may even go camping in the mountains. They will either sleep in a tent or I will build a little bunk house for them in the garden. I thoroughly believe I will have them all the time before too long, but now that I can see them for only two months out of the year I want to make the most out of it, for myself mostly, although I think I can show them a new world quite different from the streets of New York where their mother insists on living. I miss the boys pretty much, particularly the older one who was beginning to think and judge and criticize.

As for the rest I think I am fine. I have moments of rage but less and less often and it will soon fade into a memory of nightmare. It will be all right and I am at peace, without hatred and completely without longing. This is a stranger and the one I loved is dead and released and I released from her. This is not the protest that confesses the opposite. It is as near as I can judge my own feeling, and you know I would try to tell you the truth. Since we went apart I have known a great many women, perhaps fifty, not in boasting or revenge, but because the sexual energy which was dammed up while I waited and waited for Gwyn to be well again, (I thought she was ill and so did she) this energy was suddenly released and a satyric pulse overcame me so that I longed for women and I still do and I have them in great joy and exuberance. There is only one symptom of scar. I cannot sleep in the

341

same bed with them. If I try to my skin itches and if I go to sleep I have nightmares. I have become selfish in many little ways. I have a little gnawing of unknown fear sometimes and at others an utter and grey despair falls on me like a cloth. But mostly I feel well and strong (maybe you will know what this is), curiously full of dignity and sense of myself and a good myself.

In the morning I awaken to see the sun on my little garden and a flood of joy comes over me—such a thing I have not felt for many years. My material for the Zapata script is all collected now and next Monday I will go to work on it with great energy, for I have great energy again. Whether there is any talent left I do not know nor care very much. But the churning joy in the guts that to me is the physical symptom of creation is there again.

I shall not be to see you this winter. This divorce has left me 30,000 dollars short in my tax money and I must work. I still have Gwyn and the children to support. I don't care about her but I want the children well cared for. At first I wanted to kill some one or be killed, even to the extent of walking alone at night in Mexico with a bare machete in my hand but the challenge did not work. I was avoided like the mad dog I guess I was. And that is all over now and a soft benevolence is on me. And that is all of that now of me.

I did not know that the glass path was still under your feet. I thought that was all over. It is not fine to see two people determined to destroy each other. What guilt do you two carry and why can't you confess it in the dark and unload the torture and the hatred, because you do hate each other. A priest or a psychiatrist might do it if you cannot whisper your true grief into the ground. Or maybe you have learned to love pain. This is far from unusual. Pain is exciting whether with whips or with little sharp pointed thoughts barbed and poisoned. I have forgotten what it is like to love a woman. It is very strange. It is like forgetting pain or hunger. Desire I have in great and all-directional abundance, even a fine goat-like lust—but love—the softening—the compassionate thing I don't have now. I think it will come back and surely I will welcome it back. I suspect that some internal healing is going on. I would hate to be closed up and withdrawn— even unconsciously.

I do not think now I will remarry. I think I am not good at it. I want more children but it doesn't seem necessary to

342

marry to have them. Two women were turned to hatred and pain by marriage with me. And both of them would probably have been happy mistresses.

I have so much work to do. As soon as my Zapata script is finished I shall get to the large book of my life—The Salinas Valley. I don't care how long it takes. It will be nearly three quarters of a million words or about twice as long as the Grapes of Wrath. And after that I have five plays to write. And after that I should like to do one more film—the life of Christ from the four Gospels—adding and subtracting nothing. But that is for the future—maybe six years. I am so glad your windows progress and are satisfying. And I will be glad to get into my big train of a book. My blood bubbles when I think of that and I get a feeling like silent weeping. All the passion that has been drained off into neurotic and jealous women is now back and whole and ready to use for what it was conditioned to be.

My little garden, like yours, is a thing to go out to look at every morning. Some new god damned little leaf is there or a flower is curling. And the great war against snails and varmints, which are only less destructive and poisonous than us, goes on ceaselessly, I kill them and stomp on them—an enemy—and I admire them quite a lot too because they can't poison or stomp me and yet they keep ahead of me. These things I can love. And I think I could love a European woman or a negress or a Chinese but the breed of American woman—part man, part politician—they have the minds of whores and the vaginas of Presbyterians. They are trained by their mothers in a contempt for men and so they compete with men and when they don't win, they whimper and go to psychoanalysts. The American girl makes a servant of her husband and then finds him contemptible for being a servant. American married life is the doormat to the whore house. Eventually they will succeed in creating a race of homosexuals. And they will not be content with that. I am just beginning to see our mores objectively and I do not like what I see and I do not want my boys brought up by them. The impulse of the American woman to geld her husband and castrate her sons is very strong. This feeling has been brought home to me by Mexican women who are quite content to be women and who are good at it as opposed to ours who try to be men and aren't good at it at all. Well, I

343

guess I wasn't a man or I wouldn't have put up with it. But I am a man now and I don't think I will surrender that nice state. I like it and the others can lump it. I hope this does not sound like bitterness because it is not. It is anything else. So long—Write

John

On November 23, The American Academy of Arts and Letters had written to inform Steinbeck that he had been "duly elected a member."

To The American Academy of Arts and Letters

Pacific Grove
December 3, 1948

My dear Mr. Brooks:

I am extremely sensible of the honor paid me by the Academy in making me a member. Having been black-balled from everything from the Boy Scouts to the United States Army, this election is not only a great experience but for me a unique one. My most profound thanks.

Yours sincerely,
John Steinbeck

At the end of November he had written Covici:

"I did Thanksgiving very well but Xmas I will not try. I will get a gallon of wine and the prettiest girl I can find and I will forget Christmas this year."

To Bo Beskow

[Pacific Grove]
December 28, 1948

Dear Bo:

I had your good cable and thank you for it. I should have gone to spend Christmas with you but I am too broke. Christmas eve was a lonely bad time. It won't ever be that bad again. I feel that I am missing something rich and valuable in the growing of my children. It doesn't really matter, I guess, but I do feel cheated of it. The script I have been working on went to pieces too. Partly because of Christmas and partly, I am convinced, because my eyes need attention. I think I need glasses for writing and reading. Many headaches, nausea and other things could easily be eyestrain.

Funny how I had to wear the hairshirt this year. But I was trying to remember old times. I have talked with Carol on the phone but have not seen her. She sounds the same and all right, but the same.

An odd thing is that sadness does not necessarily become greater with age. I can remember desolating sadnesses when I was a child, worse probably than I have ever had since, because they came out of a black void and there was no reason for them that I could see. Things that were black were black indeed and things that were white were blinding. I do not believe now that the world is going to be destroyed by bombs or ideologies of any kind. The world has always been in process of decay and birth.

I must finish my script and I would like to get a good start on my book. Maybe when that is started I will be able to do it anywhere and maybe Stockholm would be a good place to do some of it. Maybe down on your place in the south with

345

a fine warm blonde about. My love of woman flesh and feel does not diminish. It even grows as I know more about the general and am less blinded by the particular. It was individuals who did the murdering, not the thing woman. I hope the good potters with red hearts had red wine and love this Christmas. And how I wish I could have been with all of you with a big pottery jar of wine and a plate of herring. What a nice thing is herring. I'll finish this tomorrow. I seem to have a guest arriving (see above).

Next day—I was right—it was a guest. This morning I made for me a momentous decision. I am going to spend the New Year in Los Angeles. I'll go down tomorrow and come back on the second. It will be a change of pace. I will drink a lot and make love to very pretty women. I don't care if they are not bright. They are very very pretty. And for a while I am going to be content with that. I will get this off now. The post office is going to hate all the stamps. It is more work cancelling them.

So long for now. And a good year for both of us.

Love to you all
John

To Pascal Covici

[Pacific Grove]
January 22 [1949]

Dear Pat:

I have my glasses now and print jumps out of the page at me. I only need them for reading and writing. And speaking of reading—there are some books I need Pat, to fill out my library. You see when I want to know something the local libraries either don't have it or are closed. There is no particular hurry and I don't care whether the books are new or not but I need some volumes in medicine, a Grey's Anatomy, fairly new edition, 2., a Pharmacopaea (can't even spell it).

346

This should be a new one because of the many new drugs. 3., the best standard volume in Toxicology. In this field the encyclopedia is not of much value. My books are supposed to be on the way but of course I don't know what she will let me have. I'll fill in the gap when they arrive, but I won't know until then. Also I will probably bring up most of the books from the lab which will make all in all quite a good reference library. These glasses are wonderful. It is a pleasure to write again and I was getting to dread every day's stint. Maybe I can work again. I hope. I was getting deeply worried thinking my will power was gone.

Here then is a health report. I am only interested because I must be well to work. I am tough and mean after quite a house cleaning. My closets were full of dust, of little feats, of half felt emotions. If I am to be a son of a bitch, I'm going to be my own son of a bitch. I've kicked out the duty emotions. They will snap back of course but decreasingly. I get the despondencies still. But I have learned that if you are not right with a person, nothing can make you right and if you are right then nothing can make you wrong. There is some anger at me here because I no longer have the money to solve my friends' difficulties. I stumbled on a phrase to take care of that situation: it is Fuck it! I have been the soft touch for too long. Still would be if I had it but I haven't. And probably am never going to have again.

Out of some kind of pride or weakness I have never wanted to accept anything. It gave me some self-indulging feeling to be the giver and not the receiver. It is going to be hard to learn to receive and to accept but I am going to learn. Thus when a girl in Mexico wanted to hustle for me, I wouldn't let her. She would have had some good thing if I had let her walk the streets for me—some kind of fulfilling.

It is a great fine storm in the air, wind and rain and fresh cold. It is my kind of weather and it gives me a good feeling. The rain is lashing the windows like whips and I have a good fire. Later a girl will come in and I still function well in that department. You can't want more than that—a cold night and a warm girl.

My Arabia Deserta was down at the office. I am so glad to have it. I think it is the greatest secular prose in English that I know. Doughty makes the language a great stone with designs of metal and outcroppings of preciousness, emerald and diamond and obsidian. It is good to have here to see what can be done with the language. I do not think it was easy for him to write. No such sense of ease and flow ever came without great and tearing effort.

I have some new snapshots of my children. I think I have located a boat for us to go cruising in. I told them we would sleep and cook our dinner on a boat and that seems to excite them very much just as it excites me still. What better thing is there than that?

Pat I'm getting the old ecstasies back sometimes. Thinking about a boat made the hair rise on the back of my neck. You say a good piece of writing does that to you, à chacun son goût I guess.

I went out to find little pine trees to plant about my house and they aren't up yet. But some other things are. As soon as the rain stops I will take a shovel out and get some yerba buena and some wild iris for my garden. Yerba buena is a ground crawling mint from which the old ones used to make a curative tea. I remember drinking it when I was little. It is a stomachic and it smells wonderful when you crush it—a sweet but sharp odor that pierces way back of your nose cleanly.

And this is the end. But I think you will agree that this propped up life is—what? I don't know. It still has some savor and what more could I ask of it. Women are still beautiful and desirable and things smell good and sometimes the flame burns jumping the nerve ends like little boys jumping fences.

So—
love
John

To Pascal Covici

Dear Pat:

Here it is again, another year and the first one I haven't dreaded for a long time. I just finished my day's work. It is finally going like mad, or did I tell you that? And now that it is going I don't think it will take long. And as always when I am working I am gay. I'm terribly gay. I'm even gay about what I'm going to tell you. And I want you to keep this to yourself.

I'm asking Gwyn for my books. I asked for the anthologies, poetry, drama, classics etc. which I have collected over the years. Well I didn't get them. I got an absolute minimum. I wish you would please get me, if you can, complete catalogues of Everyman, Random House and the other libraries that do such things because I do want to replace the things I actually need for work. Isn't it odd that having stripped me of everything else, she also retains the tools of the trade from which she is living? A very funny girl and I think she is headed for trouble—not from me. I did get the dictionary and the encyclopedia and a few others.

I don't know what has happened but the dams are burst. Work is pouring out of me. I guess maybe I am over the illness. Who knows? But at last there seems to be some opening at the end of the street.

Please let me hear from you. And don't tell any one about this book thing. I don't want to fight with Gwyn unless the children are involved and sooner or later I think they will be.

So long now
affectionately
John

To Elizabeth Bailey

[Pacific Grove]
March 19, 1949

Dear Godmother:

Thank you for your letter. The Academy business, unfortunately, does not impress me very much. It seems a little like
a premature embalming job—a very empty thing.

It is strange that you should have spoken of the children.
I had just written them as your letter came in. I sent them a
check for the circus in Madison Square Garden. It is very
easy to dislike this wife but her only sin is that she doesn't
like me. And that is not such a bad one. She loves the children. I can't blame her for the other because there are times
when I don't either. And even if she were bad, it would not
be good to take the children. They will be with me this summer and then I will try to make it good enough so they will
want to come back and that is all I can do. I assure you that
I have been over this problem more times than I can think.

Very hard at work now which is a saving thing. It would
be dreadful if I didn't have work.

The little house which you remember is very nice and
pleasant. And you needn't worry about anything. I will probably try again. I would surely hate to "learn my lesson." That
would be ridiculous and self-limiting and besides I like
pretty women too much. But maybe several are better than
one. That is to be seen.

Anyway, it was a very fine thing to hear from you.

Love,
John

To Gwyndolyn Steinbeck

Pacific Grove
May 3, 1949

Mrs. Gwyndolyn C. Steinbeck
175 East 78th Street
New York 21, New York

Dear Gwyn:

I am writing to inform you that, in accordance with our separation agreement, I will send for Thom and John during the first week of July, 1949, that is, between July 1st and 8th. I will let you know a little later of the exact date and time, as these will depend upon my schedule, which is not entirely definite as yet, and upon the reservations which I can get. Thom and John will, of course, be accompanied by their nurse and I will keep them with me for the full period of sixty days and will arrange for their return to you at the end of that time.

You said something to me about your leaving the house on the 1st of July. If it will be any more convenient to you and you will let me know promptly, I will arrange to take the children beginning the last week in June.

John

To Bo Beskow

Pacific Grove
May 9 [1949]

Dear Bo:

It has been too long since I heard from you and I am worried that you are not well or that some bad thing has happened to you. I know that I have been very remiss about

351

writing but I have had a lot of healing to do. Three weeks ago I had a compulsion to go to New York to see my children and I did so thinking I was more well than I was. It struck me hard, all of the unhappiness arose again but it will not be very long before I am back where I was so that will be all right. My boys were well and healthy. I shall have them with me this summer and get to know them again.

Coming home wrote three short stories and I don't know whether they are any good or not. It is long since I have worked in that form. I promptly tore up two of them because I am sure they were not very good and I don't have to put up with my own mediocrity any more. I can afford to do just what I want to do now. I have arrived at that deep security which is born in a complete lack of any security and that is a very good thing. I have been seeing Carol quite often out here and we can enjoy each other now that she has no power to hurt nor to control. And I think she enjoys that too. I think that the responsibility of hurting was one she did not like but couldn't help.

New York nearly killed me after the months of quiet. I hope I will never try to get used to it again. It is no place for me to live. Of course I love the violence of it for a little while but not for very long. I get very tired of it now and begin soon to long for the deep quiet of this little town where some weeks I do not see any one at all. Tonight for example I have a little fire going and am playing some music that I like while I write this.

One amusing thing about this free life is that everyone tries to get me married. It is almost as though they hated to see ease and wanted me to be magnificently trapped again so that I would not have this fine freedom. The papers and my friends and the dear wives of the community all conspire to get me tied up again. I will try to jump over the noose and walk around the pit. I must face it. I am not good at marriage. I find that I am a very good lover but a lousy husband and that is something I might as well accept since I do not think I will change at my time of life.

How do your windows go? I should like to see them very much and maybe I will be able before too long.

Your country woman [Ingrid Bergman] seems to be having a very good time for herself in Italy. I thought she was about to kick over the traces. She had ceased to be a person and had

352

become the small stockholder in a large corporation. I finally quarrelled with her for that reason. She could do nothing because too many people owned her. Now maybe she can be her own woman again and then I will be interested in her again.

Do write to me Bo as soon as you can. I can think that perhaps you have and that I will no sooner get this posted than your letter will arrive. It is usually that way. But do keep in touch and do not believe the stories of my impending marriage. They aren't true.

Love to all there,
red hearts and red wine.
John

The story he mentions was entitled "His Father" and sold to the *Reader's Digest.*

To Elizabeth Otis

[Pacific Grove]
May 23, 1949

Dear Elizabeth:

You know darned well you done good with the little four page story. What a price! It is next best to Air Wick. Very good news.

In the same mail with your letter, one from Ralph Henderson (Editor of *Reader's Digest*) assuring me that they bought the story because they liked it and not because of my name. Apparently you cut them deeply by asking for money as well as the honor of being published. In the light of this $2,500 for four pages—do you remember when you worked for months and finally got $90 for the longest story in the Red Pony series and forty for the shorter ones? I hardly made $1,000 on my first three novels.

Thanks for your letter. I'm going to have some more little stories before long now. They are good practice in a form I have not used for a long time.

Love,
John

To Bo Beskow

Pacific Grove
May 23, 1949

Dear Bo:

I'm glad you answered quickly. I was getting worried about you. And I am extremely glad about the girl in France. I am enjoying pretty women but I will try not to marry again.

I have my boys the two months this summer and I am going to give them some manness—by that I mean they are going to help me do things, physical things, they are going to be let to wander if they want. They are going to eat when they are hungry and sleep when they are sleepy. As much as possible they are going to be responsible for their own actions. They are going to associate with men and animals and they are going to be treated with respect—their ideas listened to and included. Maybe it is bad but it will give them some cushion against the winter and the Eton collars and showing off at parties. They can have hammers and nails and boxes to build with. Thom is old enough to take the dual control of an airplane so he can learn to fly as he learned to talk with an automatic reflex sense. And he can drive my jeep on country roads. [Thom was four.] And in a very few years, if I can afford it, I'll begin taking them to different places in the world, to Stockholm and to France and to Italy and Mexico.

I am not going with whores. I like the women I associate with. It is just that there are several or perhaps more than several, but I like them very much. Three of them are lovely

354

and two are fun and two are intelligent—and any one of them would turn into a wife instantly, and that would be over— that is, all but one would. One is really a whore and she's the sweetest and most ladylike of the lot. Strange things.

Let me hear how you liked the windows in place. And keep in touch.

John

Steinbeck had invited a new friend, Ann Sothern, the film actress, to come from Los Angeles to the Monterey Peninsula for a visit over Memorial Day weekend. It was to prove a turning point in his life.

Ann Sothern brought with her Elaine Scott, who would become the third and last Mrs. John Steinbeck. She was then the wife of the actor Zachary Scott.

The visitors stayed at the Pine Inn in Carmel. From here, Steinbeck showed them Cannery Row and entertained them in his small house in nearby Pacific Grove.

Louella Parsons, gossip columnist for the Hearst newspapers, heard about this visit and reported it on her weekly Sunday evening radio program.

To Annie Laurie Williams

Pacific Grove
[Received June 7, 1949]
Sunday

Dear Annie Laurie:

It is time for a letter to you. Not that anything has happened but a weekly report is kind of indicated. I heard the

355

[Louella] Parsons thing tonight. My taking Annie Sothern to lunch a couple of times becomes a romance. Romances must be pretty attenuated in Hollywood. I like Annie. She's a nice girl. And she was thoroughly chaperoned by Mrs. Zachary Scott which Parsons neglected to mention. As a matter of fact I kind of fell for the Scott girl. Who is she—do you know? I mean who was she? She was with the Theatre Guild. Can you give me a report on her?

I had a long letter from Gadg [Kazan] before he left saying he would be back the end of summer and then we could go into a huddle on this script. Which is satisfactory to me.

I have written Gwyn asking about her convenience about getting the boys out here but of course she has not answered. So if I do not hear by the end of next week I shall make my own plans without consulting her. I've tried to be decent.

I bought a hut for the garden for the boys to play in. Neale and I spent today putting it up and I don't think we have got it right yet. But it was fun. Today all gardening too, setting out little plants. I didn't leave the house at all.

Annie Sothern just called to ask if I was embarrassed by the Parsons thing and I had to tell her that I was only complimented. Now P. G. [Paulette Goddard] will call to rib me about it.

I got a box of silly birthday toys off to John for his birthday which is the 12th. I wanted them to get there surely on time. Let me hear from you when you can. And try to find out something about Elaine Scott. She was with the Theatre Guild for a number of years but in what connection I don't know, nor do I know what her name was but she is very attractive and very intelligent.

Love to you both,
John

His interest in Elaine Scott was reciprocated.

She was a Texan, the daughter of Mr. and Mrs. Waverly Anderson of Fort Worth; her father was a pioneer in the Texas oil fields. While a student at the University of Texas, she had met and married an-

356

other undergraduate, Zachary Scott, son of a prominent physician of Austin, Texas. With Eli Wallach, Allen Ludden, and Brooks West, they were deeply involved in civic and university theatricals. After graduation, and with some financial assistance from their families, the Scotts moved to New York with their infant daughter Waverly to begin their careers in the professional theatre—he as an actor, she in casting and stage-management with the Theatre Guild. In the early forties, Warner Brothers offered Zachary Scott a contract, and they moved to California. By the time Elaine Scott met Steinbeck, a marriage that had survived the struggle to succeed in New York was faltering under the strains of picture stardom in Hollywood.

Less than a week after their meeting Steinbeck wrote her.

To Elaine Scott

[Pacific Grove]
June 6 [1949]

Dear Miss West Forty-seventh Street
between Eighth and Ninth:

Am a widower with 10,000 acres in Arizona and seven cows so if you can milk I will be glad to have you give up that tinsel life of debauchery and sin and come out to God's country where we got purple sage. P. S. Can you bring a little sin and debauchery along? You can get too much purple sage but you can only get just enough sin.

I am really glad that you got some rest and that you feel somewhat restored. I guess it is that purple sage. I think I will try to bottle it.

Annie Rooney [Ann Sothern] called to say that the skirts had arrived [Chinese men's ceremonial skirts he had sent them as presents]. I would like one too but I ain't pretty enough. This has been my tragedy—with the soul to wear a scarlet-lined opera cape and small sword I have the physical misfortune always to be handed a hod. I have never quite got

357

over this sadness. Let me know whether you want me to get another. I have been tempted to buy the whole stock because there will never be any more. The new regime is not going to approve of them I guess and they are unique as far as I know.

I was sad when you two bugs went away. Now I haven't even a half-assed reason for not working.

I am told that darling Louella tagged Annie and me last night. This will henceforth be known as The Seven Days That Shook the Pine Inn. Running naked through the woods with flowers in your hair is against the law and I told you both but you wouldn't listen.

Sometime during the summer I will drift down your way.

[Next day]
Neale is flying a twin engine Cessna to New York on the 15th. He'll have a little vacation and bring back my kids on the 1st.

Love to you and Annie.

J.

To the novelist John O'Hara, who had just published *A Rage to Live,* he wrote, over a number of days, a wide-ranging letter, part of which is in interesting contrast to his earlier "Phalanx Theory."

To John O'Hara

[Pacific Grove]
June 8, 1949

Dear John:

Your letter made me very happy. This is a time of most profound readjustments, emotional as well as in other directions and the reassurance of a letter like yours cannot be overestimated. Everything dried up as it is bound to, and got out of drawing and with three more mixed metaphors I will have a literary boulliabaise, or how do you spell it.

I am extremely anxious to read your new book. There are lots of reasons for this. I believe that your hatreds are distilling off and that your work is all ahead of you. Maybe the training in hatred in all of us is necessary. For hate is a completely self-conscious and personalized emotion and a deterrent to a clear view but it may be as necessary to developing ability as the adjectives we later learn to eliminate. But we must first use the adjectives before we can know how to leave them out.

I've had seven months of quiet out here to try to reduce the maelstrom to tea kettle size. For myself there are two things I cannot do without. Crudely stated they are work and women, and more gently—creative effort in all directions. Effort and love. Everything else I can do without but if those were effectively removed I would take a powder instantly.

Being alone here has allowed me to think out lots of things. There is so much yapping in the world. The coyotes are at us all the time telling us what we are, what we should do and believe. The stinking little parasitic minds that fasten screaming on us like pilot fish that fasten on a shark, they contribute only drag. I think I believe one thing powerfully —that the only creative thing our species has is the individual, lonely mind. Two people can create a child but I know of no other thing created by a group. The group ungoverned by individual thinking is a horrible destructive principle. The great change in the last 2,000 years was the Christian idea that the individual soul was very precious. Unless we

359

can preserve and foster the principle of the preciousness of the individual mind, the world of men will either disintegrate into a screaming chaos or will go into a grey slavery. And that fostering and preservation seem to me our greatest job.

This will probably be a long and boring letter, but I need some one to talk to and good or bad for you, you are tagged.

You see I worked last year but it was all experiment and notes. I've been practicing for a book for 35 years and this is it. I don't see how it can be popular because I am inventing method and form and tone and context. And of course I am scared of it. It's a cold lonely profession and this is the coldest and loneliest because this is all I can do, and when it is done I've either done it or I never had it to do.

I've re-read your letter and this is another day. You know I was born without any sense of competition. Consequently I have never even wondered about the comparative standing of writers. I don't understand that. Writing to me is a deeply personal, even a secret function and when the product is turned loose it is cut off from me and I have no sense of its being mine. It is like a woman trying to remember what child birth is like. She never can.

Again I have re-read your letter. And you are quite right. A man is always married. I wonder though whether he can be married to the idea—with different people carrying the ball (oh Jesus!). I will know sometime maybe. Being married to me is a very hard thing. I am kind and loving and generous but there is always the rival (work) and to most women that is worse than another woman. They can kill or eliminate another woman but that rival they cannot even get close to no matter how you try to make them a part of it. And there's the necessity for being alone—that must be dreadful to a wife.

This maundering will probably go on for some time.

Now it is even more days later. I thought, after I stopped writing the other day, regarding your words about a wife. And do you remember in the Mabinogion, the ancient Welsh story of the man who made a wife entirely of flowers?

My boys will be with me in another two weeks and I will be glad. I deeply resent their growing and me not there to see. That is the only thing I resent now. The rest is all gone. But

360

imagine if you couldn't see your daughter for months at a time when every day is a change and growth and fascination. I saw my oldest boy turn over on his back and discover the sky and in his look of wonderment I remembered when it happened to me and exactly how it was.

That's all now. But I would like and need to keep in touch.

John

Soon afterward, when Steinbeck went south to Los Angeles for several days of conferences in connection with *Viva Zapata!*, he and Elaine Scott were able to see each other frequently. Their relationship developed with swift intensity, and it became clear that subterfuge would be necessary for a continuing correspondence once he returned to Pacific Grove. He arranged to write her in care of his friends, Max and Jack Wagner, at their Hollywood house where he had sent his first love letters to Gwyn Conger. He referred to this address thereafter as "the hollow oak." For further protection, with his penchant for drama and intrigue, he addressed his letters to "Belle Hamilton." The surname was his mother's maiden name.

To Elaine Scott

[Pacific Grove]
June 20–24, 1949]
Monday

Dear Belle:

This may seem very roundabout but sometimes that is the shortest way home. As you know, I have few if any complications. But you do have. And there is no reason to be foolish.

Maybe this method sounds silly to you but I assure you it

is not. You will just have to be and become Belle Hamilton —a separate personality. When you go east you will find another hollow oak tree and tell me that. So we will keep contact. Now—this oak tree is all right. Max is my oldest friend and even then he thinks you are Belle Hamilton. He knows there is some reason for the use of his address but he is too good a friend and too much a gentleman even to inquire what it is. But I will explain that when you call. I would like to see you solito when I go down this weekend but I will discuss that with you also when you call. If you could get free sometime perhaps Friday afternoon—I would start very early and get there in the morning. Then I could meet you at the 1401 N. El Centro address [the Wagners'] if that is convenient. And you would be completely protected. The hotels are not good. Too many people are interested in tagging me. And other friends than Max would be "interested." Anyway it's an idea.

I will leave this letter and perhaps bring it down with me. Anyway you will be calling tomorrow.

                                                    Tuesday
The other parties on my line have been chattering so maybe you got a busy signal. I must go to the bank at two. I hope I don't miss your call.

Did I tell you I bought a cute little trailer house for the boys and their nurse to live in? I shall put it in the garden where the tent is and it will be their own. It is the cutest thing you ever saw. Looks like a house, not a trailer. It has two rooms, a little kitchen, a toilet, an ice box. It is completely furnished. And—as will have leaped to your agile mind—when the boys are not here, it could have other uses—couldn't it, dear?

It is ridiculous to sit here writing to you when I will be seeing you. But it won't be the first ridiculous thing I have done. And God willing, it won't be the last.

It is brightly cold here—the way I like it—good sleeping. Could be good other things.

                                            Wednesday night
Somewhere the signals are crossed. I have only been out to buy groceries and you have not called. And I recognized the

danger signals well enough not to try to call you. That I caught. It was in the air.

Thursday night

I've spent the afternoon pleasantly making you a little Celtic or Gaelic cross and it has been good to do. I will give it to you privately when I see you and it will be up to you to explain it. Maybe you saw it in a junk store and bought it. But the story of the wood is this and it is a long one. My grandmother's father went in the 40's from Massachusetts to Palestine to convert the Jews to Christianity. He took his family, among them a very young girl—my grandmother. I don't think he converted any but he did teach some of them principles of agriculture. That was his pitch for sneaking religion in on them. They were living in Jerusalem when one night a great storm of wind and lightning arose and one of the ancient olives on the Mount of Olives blew down. We were always a family of looters. My great-grandfather cut a chunk out of the tree which was at least two thousand years old. Gradually it has been whittled away but there is still some of it left and we have always made little crosses for our children and for some others. Thus the Mother Superior in Salinas, who prayed me out of pneumonia, got one and she put it on her rosary, and because the wood is so old and dense and is always cool, she got to curing fever in children by putting the cool cross against their foreheads. I have made them for my children as my father made one for me. If there ever was a Gethsemane—the tree from which this wood was taken was there to witness it. I don't know why I made a Celtic cross and inscribed it in Gaelic. Just felt like it I guess. Anyway, rough and crude as it is, it is for you and was made for you. And maybe you will one day have someone to give it to. Stranger things have happened.

> Later, for Elaine Scott's sister, Jean Anderson Boone, he amplified his feeling about the crosses carved from this wood:
>
> "I believe that everyone needs something outside himself to cling to. Actually such a thing as I have in mind is not outside yourself but rather a physical symbol that you are all right inside your-

self. So I have made you this little cross to wear, to hold in your hand, to rub between your fingers and to feel against your cheek. I hope it can be that symbol of your own inner safety. The wood itself carries the strongest and dearest thing we know. It is older and greater than we are and yet we are a part of it. The making of it is a symbol of our love for you, and your association with it may be the promise from within yourself that what you want, with a good heart—you will have. You see—the cross, too, has an inner being which is idea and faith as well as an outer feeling which is texture and incredible age. We hope you will wear it in memory of what it has been and in confidence of what you will be."

It is very odd. I will have to pass you this letter like a conspirator and you will probably have to burn it. But maybe that is good. I nearly signed the cross Bricrin—who was the great troublemaker of Ulster because I guess I am a troublemaker but then in a burst of egotism I signed it Ollam. An ollam was the very highest class of the filid of old Ireland. The writers and poets had many classes but the ollam was the top. He had to know 350 stories of all kinds. And I think perhaps I do.

Isn't it silly to go on writing this way? But it is only nine o'clock. I have hardly been out of the yard since I have been home. I have taken great gulps of sleep and now I have no more need for it. I think if I am not sleepy at 12 or 1 or 2 I will put my clothes in the car and drive south. It is pleasant to drive at night. And if I should get sleepy on the way I can sleep in the car or roll out the sleeping bag which I now carry always. It isn't a Hemingway double, damn it. But I think two could fit in it if they were reasonably companionable. And luxury on luxury—recently I bought a rubber air mattress. My hip used to get pretty sore sometimes. I'm just rattling on. Almost as though I couldn't stop. Like the crazy time of children it is. You know about dusk when they go mad and play harder and faster and in tighter circles until they cry or get the giggles and go to sleep.

The night is so quiet here. You remember how it gets—so quiet that there is a little hum in your ears when you listen because there is nothing to hear. How very deep this is— listening for a sign, looking for omens. Everyone does it. Actually I guess it is a matter of taking one's psychic pulse.

For if one feels good the omens are invariably favorable. And I feel good tonight.

But I must make sure not to hurt Annie's feelings. There is only one thing—she has a very strong feeling about property and I am never again going to be property. I've had that twice. Once I was property to be saved and hoarded and the second time I was property to be spent. I don't want ever to be either kind again. Nor do I want to own anyone—nor anything to tell the truth. Now I have absolutely nothing but this little house. I like nice things but I don't have to own them. I used to go to the Metropolitan Museum to see that fantastic little Greek horse and the Cellini cup, but I never wanted to own them. I was always glad they were there for me to see and not to have to protect them, guard them, insure them, will them. No—I like it the way it is.

And I swear to God this is the last of this long and doleful screed. It will be a chore to read. My handwriting—never any bargain—changes at different hours of the day.

So this is the end of this. I will slip it into your hot little hand. And from then on—it's your ball—first down and ten yards to go—oops! penalty—15 yards to go.

love,
Sam

Shortly after Neale had flown the two Steinbeck boys from New York to California, Elaine Scott suggested the possibility of visiting him. By telephone, in the course of the following letter, arrangements were made for her to come to Del Monte Lodge at Pebble Beach with her friend Joan Crawford.

To Elaine Scott

[Pacific Grove]
July 10–18 [1949]
Sunday

Bellita:

I will start this and only after tomorrow will I send it. For if you are coming I will hand it to you.

I wish I knew what time you would be likely to call tomorrow. I—well, damn it, I will wait for it. The boys can just play in the street or Neale can take them someplace. I am a little razzledazzled with the crawling house but it is a healthy razzledazzle.

Tuesday

Jesus, I hope you do come up. I hope, j'espère, Espero!

I did a bad thing. The nurse just told me. John didn't even have a cake on his birthday. Reason—he had a cold! If he had been dying in my house he would have had the biggest cake. It made me feel good in a nasty way. Soooo! Thom's birthday is going to be THEIR birthday and I'm going to shoot the works. Big party. Two cakes. King's birthday. You are invited —Aug. 2. Paper hats, snappers—outside barbecue. All hell breaking loose.

Friday

Did I tell you I had a letter from Trampoline? [This was the "Mexican hustler" previously referred to.] She says—"I am working for the Banco de Mexico. We carry gold and pesos —want some?"

Saturday

This is note passing time. Thom is lying down on my bed and taking what is called a rest. This is only slightly less active than football. We went in a boat all morning—with

366

Mr. T. as skipper. He is becoming unbearably nautical. If you are leaving about eight I will compute the time and may possibly just happen to be in the bar—beautifully dressed and smelling of cologne water.

Am burned cardinal red from the water and with a little salt and rosemary could bring high prices as a steak.

I'll leave this open. Because there will probably be more note passing. But I think it would be pleasant if I were in the bar at the lodge just starting my second martini and discussing nuclear physics with the bartender when you just happened to drop in there. What do you think?

Monologue from the tent.

T: Did Willy go to heaven? [Willy was the dog.]
Me: I guess so.
T: I saw him in heaven. But where was God?
Me: I don't know.
T: Did you ever see God?
Me: Oh! yes—sometimes and often.
T: What's he look like?
Me: You.
T: Do dogs go to heaven?
Me: I don't know.
T: Do they die like caterpillars and butterflies?
Me: Yes.
T: I guess the sky falls down on them.
Me: That kind of describes it all right.
T: When are you going to die?
Me: I don't know—sometime.
T: Soon?
Me: Maybe or maybe in a long time.
T: When will you know?
Me: Never.

It's a kind of sleeplike talk, almost rhythmic. And now he's asleep.

Monday 5:15
(in the bar
at Del Monte Lodge)

My dear—this is about as complete a record as you could wish. Here I am dressed like a lily of the field—neither sow-

367

ing nor reaping but getting into a gibson and waiting for you. What a title.

Also have worked up a fiesta for J. C. I hope she doesn't try to live up to her initials.

I hope you get here before I have too many gibsons. I've only had one so far but I'm a persevering rollo. But why? I just ate the onion out of the second gibson.

5:30. New pencil. This writing is a nervous habit. I am very much excited—very much.

5:35. You are late—Ardo!

And after the visit:

To Elaine Scott

[Pacific Grove]
July 23 [1949]

My dear—

Parting is not sweet sorrow to me but a dry panic. You were kind to wire—not that I was worried but because it is like a last touch and a reassurance. One begins to distrust so much good luck. Now—8 in the evening and kids bedded down and read into the ground and I'm in the little house that has a perfume. And I have a nice weariness. Now I don't mind sleeping but before I resented it. And I don't really have any words to say.

Good night darling. I'll add tomorrow. So tired—and so properly.

Thom told a fine fantastic story tonight. I hope I remember it. It was very intense. Had to do with a little boy who left his comic books on the floor and the mother came and got angry

368

and pulled down the house and the father came and hit her and beat her up and rats ran all over everything. He lost track of the little boy in his interest in the other gaudy details.

Again good night.

Sunday morning

Oh! honey—I feel sick. I guess maybe it is the subsurface panting because you are not here.

Love—oh yes.
Cincinnatus

Steinbeck continued his habit of making almost daily entries to be mailed to Elaine Scott as they accumulated. They are presented here as the diary they actually were.

In the following letter, and with some frequency thereafter, he mentions a bird-charm from Mexico in whose magic he professed to believe. He had made a leather-covered wooden box for it. He described it in greater detail years later to Elizabeth Otis:

"The most potent [magic] I have is the Mexican humming bird in the tiny coffin. I still have it and it is still active. It has just about all the magic there is in the world. It is on the supply shelf of my work-room—a tiny black leather coffin. The witch doctor made it for me when we were shooting the Forgotten Village—a most potent affair."

To Elaine Scott

Pacific Grove
[July 25, 1949]

My dear—

Monday evening: an enormous day. Kids had their enor-mousest day of play. They have dropped as though shot. Thom wanted to know where you had gone. I told him— home. "Isn't this home?" he asked. And of course he is right.

I do make so many mistakes. I don't want to make them in this of ours. But with my long record of mistakes I suppose it is an impossible wish. I put a flower in on the bird to propitiate. This sounds as though I were abnormally super-stitious and I am to the extent that I believe that the things that happen under ladders and with open umbrellas in the house are the results of unconscious wishing and the propitiation is to the evil in one's self. And God knows there is plenty of it in everyone—dark mean imps that make us do things we don't want to do.

I was very ill yesterday—sickness used every means it could—symptoms of a cold, stomach ache, even bleeding pains in the chest. The works, and all of it the bad child stamping its foot because it could not have what it wanted when it wanted. So I spanked it soundly and it gave up and today I am more calm and the aches are gone except the lonely ones—but they are honest and not roundabout.

I shall not try to tell you anything. That has all been told, both ways and instantly and I remember the telling and hearing like phrases now on one instrument and now on another, sometimes like the notes of high humming insects and sometimes like the breathless beating of copper kettle drums. And there it is. But I am jealous of your time.

Now, referring to the Scotts' imminent departure for New York, where Zachary Scott was to make a pic-ture, he mentions the need for a mailing address there.

370

If your eastern oak is not there I shall work one out. But let me know and I think it might be better if you kept this name.

I shall send this on Wednesday. Do you know when a plane flew over today I was four feet off the ground following it? Must watch that.

One fault of such closeness is that words no longer convey much. Before—words can stimulate the senses and the understanding but after—they are pretty weak vehicles. Wherefor words are properly the tools of loneliness and rarely of fulfillment—the conveying of loss and frustration but no triumph like the closing of fingers on fingers or the pressure of knee on knee or the secret touching of feet under a table. Do you realize that language reaches its greatest height in sorrow and in despair—Petrarca for Laura, the Black Marigold. The fierce despair of Satan in Paradise Lost. L'Allegro is not nearly the poem Il Penseroso is. I suppose that what the human soul says is—"If one finds it—there is no need for words."

I want to send you some records. How can I do this? Shall I send them in care of Jack [Wagner]? They are the recordings of Monteverdi—These have some of the passion in music that the Black Marigolds have in words.

I think I may take the children to Berkeley this next weekend to see my sister Beth. I wish you knew her. She is very homely and I have seen her draw people to her and not know what she was doing. She has an incredible charm and an unbelievable energy.

Cathy and Walter [the nurse and her husband] took the kids for a ride after dinner and it is nine and they aren't back yet. Ed Ricketts used to do that when his children were restless —just put them in the car and drive. The vibration and motion soothed them and made them sleep so well. They will have to be carried to bed when they get back. And I'll wait here before I go over to my house.

Oh! and I have a present I want to get for you one day but it will take a very long time. But all good things do take a long time. The engagement ring my father bought for my mother, a good quarter of a carat, took him several years to pay for. But when he had done that he had something. I suppose that one of the troubles with having money is that beautiful things are available without effort and so the things have not the same value. I suppose nothing in the world was ever so valuable as that quarter carat diamond.

371

Words are not good to me tonight. They come out crooked and I have little faith in them. Sometimes they are much better—and once in a while they are born with small blue bows on them.

Whee! I'm up late tonight. It is midnight. For a while I thought I might go out but gave that up because where would I go?

Going to bed now darling. Neale changed the sheets, damn him. Some time with sleep—huh? That's the only thing we've not had—sleep and breakfast.

Night dear.

July 28
Thursday afternoon

My pretty quadroon—

Kids are bedded for the moment and I use the word advisedly. What a strange night was last night. I could not sleep, the kids had nightmares and today they are looking far inside and they are far away. I thought it might be a change of pressure because the air is strange and the sea is unusual but the barometer has not changed. Maybe an earthquake coming. I've felt them before. Animals are a little nuts too. Something about to happen. I wonder what. I have the excited feeling of a storm. Something has changed of course—something I didn't think ever could again and I am a little terrified but I surely would not have it any other way.

I watched the postman with gleaming eyes this morning. Once long ago when a letter with a tiny check meant the difference between dinner and not, there was a long desert time and the postman got so ashamed that he walked on the other side of the street. Finally I got to cursing him as he went by and at last I accused him of deliberately stealing mail. He drew himself up with pitiable dignity and said, "When they write them—I bring them." Poor fellow. He still works in the postoffice but they only let him cancel three-cent stamps for his spirit is broken and his armor is split and rusted.

I am going to make my world-shaking macaroni for dinner and the kids are wild with joy because it means that there will be tomato sauce all over the kitchen and all over me. My dinners are not only food. They are decorations also.

372

What macaroni. I have been heartily congratulated by macaroni-faced children.

They are at a drive-in movie beautifully dressed. But while waiting and sitting straight to keep clean—we had a conference—the old tough one. "When are you coming home to New York?" "I don't know." "You aren't ever coming back, are you?" "That seems correct." "Why not?" "I honestly don't know." "Do we have to go back?" "Yes." "Why?" "I don't know." "Why can't we stay here? We can stay in the tent—we would like it there." And Catbird—"I *like* the tent." Catbird underlines all words. There are bad times when I can't tell them anything and still am not willing to lie to them, and they are not old enough for the truth because it wouldn't make any more sense to them than it does to me. I'll have to make this start home an awful lot of fun or there is going to be bad heartbreak.

I'll put this away and finish it later tonight and post it in the morning. Don't make it too long, dear.

I've solved one thing. The two drops of Femme on the pillow make for good dreams.

Thursday night

Now a kind of ennui, darling. I wish you would call Annie Laurie Williams [in New York] and perhaps have tea with her. She's really family. I know you'll get along. Another Texan and after many years in the theater she is still starry-eyed about it. She loves me quite a lot. Also is my dramatic agent. I will write her that you may call her. Of course you need not but I would like it if you did. And I don't even know why. But it seems a right thing.

I've had a number of years of frustration and sterility. And I have work that has to be done and it should be done with violence and gaiety. And I think, God damn it, that such can be. Don't you?

I have a great humming in my ears from clenching my jaws. Isn't it odd the physical symbols we use?

The bird will have a new flower in his box for you. I should have given him to you but he might have been found and there would be no way in the world to explain him. But I hope you had the chain fixed and that you will wear the wood sometimes when you think of it. And the time will go very

373

quickly (that's a goddamned lie of course but it's the thing one says). The time will crawl like a blind snail on soft sand. And the dogs will bark pretty much too.

Do you know, I am putting off ending this letter as though the end would be the end of something I want to hold on to. That's not true of course—just a feeling like the quick one of hexing your trip so you couldn't go. The mind is capable of any selfishness and it thinks unworthy things whether you want it to or not. Best to admit it is a bad child rather than to pretend it is always a good one. Because a bad child can improve but a good one is a liar and nothing can improve a liar.

A good trip, dear, with fun. And come back after—come back. I can't write any more. But of course I will. I shall think of you.

Altoona V. Eldredge

How I hate to stop

I really feel the earthquake thing still. Or some tremendous change.

July 30
Saturday night

My Belle:

I will be restless until I have your discreet wire. So send it soon, won't you? I wasn't sick darling, except with the sickness you know. It just took symptoms on itself. I feel fine.

Do you know that the luck mark on the palm of my left hand is suddenly getting larger and darker? Isn't that interesting?

It will be a quick month, dear. It has to be. The thunder and lightning and rain came here today. I knew something was coming. That isn't all that's coming though. That's just the world symbol. All hell is going to break loose darling and it will not be your doing or mine. But it won't be easy nor soft. I would be sorry for this except that soft and easy things usually turn out to be just that— soft and easy. We've had it lucky. I don't depend on that. There must be some payment demanded. Believe it, it can't be otherwise and do you not be unhappy or uneased when the god-palm is out for its nickel.

374

Good-bye, dear. Good flight, good month, good fun and remember!

Joe Artichoke the 3rd

August 2
Tuesday noon

Darling—

I have no feeling about flying myself but I shall be very nervous until I know you are in. This is odd but not odd.

This is the interval of nap before the great party—there is a mounting hysteria in the house which will break loose at 2 o'clock. I have things that must be done now. The bakery made a mistake and put white frosting on the cakes. But the inside is chocolate anyway. My mind is split up between the party and you in the air.

[Tuesday] night

The party roared through the day. The kids are still telling jokes in bed to keep from going to sleep. They hate to let go.

The enclosed (I don't know whether you like it) is a picture of a portrait by Bo Beskow, who is the best portrait painter in Scandinavia and one of the best in the world. Gwyn has the painting of course and I don't know whether I can ever get it. I think I will try because it is the only picture of myself I have ever liked. [He was later able to get it.] If you do like it I will some day try to get you the original or have him do another. He paints me every ten years. Someday I hope you will meet him.

I have so many things to say to you and I don't know what they are. But I will. One of them is that I am deeply tired of my inferiors. It seems to me that I have spent a good part of my life reassuring insecure people. And as with a bad tennis player, it ruins your game. What is this common touch that is supposed to be so goddamned desirable? The common touch is usually an inept, stupid, clumsy, unintelligent touch. It is only the uncommon touch that amounts to a damn.

I doubt whether you can fool Annie Laurie or even that it would be good to try. She will know and approve whether you tell her anything or not. I'm sure of that. She knows everything and tells absolutely nothing. If you ever need a shoul-

375

der, she is it. I'd like her to know all about you and she'll be glad because she loves me.

This is something I want to tell you very strongly. *Don't do anything.* I am sure it will all be done for you and that will probably be much better. The most powerful magic in the whole world is working for us. Relax and let it work and make no overt moves. I know you do not like to be a mystery woman but I think it will be good for you to try for a little while.

My dear, when I asked you for a present, I think I meant something of yours, that you liked and that could be a bunch of ribbons or a glove whose mate you left in a bar. That's what I meant. I suppose it is some fetishism but not the psychiatric kind. You see? Something that feels like you and smells like you. And did you lose a little silver button that looks like braided strings? Didn't you have silver buttons on a sweater?

It's nearly time for sleep. It's been a big day and I feel fine but very tired.

Good night my very dear.

To New York:

August 16
Tuesday noon

Dear—

I thought I would tell you this when I saw you but I will now because—

As you may have gathered, there was quite a beating involved in this last thing—not so much to ego because I don't seem to have that kind of ego but rather fatalistically. You see I have never admitted that anything but dying could defeat me and stop me coming back. And then at the end of the long howl of this last thing I felt the possibility. I don't mean that I gave up but I saw for the first time in my life that I could. There was in back of the dark fringe of consciousness not only possible defeat but acceptance. Almost the words—"Well there it is and it's over and it was silly." All winter that went on. And it got in and in. As with a fighter —when he is about to go down he puts up a great flurry just on the outside chance of landing one. I think that was my life last winter—that and a drying up of the spirit and a kind of

376

dark and deathly cynicism which is the most sterile thing in the world. In that is pleasure but no joy. It is like intercourse with a condom, or stroking fine marble with a glove on.

Once when I was young I had pleural pneumonia and I was very near dying and what I remember is that in that state I had no feeling nor desire *either* for life or death. And that is somewhat the feeling I have had, fall, winter, spring. And it was so unusual for me that I had no weapons with which to fight it. There's no way of knowing but I think it was a near thing. During the war I went out definitely to be killed and this was with foreknowledge of what was going to happen. I knew it surely with my mother's second sight. I knew it and thought it would be all right to offer myself and see what the coin did. So I took really miraculous chances, with every kind of weapon and warfare and outside of getting smacked with a gasoline can I couldn't even get scratched. But that was an active creative death while, when it finally happened, it was a rusting, corroding waste away. And more horrible because there was no way to get at it to fight it. The energy, of which I have always had too much, wasted away and left me almost without strength. Of course I protested to myself and to everyone I loved that it wasn't true. But they knew and that's why they worried about me. They hadn't during the war. And I don't know of course, but I think it was a near thing. And the danger did not lie in that I was afraid but in that I wasn't. That's what I meant by acceptance.

And the reason for telling you this dismal chronicle is that it is not true anymore. It is gone and the energy is washing back into me and I'm not dried up. And I feel wonderful.

And now you know.

Good night, dear. I'll kick some worlds around now.

[unsigned]

Alarmed at reports of an outbreak of polio in New York, Steinbeck wrote his ex-wife:

377

To Gwyndolyn Steinbeck
IN NEW YORK

[Pacific Grove]
August 19, 1949

Dear Gwyn:

By now you will have had the letter written a couple of days ago. Naturally I should be very pleased if the boys didn't go back to the East until all the danger is over for this year.

Thom caught two fish today and in the excitement I dropped my rod and reel in the ocean. He dragged them home on his line and they were pretty sandy but he didn't want to eat them. Cat wanted to go back to fish just as I put them to bed.

When Thom dropped a tooth yesterday he swallowed it but the birthday mouse forgave him and put a half dollar under his pillow. He awakened me at six to show me. But there was a hole in his pocket so he lost the money and now he has worked it out that it was because he swallowed the tooth.

I shall be glad if you take the boys home yourself. But I must know your plans. I so arranged things that I could spend all of my time with them for these two months.

Do *please* let me know your plans. It is extremely necessary to me.

J

To Elaine Scott

[Pacific Grove]
August 20–21 [1949]

Fishing again today. Catbird wasn't good at it with his new rod. I tied a live fish to his line without his seeing and he caught it all afternoon. My letters are turning into a diary of a nursemaid.

Dear, my dear, the reading of Oz, the playing, the baths are over and birdlets are asleep. Your letter came this afternoon. What a good thing you are, what a double extra good thing. Oh! darling we're going to have fun at last, At Last!

Oh! darling, Thom needs a pet so badly and today one of his friends offered him a kitten and he wants it so dreadfully. He brought it up very casually and offhand—and kind of deadly. I mean in a dead manner as though he knew I would refuse to let him have it. His mother had refused. And he really needs it. And I had to make a judgment. The richness of having the kitten against the heartbreak of not being able to take it to New York with him. In the morning if he wants it, he can have it even if he does have to give it up. To refuse him would be like refusing love because you might get hurt and that's the best I can do.

Dear, I'm not afraid of anything now. And surely I won't force anything and surely I'll let it go on happening. And I know it will work out. I'm sure of it. Completely sure.

I'm covering flight 5 with the bird.

Good night, dear.

[unsigned]

"I spent the summer exclusively with the children," he wrote Bo Beskow, not quite accurately. "That is the main reason I have not written. I haven't written to anyone. The boys did not want to go back and having to make them go was not a chore that I liked very much. And you are right. I do have a girl, and a good one too, and that is a fine thing to have."

As for writing:

"I have to work on the scripts of two pictures and after that I will start on the thing I really want to do. The two pictures will make it possible for my children to be taken care of for a long time to come."

To Elaine Scott
IN BRENTWOOD

[Pacific Grove]
[October 11, 1949]
[Tuesday]

Darling—

You know sporadically I keep a kind of diary day book. It is written in a kind of Pepysian shorthand. It is valuable sometimes. Looking back through it I came to the reference to your first trip here. And it is amazing how quickly I knew. Almost immediately. I put things in it I don't even know, and only much later do I realize that they are in there. Actually it is a kind of warm-up book. When I am working it is good to write a page before going to work. It both resolves the day things that might be distracting and warms up my pen the way a pitcher warms up. It's a matter of long practice. I have made no entries all summer but now will begin it again. Very soothing to raw nerves.

Last night in one of the times I awakened I got a flock of foreknowledge that was like a landscape on a dark night suddenly created by a flash of lightning. There it was. Maybe I'll write it and put it away. But it was all there. And it was good.

Everyman [working title for what was to become *Burning*

Bright] continues to grow in my mind. My Christ! it's a dramatic thing. Now it has beginning, middle and end and that's what three acts are and that's why there are three acts. The 5-act play is still three acts. And the form was imposed by the human mind, not by playwrights or critics. This doesn't mean that external reality has beginning, middle and end but simply that the human brain perceives it so. This letter is growing pedagogic, isn't it?

October 14
Friday night

My dearest Belle:

Toby S. [Street] came in and sat with me for an hour and then went along. He is a very nice guy.

Tonight I am playing a game I have used before. It is to go over the times when I have been with you and to pick up little things that happened that were unnoticed because there was so much else at the time.

And then projection—I am so looking forward to sitting in Notre Dame with you and watching the light change through the rose window. And sitting on the steps of that ugly church on the mountain of the martyr and seeing daylight come over Paris. And of walking through Fontainebleau where Louis walked. Such places are so charged for me. The deep walls of the Conciergerie where Marie came out to go to the knife. Somehow they keep their charge. You will see. Or to sit on an island in the Archipelago near Stockholm where the Viking ships assembled to start for America before America was officially discovered.

Oh! so many things and so many I haven't seen. I sat in the room in Albany where Carlyle wrote his history. My publisher lives there now. [The famous block of flats off Picadilly usually referred to without the definite article.] But do you know—I've never been to the Tower? nor to Stratford. Fleet St. I know pretty well and the Inns of Court and the Temple which was bombed and burned. But so many I haven't seen. I want to see the house my people came from in Ireland. It's a hovel I guess. And I don't think this will be so long in the future either. My mind is popping with excitements tonight. You haven't been to Europe so you don't know how remembered things come out of the earth like gas and there you are. And only then do you realize how close we are—no matter

381

how many generations we are away from it. Funny, I can see it now in my mind—little farms in Denmark which are the picture in the Easter egg, storks and all. I wonder how I got on this. Do you suppose I am getting restless?

You said that this was my home but I have thought about it deeply. I think I have no "place" home. Home is people and where you work well. I have homes everywhere and many I have not even seen yet. That is perhaps why I am restless. I haven't seen all of my homes.

I have sat around for the best part of a year waiting for wounds to heal and the scabs to fall off. And now that has happened and I am not patient. You must know this—I am not patient. So much to do and so little time. Christ! I haven't even met Mrs. Roosevelt.

Someday before too long I will make a little cross from the olive wood for Way [Waverly Scott, her daughter]. And I will know when to give it to her.

I will mail this tomorrow my dear. And tonight I shall read a great swatch of Don Quixote and who knows—maybe I will finish the second volume sometime. I can feel it coming into the end now and with such grandeur and mature sadness. Nothing can take away the dignity then. He stands him up naked. He pins placards on his back (literally) and the enormous childlike dignity is still there. It is as though he said— "You see, if there is greatness no smallness has any effect." And suddenly it turns out that the book is not an attack on knight errantry but a celebration of the human spirit.

I'll finish this tomorrow darling. Good night. Que duermes bien.

J.

November 1
Tuesday

Darling—

So the week starts. Jules Buck got in last night and we go to work today.

> Twentieth Century-Fox had sent Jules Buck, a scenarist, to Pacific Grove to help Steinbeck with the picture form, in the preparation of the screenplay of *Zapata*. Buck later became a well-known agent and film producer.

Darling, it's going to be only notes for a while, I think. This month is going to be pure work.

Your good long letter came yesterday. It was what I was trying to say all along without making it sound cautious. I only know that if you say to hell with everything you are going to catch it from somewhere.

November 2
[Wednesday]

Now I can write a little more slowly. A good day of work and a good letter from you. Pat sent me the new Viking Portable Chaucer. It looks very fine. I am rereading Pepys in bed at night. What a wonderful thing it is. Have you ever read the uncut version? Such a good man he was.

> At that moment, Elaine Scott telephoned to report that the final break with her husband had come.

Your call came. And I assure you it was hard finishing the day's work but I did. I couldn't not do it. Jules was here.

I wish I could give you some advice or some help. But beyond what I said, I can't. But I do know this—if it will do Way irreparable harm, you will have to stick. But you always knew this. If you violated that, there wouldn't be anything for you any place. It will be most difficult on you—even terrible but you will have to stick it out to the end for your own sake as well as Way's. You cannot be a torn-up girl. It will be said that you have been unfaithful. Every means will be used to make you feel guilty. And that you must avoid. Put the rap on me if you wish. Nobody did anything. Things just happened.

The more calm you can be inside and out, the better it will be. Here I am giving advice I am not sure at all that I can take. It's going to be very bad. Please believe this.

You know that I offer you very little financial security and no inheritance. While I make a lot of money I do not get to keep much. But I am sure you know this. If I got bumped tomorrow there would be nothing except a few years of book royalties—literally nothing except this house. I will not mention that again.

383

How I wish I could help you.

You must not mind my voice over the phone. It freezes always on the phone as you well know.

Another thing you must expect is for your half-friends to turn against you. You are a set-up for that.

Now I don't want to labor this any more. I love you and you know that. If the climax comes soon you will have to go East I guess. And don't forget that the fact that you told him the truth in no way forces you to pillory yourself publicly unless you want to. And finally you must tell yourself constantly something that I know—you are one of the most beloved people in the world—not only by me but by nearly everyone you know. I am repeating these things because you are bound sometime to get to thinking otherwise. The only reason I am a little sorry it happened right now is a fear that I might lose Way's love because of its soonness—before she got used to it. Otherwise—now is as good a time as ever. It could never have been easy or soft.

Love to you, dear. It will take time. But we knew that.

J.

[November 3]
Thursday morning
It is before mail time and before Jules arrives. No call from you last night. I hope no trouble. You know how the mind leaps around and finds bad things. Mine is no different. I imagine things and for the moment they are true. And I had a strange dream. I was standing at your door. I knocked and rang and no one answered.

Now I am so anxious to know about Way. A method will be found to tell her, I think, if she doesn't pick the whole thing out of the air. And you will have to do such a good job there but being the girl she is it will be easier for her. And maybe it will not be as shocking as we think it might. Kids always surprise us.

Thursday afternoon late
Thank god that day is over. I've had to dictate all day with mice gnawing my stomach.

384

Now Elaine Scott telephoned from Brentwood to say that at her husband's insistence she was to come to Pacific Grove to discuss the future of all three of them.

My dear—I'll meet the plane Saturday. It comes in at 12:20 I think but will verify. But I know that between now and then there will be several changes. You will be ordered to come and ordered to stay, you will be commanded not to see me and ordered to see me. You will be ordered to sleep with me and ordered not to. I hope all of this does not completely sicken you. That's one of its purposes. The plan already worked out is this—It will be so terrible, uncomfortable, unpleasant, ugly, disgusting, unending, therefore it will be easier, cleaner and more decent to maintain the status quo. Believe me, this is the method.

And in all of this I have very little to offer you. And this cuts at me too. You can be sure you will not be permitted to come out of this without a beating.

I've tried to think where I have been wrong in this and I can't without reaching. It was a matter of mutual regard in all directions from the first. I would do it again instantly. And I'm too old to wear a hair shirt for pure pleasure.

I wonder whether I should send this. It might just add to your miseries. No, I think it is better to send it. There is no protection. The best protection is to be wide open to everything. It is the protected who get the worst hurt.

I know you can't write, poor dear. And it doesn't seem to me that I am backing you up very much. I will of course in any way I can or you can think of. I keep giving you advice. But you see I do not want you to get panicky nor precipitous—nor sick and tired and make mistakes that cannot be corrected.

Darling—I did not send this letter. Now it is Friday night—11:30. We just stopped work 10 minutes ago. We have worked since 9 this morning. And I think without work I would have gone a little nuts. I am so worried about you. I keep saying to myself that if things really got out of hand you would find some way to let me know so that I could do something. And now I think—what if there is no word and you are not on the plane tomorrow? I shall meet the plane whether or not I hear from you. I'm just

385

sitting here arguing with myself and planning what I will do if—. And that is crazy. I'll try to stop worrying you with my worries.

All day we worked and got much done. I think all right and Jules thinks good but how it could be with only half a mind at work I do not know. And I've got to stop this thing of building situations in my mind and then meeting them and they haven't arisen yet.

I've got to stop. Or I won't be any good to you.

> He met the plane. She was on it. It was a weekend of momentous decisions: that she would file for divorce, that after he had finished the *Zapata* script he would move to New York, and that she and Waverly would follow as soon as her interlocutory decree was granted and she could close the Brentwood house.

November 7
Monday night

Darling—

Now for the first time I can write to you as I have wished for a very long time. I adore you, I am proud of you. I want to be with you always. A long time ago when I knew the strength of my feeling I had to keep it hidden. It seemed to me that I must be non-demanding. I wanted you to come to me but it had to be out of your own mind and will—and as little as possible influenced by me. I knew there would be sorrow surely, but I did not want to add to it. I wanted you to come and maybe filled the air with it but on the surface I had to be reluctant, wise, thoughtful and even withdrawn. Even through Saturday and Sunday I had to.

And now I don't any more. And I feel that a great flat weight is lifted from me. The sorrow will still be there but now I can help with it. I want you to be my woman in all ways and permanently. You see? Now I can say it—now that you did it yourself. Sometimes I didn't know why the insistence was so great that it be this way but now I know it was right. And I feel wonderful and a whole new life opens—exciting and fun and the sorrow will recede, everyone. I swear this. I am so sorry to have made you take two steps for my one. That will never happen again from now on.

I will pray that Way will not be hurt and with that, everything will be all right, and we will live so well, so well. I love you.

John

Monday night Annex

I had just sealed that letter when the phone rang and it was Annie Laurie. She is incredible. She knew something was happening and she wanted to know what. So I told her and she cried a little with pleasure and she said things about you that should have made your ears burn. She said, "You should thank heaven. This is the best thing that ever happened to you." Which of course I do because I was about finished and now I am just beginning.

Don't please try to get a job in New York right now. When I get to the play—which will be soon—I shall want you with me or close enough so I can run to you with a page. This is our first job together and it is very important to me that you be deeply involved in it. Isn't it wonderful that I can say that now and don't have to beat about the bush? I don't have to be conservative at all. I want my woman and I want her near me.

LOTS OF TIME NOW FOR EVERYTHING

I am going to bed—wonderfully tired and relaxed—and that buzzing you hear in your ears—is me going right on talking.

I love you,
J.

By November 8, his mood was even brighter.

Darling you only know me as the Play Boy, young, daring, rich, handsome, slicked back hair and one button shirt—a beautiful dancer and the ideal fourth at bridge. You have only seen me weekends at house parties in my flannels and two-tone shoes—leaping over the net to congratulate the loser. I wonder if you would recognize me tonight—successful, graying at the temples—stern, just, a friend to cherish, an enemy to fear, incisive of speech, analytic by temperament, controlled, a thinking machine. No, I doubt whether you would know me. I have one other side. A shit. (I said it first.)

387

He sent her his mother's engagement ring, and with it, this note.

To Elaine Scott

[Pacific Grove]
[November 1949]

My dear—this is for you from me.

I wish only one thing. When Thom shall need it—will you give it to him and tell him about it? Maybe he won't be the kind of man who would want it nor understand it but if he should be—I would like him to have it.

But it is yours now.

I love you,
John

To Elaine Scott

[Pacific Grove]
November 10, 1949
Thursday

My dear—

Your letter came this morning at 8:30 and I was so glad to get it. And believe me I was wide awake. Shall I describe my morning? Jack slept in the bed at the end of the room. [Jack Wagner, who was visiting him.] At six-thirty he awakened, which waked me. He couldn't find the toilet although he had been there three times last night. Then in some way he fouled up the chain so he got splashed. I went out and fixed it for him. Went back to bed. He came in—asked if I didn't have some shaving lotion. I said about twelve bottles in the

388

bathroom. He couldn't find it. I got up and showed him the shelf full of bottles. Now he is ready to take a walk. It is 7:00. But in trying to get out the door he throws the spring lock and is trapped. I get up and let him out. He works a long time at the garden gate and manages to lock it so he can't open it. I get up and balls-ass naked go outside and let him out. It was cold. I have just got back in bed when he rings the bell. He has forgotten something. I let him in and help him out again. By this time if you can imagine it—I am not sleepy.

This was a bad time for him to come. He offers suggestions on script which are off the line—old picture tricks and we are writing a no-trick script. I hope sometimes that he gets drunk and disappears. Now I've got that out of my system. I am very impatient when I am working so hard.

I shall be with you tonight in the Way thing. Oh! Lord! I hope he [Zachary Scott] doesn't pull out the stops tonight. It will only hurt him. Kids don't like that. They don't believe in emotion in adults since they invented it themselves.

I am rushing this letter because I may have to stop it any minute. I'm so glad you like and understand my mother's ring.

It has poured rain and the country is soaked and wonderful.

November 11
Friday 6 P.M.

Tonight I shall work by myself. Tonight is dialogue and I must do that alone.

I was so pleased with your news today. I knew Waverly would handle it well. It will bother her but not too much after a little while, particularly if there is any fun. Do you think you and she could come up here? It is going to be a long month otherwise. Of course I will see you before I leave [for New York] in any case and of course we will spend Christmas together. And we'll snag the boys for some part of Christmas even if we have to have an early, separate one. I'm going to have some kind of private tree for you and me and Way and the boys even if it is in a hotel. You know very well it doesn't matter where it is if there is love and happiness. And without these no place is any good.

God I wish you were here tonight. Stay close, very close.

J.

November 14
Monday

Honey—

Jack left this morning after a last flurry of fuzziness, discontent and bumbling. He managed to get on the train, or rather was *put* on the train by Neale because at the last moment he broke his glasses.

Letter from Kazan with a P.S. "I liked your girl friend." From him that is a superlative. The fact that he remembered to say it. Neale is happy. He has had a chance to clean the house this morning. First time since Jack arrived.

November 15
Tuesday

Now it is Tuesday and two weeks ago today we started work here. Strong and active dreams and your special came this morning. Of course you should take things to New York. If you rent an apt. you will need blankets and linen, etc. Very expensive to replace as Neale and I found out when we came here.

I will be done early next week I am convinced. And then, of course, I could go anytime. I think it will be a good thing if I have Thanksgiving with Esther because probably Beth and Mary and all the nieces will be there. By the way, no word from Esther which means that she either didn't hear or is keeping her mouth shut. I've never discussed this with any of my sisters. We aren't that kind of family. They will automatically go along with me and then they will love you on your own.

When you get rested in N.Y. I am going to take you to a miraculous dinner—a real lulu. And *I'm* going to order every single item. You don't have any choice. It is going to be expensive and wonderful and I may even dress. I'm going to send my clothes on by express next week in my old footlocker. I had it all during the war. I think it still has J. S. Herald Tribune, N. Y., Paris, London painted on it in case it got lost.

I like setting a time for telephone calls. Then one doesn't have to be afraid to go out to the post box or take a bath for fear of missing one.

My very dear:

We just finished all of the 4th Act pickups and inserts and worked out the whole last half of the last act and it is going to be good. And it's only 10 P.M. so I can have a little time to write you before I go to bed. Toby Street came over about six and had a couple of drinks—not me. I'm still virgin.

I thought today how I remember you or rather scenes that have become set. One is in the Pine Inn sitting in that room waiting for the phone to ring. One is in my house with the firelight on your body when you went to get cigarettes. One is lying on a beach towel reading and one is when I had the kids in the car to take them away and I looked back and you and Way were crying. It is strange. I have no picture of you when Zack was in the room. I remember him holding Way and sitting at the head of the table. But you aren't in those scenes. In the others, it is exactly photographic. Oh! yes, and a sharp one—you and Way half running from the N.Y. plane, you carrying the large square jewel box. How sharply some things register.

And at that moment you phoned. What a job you must be doing. Ours is pretty straight line, just pound through, but you are running in all directions.

I'll stop this now and go to bed. Good night dear. Were you irritated tonight or was it just other people in the room?

November 27
Saturday

My dear thing—

I called you in the night just because I was lonely for you and for no other reason. You are right—it is a very little time and we must be very careful. It isn't much to do. I think your mother's picking it up out of your letters is very strange.

Mary is going to take my begonia bulbs and plant them next year. That way they will be kept up. And some of my bulbs are very old and fine and it would be a shame to lose them.

My God, I'm glad that I'm going Monday. I'm all cleaned up here. It would be silly to wait around.

Your sister Fran sounds wonderful and I liked the letter from your baby sister [Jean].

391

Darling, of course I'm going to like your people. They are so sound about you. And my God how understanding. Maybe Fran can come up to N. Y. before too long. I hope they won't dislike me. I will try to make it so they won't.

November 28
Sunday

Darling—

This is the last letter from here. Hasn't it all been fantastic? I think when you get away you might go into a tailspin just thinking of all the things you have done in such a short time. I am constantly amazed at your courage. You can't lose with that and we'll keep it high, too.

Lord, I wish you were going with me. Then it would be such good fun. Of course I will write you from the plane. Then I will take the sleeping pills and awaken in the morning. And I hope I don't tousle any old ladies.

Sunday 7:30 P.M.

Darling:

I am all churning inside. It's the change—change of so many things. I'm excited as well. This is the last night in this house for a while. We must come back to it often. It has been a good house always. And this time it has really done its duty. It has made me well and strong again and I first was with you here. I feel very grateful to this little house.

I'll talk to you a little later.

J.

November 29
Monday

Dearest—

wouldn't you know I couldn't finish a letter that easily? It was a dreadful long night and a lousy detective story and now I am nervous because I have to wait until night to go.

Neale is buzzing around like a bloody bug being nice. I've done all of the things I can think of that needed doing. Covered the town. Taken a bottle of whiskey to the Chief of Police and one to the mail carrier. All of these thoughts in passing. You can see that my mind is a mess. Hurry—hurry.

We've got to have a drink in the Plaza bar in the evening with the first snow falling.

Maybe there's something here I have forgotten but if there is it will have to wait. I've got a whole new beautiful life to look ahead at and I ain't going to worry about forgetting things.

Hurry, hurry, hurry!

I love you,
J.

1950 1952
1951

Steinbeck

*"...the writer
and his book..."*

1950 *Burning Bright,* novel published, play produced. Married Elaine Scott.

1951 *The Log from the Sea of Cortez* published.

ℭo Bo Beskow

145 East 52nd Street
New York
[Christmas 1949]

Dear Bo:

Your letter reached me recently and saddened me, the more so because for the first time in a very long time I am filled with hope. I have a good girl now and work and energy again, so I guess I have healed over on the wounded places. I feel that I have much writing and much living to do yet and that I am ready to do it. I have taken a very tiny apartment at the above address and although it has so far nothing but a bed and a card table, I feel good in it. Right after the first of the year I shall start the first of three plays. I hope to have them done by summer. That would make a good spring of it, I think.

I wonder how this would be! If I finished two of my three plays by June—would it be feasible to bring my two boys over there for the summer? My girl would come too and maybe we could play in the archipelago?

I miss you all very much. I have put sad things on you and frustrated things and maybe this summer could be one of joy and play and laughing. I've still got a lot of that in me whether you believe it or not. And my girl is the best girl I have known. This one is on my side and it is a very strange feeling. It is a lovely thing to have a friend in the house.

New York is exciting now. The air is crisp and cold. I walk a great deal. Indeed, from my little apartment I can walk nearly any place in the town very quickly. And it's a good town for walking. Last Christmas was a bad one without my boys. But this year I will have them on Christmas eve.

397

Gwyn has all my books and all the money and the house and the pictures—except for your portait of me. And I have one little room and a tiny kitchen and a bed and a card table and that is all I need with yellow pads and boxes of pencils. This she cannot nor ever will understand. But my new girl understands and likes it and so there we are.

Meanwhile a merry Xmas and a very good year to you.

He wrote in a similar vein to people in California, among them his niece Joan, sometimes called Toni. She was the daughter of his younger sister Mary and had recently married a Stanford University Law School student, David Heyler, Jr.:

"We had a fine Xmas. The kids were with us on the Eve and we made a good and noisy festival. They folded about 9 and I soon afterwards—and needed it. You should see my apartment—a tiny place, but it has a beautiful big terrace which will be much lived on. I will put an awning on the terrace and some plants and it will probably be the nicest terrace anywhere and most of the year will be as a huge living room. It is beautiful at night with all of the tall buildings lighted. Very Xmas indeed."

Early in the new year, he wrote to Elaine Scott's sister, in Austin, Texas:

To Frances Atkinson

Dear Fran:

The first thing I must tell you is a very simple and unadorned fact. I love Elaine. This you must accept as true.

The second thing is that I want to be with her the rest of my life.

The third—that I am sorry there had to be disruption but I am not in the least ashamed and I surely would do that or anything else to be with Elaine.

The fourth and most important thing is that Elaine seems to be happy. Happy—hell, she glows in the dark!

Apart from the matters of affection, I am sure that she belongs here rather than in that despondent paradise of Hollywood. She strides along the windy street cutting a swath of light as she goes. She is excited all of the time and she is near to the people and work she loves best of all. It may be that there will not be quite so much in a material sense although I am quite solvent, but there will be, I assure you that there will be, many other things that will more than make up for that lack.

You and Elaine are so very close. I want to know you, and as soon as possible.

There—I think that's what I wanted to say—I know it's *what* I wanted to say. I wonder whether I have said it.

I hope to meet you very soon.

My love to you
John

399

To Bo Beskow

[New York]
January 24 [1950]

Dear Bo:

Your good letter arrived at last and made me very happy. I have many things to say and ask so I will take a couple of days to write this letter so I will forget nothing. And you are right—my girl will and can take anything and love it if it is done in love. Gwyn always seemed to need more of everything than she was getting. Elaine is very different. A Texan with a soft accent but not the usual boastful Texan—the kind that can take care of itself—not like American women. She doesn't want to be a man. But you will see. She radiates warmth. I think you will like my boys. They are lots of fun and very handsome.

One thing has happened to me. I am not as shy and frightened as I was. I realize now what did it. Both of my wives were somehow in competition with me so that I was ashamed of being noticed. I am not a bit ashamed now. Elaine is on *my* side, not against me. The result is that I am more relaxed than I have ever been. And people meeting a train would not frighten me a bit. I would rather not speak because that requires preparation but I am not a bit afraid of interviews any more. You will see—after long sickness I am a well man. I am writing hard and my publishers say better than I have ever done.

So long. And this year is going so fast that it will be little time before I will be seeing you. My cabin is reserved.

Love to you
John

To Mr. and Mrs. David Heyler, Jr.

Dear Dave and Joan:

Lord! this month has gone fast and slow. With fingers crossed I am finishing my play today. That's pretty fast since I started it on Jan. 9. But that doesn't take into consideration the months of thinking about it of course. Naturally we haven't done very much else but that's not entirely true either. We saw Hepburn in As You Like It and that was a really beautiful show. I had never seen it before although of course I've read it many times. Then Saturday we went to a big party for Ethel Barrymore whom I had never met. She is charming and sharp but old and a little sick. The guest list was very strange: Bernie Baruch, Abe Burrows, Saroyan, Ray Bolger, Margo, John Ringling North with a tomato (why does he do it) Frank Loesser, Leonard Bernstein, Lillian Gish. Can you remember a crazier guest list? Anyway it ended at six in the morning with a dance contest between Bolger and Margo —she in classical Spanish and he in classical Bolger. A real good party. That's the only late one I've been to since I started. Friday we're seeing Caesar & Cleo with Hardwicke and Lilli Palmer and the Happy Time Monday and The Cocktail Party Wednesday. This is more theatre than I have seen in years. And I'm loving it. If I am going to do plays I'll have to know about them.

I know what you mean about wanting to get out of the cloisters and to work. Do you know what you are going to do? The only advice I can give you is that you must not insist on being consistent in anything but work. I mean—if one thing is not fun and rewarding, don't be afraid to reverse yourself and do something else. Joan will go along with you and it's nobody else's business. And that's my advice to you for the day—To make a little tight company composed of Joan and you—to make your plans and decisions there, to take advice if it seems good, but pressures never, and from that tight island to do exactly what you want and to hell with every-

401

body. There's only one crime in our world and that's failure and only one sin and that's weakness. And if you operate out of your tight island, you'll have neither. And my God, I've really grown a long beard in this letter—haven't I.

love
John

For the summer Steinbeck, with his two sons, a Columbia undergraduate named Jack as tutor, and Elaine Scott, moved to Rockland County where he had rented a house belonging to Henry Varnum Poor.

To Bo Beskow

[Rockland County]
Late July 1950

Dear Bo:

I was greatly relieved to get your letter. I am so glad you have broken the old slavery. I never liked the other one and I never knew why. But it was something basic; something maybe of odor beyond the conscious range. I am delighted that you have found a girl who delights you. Mine delights me.

I have my boys in the country with me about an hour out of New York in the rich green and little streams of Rockland County. It is rough and comfortable and we are having a good summer and I am getting work done too. What more can you wish? My boys are fine and brown. They are pretty good. I don't think I should want them more good than they are.

My first play [*Burning Bright*] goes into rehearsal on Sept. 5th and the second one probably in October. I am all finished

402

with the Zapata script and with a biography of Ed Ricketts for a new edition of Sea of Cortez. The second play not finished yet but should be next month. [This was abandoned.] So you can see that work has been coming out of me. I shall be done and ready to start on my long novel in October.

I have been horrified at the creeping paralysis that is coming out of the Kremlin, the death of art and thought, the death of individuals and the only creative thing in the world is the individual. When I was in Russia a couple of years ago I could see no creative thing. The intellectuals parroted articles they had read in safe magazines. It makes me more than sorry, it makes me nauseated. And of all the books required and sent to Russians who asked for them, not one arrived, and even the warm sweater and mittens for a girl, and a doll for a little girl—not even these were permitted to arrive. I can't think that wars can solve things but something must stop this thing or the world is done and gone into a black chaos that makes the dark ages shine. If that is what we are headed for, I hope I do not live to see it and I won't because I will fight it. God knows you and we are far from perfect but we are far better than that. We can make a noise even if not many people listen.

Shostakovich denounced me as a cannibal the other day. Of course he must—any man who can say that his work, written in honesty, was not true, was wrong because a committee says it was—is a liar and must have a very bad artistic conscience. He can say it was inept, badly executed, childish or immature but no artist is *wrong*. I suppose we have many people who would like to curb thought too but they have not succeeded and they must not succeed. If I seem vehement about this, it is because I saw it and see it. Here, I may not be liked for what I say but I can write it and people can read it and do and that's all I ask. And I wonder (since our species is a creative one) about the hidden artists in Russia who paint behind drawn curtains, and sing music under their breaths and write poetry and burn it or hide it. I do not think any system which uses such force can survive for long but while it does—it can ruin and maim for such a long time to come. This is a tirade isn't it?

My Elaine is a wonderful girl. I can write with her sitting in the room with me and that's the best that can be said about her calmness and benignity. It is the first peace I have had with a woman. She has great style and great kindness. She

403

doesn't want to hurt anyone for anything. I guess, in other words, she is a well adjusted girl. So that is that and I hope it is good and will be all right. I have lots of work to do and I should for once like to do it in peace. I have not had that before.

My oldest boy will be six on August 2nd. I am going in to New York tomorrow to get him some little presents. I don't know what to get him. He wants an automobile and a horse neither of which is practical. He will have to go back to his mother in October. I hope he does not have to go too many more times.

A long winter of hard work and then we will break free and if the world will let us, we will go out into it. So many people are shuddering in a planless lymph because they are afraid the world is falling apart. I do not believe that. It is changing surely but it cannot eliminate us completely. Some part of us —you in your windows and I perhaps in a sentence or two— will outwit them and go on.

Please write to me more often. I shall want to know how you are getting on.

> and affection to you
> and your girl
> John

To Pascal Covici

[Rockland County]
[Midsummer 1950]
Monday

Dear Pat:
A number of things to discuss with you so I'll write them because on the telephone I forget everything. First about Sea of Cortez. Please note down the things you might want cut or changed so I can do it all at once.

Second part—Forests [the play-novel he had been working on]. There is one disadvantage to the play-novel form. The novel has to go to press and stay that way but little changes take place in the play right up to opening night. One big change took place yesterday. Neither Rodgers, Hammerstein [producers of the play] nor anyone in this office thought In the Forests of the Night was a good title for a play. Too long, they thought, and a touch literary. They suggest and I have agreed to the title, Burning Bright. I wish I had thought of it long ago. I don't know what you will do about this since you have started the process and the thing is in page proof. Maybe just a note on the title page. I can also tell you that Mielziner will do the sets. He is crazy about the play. I am very glad of this because I think he is the very best of all.

The summer is half over and I don't know where it has gone. Nothing ever went so quickly. Elaine had to go to town to meet her daughter but she will be back tomorrow. I miss her and the boys miss her. My sister [Mary Dekker] went home. I think she was frightened. She has been living alone so long and in the past that she scuttled back. But I think she will come back and soon. It usually takes two tries when you have been boarded up so long.

If I do not mention the war it is because I try not to think of it much. It seems a screaming hysteria to me—a thing of nightmare and madness. The pattern is too recent. We seem to be forcing ourselves into a war. I do not think the Russians will fight nor will they have to. We will bleed white and all die of apoplexy.

I guess this is all. It is still cool and lovely in the country. Who could have thought it? But I am getting restive and I shall not be unpleased to be back in my little apartment with the yellow pads laid out.

I'll talk to you soon.

love
John

To Gwyndolyn Steinbeck

Dear Gwyn:

The boys are fine but bug bit. Thom especially has some very pretty mosquito bites. He scratches which makes them worse. Johnny has a tougher skin and they don't poison him so badly. The boys are both hard as nails due to constant exercise. I think they have made progress this summer. They are being very good and very good company.

Having heard small Nat [younger son of Nathaniel Bench-ley] say his prayers, they demanded to say theirs and they now know and like not only "Now I lay me—" but also the Lord's Prayer. Their interpretations of some of the words of the last one are interesting but they love the sounds of the words. Amen—has become "our men" and I can't change that, just as I can't change Oblong Cassidy and the Long Ranger. Also Johnny's remark that "Last night it was night all night," I find not only true but poetic. The boys know a great many poems and songs, some new and some they brought with them.

Thom can now dive off a board into deep water and is very proud. Johnny is still shy of swimming but that is the only thing he is shy of.

Both boys are highly manners-able (you've trained them well) and have lost the shyness with strangers. Both have remarkable ears for music but Johnny has an amazingly true pitch in singing—at four can carry a tune perfectly which is rare. Both boys want very much to go to school. Thom will learn to read this year and the moment he does, he will be into books for some time, I think.

I have completely cut off comic books this summer and they have not missed them—largely because there were not other children around reading them. I also cut off the radio. They could listen to it in the daytime but never in their room during naps or at night.

All in all they have been wonderful boys and I have enjoyed them thoroughly. They look as wild and brown as range ponies.

I should like to know when you want them back. On Sept. 5th we go into rehearsal when I will move into town.

Finally and with crossed fingers—there has not been one single cold or sniffle or stomach upset or fever all summer. They seem to be in perfect health.

Please let me know your plans so I can make my arrangements.

John

To Elia Kazan

[Rockland County]
[Late summer 1950]

Dear Gadg:

Last night Elaine read me parts of the script [*Viva Zapata!*]. She liked it very much and I must say I did too. It is a little double action jewel of a script. But I was glad to hear it again because before it is mouthed by actors, I want to go over the dialogue once more for very small changes. Things like—"For that matter." "As a matter of fact"—in other words all filler wants to come out. There isn't much but there is some. I'll want no word in dialogue that has not some definite reference to the story. You said once that you would like this to be a kind of monument. By the same token I would like it to be as tight and terse as possible. It is awfully good but it can be better. Just dialogue—I heard a dozen places where I can clean it and sharpen it. But outside of that I am very much pleased with it. I truly believe it is a classic example of good film writing. So we'll make it perfect.

Let me know what happens. After Labor Day I will be in town most of the time.

Molly [Mrs. Kazan] left her hat here.

Love to you both—
John

To Webster F. Street

[Rockland County]
August 30 [1950]

Dear Toby:

You have written me often and fully from Mexico and it occurs to me that this might be the first time you have had the leisure to write in many years. Did you like it? Did you find you could stand leisure? I can't very well. I go into a restless unhappy coma. It isn't that I want to work but that I don't want to not work. If that makes any sense. I am conditioned with a pencil until it has become a nervous tic. I can give the best advice about relaxing and not take any of it. I don't think I have ever been relaxed in my life—not for one single minute. That might be the secret of my failures. Too much tension always.

The summer is almost gone. We have one more week here. We start rehearsals on the 5th of Sept. We have a good cast. Kent Smith, Barbara Bel Geddes, [Howard] da Silva and an unknown boy who is going to make the rest of them fight for their lives [Martin Brooks]. It's a good play, strong and simple and basic with no smartness. It will either strike with a smash or not go at all. It is a morality play, completely timeless and placeless.

As a short novel—it has been turned down by every magazine in the country. The Book Clubs would not touch it. This makes me proud of them and of me. This is a highly moral story and they are afraid of it. It also gives me reason to believe that I am not writing crap. Indeed I think it might start a new trend in the theatre—partially going back to old and valid thinking and partially something entirely new. I feel some of my old vitality and courage coming back. And I do have the electric courage of a confirmed coward.

As soon as this play opens and either goes or fails I want to start on my long novel—the one I have been practicing for all of my life. It is the Salinas Valley one. I think that if I am not ready to write it now, I never will be. I am nearly fifty and I've been practicing for about 33 years. Don't these times sound incredible? How could I have lived so long? Or you. Why, in years we're verging on old age and I don't feel it at all—I'm just as crazy and randy and lacking in judgment as I ever was.

My boys have made such strides this summer. They are such good boys—really nice. They were in pretty bad shape when I got them but they have responded like nothing you ever saw. Elaine has done a lot of that just by loving them. They have some kind of security now which is all they needed anyway. I hope we have given them enough to tide them over what I suspect is going to be a tough year for them. But I will see them often this winter. Thom is old enough now to telephone me if he needs me. That makes me feel better.

I guess this is the end of this letter. It has been kind of good talking to you. Let me hear if you get this.

So long,

John

To Bo Beskow

[New York]
[September 1950]

I wish I could think of some way to help, but I don't know any. You have had this haunting for an incredible long time. And it does seem like a haunting to me—maybe tied up with a guilt feeling. Have you or have you thought of taking it to some good professional? Is it possible that finding its seat might help you to cope with it? I had always thought that a man should handle his own problems and take his own punishments but there are some things you can't handle yourself. I know that now. One might as truly say he could remove his own appendix. It is an outsize ego which refuses help. I know, because I have, or had, such a pride and I know it is wrong and unhealthy now. The moment I had deep driven into me the conviction that I was not complete and whole, I began to feel better. There was a kind of humility even in admitting it that relieved the pressure. I can only tell you about myself because that is all I know.

You have undoubtedly looked at your _____ haunting. Even in the years ago when I met her—you did not love her. But worse than not loving her, oh, much worse—you didn't *like* her. You took no health in your physical connections with her nor any joy. Indeed you practiced sex with her as though it were a sin or even a perversion. I am not making this up. You told me almost exactly this. I'm not interfering —Bo, I'm trying to help, helplessly. There is one other thing besides love which can tie two people together and that is guilt. There are so many destructive relationships—or perhaps more, than there are creative ones.

I have had two destructive ones. I think I have the other kind now. I am working at this one very hard. All of its potential is good. I know that I contributed a great deal to the destructive qualities of the other two. I must not let that happen again. Also I wonder whether your flypaper soul has caught and held a buzzing guilt. Inspect this closely and see whether you do not love the whip. I know my own tendency that way and so I probe for it in you. I know that I am not content to live my own life and think my own thoughts. I must do it for everyone about me. I must take their pains too, even when they don't have any. This I think is my prime selfish egotism. It is a thing I am fighting. It is actually one of the basic symptoms of infantilism. I have not grown up. And I am only two years short of 50. I have very little time. I would like to be an adult part of that time. There are too many disappointments for a child. The world will not give the party he has designed and so he loves no party.

I know I can't help you with my mutual wanderings *unless* I can start you to wandering in the dark forest and in this way make you find a path. I seem to see a path for me and that is what I am trying to tell you. I am trying to say that the most precious thing in the world is your self—your individual, lonely self and that you can only find it after you have given it up. I won't say that I have found it but I have seen the signs and felt a little of the light. Am I making any sense to you at all?

As for my boys—I will do the best I can all of the time. I will always be available and I will give them all the love in the world, but if I cannot be God, I will not take that blame either. This I am learning very slowly, Bo, but I am learning. It is the first symptom of adulthood—I cannot be God. My work is very important to me because I am an animal conditioned to this kind of work but it is not very important in the world. I must keep these two separate. I wonder whether I can do that. Can't you see, Bo, that I am trying to help in the only way I can?

Elaine and I will probably be married in December. Her divorce is completed on the 1st of December. Then I will have been married three times and do you know, I feel almost virginal about it. I do not feel soiled nor worn out nor calloused. I want to get a great piece of my novel done this winter so that when the spring comes we can go wandering. And I assure you that if it is humanly possible I will see you in the coming year. I think that would be good for both of us. You'll want perhaps to paint me again too for even though the usual ten years has not passed I've grown more than in another ten years.

Let me hear from you as soon as you can. I am worried about you.

Love
John

To Annie Laurie Williams

Ritz Carlton Hotel
Boston
October 6, 1950

Dear Annie Laurie—

I know you will be wanting to know how things are going. I have been working on the second act. The new build and curtain goes in tonight and the opening on Monday. I think we have a tight and dramatic second act now but I'll know more when I see it tonight. They have practically chained me by the leg to the hotel radiator.

It is the pleasantest thing working with these people. Elaine, who has had her share of troubles in the theatre is

411

astonished that anything could be so smooth. R. & H. [Rogers and Hammerstein] say they are very pleased. Business is picking up.

There is one curious thing about this play. Many people may not like it but those who do love it passionately and feel that it is somehow theirs. Katharine Cornell who came to the opening told me that this was one of the very few times she wished she were younger. "If I were 20 or even 10 years younger," she said, "you couldn't keep me out of it." Lillian Gish called me and told me not to change a line.

Now it is Saturday. The show was better last night than it has ever been. We are all very much heartened.

All of us are determined to bring in a good show. And now I think we really are going to.

love
John

To Eugene Solow
ADAPTER OF *OF MICE AND MEN* FOR THE SCREEN

New York
[October 21, 1950]
[Friday]

Dear Gene:

The critics murdered us. I don't know how long we can stay open but I would not think it would be long. But there you are. I've had it before and I will survive. But a book can wait around and a play can't. We are disappointed but undestroyed.

Now I'll get to work again. One good thing about these things—they keep you from getting out of hand but they promote no humility in me. I'll not change my address.

I wish you could have seen the play because it is a good play. I think it will do well in Europe where people are neither afraid of the theme nor the language. The sterility theme may have had something to do with the violence of the criticism. Our critics are not very fecund. Then, the universal, mildly poetic language seemed to enrage them. Garland [Robert Garland, drama critic of the *World-Telegram*]— never quite balanced—wrote a notice of unmixed gibberish. Simply nuts.

Well—there it is anyway. It can happen to anyone—and does.

John

To Jack and Max Wagner

[New York]
November 28 [1950]

Dear Jack and Max:

I must say, I get impatient with your failure ever to write a line. If one wanted to set down a description of the Wagners, one would say, "They are such and such and they do not write." That is as much as to say, "They are such and such and they have two right feet." I must think of it not as a failure or a fixation but simply as a symptom or a diagnostic. Some people write and some don't. Most people have two balls, but there are a few who have one and even fewer who have three.

We are having a very busy time. Elaine and I are going to be married Dec. 28th at Harold Guinzburg's house and then we're taking off for ten days for parts unknown and then coming back. I have a house on 72nd St. East but we will not be able to move into it until Feb. 1st. Which will be just about right. It is a beautiful little house and I think we will be very happy and productive there.

I guess it isn't that Elaine gets better all the time but rather that I knowing her better am able to see more and more of her goodnesses. She is the best girl I ever knew.

Those stains at the top are shoe polish. I have been shining some shoes.

I have not written you since my play fell on its face. And it really did. It got the shit kicked out of it. It was a good piece of work and a lot of people are pretty mad at the critics for

413

destroying it. I have thought of this a good deal. Here is a play that I, Elaine, Guthrie McClintic [the director] Oscar Hammerstein, Dick Rodgers [the producers] and many others thought was a good play. And God knows they are people who know their theatre. You would think they would know. It is very easy to blame the critics. They were not at fault.

It was not a good play. It was a hell of a good piece of writing but it lacked the curious thing no one has ever defined which makes a play quite different from everything else in the world. I don't know what that quality is but I know it when I hear it on stage. I guess we have to go back to the cliché "magic of the theatre." This thing read wonderfully but it just did not play. And furthermore I don't know what would make it play. Doctoring a play that will not play is like gagging a movie. It may make it acceptable but it doesn't make a good movie of it. I had the best possible production, the best direction and sets that would break your heart they were so wonderful. And the producers are the finest people I have ever met. I'm telling you all this so you will see that I am not the least bit angry or upset. In fact I am hard at work on my new novel—the perennial Salinas Valley and this time it is going to get done and it is going to be good. Only amateurs are destroyed by bad notices. And more and more I grow to dislike amateurs and to love professionals. There are so very few of them in the world.

Let's see—what else is news?

I see Gwyn fairly often when I go up to see the boys. She does not look well but has that kind of false gaiety you will remember. Only the boys are my business. Gwyn has never mentioned Elaine, nor asked a single question. And naturally I have never offered any information. But G. was at *Guys and Dolls* opening and she really gave Elaine a going over. And when Gwyn will put on her glasses at an opening, she is really curious.

I had a letter from Gene Solow saying that Max was in A.A. Is this so? I hope it is and that all is happy.

There it is. Our marriage will be Dec. 28th. You might write us a note of hope or good wishes or something even at the sacrifice of your principles. You were really in on the inception of this good thing.

love to you both
John

414

To Clifford Odets

Dear Clifford:

I saw The Country Girl last night, and was moved by the lines and the thinking and the sweetness. And as a semi-pro I know that the pure theatre can't be learned but I could wish that it might and that I could learn from you. I'll have to go back a few times to pick up subtleties I missed seeing square.

It is wonderful and my God it's good to see a fine clean thing in this musty time. I have just such a sense of triumph, personal triumph, as sometimes comes to me when I hear fine music.

Written with love and admiration.

John

Now, after long estrangement, the correspondence with his old friend George Albee resumed.

To George Albee

[New York]
December 19, 1950

Dear George:

I am going to get a letter off to you on the front edge of the hysteria which is about to set in. Elaine and I are going to be married on the 28th. Relatives are coming, both hers from

415

Texas and mine from California. Christmas eve I have my boys. I don't know whether you ever saw them, they are wonderful. The whole thing is fun but hectic. It's the tight top curls of a spiral.

I was interested in your remarks about success, because I have thought quite a lot about it off and on. I never had a sense of success. Good notices when the reviewer didn't know what I was talking about gave me a great sense of failure. I have a greater sense of goodness in this recent thing that closed than I have had in years. Book Review Section success is a hollow feeling like that one you get in the stomach when you have the skitters.

Of course I want the new book to be good. I have wanted all of them to be good. But with the others—all of them—I had a personal out. I could say—it is just really practice for "the book." If I can't do this one, the practice was not worth it. So you see I feel at once stimulated and scared. The terror of starting is invariable but I am more terrified now knowing more about technique than I did. There's a kind of nauseated stimulation about going ashore under fire that is not unlike this feeling. You know you're going to do it and it scares the shit out of you. I remember one night I went ashore from a destroyer in pitch darkness. There wasn't a sound. Before I got in the boat I went to the head to take a pee and my penis had disappeared. It had just retired into my abdominal cavity. I don't know whether this is common or not. Anyway it is a really shivery feeling.

Last summer I wrote a little biography of Ed Ricketts. It is a curious thing but in doing it I had to go back in my own memory to a time I had forgotten. Many things came back—warped no doubt and changed and yet strangely whole with their feelings and colorings. I would not have them back—not any of them no matter how good. And some were very good. A year ago I saw a good deal of Carol. I like her but I had forgotten why we had to separate.

I hope to see you soon.

John

To Pascal Covici

Cambridge Beaches
Somerset, Bermuda
January 5 [1951]
Dear Pat:

I haven't slept so much since I was a child—about 12 hours a day not counting naps which are pretty often. For two days we had a baby hurricane but now it is warm and calm.

I think we were both tireder than we knew. We struggle from bed to dining room to beach to bed and end up pooped. It is wonderful. And the dreams at night have been strange —a kind of autobiographical motion picture going way back and, curiously enough, in sequence, also more accurate than most dreams. Today is very warm. Elaine is on the beach getting some sun. I have to see someone from a newspaper.

Our pockets and clothes were full of rice. When we got to the St. Regis we were dripping rice. Certain nieces of mine were responsible. You know I almost wish you had tried to trail us that night. Our bags had been taken to the hotel much earlier. And we went for a long ride in the park before we went to the hotel. Didn't even have to register. I had done that earlier and had the key in my pocket. And the hotel would not have admitted that we were there. It was fun, I must say.

I thought the boys conducted themselves very well at the wedding, didn't you? There was one tragedy when they discovered that Waverly couldn't go home to live with them. They had worked that out for themselves. They were upset by that. They thought she was going to move in with them.

We'll be leaving next Monday and will be in late that night. So we may be back before you get this letter.

However, now I'm going to the beach and let the reporter find me if he can.

so long
John

They moved into their house at 206 East 72nd Street, their home for the next thirteen years. On February 12 Steinbeck began to write "the big novel," *The Salinas Valley.* He wrote it on the right-hand pages of a large ledger. Concurrently, on the left-hand pages he kept a journal of the progress of the book addressed to Pascal Covici. These notes were published posthumously as *Journal of a Novel: The East of Eden Letters* (1969).

On his birthday, February 27, Steinbeck wrote Bo Beskow:

"Elaine will have told you that we bought a nice little house in New York which we are gradually furnishing and we don't much care how long it takes. It is a pretty house with a pretty garden. I have my own work room in it—the first I have ever had. And I am at work on a novel, the longest and most ambitious and I hope the best I have done."

To Felicia Geffen
OF THE ACADEMY OF ARTS AND LETTERS

[206 East 72nd Street]
[New York]
February 20, 1951

Dear Miss Geffen:
I am sick of seeing Marc Connelly parading in regalia to make a peacock squirm while I remain as undecorated as a jaybird. Will you please send to me at the above address, any regalia, buttons, ribbons, small swords etc., as are befitting to my academic grandeur?
I'll show that upstart Connelly.

Yours sincerely
John Steinbeck

To Felicia Geffen

Dear Miss Geffen:

Many thanks for your letter and I shall treasure the buttons when they arrive. I must say I am disappointed at the lack of regalia. The French Academy meets dressed in cocked hats, embroidered vests and small swords. The Spanish academicians wear pants made entirely of bird of paradise feathers. Why can't we do something as spectacular and for the same reason—to cover with finery our depressingly small talent?

I've never been to a meeting in my life except before a judge. Maybe I will, though, one day soon.

John Steinbeck

On April 25th, Miss Geffen wrote to Steinbeck:

"Mr. Archibald MacLeish has nominated e. e. cummings and Wallace Stevens for membership in the Academy and asks if you would like to be one of the other proposers."

Steinbeck's reply, at her suggestion, was at the foot of her letter.

419

To Felicia Geffen

I am happy to join Archy in his nominations. Do I have the right to propose members for the institute? If I do have, I wish to propose Richard Rodgers and John O'Hara. Will you let me know? Archy could second for O'Hara and Deems Taylor can carry out the second in music. It is ridiculous that these two are not members. Will you please let me hear what comes of this?

Yours
John Steinbeck

And a few days later to Miss Geffen:

"I would like to go to the Ceremonial on May 25. I don't think I've ever seen a ceremonial since I was a daisy at the maypole in Salinas."

Pascal Covici had been ill, and Steinbeck, concerned, had taken him for a check-up by his friend Dr. Juan Negrin, the neurosurgeon.

To Pascal Covici

[New York]
[1951]
Wednesday

Dear Pat:

I may have spent a worse day than yesterday but I don't recall it. And when I went over the record with Juan and saw no clot, no tumor, the relief was almost unbearable. But even if there had been, there would have been plenty to do. The machine does not make mistakes.

You must have been frightened. I would have been.

I'm sorry if I was rough yesterday. I was wound up very tight and I'm afraid I would have been rougher if necessary.

But there—now I can work. I told you it was a selfish matter. I couldn't stand it if anything happened to you.

J.

The Steinbecks rented a house for the summer next to Sankaty Light at Siasconset, Nantucket, and in mid-June left New York with the boys.

It was a matter of pride with him that the move from New York had not interrupted the flow of his work on the novel which continued through the summer. References to it were almost entirely confined to the day book entries. This explains why, in much of his other summer correspondence, he mentioned the novel so little.

421

To Pascal Covici

Siasconset, Nantucket
June 18, 1951
Monday

Dear Pat:

It wasn't such a bad trip. Didn't take as long as we had thought. Got in to find the lights on, beds made and fires lighted. Very pleasant. It was cold the first couple of days but now delightfully warm but not hot and fires at night so far.

The boat is *not* here. If it is not in a very short time I am going to be angry and start burning up the wires.

Went to work this morning and got my quota done by 1 P.M. Boys and Elaine are at the beach. I am going to do a few duties and then join them. I shall be happy here if my work goes as it should. And I see no reason why it should not. Started the sequence about Tom Hamilton this morning. It will take most of this week. I will send ms. registered mail every Saturday or perhaps Friday afternoon. In any case it should be in on Monday.

We will be glad to see you when you come. Just give us a warning.

I miss the phone calls but will have to get over that.

Take your medicine and I think it is about time for you to go back and see Juan. Call for an appointment. There is another thing I have meant to discuss with you. I think you should tell Dorothy about this. I can understand your wanting to save her worry but such things usually don't save anything. I think you owe it to her to tell her. A woman marries a man for the worry as well as the other things. And now that it is better, she need not worry. But even if it weren't she deserves to know. Just imagine how it would be if she kept something like this from you for whatever reason. It's all a part of trust and sharing. You think it over. You don't really spare her anything and you rob her of something that is her right. I hate to lecture you but I think I am right about this. Love to you both and all three and remind Pascal that we expect him here this summer.

John

To Elizabeth Otis

Nantucket
June 27, 1951

Dear Elizabeth:

The work I did today, in fact for the last three days, pleases me deeply. I only hope it is interesting. It truly interests me.

We have a revolt of the children. I guess we must have it every year with the big jump from Gwyn's kind of life to our kind of life. But we're right in the middle of it. I'll let you know how it comes out because we *must* win. I'm afraid we've lost a child if we don't.

I feel excited and good. Never knew a place with more energy than here. The air is full of it. And I like the people very much and they seem to like us.

Saturday

It was a good but strenuous week. We won the first skirmish with the boys but that is not the whole war. Finished a whole section, except possibly one more episode, this week. The book does move along. Fingers crossed. Elaine says she likes this last week. I am now so completely entangled in my story that I don't know. I'm living about 75 percent in the book now. But East of Eden seems to be its title. It has settled down and seems permanent.

Bye for now,

Love,
John

To Pascal Covici

Nantucket
July 13, 1951
Friday

Dear Pat:

The ms. which I am putting in the mail at the same time I post this will be one day short. I took Thursday off and went fishing. I know it doesn't really matter that I keep to ten pages a week but it is a kind of good feeling that I can do it.

The fishing trip got no fish and I got a painful sun burn but out of it I got a whole new extension of the book. I guess I never really do stop working.

Yesterday, out on the water, I got a funny thought about you. You have been publishing things for many years and there must be a special feeling a publisher has for a book. The failure, or denunciation or attack or praise of a book would arouse an emotion but it would be a publisher's emotion. Now for the first time, although I may be wrong, I think you will have to experience writer's emotions. I think you are so close to the making of it, that an attack on the book, even a raised eyebrow will send you into a rage. You are not used to writer's emotions as I am. I think you will be more deeply hurt by attack and more proud of praise than I will be because it will be your first experience.

In your last letter, you said you liked to do the errands I ask. Will you do one more very silly one for me? Again it concerns Abercrombie & Fitch. First I would like you to go there and ask whether they have a section or a personnel which takes care of queries by mail. Second, in either the boat department or the gun department, probably the latter, they used to have small cannons for starting yacht races. They were pretty little things and they fired 10-gauge shotgun blanks. I would like you to go and inquire about them—whether they still have them. How much they cost and how much the blanks cost. Then I would like you to put this information on a separate page in your next letter to me so that I may put it aside and not show it to Elaine. My reason is both absurd and

424

good. On her birthday I would like to fire her a 21-gun salute and I don't want her to know about it. Her birthday is August 14 and she puts great stock in it. There it is, now back to work.

[unsigned]

Celebration of Elaine Steinbeck's birthday loomed large.

"Only one thing we lack," he wrote Elizabeth Otis at the end of July, "and maybe someone in the office will do it for us, or rather me. We can't have Elaine's birthday without Japanese lanterns. Could about 1 doz. of them be bought and sent to me? Just the solid color kind in various colors. I would be awfully pleased if you could have this done. Elaine thinks she is not going to have any this year."

To Mr. and Mrs. Elia Kazan

Nantucket
July 30, 1951

Dear Molly and Gadg:

Elaine has been carrying the mail for me. I, the furious letter writer, seem to have retired from the scene. Have reached the "I am well, how are you, yrs sincerely" stage.

Look what date it is! Isn't that remarkable and terrible? Half the summer is over and I can hardly believe it. I have about 600 pages of my book done and about 3 or 400 to go. At last I have a title for it which I like. See if you do. It is East of Eden. It is perfect for this book and it sounds like a very soft title until you read the first 16 verses of the 4th chapter of Genesis. The title comes from the 16th verse but the whole passage is applicable. Please don't tell my title yet. But it is

425

the one I am going to use. I think the book is pretty good. It's what I want to write anyway. It's long but it covers nearly a hundred years and three generations and you can't do that if it is short. I seem to have been writing it all my life and in one sense I have. I should finish the first draft about Hallowe'en.

We have two birthdays next month. Thom's is Aug. 2 and Elaine's is Aug. 14. Both will be observed with festivities and lanterns. I am giving Elaine the damndest presents, and don't you tell but they may amuse you because most of them are so unlady-like. 1. a genuine Dodger baseball cap to wear when she watches her team, 2. a Swedish steel bow and a rack of beautiful arrows (archery is her favorite sport), 3. a Colt woodsman .22 automatic pistol. Those are the active presents. Then a painting, and a greenhouse for the garden in New York. Also I have arranged for a 21-gun salute (a real one) to her on her birthday. But all that is the deepest secret.

I have purposely put off asking about Zapata because I know you will tell me when you can.

Love to all of you and we miss you very much.

miyagus

To Mr. and Mrs. Pascal Covici
WHO HAD BEEN VISITING

Nantucket
[August 1951]

Dear Pat and Dorothy—

I want to say that I am sorry for my beastly disposition. I guess I threw a pall over your nice dinner last night and I didn't want nor intend to. My nerve ends were spurting hot little flames and sounds crashed on me like waves. It had nothing to do with anyone but me. And I have not Elaine's strength to cover and dissemble such a feeling. I was in a nervous collapse. I'm sorry if I made you sad. Last night all night I had it and today it is better. Please believe that it had absolutely nothing to do with anything but my own insides. It is some inner confusion that comes on me sometimes with a frightening intensity. Forgive it please.

It has been good to have you here. I'm glad you have got to know the boys and they surely share our love for you both. I hope, in spite of my ugliness that you had some joy and rest here. It was a joy to have you.

A book is so long. It takes so much. It must be desperately hard to live with and I do not envy Elaine having to do it. And when it boils over, as it did last night it must be pure hell. I'm all right today. And I have no explanation.

Thank you both for everything, the lovely presents and Thom's birthday and all.

Love to you both and happy landing.

John

To Elizabeth Otis

Nantucket
August 16, 1951
Thursday

Dear Elizabeth:

The birthday is over and it was a humdinger and I think Elaine was happy with it. I am going to leave birthday telling to Elaine. I worked into Sunday and finished Book III so that now I have just one more book in this novel. And I start it after a rest and a change which is good because it is different from the rest, in time, pace, and everything. I am still not bored with it. And I should be by this time. But it is, if anything, more alive to me than ever. And I feel a hugeness in my chest out of which I hope pigmies do not come. The last book will be between 70 and 80 thousand words or roughly two more months of work if I am lucky. So it is still on schedule even though I have tried to keep schedule out of it. We have just one more month here. It looks now as though Way might be able to come, which will make us very happy. And I'll have to get ready for a whole new kind of life when this

427

book is done (if I am to live at all) because with East of Eden one part of my life is finished. But even that is fun to contemplate. It is a very big book, Elizabeth. I don't know whether or not it is very good but I am sure it is the very best and purest of which I am capable, given my faults and virtues and training. It is going down on paper and there are no complaints or excuses. It's all I have ever learned and it is really good to be out on this gigantic limb. I can't say—"I might have done better—" because I mightn't. And I'm glad.

I'll be ready to go home in a month. I miss you and I like our new house. The boys won't want to go. They have had a fine summer. Isn't it odd that I speak inside myself as though it were over. In a way it is I guess—two thirds of it. The last 10 days have been muggy and thick and foggy, old timers say the longest stretch of it in 10 years. We'll be glad of a change to storm and cold and wind.

Well, I guess that's all. I have many things to discuss with you but they aren't immediate and they are better answered in our living room with the first fires of fall burning. And that won't be long.

Love to you all,
John

To Pascal Covici

[Nantucket]
[September 11, 1951]
Tuesday

Dear Pat:

I am so punchy that I forget whether I have written to you or not. I'm saturated with story and with many outside matters. The really deep tiredness is creeping up but I'm pretty sure I have two or three months more of this kind of energy. And it is a very curious kind of energy. I have never used so much of it for so long a period. I have worked more wordage for shorter periods. I have been much longer on this for instance even now than I was on the Grapes of Wrath. I am fascinated with this week's work. As you are becoming aware, I hope—Cal is my baby. He is the Everyman, the battle ground between good and evil, the most human of all, the sorry man. In that battle the survivor is both. I have been trying to think how long it is since a book about morality has been written. That is not to say that all books are not about morality but I mean openly.

Now the summer closes. We will get up at four in the morning on Sunday and tool our way homeward. And we have had our triumphs this summer in addition to the work. Thom has taken great jumps. Elaine almost despaired a number of times but at the end of the summer Thom can read and do his arithmetic. He will start ahead of his class, and more important, he knows he can start. The block is gone. Catbird is the one who might have the trouble. He is so gifted in charm and cleverness and beauty that he will not have to go through the fire for a long time if ever. Poor Thom has it early and will have it long. But he will be fired and there is no fire without heat. We have done well this summer if you were to make a score. I do not feel ashamed. Now if I can only get a good book too, it would be fine.

Your letter came, Pat, and we'll have to take a rain check on that dinner Monday night. The boys won't be with us and we'll be so tired after moving and unpacking that we will probably fall into bed. Besides, I am going to try to get back to work on Tuesday so that I will lose only one day. The book isn't done, remember. I wish the move were over. I kind of dread it.

Anyway—we'll probably talk to you when we get in.

John

Of the work in progress, he wrote Elizabeth Otis on September 12:

"It goes on just the same. God knows how long. It comes to a terrible climax about a week or two after I get back. I had hoped to reach that point before I left here and it is possible that I may. But who knows? I can't dictate to it. It takes its own way."

429

Shortly after their return to New York in September, Steinbeck, who had been worried for a long time about Annie Laurie Williams' health, visited her at the hospital as she was recovering from a serious illness.

To Annie Laurie Williams

POSTCARD

> [New York]
> [September 1951]
> Thursday

Dearest A. L.:

I can't tell you how happy my visit with you made me. You not only looked well physically but there was something else even more important. The old fighting flash was in the eyes again and I came away on clouds. As you must know, I have been pretty despondent about you and then yesterday everything seemed to point with a very steady finger at a long fine life.

When I came home Elaine said, "I haven't seen you look so happy for a long time." We had a drink to you and last night I really slept for the first time in a long time and this morning I awakened with gladness. Now to work. Bless you.

> John

As testimony to the affection he felt for her, this is what he wrote her many years later:

"We have been through so many worlds together, you and I. Some of them didn't exist and some we saved from existing. We are old now, you and I, but I think we can say we have not let the standards down. Mean and tough and loving. And never taking

430

an unearned penny nor trusting an unearned compliment. Health to you and good spearing. Elaine sends love but I think no one knows what we have seen together."

To Bo Beskow

New York
November 16 [1951]

Dear Bo:

I finished my book a week ago. Just short of a thousand pages—265,000 words. Much the longest and surely the most difficult work I have ever done. Now I am correcting and rewriting and that will take until Christmas.

Anyway it is done and not quite all a relief. I miss it. You can't live that intimately with anything and not miss it when it dies. Such a thing must be a great strain on a woman but Elaine has stood by wonderfully. What a good wife.

Bo, I am sorry your girl and a new life did not work out and I am particularly sorry because I have such a good life now. Do you know—I will be 50 on my next birthday, isn't that amazing? I don't feel fifty. I've my contemporaries—many of them and they are old and disappointed men. I don't think I feel older than I did 20 or 30 years ago. In many ways I feel younger. The strain is off mostly. But the figures are there and at 50 one's life expectancy has dwindled considerably. So I am going to have as much fun and excitement as it is possible for me to have with the time that remains to me. In my book just finished I have put all the things I have wanted to write all my life. This is "the book." If it is not good I have fooled myself all the time. I don't mean I will stop but this is a definite milestone and I feel released. Having done this I can do anything I want. Always I had this book waiting to be written. But understand please that this is only half the book. There will be another one equally long. This one runs from 1863 to 1918. The next will take the time from 1918 to the present. But I won't start it for a year or perhaps two years.

431

I hope you will write to me soon and let me know how it is with you. I want to hear.

                                                                    John

When John O'Hara published *The Farmers Hotel* and received some bad reviews, Steinbeck hastened to write him.

To John O'Hara

                                                        [New York]
                                                        [November 26, 1951]
Dear John:
   Don't let these neat, dry, cautious, stupid untalented leeches on the arts get you down. It's a hell of a good book. I wrote a letter to the Times differing with Miss Janeway.
   They just won't forgive originality and you'll have to get used to that. Have you found too that the same people who kicked the hell out of Appointment when it came out—now want you to write it over and over?
   Hoch der Christmas

                                                        love to Belle,
                                                        John

I've got one hell of a rewrite job to do.

The manuscript of *East of Eden* was delivered to
Pascal Covici in a box which Steinbeck had carved
out of a piece of solid mahogany during the summer
in Nantucket. The letter accompanying it which follows appeared as the dedication of the book.

To Pascal Covici

[New York]
December 1951
[Christmas]

Dear Pat—

Do you remember you came upon me carving some kind of
little figure out of wood and you said—

"Why don't you make something for me?"

I asked you what you wanted and you said—

"A box."

"What for?"

"To put things in."

"What things?"

"Whatever you have," you said.

Well here's your box. Nearly everything I have is in it and
it is not full. All pain and excitement is in it and feeling good
or bad and evil thoughts and good thoughts—the pleasure of
design and some despair and the indescribable joy of creation.

And on top of these are all the gratitude and love I bear for
you.

And still the box is not full.

John

To Bo Beskow

Dear Bo:

I was getting worried to the point of cabling when your letter came—the usual thoughts of illness and disaster. We do inspire ourselves with danger. I was glad to get your letter and to be reassured that it was the windows not the winds.

The year moves frantically. I am working against time rewriting my long book. I have one third yet to go—and the hardest part. We have a ship—due to sail between Feb. 25 and March 1st. She will be 31 days to Alexandria, if that is still terra grata. I have never been in Egypt. I am learning Shaw's lines to howl at the Sphinx—"Hail Sphinx, I have seen many sphinxes but no other Caesar—." It should be a ridiculous spectacle. You should be there to see—and laugh. I shall peer into tombs not the most pleasant of which is Farouk. We shall be known as the new Hyksos and I may even build a small duplex pyramid which when ruinous and that won't take long, will be known to the Arabs as Selim al Bowery, or Steinbeck's Folly, a veritable hunting box for Ka birds in season. The Egyptians haven't been allowed to have a war of their own since Alexander's chief of staff—Ptolemy McArthur, took up squatter's rights. They are making the most of their new toy war with Israel. This means we have to go to Cyprus to get visa-ed to Israel. In Israel we will turn over the stones of our culture or perhaps some of the prophecies of our future. Then probably back to Greece where we will raise again the Eleusinean chant on the plain of Marathon. In Rome we'll buy a car and move slowly up the continent like a new Ice Age. You will know of our coming by plague and flood and famine and civil commotion. I have the distinct advantage of speaking no language, fluently and loudly. We have no plans after leaving Rome except to see everything. Simple tastes! It's an idiot's voyage and I plan to enjoy it thoroughly. The world has been coming to an end for too many thousands of years for me to hope to be in on the death

434

kick. And I remember my first story of doom. We read it in the first grade. It went:

"Henny Penny was scratching under a pea-vine when a pea fell on her tail. 'Oh!' screamed Henny Penny—'the sky is falling.' Anyway she managed to get all the chickens so upset that they formed an army and bombed the hell out of a duck-yard next door and the ducks opened up with high explosives and nearly everybody got killed and lived happily ever after. And when it was all over Henny Penny had the only pea left in the world so she started a pea cartel and right now her descendants own Manhattan Island and spend their winters in Cannes."

Seriously. I am so anxious to see you—and this time I will.

To John O'Hara

[New York]
[February 1952]

Dear John:

What a courteous memory you have. You did remember how I admired your hat. I shall wear the one you sent, and only it, on the jaunt through history we are about to make. Thank you. It should however have a plate on it and I think I will put one on, saying—

THE JOHN O'HARA MEMORIAL HAT

Thank you again. I'll wear a feather in the hat because you gave it to me.

Love and all wishes to you and to Belle and to Wiley, the serpent of the Rappahannock [their daughter].

John

To Pascal Covici

New York
[1952]
Tuesday

Dear Pat:

I have been going over the years in my mind, remembering all the things pre-publication critics have asked me to take out, things they would now be horrified at if I had.

One of the most dangerous things of all is the suggestion that something or other is not in good taste. Now good taste is a codification of manners and attitudes of the past. The very fact of originality is per se bad taste. I might even go so far as to believe that any writer who produced a book of unquestioned good taste has written a tasteless book, a flavorless book, a book of no excitement and surely of no originality. There is no taste in life nor in nature. It is simply the way it is. And in the rearrangement of life called literature, the writer is the less valuable and interesting in direct relation to his goodness of taste. There is shocking bad taste in the Old Testament, abominable taste in Homer, and execrable taste in Shakespeare.

Thinking about it, I believe that the following may be true. When a book is finished but not yet printed there is a well-intentioned urge, particularly in non-creative people, to help, to be part of it, and this urge takes itself out in suggestions for its improvement. It would not occur to me to make such suggestions to another writer because I know he must have a reason for everything in his book. But also I do not need the free creative ride. As I said, these impulses are kindly meant and they are almost invariably wrong.

And so you and I will do what we have done—listen with respect, correct the errors, weigh the criticism and then go about our business. I do not think that all the things in my books are good but all the things in my book are me. There is no quicker way to ruin any book than to permit collabora-

436

tions. Then it becomes a nothing and a bad something has a way of being superior to a good nothing. The second-hand bookstalls are loaded with good taste. No. We know this story. We've been through it together so many times.

We'll do fine.

Yours,
John

That was damn good pie

The following letter appeared as the final passage of *Journal of a Novel.*

To Pascal Covici

[New York]
[1952]

Dear Pat:

I have decided for this, my book, East of Eden, to write dedication, prologue, argument, apology, epilogue and perhaps epitaph all in one.

The dedication is to you with all the admiration and affection that have been distilled from our singularly blessed association of many years. This book is inscribed to you because you have been part of its birth and growth.

As you know, a prologue is written last but placed first to explain the book's shortcomings and to ask the reader to be kind. But a prologue is also a note of farewell from the writer to his book. For years the writer and his book have been together—friends or bitter enemies but very close as only love and fighting can accomplish.

437

Then suddenly the book is done. It is a kind of death. This is the requiem.

Miguel Cervantes invented the modern novel and with his Don Quixote set a mark high and bright. In his prologue, he said best what writers feel—the gladness and the terror.

"Idling reader," Cervantes wrote, "you may believe me when I tell you that I should have liked this book, which is the child of my brain, to be the fairest, the sprightliest and the cleverest that could be imagined, but I have not been able to contravene the law of nature which would have it that like begets like—"

And so it is with me, Pat. Although some times I have felt that I held fire in my hands and spread a page with shining —I have never lost the weight of clumsiness, of ignorance, of aching inability.

A book is like a man—clever and dull, brave and cowardly, beautiful and ugly. For every flowering thought there will be a page like a wet and mangy mongrel, and for every looping flight a tap on the wing and a reminder that wax cannot hold the feathers firm too near the sun.

Well—then the book is done. It has no virtue any more. The writer wants to cry out—"Bring it back! Let me rewrite it or better—Let me burn it. Don't let it out in the unfriendly cold in that condition."

As you know better than most, Pat, the book does not go from writer to reader. It goes first to the lions—editors, publishers, critics, copy readers, sales department. It is kicked and slashed and gouged. And its bloodied father stands attorney.

EDITOR

The book is out of balance. The reader expects one thing and you give him something else. You have written two books and stuck them together. The reader will not understand.

WRITER

No, sir. It goes together. I have written about one family and used stories about another family as—well, as counterpoint, as rest, as contrast in pace and color.

EDITOR

The reader won't understand. What you call counterpoint only slows the book.

WRITER

It has to be slowed—else how would you know when it goes fast?

EDITOR

You have stopped the book and gone into discussions of God knows what.

WRITER

Yes, I have. I don't know why. Just wanted to. Perhaps I was wrong.

SALES DEPARTMENT

The book's too long. Costs are up. We'll have to charge five dollars for it. People won't pay $5. They won't buy it.

WRITER

My last book was short. You said then that people won't buy a short book.

PROOFREADER

The chronology is full of holes. The grammar has no relation to English. On page so-and-so you have a man look in the World Almanac for steamship rates. They aren't there. I checked. You've got Chinese New Year wrong. The characters aren't consistent. You describe Liza Hamilton one way and then have her act a different way.

EDITOR

You make Cathy too black. The reader won't believe her. You make Sam Hamilton too white. The reader won't believe him. No Irishman ever talked like that.

WRITER

My grandfather did.

EDITOR

Who'll believe it?

SECOND EDITOR

No children ever talked like that.

WRITER

(Losing temper as a refuge from despair)

God damn it. This is my book. I'll make the children talk any way I want. My book is about good and evil. Maybe the theme got into the execution. Do you want to publish it or not?

439

Let's see if we can't fix it up. It won't be much work. You want it to be good, don't you? For instance, the ending. The reader won't understand it.

WRITER

Do you?

EDITOR

Yes, but the reader won't.

PROOFREADER

My God, how you do dangle a participle. Turn to page so-and-so.

There you are, Pat. You came in with a box of glory and there you stand with an arm full of damp garbage.

And from this meeting a new character has emerged. He is called The Reader.

THE READER

He is so stupid you can't trust him with an idea.

He is so clever he will catch you in the least error.

He will not buy short books.

He will not buy long books.

He is part moron, part genius and part ogre.

There is some doubt as to whether he can read.

Well, by God, Pat he's just like me, no stranger at all. He'll take from the book what he can bring to it. The dull-witted will get dullness and the brilliant may find things in my book I didn't know were there.

And just as he is like me, I hope my book is enough like him so that he may find in it interest and recognition and some beauty as one finds in a friend.

Cervantes ends his prologue with a lovely line. I want to use it, Pat, and then I will have done.

He said to the reader,

"May God give you health. And may He be not unmindful of me, as well."

John Steinbeck

440

1952 1954
1953

Steinbeck (signature)

"...sitting at Stanford
wishing I were
sitting on a rock
in Pacific Grove
wishing I were
in Mexico."

1952 Correspondent abroad for *Collier's*. *East of Eden* published. *Viva Zapata!* (film) released.

1954 *Sweet Thursday* published. Lived abroad for nine months. Correspondent for *Le Figaro*, Paris.

On assignment by *Collier's*—he to write, she to photograph—the Steinbecks left in March for six months in Europe. They went to North Africa, crossed to Marseilles, rented a car and toured in Spain.

To Pascal Covici

[Palace Hotel]
[Madrid]
April 18 [1952]

Dear Pat:

We've been nearly a week in Madrid now and go back to Seville for the great fiesta on Monday.

We have been seeing many pictures—at The Prado and today at Toledo to see the many fine Grecos. So many impressions. Maybe too many. Hard to take in in a short time, a little stunning in fact. Come in dog tired.

We did not have mail forwarded so haven't heard much of anything. Letter from Kazan saying he had testified [before the House Committee on Un-American Activities]. He had told me he was going to a long time ago. I wonder whether it made a sensation. He sent us a copy of his statement which I thought good. It must be a very hard decision to make. He is a good and honest man. I hope the Communists and the second raters don't cut him to pieces now. But they can't hurt him very much.

I haven't written anything. Going through a fallow time,

443

which, as usual, bothers me. Actually so much coming in there hasn't been time for much to go out. And my pen has gone rusty.

I'll try to write more often.

love to all
John

To Pascal Covici

Hotel Lancaster
Paris
May 12, 1952

Arrived in Paris yesterday but late at night after 28 hours on the train from Madrid. Now we are in this comfortable hotel. I have slept myself out and tomorrow morning I am going to start on my first piece about Spain. It will be a pleasure to begin putting some of it down. This is the longest stretch without writing within my recent memory. Have seen some strange and reversing things. I hope I can make some sense of it when I start writing it down. Spain wasn't what we expected. I wonder what it was! It is a completely contradictory country. Everything you say or see or think is cancelled out by something else you see. It is a country about which it is impossible to make generalities. And yet how can you write a piece about it if you don't think one way or another. Paradoxes as verities? I think the best way is to set it down just as it happened and to let the sense of paradox grow out of the material just as it has out of my seeing.

Paris is always wonderful—both recognized and new every time. This time the chestnuts are blooming and the trees are in full leaf and it is the core of spring.

Here I plan to buy a little French car (to be sold when we leave Europe) to drive to Italy and all over.

One thing will interest you. I had been told that my works were not permitted in Spain. This is not true. And it seems that they are very popular. Maybe I got a sense of self-importance by thinking my books were banned in Spain. Maybe a kind of martyr complex. Well, they aren't, so there's a good hair shirt ruined.

I do hope I'll hear from you soon and I hope you'll send me a galley. Galley hell! you'll have books in a short time.

love to all,
John

Though later the relationship as correspondent for *Collier's* proved happy, the magazine rejected his first piece on Spain.

To Elizabeth Otis

Paris
May 26, 1952

Dear Elizabeth:

Your letter this morning with Colliers' reaction to the first piece. This first piece was written to order. I won't make that mistake again. I enclose the wire specifying the kind of piece required. If you can see how I could have covered all of these fields in a whole nation in 5,000 words by any other method I'll eat it. Maybe I could have done better but not much different. It may turn out that they don't want my stuff at all but Colliers stuff with my name on it. As for its not being my kind of stuff, that's balderdash. One wants Tortilla Flat and another Grapes of Wrath. I write all kinds of stuff. I will not again follow their rules. They can accept or reject, but I will not work it over and over until it sounds like Quent Reynolds. I will send many pieces. No two will be alike. They understood this or said they did. I'm not a bit upset by this. In fact I anticipated it. They will have plenty to choose from but

445

they will have to choose, not create. If they reject, we'll try to sell it elsewhere and if no one wants it we'll throw it away.

It is certain that we have changed our plans. We changed them to match conditions we didn't know about in advance. Pat writes saying I should go to Israel, Manning [Gordon Manning, a *Collier's* editor] thinks I should go to the Slovak border. I am going to the Jura. If they think I am hanging around Paris too long—let them. I have been gathering a sense of Europe here. I know where to go now and what for. I could not have known without coming here. This is not a city desk assignment. This is no quarrel—only a restatement of an understanding.

I don't know whether the second piece I just sent off will be acceptable to Colliers either, nor the piece on the Jura but I'll do them anyway. Elaine is working hard with the camera but there is no way for her to learn. They want her to send in the undeveloped film and she never hears how it comes out. There is no way to correct a mistake if you don't know what it is. This sounds like a beefing letter and in a way it is, but now it is over.

We took a trial run in the little car yesterday (named "*Aux Armes O Citroën*") and it is very good.

We feel pretty good. There is a kind of weariness from seeing too much and trying to take in too much. But there's not any help for that.

I hope you had fun in Maine.

I'm sending a box of things for Catbird on his birthday but I'll try to send them by hand so he will surely get them.

Love and kisses to everyone,

John

Later the same day, in another letter to Elizabeth Otis, he wrote:

"I do hate the feeling of a hot breath down my neck. It doesn't bring out the best in me nor even the sweetest."

And afterward he was to be even more specific:

446

"There are two distinct crafts, writing and writing for someone. The second requires a kind of second sight with which I do not seem to be gifted. In writing you put down an idea or a story and then see whether anyone likes it, but in writing for someone you must first, during and after, keep an invisible editor sitting on the typewriter shaking an admonitory finger in your face. It is a special business and one I don't seem to learn very easily."

To Elizabeth Otis

Paris
May 27, 1952

Dear Elizabeth:

Time and space are rather terrible things. Yesterday I wrote and sent to you a very ill-natured letter. Last night we went out with the Loessers. They were fighting and for a time we caught it but saved ourselves. It was as though a kind of evil gas had spread.

This morning an angry letter from Way answering an angry letter from Elaine. By now Way has forgotten there ever was any trouble. By the time you get my bad-tempered letter, I shall have forgotten all about it and you will be irritated. New rule—"People who are more than one hour apart should never write letters."

We are not leaving until Wednesday. We are going to stay with the Frenchman in his house which he says has a toilet but no water [a school teacher and vintner in the Jura who had invited the Steinbecks to visit him]. He says we can stay at an hotel—but I would rather stay with him. He has three daughters and he says—"They have many friends who I hope will not bother you." This is a great thing for me. I will be able to see French lower middle class farmer life as I could not in any other way. I don't know how long I will stay but I will surely stay until I get a true sense of people, thinking and way of life. It is a wonderful chance.

Ridgway gets in today and every preparation is being made

447

for riots and counter riots. I will go out and see.

I am being interviewed by Combat which is a left wing Communist paper but unofficial. I have been interviewed by the Monde—conservative—so must be by the other. By the way, being interviewed is the best way of getting information. The very nature of a question can tell you a great deal.

Last night I read from the galleys of E of E and it is better than I thought. Doesn't print make a great difference though?

Have you heard about the signs in Paris? The Communists have written all over the walls AMERICANS GO HOME and crews have followed, painted "Via Pan American" and after them "Revenez Via Air France." It has completely destroyed the effect of the Communists' work.

I guess one of the reasons for my ill nature is that I am worried about money. We are not spending too much here but I can't seem to get ahead at all and it is a constant nagging worry. I think I am working as hard as I can and I can just barely keep my head above water.

Love to all,
John

To Elizabeth Otis

Geneva
June 2, 1952

Dear Elizabeth:

Now how did it get to be that date? I have the old duality —time has flown and at the same time we have been away forever.

We drove out of Paris in the little car Aux Armes. It behaves beautifully. Stayed the first night in Dijon where the streets are *not* paved with mustard. The second day we drove to Poligny in the Jura. Do you remember Louis Gibry to whom you once sent fruit trees? Well they are all growing and their branches are being used to graft other trees so that the original trees you sent are spreading all over. He lives in a little old house in a peasant street, no plumbing, no inside toilet, three little girls, two hunting dogs, flies, crumbs, bees from the hives in the yard, shouting of neighbors and birds, street full of cows, a fine dust of manure over everything. He would not hear of our going to a hotel. We had his guest room. We went into the wine caves, visited every one and were visited by everyone. If you didn't watch carefully the dogs got your dinner —the whole place crawling with children. Wines were brought in from the bottoms of cellars. We went to tiny towns famous for wines and drank the best and ate cheese and loaves of bread as long as ourselves. We heard much talk. Elaine took many pictures.

Yesterday we pried ourselves loose against protest and proceeded to Geneva. We were filthy—we do not know how to keep clean with bowl and pitcher and cold water. We and the car were deep in cow manure. And we landed in this sweet and immaculate country. In Paris we met Faye Emerson and she had just come from here. She said, "Remember how you always heard of a place where you could eat off the floor? Well, I've just seen it." As for us, we had just come from the Jura where you can barely eat off the table. We got in and began taking baths, one after another. I finally have the odor of cheese, cows, people, dogs and wine caves off me and all my clothes are being cleaned.

We both suddenly became homesick last week. It is the proper time for it. It usually happens at three months. I think it was all the children in Louis Gibry's house that did it. It surely was not the backyard toilet. However, we will get over that.

Later: We have been walking all over Geneva all day and our feet are tired and hot and now we are about to dip into a martini which is a specific for tired feet. There is one very nice thing about this city—absolutely nothing of a lively nature to do at night. The result is that we are getting some sleep. I ordered a double martini of course—half for each foot.

My French gets worse every day as it gets more fluent. A man in a shop today after listening to me a while said in well-modulated English, "What in hell are you trying to say?" I guess I was being too subtle.

449

In Paris we knew every second person we saw. Here we have not seen a soul of our acquaintance. What a joy it is, at least for a change.

I know there is no great need to keep in touch. But it does bother me. I guess it is largely the constant and never-changing sense of impending tragedy concerning the boys. I wish I could lose that. But I never have.

Last night we had a lovely dinner on the terrace of this hotel which practically hangs over the lake. It was incredibly beautiful and the evening went on for hours.

John

To Annie Laurie Williams

Hassler Hotel
Rome
June 17 [1952]

Dear Annie Laurie.

We got in here last night and your letter was waiting for us. It is very hot in Rome, I am sitting in my shorts in an open window writing this.

Gadg [Kazan] called this morning from Paris. He says he is absolutely crazy about East of Eden and wants to do it. He says he is going to talk to Zanuck about it. He says he wants to do it whether Zanuck does or not, under United Artists independently or something like that. He told me that Zapata has already grossed three million dollars. He wants to work out some kind of deal where we own a chunk of the picture and can share in the profits. I told him to call you when he gets in town. You know of course that this Congress thing tore him to pieces. He is just getting back on his feet and sounded fine on the phone. And as you know I would rather work with him than with anyone I know. We know that works. He is the very best and there is no doubt at all in my mind about that.

Well, the summer moves on and it has a kind of dream-like

450

quality. Soon it will be over and then as usual it is as though it had never been.

love to all there
john

To Elizabeth Otis

Rome
June 23, 1952
Monday today

Dear Elizabeth:

Drudi's [Gabriella Drudi, Steinbeck's Italian literary agent] office is giving a monster cocktail party this afternoon in my honor. You know how I loathe them. But I seem to have to do this one. All last night and a good part of today with the most violent stomach cramps and dysentery which does not make any kind of party seem very desirable. I shall have a number of glasses of iced tea, which looks lethal and will keep me from retching.

I have a kind of a desolate feeling of failure in this whole trip. I wish I could talk to Mr. Anthony [Edward Anthony, publisher of *Collier's*] again. I like him. What I would like to tell him is that when you have finished a long piece of work any work seems easy. You know as well as I do that I have never turned out a really easy piece of copy in my life. I wonder why I always fool myself and, through myself, other people. But I don't think I fool you. But here I am trapped again in my own upswings of enthusiasm. The easy way in which I can turn out the pretties of copy. Just interview a few people, take some pictures and there you are. Well I can't do it. These articles are going to be just exactly as hard as anything I have ever done. And it is troubling me that I have fooled people. Will you tell Mr. Anthony that? The whole thing is making me sick and putting a pressure on me that makes it impossible for me to work well. But the main thing I want you to tell him is that I will do the work and I will do it if it takes the rest of my life. I did not intentionally fool him

451

or any of them. I fooled myself. Maybe this upset is caused by a block of this kind. But I think I will feel better about it if you will tell that one man.

The first of my cool clothes are supposed to arrive this afternoon—and at that moment they did and it is such a relief.

I'm going to leave this letter open to tell you about the cocktail party. I will put on my pretty new cool clothes and get ready for the guillotine. That is exactly what I feel like.

Love,
John

To Roberto Rossellini and Ingrid Bergman

Paris
July 23, 1952

Dear Roberto and Ingrid:

We were sorry not to see you again, but you were busy and we were frantic. However, we were glad to have seen as much of you as we did and I was particularly glad at last to meet Roberto.

I hope things are easing up for you now and that there can be some relaxation for a while. You are in good hands and I must say I feel much better for you. Let Giesler do it all for you. He can and will do it well and at least you will know that you have a man who is for you, not against you.

We leave tomorrow for London and thence to Ireland, and then if we have a little more time, to Ingrid's home town for a week.

I am going to make the Ibsen play The Vikings at Helgoland in Stockholm next summer. It will make a very fine picture. You will remember I discussed it with you a long time ago. Probably make it in the archipelago. There is a great deal of enthusiasm in the Svenskfilmindustrie about it. Hjordis is one of the really great women's parts.

452

Would you be interested, Ingrid? Besides being a good part and a good picture, it might give you the chance to kick the pants of some of the people who have been kicking you in the pants for a long time. We will have a major release but the money will be private money so there will be none of that tampering with the script. Let me know whether you might be interested. It is one hell of a part.

Again, we're glad to have seen you. I think you have some of the things licked now. And you are rapidly breeding a private army which may protect you in the future.

> love to you both.
> John Steinbeck

In the manner of a Viking *skald,* Ingrid Bergman replied:

"Thou art minded I play a woman mighty as Hjordis? Set thy hand to work. . . . Now—if thou errest and thy film prate senselessly, hateful to us both it stinketh. Little dost thou know Ingrid if thou thinkest to have her help in such a deed of shame. Farewell and fortune befriend thee."

The final leg of their trip took them to Ireland in August, where Steinbeck hoped to find traces of his Hamilton ancestors.

To Mr. and Mrs. Pascal Covici

Londonderry, Ireland
August 17, 1952

Dear Pat and Dorothy:

We just got in here. We're on a hunt for the seat of the Hamiltons. The place they are supposed to have lived is not on any map no matter how large scaled but we have found a taxi driver who thinks he knows where it is and tomorrow we start out to try to find it. It should be a very interesting experience. I can't imagine any of them are still alive since the last I heard of them was fifteen years ago and there were then two old, old ladies and an old, old gentleman and they had none of them been married. However, whatever happens it will be a story to tell.

We are really tired now. Have got kind of dull to everything. Elaine has just figured out that we have been to thirty-eight different hotels since we left. That doesn't count going back to the same hotel or sleeping on boats and such.

We have just completed a drive all around Scotland. That is a lovely country, not a gay country but it is one hell of a lot gayer than England. Elaine's birthday was celebrated in the dourest little hotel by a Scottish lake. I had a magnum of champagne. The dinner was horrible. There was no way properly to ice the champagne. It was bitterly cold, believe it or not. We went to bed and huddled together and drank the whole magnum of wine, no cake, no presents, no nothing. The guests at this hotel were all British and they sat silently as we went through, sat over their papers. They whisper and look at you but look hastily away when you look up. Everybody is so busy respecting each other's privacy that there is a feeling in one of those Common Rooms like that in an undertaking parlour just before the main event. We got to giggling up in our room and probably every one of those holidaying British exchanged glances and made the mental reservation, 'Ameddicans.'

love from us both
jn

454

Back in New York, Steinbeck celebrated the birth of Pascal Covici, Jr.'s son, who had been named John after him.

To Pascal Covici, Jr.

New York
[September 9, 1952]

Dear Pascal—

Of course I am flattered. But you give me something to live up to—which maybe I won't try to live up to.

But the name is a good name. It is particularly valuable in school first because there is no rhyme for it and second because at that period when you are desperately trying to disappear into the group, John has no more emphasis than a number. It is not a name to embarrass you when you are little.

There is one other thing about it. If it is not for you, it will reject you. If you are not by nature John—it automatically becomes Jack or Johnny which are very different names, or it leaves and a nickname takes its place. I can remember wishing for a nickname but I never had one.

I hope your John will wear it in health and honor. There have been bad ones like John Lackland and Ivan the Terrible but mostly it has been a kind of nobly humble name. And I need not give you examples of that.

Thank you. It does make me feel shy and inadequate.

Love to all three,
John

Six years had passed since Steinbeck had written Carl Wilhelmson, "I haven't heard from Dook Sheffield in a long time. He seemed so touchy that I gave up. He obviously didn't want any more to do with me and I don't even want to investigate why. I think a dislikeness of experience is largely responsible with all of these things." Though a later letter to Sheffield's sister (page 708) presents a different explanation of the estrangement, there is no doubt that he felt one of its primary causes to be the contrast between the orbit of his own life, its location, interests, and associates, and that of his friend, quieter, removed, and scholarly, in Northern California.

To Carlton A. Sheffield

New York
September 10, 1952

Dear Dook:

Did I answer your card written last Feb? I think I did but I have come to put little faith in those things I think I did.

Fifty is a good age. The hair recedes, the paunch grows a little, the face—rarely inspected, looks the same to us but not to others. The little inabilities grow so gradually that we don't even know it. My hangovers are less bad maybe because I drink better liquor. But enough of this 50 talk.

We had the grand tour—six months of it and I liked it very well. I'm glad to be back. We have a pretty little house here and every day is full. Very nice and time races by. When you really live in New York, it is more rural than country. Your district is a village and you go to Times Square as once you went to San Francisco. I do pretty much work and as always —90 percent of it is thrown out. I cut more deeply than I used to which means that I overwrite more than I used to. I cut 90,000 words out of my most recent book but I think it's a pretty good book [*East of Eden*]. It was a hard one. But they're all hard. And if I want to know I'm fifty, all I have to do is look at my titles—so god-damned many of them. I'll ask Pat to send you a copy of the last one. To see if you like it or not.

In Paris I wrote a picture script based on an early play of Ibsen's called The Vikings at Helgoland—not very well

456

known—a roaring melodrama, cluttered and verbose but with the great dramatic construction and character relationships he later cleaned up. Anyway—I shook out the clutter and I think it will make a good picture.

Have three more articles to complete for Colliers to finish my agreement with them. Then I want to learn something about plays, so I'm going to try to plunge into that form this winter. You may look for some colossal flops. But I do maintain that gigantic stupidity that will let me try it.

Your life sounds good to me. I have the indolence for it but have never been able to practice it. Too jittery and nervous. And yet every instinct aims toward just such a life. I guess I inherited from my mother the desire to do four things at once.

I am gradually accumulating a library which would delight you I think. It's a library of words—all dictionaries—12 vol. Oxford, all of Mencken, folklore, Americanisms, dic. of slang—many—and then all books and monographs on words. I find I love words very much. And gradually I am getting a series of dictionaries of modern languages. The crazy thing about all this is that I don't use a great variety of words in my work at all. I just love them for themselves. The long and specialized words are not very interesting because they have no history and no family. But a word like claw or land or host or foist—goes back and back and has relatives in all directions. A negro scholar is completing a volume on all the African words in the American language. He has about 10,000 so far, some of them unchanged in meaning or form from their Zulu or Gold Coast sources. I must write to him and try to get a copy.

Just read Hemingway's new book [*The Old Man and The Sea*]. A very fine performance. I am so glad. The obscene joy with which people trampled him on the last one was disgusting. Now they are falling too far the other way almost in shame. The same thing is going to happen to me with my new book. It is the best work I've done but a lot of silly things are going to be said about it. Unthoughtful flattery is, if anything, more insulting than denunciation.

This has gone on quite a long time now.

Anyway, let me know what you think of the new work.

So long,

J

To Carlton A. Sheffield

New York
October 16, 1952

Dear Dook:

Thank you for your good letter. It warmed me and it remembered me of very many things. I guess it was the things we disagreed about that kept us together. Only when we began to agree did we get into trouble. I'm glad you like the book. The Book—it's been capitalized in my mind for so long that it was a kind of a person. And when the last line was finished that person was dead. Rewriting and cutting was like dressing a corpse for a real nice funeral. Remembering the book now is like remembering Ed Ricketts. I remember nice things about both but a finished book and a dead man can never surprise you nor delight you any more. They aren't going any place.

I guess—what may happen is what keeps us alive. We want to see tomorrow. Criticism of the book by critics has been cautious, as it should be. They, after all, must see whether it has a life of its own and the only proof of that is whether people accept it as their own. That's why most critics do not like my present book but love the former one which formerly they denounced. I have felt for some time that criticism has one great value to a writer. With the exception of extreme invention in method or idea (generally disliked by critics because nothing to measure them against) the critic can tell a writer what *not* to do. If he could tell him what *to* do, he'd be a writer himself. What *to* do is the soul and heart of the book. What *not* to do is how well or badly you did it.

I am interested in Anthony West's review in the New Yorker. I wonder what made him so angry—and it was a very angry piece. I should like to meet him to find out why he hated and feared this book so much.

The book seems to be selling enormously. I am getting flocks of letters and oddly enough, most of them have the sense of possession just as you do. People write as though it were their book. I'll speak of Cathy for a moment and then

458

forget the book. You won't believe her, many people don't. I don't know whether I believe her either but I know she exists. I don't believe in Napoleon, Joan of Arc, Jack the Ripper, the man who stands on one finger in the circus. I don't believe Jesus Christ, Alexander the Great, Leonardo. I don't believe them but they exist. I don't believe them because they aren't like me. You say you only believe her at the end. Ah! but that's when, through fear, she became like us. This was very carefully planned. All of the book was very carefully planned. And I'm forgetting it so soon.

I'm going to do a job that sounds very amusing. Frank Loesser and I are going to make a musical comedy of Cannery Row. It will be a madhouse but getting such a thing together should be great fun.

It is very good to be writing to you again. I hope we can keep it up. I think I'm changed in some ways, more calm, maybe more adult, perhaps more tolerant. But still restless. I'll never get over that I guess—still nervous, still going from my high ups to very low downs—just short of a manic depressive, I guess. I have more confidence in myself now, which makes me less arrogant. And Elaine has taught me not to be afraid of people (strangers) so that I am kinder and better mannered I think.

I think I am without ambition. It isn't that I've got so much but that I want less. And I do have the great pleasure in work —*while it is being done.* Nothing equals that to me and I never get used to it. My marriage is good in all ways and my powers in that direction are less frantic but not less frequent. This seems to be my golden age. I wouldn't go back or ahead a week.

In some things I think I more nearly resemble you than I did. I hope that isn't wishful thinking. I've always admired your ability to take stock of your assets, your wishes and your liabilities and out of them make a life that contains more elements good for you than any other. You used to have a little nagging conscience about contributing to some great world of thought or art. Maybe you have that without knowing it. Thoreau didn't know either. And you are more nearly like him than anyone I know. Elaine asked what you were like and instead I told her how and where you lived. She said you must be very wise. I don't think you are terribly wise— but I do think you have used your life well. I am caught up in the world and full of its frenzies but you are perfectly

459

placed to be a quiet, thoughtful, appraiser of your time. You used to have a crippling self-consciousness—as bad as mine. Mine made me jump in where yours made you stay out. But just as my aches have eased, so must yours have done.

The cards for you and for me have been down a long time. The thing that's natural for you, you drift towards. You drift toward peace and contemplation, and I drift toward restlessness and violence. If either of us forces toward the opposite, it doesn't last long. And we don't learn—at least I don't. I mean learn lessons applicable to myself. I am fully capable of making exactly the same mistake today I did at 16 even though I know better. That's funny isn't it? I need glasses to read now, and I can't even learn to keep track of them.

It's a grey day here. My working room is on the third floor overlooking 72nd Street which is a nice street. And I guess, by count—two-thirds of my working time is looking out the window at people going by. Didn't we used to do that in your car? But then we only looked at girls. Now I look at anyone but I still like to look at girls.

And always I feel that I am living in a dream and that I will awaken to something quite different. It's very unreal but then everything always has been to me. Maybe I never saw anything real. That's what Marge Bailey [one of his professors at Stanford] said about me once very long ago. I do go on, don't I? But it's fun.

We lead a very quiet life. Once a week or so we go out to dinner or to the theatre. Once a month or thereabouts people come in. It's much quieter than living in a small town. Very strange but true. People in the city never drop in. They always call first—a manners pattern small towns could well learn.

A fine old bum just went by as he does every day about this time. Apparently he gets drunk every night. Wakes about 3 in the afternoon and goes by eating an enormous piece of bread. I wonder where he gets the money to get drunk. He looks like death. I wonder how he stays alive or why.

I love the winters here. It gets quite cold and people are much more cheerful when it is cold. The first snow is like a holiday. Very good. We have a nice little library with a red rug and big chairs. In winter we build a coal fire in the fire-place and it is a very nice room to be in. I seem to be just flowing out words. But as I said before—it feels good to be writing to you.

460

I'd better wrap this up I guess. It looks as though it would go on interminably.

So long
John

In Adlai Stevenson's first campaign for the Presidency Steinbeck wrote scores of speeches to be delivered by supporters at rallies in the eastern half of the United States. This letter was written after the campaign before the two men had met.

To Adlai Stevenson

New York
November 7, 1952

Dear Governor Stevenson:

I hope you will have rest without sadness. The sadness is for us who have lost our chance for greatness when greatness is needed. The Republic will not crumble. But for a little while, please don't reread Thucydides. Republics have—and in just this way.

It has been an honor to work for you—and a privilege. In some future, if you have the time and or the inclination I hope you can come to my house and settle back with a drink and—tell sad stories of the death of Kings.

Thank God for the impeachment provisions.

Yours in disappointment and in hope

John Steinbeck

To Carlton A. Sheffield

Dear Dook:

There is no doubt that this will not be sent for a long time. Elections are over and we lick our wounds and try to find something good. The general has a rough future. I am told he is a very sensitive man who broods over a bad notice. Well— now they have it—let's see what they do with it. There is no excuse about a split Congress or anything.

Your dog sounds interesting and properly come by. Dogs are curious extensions of ourselves. We have two—a cocker belonging to Waverly—Elaine's daughter—a bitch of great appetite—in fact a walking stomach—greedy beyond belief, and also a big French poodle acquired in Paris—the most intelligent dog I've ever seen. I don't need dogs as I once needed them but I like them as much as ever. Once they were absolute necessities to me—emotionally. But if I lived alone I would instantly get one. A house is very dead without a dog. Here in New York we have a little garden. I have made a swinging door of plexiglass so that the dogs can go out when they wish. This removes the New Yorker's necessity of having to walk them. It also makes them much happier.

I'm coming to life again. I like the feeling of the pencil. The second finger of my right hand has a great grooved callus on it into which the pencil fits. And I have an electric pencil sharpener. I use about 200 a day. I love the smooth lead and a sharp point.

You are right about the difficulty of transposing Cannery Row to the stage. I'm not going to do exactly that. I have a whole new story. It will simply be set against the old background. You know Dook—it never gets any easier. The process of writing a book is the process of outgrowing it. I am just as scared now as I was 25 years ago.

I'm talking myself out pretty much. You say you have few friends now. The same is true of me. I have millions of acquaintances and many professional friends but no one to talk

462

basic things to and I'd like to get back to you. You don't have anything against me, do you?

I had never expected to make a living at writing. Then when money began to come in it kind of scared me. I didn't think I deserved it and besides it was kind of bad luck. I gave a lot of it away—tried to spread it around. Maybe it was a kind of propitiation of the gods. It made me a lot of enemies. I was clumsy about it I guess but I didn't want power over any one. Anyway that was the impulse. And it was wrong. But I've done many wrong things. But before I forget it—there is one thing I can do for you that isn't wrong. When you need any books—to buy I mean—I can get them through Viking at 40% discount. Remember that—will you? It makes a very great difference.

I don't have any money problems any more. After living and taxes and alimony, there isn't any left so my problem is solved. We live a good life, quite simple but we don't deny ourselves much. We see what theatre we want, and we eat well and sleep warm. I can't think of anything better. Next year we are going to start traveling more. I find I want to see many things.

I do go on, don't I? But it is good to be able to talk—very good. I hope you don't mind.

The play goes on and I'm having fun with it. This should be a danger signal.

I'm going to get this off finally.

love
John

I have named the poodle Charles le Chien, le policier de Paris. (puns yet)

The New York Times Book Review had polled a number of celebrities for their favorite books of the year, and Steinbeck had listed *Matador* by Barnaby Conrad as one of his. Conrad wrote to thank him.

463

To Barnaby Conrad

Dear Conrad:

I liked Matador for a number of reasons chief of which was that I believed it. I am not informed enough to be an aficionado but that has nothing to do with it. If I had never been near a bull ring I would still have believed it. That makes it good to me. I guess it's communication I'm talking about.

You will be amused at something that happened to me last year. I had very good seats for the week at the Feria in Seville 2nd row sombra right with the newspaper critics. A nice little business type man in a double breasted suit sat next to me all week and he was very kind in explaining many things. My questions were extremely naive and he was very nice to us. Only afterwards did I discover that the little business man was Juan Belmonte.

I am delighted that John Huston is going to do your picture. In addition to his talent, he has such integrity and intelligence that you should be pleased. Give John my greetings. He is an old and valued friend. You couldn't have better.

I am pleased that you like Eden. It is doing better than I had dared to hope. It is our tendency to think when critics do not like our work that they have a scunner. I guess I just don't bring out the best in critics. Maybe I've been around too long. The tradition is that writers of English die young. Maybe that outrages them. The pleasant thing is that people go right on reading the books.

You can't have better than Elizabeth Otis. She has the sharpest mind for story I know of. And no matter how popular you get, she'll still return a story if she doesn't like it. Still does to me. She is wonderful.

Do come to see us.

Sincerely
John Steinbeck

I have a motto you might like to share—se no quieres volar, cuidado con las alas! ("If you don't want to fly, beware of wings.")

J. S.

To Barnaby Conrad

[New York]
January 2, 1953

Dear Conrad:

This is a note somewhat in answer to your good letter of this morning. Did I tell you my wife and I are going to St. Thomas? It would be pleasant if you should come down while we're there. I'll throw a line in the water. A fish is not my destiny any more than a bull is but I can understand how either or both could be. But I have no competitive spirit. Don't even care for gambling. There's no sense in it if you don't feel tragic when you lose or triumphant when you win. I like bullfights, because to me it is a lonely, formal, dignified microcosm of what happens to every man, sometimes even in an office strangled by the glue on envelopes. In the bull-ring he survives for awhile sometimes. Also there's a fierce, unbeaten acceptance of final defeat in the bullring and I love gallantry above all virtues. It is the prime virtue of the individual and the only occidental invention, and being lost as the individual gets lost.

Do you know Annie Laurie Williams? She said a wise thing to me one time. I am reminded of it by your saying you were afraid to get away from the bulls. She said—"I can always tell the work of a young writer learning his trade because his drama is set off by an act of Nature—a storm, volcano, accident. After years he learns to find it in a simple clash of personality with experience." That's interesting isn't it?—and you can find all kinds of loopholes in it.

The bull is surely the pure symbol of dramatic fate, but within a scope, it is repetitious, purposely so just as the Hail Mary is. On the other hand chess is not. I don't favor either one over the other but you will do well with the incredible corrida where men and women battle poverty (or riches), fear, hurt, insult, triumph, and finally the great bull, Death. There's a piedras negras for you.

I'm tired. I'm going to look down into the sea and watch little animals doing it for two weeks.

See you soon.

J.S.

You're lucky in your first name. There was another good writer with your last.

To Felicia Geffen
OF THE ACADEMY OF ARTS AND LETTERS

New York
[March 1953]

Dear Miss Geffen:

Will you send me some buttons? My kids pulled mine apart to see how the crinkle got in the ribbon. I deplore it but I always wanted to know too, so I had the double pleasure of finding out and punishing them at the same time.

Have you heard of the left bank painter who fell in love and left his café and friends for his beauty?

One of the two maggots visited him and found to his horror that the girl had three eyes.

"But she's dreadful," he cried.

"Academician!" said the lover.

No offense

J. S.

To Nelson Valjean
STANFORD CLASSMATE

New York
March 13, 1953

Dear Val:

It was a very nice thing to get your letter and I am glad you like the work. I surely moved around with a manure fork, I suppose, in doing it, and I was amazed at how much I was able to remember and I suppose I didn't remember a great deal.

I have had no reaction from Salinas regarding the book, but I have had previous experience which would indicate to me that the Salinas reaction would not be good. When I wrote Tortilla Flat, for instance, the Monterey Chamber of Commerce issued a statement that it was a damned lie and that no such place or people existed. Later, they began running buses to the place where they thought it might be.

When I did Cannery Row, I had not only a charge from the Monterey Chamber of Commerce, but from the Fish Canners Association which came to the defense of Cannery Row people with a knightly intensity. They later reversed themselves, too. So I should imagine Salinas is waiting to find out what the reaction of the rest of the country is before they decide whether they will approve of me or disapprove of me. I do not think they approve of me very highly.

It occurs to me that probably the most heartbreaking title in the world is Tom Wolfe's "You Can't Go Home Again"— it's literally true. They want no part of me except in a pine box.

I am terribly interested in what you say about my father and mother. I think no one ever had more loyalty than I had from my parents. This was—or must have been—particularly painful to them, in that I was doing something that the town considered nuts and bad taste. Being intelligent people, my parents knew that my chances of making a living at writing were about one in a million—horse racing is a sure thing compared to it. A couple of years ago I came across a story about my father which I think might interest you.

467

When my first book came out, I didn't know it, but he apparently tried to get a few of my townspeople to buy a copy or so of it. They were not very much interested in so doing, but, as you know, we lived in Pacific Grove part of the time, and my father went to Mr. Holman of Holman's Store, and asked him if he wouldn't lay in a few copies of it—the book was called Cup of Gold. Mr. Holman said that if people wanted it and ordered it, he would certainly send for it, but he didn't think that he could go out on a limb and put any in stock, and so he did not. Well—many years later, Mrs. Holman began collecting my work, and she had to pay $78.00 for a copy of the book which, remaindered, could have been bought for 2c. or 3c. a copy. She blamed Mr. Holman for not having literary taste and she resents very much having to pay such a premium. It was a surprise to me that my father had tried to sell books for me. He did not succeed, but I honor him for having tried.

There is nothing I would rather do than to stop by and drink some of your grappa. Do you make it yourself? I wonder if I could still have the stomach for it. I remember we used to drink it out in Alisal and it had a distinct kerosene taste and the rule was then not to light a match within three minutes of having had a drink of it.

Thank you for writing. It's good to hear from you.

Yours very sincerely,
John

In March, while Elaine Steinbeck went to Texas for her annual visit to her family, John Steinbeck took his two sons (Thom, eleven, and John, or Catbird, or Cat, nine) to Nantucket for their spring vacation. Burgie, Miss Burgess, was a Nantucket friend.

468

To Elaine Steinbeck

Nantucket
[March 24–27, 1953]
Tuesday

Darling:

It's been busy all right but fun. Burgie and her brother were waiting for us and we got here well before dark. Fires were burning and the house warm. The days have been beautiful but at night a real winter chill sets in. Then we build big fires.

Yesterday we went to town and I ordered a jeep to be delivered today. We will go out for driftwood for the fires. We made menus for the whole week. Boys make their beds and wash and wipe dishes. They do it pretty well—sometimes three times before perfect. But they do it. Tonight we wash clothes. Yesterday we walked to the lighthouse and back. Boys want to stay up late but what with the cold air and the exercise they conk out at about 8 o'clock and I about 8:30. There has been no talk of radio, television or movies. I made my justly world famous corned beef hash last night. A dead and properly mummified seagull on the beach is being re-buried for the 8th time right now with a border of clam shells. This time he is being interred with his head above ground so he "can look out."

I love you and miss you. The jeep is coming and will have to close.

Love,
John

Wednesday

Dearest Elaine:

Your card came yesterday. I miss you very much and hope these goings away do not happen often.

Two good sunny days and today hard rain. But the boys are out in it. I have a big fire going in the kitchen and when they come in soaked and freezing I'll shuck off their clothes and

469

warm them. It is working well. Each makes his own bed—and well. Thom cleans living room and wipes dishes. Cat carries, brings coal and sweeps kitchen. I coach. Big washing today. Everyone did his socks and underwear. All hanging in kitchen over the stove.

All in all, it is going better than I had imagined it could. Boys are cooperative but incredibly thoughtless. I am going very slowly, insisting that they finish every single thing before starting on the next. We get along fine. Bed making is a singular triumph because a badly made bed lets cold air in and the nights are freezing, and I don't keep any fires. We dress by kerosene heater.

Love—and I'll be glad when you're back.

John

Thursday

Dearest:

Last night after airplane building and painting I started reading The Black Arrow of RLS. The language is that of the Wars of the Roses. The kids are fascinated by the change of word sequences. "I think me not—etc." There's a murder in the first chapter with a black arrow with the victim's name on it, so all is well.

Rain is over—sun is bright so we will go for a Moor Tour today in the jeep—collecting fireplace wood.

Thom just got up.

Later—breakfast over, beds made, dishes washed. It will be Sunday before we know it.

Gwyn is going to be very surprised. Always before the boys have come home with a bag of dirty clothes. This time, their clothes will be clean—well, pretty clean. The boys respond beautifully and they are very proud when they do a job well. They have carried logs as big as themselves. No wonder they sleep so well.

I hope you are having a good visit. New York will be in full spring before you get back. I miss you.

Love,
John

To Richard Watts, Jr.
DRAMA CRITIC OF THE NEW YORK *POST*

[New York]
April 7, 1953

Dear Dick:

I disagree with your criticism of Tennessee Williams' show Camino Real, but I don't intend to let that interfere with an old and valued friendship. There's no reason why you should like a play; there's no reason why I should not like the same play. I found in this one clarity and beauty. I listened to what seemed to me a courageous and fine piece of work, beautifully produced, and filled with excitement.

But apart from the fate of Camino Real, I think a more serious matter is involved. At least twice a year, every critic, during the dead period, writes a piece bemoaning the lack of courage, of imagination, of innovation in the American theatre. This being so, it is my opinion that when a play of courage, imagination and invention comes along, the critics should draw this to the attention of the theatre-goer. It becomes clear that when innovation and invention automatically draw bad notices, any backer will be cautious of investment, and furthermore will not playwrights stop experimenting if their plays will not be produced?

The democracy of art does not require universal acclaim. In fact instant acceptance is often a diagnostic of inferiority.

I hope you will find it in your heart to print this letter. I am not an investor, nor am I involved in the production but both you and I are amply involved in the survival and growth of the American Theatre.

See you soon, I hope. Yours in continued friendship and admiration.

John Steinbeck

In September, to be near Cy Feuer and Ernest Martin, who were to produce the musical play earlier described as an extension of *Cannery Row*, the Steinbecks rented a waterside cottage for themselves and the boys in Sag Harbor, Long Island.

The musical and the novel on the same subject that Steinbeck was writing at this time underwent several changes of title. Both were originally called *Bear Flag.* Ultimately the novel was published as *Sweet Thursday* (1954), and the musical appeared on Broadway as *Pipe Dream* (1955).

To Elizabeth Otis

Sag Harbor
September 14, 1953

Dear Elizabeth:

The time of the boys is over now. Elaine is in New York with Waverly this week and I am alone out here. The fall is coming quickly, a chill in the air and a hoarse wind blowing over the water. This is my favorite time and I couldn't be in a better place for it. I'll get my first draft of Bear Flag finished this week. That and walk and smell the good wind. I take great comfort from this wind and from the ocean. I didn't know I missed it so much. One gets so involved in New York.

Feuer and Martin are here most of the time and we work on the story line for the musical. That was, of course, one of the main reasons for coming here. They suggested it.

I have enjoyed writing this book, the B.F.

There is a school of thought among writers which says that if you enjoy writing something it is automatically no good and should be thrown out. I can't agree with this. Bear Flag may not be much good but for what it is, I think it is all right. Also I think it makes a nice balance for the weight of Eden. It is kind of light and gay and astringent. It may even say some good things.

I'll be sad to finish Bear Flag. I have really loved it. I am reluctant to start into the last two chapters. But I will. I do hope you love this book, a little self-indulgent though it may be. Try to like it.

Oscar Hammerstein took what I had of Bear Flag to England with him. He is very much interested in doing it. Now F & M have to sell the idea to Dick Rodgers. [Frank Loesser had resigned as composer.] I hope they will do it but I have my fingers crossed. That is supposed to be a secret by the way.

I keep thinking of the European trip next year and coming up with new ideas for things to write while there. I wouldn't be surprised if this should be one of the most productive times of all. It is time for me to do short things—but short things I like. I'm making a list of them.

Time goes so very quickly. Living in New York I never get a chance to write to you.

Now I'll get back to Bear Flag—refreshed and full of hell.

Love,
John

It's very late now. I just finished Bear Flag. It's crazy.

To Carlton A. Sheffield

New York
November 2, 1953

Dear Dook:

Meant to answer yours a long time ago and instead had a stretch of illness and a stretch of hard work. You say that my memory of events long past did not coincide with your memory of my original report of them. I wonder how accurate any of it is. I suspect that the most recent is the most accurate. Surely it is the most objective. I don't have to appear in a good light now, for anyone, even for myself, so perhaps it is less gilded. And I have less regard for truth than I once had with the result that I violate it less.

Anyway, a new book finished in first draft. I'm going to put it away for a few months. See whether it makes any difference in the rewrite. It should. I always want to rewrite them after it is too late.

> He wrote about this new book to the originals of two of the characters in it, who had also appeared in *Cannery Row,* Mack and Gay:
>
> "I've just finished another book about the Row. It is a continuation concerned not with what did happen but with what might have happened. The one can be as true as the other. I think it is a funny story, and sad too because it is what might have happened to Ed and didn't. I don't seem to be able to get over his death. But this will be the last piece about him."

I'm going back to Spain in the Spring. I feel an affinity there. Mexico is a kind of fake Spain. I feel related to Spanish people much more than to Anglo-Saxons. Unusual with my blood line—whatever it is. But they have kept something we seem to have lost.

It's a restless time for me between jobs. I look forward to it and then it comes and I don't know what to do with it. Once I was able to take up the slack by writing letters but that doesn't work any more. I write very few letters. There is a vast difference between writing letters and answering letters.

Then too, between jobs, the pressure is on me to write "short pieces" for this or that. It is generally considered that I can whip out a short piece—about anything you want. And damn it I can't. Or if I do it stinks. It takes just as long for a short piece as a long one.

Viking reissued six of my short novels in one volume and I happened to look at the list of my titles. It is frighteningly long. Gave me a shock at the passage of time. Lord, there are so many of them and they took so long. Recently I had an amusing lunch with six critics. They were the men who had knocked each book as it came out. Reading the books over again, they said they couldn't recall why they had got so mad. Harry Hansen said the books were so different one from another it used to make him mad because he thought it was a trick. Only now he said was he conscious of the design. Well, there wasn't any conscious design. I suppose what it boils down to is this—a man has only a little to say and he says it

474

over and over so it looks like a design. And the terrible thing is that I still don't know what it is I have to say, but I do know it isn't very complicated and surely it isn't new.

Let me hear from you.

love
John

The Steinbecks arrived in Seville in April, as planned.

"This is a lovely city," he wrote Elizabeth Otis. "The light is yellow where it is pink in Paris. The sand in the Seville bull ring is golden—the only place in the world. They take it from the river. I'll go and walk in the Court of Oranges which was laid out by the Moors in the 8th century. No doubt they had politics but they are long forgotten and only the beauty of the garden is left. It is hard to remember that this is always so."

To Elizabeth Otis

Hotel Madrid
Seville
April 21, 1954

Dear Elizabeth:

Can't seem to stay awake very much. But when luncheon is at 2:30 and dinner doesn't start until 10, it kind of cuts the day wrong for my training.

A few quotes for your pleasure. Written with black chalk on a wall—"Luisa, he who writes this is leaving you forever." On hotel porch an American woman and her little boy. Spaniard asked, "Do you like the bull fight?" Woman—"We haven't seen them but I'm sure we will like them. You see my

475

husband is a doctor so we are used to all that." Wouldn't you like to go to her husband for an office call? Over the horns with a scalpel. A new dicho or at least one I had never heard regarding drinking strong liquor. "El primero con agua, la segunda sin agua, el tercero como agua." The first with water, the second without water, the third like water. And it's true.

Am rereading Cervantes. He lived here and was in prison here and the city has not greatly changed. The little square where we drink beer and eat shrimps he mentions many times. The prison where he served was about a block from the bull ring and his window looked out on the Tower of Gold which is still there.

Also the habits of the gypsies have not changed. This morning I was sitting on a wall by the river when a gypsy asked to shine my shoes for a peseta. As he finished he caught his cloth under my rubber heel and ripped it off. It was a good trick. He then put on a new heel for 20 pesetas. Then he asked if I would like a new heel on the other shoe. It had taken me a long time to catch on. I told him one was a lesson but two would be an insult. I told him that for the first heel he would get 20 pesetas but for the second 20 days in jail. We ended good friends. In a way I love the gypsies. They are so uncompromisingly dishonest. Never for a moment do they fall into probity.

The weather continues wonderful and we are getting a little afraid it will rain for the Feria. It did last year and completely washed it out. That would be a shame.

I'm going to the Archives of the Indies tomorrow and try to get a look at the Columbian documents. They are all here. The bones of the old boy are supposed to be in the Cathedral, in a great bronze casket carried on the shoulders of bronze kings and bishops. But then, said bones are supposed to be in lots of places.

I wonder what's the matter with me? I want to sleep all the time.

Love to all,
John

Before leaving for Europe, Steinbeck had had a physical check-up with a view to taking out life insurance. In Madrid, he learned from Elizabeth Otis that the insurance had been refused.

"The insurance matter is strange," he wrote her on May 5. "Rose [Dr. Alan Rose, the cardiologist] told me only that my heart was abnormally small. I did not go to see him before we left, just forgot to. I will do as you say in Paris—find a specialist and let him give me an opinion. But I will not permit myself to become one of those heart cripples who spread their psychopathy around. It has been a good heart to me and I won't insult it now by being kind to it. That would be dreadful. I'm sorry about the insurance. That's a kind of betting game in which you bet against yourself and they have raised the odds on me—that is all. I'm sorry for my heirs but I can't help it. I'll just have to write as many books as I can."

To Elizabeth Otis

Hotel Lancaster
Paris
May 15, 1954

Dear Elizabeth:

We got in yesterday after six days of driving and it was good to get here. But the trip was fine, the car goes magnificently and the countryside is all green and gold and red poppies. We drove with the top down and the rains parted and we got only about three drops all the way. In Blois where we stayed overnight I seem to have got a mild sun stroke with a little fever. You should see our faces, just burned to a crisp. My nose has peeled four times without interval. But it was fine and for once even the driver was able to see the country.

This morning your letter came and we were very glad to get it. It seemed to us that we were cut off for an awfully long time. I was interested in the letter from your doctor. The only symptom I seem to have is shortness of breath and I think I

477

have always had that. That is the reason I was never a distance runner.

I think it has been good to be out of touch with the news. Nothing gives you more of a sense of not being able to help it anyway than not hearing news.

Elaine is so delighted to be in Paris that she is bubbling. I never knew anyone to love any place more. She hit the street this morning ostensibly to buy soap and Kleenex but really just to walk about.

That's all, dear. I'll be writing to you often now that I am a little more settled.

Love to you all there,
John

Fannie Crow, Elaine Steinbeck's college roommate, at this time Steinbeck's secretary, and Mary Dekker, were living in the Steinbecks' New York house.

To Fannie Crow and Mary Dekker

Hotel Lancaster
[Paris]
May 21 [1954]

Dear Fannie and Mary:

Elaine has been taking the rap on this trip. We got to Paris a week ago and I promptly hit the sack again with the bug, so she has had to do all of the house hunting. This morning she found a pretty little house right in the center of Paris and we will take it if we can get it. It is 1 Avenue Marigny—a very distinguished address right across the street from the President's palace—half a block from the Champs Elysées. If you want Paris—there you got Paris. It is very French and I think we will love it. Besides it has a courtyard you can drive a car

into—a covered courtyard. The kids could even play basket-
ball there in rainy weather.

The Covicis have been here. They are having a perfectly
wonderful time. You never saw anyone have better.

The Marigny house has a terrace on the roof with lots of
flower boxes so we can have geraniums and morning glories
and all such things. Oh! I hope we get it. It even has a little
study where I can work. What joy. And right beside it is a
park with ponies and a carousel and balloon men and millions of children play and the whole thing shaded with chest-
nut trees.

Tell me—did the wistaria bloom—any of it? Kazans have
bought the house three gardens down, the one with the gigantic wistarias. We'll be so glad to have them as neighbors.
Some time I am going to put trellis against our brick wall and
load it with wistaria. It is a wonderful plant for the city. So
fresh and green. We'll make it nice there some time.

Tonight our French publisher is giving a whing-ding for
us. I dread it but it will probably be fun. I won't understand
one word in 20 and that will make it all the better.

Later—just got back from my reception. Must have been
five hundred people and I had to do everything except tap
dance—and did.

We have the house. We are very excited.

[signed] Jean
(par Helène)

To Elizabeth Otis

1 Avenue de Marigny
Paris
May 27, 1954

Dear Elizabeth:
We are moved into our house now and very comfortable.
The second day, news of Capa's death which shocked me

479

very deeply. We had got to thinking him indestructible. Have been sitting with his people here, who are completely shattered. I shall miss Capa very much.

We have a cook named Rose. Our concierge is Spanish, which helps me a lot because I am helpless in French.

You know I have had an idea in the back of my mind for a long time. Here in France I get interviewed all the time. I spend hours with journalists helping them to make some kind of a story and then when it comes out it is garbled and slanted and lousy. I wondered why I did not write my own interviews and charge for those hours of time and have it come out my way. In other words, why should I not write 800 words a week for one French paper, simply called something like an American in Paris—observations, essay, questions, but unmistakably American. I asked some French newspaper men and they were violently enthusiastic. I said I would try some pilot pieces and see how they worked. Well I have three now and they go fine. Hoffman [Michel Hoffman, Steinbeck's French literary agent] will sell them to one of the big Paris papers, perhaps Figaro. Also I have made a good start on my first short story of the series. I told you I felt like working and I do. I want to turn out quite a swatch of work before the kids get here in two weeks.

Well, we gave Pat and Dorothy a farewell dinner at Vefour —damned expensive but they loved it.

Elaine is getting the house to running smoothly and it is very pleasant. The weather has finally turned warm and summer is coming in. I have a workroom with a window looking out over a garden. Couldn't want better. I intend to work in the morning and walk in the afternoon. And we hope to keep the social life down to a minimum.

Today is Ascension Day so all the stores are closed. Two days ago the President's daughter got married right across the street. Street was roped off and we had a box seat on our terrace. It will be a fine place to sit in the summer and watch Paris go by.

Love for now and I'll let you know what comes of the newspaper pieces.

John

To Elizabeth Otis

[Paris]
May 31, 1954

Dear Elizabeth:

I think it is time for me to start another letter to you. I take considerable comfort in them. Haven't much of anything to say but a great verve for saying it. I have the four pieces ready for Hoffman to sell to a Paris paper. I heard today that Figaro wants it. If the pieces do well here, do you think it would be a good idea to try them in Rome and Germany? I have got well into my first little story. And I think it is going well; a little hard at first establishing how I want to tell it so made some false starts but I think it is on the way finally.

I have been thinking a great deal about you this week and I think it is just nonsense for you not to come over here this summer. I can write you a letter telling you that it is necessary to straighten out business and for that matter Sol [Sol Leibner, his friend and accountant] could probably work it out so that I could pay your air fare. You think about this, do you hear? But don't get your mind off it the way you used to. I remember once you would have said, Nonsense. But you are changed too. I really think I am more relaxed than I can ever remember being. Every once in a while I get mad as hell at Elaine, particularly when after a few drinks she takes out after me on one of my shortcomings, but I get good and honestly mad and tell the truth about why and then it goes away and is gone. I don't think I am mean about it any more, which is a very good thing.

You wouldn't think what crazy things I have become capable of doing. On June 12, 13 and 14, there is a gigantic fete in the gardens of the Tuileries—all kinds of people are going to appear, celebrities of all kinds and the purpose is to collect money for the widows and children of the dead of General Le Clerc's army, the one which liberated Paris. I am asked to go three hours each day to sit and be looked at and probably to autograph books for his charity and I have agreed to do it and I am even looking forward to it. Isn't that something? You know I couldn't have brought myself to do that before.

Tomorrow morning I am going to the flower market at the Ile de la Cité to buy red geranium plants for our terraces. We will probably do a lot of sitting out there and having tea and all such.

This sounds as though we were on the go all the time and that is not true at all. We stay home quite a bit. Last night was the anniversary of the day I met Elaine five years ago. We drank champagne and had an era of good feeling. E. has stuck to her bed today. She says it started out as a hangover and then she got to liking it.

We are the luckiest people in the world. First in getting this house and then in finding a wonderful cook, and she is wonderful, and now we have a fine maid and the whole bunch like it with us and the house is very gay. The Spanish concierge washes my shirts and makes them just beautiful. The cook, maid and concierge are all friends and they love being together, the place rings with happiness. And my work is coming well now and that makes me feel lucky also. So you see, you will just have to come over. I'll write a couple of extra stories to pay your expenses.

And one more reason for you to come over! Think of the postage I would save.

Love to all there,
John

Richard Rodgers and Oscar Hammerstein II had taken over the writing as well as the production of the new musical. He wrote them jubilantly describing the Paris house:

". . . next to Rothschilds and across the street from the President of France. How's that for an address for a Salinas kid? Even if we were members of the F.F.S.V. (First Families of the Salinas Valley). Elaine has become Parisienne. I seem to retain some vestiges of my past because everyone tries to sell me dirty pictures."

To Elizabeth Otis

Paris
June 13, 1954

Dear Elizabeth:

Yesterday was Cat's birthday and we celebrated good. He had his birthday dinner on the Eiffel Tower as he had requested.

I had no sleep in me later so sat up and wrote a Figaro piece and part of another. The comment on the first two has been large and favorable.

I had a good and long letter from Brenner [Gertrudis Brenner, a psychologist Steinbeck had consulted in New York the previous winter.] What a good woman she is! I kind of needed it too because I had taken a deep relapse. Got crowded by all the extra-marital facets of marriage and achieved a "what the hell" feeling that was like old times. Sometimes I do seem to pay a lot for marriage. But I suppose maybe I don't give enough—only all I have. And I'm sure I'm a thankless, ungrateful son of a bitch for even thinking this. I just don't have any place to run to, it seems sometimes. Anyway, the remarkable thing was that just when I hit bottom the letter came from Brenner telling me to be not too worried if I took a dive because it was perfectly natural. She must know by the quality of progress about when it will happen—like a drunk who falls off the wagon. Anyway, it gave me hope that the backslide was not permanent. Day before yesterday I had blood tests and a new electrocardiogram. Good man too. Said my heart seemed all right for anyone who was as old and as nervous as I am. Also said he would advise against climbing Mt. Everest and that I probably smoked too much. Said heart was fast, as everyone says. After he looks at the old cardiographs I am going to have a long talk with him. And then forget the whole damned thing. I am not likely to get less nervous. I may stop smoking perhaps but that would be largely because I am disgusted with the whole process. And again I may not. I wouldn't even try to cut down. It would have to be all or nothing. I might try stopping for a week or so, just to see how hard it might be.

I've got two more Figaro pieces but haven't got to the second short story yet. Oscar Hammerstein sent me the first three scenes of the show, complete with lyrics and just wonderful. He seems happy about it and so am I.

Don't worry about my complaining in the beginning of this letter. I guess I'm just bitching. I'm a little like an automobile. Get one flat tire and you want to throw the whole thing away. Wish to God I could learn to write as I would like to write. I fall so damn far short every time. But I'll keep plugging and damn it—one day I'll maybe turn up with something. The next story might have something in it—if I ever get it written.

So long and love,
John

To Elizabeth Otis

Paris
June 14, 1954

Dear Elizabeth:

Last night was the big Kermesse in the Tuileries Garden for charity. There were literally hundreds of thousands of people standing and sitting in the rain. They carried our names on big cards and we had to walk down a long runway. There were actors and picture people. Then I went to a booth where with all of the French writers I autographed I guess a thousand books and more cards. People had to buy the books and that goes to the charity. I asked if Del Duca [his French publisher] gave the books without profit and they said no. As a matter of fact he unloaded just about a whole edition of La Flamme [*Burning Bright*]. It was a most shocking experience and at the same time very interesting. I did it for nearly four hours

484

yesterday and my hand nearly came off at the wrist.

Next week I have to go to a formal dinner being given to me by the French Academy. Don't I get to do the damnedest things?

> Love to all,
> John

To Elizabeth Otis

Paris
June 17, 1954

Dear Elizabeth:

The short stories languish. I have been thinking about them a lot, heaven knows.

It seems to me that most writers in America, and I myself among them, have gone almost entirely in the direction of the past. We are interested in setting down and celebrating old times. It is almost as though we wanted to define a past which probably never did exist. The stories of childhood, the stories of the frontier, the novels of one's old aunts, etc. This is fine but there can be enough of it. There are very few American writers, notably writing for the New Yorker, who write about today or even today projected into the future. With something of a shock I realize that I have written about nothing current for a very long time. It has occurred to me that we may be so confused about the present that we avoid it because it is not clear to us. But why should that be a deterrent? If this is a time of confusion, then that should be the subject of a good writer if he is to set down his time. For instance, the effect on young people of the McCarthy hearings is going to be with them all their lives. The responses to this spectacle, whatever they are, are going to be one of the keys to our future attitudes toward everything. If such things are not written as fiction, a whole pattern of present-day thinking and feeling will be lost. We will have the records but not what people felt about them. Do you have any thinking about this? I really wonder whether I am able to write such things. Might be very good to try.

Love,
jn

To Gwyndolyn Steinbeck
IN ROME

Paris
July 24, 1954

Dear Gwyn:

I had your letter this morning and hasten to answer so you will get this before you go away. I think it would be ridiculous, given the chance, that the boys should not see some of Italy before they go back. While they are looking, you don't think they are getting anything and then it comes out later that they got a very great deal. So of course I will send them down to Rome.

I don't think there will be any difficulty here about travelling alone, and besides the kids are getting really good about doing things. I make a practice of letting them go out in the neighborhood alone and they are very careful about streets. It gives them a great sense of responsibility and besides they are learning a lot both of French and of Paris that way. Cat has made friends in the park right around the corner from us, both American and French kids. Yesterday he strolled down to the American Embassy which is two blocks away, walked up to the Marine Guard and said, "I hope you don't mind my saying so, but haven't you got very thick glasses?" And the guard said, "Hell, son, I got to see some way."

We are getting a boat on the Seine for Thom's birthday and for his main present I got in Munich a racing car which runs with a real diesel engine. You may find that this he will want to carry in his hand but I can't help that. It is a wonderful thing. No one could resist it, and of course he doesn't know about it yet. Don't you think as long as you are going to see

486

them within a very few weeks of Thom's birthday, that a letter telling them of your plans for them and the statement that you will have a kind of second birthday for both of them in Rome, might not be the answer? Then they would have that to look forward to.

Thom has dropped some stomach, but not as much as he should. They are swimming every day and walking for miles and that probably has as much to do with it as anything else. They are fine boys and very sweet and I think the summer has been very good for them.

I do hope you will get at Thom's block against reading and writing because that is what it is, a kind of a panic. He has told me that he knows things, which he does, but that he simply cannot write them down. When it is insisted that he write answers he goes into a blue funk, but he is quite capable of reciting in great detail anything he has been told. If the block could be removed, he would be ahead of his age, not behind.

If you want them earlier than we had thought, that will be all right too. I wish I could have seen Paris and Rome at their ages.

So long, and let me hear from you.

John

To Elia Kazan

Paris
July 24, 1954

Dear Gadg:

A letter from Annie Laurie this morning with wonderful things she has heard about the film [*East of Eden*]. I am eager to see it and I probably won't until we go home in December. But it is good to have reports. Our summer is going fast and I am conscious of a stirring of restlessness. I shall not be averse to moving on when the time comes. The small short pieces I have been doing for Figaro are all right but not really satisfying. They must of necessity be so guided at the French that perhaps they suffer from a special, almost precious quality. Here we have a whole nation with its feelings hurt and doubly touchy because of it. In conquered Germany you find the treacherous slavishness that will knife you when it can. But France is hurt in its pride, hurt in its whole conception of itself. I have said some pretty brutal things in the pieces but I have coated them so that they could be received at all. And I am getting just a little tired of them. Treading lightly has never been one of my gifts. I want to build a life again and hell catch the hindmost. I am not a good diplomat. The role wears thin with me. We will have fun the rest of the time but I think right at this moment, I am a little homesick for 206.

Waverly and her friend set out on their trip to Greece in a rented car. The boys have about six more weeks with us before they have to go.

It's along in the summer now so that we begin to think Greeceward. Are you so thinking? We haven't really made any plans yet. In fact we are kind of holding up ours so they can match yours if that is possible.

I know how busy you are but I do like to hear from you and your Moll. Would you care to dig a secret tunnel between the houses? We went to a chateau the other night that has four or five of them. And we think we live in dangerous times.

So long
John

Steinbeck was fond of Dorothy Rodgers, the composer's wife, and admired her for her several successful inventions.

To Mrs. Richard Rodgers

Dear Dorothy:

I have an invention which I would like to submit for your consideration, while your husband is undertaking his various artistic assignments (surely a desirable practice but not a money maker as we more practical people understand it).

There should be several approaches to an invention. First, is it needed, second, can you make people believe it is needed, third, are replacements needed? I believe that my invention fulfills nearly all of these.

Many millions of women wash out their underwear and stockings every night usually in the wash basin of the bath rooms. A goodly number of them leave the clothing soaking in the basin so that a male getting up a little earlier, has to wash his razor in the bath tub. There is nothing glamourous about washing stockings, panties and bras.

One night having nothing to do, I put a couple of pairs of my own nylon socks in a fruit jar with one third water and a little detergent, replaced the cap and shook the jar about twenty times like a cocktail shaker. It worked very well. I then added four marbles to the thing and it worked doubly well because the marbles did the rubbing thing and greatly speeded up the process. This is the whole principle but a fruit jar is much too simple.

I have considered a plastic jar made like an hour glass with a screw cap on one of the ends, wide mouth for the introduction of the intimate garments. The narrow part of the hour glass to serve as a handle for the whole thing and also to cause the water and soap to cause a minor tornado when the whole is shaken. Instead of marbles the activators should be round balls of some semi-hard wood like beech wood, so smooth that they could not injure fabric and not heavy enough to crush. The lower part of the thing is filled with warm water, and on top of this a tiny envelope of detergent rather beautifully perfumed should be added. The top is then

489

put on and the whole thing shaken say thirty times. This will completely wash ordinarily dirty things. If they are more than ordinarily dirty the clothing may be left in the container over night, in the morning a little more shaking and rinsed in the basin.

The containers should be made of a plastic in the colors to match various bath rooms, pink, yellow, blue, green or black. The packets of soap should be distinctive, (just ordinary soap or detergent but perfumed, sandalwood, lavender, etc.). The packets should not be expensive but should be exactly the proper amount so that one envelope washed one set of clothing. This is the replacement so necessary to any paying invention. The advertising should say that you keep your hands out of soap and keep your husband from blowing his brains out. The container itself should be rather handsome so that it would be one more of those bits of clutter which we love so well.

It is that simple and darn me if I don't think it would work. A little advertising magic about the gentle swirling of water, the caressing of the soap and the clean soapless hands. It should have a gay name like the socktail shaker and the indication that the thirty shakes of the thing reduced weight and built up the bust while with the other hand one washed ones teeth.

Please give my hearty regards to Richard and Oscar and all others there. And we will see you just before Christmas.

Yours in invention
John

P.S. If you don't believe my invention, put some stockings in a fruit jar and try it.

To Marcia Ross OF THE MC INTOSH AND OTIS STAFF and Sol Leibner

Paris
August 20, 1954

Dear Marcia and Sol:

I am writing you a joint letter because there are a number of things I want to say and to ask in a number of fields, financial, spiritual, aesthetic, economic, pragmatic and you will probably add psychotic.

A letter from Sol recently said I only had forty-five hundred dollars in the bank, left out of seventy thousand that had come in this year so far. I do not think it is very good policy to scare me. I have not spent any money I could have avoided spending except possibly for the car. I could have bought one of those second hand dogs which do not work. Anyway, I went into a tailspin and for a week was so concerned with my brokeness and with the seeming impossibility of ever pulling out that I was incapable of working. In other words, the time taken out for worry about my shaky financial status took the time and more than the effort of three short stories or one long one. I imagine this could be estimated in money from previous performance.

At the end of the tailspin I pulled myself out with the following self-indulgence. OK, I had 4,500 dollars in the bank. But I have money coming in regularly. I have 24% of the movie East of Eden just finished. I have a best-selling novel which is doing very well and a percentage in the musical which will be made of it. I am not in debt except for the mortgage on the house which I am told is simple good business. I do have to pay alimony and that apparently is a permanent situation but it comes off the top before taxes.

In other words, in resources and futures I am not only in better shape than I have ever been but in better shape than anyone I know, but if I can be made to worry enough the work that is at the source of this income can be dried up *at* the source.

Now I can skimp worriedly along.

491

> It should be understood that he was living in a beautiful house in Paris, maintaining a household, of eight people including family and staff, and driving a new Jaguar.

I am getting to feel guilty if I even consider buying a pair of pliers. My glasses are mended with wire because I don't want to spend the money for new frames. I can't control the kitchen or the number of people who eat here. Do you realize that this is all a bunch of bloody nonsense? I have a life expectancy which is dwindling and I'm not having any fun. I am living in the most beautiful city in the world working my ass off. For what? For whom? And when I'm not working it off I'm worrying it off.

So I can't get insurance. My insurability is not going to be improved by worry. I have to make up my mind whether I am going to be a bookkeeper or a writer. I don't think I can be both and if I am not a writer there will not be anything to keep books about. I get a to hell with it feeling pretty often now. The more money I make the more trouble I'm in. I actually feel guilty to ask for four hundred dollars to buy a magnificent painting because I can't see any way to deduct it. I must kill this growing fixation pretty quickly or I'm not going to be around very long.

Since I am about to set out on traveling and since Elaine will have to close this house, I think the next draft should be sizable. I am gathering almost inexhaustible material and I can't buy it with peanuts.

Every trip may be the last and I'm not going to spend the rest of my life to make my heirs happy. There has never been in the history of the world enough money to make heirs happy.

I do not mean this letter to be a charge of anything or an attack on anything. I just want to let you know that I have to get rid of an attitude which is poisoning me and killing off not only my work but my desire to work.

Now that is as ill-tempered a letter as I ever remember writing but it is only aimed at a state of mind I must get rid of.

Love to all there and please don't take this too much to heart. But I also hope you will know how serious I am about it.

John

To Mrs. Richard Rodgers

Paris
August 26, 1954

Dear Dorothy:

Thank you for your letter about inventions. Maybe I'd better stick to my last or even my first. My grandfather Sam Hamilton was always inventing things and patenting them. Mother claimed he kept the family broke with fees to patent lawyers. When he got a good one it was stolen so fast it whistled. And then he kept us broke with an infringement suit which he lost through running out of money.

I think I'll go on inventing on the side. Some years ago I invented silk slip covers for the lapels of a dark suit to make it a dinner jacket. The stripe went on with straps—whole kit 10 bucks. It was for salesmen and for people who fly a lot and can't take much luggage. A lovely idea. A friend of mine in the clothing business told me it would not be popular with the clothing industry.

Then I invented stirrups for long nightgowns to keep them from climbing (unless you want them to). This just got me in trouble with the pyjama industry. My final defeat came when I invented people.

Well, Somer ben a goin oot. When we all get home—let's have a hell of a winter.

Love to Dick
John

To Pascal Covici

Paris
September 2, 1954

Dear Pat:

Everything seems to be ending at one time which is as it should be. The printed stationery is gone. The boys left for Rome yesterday and Waverly goes tonight; that leaves Elaine and me until the 9th. Then we go to London.

The boys went very gaily. We will not do what Gwyn does —that is let any sadness creep in. The night before we had a party for them and drank champagne and toasted them and they toasted us and we sang songs. In the morning we all went out to the airport with them, and made a fiesta of it. I feel sad without them but I don't want them to know it. I think it's much the better way, don't you? With Way it doesn't make so much difference. She has so many interests outside of us. And later the boys will have that too. I am not worried about them any more. They are so alive and good. They will get through just fine in spite of Gwyn and me—not because of us. I feel really good about them. I do have the habit of listening for them on the stairs but that will go away in a few days.

I have three more pieces of writing to do before I go to London. Maybe I can get started on them tomorrow. The Figaro pieces are completed in a blaze of glory. It has been a good series I think and I have liked doing it. I don't want to do anything but short things until I get home. Then I hope I will have a sharp clarity and a whole new approach toward the new book. And do you know—if I start work on it soon after the first of the year I will probably have it done by fall. I think about it a lot but I try not to think too closely about it because that would be like writing it.

Well, we put Waverly on the plane last night. Everyone a little tearful and so the summer of the children ended.

Now it's later in the day and I have managed to do a little work. But it isn't good work and must be thrown out. Too bad.

love to all
John

494

And to Elizabeth Otis:

"Time in Paris is closing up now. Filled with the restlessness of ending things."

To Webster F. Street

Paris
September 6 [1954]

Dear Toby:

Your good letter came this morning, full of news and cracks. I am answering it right away because Elaine and I are leaving Paris the day after tomorrow.

It's amazing how I have lost touch with the West Coast but inevitable. I haven't heard from anyone out there in such a long time. And why would I? There's no point of contact. New York is my home and I think Paris will be increasingly. I love it here. Maybe some time I will have a permanent apartment here. Of course I hear from my sisters regularly but all of the other contacts shrink down. I haven't heard from Dook for a very long time. I think he resents me. And perhaps I deserve it. But shoot—I only have one little life and there isn't a hell of a lot left of it and I want to have as much fun with it as I can. And associations are only kept alive if there is proximity. People change and each resents the change in the other, not thinking he has changed. And it isn't actually change either but only a non parallel existence. I have always been a mobile unit in wish if not in actuality. I thought that in middle age I would get over the restlessness—but I don't. It's just the same. I even go through the form of establishing a home. But it's only a place to go away from and to come back to. I am fortunate in that Elaine has my same restlessness. She will move at the stir of a suitcase.

I guess I don't know anyone very well any more. Right now I know Paris better than any place—and pretty soon it will be

495

Rome or as Thom spells it Roam. Maybe he has the blood too. love to you and Lois and the new generation

John

To Mr. and Mrs. Elia Kazan

Hotel Ritz
London
September 14, 1954

Dear Gadg and Molly:

Drawing a white night. Have been seeing a lot of theatre. Some good but I even like the bad. I have no taste. Wish I could talk to you. A whole revolution is going on in me. I talk and talk and I don't know whether or not it means anything. I suspect it does. I do nothing except short pieces. Good thing. I'm not ready to start yet. When I do it's going to bust a gut. It's hard to throw over 30 years work but necessary if the work has pooped out. It isn't that it was bad but that I've used it up.

Do you think I could write a play with no tricks, just he said and she said?

love to all there
John

To Elizabeth Otis

London
September 17, 1954

When a writer starts in very young, his problems apart from his story are those of technique, of words, of rhythms, of story methods, of transition, of characterization, of ways of creating effects. But after years of trial and error most of these things are solved and one gets what is called a style. It is then that a story conceived falls into place neatly and is written down having the indelible personal hallmark of the writer. This is thought to be an ideal situation. And the writer who is able to achieve this is thought to be very fortunate.

I have only just arrived at a sense of horror about this technique. If I think of a story, it is bound automatically to fall into my own personal long struggle for technique. But the penalty is terrible. The tail of the kite is designed to hold it steady in the air but it also prevents versatility in the kite and in many cases drags it to the earth. Having a technique, is it not possible that the technique not only dictates how a story is to be written but also what story is to be written? In other words, style or technique may be a straitjacket which is the destroyer of a writer. It does seem to be true that when it becomes easy to write the writing is not likely to be any good. Facility can be the greatest danger in the world. But is there any alternative? Suppose I want to change my themes and my approach. Will not my technique, which has become almost unconscious, warp and drag me around to the old attitudes and subtly force the new work to be the old?

I want to dump my technique, to tear it right down to the ground and to start all over. I have been thinking of this a lot. I think I have one answer but I have not developed it enough to put it down yet.

[unsigned]

To Graham Watson

OF CURTIS BROWN, LTD., STEINBECK'S ENGLISH AGENT

Saint Paul de Vence, France
September 29 [1954]

Dear Graham:

We have been driving very slowly, savoring the country the way you'd run wine around the back of your tongue. It is lovely. The first relaxed thing I've had in many years.

I am wearing the hat with great success. Men, prone to take it lightly as a piece of solid British frippery, are thrown into a paroxysm of admiration at the beautiful salmon flies.

I have cut off my moustache for the first time in 30 years—Elaine is not sure she likes me with a nude face. After all she does not like to move furniture. It occurred to me after all of these years that retaining a little scrap of hair as a memorial of an hairy time was silly. I think I grew it in the first place because my upper lip is so long I was afraid people would try to put a bit in my mouth. But it is more probable that I aspired to an erudition and a Latin sophistication and maturity I felt was withheld. Now that I am sure these latter are not possible I have got rid of the poor gesture. I once had a beard—but shaved it off when I found I was trying to live up to it. It's bad enough to have confused impulses but worse if you can't remember what they were.

We wish you were with us. The weather is warm and autumnal.

love to both
John

The moustache reappeared almost at once. Not many years later he grew the beard again and kept it for the rest of his life.

To Elizabeth Otis

Dear Elizabeth:

We have been driving very slowly. We have stayed in beautiful places. Last night at Les Baux and wandered in the ghost city. You undoubtedly know Saint Paul de Vence. It is above the Mediterranean in back of Nice but is a little walled medieval town. Just got in a little while ago so have only seen a little part of it. I have thought so much about the screed I sent you from London re technique [see page 497] and it seems truer to me all of the time. And the necessity for a new start is also valid. I have thought and am still thinking of the transition. Perhaps the hard discipline of play which does not have the advantage of the novelist's apology and explanation but only the iron discipline of form and the requirement that dialogue carry the whole burden not only of movement but of character. This is something I do not know and so would have to struggle with. But I have no idea in this of abandoning the novel but only of starting fresh with it. Perhaps some transition work in this form would do it. I am purposely not writing anything now. But it will not be too long before I will have to. And I would like to have some clean approach. I thought of a little playlet last night when I could not sleep. A strange little story I haven't thought of for years and which I now might be able to write. I will probably bore you with these searchings for quite a long time. Excuse it please. It is more than important to me.

Love to all,
John

499

To Elizabeth Otis

Rome
October 29, 1954

Dear Elizabeth:

I think I will start a letter to you tonight. The reception for me [at the Embassy] was quite pleasant and no strain at all. The guest list was pretty fabulous. One amusing thing happened. They wanted to make a display of some of my books. They have about 70 volumes of various titles in the library. Not one was in and they couldn't get them in, so they had to go out and buy a dozen copies.

Last night Mrs. Luce [American Ambassador to Italy] asked us to a cocktail party and then to a very small dinner party. It was pleasant and we both think she is a pretty remarkable woman.

News last night of Hemingway's Nobel Prize which pleases me greatly. He should have had it before this.

Italy is full of flying saucers. In the street the other day everyone was looking up. Thousands of people said they saw something. Clare Luce says she saw something. A football game stopped the other day and 60 thousand people saw three of them go over. I myself have not seen anything but all Italy is greatly excited. I am asked what I think about it in every interview. I have a stock answer which I may even believe. People see things. In the Middle Ages they saw angels. Later witches. Now saucers. I don't know what is there but I do know that people see things. Always have.

Strange. I have a feeling that everything has stopped and is waiting—rather like some Sunday afternoons or the hour before a party. A change is coming. I can feel it very plain. And it is a good change. This is real dope talk as far as reason is concerned but it is a skin feeling. And maybe that is as good a way as any to evaluate.

Elaine is out doing last-minute shopping (Christmas). We

have a must list as long as your arm. Seems to jump every year.

I guess that's all. I have to write to the boys.

Love,
John

To Pascal Covici

Positano, Italy
December 1, 1954

Dear Pat:

Now we're on the last lap. Tomorrow we go to Naples and Sunday get on the boat. We've had it. Both kind of worn out. It's been a long haul and perhaps we have seen too much. That is very possible. We will stop at Pompei and Herculaneum on our way to Naples though. We went to Salerno and to Red Beach where I landed ten years ago. It looks different. They have planted little pines where it was all shell holes and blood. But the place still had a kind of horrid charge for me like a remembered nightmare. I never did write what I really thought of the war. It wouldn't have been encouraging to those who had to fight it. But some of the disgust and sorrow came back on that beach two days ago. And people blithely talk about another one. You can never talk people out of fighting. Every new generation has to know by trying. Thucydides says it was true in his day.

Anyway, we'll be seeing you soon now. It is going to be very comfortable to slide under my writing board even if I just sit there and do nothing.

Elaine sends love to all.

John

1955 1957
1956

Steinbeck

"*I must say
I do have fun with
my profession....*"

1955 *Pipe Dream* (musical adaptation of *Sweet Thursday*) produced. Bought summer cottage in Sag Harbor, Long Island.

1956 Covered both national conventions for Louisville *Courier-Journal* and syndicate.

1957 *The Short Reign of Pippin IV* published. Correspondent in Europe, again for Louisville *Courier-Journal* and syndicate. Began research on Malory and *Morte d'Arthur*.

When the Steinbecks had rented the house in Sag
Harbor, Long Island, during the summer of 1953, he
was immediately attracted to the village. It was for
him an East Coast equivalent of the Monterey
Peninsula. In the spring of 1955, he bought a small
house outside the village, in an oak grove on a cove.
It marked his complete acceptance of the East Coast
as his permanent home.

𝒯o Webster F. Street

Sag Harbor
July 5, 1955

Dear Toby:

This afternoon, we are taking our boat off Montauk Point
to fish for blues. They are fine fighting fish and wonderful to
eat and they are said to be running well right now. It is about
a forty-five minute run in our boat which will do thirty-four
miles an hour if it has to. It is a sea skiff, lapstrake, twenty
feet long and eight feet of beam and a hundred horse power
Grey marine engine. I could cross the Atlantic in her if I
could carry the gasoline. Has a convertible top like a car so
that you can put it up when green water comes over the bow.
Also it only draws eighteen inches so we can take it into little
coves and very near the shore if only we watch the charts for
rocks and depth. This is fabulous boating country and fishing
country too.

We bring them home alive and cook them while they are
still kicking and are they delicious. My fear of starvation

505

disappears when I am near the ocean. I figure I can always catch my dinner. And the Atlantic is very much richer in varieties than the Pacific. Lobsters, clams, crabs, oysters and many kinds of fish. I really love it out here. Am going to winterize this little house so I can come up when it is cold. My little harbor freezes over and then you fish through the ice. The house needs double walls and an oil furnace but I'll do a lot of it myself.

I am actually losing some stomach working around here and haven't felt so good in years. Maybe I shall come to a healthy old age rather than a sickly one. Best of all, maybe I shall not come to any old age at all. I remember how Ed Ricketts used to be haunted by thought of age. He was neurotic about it. I've often thought that if he hadn't been killed he would have had a miserable time of it because I do not think he could have accepted change. In himself, I mean.

You know, Toby, I notice something in you that is also true in me. You are sharply critical of any theatre you see. I am also when I don't see much of it but I become much kinder and accepting when I see a lot of it and I become kindest when I have a show myself. Have you ever gone through the putting of a show together with all the work and hope and sweat? I guess that is why professionals are the best audience in the world. Oscar Hammerstein says that when you buy a ticket to the theatre you have more or less contracted to go along with it and furnish your part to the general illusion. God knows it is a hard enough medium and when it clicks it is just great.

The wind is coming up. We're going to have a really rough trip this afternoon and that is when I really love my boat. It is such a good sea boat, just kind of loves itself into the waves instead of fighting them. I guess it is the same hull the Vikings used and they got around.

That's all for this time. I have to write some letters of refusal. I get asked to speak more damned places and word doesn't seem to get around that I don't ever speak any place about anything.

love to you
and all of yours
John

To Mr. and Mrs. Elia Kazan
IN ISTANBUL

New York
[1955]

Dear Molly and Gadg:

We think you are writing way beyond the call of duty. The picture with the beard came in this morning—formidable. Do you think you will keep it when you get back? The trip sounds fine. I do hope you won't let any business interfere with your trip. I am taking care of all that for you. I have signed you up to direct two plays and I hope you like them. Meanwhile, I am casting and my sincere wish is that you will approve of the people I am getting. I have agreed for you to go into rehearsal on the first one, Dog Island, June 18th. You should be ready for the second one, Blindness Alley, early in September. Do you want me to take on anything else for you after that?

I've made a few changes in your office which I know will please you. I wallpapered it with a gay, flowered pattern and painted the ceiling black. Then I took out all those ugly wood cabinets and put in two breakfronts of Chinese chippendale. It makes the office seem kind of airy. I removed that curved couch which was giving me round shoulders and put in a double bed which speeded up casting immensely. Along the front (Times Square side) I put a row of windowboxes with red geraniums. It brightens the whole neighborhood.

Marie [Kazan's secretary] has made a great comeback. She was married last week and about time. I'm going to be godfather. She married a real nice boy in the artificial limb trade and she seems to be very happy. He gave her a sterling silver kneecap for a wedding present. In your absence I exercise the droit de seigneur. I hate to see beautiful old customs lapse.

Well, old pal, as you can see I'm standing in for you. Don't worry about a thing. The crack down the front of your house is not serious at all. Molly's mother just got excited about it the way women will, but I showed her how to stuff it with newspapers and practically no draft gets in now.

We both send love. This may be the last time I can catch you. Don't take any wooden drachma.

John

To Waverly Scott
ABOUT TO BECOME ENGAGED

Sag Harbor
July 8, 1955

Dear Way:

This letter is just as private as you want to make it. You can do with it what you want including what you just thought of.

Everyone in the world is going to give you advice. That is not my intention. I always suspect advice because the advisor is usually the least equipped person to give it, i.e. child counsellors who have no children, marriage helpers who have never married.

I have a feeling, although this association is pretty damned sexy that it is also pretty carefully thought out. Many times when it was considered that you were romantically stunned, you were just sleepy.

I would like to ask you certain questions and I don't want to know the answers. They are things drawn out of my own messy past. If I had known about them then I probably would have done exactly the things I did, and yet the answers to them bore little disasters.

You know of course without my telling you that no two people can ever like each other all the time under all circumstances. Also, it is equally true that if you know everything that is going to happen to you, you wouldn't get married at all.

I always thought that the marriage was between me and the girl I was marrying and that it isn't anybody's business. And this was true except that anybody makes it his business. You think you are going in as an individual, cut off and free and gradually you find that you have a trail on you like a comet and that the other party has too. You don't lose these

508

trails. There is no way to. I think the service says, "Forsaking all others—" but no one forsakes all others. And doesn't the Old Testament say that first and final loyalty is to wife and husband? That also is not possible. Families have a way of sticking around and background does too.

My questions are simple and terrible. They are not personal and they don't have to do with Jim. Therefore you can show this letter to him if you wish or if you think well.

1. After the hay, (and believe me I am not knocking it, I love it) is the other person fun? Under ideal conditions the very best time is *after* when you are fulfilled and content and open. Sex is a kind of war but the quiet time after, if there is love and interest, is about the only time when a man and woman get together and become one thing. Then they merge and their minds as well as their bodies are a unit. This doesn't happen too often unfortunately but it is one of the diagnostics of success. If it is that way then there is a chance.

2. You can get around and accept big things in another person. It is the tiny things that drive you crazy. Carol picked at her finger nails all of the time and knowing it bothered me she did it more, not out of meanness but simply because she couldn't control it. I suppose it was unconscious punishment of me for things in me that bothered her. Odors are curious things too. Elaine's skin smells to me like new grass, a lovely smell. But I knew a girl whose skin smelled like earth under an old house. It bothered me but I thought I could ignore it or get used to it, but the fact of the matter is that you can't ignore anything. Small things do not disappear. They grow. And small things in yourself grow to the other person. For instance your chewing ice irritates me. If I were marrying you it would irritate me increasingly. And being mad about something else, I might put all the irritation on the ice chewing. Do you see what I mean?

3. This question has to do with families. You may think you can get away from them but you can't. They are part of the trail of the comet. Do you like Jim's family to the point that you can associate with them indefinitely? Do they like you or do they want to change you? You see Jim is not just about to abandon his mother when he marries you any more than you are about to abandon yours. Unconsciously a mother is always a danger to a marriage whether she is or not.

4. This is a snob question but it should be asked because everybody is a snob to some degree. Do you approve of Jim

509

socially? Do you approve of Jim's family intellectually and socially? The only way you can test yourself in this question is to ask whether there is anyone in the world or any group in the world to whom you would hesitate in introducing Jim or Jim's family—Mrs. Roosevelt? Laurence Olivier? Princess Margaret? Munna [her grandmother, Zachary Scott's mother]? Mrs. Bacon [a teacher]? Adlai Stevenson?

Does Jim approve of you socially? Does his family approve of you? Would they hesitate in introducing you to anyone in any field? Don't forget your recent background is actors, gypsies and vagrants. Could they be shy and embarrassed about Zack who is an actor or me who am a writer, and both of these trades are unusual.

5. This is an outside question. If Jim should by illness or accident become incapable of sex for an extended period, would you find him attractive? Are you jealous of him? Do you resent affairs he may have had in the past? Does he resent affairs you may have had in the past? If you were ill and not capable of sex for an extended period, would he find you fun?

6. Jim has to make a living. In a way this is a large part of his life. He has to do it in his own way and within his capacities. Since you will both have to live largely on his efforts, this becomes your business too. Are you capable of going along with it, helping with it?

In the event that you should in the future find that keeping house and participating in Jim's work were not enough for you, would you be capable of taking up some other work or enthusiasm and would Jim tolerate this? There can be much more violent jealousies of interests than of people.

I hope you won't take this letter as one of disparagement. I think this marriage has as good a chance as any of succeeding and a much better chance than most. Jim is a man and that is a very great thing, to be a man, and it is a handy thing in a marriage.

There is only one thing about the wedding I could wish and that is a completely selfish one having nothing to do with your marriage but only with my own participation in the social end of it. I wish you could put it off until Christmas or a little after. We have this show with which I have to be constantly. Elaine naturally will want to be with me and it would limit our participation.

You don't have to answer this, by the way.

love john

510

The engagement did not take place.

To Webster F. Street

New York
September 23 [1955]

Dear Toby:

Summer is over and I am always glad. Now the cool weather is coming and that's my favorite time. We love our little place on Long Island but I love New York too. The show [*Pipe Dream*] is in rehearsal and Lord! it's a good show. Fine score and book and wonderful direction and cast. I was standing with Oscar Hammerstein yesterday when the lines about the Webster F. Street Lay Away Plan came up. And it occurs to me that I have never asked your permission to use your name. Do you mind? It's a lovely line and I would hate to drop it and besides it kind of ties you in with the show. You know in South Pacific Mary Martin took the name of her oldest friend. In the show within a show she says—"The dialogue was written by Bessie May Sue Ella Yeager." Well Bessie May Sue Ella Yeager used to come up from Texas every three months just to hear Mary Martin declaim her name. I hope you will let me keep your name in this show as a kind of good luck piece.

This is just a note because I am working on a book in the morning and going to rehearsals in the afternoon and it's a pretty full life. But please give me permission to use your name. You won't be ashamed I'm sure.

love to all there—
John

To Carlton A. Sheffield

New York
September 23, 1955

Dear Dook:

I'm told it is an ugly business to answer a letter right away. But if I don't, it is likely I never will. Yours came this morning and I do the ugly thing about it.

Your remarks about elastic time caught me with the same thought after a fairly quiet summer. We have a little shack on the sea out on the tip of Long Island at Sag Harbor. It's a whaling town or was and we have a small boat and lots of oak trees and the phone never rings. We run there whenever we need a rest—no neighbors, and fish and clams and crabs and mussels right at the door step. I just got it this spring and I love it. Anyway the summer zipped by. But everything zips by. The pressures come and go. Or maybe it is that sometimes they get me and sometimes they don't. Things don't change really. I am just as restless as ever. And I'm just as scared of my own craft—and attracted to it also. You say you don't know what I'm getting at. Neither do I. I just write what comes into my head and maybe sometimes it's lousy but it's the only thing I know to do. I write lots—perhaps too much but I never had any sense of proportion. I eat too much and drink too much and screw too much also. It's all part of the same pattern and I don't question it any more.

I'm starting a new book and it is fun. They are all painful fun while I am doing them. I have a show in rehearsal too. It is a musical and I love to see them put it together. It's a mystery to me how they do it. The dancers and the singers and the actors. I am very much the spectator in this one. Such pretty people—such pretty girls. We have some show girls who are perfectly exquisite. I'm not afraid of pretty girls as I once was and these kids are real warm and pleasant.

I know my life seems restless and nervous to you and maybe it is. But you were never lazy and I am so lazy that I have to work very hard. Our social life is very easy. Now and then we have people to dinner and we go to dinner now and

512

then. We have a television but never turn it on. Now and then we go to the theatre or to a concert but mostly we have conversation and reading and it's not a bad life and it's going by awfully fast.

It's been a long time since I have been west. Funny that it seems strange and a little foreign to me now. It's a kind of a sad thing to me that I don't much want to go back. You get tied to where you are I guess. And instead of the Grove cottage I have the Sag Harbor cottage. But I've never seen a national convention so next year I'm going to cover both of them—probably for the Louisville Courier-Journal—and I'll hope to see you then. We kind of plan to drive around some and see relatives and friends. I'm having fun doing some little pieces for Punch—real crazy ones but the English seem to like them and I like doing them.

Must stop and do some work. It was so good to get your letter. Do it more often—won't you?

love
John

[Marginal note] That eminence stuff is a bunch of crap.

The book he mentions was an entirely experimental work. He never felt sufficiently satisfied with it to show it to anyone else.

To Richard Rodgers
IN MEMORIAL HOSPITAL

New York
September 27, 1955

Dear Dick:

Good reports of you from Oscar and Jerry White [Rodgers and Hammerstein Production Manager]. They say the wickedness goes on behind the bandages, business as usual. I wish I could think of something to make the time go quicker for you.

We talked to your beautiful wife and to your burgeoning daughter and there is a good sign in their voices, which is better than a good report.

You will be glad to know that Elaine is doing a really adequate job in your place in Piece Pipe. She has changed some of the songs around and re-written a few lyrics, but I am sure you will approve. She had to fire three actors but she replaced them with her friends—good ambitious kids who can learn probably. Also, she has changed the ending. It takes place in a submarine putting out into the sunset with the anthem "Atoms Away, My Lads, Atoms Away." But just rest easy. Everything is being done that can be done.

Yesterday I had lunch with Helen Traubel [star of *Pipe Dream*] who, as you know, is one helluva woman. She wanted to know more about Fauna. I queried Oscar and he said it would be a good thing to do, so I dredged up some old memories, posture, voice, clothes, gestures, anecdotes, etc., and I remembered some stories about Fauna's archrival in Salinas, who was universally known and loved, by the name of Fartin' Jenny.

When I knew her she was an old woman with a patch over her left eye. She smoked black cigars and drank a mixture of whiskey and ether and late at night she would get to crying over her dead husband, Jerry, but through her tears her one eye never left the bedroom doors. Some of those girls weren't honest. Anyway, when Fartin' Jenny was a young girl, she was a cook in a whore house beside the Southern Pacific tracks in Salinas. Jerry was a gay and debonair fireman on

514

a switch engine, and as he went by the house, it was his habit to throw coal at Jenny's cat. This she took as a declaration of love. They met eventually and married and while Jerry moved up the rungs to engineer, Fartin' Jenny prospered and bought the house and her name went into song and story.

The marriage was not all enchiladas and beans. In fact, the fighting was fairly constant and usually bloody. This love fest went on for twenty-five years. Jerry died peacefully in his bed of an old ball bat wound and as so often happens, Fartin' Jenny was bereft without him; life had lost its perfume. She wanted to do something spectacular for Jerry's memory and she remembered that he had wanted to go to sea. Actually, he had said, "I'd rather be in the bottom of the Goddamn ocean than here with this bull bitch."

She decided to have him cremated and his ashes consigned to the deep. Well, she took the can of ashes and went to Monterey and rented a purse-seiner. Fartin' Jenny, accompanied by the gallant and beautiful and elite of the red-light districts of both Monterey and Salinas, together with an honor guard from the railroad brotherhoods, put out to sea. She climbed up forward, opened the can and got a handful of Jerry. She cried, "Jerry, mavourneen, I consign thee to the watery elements," and she let fly with a handful of ashes. Well, the wind caught it and brought it right back in her face. Jenny went into her famous crouch and she yelled, "You black-hearted son-of-a-bitch, I might of known you'd try to get the last word." There is a moral here somewhere.

We love you
John

Pipe Dream opened in New Haven, and the initial enthusiasm began to fade. After forcing restraint on himself, Steinbeck wrote the producers (who were also the composer and writer) a series of long letters with suggestions for the show's improvement. Again after the Boston opening, which was followed by disappointing notices, he wrote:

To Oscar Hammerstein II

[Boston]
[October 1955]

Dear Oscar:

The day after we opened in New Haven I wrote a kind of a report for you, but it wasn't the proper time. You were heavily preoccupied with getting the show open at all. Now it does seem to me to be the proper time. If changes are to be made, they must be in the works.

There are many very excellent things in Pipe Dream. If I do not dwell on them it is because you hear them everywhere and this letter purports to be a working document and not either a criticism or a flattery. I do not think this is a time to spare feelings nor to mince words. Compliments for the good things have sunk many works including my own late lamented play which you will remember with a certain horror [*Burning Bright*]. Good people came to me after it had closed and told me what should have been done, and working on it by myself I only discovered completely what was wrong a year and a half later. And the crazy thing was that audiences were telling us all the time. And audiences are telling us now. We should listen! Your face is very well known so it may be that conversations stop when you are near. But mine isn't. They don't stop talking when I go by.

Norton [Eliot Norton, Boston critic] used the word *conventional* to describe his uneasiness. I have heard others describe the same thing as sweetness, loss of toughness, lack of definition, whatever people say when they feel they are being let down. And believe me, Oscar, this is the way audiences feel. What emerges now is an old fashioned love story. And that is not good enough to people who have looked forward to this show based on you and me and Dick. When Oklahoma came out it violated every conventional rule of Musical Comedy. You were out on a limb. They loved it and were for you. South Pacific made a great jump. And even more you were ordered to go ahead. But Oscar, time has moved. The form has moved. You can't stand still. That's the price you have to pay for being Rodgers and Hammerstein.

The only thing this story has, besides some curious characters, is the almost tragic situation that a man of high mind and background and culture takes to his breast an ignorant, ill-tempered little hooker who isn't even very good at that. He has to take her, knowing that a great part of it is going to be misery, and she has to take him knowing she will have to live the loneliness of not even knowing what he is talking about if the subject gets above the belt, and yet each of them knows that the worse hell is the penalty of separation.

I have suggestions for changing every one of the things attacked in this letter, Oscar. I think they are important or I would not go out on a limb for them. Will you think about them and then perhaps submit them to some outside person who is not too close to the show, someone like Josh [Joshua Logan] or maybe Lillian Hellman, or maybe Norton, anyone who knows theatre, whom you respect and whose word you can trust. I hope you will do this. I think we are in danger, not of failure but of pale and half-assed success which to me would be worse than failure. In a word we are in grave danger of mediocrity.

Should I run for the hills now?

yours in the faith
John

Appended were specific, scene-by-scene, often line-by-line suggestions.

To Elia Kazan

New York
December 3, 1955

Dear Gadg:

Well, thank God that is over. We didn't get murdered but
we got nibbled pretty badly. I guess that was the coldest-
assed audience I ever saw. They dared us and we lost. Then
the notices said just exactly what I have been yelling about
for six weeks and I think were completely just. R. and H.
thought they could get away with it. And do you know, for the
first time in their history, they are going to make some cuts
and changes. The crazy thing is that I have written all the
changes weeks ago and have turned them in. I don't know
whether they will ever look at them, but they are there.

What really is the trouble is that R. and H. seem to be
attracted to my kind of writing and they are temperamen-
tally incapable of doing it. The burden of most of the reviews
was that they had left the book.

Tickets are still being bought and so far there are no returns. I don't understand this but it's true. I think the thing
will run for a while. Another crazy thing is that this is a
better show than most of the musicals running now. It just
isn't good enough for R. and H. I told them this in writing in
New Haven. Even told them the story of Pickles Moffett in
the fifth grade. He was a nice but illiterate little boy and my
best friend. When we got the assignment to write a four line
poem he went into shock and out of kindness I wrote two
instead of one and gave one of them to Pickles to save his
sanity. Well he got an A and I got a B. This outraged me
because the verses were of about equal quality so I went to
the teacher and asked her why. She said, and I remember her
words very well, "What Pickles did was remarkable for Pickles, but what you did was inferior for you."

We're going to the country on Monday for about three days.
I want to get the reek out of my nose. I could do with some
solitude. And I could do with some good solid work of my own
kind. There are too damned many personalities and egos

518

involved in theatre. I guess I am really tired. And disappointed actors—the poor things. I feel so sorry for them. They can't work unless we do something. It is the worst of crafts, I guess. Hell, I could take a nail and go out and scratch words on a limestone cliff and have some kind of fun, but actors can't.

I'm going shopping with my kids this afternoon down to a war surplus store. They want tents and sleeping bags and I understand the impulse very well. They want to run away and hide too and that is their symbol.

We go out to the country this afternoon. I guess I had better stop this now. Hope the picture goes well,

love to all there
john

The Steinbecks flew to Trinidad for the New Year's holiday, were joined by their friend, John Fearnley, of the Rodgers and Hammerstein staff, and sailed through the Windward and Leeward Islands. They took Calypso names: Inside Straight (Steinbeck) Queen Radio (Elaine Steinbeck) and Small Change (Fearnley).

OLD STYLE AND NEW STYLE ELAINE

Calypso written in honor of Trinidad,
New Year's Eve [1956]
and my darling Elaine

By that new and elegant
CALYPSIST * * * * *
INSIDE STRAIGHT

Note
This is a happy wedding of
the Trinidad and the Texas schools

Old style Elaine in a time gone by,
Got a red hot yen for a lukewarm guy,
She sit up river in Astolat
Singing the blues for Sir Launcelot.
She love him good and she love him here,
But he buzzing the Queen Bee Guinevere.

Lancy signs for the horse event,
Got a two-squire outfit and a purple tent.
Two-to-one favorite in a jousting bout
A big dam purse and the house sold out.
But the champ sit fidgeting with Guinevere,
Say "What I'm doing a mouldering here?"
The Queen she say, "What I hear tell—
You got you a pigeon and she raisin' hell."

Old Miss Elaine make a bad erreur
Got her a man but he ain't got her.
She a broke heart dame and she die real loud
And they float her down the river in a lace-line
    shroud.
Lancy get the message and he say real plain
"I rather be a shroudin' with Sweet Elaine."

Sugar Hill Guinevere she up her nose
Give the real royal treatment 'til he dam near froze.
Say "Don't clank around, you poor tin thing.
I got me a certify guarantee King.
He top stock holder and Chairman of the Board
With solid-gold armour an' a platinum sword,
And you, Sir Honey, you can paw the ground,
But I got another Knighty on the Table Round."

Guinevere a queen and she act like same
But she also a qualified female dame.
Say, "Got me a king and what you got?
A real dead lady at Astolat,
A show boat funeral in a ten foot scow,
Guess I'll get me to a nunnery now."
Lance win the title but he feel bad
So he pass on his gauntlet to Galahad.
'Cause love is a double-joint two-way thing
And he shouldn't made a pass at Mrs. King.

NEW STYLE ELAINE

Now *my* Miss Elaine got a new-style set,
She a high-breasted deep-breathing growed-up bru-
    nette.
She tuck her behind in and she walk real proud,
Got a B flat baritone C sharp loud.
Say, "Listen, you rounders, and you'll agree,
I got me a man and he got me."
She rustle up her bustle and the folks concur,
That she branded her a wrangler and he ear-
    notched her.
                    Signed
            INSIDE STRAIGHT

To Pascal Covici

Sag Harbor
[February 1956]
Wednesday

Dear Pat:

I guess you are going to get bombed with notes from out here. I imagine the reason is that a kind of peace is settling over me. Seems to me that I have in the past few years been so nibbled and pushed by light minds and troubled by tiny things that I have been constantly off balance. Large things I can stand up to. I think most people can—I believe that men are destroyed by little things—so little that they can't be got at or even identified—the nibbling of ducks. A large demand may stimulate—a thousand small ones only confuse and erode.

Out here I get the old sense of peace and wholeness. The phone rings seldom. It is clear and very cold but the house is warm. Elaine is ecstatically happy out here. She cooks and sews and generally enjoys herself. You can't imagine the change in disposition and approach in both of us.

And it seems to be getting into my work. I approach the table every morning with a sense of joy.

The yellow pages are beginning to be populated both with people and with ideas. This book with its new approach is not going to be long. It is only a practice book because in the back of my mind there is arising a structure like those great cumulus clouds you see over high mountains.

I can feel this rising and preparing the way weather prepares—a long time in the future and far away—a pressure area that breaks up in Greenland and will weeks later influence a rain storm in Manhattan.

Technique should grow out of theme—not dictate it. I think I told you that I want to leave the past and the nostalgic. It is the disease of modern writing. In the work I am doing, the past is used only in so far as it affects the present. Anyway it is a very pleasant thing to be doing. I want to get maybe fifty or a hundred pages done before you see it—otherwise

521

my method will not be apparent.

Meanwhile if you should see a second hand big Oxford 12 vol.'s—I would like to have it for out here. I know no book I use more—nor value more. I hate to be away from it.

Another request. Does Viking still subscribe to that service which answers questions—you know the one which will do any kind of research? I want to ask it a question. Maybe you will do it for me. I want to know how soy sauce is made. I know it is fermented from the soy bean but I want to know the exact method—step by step and like a recipe so that from the directions it could be made. I promised this to some people in Dominica. I'm always giving you odd requests.

Well all of this is keeping me from my book. But it is fun and you see? I have time. Isn't that wonderful? No gnawing that I should be doing something else. For six hours every day I have nothing to do but think and write. May it go on for a long time. I seem to be reborn.

See you Monday at 12—noon.

love
John

Peter Benchley, son of Steinbeck's friend Nathaniel Benchley, wrote from Exeter asking for a contribution to a special issue of the school newspaper. Steinbeck replied:

"Here are some lines. You're welcome to them if you want them. In a first draft I usually put in lots of generalities and in rewriting hunt them down and kill them."

To Peter Benchley

[Sag Harbor]
[1956]

A man who writes a story is forced to put into it the best of his knowledge and the best of his feeling. The discipline of the written word punishes both stupidity and dishonesty. A writer lives in awe of words for they can be cruel or kind, and they can change their meanings right in front of you. They pick up flavors and odors like butter in a refrigerator. Of course there are dishonest writers who go on for a little while, but not for long—not for long.

A writer out of loneliness is trying to communicate like a distant star sending signals. He isn't telling or teaching or ordering. Rather he seeks to establish a relationship of meaning, of feeling, of observing. We are lonesome animals. We spend all life trying to be less lonesome. One of our ancient methods is to tell a story begging the listener to say—and to feel—

"Yes, that's the way it is, or at least that's the way I feel it. You're not as alone as you thought."

It is so hard to be clear. Only a fool is wilfully obscure.

Of course a writer rearranges life, shortens time intervals, sharpens events, and devises beginnings, middles and ends and this is arbitrary because there are no beginnings nor any ends. We do have curtains—in a day, morning, noon and night, in a man's birth, growth and death. These are curtain rise and curtain fall, but the story goes on and nothing finishes.

To finish is sadness to a writer—a little death. He puts the last word down and it is done. But it isn't really done. The story goes on and leaves the writer behind, for no story is ever done.

[unsigned]

To Webster F. Street

Dear Toby:

We've been out here on the end of Long Island during this storm which you may have read about. It was beautiful and violent—18 inches of snow and high drifted by the wind.

Two weeks ago, Jimmy Costello [Editor of the Monterey *Herald*] called me and told me Ritch [Lovejoy] had been operated on for a brain tumor and had very little chance to live and if he did live had no chance of regaining his mind. I wrote to Tal but of course have had no answer. We are getting to the age when the obit pages have a great deal of news. And this has been a bad year in the loss of friends. About seven in the last few months. Two days ago Fred Allen. A wonderful man and one of the true humorists I have ever known. He was Catbird's godfather and took it very seriously. I guess it is a symptom of our ages. But it seems to me a lot of what I think of as the young ones of my friends have toppled over—like John Hodiak and Lemuel Ayers. In some cases, one feels a little guilty for being alive. But that is silly too.

I've finally got my life in shape to go to the National Conventions. I have about 12 papers I will file for. And I intend to have fun with this writing. I am going out with the attitude of a Curse on Both Your Houses and I will do no punditry so Walter Lippmann need not shudder in his elevated position. Also I am going to the Kentucky Derby this year and I've never seen it. The editor of the Louisville Courier-Journal has invited us.

I started out gaily on my novel and then, without warning an idea happened that so charmed me that I couldn't shake it out. It seemed easier to write it than to lose it. It is the wrong length, the wrong subject and everything else is wrong with it except that it is fun and I could not resist writing it [*The Short Reign of Pippin IV*]. I must say I do have fun with my profession, if that's what it is. I get real cranky when too many things interfere with it.

I guess I'd better get out and shovel some snow now. Maybe I can get into town tomorrow.

All the best
John

Mark Ethridge, the publisher of the *Courier-Journal* of Louisville, Kentucky, and Steinbeck had become acquainted on a trans-Atlantic crossing, and in the correspondence that followed, "Steinbeck confessed to an ambition to cover the conventions." He was hired by the *Courier-Journal* which then offered his dispatches to its syndicate. About thirty-four newspapers accepted, from the *Arkansas Gazette* to the Washington *Post,* and, as Steinbeck wrote Ethridge and James S. Pope, Editor-in-Chief of the *Courier-Journal:*

"I am composing a letter to the papers which have done me the honor of accepting my highly speculative copy. When it is finished I will send it to you and hope that you will send it out to them."

To the Syndicated Newspaper Editors

Sag Harbor
April 1956

Thank you for accepting my convention copy sight unseen, but I think I owe you an explanation and an out. I have never been to a National Convention. That is my main reason for wanting to go.

When I first suggested that I go conventioning I was told that I had no training as a political reporter. This was true

and I began to study the techniques of my prospective col-
leagues who were so trained. I was particularly interested in
the analysis of one paragraph of a Presidential news conference by four politically trained reporters. Each one experted
it differently. Walter Lippmann, the Alsops and David Lawrence have nothing to fear from me.

I have no sources—dependable or otherwise. If I should
make a prediction, it will probably be assembled out of information from the wife of the alternate delegate from San José,
California, plus whispers from the bell-hop who has just
delivered a bucket of ice to "usually dependable sources."

A new political phrase is "running scared." This is pre-
sumed to be good because it means the candidate is running
hard. Well, I'm writing scared. A good writer always writes
scared.

I have promised to give you printable copy. I think I can,
but if this boast should turn out to be so much grass roots, I
don't think you should take the rap. I shall write what I see
and hear and what I find amusing or illuminating. If you do
not find it so, all bets are off. If on the other hand I succeed
in interesting you and your subscribers, I shall insist, in addition to the simple money agreed on, that I be given honorary
police, military, social, civic and tree planting honors.

Yours very truly,
John Steinbeck

Steinbeck stated his view of journalism in a letter to
John P. McKnight, of the United States Information
Service in Rome:

"What can I say about journalism? It has the greatest virtue and the greatest evil. It is the first thing the
dictator controls. It is the mother of literature and
the perpetrator of crap. In many cases it is the only
history we have and yet it is the tool of the worst
men. But over a long period of time and because it
is the product of so many men, it is perhaps the
purest thing we have. Honesty has a way of creeping
in even when it was not intended."

Pascal Covici, Jr., at Harvard, wanted to do some critical writing and had sent Steinbeck some samples of his work.

To Pascal Covici, Jr.

New York
[April 13, 1956]
Friday

Dear Pascal:

We're running to Washington this morning. Haven't been there since the war. I do hope they have cleared the rubble.

I had your letter yesterday and that is exactly what I mean. But say it as roughly as you have in the letter. Make your point and make it angrily. I think of a number of pieces which should be done but that I as a novelist can't or should not do. One would be on the ridiculous preoccupation of my great contemporaries, and I mean Faulkner and Hemingway, with their own immortality. It is almost as though they were fighting for billing on a tombstone.

Another thing I could not write and you can is about the Nobel Prize. I should be scared to death to receive it, I don't care how coveted it is. But I can't say that because I have not received it. But it has seemed to me that the receivers never do a good nor courageous piece of work afterwards. It kind of retires them. I don't know whether this is because their work was over anyway or because they try to live up to the prize and lose their daring or what. But it would be a tough hazard to overcome and most of them don't. Maybe it makes them respectable and a writer can't dare to be respectable. Anyway it might be a very interesting little essay. The same thing goes for any kind of honorary degrees and decorations. A man's writing becomes less good with the numbers of his honors. It might be that fear in me that has made me refuse those L.L.D.'s that are constantly being put out by colleges. It may also be the reason why I have never been near the Academy even though I was elected to it. It may also be the

527

reason I gave my Pulitzer Prize money away. I think you might well make a good piece of it.

It is usual that the moment you write for publication—I mean one of course—one stiffens in exactly the same way one does when one is being photographed. The simplest way to overcome this is to write it *to* someone, like me. Write it as a letter aimed at one person. This removes the vague terror of addressing the large and faceless audience and it also, you will find, will give a sense of freedom and a lack of self-consciousness.

Consider also writing some criticisms of critics. The few pieces I have written against critics have been gobbled up. And it is not considered sporting for a novelist to attack his critics. But it would be perfectly valid for you to do it.

I am in a rush but I did want to get this off because your letter was very good.

Love to you all
jn

James Pope had mentioned that he had to write a commencement address for delivery at Emory University. Alone one evening in Sag Harbor, Steinbeck amused himself by dashing off a letter to Pope and a commencement address for him to deliver.

To James S. Pope

Sag Harbor
May 16, 1956

Dear Jim:

The Lillymaid has gone to Astolat for a couple of days to do for her daughter what her daughter had better pretty soon learn to do for herself or this marriage isn't for eternity [Waverly Scott's forthcoming marriage to Francis M. Skinner]. Also she has a yen to get her hair washed. Ain't she a doll? I *like* that dame. But being left alone, this mouse got to playing and wrote twenty-five pages of dialogue today. It was raining anyway.

A letter from Alicia [Alicia Patterson, publisher of *Newsday,* wife of Harry Guggenheim] today enclosed an interview with Bill Faulkner which turns my stomach. When those old writing boys get to talking about The Artist, meaning themselves, I want to leave the profession. I don't know whether the Nobel Prize does it or not, but if it does, thank God I have not been so honored. They really get to living up to themselves, wrapped and shellacked. Apparently they can't have any human intercourse again. Bill said he only read Homer and Cervantes, never his contemporaries, and then, by God, in answer to the next question he stole a paragraph from an article I wrote for the Saturday Review eight months ago. Hell, he's better than Homer. Homer couldn't either read or write and the old son of a gun was blind. And Cervantes was broke, a thing Bill never let happen to him while he could go to Hollywood and turn out the Egyptian. THE ARTIST—my ass! Sure he's a good writer but he's turning into a god damned phoney. I guess that got rid of my nastiness and Elaine wouldn't approve of my saying it. That will teach her not to go away.

It's late but I'm not sleepy so I might as well write you a commencement speech, what the hell! Of course if I had to do it myself I'd cut my throat.

I see you sitting in the front row, robed in academic splendor. It is pretty hot and you are sweating under that cape. You sat on your back tassel and pulled it off and shoved it in your pocket and that got your robe caught in your pocket and you can't get it out so you yank at it and out come your keys and a handful of small change. You keep thinking the tassel of your mortarboard is a fly and you swat at it every time it swings in front of your eyes. You wish you hadn't worn nylon drawers. You itch.

Then you hear the President announce.

"And now, I have the honor to present our honored guest, William D. Pope, who has consented to address you."

As you stand up you try to work the nylon drawers out of your crevice by dragging against the little hard chair but it sticks. So you say to yourself, "The hell with it," and you try

529

to get your notes out of your pocket under all the harness you are wearing and you realize that if you did manage to dig them out, you would have to throw your skirts over your head. So what do you do? You advance to the front of the stage and deliver the address I am about to write for you.

COMMENCEMENT ADDRESS BY JAMES S. BISHOP

"President Onassis," you begin. "Honorable Regents, members of the Faculty, without whose loving care this day could not happen (laughter), ladies and gentlemen:"

(Now draw a big deep breath because it is the last one you are going to get as you become caught up in the fire and thunder of your address. And you don't really have to go to the bathroom. It is just your imagination.)

"I suppose you think I am going to give you one of those 'You are going out into the world' speeches. (Laughter and cries of 'Hear, Hear.')

"Well, you are perfectly right. You are going out into the world and it is a mess, a frightened, neurotic, gibbering mess. And there isn't anyone out there to help you because all the people who are already out there are in a worse state than you are, because they have been there longer and a good number of them have given up.

"Yes, my young friends, you are going to take your bright and shining faces into a jungle, but a jungle where all the animals are insane. You are going from delinquency to desuetude without even an interlude of healthy vice. You haven't the strength for vice. That takes energy, and all the energy of this time is needed for fear. That takes energy too. And what energy is left over is needed for running down the rabbit holes of hatred, to avoid thought. The rich hate the poor and taxes. The young hate the draft. The Democrats hate the Republicans and everybody hates the Russians. Children are shooting their parents and parents are drowning their children when they think they can get away with it. No one can plan one day ahead because all certainties are gone. War is now generally admitted to be not only unwinnable but actually suicidal and so we think of war and plan for war, and design war and drain our nations of every extra penny of treasure to make the weapons which we admit will destroy us. Generals argue with Secretaries about how much *they*'ve got and how much *we*'ve got to fight the war that is admitted will be the end of all of us.

530

"And meanwhile there is no money for the dams and the schools and the highways and the housing and the streets for our clotted and festering traffic. That's what you are going out to. Going out? Hell you've been in it for years. And you have to scrape the bottom to avoid thinking. Some of us hate niggers and some of us hate the people who hate niggers and it is all the same thing, anything to keep from thinking. Make money! Spend all of your time trying to avoid taxes, taxes for the 60,000,000,000 dollars for the weapons for the war that is unthinkable.

"Let's face it. We are using this war and this rumor of war to avoid thought. But if you work very hard and are lucky and have a good tax-man, then when you are fifty, if your heart permits, you and your sagging wife can make a tired and bored but first-class trip to Europe to stare at the works of dead people who were not afraid. But you won't see it. You'll be too anxious to get home to your worrying. You'll want to get your blown prostate home in time for your thrombosis. The only exciting thing you can look forward to is a heart attack. And while you have been in Athens on the Acropolis not seeing the Parthenon, you have missed two murders and the nasty divorce of two people you do not know and are not likely to, but you hate to miss it.

"These are your lives, my darlings, if you avoid cancer, plane crashes and automobile accidents. Your lives! Love? A nervous ejaculation while drunk. Romance? An attempt to be mentioned in a column for having accompanied the Carrot Queen to a slaughter house. Fun? Electric canes at a convention. Art? A deep seated wish to crash the Book-of-the-Month-Club. Sport? A television set and a bottle of the proper beer. Ambition? A new automobile every year. Work? A slot in a corporate chain of command. Religion? A private verbal contract with a Deity you don't believe in and a public front pew in your superior's church. Children? Maybe a psychiatrist can keep them out of the detention home.

"Am I boring you, you nervous sons of bitches? Am I keeping you from your mouldy pleasures? And you, President Booker T. Talmadge, are you restless to get to your rare roast beef? Regents, are you lusting for the urinal? And you, Professors—are you cooking up some academic skullduggery for the Faculty Club?

"Now, you say hopelessly, he is going to give us his science lecture. And you are right again, but it is the last time you will be right.

"Your professors will squabble about how many milleniums ago it was when a man picked up fire and it burned him, and he picked it up again and it burned a forest and he brought it home and it burned his shelter and he threw it on a pile of bones and learned to cook and he found a piece of shining metal under a bonfire and wore it for a while and then hammered it to a cutting edge. It took him hundreds of thousands of years to get used to fire. The very concept of fire so frightened him that he refused to think about it. He called it a god or the property of a god, and gradually over hundreds of thousands of years he reluctantly evolved a set of rules and techniques and mores for thinking about fire. Then he loved it finally and it was first lord of the hearth, the center of his being, the symbol of his ease and safety. Many more people got warm than got burned and so he gradually inspected this extension of himself, this power and found what made it do the things it does. But that was the end of the process, not the beginning. And meanwhile there must have been a good number of men who seeing a forest burning shrieked out that this devil would destroy the world.

"Do you know what is wrong with you? It isn't niggers or Democrats or Russians. The Quantum Theory tumbled your convictions about order, so you refused to think about it. The Expanding Universe blasted your homocentric galaxy, and then the fissionable atom ripped the last of your fire-minded world to ribbons. For the first time you have unlimited power and an unlimited future, the great drama of magic and alchemy. And are you glad? No, you go groveling to analysts to find out what is the matter with you. You will not inspect the new world that is upon you.

"Wouldn't it be wonderful if you could look at your world and say, and hear yourself—'This was once true but it is no longer true. We must make new rules about this and this. We must abandon our dear war, which once had a purpose, and our hates which once served us.'

"You won't do it. It will have to slip up on you in the course of the generations. But wouldn't it be wonderful if you could greet the most wonderful time in the history of our world with wonder rather than with despair?"

Now you bow coldly and try to get out alive. The audience is silent and as you walk up the aisle working at your suffering crotch you hear whispered comments. "The old fart. Who does he think he is?" "Nigger lover." "Did you hear him say those Communists weren't dangerous? He must be one."

Say—I like that! I may make that speech myself—from a helicopter. But you may borrow it if you like. And invite me to hear you deliver it. I'll cover your exit and bring a few of the boys.

Oh, Elaine will be so mad at me!

yours
John

I told you I was a spastic writer—

To Graham Watson

Sag Harbor
July 2, 1956

Dear Graham:

Your good letter coincides with a genuine homesickness for London. Not that it is going to do any good for quite a long time. Our daughter is getting married on July fourteenth, and this astonishing occasion is being produced only a little less splendidly than Billy Rose's Aquacade. You can't imagine how many clothes you have to put on a girl when the sole purpose is to get them off.

Meanwhile I have been trying to finish a little book which could be amusing and could get me guillotined also, but the interruptions of more important, i.e. wedding things have made it very difficult. Now my kids have gone to camp and Elaine is running back and forth to New York to stage manage the pageant. Women are very touchy about this. I smiled when they were talking veil and caught hell, and I was so stupid as to suggest that they bring back the kerchief and sheep's blood symbol, but they found that bestial. I wish I had the sense to shut up. If only the intensity of the wedding could guarantee that she would stay married, it would be

533

more than worth it. Do I sound bitter? Well I am a little but I am also philosophic.

>To James Pope, at the same time:
>
>"Where do you seat the grandparents of the bride when the bride's father has gone to England and the grandparents hate the stepfather for having stolen the bride's father's wife? If I can get by this wedding I think the conventions will be a breeze.
>
>so long . . .
>
>Where the hell would you put the chrysanthemums on the St. Regis Roof if the bride's uncle-in-law owns the King Ranch?"

In the spring we shall go back to Europe. I am going to take Elaine to follow the spring up Scandinavia. I want her to be perhaps in Dalerna for midsummer where they dance and play the violins and do the summerpoles and the wreathes and drink one hell of a lot of schnapps. I find that after six or seven I can sing in old Norsk. At least it sounds like old Norsk. But Elaine says that everything I say after even four akvavits sounds like old Norsk.

We want to see you. Consider very carefully meeting us in Florence. We know lots of people there and places where you can eat little birds and we'll take you to Castle Broglio where the Chianti is golden for a change and twice as strong. Wouldn't that be fine?

yours
John

To James S. Pope

[Sag Harbor]
[July 1956]

Dear Jim:

If I feel like wringer-juice, what do you think Elaine is like? That's the tiredest white girl I ever saw. I've put her on a diet of bed and vitamins. The wedding was very pretty, the bride truly radiant, the groom handsome and properly frightened, the reception a gala of the youth and gallantry and beauty of Texas and Manhattan. I think I handled myself with the proper mixture of gruffness and tears—a regular Lionel Barrymore. Seemed to me that Elaine was prettier than the bride. Good show from beginning to end and now over, and E. and I alone—really alone for the first time in our lives. I feel new-married myself and when she gets rested up I'm going to make the Lily Maid feel the same way. Chicago will be a kind of wedding trip for us.

Meanwhile, it is so lovely out here with sun and breeze and water that the flowers in the garden are yawping like coon hounds on a moonlight night. What joy! The deadline on my little book which I had hoped to finish before Chicago, I probably won't make. It was my own deadline anyway—but that is the toughest kind. I guess I am telling you all of this out of a kind of effusion.

Meanwhile—the conventions. I'm going to keep the title "O' Both Your Houses." I like it and it kind of sets the tone.

I guess that's all. I want to thank you for the lovely letter you wrote Elaine. It bloomed her all up and made her happy. Now we have three weeks to rest and kind of get acquainted and that's the very best of all. And I won't be quite so hysterical from now on.

Best to all of you there.

John

On receipt of a photograph of himself to be used for the syndicated stories from Chicago:

To James S. Pope

[Sag Harbor]
[July 1956]

Dear Jim:

I guess I never saw a more villainous face. The expression seems to be one of planned lechery. It has the open honesty of the weasel and the trustworthiness of the mink. The lumps and erosion are almost geologic as a record of a virtuous and uneventful life. In fact why anyone would want it except for a dart game or a rogues' gallery I don't know.

Working furiously on my French History [*The Short Reign of Pippin IV*] and there's just a teensy-weensy chance I may finish it before Chicago. To this devout end address your prayers, please!

Yours
John

To James S. Pope and Mark Ethridge

San Francisco
August 23, 1956

Dear Jim and Mark:

I have just finished my last copy which will be filed tomorrow. I have had fun, some of which I hope communicated. And I'm very tired because regardless of the irresponsibility of the copy, I have missed very little and have stood still for every nuance of these fantastic rituals of complexity. I'm

536

pretty sure I shall not want to see another one. Like a fighting bull once fought I know too much and my innocence is being swept up from the floor of the Cow Palace along with the posters.

I've made a lot of new friends and renewed old friendships with press people. They are not resentful of me once they know I am not competing with them. On the contrary they have been kind and helpful and amused at this dog walking on its hind legs. I've been scared in the matter of copy and hopeful that it might be better than most has turned out. But I guess that's the story of a writer's life. And it was the very best I could do.

Tomorrow we're going down to Monterey for a few days to see my sisters.

Finally—thanks for everything.

Yours,
John

To Pascal Covici

[Sag Harbor]
[1956]

Dear Pat:

I suppose you will be asked why I wrote The Short Reign of Pippin IV. Maybe you will ask it yourself. As an answer I recall a beautiful lady of my acquaintance who was asked by her two young daughters where babies came from. Very patiently she explained the process to them and at the end asked—

"Now—do you understand?"

After a whispered conference, the older girl reported—

"We understand *what* you do, but *why* do you do it?"

My friend thought for a moment and then retired into the simple truth—"Because it's fun," she said.

And that's the reason for this book. Because it's fun.

Anyone who can go along with it in a spirit of play may have some of the pleasure I had in writing it. On the other

537

hand, the searchers after secret meanings, the dour priesthood of obscurantist criticism and the devout traffic cops of literature will neither like nor approve of The Short Reign.

But anyone who in our humorless times has concealed a sense of play, can, I believe, get an illegal chuckle from this book. In our scowling era, laughter may well be the only counter-revolutionary weapon.

I can imagine that future critics, if any survive, may view our ridiculous antics with hilarious laughter. And to that desirable end, The Short Reign of Pippin IV is dedicated.

Yours conspiratorially
John

Dennis Murphy, the writer-son of Steinbeck's old school friend, John Murphy of Salinas, was in the middle of his first book, *The Sergeant,* and had apparently written Steinbeck about certain difficulties.

To Dennis Murphy

[Sag Harbor]
September 21, 1956

Dear Dennis:

I'm sorry you had an argument with your father. But from where I sit, and I sit a little bit along the road you are travelling, you have only one thing in the world to do. You *must* finish this book and then you *must* finish another. If anything at all, saving your own death, stops you, except momentarily, then you are not a writer anyway and there is nothing to discuss. I do not mean that you should not bitch and complain and fight and scrabble but the one important thing for you is to get your work done. If anyone gets hurt

538

in the process, you cannot be blamed.

But don't think for a moment that you will ever be forgiven for being what they call "different." You won't! I still have not been forgiven. Only when I am delivered in a pine box will I be considered "safe." After I had written the Grapes of Wrath and it had been to a large extent read and sometimes burned, the librarians at Salinas Public Library, who had known my folks—remarked that it was lucky my parents were dead so that they did not have to suffer this shame. I tell you this so you may know what to expect.

Now get to work—

> Yours
> J.S.

David Heyler, Jr., was beginning a collection of Steinbeckiana.

To Mr. and Mrs. David Heyler, Jr.

> New York
> November 19, 1956

Dear Dave and Joan:

Today I packed up a bunch of junk and put it in a box and as soon as some one can get over to the post office it will go off to you, oddities and several manuscripts that have never been printed.

Hope you are all well and happy. We are studying Italian, getting nowhere but it is kind of fun and a kind of discipline which I am not used to these many years. A professor comes twice a week and Elaine and I find ourselves fighting to recite when we know the answer and pretending to be busy when we don't. I guess you don't grow up at all. And all the

Italian we will learn you can put in you know what. I am trying to get sounds by trying to memorize some of the sonnets of Petrarca. I find that poetry gives you a much better sense of the flow of words than the inkwell of Catarina Rossi, whom I am beginning to detest. We are studying because about the first of April we are going to Florence for a couple of months and I want to know a few words so that as in French I can ask a question even if I can't understand what the answer is.

I finished my little book. Now I am engaged in another thing and I must ask you not to speak about it for reasons that will be obvious. I've thrown out the novel I was going to write because it did not go well and because it arose from a wrong premise. And because I must go on working because I get unhappy when I am not working, I am taking on something I have always wanted to do. That is the reduction of Thomas Malory's Morte d'Arthur to simple readable prose without adding or taking away anything, simply to put it into modern spelling and to translate the obsolete words to modern ones and to straighten out some of the more involved sentences. There has not been an edition of this since 1893, the Dent edition of Caxton, except for a cut version called the Boy's King Arthur in about 1900 which was the one I cut my teeth on. And there is no rendering of it into modern English. In 1934 the Winchester ms of Malory was discovered and is now available in Oxford University Press, three volumes. And the Winchester is much more interesting and indicates some things which Caxton edited out.

It was the very first book I knew and I have done considerable research over the years as my work will show. I loved the old forms but most people are put off by the spellings and obsolescences and the result is that all they have to go on is Prince Valiant and the movie versions. This is odd because I don't know any book save only the Bible and perhaps Shakespeare which has had more effect on our morals, our ethics and our mores than this same Malory. So that is what I am up to and I should be able to have it pretty well in hand before we go to Italy. However, if it is not completely done by then I will put it aside because I would want it to be beautifully done or not to do it at all. I want to make it as simple as possible but not to leave out anything and not to sweeten nor to sentimentalize it.

540

Anyway, I'll get the box off to you as soon as I can. Love to all there,

love
John

To Elizabeth Otis

New York
November 19, 1956
Monday

Dear Elizabeth:

I've finished now the Short Reign. Pat is coming for it to-day. There's a great unease about it at Viking, but there's an unease all over and maybe one thing transmits to another. Meanwhile, I have been dipping into the Malory. And with delight. As long as I don't know what is going on in the world, I would like to have a try with this.

Now as to method. I am in some wonder about this. When I first read it, I must have been already enamored of words because the old and obsolete words delighted me. However, I wonder whether children now would be so attracted. They are more trained by picture than by sound. I'm going to make a trial run—not removing all of the old forms, nor all the Malory sentence structure, but substituting known simple words and reversing sentences which even now are puzzling.

When I have some of it done, I shall with an opening essay tell of my own interest in the cycle, when it started and where it went—into scholarship and out again on the other side.

Now as for title—I should perhaps like to call the book The Acts of King Arthur. Of course I would explain this in the introduction—the Book is much more Acts than Morte.

Do you have a Caxton edition? I should like you—as you read my version—to compare it, so that recommendations can be made.

Next, what would you think of Chase as a kind of Managing Editor? [Chase Horton, owner of the Washington Square

Bookshop and friend of Elizabeth Otis.] His knowledge and interest seem to be great and he could be of help to me when I come a cropper. It would be good to have someone to consult with. And he might have an opening essay to precede mine. Let me know about this.

Let us keep this project to ourselves until I am well along. I don't want Pat or Viking nudging me.

There it is anyway and I find I am anxious to get into it. It could be a peaceful thing in a torn world.

Love
John

To Roland Dickey
DIRECTOR OF THE UNIVERSITY OF NEW MEXICO PRESS

New York
December 7, 1956

Dear Mr. Dickey:

I have read with very much interest the book, Steinbeck and His Critics, particularly since I have not seen most of the material before.

It is always astonishing to read a critique of one's work. In my own case, it didn't come out that way but emerged little by little, staggering and struggling, each part alone and separated from the others. And then, after the fact—long after—a pattern is discernible, a clear and fairly consistent pattern, even in the failures. It gives me the pleased but uneasy feeling of reading my own epitaph.

So many of the judgments and arguments in this book of opinions seem to me to be true. I only wonder why I didn't think of them myself. I guess I was so lost in the books I couldn't see the long structure. Of course, in this river of opinion there are special pleaders—men who were backing their own particular horses—but also there seem to me to be many accuracies.

This book does make me aware of how long I have been at

542

it. Good God, I must have been writing for hundreds of years. But I must assure you that it fails to make me feel old or finished or fixed. Perhaps my new book falls into the pattern, and perhaps the two books in process will drift in the inevitable stream—but to me they are new and unique in the world and I am as scared and boastful and humble about them as I was a thousand years ago when I began the first one. And it is just as hard and I am just as excited as I was. The approach to a horizon makes the horizon leap away. And the more one learns about writing, the more unbelievably difficult it becomes. I wish to God I knew as much about my craft, or whatever it is, as I did when I was 19 years old. But with every new attempt, frightening though it may be, is the wonder and the hope and the delight. As the angels said in Petrarca, "Che luce è questa e qual nova beltate?"

> Yours sincerely,
> John Steinbeck

To Elizabeth Otis

Sag Harbor
January 3, 1957
(I think it is Jan. 3,
pretty sure in fact.)

Dear Elizabeth:

Just reading and reading and reading and it's like hearing remembered music. The bay is nearly all frozen over with just a few patches of open water and as the tide rises and falls the crushing ice makes a strange singing sound. I've moved my card table to the front window with the telescope beside it so if anything goes on I can tompeep it. Two seagulls right now trying to walk on the ice and falling through every few steps and then looking around to see if anyone noticed. I have a feeling that seagulls hate to be laughed at. Well, who doesn't, for that matter?

Remarkable things in the books. Little meanings that peek

543

out for a moment, and a few scholars who make observations and then almost in fright withdraw or qualify what they have said. Somewhere there's a piece missing in the jigsaw and it is a piece which ties the whole thing together. So many scholars have spent so much time trying to establish whether Arthur existed at all that they have lost track of the single truth that he exists over and over.

It is very easy to see how Malory, steeped as he must have been in the church, could unconsciously pattern the brotherhood after the twelve apostles. That was what people understood. Twelve was the normal number for any group of followers of a man or a principle. The symbolism was inevitable. And whether the Grail was the cup from Golgotha or the Gaelic cauldron later used by Shakespeare doesn't in the least matter since the principle of both was everlasting or rather ever-renewed life. All such things fall into place inevitably but it is the connective, the continuing line with the piece missing in the middle that fascinates me.

Another beautiful thing is how the straggling sentences, the confused characters and events of the early parts smooth out as he goes along so that his sentences become more fluid and his dialogue gets a sting of truth and his characters become more human than symbolic even though he tries hard to keep the symbol, and this I am sure is because he was learning to write as he went along. He became a master and you can see it happening. And in any work I do on this thing I am not going to try to change that. I'll go along with his growing perfection and who knows, I may learn myself. It's a lovely job if I can only lose the sense of hurry that has been growing in me for so long.

Last night when I could neither sleep nor channel my attention on my reading, my nerve ends got to whipping like the whitecaps on the bay and darkness seemed to come close and then to recede and then come close again. This was not only nonsense but fatuous nonsense. And it occurred to me that what was good for squirrels and bears might be good for me so I went out to walk and the cold got through my skin and then through my meat and then right into the center of my bones, and do you know it worked? A soothing and a quieting it was. It was about six above zero and the deep freeze acted like an anaesthetic as of course I knew it must. When I was cold clear through I could come back and read again. I think these squirrels and bears have something. I don't know

544

whether it was fortunate or unfortunate that I didn't find a hollow log and crawl in for the winter.

Charley is having a wonderful time trying to walk on the ice. He falls through at every step and looks puzzled every time. One day soon it will support him and then he'll give those seagulls hell.

That's all for now. I'll get back to my Legend and I'll bet it turns out that it isn't a Legend at all any more than any dream is.

Love
John

To Chase Horton

Sag Harbor
January 12, 1957

Dear Chase:

I come from a line of inventors. Several years ago in a Midlands, I think Birmingham, newspaper I read a bitter request from the local public librarian, asking the subscribers *not* to use bacon or kippers as book marks because the grease soaked through the paper.

I have never used book marks no matter how pretty or ingenious they were. Therefore you may believe me when I say I was surprised to find I was using your very pretty cloth ones. I couldn't figure why and so I watched myself and do you know why? I found that I was wiping my glasses with them. They aren't very good for that but it was better than getting up and finding a kleenex. Hence my invention—a book mark made of cloth designed to wipe glasses, perhaps impregnated with one of those silicate compounds which coat the lens. These could be in bright colors, could have pretty designs, and perhaps an indication of their use such as:

A DOGGE EERED BOOKE YS IYL BE SEYNE
I KEPE HIR BOOKES AND GLASYS KLENE.

545

Such a book mark could also have printed on it advertising of publisher or book shop which would remind the reader where he got it. What do you think of this? Want to go partners in it?

And by the way, if in your wandering you should see a stuffed owl—I want one. I need it for a birthday present this summer—almost any kind of owl, screech, barn, fence post, ground, hoot.

Yours,
John

To Arthur Larson
DIRECTOR OF THE UNITED STATES
INFORMATION AGENCY

[New York]
January 12, 1957

Dear Mr. Larson:

The following notes arise out of a genuine concern about our communications with our neighbors.

Recently the President asked William Faulkner, perhaps the dean of American writers, to form a committee to recommend techniques for what Mr. Eisenhower tellingly called "a People to People program."

It has been our misfortune to dangle our freedom in front of our neighbors and then to refuse them even the simplest hospitality. Our closed and suspicious borders have not reassured our friends and have given our enemies magnificent propaganda fuel.

Our refusal of a passport to Paul Robeson, for example, was stupid. An intelligent move would have been to let him travel and to send Jackie Robinson with him.

The second item grows out of our uneasiness that we are constantly re-converting our friends who do not need it, and ignoring our enemies who do. In this, of course, we are driven by our hysteria about security.

I believe that commerce is not only the mother of civiliza-

546

tion, but the teacher of understanding and the god of peace. And I mean all kinds of commerce—movement of goods and movement of ideas. The first act of a dictator is to close the borders to travel, goods and ideas. It is always a matter of sadness, and of suspicion to me, when we close our borders to any of these.

In 1936, I went as a tourist to Russia and what were then called the Balkans. In 1947, with Robert Capa, I toured Russia and some of the satellites for the Herald-Tribune. We asked many people who had been kind to us what we could send them. The invariable answer was "books." On returning, we sent books. They never arrived. We sent them again—and again they failed to arrive.

Next—I have had a number of letters from East German students who crossed into West Germany, ostensibly to take part in Communist rallies. These letters asked for books, gave Berlin addresses to which they should be sent, and guaranteed wide distribution. One student said, "I can assure you that at least a thousand people will read each book you send." Naturally, I sent the books—not only my own books, but many others.

Now—My conclusion is that the book is revered. The book is somehow true, where propaganda is suspected. Denial of the right to read whatever they want to is one of the most bitterly resented of all of the Soviet's tyrannies.

You will remember the Army editions of books sent to troops during the last war. They were small, compact—designed to fit in the shirt pocket. They were distributed by the millions. Publishers and authors contributed their services. Where are those plates? Could they be reprinted? They could be moved over borders in various ways—by Underground, as the East German students suggested, by balloons as Radio Free Europe has flown pamphlets, and by the inevitable movements across borders, no matter how closed they are. A packet of books thrown over the barbwire fence and picked up by a border guard *might* be burned, but I swear it is more likely that the books would be hidden, treasured and distributed. During the German occupation of Norway and Denmark, my own books were mimeographed on scraps of paper and distributed.

Now—What kind of books?

Any kind. Poetry, essays, novels, plays—these are the things desired and begged for. Pictures of how it is in Amer-

547

ica—good and bad. The moment it is all good, it is automatically propaganda and will be disbelieved.

These are some of the conclusions of the best writers in our country, and they are offered out of a simple desire to help in your very difficult task.

Yours very sincerely,
John Steinbeck

To Alexander Frere
THEN DIRECTOR OF HEINEMANN, LTD.,
STEINBECK'S ENGLISH PUBLISHER

New York
January 18, 1957

Dear Frere and Frau:

Your letter arrived with its charming news that we can lay down our heads at the Dorchester.

First, I and later we have been to Sag Harbor. I've been doing some concentrated reading—a lovely thing—and not done by me in recent years. To read and read in one direction night and day; to pull an area and a climate of thinking over one's head like a space helmet—what a joy that is! No telephones, no neighbors, no decisions except great ones—that is a good way to live for a time.

Working on the Malory is a thing of great joy to me, like coming home. I am having a wonderful time. The Morgan Library has opened its arms and its great manuscripts to me, and I can touch and feel, put a microscope on the vellum. I think I will write a small essay on what one finds on a monkish manuscript under a powerful glass. I am convinced that with practice I could tell when the copyist had a hangover. Every sharpening of the quill is apparent and since cleanliness was not a monkish virtue, the pages are rich—even racy—with fingerprints and smudges and evidences of pork pasty on fingers hastily wiped on nut-brown robes. It is fascinating and some of the scholars down there are a little puzzled and aghast at my own in-

548

spection with a sixty-power glass, but they are fascinated too. I haven't yet dared ask permission to take scrapings for analysis, but maybe later when they find I am not a crank, they may permit it.

Later he wrote:

"The Morgan Library has a very fine 11th century Launcelot in perfect condition. I was going over it one day and turned to the rubric of the first known owner dated 1221, the rubric a squiggle of very thick ink. I put a glass on it and there imbedded deep in the ink was the finest crab louse, pfithira pulus, I ever saw. He was perfectly preserved even to his little claws. I knew I would find him sooner or later because people of that period were deeply troubled with lice and other little beasties—hence the plagues. I called the curator over and showed him my find and he let out a cry of sorrow. "I've looked at that rubric a thousand times," he said. "Why couldn't I have found him?"

I am having the time of my life with the work, and although I have a fairly good background, I am learning much in supplemental reading.

My love to your darling wife and whatever you can get for yourself.

Yours,
John

To John Murphy

[New York]
February 21, 1957

Dear John:

After talking to Elizabeth Otis, one of the best judges in the country, who has seen the beginning of Dennis' book [*The Sergeant*], I shudder to tell you what I have strongly sus-

549

pected—that you have a writer in the family. This is sad news, but I can't think of a thing you can do about it. I can remember the horror which came over my parents when they became convinced that it was so with me—and properly so. What you have and they had to look forward to is life made intolerable by a mean, cantankerous, opinionated, moody, quarrelsome, unreasonable, nervous, flighty, irresponsible son. You will get no loyalty, little consideration and desperately little attention from him. In fact you will want to kill him. I'm sure my father and mother often must have considered poisoning me. There will be no ease for you or for him. He won't even have the decency to be successful or if he is, he will pick at it as though it were failure for it is one of the traits of this profession that it always fails if the writer is any good. And Dennis is not only a writer but I am dreadfully afraid a very good one.

I hasten to offer Marie and you my sympathy but I must also warn you that you are helpless. Your function as a father from now on will be to get him out of jail, to nurture him just short of starvation, to watch in despair while he seems to be irrational—and your reward for all this will be to be ignored at best and insulted and vilified at worst. Don't expect to understand him, because he doesn't understand himself. Don't for God's sake, judge him by ordinary rules of human virtue or vice or failings. Every man has his price but the price of a writer, a real one, is very hard to find and almost impossible to implement. My best advice to you is to stand aside, to roll with the punch and particularly to protect your belly. If you are contemplating killing him, you had better do it soon or it will be too late. I can see no peace for him and little for you. You can deny relationship. There are lots of Murphys.

This is a strange phenomenon—No one understands it. In the Middle Ages they ascribed it to evil spirits or the devil and they may not have been far wrong. But there is a heavy penalty for excellence. I have tried to explain this to Dennis—and I think he knows it but knowing some things doesn't make it easier. And out of all the mess sometimes comes great beauty—the only thing that survives in our species.

We're on the move again. We go to Italy March 25 and to Japan in September. If I have any complaints with my life, one of them can surely not be that it is dull.

550

Again my condolences to you and Marie—but you're stuck with it.

Yours,
John

In the spring, on the first of three Arthurian "questes," the Steinbecks and his sister Mary Dekker sailed for Italy, in search of material not available elsewhere on Sir Thomas Malory. Steinbeck believed Malory himself had gone to Italy at one point as a mercenary. Furthermore, as he wrote McIntosh and Otis, he wanted to go to the Florentine archives—

"since the economics of fifteenth century England were dominated by Florentine bankers."

At the same time, as he wrote James Pope and Mark Ethridge, for whom he was going to write a series of travel pieces:

"I should like to be accredited to the Courier-Journal and to have a cable card. This is for my convenience and self-importance. I will report ship sinkings and keep the paper informed on the Guelph-Ghibelline matter. I promise not to send anything day rate short of the return of Christ to Eboli."

On arrival in Florence he wrote a happy letter to Elizabeth Otis:

"We got in last evening in a state of collapse. Farewell parties on the ship lasted three days and did us in. Our apartment looked like Forest Lawn with flowers from Florentine friends and we fell into the mood by going to bed and dying for twelve hours. Yesterday in Naples I told the press that for the first time in two years Naples had a ruin second only to Pompeii, namely me. This remark so delighted them that they forgot to ask me which Italian writers I liked best."

After three weeks in Florence they went to Rome. He wrote Covici:

"A couple of days ago I went into the Vatican Library and archives—what a place! I guess the most exciting I ever saw. Manuscripts by the acre and all beautifully catalogued. I am accumulating a huge fund of Maloryana. I wonder whether I will ever get it written. It is such a huge job and sometimes I get very tired. Sometimes I think I have written too much. But, hell, it's kind of a nervous tic by now."

To Elizabeth Otis and Chase Horton:

Rome
April 26, 1957

Dear Elizabeth and Chase:

I have been reading all of the scholarly appraisals of the Morte, and all the time there has been a bothersome thought in my brain knocking about just out of reach, something I knew that was wrong in all of the inspection and yet I couldn't put my finger on it. Why did Launcelot fail in his quest and why did Galahad succeed? What is the feeling about sin, the feeling about Gwynevere? How about the rescue from the stake? How about the relationship between Arthur and Launcelot?

Then this morning I awakened about five o'clock fully awake but with the feeling that some tremendous task had been completed. I got up and looked out at the sun coming up over Rome and suddenly it came back whole and in one piece. And I think it answers my nagging doubt. It can't be a theory because it won't subject itself to proof. I'm afraid it has to be completely intuitive and because of this it will never be very seriously considered by scholars.

Malory has been studied as a translator, as a soldier, as a rebel, as a religious, as an expert in courtesy, as nearly everything you can think of except one, and that is what he was—a novelist. The Morte is the first and one of the greatest of novels in the English language. And only a novelist could think it. A novelist not only puts down a story but he is the story. He is each one of the characters in a greater or a less degree. And because he is usually a moral man in intention and honest in his approach, he sets things down as truly as he can.

A novel may be said to be the man who writes it. Now it is nearly always true that a novelist, perhaps unconsciously, identifies himself with one chief or central character in his novel. Into this character he puts not only what he thinks he is but what he hopes to be. We can call this spokesman the self-character. You will find one in every one of my books and in the novels of everyone I can remember. It is most simple and near the surface in Hemingway's novels. The soldier, romantic, always maimed in some sense, hand—testicles. These are the symbols of his limitations. I suppose my own symbol character has my dream wish of wisdom and acceptance.

Now it seems to me that Malory's self-character would be Launcelot. All of the perfections he knew went into this character, all of the things of which he thought himself capable. But, being an honest man he found faults in himself, faults of vanity, faults of violence, faults even of disloyalty and these would naturally find their way into his dream character. Oh, don't forget that the novelist may arrange or rearrange events so that they are more nearly what he hoped they might have been.

For example, if Malory had been at Rouen and had seen the cynical trial, the brutal indictment and the horrible burning, might he not be tempted in his novel to right a wrong by dreaming he had done it differently? If he were affected by the burning of Joan and even more by his failure to save her or even to protest, would he not be likely to have his self-character save Gwynevere from the flames? In a sense he would by this means have protested against the killing of the falsely accused but he would also in a sense have cured it.

And now we come to the Grail, the Quest. I think it is true that any man, novelist or not, when he comes to maturity has a very deep sense that he will not win the quest. He knows his failings, his shortcomings and particularly his memories of sins, sins of cruelty, of thoughtlessness, of disloyalty, of adultery, and these will not permit him to win the Grail. And so his self-character must suffer the same terrible sense of failure as his author. Launcelot could not see the Grail because of the faults and sins of Malory himself. He knows he

553

has fallen short and all his excellences, his courage, his courtesy, in his own mind cannot balance his vices and errors, his stupidities.

I think this happens to every man who has ever lived but it is set down largely by novelists. But there is an answer ready to hand. The self-character cannot win the Quest, but his son can, his spotless son, the son of his seed and his blood who has his virtues but has not his faults. And so Galahad is able to win the Quest, the dear son, the unsoiled son, and because he is the seed of Launcelot and the seed of Malory, Malory-Launcelot has in a sense won the quest and in his issue broken through to the glory which his own faults have forbidden him.

Now this is so. I know it as surely as I can know anything. God knows I have done it myself often enough. And this can for me wipe out all the inconsistencies and obscurities scholars have found in the story. And if the Morte is uneven and changeable it is because the author was changeable. Sometimes there is a flash of fire, sometimes a moody dream, sometimes an anger. For a novelist is a rearranger of nature so that it makes an understandable pattern, and a novelist is also a teacher, but a novelist is primarily a man and subject to all of a man's faults and virtues, fears and braveries. And I have seen no treatise which has ever considered that the story of the Morte is the story of Sir Thomas Malory and his times and the story of his dreams of goodness and his wish that the story may come out well and only molded by the essential honesty which will not allow him to lie.

Well, that was the problem and that was the settlement and it came sweetly out with the morning sun on the brown walls of Rome. And I should like to know whether you two find it valid at all. In my heart and in my mind I find it true and I do not know how in the world I can prove it except by saying it as clearly as I can so that a reader may say—"Of course, that's how it had to be. Whatever else could be the explanation?"

Please let me know what you think of this dizzying inductive leap. Does it possibly seem as deeply true to you as it does to me?

I shall dearly like to know what you think.

Love to all there,
John

554

To Pascal Covici

Florence
May 16, 1957

Dear Pat:

Spring has finally come, and late spring at that. The rains have stopped and the sunshine is beautiful, almost painfully beautiful so that in the morning you look out and take a quick breath as you do when you are quickly, sharply hurt. This afternoon I walked for quite a long time by the Arno and repeopled it. And I can now. I know what the people used to wear and to some extent how they thought, at least in so far as any age can get near another. But I told you I felt that I understood.

Thanks for sending Atkinson's letter on to me. [Brooks Atkinson, drama critic of *The New York Times*.] I have answered it.

> The House Committee on Un-American Activities had investigated Arthur Miller. Steinbeck had written a defense of him published in *Esquire.*

I feel deeply that writers like me and actors and painters are in difficulty because of their own cowardice or perhaps failure to notice. When Artie told me that not one writer had come to his defense, it gave me a lonely sorrow and a shame that I waited so long and it seemed to me also that if we had fought back from the beginning instead of running away, perhaps these things would not be happening now. These committee men are neither very brave nor very intelligent. They would not attack an organism which defended itself. But they have been quite brave in pursuing rabbits and in effect we have been like rabbits. McCarthy [Senator Joseph McCarthy] went down not because Eisenhower faced him. That is a god damned lie. Eisenhower was scared of him. It took one brave man, Ed Murrow, to stand up to him to show that he had no strength. And Artie may be serving all of us. Please give him my respect and more than that, my love. You

555

see, we have had all along the sharpest weapons of all, words, and we did not use them, and I for one am ashamed. I don't think I was frightened but truly, I was careless.

Only two more days in Florence. I've had a large and good time here with too much work perhaps but very valuable.

love to all there,
john

Steinbeck's feeling for Arthur Miller was reflected in a letter written the year before to Annie Laurie Williams:

"Did you ever hear the poem I wrote for Artie Miller? I guess he is the most peaceful man in the world and one of the gentlest. Anyway one time when I was going into Mexico, he asked me to bring him a machete. You know in Oaxaca they make the most beautiful in this hemisphere. The makers are in fact direct descendants of the sword makers who went from Damascus to Toledo in Spain and then brought their secrets to Mexico. They make the great blades which can be tied in a knot and then spring back straight. Arthur wanted the machete, not for murder but to cut brush on his country place. Anyway I bought a beauty and since most of these have some noble statement etched on them I had etched on this blade the following poem which I think is funny, if you know Artie:

> Who dares raise war 'gainst Arthur Miller.
> Destroys the Lamb, Creates the killer.
> Then Leap, Sweet Steel, release the flood,
> Until the insult drowns in Blood.

Artie loved it and perhaps even once or twice got to believing it."

The Steinbecks next went to Manchester to meet the eminent scholar and leading authority on Sir Thomas Malory and the Fifteenth Century, Professor Eugène Vinaver, who held the chair of Romance of the Middle Ages at the University of Manchester.

556

To Professor and Mrs. Eugène Vinaver

The Lord Crewe Arms Hotel
Blanchland [England]
July 20, 1957

My dear Professor and Madame Vinaver:

I cannot tell you what pleasure and stimulation I had in meeting and talking with you. I carry a glow from it in the mind as well as well-defined gratitude for your hospitality which was princely. Just as Launcelot was always glad and returned to find that a good fighting man was also a king's son, so I am gratified to know that the top of the Arthurian pyramid is royal. Having read you with admiration, I could not have believed it to be otherwise for I have been fortunate in meeting a number of great men and it has been my invariable experience that in addition to eminence, superiority has two other qualities or rather three—simplicity, clarity and generosity.

It could not be otherwise with you and is not. There is a final ingredient in the recipe for greatness—enthusiasm—which you have to a superlative degree. I shall carry this glow for a long time.

I hope you will not be bored with me if I write to you occasionally and, if I know myself, at great length, and even presume to ask questions both of fact and of intuition.

Elaine joins me in compliments and gratefulness. Nothing would give us greater pleasure than to be allowed to entertain you in our own querencia.

Finally, my deep thanks for your kindness, your hospitality and your encouragement. It provides a noble pediment for work which I dearly hope will not embarrass you.

Yours in pleasure
John Steinbeck

1957 1959
1958

Steinbeck (signature)

*"...taut as
a bowstring..."*

1957 Attended P.E.N. Congress in Tokyo.

1958 *Once There Was a War* published.

To John Steinbeck IV

ELEVEN YEARS OLD, AT EAGLEBROOK SCHOOL,
DEERFIELD, MASSACHUSETTS

Sag Harbor
August 7, 1957

Dear Catsell:

Finally I got your long and beautiful letter and was properly impressed. There was a laugh in every line. Nancy Brown must be a killer, even if she is "shear jelousy." Please don't marry her right away unless she can support you, in which case grab her up even if her name does sound like an item on a police blotter on a Saturday night. As for your ducking of DeeDee Snider in the pool, I seem to detect some catbirdian technique for keeping Nancy off balance. And it is a tried and true method. Don't ever forget it. And I wonder whether some more of the "shear jelousy" is not attributable to certain catbirdiana. Just remember that you are a poor kid with no prospects and no fortune—in fact a brave but pitiful character. That way you will be loved for yourself rather than for financial tangibles. You had better learn from the experience of others, namely me. Solvency never made a girl less attractive and has been known to improve the appearance of a clubfooted harelip.

I hasten to tell you that our beloved government charges duty or customs on items sent in from outside the country. The twelve dollars duty on the microscope was just such a thing. I am interested in your remark that you had paid for it. I had understood that your grandmother and also your mother paid it so that makes $36 already and since I will inevitably pay it $48 seems to be the final figure. But I will settle for $12 just as soon as I find out who actually disbursed the money.

561

It strikes me that having a rich brother may be setting you back emotionally so tuck the enclosed bill in your pocket and invest it as you see fit in Nancy Brown, but don't give her the impression that this is going to last.

Please give my love to Thom and tell him that next year is Geo-Me year

with love from your
Fa.

Though ostensibly to Annie Laurie Williams the following letter is really addressed to the creators of a musical play based on *Of Mice and Men* which was eventually produced off-Broadway. It was adapted by Ira J. Bilowit and Wilson Lehr, with lyrics by Bilowit and music by Alfred Brooks.

To Annie Laurie Williams

New York
August 28, 1957
Wednesday

Dear Annie Laurie:

With reference to the Mice and Men music and plans we heard the night before last—I would not presume to give advice to creative people, which means of course, that I will inundate them with advice.

The company must add a freshness to my play which may well suffer from a kind of mustiness.

First, I like what I heard. I know the pressure they are under and they did it very well and I am grateful. There was freshness and force in what they did. M & M may seem to be unrelieved tragedy, but it is not. A careful reading will show that while the audience knows, against its hopes, that the dream will not come true, the protagonists must, during the play, become convinced that it will come true. Everyone in the world has a dream he knows can't come off but he spends his life hoping it may. This is at once the sadness, the greatness and the triumph of our species. And this belief on stage must go from skepticism to possibility to probability before it is nipped off by whatever the modern word for fate is. And in hopelessness—George is able to rise to greatness—to kill his friend to save him. George is a hero and only heroes are worth writing about. Boileau said that a long time ago and it is still true.

The other night the word "corn" came up and I said not to be afraid of corn. I want to amend that now. In an otherwise lovely song the words occur "It wasn't meant to be." To me this is fake corn. It implies a teleology not inherent in this play. You will find any number of things were not "meant to be" in a lot of successful plays and songs and I hate every pea-picking, Elvis Presley moment of them.

On the other hand a sense of fate expressed as I have heard it "Everything in life is 7 to 5 against"—is good corn. If the protagonists leave a feeling that they never had much of a chance—and in this play that is perfectly true—let them sing that the deck was stacked, the dice shaved, the track muddy, there was too much grease on the pig—corn, sure, but make it corn in the vernacular. I like the idea of a little party when the girl comes to her new home. Let it almost work! Almost! and let the audience feel that it might.

I like the idea that George might get the girl or at least that he might want to get the girl. This would enrich. And also you might let the girl feel that she might want George—all good and all possible.

Now let me finally speak of music. I am pleased with the freshness and unhackneyed tone. I like the hint of the blues. Remember, please, though that music can pull the guts out of an audience. Consider then—hinting at the known—the square dance, the ballad, the ode, again the blues, even the Moody and Sankey hymn form. These are part of all of us and we rise like trout to mayflies to them. Hint at them—because after all this is a ranch. Let your audience *almost* recognize something familiar and out of that go to your freshness.

My friend Abe Burrows told me a very wise thing once about theatre and I believe him. He said—"Your audience is usually ahead of the play. They get impatient if you tell them something they have already got. Give them a signal and let them do it." My own plays, most of which have failed, have failed because I told audiences things rather than let them move along. A good mule skinner simply indicates to his lead pair what he wants by a twitch of the jerk line. And the mules do it.

Now finally—I am pleased and excited with this project. I think it can have stature as well as uniqueness. I know the old feeling about never letting the author backstage but I think you will find me a different kind of author. I have no wish to protect my "immortal lines," I want a play and I'll go along with anything that works—and help with it too. Just let's keep it hard and clean and very, very sparse. The emotion is in the situation. Let the audience emote and let the players simply twitch the jerk line.

And there is the advice I said I wouldn't presume to give you. Believe me please when I say that if I were not stimulated by what you have done—I wouldn't bother.

Good luck and thanks—

John Steinbeck

Having been invited to attend the P.E.N. Congress in Tokyo in September, Steinbeck wrote William Faulkner for advice about Japan. Faulkner replied from Charlottesville:

"The thing to watch for is their formality, their excessive prolongation of mannerly behavior; I had to watch myself to keep from getting fretted, impatient, or at least from showing it, with the prolonged parade of social behavior, ritual behavior, in even the most unimportant and unscheduled social contacts. They make a ritual of gift-giving—little things, intrinsically nothing. I was always careful to accept each one as if it were a jade Buddha or ivory fan, and return in kind, I mean with the same formality, giving the same importance not to the gift but to the giving, the act.

"That's all you need remember. A culture whose surface manners is important to them; a people already sold in our favor; they will know your work by the time you get there much better than you will ever know theirs. They will really make you believe that being a writer, an artist, a literary man, is very important. Probably the nicest gift you can give is an inscribed book of your own."

To William Faulkner

New York
February 20, 1957

Dear Bill:

Thank you very much for your advice.

I think possibly I knew these things but it is good to have them underlined. I know what you mean about the continued formality, and it makes me itch a little bit, but I think I will get by with it.

I am particularly glad about the advice about taking books. I get so damned sick of them before they are out that giving them to someone seems a poor present. But if that's what they want, that's what they'll get.

I read in the papers that you are considering going to Greece. I hope you do. Nothing has ever given me the emotional impact like that little country—an earthquake feeling of coming home, a recognition of everything. And the light makes it seem that you can look into the surfaces of things and see them in depth. I have never been quite so moved as I was by my first experience in Greece, and it doesn't get any less moving. They are wild, crazy, disrespectful, independent people and I think you'll love them.

I was asking the brother of the Queen something about peasants and he told me a story of walking with the King in the countryside and stopping where a man was tilling a field. They asked him what kind of fertilizer he was using. The man straightened up, looked in the face of his sovereign and said: "You stick to your kinging and let me stick to my farming."

Again, thanks for your advice. I shall try not to disgrace us and if I succeed in doing that, it will be a success.

Yours,
John Steinbeck

To Elaine Steinbeck

Imperial Hotel
Tokyo
September 1 [1957]

My darling,

We arrived under a barrage of cameras usually reserved for M. M. [Marilyn Monroe] Good room here with air conditioning and the courtesy immaculate. Thirty-eight hours flying. Wake Island a hell hole of heat. Honolulu—Glendale in the Pacific. Hersey and Dos Passos wonderful traveling companions. Typhoon on the way but that means hot weather. If the reception last night at 10 P.M. is an indication, this is going to rival a Roman triumph, including the arches. I'll write a little to this here and there as I go along. Phone is ringing, phone is ringing.

Later—I have been interviewed unendingly all day long. And to put it delicately, my ass is dragging. Remember that piece about how many newspapers there are in Japan? It was an understatement. I must admit one thing though—the men they send are of a much higher caliber than any I have ever experienced. The questions are intelligent and the discussions a pleasure. But it is wearing.

I find now that they have scheduled me for a speech tomorrow. I was not told about this. You can be sure it will be the shortest speech on record.

The beer is excellent and I am sticking to it. The maids fold the end of the toilet paper with a neat little point every time I leave the room—like paper napkins in an Italian restaurant. I'll show you how to do it. Mighty pretty. I may end up as a toilet paper folder.

I am told that the Emperor has expressed a wish to see me and that I would like to do. He is a darned good marine biologist among other things. Hissing is no longer done socially but bowing is constant. I have bowed so much that my waistline is going down. For the time being I am substituting for Fujiyama as a tourist attraction. Heard a story about a professor, which I am stealing to use on the Ike administration. It was said of him that he was "a sham giant surrounded by real pygmies." I told a newspaper man that I loved Japanese lanterns, paper fish and kites, and I suspect I am going to be given a crate of them. Never mind. I'll love them. Someone sent me a plastic pencil box with 6 pencils. A newspaper sent me a box of calling cards with my name on *each* side. English on one and Japanese on the other. The typhoon has not arrived yet but everyone expects it with a certain pleasure. I am following advice to rest every moment I can. There aren't many. It will take me months to get the smile off my face and this noon I caught myself bowing to a samovar in the dining room. For your private ear—Elmer Rice is a fool. He is so afraid of doing something wrong that he is going to end up doing nothing, which is the story of all such meetings. I have a little sneaking suspicion that he resents me. So I guess I'll have to make a pet of him. Egos are in bloom as you might well suspect. And this might well be the worst thing I have ever done. I wish to God the typhoon would strike.

I'll close this now. It isn't very gay.

Love,
J

[September 3]
[Tuesday]

Now it's Tuesday the third of Sept., of the longest week in the world. Yesterday morning I was in the tub reading the paper when I discovered to my horror that I was to make the closing address of the opening session. They had not told me. I went into a blind panic, sat on the stage under blinding light. The Mayor of Tokyo spoke half an hour. The Prime Minister three-quarters of an hour—I thought, in Japanese, but was told later English. The international president of PEN (French) gave an impassioned address, shadow boxing the while. An Indian lady delegate intoned a long prayer in the bell tones of a red coon hound and then there was me, down front and lighted with enough candle power to illumine all Japan. I got a bowling ball grip on the lectern to keep from falling on my face—and plunged. I enclose my address. This is not an excerpt. It is the whole damn thing, accurately quoted. It took, with interpreter, not more than 3 minutes. And at the end all hell broke loose, probably out of relief at its brevity. Every paper has printed it. It has been compared to Japanese poetry and someone has set it to music. Anyway, thank God I didn't know, or I might have worried up an address and that would have been dreadful.

I'll have to finish this note later.

[September 7]
[Saturday]

Later is right. It is now the following Saturday. The roof fell in on me. I couldn't keep down things I swear I never ate. Everybody sent doctors. The U. S. Embassy sent a Colonel of Army Medical. So I had to come 7,000 miles to get Asiatic flu. I'm still not sure it wasn't better than the speeches. I'm up now but weak as 8 cats and the suggestion of a Japanese dinner of raw fish brings hot flashes. The Congress has moved on to Kyoto. My room looks like a combination of Forest Lawn and a garbage dump. I've subsisted on tomato soup (Campbell's) for four days. The only thing I could keep down. I've been a perfect guest because I couldn't get away. From 8 to 12 smiling Japanese hosts have observed my most delicate moments—and they have been real delicate. At some moment of fever I wrote 64 analects on a yellow pad in the manner of Confucius.

Now hear this—I get on the plane at 6:30 P.M. Tuesday the 10th and I arrive in San Francisco 24 hours later at 6:30 P. M. Tuesday the 10th. Don't think about that. It will just make you mad.

The doctor let me up for two hours yesterday and I bought you two beautiful pearls for earrings—10 1/2 centimeters and flawless. And I was very happy to get back to bed as he told me I would be. I plan to spend the weekend opening a bale of letters, mostly in Japanese and one in Japanese braille. The poor things have read my stuff in Japanese and the idea that I didn't write it that way has not penetrated.

Hersey and Galantière have been wonderful to me. They

just phoned from Kyoto 8 hours away to see how I am. We will be on the plane together Tuesday. Dos Passos has been an angel also. What a nice bunch of people.

I'm sorry I didn't get this letter off to you but I've been a little off my rocker. You know what fever does to me.

Typhoon Bess has been raising hell in Japan. She is supposed to strike Tokyo tonight sometime but kind of weakened —only 70 miles instead of 115. It has been raining dogs and very hot and sultry. Anyway the Governor of Tokyo promised us a typhoon and he'd better deliver. It's kind of dull here with everyone away in Kyoto. I'll try to save a copy of my analects but they are pretty much in demand. Dos Passos read them to the Congress and apparently they caused a sensation. Congresses aren't very humorous bodies and some of my dichos are pretty sharp. Anyway, I saw enough of this first Congress to know it is my last. I guess some people just aren't cut out for them. Another bundle of mail just arrived. I've got to open it sometime. The ones I have looked at begin, "I are Japan girl higher student which like you bookings." Mostly they enclose photos and pretty cute too. I could be a real heller with Japan girl higher student if I having impulse. But not soooo. Hai! I'm going to hit the sack now.

Damndest people. Phone just rang and a man told me a long story in Japanese. When he paused, I said, "Hai" and he hung up. I wonder what Hai means?

Anyway I love you—what's left of me. And you wouldn't want the part I threw away.

Yours,
Tokyo Rose

Oh! Lord! a letter eight feet long has just come—Japanese. Looks like poetry. Very beautifully written. I'm going to have to send lots of books in English when I get home. I should have brought a suitcase full. They want them in English.

After lunch now (Saturday night). I can't sleep and I miss you. Miss you like the devil. I've looked for wind-bells but can find only little ones. Have decided to make my own. I'll bet I can. I bet I can even pitch them. I'll copy the little ones bigger—maybe even use plate glass if I find it has a good tone. Or brass tubing might be nice. You can see that I'm getting well. I'm making plans. I'm anxious to get home now. But then, I wasn't anxious to leave.

569

Four more vases of flowers came this evening. There's not much room left for me. It stays hot and muggy and they promised that when the typhoon passed it would cool off. Bess went and missed us so no flying rooftiles or anything, but the southern cities were beat up and the southern rice crop ruined. I saw a 600-year-old cypress a foot and a half tall. Beautiful thing. Haven't seen the Emperor. He's tied up with Yugoslavs.

I've got to stop this nonsense now but I do miss you.

Love,
Abata Watabe

September 8
Sunday

Honey:

I'll write this and then race across the Pacific and try to beat it to America. Let's don't move to Japan. It is charming but I'm fed up with charm. I've done the turn, I've had the boneless chicken, the tea ceremony is fine but I don't understand much of it. The Imperial Palace is lovely. It is surrounded by a moat. I asked a Japanese how deep it was and he said deeper than a cab. He knew because he saw one taxi go in and it disappeared.

_____, the British delegate, made a long, impassioned speech in a high girlish voice. His interpreter, a real girl, had a low voice. It went on radio and the Japanese are still wondering how it is that the girl spoke in English and the man in Japanese. Is certainly a puzzlement.

The _____ delegation was nearly 100 percent queer. The Americans—Hersey, Dos Passos and me—shockingly masculine. Rice is an old lady but a masculine old lady. Galantière would make passes at a lady streetcar. All in all, we have given P. E. N. a bad name.

I should go out and walk around and I dread it. It's like swimming in warm blood, humidity 300 percent. You don't breathe, you bubble. I'm sorry to have to tell you this and crush your hopes, but we will *not* live in Japan. You can grow your chrysanthemums at home.

Love,
Watanabe

Darling:

Back at the old stand. The morning paper says the epidemic has broken out again in Tokyo and schools closing for lack of customers.

The feeling about the bomb is something. It is strange and submerged and always present. It isn't quite anger and not quite sorrow—it is mixed up with a curious shame but not directed shame. It is an uncanny thing—in the air all the time. The typhoon rain is reported to have an all time high of radioactivity. Every bomb test is salt in the wounds.

[September 10]
[Tuesday]

Next morning—The hall boy whose name is Yoshiro is a friend of mine and has taken care of me. He came in at about 8:30 and said a girl wanted to see me. I told him that is ridiculous at this time in the morning. He said, "Please see her because she came in from the country to see you and she has been waiting two days. She brought you a present." So I said, "O. K. Bring her in." She had a perfectly flat face and rather poor clothes and they were torn. And she was weeping. Her name is Mifuyu Nishikawa. The hotel people would never let her in because of her poor clothes. So this morning she tried to get in through a back entrance and they put up barbed wire and she got caught in the wire and Yoshiro got her loose and brought her in secretly. She brought me two carved figures she made herself. She cried the whole time. I gave her a ballpoint pen and a letter which she particularly asked for and she wouldn't take any money. She had brought a copy of Grapes in Japanese she wanted signed. Then I got on clothes and took her out through the lobby so she wouldn't have to go through the wire again, and she cried the whole time.

About 10:30 the President of Tokyo P. E. N. visited me with a bouquet bigger than he was.

A Japanese girl who has been helping us told me that Kyoto was once the capital of Japan and was very beautiful. I asked her why they had moved the capital to Tokyo and she said Kyoto has rowsy crimate. And I guess it has but I can't

571

see how it could be rowsier than Tokyo. The air is full of damp feathers.

Love,
Tokyo Joe

To Mrs. Donnie Radcliffe
OF THE STAFF OF THE *SALINAS-CALIFORNIAN*

New York
December 22, 1957

Dear Mrs. Radcliffe:

The blinding flash and mushroom cloud of the suggestion that a Salinas school be given my name is shattering as a compliment, and I love compliments as well as the next man —maybe better. A heartwarming honor it is, even as a suggestion.

So far only my first name has been given to an institution.

Perhaps it is well to inspect honors in the light of cool reason lest the footprint in the concrete disclose a bunion. Do the proposers of this naming wish to subject my name to the curses of unborn generations of young Salinians? Think of the millions to whom the name Horse Mann is a dirty word.

But the danger of the situation is not only aimed at me. Consider, if you will, the disastrous result if some innocent and talented student should look into my own scholastic record, seeking perhaps for inspiration. Why his whole ambition might crash in flames.

In view of these sober afterthoughts, and being still shaken by the compliment implied, I hope the Board of Trustees will think very carefully before taking this irrevocable step.

If the city of my birth should wish to perpetuate my name clearly but harmlessly, let it name a bowling alley after me or a dog track or even a medium price, low-church brothel —but a school—!

In humble appreciation,

John Steinbeck

At the foot of the page, in his own handwriting, he added:

Dear Donnie: This is a copy for you. And of course you may print it in any way you see fit. What fun! Twenty years ago they were burning my books. Makes me feel old and pretty dead and I assure you I am neither.

> Yours,
> J. S.

Joseph Bryan III, the writer, had been a friend of the Steinbecks ever since their meeting in Spain in 1954. He lived in Richmond, Virginia.

To Joseph Bryan III

New York
[December 17, 1957]

YES, JOE, THERE *IS* A SANTA CLAUS IF YOU BUT LOOK ABOUT. HE IS:

In the wistful eyes of a general writing Santa for one more star;

In the homeward tread of a call girl whose date wanted to dance;

In gay, song-driven garbage men;

In the earnest loft burglar with twelve fur coats for his mother;

In the selflessness of Richard Nixon and of his wife Pat and of his children whose names I do not know.

SANTA IS ALWAYS THERE IF YOU HAVE EYES TO SEE. YOU WILL FIND HIM:

When you hit your funny bone on the bathroom door, Kris Kringle is nigh;
He dwelleth on the top floor of the FBI Building at 69th and Third Avenue;
You will glimpse him in the subway at 5:15;
His cheery hand reaches for the cab door you thought you had;
When your show closes out of town—look for reindeer droppings;
Santa speaks in the kindly voice of the income tax collector;
He lurketh under the broken filling—peereth from behind the ulcer and caroleth in the happy halls of Mattewan.
Yes, Joe, there *is* a Santa Claus if we but seek him—BEFORE HE SEEKS US.

MERRY CHRISTMAS TO ALL
AND
GOODNIGHT

When you slip in the bath tub and land on your ear
hallelulia in excelcis
Kris Kringle is near
(Sorry, Virginia)

J. and E.

Throughout this winter the *Morte d'Arthur* was never far from his mind.

574

To Elizabeth Otis

New York
March 1958
Friday

Dear Elizabeth:

I enjoyed the other night at dinner very much. Lots of laughter and fun. I do feel to myself as though I were drawn taut as a bowstring and might snap, and I'm afraid I communicate that feeling. I find it almost impossible to discuss the Morte and the more I read the more that is so. It has tunneled so deep in me that I can hardly dredge it up to the word level.

I can't tell you what solace I get from the new boat [at Sag Harbor]. I can move out and anchor and have a little table and a yellow pad and some pencils. I can put myself in a position so that nothing can intervene. Isn't that wonderful? I bought a little kerosene lantern with a mantle today so I can even work at night on board. And also a tiny heating thing that works with alcohol which can warm the cabin in the coldest weather. I'm beginning to take health from it long before it is delivered.

To Elizabeth Otis and Chase Horton

[New York]
March 14, 1958

There seems to be something necessary about pressures. The other night I was lying awake wishing I could get to Malory with a rolling barrage of sling-stones and arrows—which isn't likely to happen—and suddenly it came back to

575

me that I have always worked better under pressure of one kind or another—poverty, death, emotional confusion, divorces—always something. So maybe I had better pray not for surcease but for famine, plague, catastrophe, and bankruptcy. Then I would probably work like a son-of-a-bitch. I'm comparatively serious about this.

A curious state of suspension has set in, kind of a floaty feeling like the drifting in a canoe on a misty lake while ghosts and winkies, figures of fog go past—half recognized, and only partly visible. It would be reasonable to resist this vagueness, but for some reasons which I will set down later, I do not.

It is all very well to look back at the Middle Ages from a position of vantage. The story, or part of it is finished. We know—to a certain extent—what happened and why and who and what were the causes. This knowledge of course is strained through minds which have no likeness of experience with the mind of the Middle Ages. But the writer of the Morte did not know what had happened, what was happening, nor what was going to happen. He was caught as we are now. In forlornness—he didn't know finally whether York or Lancaster would win, nor did he know that this was the least important of problems. He must have felt that the economic world was out of tune since the authority of the manors was slipping away. The revolts of the subhuman serfs must have caused consternation in his mind. The whisperings of religious schism were all around him so that the unthinkable chaos of ecclesiastical uncertainty must have haunted him. Surely he could only look forward to these changes, which we find healthy, with horrified misgiving.

And out of this devilish welter of change—so like the one today—he tried to create a world of order, a world of virtue governed by forces familiar to him. And what material had he to build with? Not the shelves of well-ordered source books, not even the public records of his time, not a single chronological certainty, since such a system did not exist. He did not even have a dictionary in any language. Perhaps he had a few manuscripts, a missal, maybe the Alliterative Poems. Beyond this, he had only his memory and his hopes and his intuitions. If he could not remember a word, he had to use another or make one up.

And what were his memories like? I'll tell you what they were like. He remembered bits and pieces of what he had

576

read. He remembered the deep and terrible forest and the slime of the swamps. He remembered without recalling stories told by the fire in the manorial hall by trouvères from Brittany; but also in his mind were the tellings in the sheep byre in the night—by a shepherd whose father had been to Wales and had heard Cymric tales of wonder and mysticism. In his mind were perhaps some of the triads and also some of the lines from the poems of hidden meaning which survived in him because the words and figures were compelling and spoke to his unconscious mind, although the exact meaning was lost. The writer had also a sky full of cloud-like history, not arranged in time but with people and events all co-existing simultaneously. Among these were friends, relatives, kings, old gods and heroes, ghosts and angels and devils of feeling and of traditions lost and rediscovered.

And finally he had himself as literary material—his vices and failures, his hopes and angers and alarms, his insecurities for the future and his puzzlement about the past. Everyone and every event he had ever known was in him. And his illnesses were there too, always the stomachache, since the food of his time was inadequate for health, perhaps bad teeth —a universal difficulty, maybe arrested syphillis or the grandchildren of the pox carried in distorted genes. He had the strong uninspected fabric of the church, memory of music heard, unconscious observation of nature, since designed observation is a recent faculty. He had all of the accumulated folk-lore of his time—magic and sooth-saying, forecast and prophecy—witchcraft and its brother medicine. All these are not only in the writer of the Morte—they are the writer.

Let us now consider me—who am the writer who must write the writer as well as the Morte. Why has it been necessary to read so much and to accumulate so much—most of which will probably not be used? I think it necessary for me to know everything I can about what Malory knew and how he might have felt, but it is also necessary for me to be aware of what he did not know, could not have known, and could not feel. For example—if I did not know something about contemporary conditions and attitudes toward medieval villeins and serfs, I could not understand Malory's complete lack of feeling for them. Actually, without considerable study on the part of a present-day man—if he were confronted by a fifteenth century man—there would be no possi-

577

ble communication. I think it is possible through knowledge and discipline for a modern man to understand, and, to a certain extent, live into a fifteenth century mind, but the reverse would be completely impossible.

I don't think any of the research on this project has been wasted because while I may not be able to understand all of Malory's mind, at least I know what he could *not* have thought or felt.

[unsigned]

To Eugène Vinaver

New York
March 10, 1958

Dear Eugène Vinaver:

It will not have escaped your notice that a mule has foaled in Cornwall, that there has been an unusual appearance of the northern lights, that the weather has been strange and that there have been meteorological manifestations which, in a more enlightened age, would have been justly considered portents.

Those portents refer to Elaine and to me.

We are arriving in London about June 1st and will be at the Dorchester. We will be staying in England for the month of June.

I have read until I am blind with reading. I think I have some emotional grasp on the 15th century. And as is natural —the field has widened faster than I could go so that the only thing which has increased is my own ignorance. But there must come a time when one says to oneself: "If I go much further, I will know nothing." Now, I must feel and taste some few more things—Colchester, Bamburgh, Cornwall. These are stimulations to intuition.

My profound hope is that some time during the month of June, you might be able to join us in a walk about—perhaps to let imagination run free. My associate, Chase Horton, is going to join me.

578

Elaine sends her finest to you and to your charming wife Betty and so do I.

Yours,
John Steinbeck

To Joseph Bryan III

[New York]
March 15 [1958]

Dear Joe:

This is the kind of letter you write when you just want to talk and haven't anything to say. Snowing hard outside. Typewriter clacking in the other room with a good girl copying long sections of an article in Speculum—mostly in Latin of the 15th century. That's one reason for the hand writing. The other is that it is the only kind of writing that comes naturally to me.

Elaine is doing very well [after surgery]. Next Monday she will get out for the first time for Tamara Geva's birthday. Meanwhile she has the telephone and squads of visitors. It is snowing today—big pieces like white cow flops and the streets a mess already.

I envy you being able to talk with Graves. I have never met him but I want to. Have been going over his White Goddess again. What a man! He knows more about what I am trying to get at than anyone. Scholars have a way of parenthesizing periods and then slipping in behind the safety of the parenthesis. Only Graves seems to have a true sense of continuity. It doesn't stop on century changes nor tidy up with descriptive drawstrings. One thing grows out of another while keeping a great part of what it grew out of. The American Western is not a separate thing but a direct descendant of the Arthurian legend with all the genes intact and drawn to the surface by external magnets. Nor was the legend ever new. Anyway, I am not going to belabor you with scholastic frustrations. Just tell Mr. Graves, please, that I admire and wish to God I could talk to him.

579

So many of these scholars are full of holes. Also—they, some of them anyway, are incredibly vain. Also they cover for one another.

But enough of this faculty club bickering. I simply want to know what happened insofar as it can be known.

I'm making a dedication of the Malory work to my sister Mary, who was deeply involved in it. I wrote the opening the other day—funny to write a dedication before anything else. I enclose a copy which I think might amuse you. But it isn't meant to be funny. It is deadly serious and damned good Middle English, I think you will agree.

For yourself the best. Why don't you start a boarding house on your inheritance? Might be a new Tom Wolfe.

so long,
J. S.

WHAN AS CHYLDE NINE WYNTRE OF
AGE I TOKE SIEGE AT ROUNDE TABLE
MONGST ORGULUS AND WORSHYPPFUL AND
DOUGHTYEST KNYGHTS OF KYNG ARTHUR'S
COMPAGNY—GRATE LACK WAS OF SQUYRES
OF NOBLE BIRTH AND HARDYNESSE TO
BEAR SCHYLDE AND LAUNCE, TO BOCKLE
HARNYSS, TO SALUE PROWYSS AND
SUCCOURE FALLEN.
    THAN YT CHAUNCED THAT SQUYRE-
LYKE DUTIS FELL ON MY SYSTIR SIX WYNTRE
OF AGE THAT FOR JANTYL HARDYNES HAD
NO FELLAWE LYVYNGE.
    SOMTYMES YT HAPS IN SADDNESSE
AND PYTIE THAT WHO FAYTHFULL SERVYS
YS NOT FAYTHFULL SEEN—MY FAYRE AND
SYKER SYSTER-SQUYRE DURES STYLLE
UNDUBBED.
    WHEREFORE THYS DAYE I MAK
AMENDYS TO MY POWER. I MAYKE HIR
KNYGHT AND GIFF HER LONDIS.
    AND FRO THYS HOWER SHE SHALL BE
HIGHT—SIR MARY STEINBECK OF THE VALE
SALYNIS.
    GOD GYVE HIR WORSHYPP SAUNZ
JAUPARDYE.

A reminiscence of "Sir Mary" occurs in a letter to Mrs. Waverly Anderson, Elaine Steinbeck's mother:

"My youngest sister when she was a little girl didn't want to be a girl at all. She felt it the greatest insult that she was a girl. And when you consider that she rode like a cockleburr, was the best pitcher anywhere near her age on the West side of town, and was such a good marble player that the season had to be called off because she had won every marble in town, you can understand why she felt that it was unjust that she should wear little skirts. This all gets back to a magic she designed. One that didn't work—to her sorrow. She felt that if she went to sleep in just such and such a position, she would be a boy when she awakened. For a long time she experimented with positions but she could never arrive at the right one and every morning—there she was, still a girl. This was great sadness to her. And then her girlness crept up on her and she became lady-like. She threw a ball with that clumsiness girls have, she ran with little stumbling steps, she cried a great deal—in a word she became a dame."

To Elizabeth Otis

[Sag Harbor]
April 6, 1958

Dear Elizabeth:

This is really heaven out here. There is only one drawback to it. If there are guests or children here I have absolutely no place to go to work or to be alone. My stuff gets stuffed into closets and drawers and it sometimes takes me several days to find it again. Right now Thom is with us. I am going to build a little tiny workroom out on the point, too small for a bed so that it can't be considered a guest room under any circumstances. It will be off limits to everyone. I can take electricity out there on a wire which can be rolled up when we are not here. It doesn't

581

need plumbing of any kind. I designed a cute little structure, six-sided, with windows looking in all directions. Under the windows will be storage space for paper on three sides and the other two will be a desk so that it will need no furniture except a chair and I will use one of our canvas deck chairs for that. It will look like a little lighthouse. I'm going to get to it right away because Elaine gets too lonely without guests and with no place to go guests throw any work I want to do sky high. I will build most of it myself and then with that and the boat I will have some semblance of privacy. One of its main features will be an imposing padlock on the door. I think I am going to name it Sanity's Stepchild.

I'm afraid I can't concentrate today. A thirteen-year-old boy who paces, can't sit still, doesn't read, picks up things and puts them down, rattles things and can't go outside because it is raining and probably wouldn't want to anyway, is slowly driving me to distraction if I am trying to concentrate. Sanity's Stepchild looks very good to me at this point.

So that is that.

Love,
John

Sanity's Stepchild was only a temporary name. Following his Arthurian bent he soon christened the little work-house Joyous Garde, after the castle to which Launcelot took Guinevere.

To Elizabeth Otis, Chase Horton, and Shirley Fisher
A SENIOR PARTNER AT MCINTOSH AND OTIS

Dorchester Hotel
London
June 5, 1958

Dear Elizabeth
and Chase
and Shirley:

The loveliest weather you can imagine and every flower screaming with joy and splashing color about. Even the British grudgingly approve. This is the nicest trip we have ever had—no press, no telephones, no appointments. We have wandered about, to Pyx and Muniment rooms of the Abbey, to the London Museum in Kensington Palace to see the models of the city down the ages from wattle on a mud flat, to Roman camp to Caesar's ill-erected Tower— and in the streets following the line of old walls, and the dream memories of the street names, along the Embankment. You have only to squint your eyes a little to see it all in all periods.

I have written John Forman [headmaster of the Forman School, where Thom was enrolled] a letter of such consummate treachery that any way he turns he will be trapped. I will be interested to see what he has to answer. It is a deadly and jesuitical letter. I wish I could send you a copy but I had no carbon.

Elaine has gone out this morning to tombify. When she gets home we can scrape her for graveyard dust.

Kenneth Galbraith, the economist, came through the other night from lecturing in Warsaw. He had many stories, particularly the jokes being told within the party. My favorite is a solemn definition. A student said: "Under Capitalism man exploits man, whereas under Communism it is just the reverse."

The month is moving along steadily. It will be time to leave before we know it. But it is a wildly pleasant trip and good even if it were of no value.

I think I'll go out and walk and look now. I like that.

> Love, to all,
> John

This is "the deadly and jesuitical letter" to the Head-master of Thom Steinbeck's school. It dealt with a problem that had come up before. An anonymous letter-writer, signing himself FBI, had called Mr. Forman's attention to the sentence in *Cannery Row* in which Steinbeck mentioned that some of the girls in Fauna's house were Christian Scientists.

To John Forman

[London]
June 3, 1958

My dear Mr. Forman:

Your letter of May 31st arrived this morning and I have considered it very slowly trying to understand both what it says and what is perhaps implied. In this response I hope to leave no room for interpretations.

When I visited the Forman School and enjoyed your hospitality I was quite well aware that you and Mrs. Forman were Christian Scientists. And surely your feeling that there was no hostility was keen and accurate. Indeed the opposite was true, for it seemed to me that we were in agreement that the Christian fabric is a strong and ancient tree out of which a number of branches grew, and that one must know the tree before one is capable of climbing to his own personal branch. I wish my son to know the tree. The branch he chooses will be what his feeling, his thought and his nature make desirable and necessary. In this I think we agreed and I still believe that to be so. But I would no more interfere with his choice than I would rob him of any other freedom so long, at least, as his choice is not dictated by fear or ignorance, or social or economic gain. However, he must have the tools of choice—knowledge, understanding, humility and contemplation.

I have never felt or uttered contempt for any religion. On the other hand, in religion as in politics I have attacked corruption and hypocrisy and I think in this I have the indisputable example of Jesus, if authority be needed.

Let me now go to Page 17 of Cannery Row. I dearly hope that neither you nor your friend read it out of context. The statement that a number of the girls were Christian Scientists was neither contempt nor satire but simply a statement of fact. For eighteen years I lived and worked in that laboratory. The book is only fiction in form and style. I do not know what the organized church felt about it but these girls took comfort and safety in their faith and I cannot conceive of any Christian organization rejecting them. There is no possible alternative interpretation of Jesus' instructions concerning Mary Magdalene. His contempt was reserved for the stone throwers.

Cannery Row was written in compassion rather than contempt, and a bartender who reads Science and Health (and he did) seems to me no ill thing. Few heroes and fewer saints have sprung into being full blown.

In only one book have I tried to formalize my own personal branch of the ancient tree. That was East of Eden, and while it is long, it is precise.

Finally, I am content that you can and will help my son in the always agonizing search for himself, for I felt that the tone and the overtone of the school were good. And while I am not inclined to be critical, I do feel saddened by the man who, calling himself FBI, used as a weapon a misinterpretation of one sentence of a lifetime of work. It seems to me that it was an unkindly and therefore unChristian impulse.

John Steinbeck

Toward the end of the month, he reported to Elizabeth Otis:

"A letter from Forman says—'What a lovely letter. I feel very happy now about having Thom with us next year. I hope we are going to have the added pleasure of seeing you as time goes on—'

"I think that took some doing after my letter and it makes me think that he is a better man than I might have. Mine was a tough letter to answer, I think you will agree, and he did it well."

To Elizabeth Otis

London
June 13, 1958
Friday

Dear Elizabeth and I guess Chase, if he hasn't taken off before this arrives:

We just got back to London this afternoon. Went by train to Glastonbury on Tuesday. Stayed in Shirley's pet George and Pilgrim in the room of Henry VIII from the window of which he is supposed to have watched the sacking of the Abbey. We climbed the Tor and sat for a very long time up there seeing how it was and talking to an old Somerset man and a little boy. A lot of time in the Abbey close, just watching. Bought all of the local books and their theories and read them, walked about and more looking. Then the man who wrote the current London hit play Flowering Cherry [Robert Bolt], who teaches school nearby, took us to village cricket and afterwards, with the teams or elevens if that's what they are called, for beer and skittles in the village pub and we learned a lot: Of pixilated fields where people will not walk, of witchcraft still practiced so that only last year a man was tarred and feathered as a witch for casting spells. And it is a magical country and it does seem to me that the Somerset people don't look like the others. They have cats' eyes, both men and women, and they hide behind their eyes like sleepy cats. I asked for and got some cuttings from the Glastonbury Thorn which flowers at Christmas, and I am going to try to root them. Maybe I can. If Joseph of Arimathea could root his staff I should be able to root a fresh cutting from his staff.

Love to all there,
John

He was. It still grows in the Sag Harbor garden.

To John O'Hara

London
June 14, 1958

Dear John:

Yours was a good letter. I can't tell you how glad and warm I felt to get it. There was kindness in it and wisdom and besides it was god damn good writing. I am glad also to see that maturity, which is ordinarily a process or even a synonym for erosion, has not eliminated ferocity in you. I have a very strong feeling that you are about to shoot the moon.

I knew the shock of Belle [O'Hara's first wife who had died in January 1954] and I was speechless hoping that you would understand that my inability to trap words into a pattern was somehow a measure of my sorrow. But you have a little girl to keep you linked securely to past and future, and a big girl [his second wife, Katherine] to relate future and present. Hell, man, they drive us—else I suppose we wouldn't move at all.

My boys are moving into the smelly, agonizing glory of manhood. I won't know the world they will inhabit. I just get glimpses of the life they live now. But the incredible gallantry of a child facing the complication of living with no equipment except teeth and nails, and accumulated instincts and memories that go back to the first activated cell in a house of plasm, never fails to astonish me. And I am amazed at their beauty, pure unadulterated loveliness. My boys have been going through the horror of disintegration about them and handling it with more wisdom and integrity than I could whistle up.

I am springing them from Walpurgis on the East Side this fall. They are going away to school, a new and frightening life also but without the pattern of decay which has been their sentence for the last few years. There is little communication between father and son but a deep and wordless love creeps through I think from both sides of the barricade. I wish we benighted gentiles had a bar mitzvah—a moment when the community accepts them as men—important, responsible and free. The two boys and I had a small Irish version of it recently when I welcomed them as men, told them it was a painful thing and magnificent—tried to explain the slavery of freedom. But I think they know. They have had secretly to wear the toga while pretending to be babies.

I think they need eagles now, the external physical symbol of truth and gallantry with which to identify themselves. I'm having massive signets carved which aim to be the standard of themselves, to tie them to the line and to introduce them to truth and virtue. It must be intensely personal and at the same time relate them. It may be what used to be called corny and probably now has another name but means the same. So I have decided to tie it to the most personal thing we know—our name.

Our name is an old one from Westphalia or the Saxon Baltic before they moved on England. Stein still means a stone but beck is exclusively English as a word. Some time in the 13th century my blood people moved down the map instead of up and got fancy. Probably put a chain across the Rhine and charged toll against the poor bastards who simply wanted to transport goods. This benefaction naturally ennobled them and they began wearing a "von" to prove—whatever they wanted and/or had the power and weapons to prove. However, that was all dropped not because of democracy but because it was too damned hard for their neighbors to spell. But the name in old English and disappeared Saxon means stone stream—or brook or beck. I can't draw—but the seals are a rapid stream taking the reverse curve of an S and in the stream at the belly of the S a large rock with the water flowing around it on either side and the motto "Aqua petrum vincit." Poor kids have water and rocks in themselves as well as their name and I think it's no bad thing for them to know that water does defeat rocks.

We are here for a month. I'm doing final research before beginning a very long and to me a satisfying job.

I hope all is well with you. Your letter had a glow that would have shattered a Geiger counter and I take that to mean that you are deeply at work and you can't want better than that.

Thank you for the picture. It has gone up in good and proper company. I shall do the same if I ever get one that makes me feel pretty but right now I don't feel glowy. Maybe that's because I am going to work but am not actually in the furnace.

We'll be back July 1st and hope to see you.

Thank you for writing. It is a letter for keeping and going back to.

Yours and with love from both of us to both of you.

John

To Eugène Vinaver

London
June 22, 1958

Dear Eugène:

I had just finished the enclosed and moved some papers and found your gifts which had been placed there while we were away—and your wonderful letter. I love compliments, even, I suspect, if they aren't true. My father, who was a wise as well as a taciturn man, tried to instruct me and failed as all fathers fail. In defamation, he said, inspect the purpose and the source. In a compliment do the same. And I think he could have found no fault with this except perhaps in my unrestrained pleasure. Your letter goes with a very few other precious ones—which make me alive and proud—a kind one from Mr. Roosevelt on the birth of my first son; a private letter of commendation from General Arnold, commander of our wartime air arm; a letter from a Danish bookseller telling of a woman who rowed a boat in from the outer islands to trade two chickens for one of my books. Those aren't very many but they are very good to have, and they bridge the times when self-love is at low ebb. Thank you.

A year earlier Steinbeck had written to Pascal Covici from Florence:

"At a cocktail party I met an Italian man from the underground, a fugitive not only from Mussolini but Hitler. He told me that during the war he came on a little thin book printed on onion skin paper which so exactly described Italy that he translated and ran off five hundred copies on a mimeograph. It was The Moon Is Down. He said it went everywhere in the resistance and requests came in for it from all over even though possession was an automatic death sentence. And do you remember the attacks on it at home from our bellicose critics?"

A long time ago I learned a trick—or perhaps it might be called a method for writing. I stopped addressing my work to a faceless reader and addressed one person as though I had only that one to talk to. I gave him a face and a personality. Sometimes I told a book to a real person. Several to Ed Ricketts. East of Eden was addressed to my sons to try to tell them about their roots, both in a family sense and in a human sense. I should like to hold you in image in this new work. You would then be the focusing point, the courts, the jury. Also the discipline of your great knowledge would forbid nonsense while the memory of excited exchanges would keep alive the joy and the explorations. This would be very valuable to me. And I hope you will not forbid it.

Yours,
John

To Professor and Mrs. Eugène Vinaver

London
June 27, 1958
Friday

Dear Eugène and Betty:

Back in Londunium after a successful queste. The defeated should begin trooping in to pray you mercy at any moment now. First to Chester and circumambulated the walls—extra, super et intra, walked in the Rows and peered into crevices and holes, a noble and strange city captured between the warp and woof of Roman and medieval patterns with only a patina of sterling area. Then on by car to the dragon lake and found there our old friend Ingrid Bergman making a Chinese film, a different kind of dragon surely and it did seem odd that neither she nor any member of the company knew that they were living where the dragons fought. Then on to Caernarvon and again the walls and towers and trying with all of my might to rip off the dust-covers of time. It is not hard to do. Then on to Conway and there took our rest until next day at howre of prime. Then across Englonde and to Durham to bend knee to St. Cuthbert and to bow respect to the bones of Bede, and to shudder a little at that mailed and military bishopric, a See of iron. Then back to Alnwick with the sweet meadows behind, sheep in the moat and cows in the bailey, and then finally to the end and the proper end to Bambrugh. The rain was black and then it opened like a torn curtain and the streaks of sun exploded on the battlements as though the original Ina the flame-bearer had come back. In all of these it is necessary to see into and under and around as one must the beast in Peer Gynt. Of course I think I can but that may be self-delusion.

I, as a novelist, am a product not only of my own time but of all the flags and tatters, the myth and prejudice, the faith and filth that preceded me. I must believe that it was the same with Malory. And to understand his stories and his figures, I must, as much as is humanly possible, subject myself to his pattern and background, in all directions. A novel-

591

ist is a kind of flypaper to which everything adheres. His job then is to try to reassemble life into some kind of order.

To people of our time, unable or unwilling to project into the past, a castle is a kind of lovely dream and armour the clothing of a pageant. But in Malory's time armour and castles had one major purpose, to protect lives and to serve as a base for counter-attack. The sword was not an ornament. It was designed to kill people. If the towers and curtain walls are beautiful, it is because strength with economy and purpose usually turn out to be beautiful. We do not know it now, because like purposes are involved, but the shape and line of the guided missile will be found to be lovely. It does seem to me that our time has more parallels with the fifteenth century than, let us say, the nineteenth century did, so that we may be able to understand it more nearly accurately than the Pre-Raphaelite guardsmen of the Victorian round table. For we are as unconsciously savage and as realistically self-seeking as the people of the Middle Ages.

We got back at three this morning and I have a great packet of things to remember.

I forgot to hand you some of the vellum we bought. I shall enclose it with some books I have ordered to be sent to you.

I tried soaking some of it in detergent and found the ink comes out readily. I suppose that it should then be ironed dry with a warm iron or boned to smoothness. I am taking some sheets home with me and will experiment with it to recover its original surface.

I hope in the many months to come when this work comes borning that you will not mind my asking for advice and criticism. That is the time when it has value, in the process.

And again our thanks for being so good to us.

yours,
John

To Elizabeth Otis

Sag Harbor
July 9, 1958

Dear Elizabeth:

Yesterday I started the translating, starting from scratch, and continued today.

You remember when I started talking about it, I wanted to keep the rhythms and tones of Malory. When he started, he tried to keep intact the Frenssche books. But as he went along he changed. He began to write for the fifteenth century ear and the *English* mind and feeling. And only then did it become great. The twentieth century ear cannot take in the fifteenth century form whether in tone, sentence structure or phraseology. A shorter and more concise statement is the natural vehicle now.

An amazing thing happens once you drop the restrictions of the fifteenth century language. Immediately the stories open up and come out of their entombment.

I can give you many examples. Let us take the word worship in the Malorian sense. It is an old English word *worth-ship* and it meant eminence gained by one's personal qualities of courage or honor. You could not inherit worship-fulness. It was solely due to your own nature and actions. Beginning in the thirteenth century, the word moved into a religious connotation which it did not have originally. And now it has lost its original meaning and has become solely a religious word. Perhaps the word honor has taken its place or even better, renown. Once renown meant to be renamed because of one's own personal qualities and now it means to be celebrated but still for personal matters. You can't inherit renown.

Anyway, I am started and I feel pretty fine and free. I am working in the garage until my new workroom is completed and it is good. Thank God for the big Oxford dictionary. I find myself running to it constantly. And where Malory uses often two adjectives meaning the same thing I am using one. For on the one hand I must increase the writing—on the other I must draw it in for our present day eye and ear. It may be charming to read—"to bring his wyf with him for she was called a fayre lady and passing wyse and her name was called Igrane." But in our time it is more communicating to say—"to bring his wife, Igrane, with him for she was reputed to be not only beautiful but clever."

I do hope this doesn't sound like vandalism to you. If it or rather they (the stories) had been invented in the fifteenth century, it would be another matter—but they weren't. If Malory could rewrite Chrétien for his time, I can rewrite Malory for mine. Tennyson rewrote him for his soft Victorian audience and pulled the toughness out. But our readers can take the toughness. Malory removed some of the repetition from the Frensshe books. I find it necessary to remove most of the repetition from Malory.

It is my intention to write to you regularly in this vein. It is better than a day book because it is addressed to someone. Will you keep the letters? They will be the basis for my introduction.

Catbird is acting up over at camp. I will have to go this afternoon and try to straighten him out.

Big thunderstorm and rain last night and the wind blew big.

I can't tell you how happy I am to be at work. Makes me want to sing and I will.

Elaine is fine. Working like mad in her garden.

Love,
John

To Elia Kazan

[Sag Harbor]
[October 14, 1958]
Dear Gadg:

Many thanks for your letter. It was a thoughtful thing to do. One of my main faults is that I take myself too seriously but I have other faults which will run it a close second and third and fourth.

Elaine was sad that you and Mollie saw and heard us blasting away destructively at each other. It doesn't happen very often and we get over it. It is as though imps got in and took over. They ride on alcohol. I always think I am braced to withstand it and then a school teacher tone comes into Elaine's voice and I go mad. She gets me every time. Maybe a memory of my Presbyterian grandmother who was always right. I just literally go insane when I hear that didactic tone of voice. But I have learned some things. Such a fight is a kind of purge to a woman. She comes out of it feeling fine. A man is likely to brood about it. And I have learned to brood as little as possible. It's just imps. And maybe we play into each other's hands. If I didn't get mad, Elaine would have to keep trying until I did. Maybe it's better just to blow up. But E. being more a social creature than I am, hates to have anyone hear it. I'm sorry if we made you unhappy. I just want to assure you that we like each other more than we ever have, if that is possible. And the fights get rarer and rarer. It might be really dangerous if they should stop.

Do you and Mollie ever come to open fighting? We wouldn't without drink. Maybe it's better than leaving things bottled. I don't know.

My work moves on slowly. I kind of like the way it is going down now. I threw out everything I read to you and started fresh before I got your letter. Reading it aloud to you made me aware of things I didn't like.

I don't know why I keep on. I have plenty of books for one lifetime. But perhaps because of long conditioning I go right on whether it is lousy or not. The great crime I have commit-

595

ted against literature is living too long and writing too much, and not good enough. But I like to write. I like it better than anything. That's why neither theatre nor movies really deeply interest me. It's the fresh clear sentence or thought going down on paper for the first time that makes me pleased and fulfilled. All the rest—rewrite and by-products are mechanical to me but there is nothing mechanical in the joy of the first time.

Did any of your pictures turn out well? I like the way you take them—so casually. If there is a good half humorous and half dignified one, I should like to send it to my boys.

That's all—thanks again for your nice and helpful letter. There's nothing wrong with us or our relationship, believe me. Just two brute humans.

love
John

To Pascal Covici

Sag Harbor
October 17, 1958

Dear Pat:

Wyntre ben y commun in loud sing cookoo

Comes time pretty soon to move into town. I love this season but the city will be good too. How very fortunate I am that I can have both and each one as it is needed.

This is the time to put things away. It is strange. In spring and summer we work over the earth as though it belonged to us—plant lawns and cut them, flowers, trees, put in water pipes. We are proprietors. And then the fall comes and the frost and the ice and it is too much for us. We lose our ownership. We scurry to put things away out of danger, drain water, let the leaves be as they fall. The strong forces creep back and we burrow down like moles to wait it out until we can take control again. It's a fine lesson every year—a lesson in humility. I can sit in my little house on the point and watch the winter come and I guess I am a traitor to my species because I get a sharp sense of joy to see the older gods move back in. I am for them. The wind and the ice taking command again. We can't fight it. We must retreat as we always have. Almost my favorite season. For some reason it brings a kind of happy energy back to me. It is almost as though I go back to old loyalties. The birds are flocking and flying. The geese go over at night very high. And the air has muscles.

We will be coming in about the 1st of Nov. This place though will be waiting. I can come out any time when I need a change from the city. I love the winter storms and the cold. They are much more my friends and relatives than the summer with its lawn mowers and the brown girls greasy with sun tan oil.

My life is coming back now. Strange isn't it how periodically my life force goes into hibernation very like death and then it stirs very drowsily to life and one day the words begin to rush out and every other consideration dissipates like mist. I am very fortunate in so many ways.

Well, this is nearly all. The words are beginning to flock and fly again like the night birds. I wonder where they will go this time.

> See you soon
> John

His delight in the Sag Harbor property was pervasive. As he wrote O'Hara:

"I grow into this countryside with a lichen grip."

And to Shirley Fisher:

"It is getting lovely and cold out here now. Tonight the bay is smooth as milk and little curls of mist, millions of tiny white pin curls are rising about a foot in the air. It looks a little like a burning stubble field. And in this curly thicket the ducks are hidden, and they speak up now and then in conversational tones and then a fish jumps and plops back. Elayne the Fayre [his boat] is riding so high in the water that maybe she isn't in at all but hanging a few inches

597

above the surface. And it is so clear that the sky is porcupiny with stars and yet it is a black night. It's very late but I am wakeful."

For some time he had been troubled about his inability to find the exact tone for his Arthurian translation. It is possible that this is why he had taken a step unprecedented for him—submitting it for Elizabeth Otis's and Chase Horton's opinions, or reading it aloud to Elia Kazan.

To Chase Horton

[Sag Harbor]
October 21, 1958

Dear Chase:

I realize that after all of our months of work together, for me to cut myself off as I have must seem on the prima donna side. And I haven't been able to explain it simply, not even to myself. Kind of like an engine that is missing fire in several cylinders and I don't know quite what is causing it. The only thing that will be applicable to you is that the engine doesn't run. The whole thing must be a little insulting to you and I don't want it to be. It grows out of my own uncertainties.

You will remember that, being dissatisfied with my own work because it had become glib, I stopped working for over a year in an attempt to allow the glibness to die out, hoping then to start fresh with what might feel to me like a new language. Well, when I started in again it wasn't a new language at all. It was a pale imitation of the old language only it wasn't as good because I had grown rusty and the writing muscles were atrophied. So I picked at it and worried at it because I wanted desperately for this work to be the best I had ever done. My own ineptness and sluggishness set me back on my heels. Finally I decided to back off and to try to get the muscles strong on something else—a short thing, perhaps even a slight thing although I know there are no slight things. And that didn't work either. I wrote seventy-five pages on the new thing, read them and threw them away. Then I wrote fifty pages and threw them away. And then it came to me in a quick flash what that language was. It had been lying around all the time ready at hand and nobody had ever used it as literature. My "slight thing" was about present day America. Why not write it in American? This is a highly complicated and hugely communicative language. It has been used in dialogues, in cuteness and perhaps by a few sports writers. It has also been used by a first person telling a story but I don't think it has been used as a legitimate literary language. As I thought about it I could hear it in my ears. And then I tried it and it seemed right to me and it started to flow along. It isn't easy but I think it is good. For me. And suddenly I felt as Chaucer must have felt when he found he could write the language he had all around him and nobody would put him in jail—or Dante when he raised to poetic dignity the dog Florentine that people spoke but wouldn't dare to write. I admit I am getting a little beyond my peers in those two samples but a cat may surely look at a Chaucer.

And that is what I am working with and that is why I have times of great happiness as well as times of struggle and despair. But it is a creative despair.

Love to you and
to Elizabeth,
John

To John Steinbeck IV
TWELVE YEARS OLD, AT SCHOOL

New York
November 6, 1958

Dear Cat,

Of course I was terribly pleased to get your last letter and to hear that you had the second highest mark in "Bugby". I didn't even know you were taking it. It sounds fascinating. That and your triumph in mathematics seem to have set

599

your handwriting back a little bit, but we can't have every-thing. I have often told you that spelling was fairly unimportant, except that sometimes it can be a little confusing. You said, for instance, that the "wether" up there is cold. A wether is a castrated sheep and I'm sorry he's cold but there is nothing I can do about it from here. I am also sorry that I will not see your crew cut in full flower, but maybe it will be rather pretty when it leafs out.

The last line in your letter indicates that you want something and by an intuitive approach we believe it says hair tonic. I can't imagine letting you go without hair tonic, particularly now in these critical days of the crew cut, and Miss Astolat says that she will put some in the mail for you. It's a little surprising to me that Eaglebrook School dispensary hasn't any bear's grease to rub in your hair.

It won't be long now till we'll be up to see you, and we'll have a celebration. And believe me I am pleased that you're trying. That's all that's needed—is just to try and the marks will come. Don't necessarily try to beat the world in one week. But try pushing at it a little bit every day. That way everybody will be happy, you particularly. We love you and we'll see you very soon.

Fa

To Thom Steinbeck
FOURTEEN YEARS OLD, AT THE FORMAN SCHOOL,
LITCHFIELD, CONNECTICUT

[New York]
November 10, 1958

Dear Thom:

We had your letter this morning. I will answer it from my point of view and of course Elaine will from hers.

First—if you are in love—that's a good thing—that's about the best thing that can happen to anyone. Don't let anyone make it small or light to you.

Second—There are several kinds of love. One is a selfish,

mean, grasping, egotistic thing which uses love for self-importance. This is the ugly and crippling kind. The other is an outpouring of everything good in you—of kindness, and consideration and respect—not only the social respect of manners but the greater respect which is recognition of another person as unique and valuable. The first kind can make you sick and small and weak but the second can release in you strength, and courage and goodness and even wisdom you didn't know you had.

You say this is not puppy love. If you feel so deeply—of course it isn't puppy love.

But I don't think you were asking me what you feel. You know that better than anyone. What you wanted me to help you with is what to do about it—and that I can tell you.

Glory in it for one thing and be very glad and grateful for it.

The object of love is the best and most beautiful. Try to live up to it.

If you love someone—there is no possible harm in saying so—only you must remember that some people are very shy and sometimes the saying must take that shyness into consideration.

Girls have a way of knowing or feeling what you feel, but they usually like to hear it also.

It sometimes happens that what you feel is not returned for one reason or another—but that does not make your feeling less valuable and good.

Lastly, I know your feeling because I have it and I am glad you have it.

We will be glad to meet Susan. She will be very welcome. But Elaine will make all such arrangements because that is her province and she will be very glad to. She knows about love too and maybe she can give you more help than I can.

And don't worry about losing. If it is right, it happens—The main thing is not to hurry. Nothing good gets away.

Love
Fa

To Stuart L. Hannon
OFFICE OF THE DIRECTOR, RADIO FREE EUROPE

New York
November 6, 1958

Dear Mr. Hannon:

Thank you for your very kind letter. You may use any part of the following statement you wish or all of it.

The Award of the Nobel Prize to Pasternak and the Soviet outcry against it makes me sad but not for Pasternak. He has fulfilled his obligation as a writer, has seen his world, described it and made his comment. That the product of his art has found response everywhere in the world where it has been permitted to be seen must be a satisfaction to him.

He is not to be pitied however, no matter how cruelly he may be treated. My sadness is for the poor official writers sitting in judgment on a book they are not allowed to read. They are the grounded vultures of art who having helped to clip their own wings are righteously outraged at Flight and contemptuous of Eagles. These are the sad ones at last, the crippled and distorted ones, and it is quite natural that they should be hostile toward one who under equal pressures did not succumb and did not fail. They are the pallbearers of Soviet Literature, and they must now be aware of the weight of the corpse.

No matter how they may quote Pasternak in his absence, no matter what groveling may be reported, his book is here to refute them now and always. The real traitors to literature are Pasternak's judges, and they will be punished as were the judges of Socrates—their names forgotten and only their stupidities remembered.

Yours,
John Steinbeck

To Henry Fonda

Dear Hank,

It is strange but perhaps explainable that I find myself very often with a picture of you in front of my mind, when I am working on a book. I think I know the reason for this. Recently I ran a 16 mm print of The Grapes of Wrath that Kazan had stolen from Twentieth Century Fox. It's a wonderful picture, just as good as it ever was. It doesn't look dated, and very few people have ever made a better one—and I think that's where you put your mark on me. You will remember also that when I was writing Sweet Thursday I had you always in mind as the prototype of Doc. And I think that one of my sharp bitternesses is that due to circumstances personality-wise and otherwise beyond our control you did not play it when it finally came up. I think it might have been a different story if you had.

Now I am working on another story, and again I find that you are the prototype. I think it might interest you. It will be a short novel and then possibly a motion picture, possibly a play—I don't know. But it's just the character and the story that remind me so much of you that I keep your face and figure in mind as I write it. I don't know whether you're in town or not—but if you are I wish you'd come over some evening, and maybe we can talk. I'd like that very much. And you might be very much interested in the story I am writing. It seems made for you. In fact it's *being* made for you—let's put it that way.

Yours,
John

The story was *Don Keehan*, one of the two modern works he was using to get distance from Malory. This may have been a contemporary version of *Don Quixote;* in any case it was abandoned.

To Professor and Mrs. Eugène Vinaver

New York
November 30, 1958

Dear Eugène and Betty:

When one is as neglectful as I have been of you since the wonderful June, it must be obvious that it is not carelessness. It is either guilt or confusion or a combination of both. Actually the second is the more compelling of the two—I came back crammed with Arthur and the flashing lights you did so much to ignite. I sat down lightly and gaily and like our giant missiles, I didn't get off the ground. I was too full of too much recently absorbed. Digestion had not occurred. Nevertheless, I drove myself like a reluctant mule. It was no good. The lump remained undigested.

Finally, thank heaven, I put it away, back into the dark places of mind and feeling, put it in my personal cave like a wine or a cheese, to mature.

You remember, Eugène, how the wine masters in France say that in the winter the wine sleeps—but when spring comes and the vines cluster with flower then the wine remembers its flowering and it grows restless for a time. It heaves and referments a little—memory of the flower. And if it does not—the wine is dead. And this is so. At that season one can taste the little anguish in the wine. And we have learned no technique nor ingredient to take the place of anguish. If in some future mutation we are able to remove pain from our species we will also have removed genius and set ourselves closer to the mushroom than to God.

Elaine the Fair who is good and loving but more wise than her cousin of Astolat, said very recently, "Are you troubled about not working on Malory?" and I said, "Of course. Always troubled, even when I have explained it to myself."

Then she, that wise one, said, "Could it be that the dissonance created by the clash of 15th and 20th centuries is making trouble?" My words but her meaning. And I said, "That is certainly part of it. Too many friends, relations, children, duties, requests, parties. Too much drinking—telephones—play openings. No chance to establish the slow rhythm and keep it intact."

Then she said, "Would it be good to go away—say to Majorca or Positano?"

"Yes."

"Where would you like to go?"

And I said, "One place. Where it happened—to Somerset."

And this pleased Fair Elaine. We are moving on it now—asking about renting a small farmhouse in Avalon. Something very simple—kitchen, sitting room, two bedrooms and a cubicle for work. We plan to stay here and finish the little work and in March to move with books and microfilm and all the squirming ferment in my head to Somerset, there to center and to remain until the work is done. We will rent a small car because I will want to move about now and then—to Worcestershire, to Manchester, to York and Durham, to Bamburgh and Alnick, to Sandwich and all of the haunted places in Cornwall. To hear the speech and feel the air, to rub hands on the lithic tactile memories at Stonehenge, to sit at night on the untouristed eyrie at Tintagel and to find Arthur's mound and try to make friends with the Cornish fayries and the harsh weirds of the Pennines. That's what I want, so that my book grows out of its natural earth.

Do let me know what you think of this. I'll want to know.

Our love and greetings to you both.

Affectionately,
John

Elaine sends double-love and she can afford it. She's rich in love.

To Elizabeth Otis

[New York]
December 7, 1958
Sunday

Dear Elizabeth:

We never seem to get things talked out. Every time I have been with you I remember a hundred things I wanted to say or to ask. And as usual I get frantic when I try to do or think more than one thing at a time.

I think the Somerset plan is good. I know it is self-indulgence, but if it works, it is worth it.

There's the matter of money and in this you and I are very much alike. First I never expected to make any and you didn't expect me to. When outrageous amounts of money began to come in, both you and I took a very simple course. We didn't believe it. And we still don't. There is nothing real about this money. On the other hand we are well prepared for poverty. Our only reaction to money is a kind of panic that we won't have enough at tax time.

I live in two houses. The expenses are enormous by our old standards. Sometimes I break out in a cold sweat at the size of the monthly bills, but mostly I don't even think about it. Then if I haven't worried enough I make it up, wondering how I am going to leave some for the boys. And I do this right alongside of being sure that the worst thing I could do for the boys is to leave them money. And my expenses aren't enormous at all. I can even whip up a guilt about owning a 22-ft. boat. People with one quarter of my recent income have a 40-ft. boat and want a bigger one. It all goes back to our basic disbelief in the stuff.

Right now I am pounding away at Don Keehan, working much too hard and too fast, and maybe it is because I feel guilty about putting the Malory off.

Now let's move into the loyalties division. Not the loyalties to you because I don't have any. I might as well say that I was loyal to my right arm or my heart as to you. No, I feel a responsibility toward Harold. Harold bought my contract to make money. His sense of loyalty has never for one second interfered with Viking's intention of making a profit. And I feel responsible for Pat. He may love me dearly as I do him but that hasn't limited his endless attempts to con me. He worries about me if I am not writing and even more if I am writing something which won't sell. But do we ever think of getting some competitive bidding from other publishers? Never. We are loyal. I'm not against this, Elizabeth, but by every standard of practice in this period we are nuts. Quixotic and crazy. I am not suggesting that we change because I know that even if we decided to, we wouldn't.

But I wouldn't mind it if you stirred them up a little. For instance, if you wanted to indicate to Pat and to Harold that I was bravely and secretly nursing a broken heart over the fact that so many letters come in saying my books are out of print. You can say, if you wish, that I asked you how it is possible for France and Italy and Denmark and Norway to keep them in print while American know-how lets them lapse. Also, we might suggest that the lapsed titles might be of interest to another firm. I was quietly visited by a representative of a rival publisher who wished to publish a complete list. There's not a word of truth in this of course but we could cause it if we wished.

Now I've told you that I had a double life. I must live as though I were going to live forever and at the same time as though I were going to die tomorrow. That's quite an assignment. And with your knowledge and permission I am going to make some conscious and earnest attempts to change some of my attitudes. I am going to try to abandon my feeling that I am poverty stricken. And I hope you will encourage me in my attempted new attitude. I know that I am not bright about money but one of the real unfortunate tendencies I have is a feeling that I should put in a time of worry about doing something I'm going to do anyway. I would have more time for writing if I gave that up. Anyway, I'm going to try.

I'm taking most of Sunday composing this letter because I think it is important for me to say. Sometimes a kind of quiet weariness settles on me—a listening and a waiting. And when the clamoring from outside goes on too long and too stridently and too repetitiously, the weariness gets sometimes a kind of hunger in it. I've heard it too often, like the letters from schoolchildren, or the requests for essays from little magazines which can't pay—just write anything—you know? So many things are beginning to sound like refrains. This isn't always. I can get as excited as ever about a high velocity word or a supersonic sentence that comes flying in, unbidden but welcome. But at night too often when sleep does not come, the yammer comes in my ears and I grow lonesome for death. That must happen to everyone. I think I remember it in my father's eyes. But then the new and exciting comes back and I get up and write the little poems that must and should be thrown away as this letter should be if it were to anyone but you.

One of the hangovers from the old poverty that never loses its impact is a hatred of waste. Locked up and unused and unenjoyed, Sag Harbor represents waste to me. And this did occur to me. The people in your office—they take vacations and they need them. Would it be a good thing if they could use the Sag place? I haven't discussed this with Elaine but I know she would approve. She doesn't have my sometimes sense of privacy and possession. I'm going to offer Shirley the use of the boat because she loves it and I trust her with it completely. Maybe some of the people in your office might have a frantic need to dig in a garden. I get that sometimes, a hunger to put my fingers in the soil. It's such a wonderful place and it should not be locked up if it could give as much joy to someone else as it gives me.

I think that's all. Maybe this scribbling will be the basis for some good constructive thinking on the part of both of us.

Love,
John

To Pascal Covici

Dear Pat:

You and I have had crises enough over the years so that a small one is not likely to throw either one of us. I do not intend to finish nor to publish the little book you have been reading parts of.

It isn't a bad book. It just isn't good enough—not good enough for me and consequently not good enough for you. It is a nice idea—even a clever idea but that isn't sufficient reason for writing it. I don't need it. The danger to me lies in the fact that I could finish it, publish it, and even sell it. The greater danger is that it might even enjoy a certain popularity. But it would be the fourth slight thing in a series.

It would bear out the serious suggestion that my time for good writing is over. Maybe it is but I don't want that to be for lack of trying.

Frankly this is a hack book and I'm not ready for that yet. To be a writer implies a kind of promise that one will do the best he can without reference to external pressures of any kind. In the beginning this is easier because only the best one can do is acceptable at all. But once a reputation is established a kind of self surgery becomes necessary. And only insofar as I can be a more brutal critic than anyone around me, can I deserve the rather proud status I have set up for myself and have not always maintained.

Anyway, we come to the final thing. In the time left me, I want to do the best I can and I shall look with a very sharp eye on what it is I do. I know you will be glad of this since over the years we have come to be woven of one pattern.

I know that a publishing house must show a profit, but when a writer does, he should be doubly inspected. It's a strange business. Maybe the fires burn out—surely they burn differently, but in me they *burn*. I take a very long time with everything. How many years it has been before any decent thing could bear fruit! You remember them—the false starts,

609

the endless searching. And what has emerged may not have been the best but at least it was the best I could do.

It has been a good Christmas. The boys are coming along more satisfactorily than I could have hoped. We have spent too much money, eaten and drunk too much and in every way displayed the intemperance of the season.

Now there will come a little time of getting ready and then we will go to England and there will be quiet and peace I hope and a chance to bring out and inspect the wares I have accumulated. Anyway we'll see. It's always that—we'll see, but we'll also look.

love to you
John

Later he went a step further to Covici:

"This is a lonely business. The difficulty comes when you begin to think it isn't. It's not a social racket at all. It has nothing to do with conversation or criticism or even compliments. It has nothing to do with family or marriage or friends or associates or pleasures. It is and should be the most alone thing in the world. I guess that's why writers are hard to live with, impossible as friends and ridiculous as associates. A writer and his work is and should be like a surly dog with a bone, suspicious of everyone, trusting no one, loving no one. It's hard to justify such a life but that's the way it is if it is done well."

And to Elizabeth Otis, about the same time:

"Why this terror of being through, since everyone will inevitably be one day? Is it a race against remaining time, and if so, is it well to race in an inferior machine? Is it an unadmitted passion for immortality? If so, an inferior vehicle is not the answer. Or is it the fumbling motions of a conditioned animal, the dunghill beetle, robbed of his egg which ploddingly pushes a ball of fluff about simply because that is what dunghill beetles do."

To Elizabeth Otis

New York
January 3, 1959

Dear Elizabeth:

I know that what I am going looking for in Somerset I can find right here. What I am wishing for is a trigger rather than an explosion. The explosion is here. But in the haunted fields of Cornwall, in the dunes and the living ghosts of things, I do wish to find a path or a symbol or an approach. And please do know that in turning over the lumber of the past I'm looking for the future. This is no nostalgia for the finished and safe. My looking is not for a dead Arthur but for one sleeping. And if sleeping, he is sleeping everywhere, not alone in a cave in Cornwall. Now there, that's said and done and I've been trying to say it for a long time.

There's no way of knowing whether the new course is good or bad because the sea is uncharted and a compass is of little use if you don't know where you're going. Old navigators, when they had lost a headland for a point of reference, and when wind direction could only be judged by sunrise and set, had then to watch for flights of birds, weed and bits of wood floating in the sea and the high cumulus clouds that signaled land. It wasn't very accurate but it got people to strange places and there was no turning back because which is back?

If this does seem to be taking a trip to Southernmost England very seriously it is so because it is much more than that to me. There are no figures of speech for what I am trying to say—the "path" but a path on water. Do you see what I'm trying to say at all, or is it all lost in vagueness? Because in my mind it isn't vague at all.

And now I've used you as a well. As I always have.

Love,
John

1959

Steinbeck

"In the
Vale of Avalon…"

1959 Spent most of year in Bruton, Somerset, England, working on *Morte d'Arthur*.

In early March, John and Elaine Steinbeck arrived in England, took delivery on a Hillman station-wagon and drove to the house that Robert Bolt had found for them—Discove Cottage, near Bruton, Somerset.

𝒯o Mr. and Mrs. Graham Watson

Discove Cottage
Bruton, Somerset
March 14 [1959]

Dear Graham and Dorothy:

Finally—finally we are settling. I am getting over my beast of an influenza cold. The house is warm and cozy, the telephone is on. Elaine romps happily with tradesmen. I have a fine little room in which to work—overlooking fields and hills and some forest. All in all a very comfortable and happy spot. The little Hillman is a good and gallant sort. Only fly in the jam has been the lousy press. Never have they been so arrogant and rude. The reign of terror seems to be over now, at least for the time being.

Now, I want to grow calm and slow and gradually to start to work. We couldn't have found a more perfect place. Gradually I will get my equipment working. There is a small garden in front, hedged against a pasture and a very large space for vegetables in back with black lovely-looking soil. It rains today but we had sun two days and a half running. I will get to turning over the earth in a very short time. It seems an early spring.

Now it's Monday. Yesterday, cows in the garden—a giant 7 A.M. cow hunt in bathrobes and boots. Shades of the old west. Comes the shout in the dawn "Cows away! Cry Havoc, Cry Riding" and up we spring to the defense. Meanwhile our little garden has become a morass or moreass. It's fun. But when we are planted and neat, then will be quite another story. Then will the cry be for revenge. Must speak to the farmer about this. Some very ancient laws of impound apply. I'm sure he will be happy to fence properly. Either that or there's going to be beef in our refrigerator.

As I knew she would, Elaine is seeding Somerset with a Texas accent. She's got Mr. Windmill of Bruton saying you-all. At this moment she is out in the gallant little Hillman, calling on the Vicar and getting in some booze. She'll probably bring both back with her.

It feels good here now that the press war is over. Feels right. Country people are always skeptical of strangers, particularly foreigners. But we know a trick that always works. We ask, and it's a mean, no-good bastard who won't respond to a civil question as a request for help and we haven't found any such here yet. I am becoming expert with the Rayburn stove, can build a fire with wet unseasoned wood. Haven't yet asked about the fishing but am equipped for a little poaching if I can't beg or purchase or hire some trout water hereabouts.

I think it won't be very long before I shall get down to work. The house is beginning to run nicely. We will this week meet the local antiquary. A little later I may need some books but right now am all right. No ghosts yet in the cottage but then April isn't here.

I'm just settling back and back and I think all will be well. And surely we have had beautiful weather to welcome us.

This is just a kind of a token letter. More in a little.

Yours
John

Paragraphs from other letters reflect his happiness.

To James Pope he wrote:

"We have a cottage that was occupied at the time of Edward the Confessor and was old when it was listed in Doomsday Book. It has stone walls three feet thick and a deep thatched roof and is very comfortable—out in the country with fields and big oaks and the fruit blossoms just about to pop. The people here are strong and tough and like the way they are living, and I'm going to let them. Not having American know-how doesn't seem to have hurt them a bit. They have heard that America is off to the right as you face south, but beyond that they are not greatly interested."

And to the Covicis:

"We've only been in a little over a week but we are deeply in. It is a stone cottage. It is probable that it was the hut of a religious hermit. It's something to live in a house that has sheltered 60 generations. My little work room on the second floor overlooks hills and meadows and an old manor house, but there is nothing in sight that hasn't been here since the 6th century. If ever there was a place to write the Morte, this is it. Ten miles away is the Roman fort which is the traditional Camelot. We are right smack in the middle of Arthurian country. And I feel that I belong here. I have a sense of relaxation I haven't known for many years. Hope I can keep it for a while. I've really started to write, slowly and happily. How fine that is.

"The whole thing is dream-like and I like the dream. I've had enough of so-called reality for a while. A few months of this and I will be a new person."

To Elizabeth Otis:

"We have been here less than two weeks and it seems as though we had lived here forever. Everything is recognizable and recognized. I shall probably be less talkative in the future. I am just so pleased that I am babbling, I guess. But that isn't a bad way to be.

"Of course it isn't amazing, but it is surely gratifying how wonderfully Elaine is doing it. She says she has never been happier in her life and she is all over the place. The cooking facilities aren't skimpy. It is just getting used to them and now we have them under control. Vegetables are almost non-existent at this season which is very strange. We may have to make a contact in London because we are not used to meat and bread and potatoes. There isn't even a cabbage to be had or a rutabaga. I don't know where the stored turnips and carrots are. I'll have my own vegetables later in the season. There's a fine plot of black earth for them but it is still sticky with mud. I'm going to do some work outside for health's sake but my main job is manuscript and I'm not going to forget it. My duty in the house is to keep the fires and the hot water and the fuel. To fix anything that breaks, to carry coals and empty ashes, fill hot water bottles. Yes, we use them. And you would be surprised at how comfortable we are. It is going to be and is a very good life. And out of it I hope will come some good work."

And finally, to Graham Watson:

"I'm going out for dandelions this afternoon to cook for greens for supper. They are delicious. Do you ever eat them? You cut the little plants at the place where the root branches out to a white bundle of stems—wash them and cook them slowly and for a long time with pieces of bacon. Don't taste them while they are cooking because they will be bitter, but when they are done, they are most delicious. We need greens, being Americans and the young dandelions are among the best. When my soil gets a little more friable I shall plant mustard and turnips both for greens and also chard which I love when it is picked young and tender. Field mushrooms we shall not have until July, but the meadows are filling up with interesting things, many of which I don't know —but I will. I may even try some of the climbing strawberries. The idea of them fascinates me. Besides, they should be pretty—maybe in pots against our sunny front wall and trained up the stones on strings. They would get a maximum of light and warmth there."

To Eugène Vinaver

Dear Eugène:

Good letters from you and from Betty this morning. What a fine related feeling to get them. Now the work seems to begin to churn. "Hit befel in the dayes of Uther Pendragon when he was Kynge of all England—" And my little room looks out over the meadows and forests of the England he was kynge of. And the pace hasn't changed much here. Never any manufacturing. Still cows and pigs and some sheep. The Somerset speech is Anglo-Saxon with a lacing of Celtic—it is even pronounced in that way. For right here the two met and fought and later mingled. The Norman never really took hold here. I feel at home here and why—? My mother was of pure Celtic stock if there is any such and my name Steinbeck is not German in the modern sense. The two bloods meet in me just as they met here in the Pennine Hills and so there is every reason for me to feel that I have come home.

I brought very few source books. For the moment I have read all I can take in. But words I need. I have sent to London for dictionaries—lots of them. I didn't bring them. They are too heavy. Dictionaries of old and transition English, of later —classical and medieval, of Welsh, Cornish, of Anglo-Saxon and of Old Norsk—Words are very important to me now. A Somerset man in Bruton said disparagingly of another—" 'E be mean-like. 'E be 'thout worship." Still the word "worship" and used in its oldest sense. And the Anglo-Saxon syllables are all pronounced here. Great is said gre-at, meat is me-at. I am learning much and there is so much to learn. But the earth is full of it. Last night the moon through the mist on our meadow—and time had disappeared—and night birds whirring so that past and present and future were one. In the Vale of Avalon, the waters have receded, but in these Mendip Hills nothing has changed. The hill forts are still there and the oaks and the hedges.

We have mastered the cottage as I knew we could. I keep the fires. Elaine runs the house and it is warm and cozy and the dreams float about. This is right. This is good. Yesterday I cut dandelions in the meadow and we cooked them for dinner last night—delicious. And there's cress in the springs on the hill. But mainly there's peace—and a sense of enough time and a shucking off of the hurry to get to the moon. I don't want to get to the moon—do you?

I am very anxious to see your new book. It takes years to publish. Is there any chance that I can see it in manuscript?

I have no suggestions for change of method in your new edition of the great Malory. But I would be interested to know what new thoughts and findings had come to you since the first edition. Oh! wouldn't it be fine if another ms. should turn up? Two isn't enough for any scientific approach. I wonder whether I could put a bomb under the Duchess of Buccleuch —to turn out her libraries. Not that she would read anything, but they must have book men in their holdings. And if the history of Prince Arthur could hide in Winchester, think what might be lurking in the ducal bookshelves. I'm going to give it a try.

I am so anxious to see you both. As soon as my foot is in the door, and the full spring comes—maybe you can come down here and walk our Camelot with us. That would be a good thing—

It is not cold now. The moment the wind switched to the west, the sweet warm air of the Gulf Stream came in. Today is gloriously sunny.

I am very glad to be here. Very glad.

As always,
John

To Graham Watson

Discove Cottage
[March 1959]

Dear Graham:

My work is going beautifully and I didn't expect that for a long time—at least a month. But then it crept in on little goat's feet. And good too, but then I have to believe that. I don't have any choice. But I believe it thoroughly.

I hope you are having this wonderful day in the country. The most golden and lovely day. It makes me want to get out in it. Our garden is overgrown and full of trash but with the help of a school boy on vacation I am getting it cleared. And I have a fine scythe (borrowed) and a sickle (owned). I shall soon have it cleaned and clipped and then our area for planting will be ready. But it is still a touch sticky. I have the gardener at the Manor house as advisor—a hard-bitten, red faced Somerset-born man who can make orchids grow on Mars. He is teaching me local gardening but what he doesn't know is that he is teaching me local speech and many things he has forgotten he knows. A mean, crusty man and one I trust. When I asked to borrow a scythe he said cynically— "Thu be a scythe-hand?" "Once was," I said. Then he watched me use the scythe in the grass and his whole attitude changed. You can't fake it if you don't know the rhythm of the scythe any more than you can fake the clean use of an axe. My God! What a lovely day it is. It's almost time for me to go to work. And it comes easily and right. I *am* so pleased. Never could I have hoped for so much so quickly. I'm having to hold down the word rate to keep it from going beyond the speed I wish.

We are painting the old cow byre which is just off our sitting room and it is going to make a delicious little guest room. It has its own outside entrance and privacy and easy access to the bathroom. As soon as it is ready, maybe you and Dorothy will come down and see how we country people live.

I ate too much rhubarb last night, forgetting its secondary properties which promptly became primary and it is keeping

621

me jumping today. No wonder it had such a place in medieval medicine. It works.

Love to you both. We are comfortable and happy.

John

Referring to the painting of the cow byre, he wrote Elizabeth Otis a few days later:

"The byre is just about finished as a guest room. I am making a small sign in Caxton black type saying KYNNE SLEPPEN HEERE. And they did, you know, and pigs and chickens too."

To Elizabeth Otis

Discove Cottage
March 30, 1959

Dear Elizabeth:

I have forgotten how long it is since I have written you. Time loses all its meaning. Work goes on with a slow, steady pace like that of laden camels. And I have so much joy in the work. Maybe the long day off is responsible or perhaps it is only Somerset but the tricks are gone. Instead, the words that gather to my pen are honest sturdy words. There are many more than I will ever need. And they arrange themselves in sentences that seem to me to have a rhythm as honest and unshaken as a heart beat. The sound of them is sweet in my ears so that they seem to me to have the strength and sureness of untroubled children or fulfilled old men.

I move along with my translation of the Morte but it is no more a translation than Malory's was. I am keeping it all but it is mine as much as his was his.

622

Meanwhile I can't describe the joy. In the mornings I get up early to have a time to listen to the birds. It's a busy time for them. Sometimes for over an hour I do nothing but look and listen and out of this comes a luxury of rest and peace and something I can only describe as in-ness. And then when the birds have finished and the countryside goes about its business, I come up to my little room to work. And the interval between sitting and writing grows shorter every day.

Yesterday, Easter, we went to services in the Bruton church. I found it nostalgically moving because I knew it all from my childhood, but also I found again that there is nothing in it that I need or want. Elaine both needs and wants it and so she may have it. But I'll take my birds any day and the processional of the sun. This letter is a mess. I haven't told you any news. But that's what news I have. That's all of it.

Love,
John

Elaine Steinbeck, writing to Shirley and Jack Fisher, confirmed his delight:

"John's enthusiasm and excitement are authentic and wonderful to see. I have never known him to have such a perfect balance of excitement in work and contentment in living in the ten years I have known him. He wonders aloud every day why he has had so much trouble writing the last eighteen months. The impatience, and the alternating black moods and wrought-up-ness are gone. He goes out and cuts the long grass with a scythe and thinks. (Frere says he's going to cut off both feet if he scythes and writes at the same time.) Last night he read me the first section and it is just fine. *That* nightmare is over, I think. Hooray and thank God."

And Steinbeck himself was writing Joseph Bryan III:

"I wonder whether the words I have written can convey to you my joy and peace and almost shrieking sense of fulfillment. If this should be my last book—this is what I would want it to be."

Similarly, to Elia Kazan, whom he had once described as "a nervous, restless, despairing and passionate Greek torn from his city. His talent is a hair shirt":

To Elia Kazan

Dear Gadg:

I have your letter this morning and I shall start this, although when it may be finished I do not know. A typewriter stands between me and the word, a tool that has never become an appendage, but a pencil is almost like an umbilical connection between me and the borning letters.

You ask, parenthetically, why I should be interested in your soul. I shall put aside the implications in the fact of your asking. I do not even use the usual reasons, although they are true—that you are valuable, that you are the one continuing triumph of our species, the creative man. No, the reason I am implicated with your soul is that it helps relate me to my own. We must constantly check our evaluations against those of our peers. And I have very few peers and you are one of them. What happens to and in your soul is a kind of map of the countryside of mine.

You say that success is like a candy—quickly eaten. But the analogy is closer. The first piece is wonderful, the second less so. The fifth has little taste and after the 10th, our mouths long for a pickle to clear the sweet cloy away. When people ask me if I am not proud to have written certain things, I reply that I am when the truth is that I am not at all. I don't even remember them very well and very deeply. Now here comes your soul again, because it parallels mine. Two years ago, as you will remember, I discovered that writing had become a habit with me and more than that, a pattern. I had lost the flavor of trial, of discovery, of excitement. My life had become dusty in my mouth. What I did was not worth doing because it gave me no delight. And you remember that I stopped writing. It was very hard to do because I had become a conditioned animal and it was easier to follow the road of my habit than to set off into the bewildering brush country of what is called idleness. Because Elaine's mind deals only with healthy exactnesses, with faces and names, she would say, "What are you doing?" And I would say "working." "No you aren't," she said. "I know when you are working." But even she can be wrong because it was some of the hardest work I ever did, sitting still in a busy world, aching for nothingness or the meaning that could only grow out of non-participation. Here still we are parallel.

Now hear me out because I must go into figures of speech to try to explain. Externality is a mirror that reflects back to our mind the world our mind has created of the raw materials. But a mirror is a piece of silvered glass. There is a back to it. If you scratch off the silvering, you can see through the mirror to the other worlds on the other side. I know that many people do not want to break through. I do, passionately, hungrily. I think you do also.

I wanted peace from the small and to me old or repetitious tensions—the day's breakage in the house to be repaired, the crystal system, very like the solar system, of friendships, responsibilities, associations, mores, duties, empathies all revolving and held in orbit by me, by the fact that I existed, but all of these orbiting at different rates, at different speeds and with no two parabolas the same. And what I wished was to be relieved of this power, this *me*—to sit apart, untroubled with satellites and watch and see and perhaps to understand a world which had blinded and dizzied me. You say you are not tired. Neither am I—only bewildered.

Then there is another place where you and I are very alike. We are blindingly clever. We can twist up a ball of colored yarn, put glass beads in it, hang it from a string, and whirl it so that it seems a real world to many people. Sometimes we even get to believing it ourselves, but not for long. For cleverness is simply a way of avoiding thought. Do you see now why your soul is important to me? It is a pattern of my own.

I had to make a physical sacrifice, a bodily symbol of change and revolt against what was killing me, or rather smothering and turning me down like the damper of a stove. And so I prepared to go away from everything I know and by that means to try to find my way home. When Elaine would say with compassion—"I know you are miserable. What do you want to do?" I could not say the truth which was that I wanted nothing, and wanted to want nothing. That would have made no sense to her. Nothing is an horror to her. Odd that two people could be so different because I thirst for nothing, but because I cannot have that yet I must substitute understanding for a little while. But understanding was warped all out of shape by those rotations of a thousand satellites I spoke of.

And so I came here, to the hills near Glastonbury which has been a holy place since people first came to it maybe forty thousand years ago. Maybe I am telling you this because it seems to be beginning to work. The seed is swelling and the tip is turning green. I feel more at home here than I have ever felt in my life in any place. I perceive things that truly pass all understanding. Sixty to seventy generations have been born and lived, suffered, had fun and died in these walls. The flagstones on the lower floor are smoothed and hollowed by feet. And all of those generations were exactly like me—had hands and eyes, hunger, pain, anxiety and now and then ecstasy. Under my feet there is a great stack of men and women and I am sitting on the top of it, a tiny living organism on a high skeletal base, like the fringe of living coral on the mountain of dead coral rising from the sea bottom. Thus I have the fine integrity of sixty generations under me and the firm and fragrant sense that I shall join that pediment and support another living fringe and we will all be one. I've never known this sweet emulsion of mortality and continuum before.

At about six in the morning a bird calls me awake. I don't even know what kind of bird but his voice rises and falls with the insistence of a bugle in the morning so that I want to answer, "I hear and I obey!" Then I get up, shake down the coal in the stove, make coffee and for an hour look out at the meadows and the trees. I hear and smell and see and feel the earth and I think—nothing. This is the most wonderful time. Elaine sleeps later and I am alone—the largest aloneness I have ever known, mystic and wonderful.

Everyone is related to the world through something. I through words—perhaps inordinately but there it is. But

626

before I stopped writing, words had become treacherous and untrustworthy to me. And then, without announcement they began assembling quietly and they slipped down my pencil to the paper—not the tricky, clever, lying, infected words—but simpler, stately, beautiful, old with dignity and fresh and young as that bird who wakes me with a song as old as the world, and announces every day as a new thing in creation. My love and respect and homage for my language is coming back. Here are proud words and sharp words and words as dainty as little girls and stone words needing no adjectives as crutches. And they join hands and dance beauty on the paper.

This is true—as true as I can think and if you do not believe me, or think this is an effusion you can go fuck yourself. But if you do believe it or feel that it is so, because we are related, you and I—then you will know that somewhere you will find your home also. That does not mean you must remain in it. Finding it, feeling it and knowing it is there—is more than you can conceive and is enough.

If I could influence you I would tell you to go to Greece or Turkey—to Delphi, Argos, Epidaurus, Lesbos—go alone and see if that is your home. But go alone, so that when the eagles of Zeus fly out from the cliffs above Delphi, they fly for you. I am alone here. Elaine quickly builds a life of neighbors, children, tradesmen, household duties and pleasures and despairs—of friendly, unpoisoned gossip and of endless talk and talk and talk. And because I love her and do not want always to be alone, we meet and associate and enjoy and then each goes to his private home again without anger nor jealousy.

Lift up your mind to the hills, Gadg. Criticise nothing, evaluate nothing. Just let the Thing come thundering in—accept and enjoy. It will be chaos for a while but gradually order will appear and an order you did not know. No one survives in other people more than two weeks after his death unless he leaves something he has much more lasting than himself.

This is a long letter of talk. What difference? I can afford the time and even the possibility of boring you. Your soul? I've been talking about mine and it is the same as yours—not identical but like.

And I watch the words of my translation go down and god damn, I think they are good. They are clean, hard, accentless English prose, exquisitely chosen and arranged and I am

627

overwhelmed with joy because something in me has let go and the clear blue flame of my creativeness is released. I am uplifted but not humbled because I have paid for this with the currency of confusion and little sufferings and it is mine, sealed and registered. And on that whole stack under me, no one could do it as I am doing it. It makes me want to scream with a kind of orgiastic triumph.

Go to Greece, but come by here on your way. The shield of Achilles was made of bronze compounded from the tin mined in the hills of which the diggings are still visible. The Camelot of King Arthur is only four miles from here—a great and frowning fort built thousands of years before there could have been an Arthur, and there are stone rings hereabouts which like Stonehenge bear the crossed axes which prove that the builders came from your own native Anatolia wherefrom the mysterious genius of the Hittite people spread out over the world.

Come to visit me in the place I have come home to. I will not go away from here until Thanksgiving at the earliest. That is a secret between us. I suppose most of this letter is secret between us but largely because who else would understand it? I have spoken to you as I would talk to my own heart.

Yours
John

To Elizabeth Otis on April 5:

"My vegetable ground—a big patch is just now ready for preparing. And I am doing it after work. No wonder we go to bed at nine o'clock. I want to get my vegetables in. Elaine is attacking her flower garden as though it were an enemy. She always gets half angry at weeds. Luckily there is a hedge between our two gardens because Elaine would not tell her grandmother how to suck eggs; she would be too busy telling the hen how to lay them. She has stage-managed too many shows to allow me to plant a cabbage without direction. Right now she is at

628

church and God is getting his instructions for the coming week."

To Eugène Vinaver on May 1:

"Yesterday I climbed to Camelot on a golden day. The orchards are in flower and we could see the Bristol Channel and Glastonbury too, and King Alfred's tower and all below. And that wonderful place and structure with layer on layer of work and feeling. I found myself weeping. I shall go up there at night and in all weather, but what a good way to see it first. I walked the circuit of the ramparts and thought very much of you and wished you were with me."

His gratitude to Robert Bolt for having found Discove Cottage took the form of a gift of the thirteen-volume *Oxford English Dictionary*. He wrote on the flyleaf of the first volume:

To Robert Bolt
IN LONDON

Discove Cottage
April 8, 1959

Dear Bob:

I wish you joy of these noble books and I can think of no more precious gift for a writer. For here is the whole structure and life story of the most glorious of languages—sensitive, subtle, strong, catholic, intuitive and formidable. It can truly roar like a lion or sing sweetly like a dove.

These books make me feel very humble against the giant architecture of our speech, astonished at its size and multiplicity, but, looking closer, the life story of each word makes me also feel that it is close and dear, for they are my family and yours. And words are truly people, magic people, having birth, growth and destiny.

May you, in your writing life, add to this glittering tower which was made, added to and kept alive by people like

629

you and me. Good luck and looting and with thanks to you
and Jo

from
John Steinbeck

To Elia Kazan

Discove Cottage
[1959]

Dear Gadg:
Don't think you were the only immigrant. I was a stranger
in Salinas and always felt alien. I didn't want, nor think, nor
admire the things my people did and when I tried to be like
them, I was simply ridiculous. As for being rejected by
women—I was also, by some. And like you I was accepted by
many, maybe more than my share, good women, lovely
women and girls. I would be graceless not to remember them
because some others did not find me acceptable. Why, that
would be like asking that everyone like my books.

You say that you feel guilty about Chris [Kazan's son]. Don't
let yourself, or call it by its name. I know there is a strange-
ness here—as though you two were not related and were
trying to make it so. My boys and I are deeply related—so
closely that it is probable we will not like each other. If you
are able to build a guilt about Chris—you can be sure that
there is something you don't understand or don't want to
understand. Or you might be seeking to chain him to you
with your guilt. Set him free! Only then can you be friends.
Jesus, the cruelties we inflict in the name of virtue.

I have a letter from Elizabeth Otis after seeing Sweet Bird
of Youth. She says—"I wonder what it would be like to live
in Mr. Williams' mind. I don't think I would like it."

Well, a writer sets down what has impressed him deeply,
usually at an early age. If heroism impressed him that's what
he writes about and if frustration and degradation, that is it.

Maybe somewhere in this is my interest and joy in what I
am doing. There is nothing nastier in literature than Ar-

630

thur's murder of the children because one of them might grow up to kill him. Tennessee and many others would stop there saying—"There—that's the way it is." And they would never get through to the heart breaking glory when Arthur meets his fate and fights it and accepts it all in one.

The values have got crossed up. Courtesy is confused with weakness and emotion with sentimentality. We want to be tough guys and forget that the toughest guys were always the wholest guys. Achilles wept like a baby over Patroclus and Hector's guts turned to water with fear. But cleverness has taken the place of feeling, and cleverness is nearly always an evasion.

God almighty, I'm reading you a bloody lecture. But all right, so I am. I will finish it by saying that you should resist letting self-analysis become self-abuse. Perhaps you did get a sense of power from directing but you also put love and loyalty into it. I just don't believe it is that simple and neither do you. My own analysis would be that you are fighting the symptoms of your own greatness out of a curious shyness. And I would strongly suggest that you let yourself go. Stop building the work of limited men where there are giants to play with. I would like to see you direct Medea or The Trojan Women, or turn loose a *real* Othello. You claim not to like Shakespeare and I think that isn't true. It would be like hating the moon. If you want grandeur of disillusion, do Timon of Athens. I've never seen it produced. I am having a time because I am working with a great man and perhaps catching some of it. That is just as infectious as littleness.

The spring is lovely here and exciting as though it had never happened before.

What am I trying to say? I don't know. Maybe—"Come off it!" Open up and enjoy. Remember those girls who accepted you. Take one whole day as a gift rather than a sentence. But first you will have to be alone.

I hope to be able to go back and still keep something of what I have here.

That's all.

with love
John

To Elizabeth Otis

Discove Cottage
May 5, 1959
Tuesday

Dear Elizabeth:

The weekly Progress Report and News Letter.

We had a profound shock this week from which it will take some time to recover. Catbird's marks came in from school. He had a I in math—that is good and he passed in everything else. It's not nice of him to put us through this—not friendly. He hasn't ever passed anything in his life—but a I in math is going too far. I have written him a bitter letter about this.

Mary [his sister, who was visiting] and Elaine continue to cover the countryside and for the first time since the War and Bill's death, Mary seems to be coming alive. I think this is largely Elaine's doing and it is wonderful to see. She is going to London tomorrow a new person. I do hope it survives.

Waverly wrote that she was flying to Mexico last weekend to get her divorce.

The last part of the Merlin should be in type today and I will get a carbon off to you right away by air mail. I shall be on needles to know what you think of it.

Now it is afternoon and the Merlin typescript has come back. I think I will go to Bruton a little later and mail it to you because I fervently want you to see it. Am I off on the wrong foot? It seems right to me but I can be very wrong. There must be some reason why no one has done this properly. Maybe it is because it can't be done—but I don't really believe that. I think the reason is that they tried to make it costume instead of universal. Well, anyway, you will know. And good or bad, I have a feeling that the prose is good.

The Post Office is going to go mad when I send it air mail. They think we are terribly extravagant anyway.

Love to all there. I'm sorry I'm so nervous about this but after all, I've been at it a long long time and this is the first and acid test—the hardest story and the first.

John

632

To Elizabeth Otis and Chase Horton

Discove Cottage
May 13, 1959

Dear Elizabeth and Chase:

Your comments and Chase's almost lack of comment on the section sent to you. To indicate that I was not shocked would be untrue. I was. Let me say first that I hope I am too professional to be shocked into paralysis. The answer seems to be that you expected one kind of thing and you didn't get it. Therefore you have every right to be confused as you say and disappointed. All the reading and research is not wasted, because I see and I think understand things in Malory I could not have seen before. Finally, I have had no intention of putting it in 20th century vernacular any more than T.M. put it in 15th century vernacular. People didn't talk that way then either. For that matter, people didn't talk as Shakespeare makes them talk except in the bumpkin speeches.

I know you have read T. H. White's Once and Future King. It is a marvelously wrought book. But that is not what I had wanted and I think still do not want to do.

Where does the myth—the legend start? Back of the Celtic version it stretches back to India and probably before. The people of legend are not people as we know them. They are figures. Christ is not a person, he is a figure. Buddha is a squatting symbol. As a person Malory's Arthur is a fool. As a legend he is timeless. You can't explain him in human terms any more than you can explain Jesus. At any time in the story he could have stopped the process or changed the direction. He has only one human incident in the whole sequence—the lama sabachthani on the cross when the pain was too great. It is the nature of the hero to be a fool. The Western sheriff, the present literary prototype as exemplified by Gary Cooper, is invariably a fool. He would be small and mean if he were clever. Cleverness, even wisdom, is the property of the villain in all myths.

It has been my intention in all of this and still is, to follow each story with an—what can I call it?—essay, elucidation,

633

addendum. I do not know that Merlin was a Druid or the memory of a Druid and certainly Malory never suspected it. In the studies I can speculate that this may have been so, although I suspect that the Merlin conception is far older than Druidism. His counterpart is in every great cycle—in Greece—in the Bible, and in the folk myths, back to the beginning. Chase says wisely that Saxon and Saracen are probably the same thing. Foreigners from far off. They always occur.

Very well, you will say—if that is your intention, where are those comments which intend to illuminate? Well, they aren't written for two reasons. First I'm learning so much from the stories and second I don't want to break the rhythm.

But there are some things I don't understand. You say the killing of the babies is an unkingly retelling of the Herod story. But that is the theme of the whole legend. The Herod story is simply another version of the timeless principle that human planning cannot deflect fate. The whole legend is a retelling of human experience. It is a version of "Power Corrupts."

You will understand that what saddened me most was the tone of disappointment in your letter. If I had been skeptical of my work, I would simply have felt that you had caught me out. But I thought I was doing well, and within the limits I have set for myself, I still do.

Love,
John

To Elizabeth Otis

Discove Cottage
May 14, 1959

Dear Elizabeth:

Now I have thought a day and throbbed through a night since I wrote the letter. I still feel about the same. Maybe I am not doing it well enough. But if this is not worth doing as I am trying to do it, then I am totally wrong, not only about this but about many other things, and that is of course quite possible. Alan Lerner is making a musical about King Arthur and it will be lovely and will make a million-billion dollars —but that isn't what I want. There's something else. Maybe in my rush to defend myself I've missed what I wanted to say. Maybe I'm trying to say something that can't be said or do something beyond my ability. But there is something in Malory that is longer lived than T. H. White and more permanent than Alan Lerner or Mark Twain. Maybe I don't know what it is—but I sense it. And as I have said—if I'm wrong then it's a real whopping wrongness.

But, can't you see—I must gamble on this feeling about it. I know it isn't the form the present day ear accepts without listening but that ear is somewhat trained by Madison Avenue and radio and television and Mickey Spillane. The hero is almost bad form unless he is in a western. Tragedy—true tragedy—is laughable unless it happens in a flat in Brooklyn. Kings, Gods and Heroes—Maybe their day is over, but I can't believe it. Maybe because I don't want to believe it. In this country I am surrounded by the works of heroes right back to man's first entrance. And if all of this is gone, I've missed the boat somewhere. And that could easily be.

I feel sad today—not desperate but questioning. I know I'll have to go along with my impulse. Maybe it will get better as Malory got better—and he did. If then I've worked the summer away and the fall—if it still seems dull, then I will stop it all, but I've dreamed too many years—too many nights to change direction. I changed myself because I was sick of myself. A time was over, and maybe I was over. I might just possibly be wiggling like a snake cut in two which we used to believe could not die until the sun set. But if that's it, I'll have to go on wiggling until the sun sets.

Nuts! I believe in this thing. There's an unthinkable loneliness in it. There must be.

Love,
John

To Chase Horton

Dear Chase:

Thank you for your letter of confidence. One can go on in the face of opposition, but it is much easier not to. I am learning something new every day. It is like the wood carving I do—the wood has its way too—and indicates the way it wants to go, and to violate its wishes is to make a bad carving.

I am a bad scholar and moreover have not many references at hand and beyond that find myself sceptical of many of the references that are *blandly accepted* just because they have been printed. Sometimes a truth lies deeper in a name than anywhere else. Now here is a premise, a kind of inductive speculation that should delight your heart. It came to me in the night, dwelling on the fact of Cadbury. Look at the place names—Cadbury, Caddington, Cadely, Cadeleigh, Cadishead, Cadlands, Cadmore, Cadnaur, Cadney, Cadwell. According to Oxford "Place Names" the first element refers to someone named Cada—

Then there are the Chad places—beginning with Chadacre and lots more ending with Chadwick. These are attributed to Ceadvalla—the Celtic counterpart. There are many other variations. Now look at the cad words in the dictionary and see where so many of them point, Caddy, cadet, caduceus. Cadi is Arabic and you come back to Cadmus, a Phoenician, founder of Thebes, bringer of the alphabet to Greece. Caduceus—symbol of the herald, later of knowledge, particularly medical, and the snake staff still used on license plates. Cadmus sowed the dragon's teeth also, which may be another version of the tower of Babel, but the main thing is that the myth ascribes his origin to Phoenicia. Were the Trojans forerunners of the Phoenicians?

But let's go back to the Cads. We know that in 1,500 to 2,000 years the only foreigners to come to these islands were Phoenicians, that they brought design, probably writing and certainly ideas straight out of the Mediterranean. They also concealed these islands from the world so that their source of metals was not known—this to protect their monopoly of the tin which made all of the bronze in the then known world. And where did these Phoenicians come from? Well, their last stopping place and probably their greatest outland port was Cadiz—a Phoenician word which has never changed.

Is it beyond reason to conjecture that the Cad names as well as the Cead words, the Cedric words, came from Cadiz which came from Cadmus who is the mythical bringer of culture from outside? Why would not these rich and almost mythical people who came in ships and brought curious and beautiful things have names of their origin—the people from Cadiz, the people of Cadmus, the bringer of knowledge, the messengers of the Gods! They must have been God-like to the stone-age people. They would have brought their gods, their robes of Tyrrhenian purple; their designs are still *on* early British metal and jewelry. Their factors would have lived with the local kids and their memory seeped into the place names. There is little doubt that they brought Christianity to these islands before it even got a start in Rome.

In none of my reference books can I find even a hint of this thesis. It is supposed after fifteen hundred years of constant association with the West Country the one bright and civilized people disappeared, leaving no memory. I just don't believe it. I think the very earth shouts of them.

What do you think?

Yours
John

It's interesting anyway, isn't it?

To Eugène Vinaver

Discove Cottage
[May 1959]

My dear Eugène:

Sometimes I simply want to talk to you, and not having you here, a letter is the next best. I do feel that I much impose on your time, so taken with your work and midge-bitten with undergraduates.

It is my custom, before going to work in the morning, to do some writing, much like an athlete warming his muscles for a match. This I have always done—sometimes notes and sometimes letters. But please to remember, they are not traps for answers.

I always write by hand and my fingers are very sensitive to shapes and textures. Modern pencils and pens are too thick and ill-balanced, and you will understand that five to eight hours a day, holding the instrument can make this very important. The wing quill of the goose is the best for weight and balance, curve and the texture of quill is not foreign to the touch like metal or plastics. Therefore I mount the best fillers from ball points in the stem of the quill and thus have, for me, the best of all writing instruments. When I find some particularly fine quills I will send you one. Besides, some of the finest of writing has been done with a quill. For a time I cut my pens but I don't like the scratching sound. No, this is best and I will like making one for you but I must find a perfect feather from a grandfather goose.

I'm afraid I have fallen a little afoul of the publishing end. Sending some copy to New York I have aroused disappointment. I think they expected something like T. H. White, whose work I admire very much but it is not what I am trying to do.

I am working now on Morgan le Fay—and the plot against Arthur's life—one of the most fascinating parts. And, while it may seem to be magic, it is based on a stern reality. Morgan learned necromancy in a nunnery. What better school for witches—lone, unfulfilled women living together. We can conjecture what must have happened in such places but we don't have to. In my notes I have a number of charges after visitations by inspecting bishops, charges not only of sexual abnormalities but also several demanding the study of magic and necromancy and the celebrations of obscene rites. There were definite reasons for locking the covers of the fonts.

So much to do and think about. A day is ill-equipped with hours. I have been happily digging in the foundations of one of the five cottages of Discove Manor of which the one we live in is the last remaining. I believe that Discove was a Roman religious center, possibly dedicated to Dis Pater and perhaps built on an older ring. Now I know how cottages were built and still are. When a structure burned or was destroyed in war, the stones and bricks and tiles were taken to build something else. Just picking in the foundation of the burned cottage and quite casually, I have found bricks from five different periods, some hardly burned through and some hard, thin, and red, possibly Roman. A hearthstone, coated with modern (last hundred years) cement, when I chipped the coating off, was a shaped stone with just a hint of shallow inscription. Drops of glass, raindrop-shaped, the result of fire but not this recent fire, since they were below the foundation level. Curious stones, some with marine shells and fossils. And these just with my fingers. And when I go down deep— who knows what I shall find? It makes my mind squirm with delight just to think of it.

Now I have done what we call in America bending your ear. I've taken enough of your time.

Love to Betty from both of us. Elaine says she is writing to her.

Yours,
John

To Elizabeth Otis

Discove Cottage
[June 7, 1959]

Dear Elizabeth:

Yesterday the work seemed to grow wings and start to fly for the first time. This may not show. It is just what I felt. And this morning early I was drawn to work and it continued— the feeling of getting off the ground, I mean. The only proof will lie in what comes out.

I can tell you one thing I have finally faced though—the Arthurian cycle and indeed practically all lasting and deep-seated folklore is a mixture of profundity and childish nonsense. If you keep the profundity and throw out the nonsense, some essence is lost. These are dream stories, fixed and universal dreams, and they have the inconsistency of dreams. Very well, says I—if they are dreams, I will put in some of my own, and I did.

A number of boys from Kings' School Bruton came to see me yesterday—boys working in geology and archeology. Every Wednesday afternoon they excavate on Creech Hill about five miles from here—real knowledgeable boys 15 to 17. They invited me for next Wednesday and I wouldn't miss it.

Now here comes Elaine from church. I can see her halo through the window. I'll join her for a cup of coffee and then go back to work.

Mary Dekker is restless as a ghost. She has no place in the world, in fact won't allow herself to have a place. I had long talks with her trying to break into her closed circuit but I don't think I made it. Her world is so full of fancies and so loaded with untruths—not lies—just things that have no relation to any reality that she seems impossible to reach. And she can't be helped because she doesn't want to get well or to be happy or even to be content. There seems to be some Presbyterian self-punishment there. I wanted her to try to see Gertrudis [Brenner] because some of her time-bomb questions might blast out a wall, but Mary said she couldn't be

640

cured and there was no point in it. I said, "Cured be damned. You could maybe be less lonely." And she said, "Maybe I want to be."

Now I've talked about myself steadily for months. How are you? More than anything I can think of I wish you could slip over here and settle into the Byre which is a very pleasant room. I have sat sometimes arguing with you, even wrestling with your mind and trying to topple your arguments. "Nonsense. It's expensive. I don't like the country. I have no reason to go." "Well, it isn't nonsense and it isn't even expensive. It isn't really country. It's the most inhabited place you ever felt and there's a goodness here after travail. There's something here that clears your eyes." And then you toss your head like a pony the way I've seen so often and you set your chin and change the subject. "Then you won't consider it?" "No." "I'll keep after you. There's a power here I'll put to work on you." "Go away." "Well, I won't. I'll wait until you are asleep and I'll send a squadron of Somerset fairies to zoom around you like mosquitoes—real tough fairies."

I won't stop. One morning you'll wake up all decided and you won't even know how it happened.

Love,
John

To Chase Horton

Discove Cottage
June 8, 1959

Dear Chase:

I have been thinking about E.O. [Elizabeth Otis] You know in the many years of our association there has been hardly a moment without a personal crisis. There must be many times when she wishes to God we all were all in hell with our backs broke. If we would just write our little pieces and send them in and take our money or our rejections as the case might be and keep our personal lives out of it. She must get very tired of us. If she should suddenly revolt, I wouldn't be a bit surprised. Writers are a sorry lot. The best you can say of them is that they are better than actors and that's not much. I wonder how long it is since one of her clients asked her how *she* felt—if ever.

Now back to Malory. As I go along, I am constantly jiggled by the arrant nonsense of a great deal of the material. Two-thirds of it is the vain dreaming of children talking in the dark. And then when you are about to throw it out in disgust, you remember that knight errantry is no more crazy than our present day group thinking and activity. Then when I am properly satiric about the matter I think of my own life and how I have handled it and it isn't any different. I am brother to the nonsense and there's no escaping it.

When a knight is so upset by emotion that he falls to the ground in a swound, I think it is literal truth. He did, it was expected, accepted. And he did it. So many things I do and feel are reflections of what is expected and accepted. I wonder how much of it is anything else.

I'm trying to shoot a rabbit from my window. Poor little thing is so innocent and sweet. But he is destroying the lettuces I raised and planted. And so I must kill him or go lettuceless. If I could tell him to go away and he would be safe from me it would be well.

We are living here very happily and simply. I don't remember ever being so content and at home. To a large extent our contentment grows out of a *lack* of *things*. Last night in front of the fire I built myself with wood I chopped myself, we were speaking of this, of how the things we think we must have are the causes of most of our unease.

I'll put this aside and mend my fires and prepare us against the night—wood, coal, onions and radishes from the garden, gooseberries fresh picked and tender garden lettuces which I will get before the rabbit gets them. He must know I am watching for him with a gun because he has not come out today and so he has another day and night to live. And so have I.

Yours,
John

To Elizabeth Otis

Discove Cottage
June 17, 1959

Dear Elizabeth:

This is going to be a short letter by my standards. The trip up Creech Hill with the boys was good and bad. I think the directress grew to dislike me intensely.

I asked her—"Is it not true that in working on these hill forts, you find quantities of shards of pottery and broken stone tools in the ditches of the outworks but no metals, no bronze or coins or bits of iron?"

She leveled at me and said, "How do you know that?" and she was a little angry with me. I said, "Well, it just occurred to me that over the ages the outer ditches would be the garbage disposal, for everything that couldn't be reused. Even broken metal could be remelted but a broken pot is useless." She was pretty huffy with me. I wanted to tell her to look for hoards not inside the walls but outside, preferably to the right of the entrance going out and low down.

My hoard theory is based on what I would do in case of siege, and all these places have suffered many sieges. I would take my things outside the walls, knowing the inside would be thoroughly searched. I would take it far enough out so that I could creep back and get it. I would do it at night and alone. In the dark, a man leaving a road almost invariably turns to the right, particularly if he is carrying something heavy in his right hand. Twenty to thirty steps is the minimum for safety, and my instinct would tell me to place it on the up side and about chest level and under a large outcropping of stone to prevent water from uncovering it. And even if the fort was lost, I could possibly come back in the dark and get it. If any two permanent features lined up against the sky I would choose that place so I could find it again in the dark.

The night of the 24th, that's next week, we will spend the best part of the night at Cadbury [Camelot]. The tradition, held very widely here, is that Arthur rides that night, the longest day in the year and that certain people can see him.

Quite a few people will be there and I wouldn't miss it. You can't imagine how deep this thing is in people's minds. They still believe the hill is hollow and that there is a great cavern underneath. I have letters from people who say they have seen a post sink into the hill in one year, and that a shout in a well on one side can be heard in a well a quarter of a mile away.

The other night I discovered that fifty feet from our house, through a break in the trees, you can see St. Michael's Tor at Glastonbury. Elaine didn't believe it until I showed her and she is so delighted. It makes this house so much richer to have the Tor in sight. Am I in any way getting over to you the sense of wonder, the almost breathless thing?

And now to work and gladly.

Love,
John

June 23, 1959

Dear Elizabeth:

I have an idea for a little book that could be valuable, could be profitable and would be easy. The idea grows out of our experience here. If you go shopping in Italy or France, you have a little dictionary with the names of things. But there is none for here, and there is hardly a thing in England that has the same name as in America. What I am proposing is an English-American, American-English Lexicon—arranged by subjects and alphabetically—household hardware, foods, meats, sports, clothes, automobiles, telephones, electricity, hotels. To get a double socket I have to describe what it does and it is called, when I find out—a multiple outlet adapter. An electric wire is a flex.

Elaine has only now learned to order a ham for baking. It is of course a smoked gammon. Cheesecloth is butter muslin, hamburger is minced beef, a pot is a basin, a battery is an accumulator, a flashlight is a torch.

I am going to suggest to Bob Wallsten, a good and careful worker whom I am going to see soon, that he do the compiling or oversee it. I would write introductions and it could go out as a collaboration. In that way I wouldn't have to interrupt my work and we would still have a profitable venture.

644

[July 1959]

Dear Elizabeth:

Now let me tell you about a miracle, of the kind that happens here. Day before yesterday I was writing about a raven, quite a character and a friend of Morgan le Fay. Yesterday morning at eight I was at my desk and there was a great croaking outside my door. I thought it was a giant frog. It awakened Elaine sleeping upstairs. She looked out the window and there was a huge raven pecking at my door and croaking—a monster bird. The first we have seen. Now how do you account for that? I wouldn't even tell it if Elaine the Truthful hadn't seen it also.

July 4, 1959

Dear Elizabeth:

Happy Independence Day! I guess we are the only people in Somerset who know about it. We are going to celebrate it by going to two church fetes, Bruton and one in a neighboring parish. We will do the coconut shies, muttering quietly and cautiously under our breaths "Dirty Redcoats, That's for Concord! That's for the Boston Massacre!" And we will donate 5 quid to the war against the death watch beetle, much more serious here than a revolution which took place 200 years ago. Now this is very interesting and I want you to remember it in case you put too much stock in progress and comfort. These churches have been here since the 14th century. And the death watch beetle has been here even longer. Every summer the beetle ate away at the oaken beams and every winter they died of cold and actually they didn't get very far. Then fifty years ago people became conscious of cold feet. The churches all put in heating systems. The result? No slack period for beetles. Extra generations and no time off. In fifty years they have been able to accomplish what they had failed at in the previous 600 years. Put that in your pipe and smoke it! Down with the dirty redcoat beetle. Arise ye prisoners of bad circulation. Up gangrene! I am full of fervor on this glorious Fourth, but you can see the direction is a little confused.

We drive some after work. Went to see the prehistoric giant carved in the chalk above Cerne Abbas. The next village is named Godmanstone. Isn't that wonderful? Then to the Maiden Castle near Dorchester, the greatest prehistoric

645

earthwork of them all. Tell Chase please that the name Maiden Castle has always bothered me. There are several of them and all of them are very old. I don't think they mean maiden which is a Teutonic word and couldn't have been around when they were built. So let the sound maiden get in your ears. I looked the whole sound up. Sanskrit has a root *mei,* pronounced *may*—which means change or changed. From it we get make and the past tense made. We also get midden—which means not only refuse but anything heaped up. Now these are great earthworks. The one at Dorchester has eight huge ditches, some of them 6o feet deep. Could not the Saxon seeing these have called them either heaps or midden or maden? Things made by men rather than natural hills? This is far more reasonable than to suppose they referred to maidens.

We go to London on Tuesday, then to Sussex and will be back Sunday. I shall take my work with me. Elaine is busy collecting words for our lexicon and so am I. It's fun and we do it while driving.

Love to all there,
John

In search of further Arthurian background, the Steinbecks and their house guests, Robert and Cynthia Wallsten, took a motor trip into Wales, through the Wye Valley to Caerleon and Usk.

To Shirley Fisher

Discove Cottage
August 10, 1959

Dear Shirley Elfinheimer:

We couldn't resist sending the wire from Usk ["Happy Birthday to Yousk from Usk"] and were afraid some one would correct it on the way. But once bitten with the silly joke, we were committed. It was like with Erskine Caldwell. I couldn't resist addressing him at Claridges as Erskine Caldwell, Ersk. Who could?

I don't know whether you have read my first book of Lancelot. I hope so. It's a crazy thing but mine own. You see I *like* Lancelot. I recognize him because in some ways he is me—corny and fallible. Then consider Guinevere. No one has ever made the point that you had to like a guy pretty much to be unfaithful with him because if you got caught, you got burnt and you knew it. The danger wasn't getting divorced or pregnant, it was getting up on a bonfire. It took some courage, did infidelity.

But it's a hard story because you have to believe the enchantments or it is all nonsense. You had to believe it as much as we believe psychiatry and much the same way. I'm trying to write it so that the reader doesn't question necromancy. It is an every day matter. Then you take treason against the king. To Lancelot—that wasn't a crime, it was a sin—the worst a man could commit. When he feels bad toward Arthur it is because he has committed the dirtiest sin he can conceive.

You know, perhaps it is your inspiration but I have been practicing on the harmonica very hard. I could always pick out a tune but not really play. Now I'm trying to learn to play and it's fun. When I get back I'm going to hunt Larry Adler out and ask him to give me some instruction about control of tones.

On the way home from the Wye Valley, we stopped at Berkeley Castle where Edward II was murdered. This is not National Trust but just the Berkeley family. No guides, you are free to walk about but there is a sign asking visitors to respect the property and it ends up with a line I like. It says —"It is the duty of a host to make a guest feel at home. It is the duty of a guest not to." Isn't that fine? The moment a guest feels at home the host has lost his property.

I hope you had a fine birthday and we are waiting to hear about it. If you are around a music store, will you see whether there is a compendium on harmonica playing?

love
John

To Eugène Vinaver

Discove Cottage
August 27, 1959

My dear Eugène:

This field and subject is so huge, so vague, so powerful and eternal, that I can't seem to mount it and set spurs. I need badly to talk to you. For the deeper I go, the more profound the subject becomes, always escaping me, so that often I feel that I am not good enough nor wise enough to do this work. I have a dreadful discontent with any efforts so far. They seem puny in the face of a hideous subject and I use the word in a Malorian sense. How to capture this greatness? Who could improve on or change Launcelot's "For I take recorde of God, in you I have had myn erthly joye—" There it is. It can't be changed or moved. Or Launcelot's brother Ector di Maris—"Thou were the curtest knight that ever bare shelde! And thou were the trewest frende to thy lover that ever bestrayed hors and thou were the truest lover of a synful man that ever loved woman—" Good God, who could make that more moving? This is great poetry, passionate and epic and with also the stab of heartbreak. Can you see the problem? Do you know any answer?

Oh! I do need your opinions before I fly to pieces with frustration.

648

This perplexity is like a great ache to me. You see a writer
—like a knight—must aim at perfection, and failing, not fall
back on the cushion that there is no perfection. He must
believe himself capable of perfection even when he fails.
And that is probably why it is the loneliest profession in the
world and the most lost. I come toward the ending of my life
with the same ache for perfection I had as a child. That
doesn't change nor does the soul grow calloused to pain—it
only perceives more channels of suffering—as when Launcelot perceived that his courtly love for Guinevere was not that
at all and still could not help himself.

Now, I have jawed you into boredom howling this little
picayune agony.

Will you let me know your plans and the timing of them?
Time creeps on me.

Affectionately,
John

To Joseph Bryan III

Discove Cottage
[September 28, 1959]

Dear Joe:

It doesn't march because it doesn't jell. If I knew less it
would be easier. If I knew more it would be increasingly
difficult. This has been a good time—maybe the best we have
ever had—not wasted at all. But my subject gets huger and
more difficult all the time. It isn't fairy stories. It has to do
with morals. Arthur must awaken not by any means only to
repel the enemy from without, but particularly the enemy
inside. Immorality is what is destroying us, public immorality. The failure of man toward men, the selfishness that puts
making a buck more important than the common weal.

Now, next to our own time the 15th century was the most
immoral time we know. Authority was gone. The church
split, the monarchy without authority and manorial order
disappearing. It is my theory that Malory was deploring this

649

by bringing back Arthur and a time when such things were not so. A man must write about his *own* time no matter what symbols he uses. And I have not found my symbols nor my form. And there's the rub.

Language changes fascinate me. We have collected some cockney changes. Elephant and Castle, you know is Infanta de Castile but do you know Goat and Compass—God Encompasseth Us. You know Bloody is By our Lady but do you know Charing Cross, the last stop of the funeral procession of Eleanor of Castile? It is Chere Reine. I love these changes. Some words describe a full circle also. Husband for example is house bound or a hand servant who served in the house. Later he became a farmer and husbandry is still current and now the ordinary husband has become a house servant again —full circle.

Our time here is over and I feel tragic about it. I feel like an egg about to be tossed into an electric fan. The subject is so much bigger than I am. It frightens me. You can call it divine discontent if you want but to me it is divine scared shitless. Maybe I'll find a simplicity somewhere. It must be a simplicity because the whole cycle is getting lost in cleverness and scholarship. Every once in a while I think I have it and write three or four hundred pages and it isn't right.

Maybe I should choose someone to tell it to, a child or better a growing boy—looking desperately for his moral clothing and address it to him with explanation when necessary. I hope I can bring something off. If I can't—I'll break my brushes, and call it a day. The flame can go out, you know. It has happened. But it must be abysmal pain when it does. And faced with the great theme—what sadness. Not that I am going to stop trying. When my brushes break, my heart will go with them. Let us hear from you.

Yours
John

Last days Somerset

650

To Professor and Mrs. Eugène Vinaver

The Dorchester
London
[October 1959]

Dear Betty and Eugène:

Now we go both sadly and gladly. My pencil is very restless.

Today I have sent you some books. I hope they may divert you. Perhaps it is vanity to send my own books, but out of a welter of living they are what I have and I must believe the best I have.

In November there will be delivered to you a Glastonbury thorn. I hope it may be planted in some corner, perhaps by the pond at "Malory." It should blossom at Christmas, this thing from the staff of Joseph of Arimathea.

This journey has been a joy and the fifteenth century, neither a dark nor a dead age but living and lusty thanks to you.

"Then my fayre felowys—I must departe oute of thys moste noble realme."

Yours,
John

To Adlai Stevenson

New York
[November 5] 1959
Guy Fawkes Day

Dear Adlai:

Back from Camelot, and, reading the papers not at all sure it was wise. Two first impressions. First a creeping, all-pervading, nerve-gas of immorality which starts in the nursery and does not stop before it reaches the highest offices, both corporate and governmental. Two, a nervous restlessness, a

651

hunger, a thirst, a yearning for something unknown—perhaps morality. Then there's the violence, cruelty and hypocrisy symptomatic of a people which has too much, and last the surly, ill-temper which only shows up in humans when they are frightened.

Adlai, do you remember two kinds of Christmases? There is one kind in a house where there is little and a present represents not only love but sacrifice. The one single package is opened with a kind of slow wonder, almost reverence. Once I gave my youngest boy, who loves all living things, a dwarf, peach-faced parrot for Christmas. He removed the paper and then retreated a little shyly and looked at the little bird for a long time. And finally he said in a whisper, "Now who would have ever thought that I would have a peach-faced parrot?"

Then there is the other kind of Christmas with presents piled high, the gifts of guilty parents as bribes because they have nothing else to give. The wrappings are ripped off and the presents thrown down and at the end the child says—"Is that all?"

Well, it seems to me that America now is like that second kind of Christmas. Having too many THINGS they spend their hours and money on the couch searching for a soul. A strange species we are. We can stand anything God and Nature can throw at us save only plenty. If I wanted to destroy a nation, I would give it too much and I would have it on its knees, miserable, greedy and sick. And then I think of our "Daily" in Somerset, who served your lunch. She made a teddy bear with her own hands for our grandchild. Made it out of an old bath towel dyed brown and it is beautiful. She said, "Sometimes when I have a bit of rabbit fur, they come out lovelier." Now there is a *present*. And that obviously male Teddy Bear is going to be called for all time MIZ Hicks.

When I left Bruton, I checked out with Officer 'Arris, the lone policeman who kept the peace in five villages, unarmed and on a bicycle. He had been very kind to us and I took him a bottle of Bourbon whiskey. But I felt it necessary to say—"It's a touch of Christmas cheer, officer, and you can't consider it a bribe because I don't want anything and I am going away." He blushed and said, "Thank you, sir, but there was no need."

I should love to see you when you have the time. I remember with such pleasure the day on Camelot. And didn't the

652

Fayre Eleyne put up a proper salmon? But next time the subject of politics will not be taboo. Someone has to reinspect our system and that soon. We can't expect to raise our children to be good and honorable men when the city, the state, the government, the corporations all offer the highest rewards for chicanery and dishonesty. On all levels it is rigged, Adlai. Maybe nothing can be done about it, but I am stupid enough and naively hopeful enough to want to try. How about you?

Yours,
John

To Dag Hammarskjöld, who had become Steinbeck's friend after an introduction arranged by Bo Beskow, he wrote in a similar vein:

"I arrived at home for the culmination of the TV scandal. Except as a sad and dusty episode, I am not deeply moved by the little earnest, cheating people involved, except insofar as they are symptoms of a general immorality which pervades every level of our national life and perhaps the life of the whole world. It is very hard to raise boys to love and respect virtue and learning when the tools of success are chicanery, treachery, self-interest, laziness and cynicism or when charity is deductible, the courts venal, the highest public official placid, vain, slothful and illiterate. How can I teach my boys the value and beauty of language and thus communication when the President himself reads westerns exclusively and cannot put together a simple English sentence?"

All these feelings would become the theme of *The Winter of Our Discontent.*

To Lawrence Hagy
AN OLD FRIEND IN AMARILLO, TEXAS

New York
November 24, 1959

Dear Hagy:

It occurred to me to wonder whether during the coming summer vacation there might be a job for Thom on your new ranch. Please say no if there is not because a made job is worse than none. I should want him to do a man's work and take a man's responsibility and get a man's pay if he earns it. I would be very glad privately to pay that salary because I think something like this is so important right now.

When I was sixteen I differed with my parents and walked away and got a job on a ranch where they didn't give a damn whether I was sixteen or not. I slept in the bunk house with all the other hands, got up at four-thirty, cleaned my stall, and saddled or harnessed my horses depending on the job, ate my beefsteak for breakfast and went to work, and the work day was over when you could no longer see. I learned a great deal on that job, things I have been using ever since. I got a sense of values I have never lost but above all I became free. Once I could do that, make my own pay with my own hands, nobody could ever push me around again. Also I learned about men, how some are good and some are bad, and how most are some of both. And I learned about money, and how hard it is to get. On that ranch there wasn't one soul who knew me or my family or gave a damn. It wouldn't have been as good if there had been. I think that until a boy is put out on his own, he hasn't a chance to be a man. A kind of pride comes with it that is never lost again and a kind of humility also. I think the best gift I could give my son is that fierce sense of independence. Very few American kids ever get the chance to have it. They are always able to come up with excuses. But there aren't any excuses on a man's job. You do it or you don't.

This is a crucial summer for Thom and I am going to see

that he does something about it, something that will make all the difference in his whole life.

yours
John

On the Sunday after Thanksgiving, John Steinbeck suffered an attack for which Elaine Steinbeck was never given a diagnosis. He felt ill and went to bed. She left him resting and went downstairs to the kitchen. Something impelled her to return to the third floor, where she found he had lost consciousness and dropped a lighted cigarette which had set fire to his pyjamas and sheets. She was able to put out the fire and send for help. By the time it arrived and Steinbeck was taken to the hospital, a brief impairment of speech and hand had passed. Mrs. Steinbeck is convinced that he had had a small stroke, not unlike a previous incident in Blois which had been called "sunstroke."

In any case, he was hospitalized for a week or ten days, returned home to 72nd Street for Christmas, and went out to Sag Harbor for recuperation afterwards.

For Steinbeck, thinking about it later, it was an experience with much more interior or spiritual significance than a bare description of symptoms could suggest.

"I was pretty far out, regarding my disappearance with pleasure," he wrote a friend three months later. "The real battle they couldn't see nor test. It was whether or not I wanted to live and I knew I had the choice. One who has lived in the mind as much as I have does have a choice which he can enforce. When I closed the door, I knew it wouldn't open again. The half-informed medic will smile and believe a mild coronary but the men who took care of me don't believe that. Elaine, like most people who put great value on the soul and its immortality, doesn't really believe it is as powerful an organ as I know it to be. She prefers to believe that I was sick in my body because that is easier."

To the Vinavers:

"Privately I think my recent illness was largely contributed to by the frustration of not being able to do what I wanted to do with the book. Such things happen. And nature has a way of using shock therapy. I reached a state of confusion out of which there was no exit except a dead stop. Perhaps I know parts of my theme too well and parts not well enough. I have tried to put the whole thing out of mind for a while, perhaps to get a new start. Arthur is a terrible master. If you don't give him your best, he wants no part of you. And so I guess I rest panting like a spent runner to get the strength to run again, for unless this can be better than I have ever done, I should not want to do it at all. I haven't been able to reach down into the great water for the timeless fishes. Now and then I see a certain glow like aurora borealis but it shifts and wavers. Sometimes it seems that this is not a matter for effort but for prayer."

To Elizabeth Otis

Sag Harbor
December 30, 1959

Dear Elizabeth:

I'm sitting out in Joyous Garde and the deep snow is all around and I feel rested and unraveled. In a way, I'm sorry I didn't see you privately but in other ways it is probably better because I had nothing really to say. It takes time to work things out. I can tell you that although I have been in shock I haven't been in fear.

The hospital found many small things wrong with me but they couldn't find the big thing. It doesn't show on X-ray film. I think I know what it was or is better than anyone but still perhaps not enough to describe—even if that would be good. I don't know whether or not I expected too much of myself. It was when I realized all in a moment what I had got, that the shock set in, and not what I had got recently but over 12 to 15 years. It was no one's fault but my own that I lost command. I relinquished it slowly and imperceptibly. Command is a curious matter. I'm still pretty weak and lacking in energy but I do know now that I have only two ways to choose —either to take back command or to bow out. The third— remaining the way I have been—I won't have.

I'm going to do what people call rest for a while. I don't quite know what that means—probably reorganize. I don't know what work is entailed, writing work, I mean, but I do know I have to slough off nearly fifteen years and go back and start again at the split path where I went wrong because it was easier.

True things gradually disappeared and shiny easy things took their place. I brought the writing outside, like a cook flipping hot cakes in a window. And it should never have come outside. The fact that I had encouragement is no excuse. That same cook in a window can draw a crowd too but he is still making hotcakes. I tell you this because if I am able to go back, the first efforts will be as painful as those of a child learning to balance one block on top of another. I'll have to learn all over again about true things. I don't have any other choice.

In the hospital I must have hit bottom or at least a very low level. For one thing, I got over mourning for lost time because I grew to know that time can't be lost—only people can be. Also I seemed to survey all literature with clarity and to understand not only where I went wrong but where so many have in the last hundred years, and I remember and it seems valid. But mostly I found one thing that clings to me so that I think about it nearly every hour. When the door opened, and it did—I ran to it with longing. But I didn't go through. When I didn't go through, the door closed but the sure thing to me is that having refused it, it will never open again.

Now Elaine knows all this because I have told her. And she is wonderful. But she, as do most people, considers this a warning to me to take it easy. And that's not the way it is at all. That's the thing which makes invalids. It's not taking it easy that matters but taking it right and true. The mind does not tire from true work nor does the body moving efficiently. Only frustrations weary one to death—a blunt axe, a dull saw, or a false premise. Those are the killers unless one sharpens the tools and straightens the line. It is true that bad architecture is ugly but more important, with bad design a building falls down—and so does a man. And that's not a bad lesson nor too great a price to pay for learning it.

I will not take it easy. That would be sick. But I will throw everything I possess against whatever world I can move, in the effort to take it right.

And do you know—I have a sense of dignity again. And I am not afraid.

Love,
John

1960
1961

Steinbeck

*"I'm still a man,
damn it."*

1960 Traveled through America, collecting material that would become *Travels with Charley*.

1961 *The Winter of Our Discontent* (last novel) published; Book-of-the-Month Club selection.

To Robert Wallsten

[New York]
[February 19, 1960]

Dear Robert:

I hear via a couple of attractive grapevines, that you are having trouble writing. God! I know this feeling so well. I think it is never coming back—but it does—one morning, there it is again.

About a year ago, Bob Anderson [the playwright] asked me for help in the same problem. I told him to write poetry—not for selling—not even for seeing—poetry to throw away. For poetry is the mathematics of writing and closely kin to music. And it is also the best therapy because sometimes the troubles come tumbling out.

Well, he did. For six months he did. And I have three joyous letters from him saying it worked. Just poetry—anything and not designed for a reader. It's a great and valuable privacy.

I only offer this if your dryness goes on too long and makes you too miserable. You may come out of it any day. I have. The words are fighting each other to get out.

Can I help in any way? I know the pain and bewilderment of the thing.

love to you
John

To Elizabeth Otis

Dear Elizabeth:

I am sitting in this good little house on the point. Poor Harry, the giant blue heron, is wading past looking for soft clams and the wrinkled water moves in as though I were on the bridge of a ship. I could want no better place to sit and contemplate and turn over the rocks of what mind I have left. I know some of the wrong turnings now but they may not have been wrong, only indirect. Once I trusted the persuasions of whatever force it was that directed me and it was easy because no one else gave a damn. But then I became what is called eminent and immediately many people took over my government, told me what I should do and how, and I believed many of them and gradually tried to be something I am not and in the process became nothing at all. It is a sickeningly common story.

I remember once, long ago, I wrote you ten titles for un-written stories and asked which one I should write, and you replied—"Write all of them." And that was correct. What's to stop me except the traffic officers of criticism and I don't mean only the external ones. I should have written every-thing—absolutely everything. And it's back to that I must go. What have I to lose except sadness, and anger and frustra-tion? I should imagine that the only evidence of interest and value is copy. And that's the way it should be. Otherwise, it's like the patient in a hospital who fancies the doctor is really interested in him or her when what the doctor is interested in is himself, his art, his science and his success or fail-ure. He wants to cure the patient, as you doubtless would like me to be cured, but the important thing—to every-one—is the cure, not the patient. And so we'll leave it that way. The hell with the symptoms. Everyone has them if he cares to look but it's healthier if he doesn't look. And that should be a relief to you. The role of wet nurse was never anticipated in our unspoken agreement.

I forget what day we are going in to town but it's probably next Monday. Thanks for your letter.

Love,
John

To James S. Pope

New York
March 28, 1960

Dear Jim:

This is a kind of pass-the-time-of-day letter, not to be taken too seriously if you are wise, and you are. I shall enquire about your health later in the letter. That proves that I don't want anything. If I did, there would be a note of solicitousness for your well-being in the first paragraph. At least that's the way my sons work it and it usually works for them.

I'm afraid I have joined your school of political thinking— what might be called the Old Curmudgeon School, and I have some desire to sit at the feet of the master. The present sad scene of candidature is ridiculous when it isn't disgusting. Would you mind moving over a little and letting me sit on the bench with you? Maybe the country has been in as bad a state before but the only times I can think of are the winter of Valley Forge and the glorious days of Warren Harding. The candidates are playing them so close that they have Ace marks on their shirt fronts. The mess in Washington now resembles a cat toilet in Rome. It isn't that the Administration is cynical—I honestly believe it doesn't know any better. And the Democrats, Jesus, the Democrats—fighting over a dead colt before it is foaled, no guts, no ideas, no plan, no platform. If I had any sense I'd go back to Europe and let the thing rot. I have never held with those who somehow find the rat that leaves the sinking ship ignoble. Wouldn't it be a stupid rat that didn't?

I don't suppose you would be interested in some Old Curmudgeon pieces. I'm in the middle of a book [*The Winter of*

Our Discontent] and it is going swell and I wouldn't interrupt it for anything, but there is always that early morning when cantankerousness is the better part of valor.

Have any more capes been draped about your shoulders? I had to turn down another honorary degree the other day with my hackneyed excuse that so long as I had no legitimate degree from my own university, it seemed a little silly to assume a fake one. It's my last virginity, that and television. But then I got badly bit with a prize one time. It was a number of years ago when I was pushing starvation pretty hard. The Commonwealth Club of San Francisco awarded me a gold medal for a book. It was a right sizeable medal and I judged that melted down it would come to something like fifty bucks even if the gold was sort of thinned out with baser metals. I felt real good about it and put it away because it represented about four hundred-pound sacks of beans and enough side meat to go with it to live safely for six months. That medal was a real wolf-chaser and kept me pretty happy and with a sense of security I hadn't felt for a long period. Well—the time came and I took my medal up to the jeweller to convert it into cold cash and thence into beans, and the jeweller said that if he could get the plating off at all it would be worth about thirty cents. And since then I have been suspicious of honors other than pure money in small denominations and unmarked bills.

But honorary degrees are even worse. They mean nobody's scared of you any more. You can't bite the hand that sets a mortarboard on your head. And my trouble is that I am not a jolly old fart watching the passing show. My poison glands are still producing a very high test kind of venom and I'll resist being a classic until they plant me at which time I will automatically cease to be one.

I would like to hear from you, Jim. It would be good to know that somewhere, somebody cared—or didn't for that matter.

Yours
John

The fair Elaine is fairer and Elainer than ever. What a dame. When I'm counting my blessings I can stop right there with a profit.

To Adlai Stevenson

POSTCARD

New York
April 12, 1960

Dear Adlai:

Welcome home and well come. Your pictures look healthy and full of beans and we could use some of those instead of this product which has been the campaign so far. For God's sake come out for something real. Both candidates constitute a Popish plot.

You know, I rather liked Nixon when he was a mug. You knew to protect yourself in a dark alley. It's his respectability that scares hell out of me.

Good hunting.
Yours,
John

All the female pet-names in the following letter refer to the new Mrs. Frank Loesser, the musical star, Jo Sullivan, then traveling abroad with her husband. Pet-names were very much in Steinbeck's mind at this period, as proved by the great number of them in *The Winter of Our Discontent* which he was writing. But already he was looking ahead to the trip around the United States that would provide material for *Travels with Charley.*

To Mr. and Mrs. Frank Loesser

Sag Harbor
May 25, 1960

Dear Frank and Fatima:

Soraya's letter arrived and about time. I wanted to have intercourse with you, i.e., communication, but somebody gets screwed. Somehow I can't imagine the toy Brunhild in a yashmak. Yes, I do know Marrakech. I spent some disreputable time there during the war. The smell of piss of a thousand years plus a thousand years of saffron that has passed through the Arab body can be smelled deep in the Atlas—but isn't that city wall in the sunset something to see?

I have been in wonder at the word Frank—First a javelin, then a German, then a Christian, then a Western person, once a sty where pigs are fattened, then fat, then pure or good like frankincense, then open, honest, outspoken, bold—in a word Franc or Frank. And now the name describes a little, mean, crooked, evil-eyed, devious, conniving, dark-browed gnome of Jewish extraction. Grimm's law of language mutation will not take care of this situation.

I am delighted that your pocket Valkyrie is loving the trip. And if in the future a bunch of Ayrabs come up with a Middlewestern accent, I wouldn't be surprised.

My new book is known to no one except Elaine. I have told only the title, a great one, I think. The Winter of Our Discontent. It's a strange book that is taking its own pace—part Kafka and part Booth Tarkington with a soup-song of me. It's writing along and I am following mostly amazed. I hope to finish it this summer.

In the fall—right after Labor Day—I'm going to learn about my own country. I've lost the flavor and taste and sound of it. It's been years since I have seen it. Sooo! I'm buying a pick-up truck with a small apartment on it, kind of like the cabin of a small boat, bed, stove, desk, ice-box, toilet —not a trailer—what's called a coach. I'm going alone, out toward the West by the northern way but zigzagging through the Middle West and the mountain states. I'll avoid cities, hit

666

small towns and farms and ranches, sit in bars and hamburger stands and on Sunday go to church. I'll go down the coast from Washington and Oregon and then back through the Southwest and South and up the East Coast but always zigzagging. Elaine will join me occasionally but mostly I have to go alone, and I shall go unknown. I just want to look and listen. What I'll get I need badly—a re-knowledge of my own country, of its speeches, its views, its attitudes and its changes. It's long overdue—very long. New York is not America. I am very excited about doing this. It will be a kind of a rebirth. Do you like the idea? I'm not worried about being recognized. I have a great gift for anonymity.

Frank, when you are in Paris, please show your bride John's Elysée. After that I won't even mind if you take her to the Tour F.L.

And a belated congratulation on M.H.F. [*Most Happy Fella*]. We hear from Londoners that it is terrific and a wild crazy smash. Isn't that a hell of a way to refer to a damn fine piece of work?

Anyway, have fun and write if you don't get work.

Love to you both,
John

Elizabeth Otis had long urged Steinbeck to make a trip around the United States, but his choice of transport worried her. Along with Elaine Steinbeck and others, she was apprehensive about his making the trip alone in a car.

To Elizabeth Otis

Sag Harbor
[June 1960]

Dear Elizabeth:

I've put off answering your other letter about Operation America until last. I have thought of little else all weekend or since I got it. So I will try to tell you what I think about it.

Frequently, of late, I have felt that my time is over and that I should bow out. And one of the main reasons for this feeling is that—being convinced in myself of a direction, a method or a cause, I am easily talked out of it and fall into an ensuing weariness very close to resignation. Once I was sure I was right in certain directions and that very surety made it more likely to be right. But now my malleableness makes it more likely that I am wrong, and one does not fight very hard for a wrongness. Now, concerning my projected trip, I am pretty sure I am right. I only hope I do not succumb to better judgments, and in so doing tear the whole guts out of the project.

I can of course answer every one of your arguments and probably will.

Let me start with your statement that people travel by bus and talk to each other. That they stay in motels. So many of them do but while they are so traveling they are not what I am looking for. They are not *home* and they are not themselves. There is a change that takes place in a man or a woman in transit. You see this at its most exaggerated on a ship when whole personalities change.

Motels and bus routes are on the main highways. One cannot leave the highways. At a motel or tourist house you have made an inroad—your coming is noted—your name registered, your intentions and plans subject to question or curiosity.

I chose a truck for several reasons. First, a truck is a respectable and respected working instrument as apart from a station wagon or an automobile or a trailer. Second—in a truck I can get into a countryside not crossed by buses. I can see people not in movement but at home in their own

668

places. This is very important to me.

Now my reason for wanting to be self-contained is that I also will be at home. I can invite a man to have a beer in my home, thereby forcing an invitation from him.

Next—Any stranger in a rural community is suspect until his purpose is understood. There is one purpose that is never questioned, never inspected and that causes instant recognition and sympathy—that is hunting and fishing. If in my truck I have two fishing rods, two rifles and a shotgun, there will never be any question of my purpose.

Next, I would like it fairly comfortable, if you call a bunk, a butane stove and an ice-box comfortable. If you are driving 10 or 12 thousand miles, it is no sin not to want to break down. I moved about the Okie camps in an old bakery truck with a mattress in it but that was a matter of four counties, not many states.

Next, I do not want to take a sampling of certain states as you suggest—I want the thing in context against its own background—one place in relation to another. My clothing will be khaki hunting clothes, a mackinaw and a Stetson hat. This is a uniform that will get me anywhere.

In your letter you say I should not go as J.S. novelist or journalist but as J.S. American. What I really hope for and believe I can do is to go as nobody, as a wandering car and eye. And the means I have chosen is designed to make it unnecessary for anyone to ask my name. The people I want to listen to are not the high school principal nor the Chamber of Commerce, but the man in a field who isn't likely to know my name even if he heard it, and there are millions of those. By the very mobility I could be gone before my name caught up with me. Besides this, while it is true that my name is fairly widely known, in America it is not, outside of certain cities and certain groups.

Now I feel that what I have written here is true and right. I know it is right for me. But I fear the weariness that might succumb to better judgment.

I am trying to say clearly that if I don't stoke my fires and soon, they will go out from leaving the damper closed and the air cut off.

It is so seldom that you and I disagree that I am astonished when it happens. Between us—what I am proposing is not a little trip or reporting, but a frantic last attempt to save my life and the integrity of my creative pulse. An image of me

669

is being created which is a humbling, dull, stupid, lazy oaf who must be protected, led, instructed and hospitalized. The play will have been stage managed out of existence.

If there is a seething in this letter—do not mistake it for anger. It is not. I don't know that my way is right but only that it is my way. And if I have had the slightest impact in the world, it has been through my way.

> The stilling mind
> Cries like a kestrel in the window crack.
> The house layered with shining cleanliness
> Is set and baited for new guests,
> And the sloven heart of the king in name
> Is dusty as a beaten rug in its beating.
> How much is required! How little needed!

Love,
John

To Elizabeth Otis

Sag Harbor
June 1960

Dear Elizabeth:

Your letter made a very great difference. Many thanks. The thing isn't really Quixotic. It undoubtedly is selfish but there are times for that too. Elaine, with your backing, which in our house amounts to public opinion, was dead set against my going until your letter.

My book is moving rapidly now. It's as though the pressures were removed from it. I don't know whether or not it is good but surely it is moving and moving fast. Such an odd book to be coming from me, or maybe not.

Thanks again for your letter. It made all the difference.

Love,
John

670

He wrote to many people about the coming trip, and as time passed he refined and expanded his plan. One day, as Elaine Steinbeck recalls, he said, "I have a favor to ask of you. May I take Charley?" The poodle had been a present to her from him. "O.K.," she remembers saying, "he'll take care of you." And her final reservation disappeared.

On June 16, Steinbeck described his vehicle to James Pope as

"a pick-up truck with a camper top, rather like the cabin of a small boat or the shell of a learned snail. I shall take my dog and that's another reassurance that I am not either dangerous or insane. I shall take no polls and ask no questions except 'How are you?' I used to be pretty good at this."

To Pascal Covici

Sag Harbor
June 20, 1960

Dear Pat:

Nearly every one I know feels, whether he or she admits it or not, that neglect in favor of my work is a kind of unfaithfulness. I think you are one of the very few exceptions. I think my work to you is me.

I haven't written because I have been writing. Now there's a sentence that could only be said in English.

Winter progresses, often becoming so much more real than any daily life that I seem only to be awake at my desk.

My truck is ordered for the trip I spoke of about the country. It will come in the middle of August. I plan to leave after Labor Day. I know you approve of the trip and know how necessary it is to me but there are others who find it so Quixotic that I am calling it Operation Windmills and have named my truck Rocinante. But regardless of advice, I shall go. Sure I want to go and am excited about it, but more than that—I have to go. And only I can judge that necessity. I know you understand this. I don't know what I shall find nor feel about what I shall find. For that reason I am making no literary plans in advance to warp what I see. As again in the Sea of Cortez—a trip is a thing in itself and must be kept so.

There are people who would like to contract for writing about it in advance. But since I don't know what it will be, I think any agreement might have a governing effect and I should want to see and hear what is there, not what I expect to be there. I nearly always write—just as I nearly always breathe. So there will be writing in it but I don't know what. That's one of the reasons I am so excited about it. I will not shape it. It must make its own form.

It is still very early in the morning. I get up at dawn, make a thermos of coffee and come out to my little work house on the point where I stay until I am finished. I never answer the phone and rarely answer a letter.

One thing is so—I must finish Winter before I start on Windmills. That is fixed. And I will, barring the unforseen.

That's all, Pat. I'm not good nor thoughtful but I do work and am working.

love
John

To Frank Loesser
IN LONDON

[Sag Harbor]
June 21, 1960

Dear Frank:

At the risk of being impertinent, I am well. How are you?

My book goes ahead. Books are such strange animals and this one particularly strange and willful. Sometimes it surprises and shocks me. I'm pleased with it but I don't want anyone to see it before it is finished.

I got that far and went to my yellow pad of pain and behold it was another day. And a new letter came in from you on the paper of the Lancaster which did give me a wrench in the stomach of longing for Paris. But I know now there's going to be no respite in my life for this longing to be one place or another. There it is like a lumpish *"thing."* What was the name of the "thing" in Peer Gynt? Always in the path. You couldn't go over nor under nor around. There are so many of those things in the path. Sometimes I weary deeply because many of the things in the path have no business being there at all except for their own advantage.

I hope you liked Copenhagen. I love that town and have many fine friends there. I'd rather sit in Tivoli than almost anywhere I know, and to come sailing into Elsinore or Helsingör in the early morning is a fairy experience full of dream reality. Once I saw Hamlet there—in 1936 with a budding Olivier and a dewy-faced Leigh, and it rained and they got wet and called the show and I and four thousand Danes demanded our money back.

I am very much interested in your darting thinking about the something of great price [*The Pearl,* another Steinbeck work that Loesser was contemplating turning into a musical]. It is so strange because you have to make another language. If I write whatever it is I write and do it well, the show goes on in back of the reader's eyes and I can use his experience for sets and his memories for props and his desires for certain lines. But once you put it on stage, the audience makes you prove everything. And you are right—faces they can't see—lines they only half listen to and you must force their attention and keep it through rustle and cough and what dinner they ate and can they get to a bar and back at intermission and can they lay the girl they brought. It's tough. But when it works, you have them as they are not had in any other medium.

I used the gesture of stroking the braid of hair because once in Mexico I saw a fine fierce man sitting on the steps of a straw jacal. A girl lay on her back, her head in his lap and with such an infinite tenderness and yet with great skill, he combed the black and shining waterfall of her hair. Her mouth was half open with pleasure and her eyes closed, and it seemed to me I had never seen nor felt anything so beautiful and I wished that some day I could be a part of such a closeness, but of course I never can nor will. Maybe it's enough to have seen it. Some things there are that continue happening forever. I can see them now, his left hand supporting the hair, his right hand combing, and I can see her

673

breast rise high and fall as though the air she breathed had taste and texture, as though the light around them was beloved. That hair was combed over twenty years ago and it is still being combed. There *are* immortal things you know.

I read in the paper that a Beefeater on battlement duty at "Caesar's ill-erected tower" was apprehended playing "It must be jelly 'cause jam don't shake like that" on a guitar. How I would have loved to see that. I'll bet he played it lousy. Once in Green Park I heard the regimental band of Irish Grenadiers play "St. Louis Blues." It was a strange, puzzling performance. One wonders why it was chosen.

Why don't you go down to Somerset where we lived last year? Glastonbury is one of the most moving places I know.

You can see the restlessness I know now I'll never get over. I want to be everywhere at once. Perhaps I am lucky in my trade because in a way I can be. Just now I saw the half-arches of Glastonbury rising to be completed by the eye.

I like your letters. They dart like chipmunks but they tell me what you want to say. And there's no greater joy than what you're doing—putting together something new, something the world never said before out of the rubble of the world. I'm doing the same thing. Why should I envy you?

Love to Ducks,
John

To Adlai Stevenson

Sag Harbor
June 29, 1960

Dear Adlai:

Forgive the pencil as I forgive those who trespass against me.

Two little sequences occur to me.

"Harding had his Teapot Dome; Eisenhower his Kishi; and Richard Nixon—('Treason!' cried the Speaker)—may profit by their example. If this be treason, make the most of it."

674

"He was close and secret, a deep dissembler, lowly of countenance, arrogant of heart, outwardly companionable when he inwardly hated, not letting to kiss whom he thought to kill; despitious and cruel, not for evil will always, but after ambition and either for the surety or increase of his estate." No, it's not Poor Richard. It's Holinshed on Richard Crookback. Perhaps it is an accident that the names are the same —but the theme of Richard III will prove prophetic—Blood will get blood and evil can only father evil. Damn it, those boys knew what they were talking about.

About every two years I rediscover the Sonnets with wonder. Always fresh, always with increased meaning. May I suggest for your refreshment and a kind of shining joy that you go alone and read aloud to your listening heart #54.

Oh how much more doth beauty beauteous seem
By that sweet ornament which truth doth give!

or the great 29, "When in disgrace—" or 25, "Let those who are in favor with their stars—" or 6 or 14. But as you know, it's like a dictionary, one leads to another.

Do you not find that in the litter of a day, it is a kind of poultice to go back to beauties beautifully arrived at? I had from my father a tiny volume of Marcus Aurelius, the sovereign Meditations. It was pocket size and had been so pocketed that the title was worn off and the edges of the covers soft as sponge. In the insanity of divorce, my wife who was not insane, kept all my books. I got to brooding about that one. A new copy would not do, and one day, visiting my boys, I stole it from the shelf and stuffed it in my pocket. I have many sins but theft is not one of them. I guess it is the only thing I remember to have stolen since apples long ago. And I feel little guilt. In the fly leaf in my father's hand is written— "John, when you are troubled, open this anywhere." And if I were in New York I would try to find you a small pocket copy. I know you have one but this is a dear book of the mind and very good to carry with you, a strong drink after a weary day, and a reassurance that somewhere in us there is a noble taint.

If I am solemn today, it is because I have a litany to write, and somehow jokes glance off an holy shield.

But tomorrow I'll be a mug again.

You do sound free. It's wonderful.

Yours,
John

675

To Pascal Covici

Sag Harbor
July 1, 1960

Dear Pat:

I guess it is characteristic that I am writing a book called Winter in July. But, maybe it's all right because the line goes, you remember—Now is the winter of our discontent made glorious summer by this sun of York.

The scene I work on today falls on July 1st, 1960. The date of the last and final scene will be July 10, 1960. I've never done that before. I am writing not only about this time but this time to the exact day. This is no trick. The story hinges on this date. And the date has fallen right into my lap.

I appreciated your letter. Few people know how completely the attention must be concentrated, and it is. Family, friends, duties must be put aside for the time being. I go through the motions of being a husband, father, man, householder like a sleepwalker. It must be very hard to live with but Elaine is very patient with me. It's a dreadful thing to say, but if it happened that she weren't—it wouldn't change anything. I have thought that perhaps the failure of my first two marriages might have been caused by the fact that most women can't live with a Zombie.

I've made a little change in method which is very great. I used to get the papers in the morning and read them before I went to work. Now I get up at six, hear fifteen minutes of news and go directly to work unconfused and undeflected. This simple thing works so well that I shall never go back to the other. I read the papers in the evening, after work.

This is an egocentric letter but I thought you might like to know these things. You say it isn't a novel. Maybe you're right. It's not a novel like any I have seen or read or heard of, but as far as I know a novel is a long piece of fiction having form direction and rhythm as well as intent. At worst it should amuse, at half-staff move to emotion and at best illuminate. And I don't know whether this will do any of those things but its intention is the third.

That's all. Write to me.

yours
John

John Steinbeck's departure on Operation Windmills in the truck Rocinante was delayed by Hurricane Donna. At last, on September 23, he set off with Charley. For his first overnight stop, he camped near his son John's Eaglebrook School at Deerfield, Massachusetts, whose headmaster was Thurston Chase.

To Elaine Steinbeck

Saint Johnsbury, Vermont
September 24, 1960
Sunday evening

Dear Bogworthy:

I didn't get you written last night as I thought I might. There was the yearly Pow-Wow when the new boys are taken into the two tribes. It was beautiful—big bonfire, and Thurston Chase in a war bonnet looks exactly like Thurston Chase in a war bonnet, glasses and all and speaking Longfellow Indian. I swear it. He wrote it himself in Hiawatha hexameters, and it was as sublimely dreadful as anything I ever heard.

The first boy I saw on arrival was Cat [now fourteen]. Rocinante was in the parking lot and everybody came to it—all the teachers and Mrs. Chase, and I made them coffee. It was fine. John acted as master of ceremonies, passed cups and canned milk. At one time there were twelve people—three on each side of the table and six standing. Then I was asked to lunch and went, sat at John's table.

He told me he was working hard, and he said he was beginning to enjoy it. He loves biology, and he kept talking the kind of French we did at Sag, and when we sent you the photograph he wrote the French himself. We talked well and easily and he was genuinely glad I had come. I got him back at 3 for soccer practice and watched that.

Charley and I had onion soup in the truck and after the Pow-Wow they let John go out with me. We went to a doleful little roadside place and had a steak—a bad one. I got him back at 9:30 and went up and camped in an orchard at the hilltop farm. Went to sleep and overslept so that I barely made church.

I think John was pleased and proud that I came. For one thing he had just been elected head of the band committee and was wearing his red eagle—the first one he ever got, and then he knew that he has been doing well in school. We liked each other and were easy together and that's the best. And so I left him with good feeling all around and I'm crazy about him.

I've had a reluctance about writing about the trip so far but I know now it was because the trip hadn't started until this noon. John is nuts about you. I think notes from you will be very valuable to him. I am going to write him every few days. He feels very close now and needs to.

And of course I adore you.

The country up here is just beginning to burst into flame. It was thirty here last night—in Vermont, I mean. Tomorrow I'll get as close to Deer Isle as I can without pounding. Talking with people is easy because everyone loves the truck. And Charley is a big hit. He takes his guarding very seriously and sticks very close. And he prances around like a puppy. As I get farther out, people have more opinions. But it isn't "talk back to the Russians"—it's more—"Let's figure what they're up to before we talk back." And this is healthy.

I've been gone just two days and it seems forever.

That's all for now, my love.

Charley sends a wag. And me too—

Me

To Elaine Steinbeck

Boggins:

Stopped early today—about four—right on the border between New Hampshire and Vermont. Been driving the log-
ging roads of Maine and N.H. all day and those roads are
rough and twisty. So Charley said it was all right to quit
early. Besides, we are camped on a stream which he likes. I
can't call you tonight. There isn't a soul around anywhere. I
think I'll make my famous Spanish rice tonight. Feel much
less hopeless and what am I doing here than last night in the
rain. I got too tired for one thing and then it got dark and I
couldn't find a place to stop until I got into that space behind
the bridge. Feelings get very volatile in the rain anyway.
Tonight I feel so good I might even have a drink later. But it
will be with a feeling of sin. There isn't a soul anywhere
about, to invite to join me. You'd be amazed how deserted
much of this north country is. I had heard this and how the
game was coming back. I've seen two cow mooses by the side
of the road and today I had to stop because a doe wouldn't get
out of my way. She wandered off after giving me a long and
scornful look.

I don't have any thoughts at all. Maine seems a big empty
place where people have been—and gone. And near the
towns it's mostly trash—miles of junked automobiles. I hear
the news on the car radio. Khrushchev's pounding and
chanting seem incredible and inexplicable to me. I guess I
was crazy to leave New York just at this time. I might even
have seen the table pounding but can't have everything and
I hope this is valuable.

Nixon invaded Maine today and made his usual speech. I
heard it on the car radio. He can hardly talk for unmelted
butter in his mouth. I do hope I can find some opinion somewhere. The Down Easters don't give out much if they don't
know you. And as I told you there are no bars. I've haunted
roadside coffee shops, drunk gallons of bad coffee but mostly

they stare into their cups and don't even talk to each other. It's as though they knew each other's thoughts and had no need to say them. I wonder if I will find the whole country like that. But worried they are.

It's very odd—I haven't been very far from New York yet but I seem to have been on another planet. So much of Maine is solitary and deserted. Of course there are islands of neat, white-painted prosperity and lots of new cars but what I remember are all the houses finally crushed by the weather and deserted—big houses, and the forest has crept back. The milltowns are humming—the paper towns with their sour smell of fermenting wood pulp, but it's like a quick cancerous growth, and on the outskirts the woods creeping back. It's something very strange. Now I'm about to hit the ragged centers, the Youngstowns and Detroits etc., crawling with production. I can't avoid them. There they are—right in the way. I only know they make me nervous.

Nixon says, "Hi there. So nice to see you. I see you've got California weather for me." How we laughed because it was pouring. Then he went on to say it was pretty good for a country to be able to rain like that and he wasn't one to run down rain. But on the other hand he didn't come out for it either.

This letter goes on and on. It comes of stopping driving before I am exhausted. I guess I shouldn't do that. It has fooled Charley. He thinks it is bedtime and the sun isn't even set yet.

Later—My lima beans smelled so good that I had them again instead of my fabulous Spanish rice. It wouldn't have been so fabulous without you to ooh and aah it anyway. Now, I've had dinner, peed Charley, read a little Robert Graves and I completely forgot the drink I was going to have. Too late now I guess. Late meaning it is 7:30 or quarter of eight. A dark, clear night and a little chill but not cold enough for the scarlet underwear.

And that, my fair, is about that. Tomorrow night I will probably put up at a motel for the sake of a bath and if I can find one with a phone I will call you.

Good night, darling.

[unsigned]

To Elaine Steinbeck

On the road
October 1, 1960

Dear Whamfort:

Writing this sometime after talking to you this evening. And I must say I am glad I will be seeing you soon. I said I had no thoughts but I have impressions. One is of our wastes. We can put chemical wastes in the rivers, and dispose of bowel wastes but every town is ringed with automobiles, machines, wrecks of houses. It's exactly like the Christmas Eves I described—opened and thrown away for the next package.

Tonight I pulled into this trailer park. Run by a square-jawed, crew-cut, National Guard officer. I asked him to have a drink. He never touched the stuff. I asked him for coffee. His wife was the coffee maker. He lives in a red trailer about the size of our house, only longer. I phoned you from one of the rooms. There must be six. All through my travels I've seen thousands of these trailers. People live in them. They don't move them. Build them up with cement blocks. This man tonight told me one out of four new houses is a trailer. Made of aluminum and plywood. I asked him if he thought it was a lack of permanence. He said, no. They want to see what's coming out next year. They trade them in like automobiles. They're called Mobile Homes—only they aren't mobile. They can't move legally on the highways (except by permit). I've seen them with big overhangs of jalousies and awnings. They are cheaper to buy than houses.

He is a young man who has quarreled with his father and gone into the trailer-court business. His wife says he is in training for something but she doesn't know what. Apparently he doesn't touch *that* stuff either. His trailer is 20 miles from where he was born. This trailer business is very important. It means you will throw away a house the way you consign a car to the junkyard.

These are Martians. I wanted to ask them to take me to their leader. They have no humor, no past, and their future

683

is new models. Their present is exactly that of the White Leghorns that produce the eggs in batteries. Maybe I've finally found it. We live in batteries and any product is no better than the chemicals we take in. I wish I had a week with this young man. It would take a week because he can't talk.

If I ever am looking for a theme—this restless mobility is a good one. Just now I went out in the moonlight to pee. A picture window was clear, looking like a quarterdeck. I said to the owner, "That looks like an architect's office." He said, "It's my home!" That's dreadful! A home accumulates. A home has a roof of hope and cellar of memories. That's our kind of home. But there's a new kind. That man meant it. That plywood and aluminum thing is his "home."

It's quite a cold night—maybe one for my space suit underwear. It was brilliant of you to make me bring it.

I begin to think if you were in Chicago Wednesday or Thursday it would be fine. And I would be ready for a break too. Then I wouldn't start west until the following week.

Love,
Merlin

To Elaine Steinbeck

On the road
October 10, 1960
Monday

Dear Flouncefoot:

I'm very glad you came out and it was a good time wasn't it? It took the blankness off a lot.

Today I wafted up out of Illinois and into Wisconsin and am encamped right now near a place named Manston, about halfway between Chicago and Minneapolis. Came through the Wisconsin Dells, a beautiful and strange country. And all of it very rich, black soil and corn, but forests too and round hills not unlike Somerset. I find I brought the hotel key but forgot to bring the ash tray I stole. So it's still a coffee can. I can't seem even to be properly dishonest. I am camped in a cornfield behind a truckers service place and coffee shop. Talk was all of baseball and little else. I heard the game on the radio and it was a fine one. There is great joy here in the Pirates. No politics, just baseball. This is cow country, so Rocinante is full of flies. I have put Charley in the cab while I sprayed them dead. It gives him the wheezes.

It's easy to see how this part of the country is important. Good lord, it is so rich—corn and pigs and cows and cheese everywhere—cheese centers, cheese stores, cheese ice cream, I guess. I'm too well fed after the weekend to take advantage of it. I'm going to have a bowl of soup and hit it. But I do have a good feeling now and I'm not so lonesome. Probably will be by the time I hit Seattle.

From here I'm aiming an angular course for Fargo, North Dakota. I can't tell you why except I have heard of the weather in Fargo all my life. When it is cold, it is said to be colder than the North Pole. Also it is almost exactly in the center of the country. I mean if you fold a map of the U.S., Fargo will be in the crease. You can see how important this is. Maybe this whole trip is just as silly. It is odd that everyone except you tells me how I should do it.

Of course one of the reasons for it must have occurred to you—I nearly told you that one in Chicago. American men of a certain age are very likely to get the George Albee disease. They become habitual sick men. After my illness I have had every chance to develop this state. It's so nice to have things done for you, to have loving people take care of you. Then you begin to take care of yourself and gradually you have the George Albee disease for good. If this trip does nothing else, it will remove the possibility of that trouble. You see, I *can* read a map. I *can* drive a truck, I *can* make do. And I *can* stand the loneliness as you can. There it is. It's an antidote for a poison that gets into very many men of my age and makes them emotional and spiritual cripples. But we're not going to have that, are we? I'm still a man, damn it. This may seem silly but to me it isn't. I've seen the creeping sickifying creep up on too many. But you married a man and I'm damn well going to keep him that way.

That's all for tonight. I love you.

Charley's uncle.

685

During one of the telephone calls he made to Elaine Steinbeck along the road, she told him she was enjoying his diary-letters. "They remind me of *Travels with a Donkey*," she said. "I think of them as *Travels with Charley*." He replied, "You've just given me my title."

To Elaine Steinbeck

Not far from
Detroit Lakes, Minnesota
October 11 [1960]

Dear Monsoon:

Seems impossible that you went yesterday morning. It seems very much longer ago than that. I've been through so many kinds of country. I'm camped in a row of great cattle trailers—longer than box cars. Got to talking to the man at the gas pump and he invited me to stay. These big trailers have taken it away from the railroads. This is also turkey country. Just below this hill the earth is black with them. There must be ten thousand turkeys in the one flock.

I guess Wisconsin is the prettiest state I ever saw—more kinds of country—hills and groves like Somerset, and the Dells a strange place of water and odd mushroom-shaped rocks. Lousy with tourist places but nearly all closed now with signs saying—"See you next spring." Then I got into St. Paul and Minneapolis. There must be some way to avoid them but I didn't make it. Crawling with traffic. Took a good time to get out of that. So I've been in Minnesota all afternoon and now am not far from the North Dakota border. At breakfast a trucker told me how women drove the big trucks during the war. I said, "My god, they must have been Amazons," and he replied, "I don't know. I never fought one." I've talked to lots of people today. Stopped quite a lot. One argument— did you know if you bake a doughnut, it will float? I'm just repeating what I heard. And I heard that Dag Hammarskjöld could easy be President. When I suggested that he was a

Swede the reply was—"What of it?" I think I'll write that to him.

I know you think just because I'm away from you and you can't check on me, that I make up things. I'll just have to ask you to believe there is Swiss cheese candy. No, I didn't taste it, I just saw the sign. Also that the largest collection of Sea Shells in the world is on Route 12 in Wisconsin. Who could make up things like that? Who would want to?

I know E.O. wouldn't approve of the speed with which I am covering ground but I'm sure seeing lots and hearing lots. People don't talk about issues. They talk about how you bake a doughnut and it will float. There's lots of local politics talked but I can't see much interest in the national. But plenty in the U.N. Washington is so far away. A man today looked at my license plates and said, "Clear from New York." But mostly it's hunting and stories about hunting. The bombardment against ducks starts at dawn.

I went from maple country which is flame red to birch which is flame yellow. You would have oohed quite a lot, aahed some. I stopped at a sign that said "home made sausages," and bought some. I'm cooking it now and it smells really wonderful. And at another place I got apples that just explode with juice when you bite them. There's no doubt that frost does something to them. But it's stopping like this that gets talk going. Everyone wants to see the inside of the truck. I even do the floors with Lestoil and I keep the stove shined. When they see the guns they say, "Oh, going hunting!" and never ask another question. Because of the cap and beard they usually take me for a retired sailor and make jokes about do I get car sick. I say I sure do. On the Duluth and Minneapolis radio there is a great block of advertising for Florida real estate. I listened carefully and all it promises is that it is in Florida.

I'll go through Fargo tomorrow morning and by the time I call you tomorrow night I'll be deep in North Dakota. From now on there will be long stretches less populated. In two days I'll be climbing toward the Rockies.

Well, I had the sausage and it was just as good as it smelled. And I didn't even splash grease on this letter.

They're loading cattle outside with floodlights. Must get out to see that. The truckers are a set-apart bunch of men. The long distance ones are exactly like sailors. I suppose they have homes but they live on the road and stop to sleep.

Well, I watched. Two truckloads of yearlings. Going south to be fed—but bull calves. The beefers are kept for milk. There is too Swiss cheese candy.

I miss you already. Time gets all out of kilter.

Good night my love.

Tobit

To Elaine Steinbeck

Beach, North Dakota,
but why Beach?
Columbus Day [1960]

Honey:

I was so glad to hear you tonight.

I should write to you in the mornings. I get a little tired, particularly tonight. The roads were very rough and the wind high. The Badlands are moody things—really as though someone were being bad. But I can see how it would be possible to fall in love with them.

I listened to the game. When the Pirates lose they sure lose big, don't they?

I'm staying in a motel called the Dairy Queen. Reason? The only public telephone in forty miles.

The Dairy Queen has a large, beautiful tub and I'm going to get into it almost at once. Beach has a bar. I went in and there was nothing talked but deer hunting. I've seen about six go by on car fenders today.

I think I'll get in the tub and then wash shirts and sox. Maybe that will freshen me. I started out at 6 this morning. North Dakota is like the great plains anywhere, and then— Wham! the Missouri River, and instantly it becomes the West, brown hills and then the moon country of the Badlands. And what they call painted canyons—all blue and red. It was rainy at first and then the sun burst out and whopped

688

it up. Charley has had his dinner now and peed a Badland. And I feel a little peaked and tired. So I'll have the bath and see what it does.

That was yesterday. I went to sleep like a shot. So pooped I guess. So much to tell you. I crossed into Montana today. Where the Badlands are naughty—Montana is grand. What grandeur! It's like coming out into the north of England— huge and largely impractical. Lots of sugar beets. Lots of small bars in the towns. I stopped in about six. Little square, burnt-up men with little speech, all bent and warped with riding and sun and also cold, faces very red. I know the price a steer will bring and it's pretty good if it's local.

And it, the road I mean, looks level, but it isn't, you're climbing all the time, and you just think your car isn't doing very well. Been snow in the Rockies and more predicted so I came on over. I'm outside of Bozeman now and it's the coldest it's going to be. Tonight I wear the red pyjamas. There's a great snowy mountain beside me and the slender fir trees all look like what we try to do with soap at Christmas. I'm in a trailer park and I've talked with the people and they like the trailers because they are warmer and more comfortable.

I have two lamps on and my house is warm now. Also I had the good sense to buy a bottle of booze—namely Vodka, the first I've had since I left you and it comes in handy. It warms my feet. I've had two and I'm going to have another before I hit the bag. I'm having Jack Wagner's Pissoli tonight [A can of chile and a can of hominy].

It's been a wonderful day for looking and hearing. More historical markers. I shed a tear for Custer (the dumb bastard) at the field of Little Big Horn. And Charley peed a tear also.

I bought a hat today, an old-fashioned, narrow-brimmed stockman's hat. The naval cap causes too much attention this far from the sea. It was contrary to my purpose. The hat I bought is the one Sam Hamilton probably wore. Stetson called it a stockman's hat and it is not the movie version, just a plain hat. No one has looked at me since I bought it. Must remember this.

There are a few little air leaks—like behind the refrigerator but I've plugged them with Kleenices. I remember at Tahoe one time when a keyhole let in so much cold that I put a cork in it. The tropical plant is all curled and shivery. I don't know whether or not it will survive. It's got its leaves crossed like a lady in a wind tunnel.

From the smell, the pissoli is ready. I'll eat and then complete this and then have a shot of Vod and hit the blankets. Curfew shall not ring tonight.

I do miss you, you know.

Tomorrow I'll be moving toward Idaho but I don't know if I'll make it. Montana is very big to cross and so beautiful and grand that I drive slow for to look at it.

Love to my Mouse who has never been in a nose cone—so far.

Wonderful about Way's new job and Thom's A's and Cat's study hall.

Love from your true adorer.

I wish you were here, only your feet would be colder than mine and I couldn't take them.

Because Elaine Steinbeck joined him for a few days at a time along the way, the letters to her stopped. After coming down the West Coast he crossed the country through Texas and Louisiana and returned to New York.

To John F. Kennedy

New York
January 23, 1961

My dear Mr. President:

I thank you for inviting me to your inauguration. I was profoundly moved by this ceremony which I had never seen before and even more moved by your following speech which was not only nobly conceived and excellently written and delivered, but also had that magic undertone of truth which cannot be simulated.

Personally, of course, I am honored to have been invited, but much more sharply felt is my gratification that through me you have recognized the many good members of my profession as existing at all. A nation may be moved by its statesmen and defended by its military but it is usually remembered for its artists. It does seem to me that you, sir, have discovered or rather rediscovered this lost truth.

Again my thanks, my pledge and my passionate hope that your words may become history. And I believe they will!

Yours gratefully,
John Steinbeck

The President responded with a letter of thanks:

"I only regret that it was not possible for me to meet personally with you and other distinguished artists who were kind enough to be in Washington."

Handwritten below the typed letter, appeared the words:

"No President was ever prayed over with such fervor. Evidently they felt that the country or I needed it—probably both."

Steinbeck made his own comment to his friends the Howard Hunters:

"I had never seen this ceremony. I found it very moving when they finally got through the prayers to it. As Elaine says, most ministers are hams but they haven't learned the first rule of the theatre—how to get off. When Cushing got to whumping it up I thought how I'd hate to be God and have him on my tail. The good Cushing didn't ask, he instructed; and I bet he takes no nonsense from the Virgin Mary either nor from the fruit of her womb, Jesus."

Adlai Stevenson, by now United States Representative to the United Nations, wrote President Kennedy on January 3, 1962:

"I am loath to request your personal attention to a question that is manifestly political patronage. Yet I have a feeling you will want to see the attached excerpt from a letter from my long-time friend, John Steinbeck. After all, we are in search of initiatives in the foreign field and this seems like one of the most promising I have heard of!

" 'I want to be Ambassador to Oz. Don't smile that way, please. Glinda the Good has a mirror which makes all of our listening and testing devices obsolete. I don't know whether I could bring Oz into NATO right away, but at least the U.N. might benefit by its membership. You will remember also that the Wicked Witch melted and ran down over herself. If I could get that secret, we could handle quite a few people who would look better melted down. Then, too, we could dye different countries different colors so that we would be able to know whether we hated them or not. There is only one great danger that I can think of. In Oz they have a wizard who openly admits that he is a fake. Can you think what that principle would do to New York politics alone, if it should spread, I mean.' "

Steinbeck had been writing a series of letters to Stevenson, which he had prefaced, some time before, as follows:

"You might come to know these effusions as The Stevenson Letters, if I tell you a story Jack Ratcliff told me. When he was a child, his paternal house was haunted by an ancient crone, his grandmother, mean, fierce, mustached and with the disposition of a disappointed mink. She was old beyond credence and was generally and sadly considered immortal. She was not rich but she had a treasure which she used like a whip over the family. This was The Lincoln Letter. She kept it in a black metal japanned box which was locked. No one had ever seen the Letter but the beldame threatened them, saying— 'You—or you—or you—will not get The Lincoln Letter when I die.'

"She lived an unconscionable time, but finally she did breathe her last. Jack says that when the doctor folded his stethoscope, the family as one rushed for the black box. They pried it open, and there on top was The Lincoln Letter. It was not *from* Lincoln but was one the grandmother had written *to* Lincoln. She had never mailed it."

To Adlai Stevenson
IN NEW YORK

Sandy Lane Hotel
Barbados
February 15, 1961

Ambassador Adlai Stevenson:

Your Excellency, honey—Dear Adlai: I am at a loss about how to address you. In my country Hon. means you have been paid public money legitimately, while Honest—Honest John, Honest Jim—means you have stolen public money.

I had dinner with Marietta the Naughty [Marietta Tree, United States Representative to the Human Rights Commission of the United Nations] two nights ago. I told her I had stopped Stevenson letters because of the sensitiveness of your present position and because I am by no means sure that I could be cleared as a guilty association. She said, "Bosh! Continue them because I want to read them too." You must admit that's pretty flattering.

What a lovely place this is. The Fayre Elayne progresses from high yellow to octoroon. I simply slough skins like a snake.

No Stevenson letter is worth its ink without advice. I have a plan which is not as silly as it may seem. May I tell it to you? It seems very likely that Mr. K. [Khrushchev] will be coming to your club before long. What I propose is this. I know that all delegates carry attaché cases on the upper levels and briefcases on the lower. I suggest that your delegation and as many others as you can persuade, on the day Mr. K. takes his seat, have in each piece of diplomatic luggage a shoe. If you still have your famous shoe with the hole, it would be perfect. I suggest that when Mr. K. takes his seat each member should place a shoe on his desk. Probably no comment would

693

be necessary but if it seems advisable, you or perhaps the representative of a small nation should announce that on a previous occasion we had been ignorant of Soviet parliamentary procedure, but that the democracies out of courtesy for Soviet conventions were determined to go along.

Now that is not a joke. In spite of all his jokes I think Mr. K. is a humorless man. I think if this could be done in a tense moment, and there is bound to be one, it would throw him sky high and deliver against him the most terrible weapon in the world, laughter.

We will be here until March 4th. I've been asked to go with Project Mohole—to take a core off the coast of Mexico at 12,000 feet. I have accepted with fantastic joy. I'll go March 15th for one month. The whole undisturbed history of the world in one core. I can't resist it. Besides, many of my old and abominable friends will be there—good men, good minds, good scientists.

This is a short Stevenson letter. Please let me know whether or not they could embarrass you or the important work you are doing.

Elaine sends love.

Yours,
John

On their return from Barbados, the Steinbecks found Thom and John Steinbeck IV, then sixteen and fourteen respectively, sitting on the doorstep of the 72nd Street house asking to be taken in. From then on the boys lived with their father and stepmother.

Soon afterward, Steinbeck flew to San Diego where the Mohole Expedition's ship, the *Cuss I,* was being fitted out. As he wrote friends:

"I was picked as historian of the expedition not because I am a superb oceanographer but simply because I seem to be the only American writer who is one at all. This is a most fascinating job, a whole new world being discovered for the first time. With

694

these cores and some more in the future, we will know much more about what the earth is made of, how old it is and what has happened to it during its five billion years, how long life has existed and very possibly how it came to be at all."

And to Elaine Steinbeck on March 21:

"This is like a show on the road, a little world, self-contained and self-sufficient."

To Elaine, Thom, and John Steinbeck

San Diego
[March 23, 1961]

Dear Elaine and Dear Thom and Dear John:

I don't think you ever heard noises like those that are going on around me. Triphammers going and pounding on the steel hull with sledge hammers and the engines all running, hundreds of them. People rushing about with cables and bits of steel and new electronic equipment. We are supposed to sail at dawn and all this has to be cleared by then, and I don't see how in the world they are going to do it. Sailing is a laugh. We are going to be towed by a navy tug and when we turn across the waves we wallow like you couldn't believe. The crew aboard is as crazy as everything else—geologists, zoologists, petrologists, oceanographers, engineers of any kind you want to imagine, and on top of this the toughest crew of oil riggers you ever saw. They look like murderers and have the delicate movements of ballet dancers, and they had better have, because to lower drill string from a heaving ship takes some doing. I watched them work on the experimental hole and they are quite some men. The lightest slip and they kill someone. I wouldn't think of going on deck without a hard hat on. In fact you feel naked without one. Mine is bright yellow and I am getting so fond of it that I may bring it home to go on the hat rack with the other hats.

I know my typing isn't so good but it is worse right now

because the ship has a ten-degree list. They are doing something on the port side and so have flooded the starboard tanks to bring her over, so I am writing up hill and my chair which has wheels on it is sliding downhill.

Boys: I hear really fine reports from the Fayre Elayne about you, and it makes me so very glad and happy and relieved to know that you are taking good care of Elaine about whom I have rather strong feelings as I do about you. It is a very nice feeling and makes me want to go home very much. I don't know when I will make it but I will as soon as possible. But it would be a shame to miss this opportunity to see something entirely new in the world. If I don't get back before you go to Sag I will join you there just the moment I can.

It is almost impossible to write with all this noise going on.

Love to all and I will see you very soon and want to dreadfully.

John

To Elaine, Thom, and John Steinbeck

At sea
March 25, 1961

My dearest darling family:

We are at sea now since last night, a heavy swell, towed by a tug and heavy weather on us. We are rolling like an old sow pig. We are about 90 miles west of San Diego traveling at about 4 knots. It will be twenty-four hours before we are on station where the buoys have already been set up. Finally I have found my place, the gyroscope room just under the bridge. No one ever comes here except occasionally to throw a switch. I've tied my chair to the stationary table legs, else it would slide out from under me. I started the piece for Life and will continue it as we go along, in the form of a log. More immediacy I think in that way.

All over the ship there are signs "Danger High Voltage, Danger Explosives, Danger Gasoline, etc." So I have made a sign for my door which says—Danger Cerebration Area. It looks very pretty in red.

Saturday morning

We've shifted course now and going with wind and wave. We have to put out 12,000 feet of drill string before we even touch bottom. We have to hold a position over the drill hole without anchoring, by sonar and radar; if there is the slightest drift the outboards in the direction of drift speed up and keep it on the spot over the hole. It is a great and new piece of engineering. If you want to know how precise it is, try taking a six foot piece of thread and holding it at the top, then try to thread a needle on the floor. Of course if we should, through engine failure, lose a hole, we could never find it again.

The rest of today and tomorrow morning will be the last of leisure. The moment we are on station we will start the drill string down. And then I'll have to be there day and night.

[Sunday]

Darling and darlings:

It is Sunday afternoon and we are still about thirty miles from our station. The wind and the weather have all delayed us. Everybody getting a little nervous and overwrought because we should have been drilling yesterday. We will go on station we hope before dark and will start the drill string down right away.

I want to tell you what I should do. Four holes are contemplated, but I should not have to be here for more than two of them. I will get out by air as soon as I can after the second hole. I will telephone you there as soon as I get to San Diego. I'll stand by for the first jet and will get on it. Then I will telephone you from Idlewild. I wish I could tell you how soon, but I can't. I love you and will hie me home the moment I can, no more to rooooaaaammmm.

love, love, love,
Pappy Poseidon

To Elizabeth Otis

Sag Harbor
June 26, 1961

Dear Elizabeth:

The reviews of Winter have depressed me very much. They always do, even the favorable ones, but this time they have sunk me particularly. Of course I know the book was vulnerable. And I don't know why this time I feel so bad about them. But I do. Of course I'll climb out of it. Maybe as the future shortens, the optimism decreases. I don't know. I wish I did.

Funny thing. Esther telephoned to tell us further news about Beth. [His sister, Mrs. Ainsworth, had broken her hip.] And she said she was canceling her subscriptions to Time and to Saturday Review. I told her she must not but she said quite firmly that they didn't tell the truth. I haven't read either Time or the SRL so I don't quite know what she is talking about. And I don't think I will read them right yet. I feel too badly about the good ones to rub my nose in the bad ones. It's just been one of those weeks—I'll snap back right away. Just feel a little raw now. And so I suppose I'm taking it out on you. The usual letters are beginning to come in. I can't find the energy to answer them. The whole thing has gone into what feels like very painful pleurisy and is probably as Elaine points out, simply psychological. But, I think I said I would probably snap back in a day or so and be as high as I have been low. A pure manic depressive, I guess.

That's all for now.

Love,
John

Before Project Mohole he had started writing *Travels with Charley* from letters and notes written during the trip. Now he resumed this work at Sag Harbor.

To Pascal Covici

Sag Harbor
June 28, 1961

Dear Pat:

I am past the usual crisis of fighting back at the critics, even in my mind. It's just a part of the rather tiresome quadrille. It never changes. One Middle Western reviewer said a little sadly about Winter, "I suppose, as usual, the faults we point out as making this book less than a work of art, will in the future turn out to be the factors of its excellence." At least there was a man who remembered or reread the earlier criticisms.

Two nights ago, I had a singular experience I want to tell you about. As you must know, I am having great difficulty getting back the rhythm and flow of the Travels piece. Every day I have fought it and with no sense of getting anywhere. This is not a new experience with me and it has a painful ally that comes at night. I lie in bed and in the dark try to work out the difficulty. Then other difficulties enter. The worries about John and Thom and Waverly and Elaine and her mother and her aunt—all matters impossible of solution but in the dark they grow to intensity until the skin of my mind begins to crawl and itch. And all sense of proportion disappears. Then I know there is to be no sleep that night. It is a kind of silent ballet of frustration.

Well, two nights ago I went through this silly process and it continued until just before dawn, when I heard a voice. Now I've heard voices before, have been suddenly called sharply—a common experience. This was not like that. I heard it but it was not as though it spoke aloud, although I could hear the tone and timbre. It was a voice which was kind but at the same time heavy with authority. I remember the words very clearly. The voice said—"What difference does it make? You've worked enough. You have twenty-six published book titles and God knows how many stories and essays. That ought to be enough. What are you struggling for —or against? You don't own the world." It was just like that. Now I can understand this and its origin and its reason but what followed was one of the most remarkable things that ever happened to me.

When the voice stopped I was flooded with a great smooth sense of ease and rest. I don't think I remember such a feeling of well being. Every muscle in my body stretched and felt good and I went to sleep. My alarm awakened me at 6:30 as usual when I go to work. The words were still with me. I turned off the bell and slept two hours more, and awakened more refreshed than I have in a long time. When I came out to my work room I didn't care whether I worked or not. I felt good all day and that night which was last night and I still do today. These words are true. I have no doubt that they came from my beaten and aging tissue and were delivered as a warning. Because, you see, I have never permitted myself the license of comfort. If work did not come, I had to exert just as much force against the page—perhaps more. And it is true. What am I fighting so hard for or against?

And I don't own the world; but apparently I have permitted it to own me. And the feeling of comfort has persisted. The very feeling—"There is a page—but I don't have to fill it" is comforting. In fact a blank page is a very pretty thing. But I have been straining and leaning under the whips. Let's see what this means. When you whip a horse he leans full strength, maybe more than his full strength, into the collar, not to get ahead but to get away from the stinging of the whip. And I have had not one whip but several. First the whip of duty—this is more like a club or a goad than a whip. Second, the whip of inadequacy. I have always recognized that I did not have great talent but rather relied on the whip to make me over-leap my limitations. And third the whip of flattery. This is as delicate and painful as a limber buggy whip with a striker of sharp knotted string. It is applied to me by the wishes and the desires and even the needs of those around me who by expecting of me more than I am, force me to do better than I can. The only whip I do not think I am subject to is that of ambition. I don't think I have that. Vanity yes, but not ambition.

Is this a long and tiresome essay? It may be but if so you are in the path of it and have no more choice than a man in an intersection, run down by a mad car driver. And knowing you are helpless I shall continue.

In the time I have left and that, by the large law, is not a very great amount of time—it would be a pleasant thing if I came to my work moving toward something rather than trying to escape from something. The carrot on the stick rather than the whip on the ass. Perhaps the carrot has no more validity than the whip but it is more pleasant.

I think I've overworked my engine and maybe the voice I heard was telling me so. When the invasion barges started for the beaches during the last war—full of huddled frightened men, the sergeants and officers did not address soldiers saying—"Go forth and fight for glory and immortality!" No, they said, "Hit the surf! Do you want to live forever?"

And it does occur to me that those critics who so belabor me for my inadequacies are trying to force me to want to live forever. And I don't. The voice I heard two nights ago was the more valid critic.

In all of this I hope I have not indicated that I will not face the empty page any more but that I hope I will keep the comfort I have now and that some joy will come back. I really hate publication dates very much. They throw the whole thing out of drawing. Do you know what it reminds me of? It is like a baseball game at Yankee Stadium. Let us say it is a perfect game, a tight, precise game, perhaps a no-hitter— and then comes the last out of the last inning and the spectators pour out on the field and convert the preciseness into a meaningless ant hill. And that's exactly what a publication date is to me, crowded with people all getting in the act and milling about like ants, hacking up the turf and spoiling the diamond.

And there you have in this letter a kind of ant hill, if you wish.

yr hble svt.
John

To Pascal Covici

Sag Harbor
[July 1961]

Dear Pat:

Another week and into thick summer. We have the breeze of course but the air is heavy. Summer is far from my favorite time. The village fills up with hot angry people, strangers with all the overbearing shyness of strangers. And the highways crawling with aimless cars. The vacationers don't have much fun if any, or if they do it is by contrast with an even more dull and doleful life. And so I go very seldom off my point of land and spend even more hours than usual in Joyous Garde.

And the little book of ambulatory memoirs staggers along, takes a spurt and lags. It's a formless, shapeless, aimless thing and it is even pointless. For this reason it may be the sharpest realism because what I see around me is aimless and pointless—ant-hill activity. Somewhere there must be design if I can only find it. I'm speaking of this completed Journey now. And outside of its geographical design and its unity of time, it's such a haphazard thing. The mountain has labored and not even a mouse has come forth. Thinking and thinking for a word to describe decay. Not disruption, not explosion but simple rotting. It seemed to carry on with a weary inertia. No one was for anything and nearly everyone was against many things. Negro hating white. White hating negroes. Republicans hating Democrats although there is little difference.

In all my travels I saw very little real poverty, I mean the grinding terrifying poorness of the Thirties. That at least was real and tangible. No, it was a sickness, a kind of wasting disease. There were wishes but no wants. And underneath it all the building energy like gasses in a corpse. When that explodes, I tremble to think what will be the result. Over and over I thought we lack the pressures that make men strong and the anguish that makes men great. The pressures are debts, the desires are for more material toys and the anguish

702

is boredom. Through time, the nation has become a discontented land. I've sought for an out on this—saying it is my aging eyes seeing it, my waning energy feeling it, my warped vision that is distorting it, but it is only partly true. The thing I have described is really there. I did not create it. It's very well for me to write jokes and anecdotes but the haunting decay is there under it.

Well, there was once a man named Isaiah—and what he saw in his time was not unlike what I have seen, but he was shored up by a hard and durable prophecy that nothing could disturb. We have no prophecy now, nor any prophets.

[unsigned]

To Pascal Covici
AFTER A WEEKEND AT SAG HARBOR

Sag Harbor
[July 1961]

Dear Pat:

Before I am tempted into civility, let's get one thing straight. It made me proud to see how here at New Discove you resisted rushing to cut the lawn and plunge your arms into the soil. Marvelous example of self-control. I could see your knuckles pressed white on your Vodka glass while your whole being cried out for hard physical labor.

The first thing we heard of Ernest Hemingway's death was a call from the London Daily Mail, asking me to comment on it. And quite privately, although something of this sort might have been expected, I find it shocking. He had only one theme—only one. A man contends with the forces of the world, called fate, and meets them with courage. Surely a man has a right to remove his own life but you'll find no such possibility in any of H's heros. The sad thing is that I think he would have hated accident much more than suicide. He was an incredibly vain man. An accident while cleaning a gun would have violated everything he was vain about. To

703

shoot yourself with a shot gun in the head is almost impossible unless it is planned. Most such deaths happen when a gun falls, and then the wound is usually in the abdomen. A practiced man does not load a gun while cleaning it. Indeed a hunting man would never have a loaded gun in the house. There are shot guns over my mantle but the shells are standing on the shelf below. The guns are cleaned when they are brought in and you have to unload a gun to clean it. H. had a contempt for mugs. And only a mug would have such an accident. On the other hand, from what I've read, he seems to have undergone a personality change in the last year or so. Certainly his last summer in Spain and the resulting reporting in Life were not in his old manner. Perhaps, as Paul de Kruif told me, he had had a series of strokes. That would account for the change.

But apart from all that—he has had the most profound effect on writing—more than anyone I can think of. He has not a vestige of humor. It's a strange life. Always he tried to prove something. And you only try to prove what you aren't sure of. He was the critics' darling because he never changed style, theme nor story. He made no experiments in thinking nor in emotion. A little like Capa, he created an ideal image of himself and then tried to live it. I am saddened at his death. I never knew him well, met him a very few times and he was always pleasant and kind to me although I am told that privately he spoke very disparagingly of my efforts. But then he thought of other living writers, not as contemporaries but as antagonists. He really cared about his immortality as though he weren't sure of it. And there's little doubt that he has it.

One thing interests me very much. For a number of years he has talked about a big book he was writing and then about several books written and put away for future publication. I have never believed these books exist and will be astonished if they do. A writer's first impulse is to let someone read it. Of course I may be wrong and he may be the exception. For the London Daily Express, I have two lines by a better writer than either of us. When they call this morning, Elaine will dictate them over the cable. They go—

> He was a man, take him all in all,
> I shall not look upon his like again.

And since he was called Papa—the lines are doubly applicable.

That's all today. I got up at five. Now it's time to work.

And I did work and got a goodly part of a thing done. So I will send this.

Prosit
John

To Frank Loesser

Sag Harbor
The Glorious Fourth, 1961

Dear Frank:

Your description of overcoming your son has to be true in detail—I know every instant of it. I am glad to have you available for proof. A number of our childless friends, on hearing of the peccadillos of our offspring, are prone to say —"But these are monsters." But they're not. They are just ordinary kids.

You are now in a position only recently removed from us. Just as the boys had got used to our way of living, they went to Gwyn. They found it a rich field for various kinds of blackmail and a very Ft. Knox for excuses for any kind of conduct. I am not saying that Gwyn's plateau is higher or lower, better or worse than ours but there is no doubt it is different. If, when Gwyn was divorcing me, I had had any experience, knowledge or even kindness, I should have insisted—All right, if you want the boys, take them and I will disappear. If you don't, give them to me and you disappear. And now I see you, with the best intentions in the world, doing the same things at the same cost. You can make arrangements with a dead parent. But a living and absent but available parent does untold harm and no possible good.

I think this will amuse you. For the last little while Thom has been denying that I am his father, when he meets new people. Sometimes his father is a doctor and sometimes he is adopted. I expect that this is one of the commonest of all adolescent practices—I think I have found its origin and it isn't limited to children. World myth is full of it. Let us say you want to be a hero. A hero can't have a common origin. One's parents are common no matter who they are. And since one feels different from one's parents, one can't be their child. All the world's heros have magical or mystic origins—Christ, Hiawatha, Zeus, Achilles. Even Lincoln has the mysterious illegitimacy in his background. So perhaps what Thom is telling himself is this—"I am special. My father is a tiresome fellow. Therefore he can't be my father, therefore he isn't my father. Now—that frees me. Who would I like for a father—?" My so-called ability or celebrity has nothing to do with it because Thom knows I am a dull fellow. The reddish smudges on this paper are from jeweler's rouge. I have been polishing a knife blade.

Thom solos this week I think. He is very excited. He spends about twelve hours a day at the airport. They pay him for eight. He cleans aircraft and services them and works on motors and next week he's going in the tower. I go on plugging at my travel piece. One day I'll stop writing and that'll be the day.

Now—back to the pad.

So long
John

To Frank Loesser

Sag Harbor
August 1, 1961

Dear Frank:

A wee mousie got into my little work house on the point. Now on the bottom shelf behind a curtain there sits a saucer of goodies. There is a sign on the plate which says "Welcome Visiting Mice. Register here!" You will have guessed that these mouse d'oeuvres are actually Mouse Mickeys.

Our little friend had a nibble and a martini and put on his

badge. Suddenly he was too dizzy. He staggered and fell, got up, staggered and fell. Yesterday, some weeks later, I found him. He was lying with his head on the enclosed letter written by me to you some weeks ago. I think the spots are tears.

This is no new thing. Only about one tenth of the letters I write get sent. In the long run this turns out to be a very good thing.

Thom is still working at the airport. John comes back from Amherst Music Center. I expect him to join a hippie band any moment. Thom goes on with his dreary love affair, suffering every step of the way. God, the loves of the young are dull. Waverly got married last week to a nice guy, a U.P.I. photographer [Paul Farber]. We know him and like him. It takes a great weight off Elaine and I hope to God it sticks.

Elaine is fair blooming but the hot weather gets her down, as it does me. She has a birthday on the 14th. Bastille Day in August. If you think of it, drop her a card, will you? She adores her birthday and loves to have something made of it. I fire cannons and such-like things.

When I finish the travels I don't know what I'll do. Sooner or later I want to get back to the Arthurian stuff. But not sure this is the time. I'd like to write a few short stories but they are very hard. They knock the daylights out of me.

> Love to your tomato,
> John

Among the letters he received after publication of *The Winter of Our Discontent* was one from Duke Sheffield's sister.

To Marion Sheffield Adams

Dear Marion:

I write few letters now and answer even fewer. The result is that my post box is daily choked with mail from strangers. Therefore, it was a pleasure to get yours and while my eyes have slipped, I still have a 20–20 memory, sometimes too good, too harsh, and too critical.

I used to wonder what had happened between Dook and me. Perhaps there were many little things, but I believe now that the most powerful force was simple drift. Over the years both of us made timid and futile attempts to reestablish something which was once good and true, but the process ground to a halt every time, and the fact would emerge that due to drift, we had become strangers.

I have always admired Dook's choice of a life for himself and his rugged defense of it. He has been far more successful than I have, in making his own kind of life, while I have been pushed and blown by people, circumstances, and emotions, some valid and others rather tawdry and not to be dwelt upon with pleasure and satisfaction. But always my intentions were the best paving material, at least I thought at the time they were. One thing, however, has never changed in me. The meaningless, pointless endless restlessness is just as powerful as it ever was, and that, I know now, will continue to the end.

That's an awful lot about me, but because much of it concerns your brother, I thought you might like to know. Long ago, I knew perhaps that mine was not a truly first rate talent. I had then two choices only—To throw it over or to use what I had to the best of my ability. I chose the second and I have tried to keep it clean.

I am married for the third time to a wise and gracious woman whom I love very much. My two sons by my second wife now live with us. They are 15 and 17 and they have all of the faults and some of the graces the race is subject to.

They are bright and intelligent and they fail in school. They are slaves of love for everything that walks upright and some things that do not. They are young agonies and very beautiful.

About a year ago, I got the light tap on the shoulder, that must come to everyone so that I began to wonder what I could do for my boys that would have surviving meaning and value to them. And suddenly it seemed very clear. I would give them a large part of the world and fortunately, for the time being at least, I can afford it. Early in September we will start out and travel slowly around the world taking ten to twelve months to do it. A young Irish tutor will go along so that their school work can go on. Some of the world I've seen but much I haven't, so in a large part, we will discover it together. Of course they may resent it at first because it may take them away from the particular teen-age squaw-lings of their dreams of the moment. But I think in the future, what they hear and see and feel will more than repay them. Geography doesn't mean much until you've moved over it and one bicycle trip along Hadrian's Wall makes you know the Roman Empire as you never could otherwise. And we'll hear the music of the world, and about music both boys are passionate. It's about the only thing they truly believe in and quite properly. You can't fake music really. One thing I insist on and that is that we don't move constantly. Here and there we will sit down for a week or a month. I know how that is. I spent ten months in Somerset two years ago counting grasses in a meadow. At the end of a year, I think I will have carved very deeply in them the one thing I truly believe—that all that is is holy, with its sub-heading—a penny has two sides.

Your news that Dook had taken a job surprised me. He had so successfully geared his wants to his income in a high classical sense. I can only suspect that an inflationary economy and a fixed income have got to quarreling. That would be a shame. With the years of reading omnivorously and in many directions, what knowledge he must have accumulated.

Marion, strange things happen. I think I know the beginning of the break between Dook and me—the point from which no return was possible. It was due to a stupidity of mine but I have been guilty of many. I'll tell you about it. I don't think I've ever told anyone else because of a flood of shame at my own lack of sensitiveness.

There were the years of the rejected work and the published books that were financial flops and they went on so long that it became the normal life. Then without warning my books began to sell and money began to come in. It scared the hell out of me because there was not and is not any payment which relates to the work in a book. So I gave the money away in all directions. And then I got my ill-conceived plan, and I worked it out in detail by myself. Dook was to go on with his formal education—Oxford or Cambridge for a Master's and the University of London for his Doctorate. It seemed so simple. I had the money. It didn't seem to be my money. Dook was broke. He was academic material and I wasn't. Well, I took the finished plan to him stupidly thinking he would be glad. His rage was cold and fierce. I see it now, and I see why now. But I swear to you that I had no feeling of charity, only of sharing. And a coldness set in that has never been overcome. Oh! I see now how he felt. From my misguided impulse both of us got hurt feelings and suspicions. He felt insulted and I felt slapped down. And there were no words for either of us for the truth. And by the time we were ready for truth, the drift had taken place and you can't do anything about drift. If we hadn't both been bruised, we might have fought against it.

And I think that's where it started—in my clumsiness. Since then I've learned what a dreadful weapon or tool money is but then, I'd had no experience with it. It was bright stuff and I wanted to spread it around, overlooking the brighter stuff of human feelings. Isn't it remarkable how suspect good intentions must be? If I had it to do again, I think I would still find the plan good and valid but perhaps I will have learned the technique of giving without wounding. Of course Dook had the much harder row—that of receiving and he wasn't any more prepared for receiving than I was for giving. It seems to me a little sad that we are only prepared to live at about the time of leaving life. Now I don't think I have ever told that to a soul before because I was ashamed and when one is ashamed, he builds a wall of defenses and justifications. And on such small ineptnesses and accidents lives are changed and destinies directed.

I would not have you think I am complaining. I've had a good, full, painful life. I've thoroughly enjoyed my work. I believe that is one of the critical charges leveled against me. I've tried to write the truth as I saw it and I have not held on to a truth when it became false. When the tap came, I was ready—too ready—even anxious. But on inspection this seemed wrong to me and I closed that door and I can't ever open it again. And it hasn't seemed long, but sometimes it seems endless. And then the radishes come up and there are baby rabbits on the lawn and a small delighted conceit becomes a sound of a book and the whole world is fresh and new and wonderful again. So if there is any overtone of regret in this letter, ignore it. I regret my stupidities but only as I might regret my big ears and shapeless nose. They are all a part of me and I could no more cut off my stupidities than my nose to spite my face.

This, which intended just to be a note—has turned into a sluggish muddy essay. But thanks to you for writing. Your letter opened a room which needed airing.

Love to you
John

1961 1963
1962

Steinbeck

"...I don't belong anywhere."

1961 Began ten months' trip abroad with his family.

1962 *Travels with Charley* published. Steinbeck received Nobel Prize for Literature.

In September 1961, the Steinbecks set out on what they planned as a round-the-world trip with Thom and John. They took with them as tutor for the boys a recent Columbia graduate named Terrence McNally, who would later become the well-known playwright. He was at this time a student in the playwriting department of the Actors Studio. Here he had come to the attention of the Kazans, who had recommended him to the Steinbecks.

To Elizabeth Otis

The Dorchester
London
September 19, 1961

Dear Elizabeth:

News of D.H.'s [Dag Hammarskjöld] death so devastating it's hard to think. Two weeks ago last night I had dinner with him.

My hand is shaking pretty badly, isn't it? Guess Dag's death hit hard. I'm all shaky inside. Have been reading the appraisals of his character in the paper and I guess I knew a different man than they did. He was neither cold, cool, dispassionate nor neutral. He was a man passionate about what he was doing. He wrote letters all over the world to people he wanted me to talk to. That last night I asked him what I could do for him and he said, "Sit on the ground and talk to people. That's the most important thing." And I said, "You keep well. That's the *most* important." He said, "I'm all right. Don't worry about me." And as I was leaving he repeated that—"I'm all right! Don't you worry!" Is that a cold man?

I just can't seem to write a coherent letter today. I'll do better later. I'm all shook up.

Love to all there,
John

To Adlai Stevenson

London
September 23, 1961

Dear Adlai:

I had a letter from a friend today which ended thus—"Poor Mr. Stevenson—he must feel like God's Last Good Man. Wish I could send him a word of cheer." And so do I. And so I try.

You must have awakened with a sentence in your mind as though it had been spoken. The night after the crash I had such an experience and the words were odd—"Baldus is dead! Loki has won again—but Baldus does not remain dead."

Once Emiliano Zapata, the Mexican revolutionary, said, on being warned that he would be assassinated—"Then that's the way it must be and perhaps better, for some men find their real and permanent strength there. I think," he continued, "of Benito Juarez, of Abraham Lincoln, of Jesus Christ. Death only kills little men." And he was illiterate.

Friday next we start our wandering. But if you have some small wish for service from me, I can be found through Elizabeth Otis.

Yours,
John

To Elizabeth Otis

The Blue Ball
Bruton, Somerset
October 1, 1961

Dear Elizabeth:

Sunday today and Elaine and the boys churchifying. Wonderful to come back to Somerset.

Terrence is locked in mortal combat with Thom who has brought out his great arsenal for resisting learning anything. I don't know who is going to win but he can't escape a good try this time. But it's a sad thing to watch.

The weather is that fine combination of sun and rain, probably the best time of the year. We had lunch at Discove yesterday and after went up to our cottage. It looked very pretty and we were very emotional about it. Kai Leslie [of Discove Manor] laid on a great luncheon of Scotch grouse and farmhouse cheddar. The whole thing is like coming home.

The car we have rented is a Ford station wagon but even then we have too much luggage. We shall be out of touch to a certain extent for a time. We are going to try to reserve at Chagford on the edge of Dartmoor on next Wednesday. Tomorrow we will all go to Glastonbury and Wells and the next day move down toward Cornwall.

Love,
John

To Mr. and Mrs. Frank Loesser

Dublin
October 17, 1961

Dear Frank and Jo:

In the dark the other night I wrote in my head a whole dialogue between St. George and the Dragon. Very close relatives those two. Neither could exist without the other. They are eternally tied together—actually two parts of one whole. I guess the Greek had the truest conception of that in the centaurs, the man only partly emerged from the beast. But you will notice that centaurs steal and screw only women, never fillies. So the urge is toward man and away from beast. So St. George must always kill the dragon and it must be repeated because if the dragon were finally killed, there would be no St. George—only a lonely man looking for something to do.

I still want to write a story about Greece. Maybe you Frank, might like to help. It's about something that happened a little while ago. Some strange fishermen at a harvest festival stole Miss Grape Leaf of 1956 with her help. But she was engaged to the local strong boy. Well, he got his friends and his creditors and his relatives together because not only were his feelings hurt but who could feel safe when strangers steal your dame? So they went to the island where those sponge divers lived and after a lot of pretty dirty fighting they tore the place apart and got the girl back and so right triumphed and everybody got destroyed. And it was fine.

Then there is another one I started a long time ago. Max Anderson and Kurt Weil and I worked on it together but we never got it finished. It's about a negro soldier demobbed in the north and he wants to go home only the Okefenokee Swamp is in his way. He meets a little old conjure woman and he meets a big son of a bitch with one eye and he meets a pretty nice yellow girl but he still wants to go home. And he does and nobody knows him but a coon hound. Kurt started to write the music of an ode to a hound dog but he never finished it. And Max went haywire and both of them died. But it was my idea in the first place.

So maybe you and I should do it. You always like to do wandering stories and you've got the call away in everything you do. But if you *are* away, the call would be for home. The call is always for where you aren't. Would you like to do that? You've got a great big hit now and if you're anything like me, and you are a little, you'll have to do penance for it. Whenever a book of mine gets too biggety, I feel I've failed some way. This doesn't mean I don't like hits. I love them but I don't trust them. They carry a poison gland. Anyone can survive a flop but a great big hit has to be paid for with humility and grandeur.

And as you can feel from all this, I do hear the low rumble of poetry. The greatest stories are the oldest ones because they didn't fall down. We go to see cathedrals, great, free-standing marvels, but there were lots of others that fell down and aren't there to see. And there's never been anything truer than Hector coming out to meet Achilles with all the women on the walls watching. And suddenly he got scared and he turned and ran away and Achilles killed him. But that only happened when he found he couldn't get away and turned to fight. It happened to me when I was a little kid. There was a big black parson's boy named Laguna and he was after me. I used to sneak home from school to get in our house but I made a wrong turn and he cornered me in our side yard where there was no exit. I was so scared of him that I went mad with fright. My sister Beth pulled me off him. I was on top of him hitting him on the head with a half brick. And if Beth hadn't saved me, I would have killed him out of pure fear. So I can understand Hector very well. Homer said his blood turned to water, and so did mine. And I guess everyone has lived all of the great stories and that's why they are great.

Love to you both,
John

To Elizabeth Otis

Dear Elizabeth:

We had a note from Tom Guinzburg [son of Harold Guinzburg, Steinbeck's publisher] this morning saying that Harold
was dying. We've just called Tom and he says it is very soon,
perhaps in twenty-four hours. This is a numbing thing. I
can't grow used to the thought. In March we went diving
with aqualungs. I guess it's the speed of the thing. There is
no milestone for comparison. It seems uncalled for. But I
realize that none of those sentences make any sense whatever.

The fact of the matter is that people of our generation are
coming of the age to die. Nothing strange or unusual about
that unless we find it strange. The boys had a serious and
private meeting and reported that if we wanted to fly home,
they would carry on. And they would and would do it well too.
Of course the main worry is for Alice [Mrs. Harold Guinz-
burg]. She has little experience in taking care of herself. Only
I suspect that she is much tougher than she looks or seems
to be.

[unsigned]

To Pascal Covici

Dublin
October 17, 1961

Dear Pat

We had the appalling news about Harold this morning and
it has stunned us. Of course we knew long ago it was inevitable but the speed and ferocity of the attack was not an-

ticipated and we haven't even come by a way to think about it yet.

We came across to Dublin where we have never been. It's a city of smells and darkness and now we'll never know how much of the darkness we have brought to it. We talked to Tom this morning and he told us it would be very soon. There doesn't seem to be any way to prepare for it. People in the Middle Ages surrounded themselves with the symbols of death and I wonder whether they succeeded. But this particular opponent seems to fight like an enemy. It would be good if one could fight back. Failing that one is left with a kind of rage.

Elaine bewails the fact that we are not there to help. I can't think what we would help with but probably she would find a way. I guess it's just putting one foot in front of the other and moving on. That's the way it's done until it is over. But here we seem cut off and very far away.

love
John

To Mrs. Harold Guinzburg

The George
Chollerford,
Northumberland
October 23, 1961

Dear Alice—

The times of the most agonizing need for communication are those when there is nothing that can be said in words.

You know how much we are with you and have been, and that the wounds are mutual. I can't offer any of the usual sops. They don't mean anything. We love you is about the only thing that has any meaning, even if a small one.

But we do, as you must, honor Harold with a courage approximating his own, and an integrity and honesty he could approve. There isn't any easy way, dear Alice, dear

Alice. No easy way at all. You know how much we wish you could be with us or we with you. And we do love you with everything we have, and that is even more now than it has been before.

May you have some peace soon and may you accept it when it offers.

Love as always,
John

Later he wrote her:

"I know that one seems cut off and alone before one picks up a little thread and draws in a string and then a rope leading back to life again."

To Elizabeth Otis

[Chollerford,
Northumberland]
[October 23, 1961]

Dear Elizabeth:

Your letter this morning. Thank you for sending the flowers. We had been in communication but had not done that. We feel very bruised about it, even though we knew it must happen. I had a short letter from Pat this morning—rather a formal one except for the last line in which he said he felt that he was waiting for Godot. Yes, this must cut the ground from under him.

Thanks for sending the obits. We wouldn't have got them. I didn't know Harold was involved with so many things.

We are loving these few days of quiet. There's a great rain

and wind and the Tyne is swollen with brown peat water. Then there are splashes of blinding sunlight. There's a great Roman fort near here and a section of the wall we haven't seen so we'll probably walk there this afternoon.

Love to all,
John

To Mr. and Mrs. Robert Wallsten

Chollerford,
Northumberland
I think it is about
October 26, 1961

Dear Wallsteaux:

In this sad and mixed up time of Harold's death, we have lost track of things and time. The boys went on their own to Edinburgh while we stayed here for a few days at Chollerford-on-Tyne to lick our wounds.

Something has just occurred to me—kind of in the nature of a law. The effectiveness of a man's life can be measured by the depth of the wounds his death leaves on others.

We depended on Harold for so many things and mostly to be there. It's something like having a navigational star removed. No set of course until you find another point of reference.

So if we have been neglective, that's why. We went to Dublin. A sad place we thought. Joyce described it. The boys loved it. We are learning every day—our joys and theirs are on a seesaw. This is another law. If we love a place they are forced by a high morality to hate it.

They will come back from Edinburgh today having found it the most, the greatest, the noblest—why? Because they found it themselves. Now that's not a very complicated lesson. But we've taken a long time to learn it.

This place—"The George," Chollerford, is one of the very most places in England. We look out on Tyne and a wide horizon and the rains and suns chase each other.

love to both
John

To Elizabeth Otis

Nice (my ass)
I think it is
November 23, 1961

Dear Elizabeth:

We are staying at the Brice-Benford, a dismal hotel which required great genius to have everything in bad taste. To the worst of the 19th century they have added the worst of the 20th, stainless steel and plastic. We stopped so the boys could see Vence and St. Paul de Vence. I didn't go. I stayed in today and it rained. They aren't back yet. When they came to do the room I wouldn't move so they dusted my feet. I mean it. They dusted my bare feet. What service. I ache now to get out of France—The new look in girls is disgusting to me. The boys find them incredibly smart with their gray lips and charnel house complexions. I have not been drawn to the Lichen Look.

What a dreadful place this is. If Matisse hadn't stopped his wheel chair near here we might be in Portofino this moment. Now onward to Milano. The Mondadori rascals are going to remember this year. Nothing like it has happened since Attila swept in.

In some ways I am perfectly resigned. I attribute this to hitting my head on an iron bar in Avignon. It was a window and I struck right on the right temple. It has changed my whole life. If I ever even begin to get better I shall hit myself on the head again.

Everyone says, "Why didn't you *say* you didn't want to come to Nice?" And I say, "I did." "But you didn't say it loudly enough or soon enough or often enough." So we are in Nice. At least I am. They are at Vence and it is raining and beginning to get dark. Did any of you ever have your feet dusted? I just sat still and they dusted my toes with a feather duster.

I suppose you know it here. All the hotels have English names. The Promenade des Anglais is a bitter windswept place with old men taking their exercise. In a shop around the corner they sell vests made of alley cat skin—very pretty. That's true. I haven't priced them but they look very warm; calico cats and tiger stripes and angoras—just ordinary cats. I wonder why no one has ever done it before. Certainly there are more cats around here than anyone needs.

Tomorrow the movement starts. It takes two taxis to take us and our luggage to the station. If there are more than five pieces of luggage you must get two porters and they get pretty mad if you carry your own. I think we are down to 12 pieces with John's trumpet and Terrence's typewriter. We started with 19. But we have worked out a system when we arrive at a station. Two of us leap out and the others throw the baggage out the window. French trains have no luggage room except over your head, and for us to get eleven pieces over our heads plus coats, hats, etc. is something. One good hard lurch and everyone would be killed.

Now it's even darker and rainier. Maybe they're lost. No. That would be too simple.

Well, anyway, happy Thanksgiving. And now I think I'll go and bang my head again. I can't explain how wonderful it is.

Love to all,
John

He had warned his Italian publishers, "the Mondadori rascals," of the family's imminent descent on Milan:

"With our two sons, fifteen and seventeen, we are travelling very slowly around the world, taking ten months to do it. Their interests are wide and healthy. They like girls and music

725

and Leonardo and girls and automobiles and girls and all machines and girls. I find this encouraging. For myself, I find I like girls also even in my antiquity."

Toward the end of November in Milan Steinbeck suffered what was later diagnosed as a small stroke or heart failure. Doctors and nurses were in daily attendance in what Elaine Steinbeck recalls as a gloomy hotel. Terrence MacNally and the boys continued their travels in the north of Italy while the senior Steinbecks stayed on quietly in Milan. In a short letter to Elizabeth Otis he described himself as "truly weary," and ended—

"This is no letter. It never intended to be. It's just mist on a mirror."

To Elizabeth Otis

Pensione
Tornabuoni-Beacci
Florence
December 7, 1961

Dear Elizabeth:

I'm afraid I scared Elaine and maybe she scared you. I can't explain it. My energy just seemed to run out, like pulling the plug of a bath tub. I'm perfectly all right now. And never did show anything in tests. It's just like an overpowering weariness. These ten days in Florence should pick me up.

With Harold Guinzburg's death, the presidency of The Viking Press passed to his son, Thomas Guinzburg. Elizabeth Otis wrote of a conference about *Travels with Charley*; Viking had been advised against the use of the obscenities that Steinbeck had reported in the episode about the black child going to school in New Orleans.

I'm glad you got along with Tom G. I've always liked him. And as for the use or non use of the words in New Orleans, I don't really care. I think I protected the thing pretty well but I also don't think you can get a sense of the complete ugliness of the scene without the exact words. But then we have protected ourselves from this kind of experience for so long. No, I really don't care much—and that's a bad sign. You were very right not to send on the galleys of the last section. It's a thousand years behind me now.

This afternoon Elaine and I are going over to look at David. Just that one. I can only see one thing at a time but that's not new. It has always been that way. We had a card from Terrence saying Thom had decided to live his life in Venice. He fell madly in love with the city.

I seem to have stopped there in a kind of tiredness and now it is the 9th of December. My mind is lazy and doesn't seem to want to work for me much. Then a few minutes ago your letters came and I have to stir myself. The boys came back yesterday and I think some big change has happened. They are suddenly full of enthusiasm. It makes up for my sluggishness. They've been out all morning sniffing the city like morning dogs. The sun is bright. Elaine has rushed out to pictures. I'm perfectly all right and not weak or anything, only very lazy.

I'm going to get this off right away. Sorry we alarmed you. Everything is all right now. I'll be fine as soon as energy comes back and it always does.

Love to all there,
John

To Elizabeth Otis

Hotel de la Ville
Rome
December 20, 1961

Dear Elizabeth:

Of course we will try to phone you on party night but I know how that comes out. "I am fine. How are you?" "Fine, but how are you?"

I will try to put down some of our adventures. Our trip to Rome was pleasant. Then we went to the hotel—the Legazione, presided over by an Ethiopian girl, a serpent of the Nile, an asp, even a half-asp. The halls were beautiful with plants and marble, oh! prince's daughter, the rooms senza heat, were such as to have given monks pause about religion. But we had a bathroom of bathrooms. Vulgar as it may sound, its technique made it beautiful. To take one's seat, one slipped sideways under the basin and rested one's elbow in the basin. This hotel had one great quality. Everybody hated everybody. The asp was the worst. Nearest I have come in years to striking a woman smartly with my bastone (walking stick). So we moved to this hotel which we know from old times and where we are loved. Elaine and I have a sitting room where we can assemble. We will put up a tree here and decorate it. The boys and Fair Terr are writing Christmas revels, I believe all in verse, and allegorical too. There will be music, poems and recitations. They have worked long and hard on it. Meanwhile, we hope you will have a very happy Christmas. We have eliminated presents mostly this year except sillies.

Now to the boring subject of my health. The professore finds that I have a fine body. He uses the most hopeful and encouraging words for saying that the organism is wearing out. I must rest—take it easy, not exert myself. If he could take command he would send me home but anyway etc. The liver—she is not diseased but she do not function with complete felicity. The circulation circulates but tends to be excitable. I must not excite myself. I must control my diet, not

728

smoke nor drink nor do other things of an exciting nature. Thus and so, I will have many happy and contented years of life. And so I go back to think about those many happy years. And I remember the last fifteen or twenty years of John D. Rockefeller. He subsisted on human milk and predigested oatmeal. And I'm sure that he was very happy.

Nuts. I cannot conceive it on a quantitative basis. It must be qualitative. I'm not about to change. To go home just now when the project seems to be working, would be nonsense and very unhealthy. We will make fewer one night stands, will choose a center, and let the boys radiate. They are learning so much you can't believe it. After the eastern Mediterranean we will reappraise. But I will sit at Delphi and regard the sea below. And I will see whether there is any prophecy left in the Oracle there. No one has asked for a long time. And I utterly refuse to be a sick and careful old man nursing his little restricted time. It isn't worth it. I believe too deeply in Ecclesiastes: "There is a time to be born and a time to die," etc. And that's enough of that.

The weather here is clear and sparkling. The wind is from the north blowing over the snow. But the sun makes the city a wonderful pale gold. The boys are out tumbling over the centuries like kittens. They are being very helpful. I'm afraid they will have to grow up now. The baby time is over. And it's overdue but I know now that they can do it. We are going to have a very gay and happy Christmas, and I do hope you all will.

> Love to you and to you all,
> John

Robert and Cynthia Wallsten, worried by Elaine Steinbeck's reports of her husband's health, wrote suggesting that it might be wise to abandon the full round-the-world trip that had been planned and to return to the United States.

To Mr. and Mrs. Robert Wallsten

Roma
December 20, 1961

Dear Wallsts:

And a very merry Christmas to you. I haven't written for quite a long time but I have engulfed your letters. In recent times, too much space has been taken up with "my health." Let's forget it. I intend to ignore it.

It has been a curious and unreal time. The illness was not really an illness and yet it was. Hard to understand. We and particularly I am grateful for your concern. It may be that I will find it impossible to continue at some later date. However, the gains are so great and the rewards even greater that I cannot discontinue right now. The boys are growing by leaps. And I think their understanding is also. To stop now for any reason would be to cut the process in two.

This is a very private letter. I must tell you that next February I shall have had sixty years with more joy and more sorrow than is given to most people. I am a fortunate one. I have never been bored and I have always been curious. Therefore I cannot find any reason to complain. No one has ever had more love given nor taken than I. What other product can make this claim? You are not to take this as a giving up nor as a dalliance with the past. It is simply an evaluation. I have whomped a small talent into a large volume of work. And now I see the boys making such strides I am filled with wonder. With the very large help of Elaine and Terrence they are developing that hungry curiosity without which the human is worthless. They are gobbling up knowledge they can never lose and they are beginning to love it for itself. Beginning, I say—but that beginning is the best Christmas present a father could have. And I think you will understand how unthinkable it would be to run home now and fall back to where we started.

We have a little Christmas tree. Elaine and the boys are out getting ornaments. Tonight we will decorate.

I have no present for Elaine. My mind seems to have gone

dead. She says she needs and wants nothing. I've whipped my brains for a fancy thought and so far have come up with nothing. Wish you were here to consult.

This is all by way of wishing you a fine Christmas and the best of years. And you will have it. But I wish we could be together.

Love to you both. You help so much.

John

But after the New Year travel plans were changed.

To Mr. and Mrs. Robert Wallsten

Roma
January 9, 1962

Dear Robert and Cynthia:

Your very dear letters moved me very deeply as they should have done, for it is a rare and to be savored thing to have such friends. I've had to face many things these last few weeks of ceiling staring and one is my sin of pride. I have never before permitted myself the simple admission that there were things I could not do so only my will held out. But here I have an opponent against whom will has no terror. I think I could continue the course I set. Whether I could complete it and at what cost to others is another matter. The giving it up was the hardest thing. Once that was accomplished, other things fell into place. It is very good to have friends but even better, knowing this, not to have to test them. Thank you with all my heart.

I'm sure Elaine has told you of our adjusted plan and how we intend to settle in the sun on Capri for a time. Meanwhile the boys will range about on many side trips and use us for a center. In one way it is perhaps better. They will know a small part of the world much better. Maybe the whole world is too much to gulp down. And they do not seem in the least perturbed at the change in plans. As you said they would, they took it in stride. Right now they range this city like pointers and it is amazing how much they are learning to read, and to like what they are reading.

Elaine, of course, has carried the ball while I languished in a kind of impatience. Well, maybe I can help from now on. Some energy is coming back. And I feel that if I can just look out at the sea for a time certain adjustments may take place.

The last section of Travels With Charley has been giving the publishers trouble. It deals with some rough things in the south. Of course, Holiday will clean it up and even then think they will get cancelled subscriptions. But Viking wants to keep it tough and still not be sued. And I have been so bloody weak that I just don't give a damn. It seems to me that everybody in America is scared of everything mostly before it happens. I finally sent word that what reputation I had was not based on timidity or on playing safe. And I hope that is over. What I wrote either happened or I am a liar and I am not a liar. And I know that truth is no defense against libel. But there is no way of being safe except by being completely unsafe. And in the succeeding months I don't think that being careful of my health is likely to improve it. Rather it will give me another sickness called self-preservation. And that's our national sickness, and I hate it. The whole world is torn up, if the papers tell the truth and the papers themselves may be the paper tiger we hear so much about. Everywhere are paper tigers.

I wish we could see you. I've lost all rhythm of words and flow of images. Maybe it's the boys' struggles not to understand but to know that is throwing me. Even Terrence I keep forgetting is 23 and at that age understanding is not enough. One must be right as opposed to wrong and white against black. I remember it all so well.

Now as to you. Is there any chance that you might come out to Capri and to Greece? Robert I know has a double job now and how much better that is than not having enough to do. I can imagine no hell like that of an actor waiting by a telephone. I'm glad of anyone who has more than he can do. I am not working on anything and this may well be a large part of my illness—the "doctor, heal thyself" business.

When work is not in me, I think it will never come again. It is always so. And I've been in a black funk about it. My pencil has wavered and my hand has been shaky. I know it doesn't matter a damn whether I ever write another word but it matters to me. For I would be a gelatinous mess without that hope that one time something really and truly good would come of it. And the odds against that, however great, have no effect on the hope for it or the despair of it.

I haven't said any of the things I intended, I guess. Maybe I implied them. Maybe best said—I value you and I am glad of you.

Let that carry all the charge it can because it is true and you cannot overload the truth. Love to you both,

John

I'm ashamed of my weakness in that last few weeks but there it is. I *was* weak and very weary and I couldn't seem to bring up any reserves. But I do feel a small return of vitality.

To Elizabeth Otis

Villa Panorama
Capri
February 1, 1962

Dear Elizabeth:

The north wind seems to have blown itself out and this morning is serene and beautiful—silver olive trees on the hill behind us and the glowing oranges below.

Yesterday I got a letter from Pat crying his eyes out about how much money I am going to lose in lawsuits and indicating that I will have to carry it alone, which is probably true.

What has happened here is what has happened all over America. Caution is King. What started out as a simple piece of truth now wears all the clothing of sensationalism and has

733

lost every vestige of its purity. It doesn't feel clean to me any more. The only value of the passage lay in its shock value. Now it has become that book with the dirty words and by a magical turnabout the dirty words are no longer the cheer leaders' but mine. When I get the galleys I shall see what I want to do. I know that by simple suggestion I can make them much uglier without saying them. Do you remember when the B.O.M. [Book-of-the-Month Club] suggested the removal of certain words from The Wayward Bus and when I agreed, it was discovered that the words weren't there? Thousands bought Ulysses for the privilege of seeing one single word in print and didn't read the rest.

The quiet here is very soothing and healing. It has been so cold that we have simply gone to bed after dark but that has changed now. When the wind stopped, the air grew much warmer.

We are going to walk down to the Piccola Marina this afternoon and get the bus back.

That's all now—love to all there,

John

To Pascal Covici

Capri
February 10, 1962

Dear Pat:

By now the galleys will have been returned and the old process continued.

The weather here is uncertain which makes me like it more. A few chilled and forlorn tourists come over on the daily boat and wander about disconsolately until the boat takes them back. Meanwhile the shops and workrooms here are going full swing making the things they will sell to the tourists who engulf the Island in the summer.

We live a life of incredible quiet. Although somewhat troubled by vestiges of a Presbyterian conscience, I have succeeded in doing nothing whatsoever, and it seems to be working because I feel much better. We rise late, take a walk, read the papers. Sometimes we have dinner in and at others eat at little restaurants deep in the thick and Moorish walls of the old buildings. At our favorite place, we have a table in front of the opening of the pizza oven which serves instead of a fireplace.

This is no tropic place in the winter. The climate is about northern California. The storms come and the wind blows and then suddenly comes a golden day—very like Monterey. The people here are not like other Italians. They seem to be a separate breed. They are very kind and friendly, physically short and wide and with enormous muscular development from climbing the hills and carrying and pulling loads. There are few motors here because there are only three roads, and no cars are allowed in the town. The result is no noise and absolutely pure air which few people living have ever smelled. I wonder if it could not be shown that most urban populations are systematically poisoned with carbon monoxide. That could easily account for the lung troubles as well as others.

Elaine is loving the life here. As usual she knows everyone and everyone loves her. Also her Italian is growing by leaps and bounds. Our plans are still to remain here until the end of April by which time my health should be well back. There is something very soothing and benign here.

My 6oth birthday is this month. I don't know how it happened but there it is. And I must say I never expected to make it. Carola Guinzburg [Carola Guinzburg Lauro, Thomas Guinzburg's sister] and her husband are coming over for it and we will cook a big fish.

Ken Galbraith asked us to go to India but we are refusing. Maybe some other time but not now for I know now I cannot do everything. It is enough to be able to do anything.

love
John

Robert Wallsten wrote Steinbeck that he was experiencing a kind of stage fright about actually starting to write a biographical work, which he had been researching for a long time, on the actress Dame Judith Anderson.

To Robert Wallsten

Villa Panorama
Capri
February 13–14, 1962

Dear Robert:

Your bedridden letter came a couple of days ago and the parts about your book, I think, need an answer. By the way, Elaine has a better title than mine. Hers is—There is Nothing Like a Broad, by Dame Judith Anderson.

Now let me give you the benefit of my experience in facing 400 pages of blank stock—the appalling stuff that must be filled. I know that no one really wants the benefit of anyone's experience which is probably why it is so freely offered. But the following are some of the things I have had to do to keep from going nuts.

1. Abandon the idea that you are ever going to finish. Lose track of the 400 pages and write just one page for each day, it helps. Then when it gets finished, you are always surprised.

2. Write freely and as rapidly as possible and throw the whole thing on paper. Never correct or rewrite until the whole thing is down. Rewrite in process is usually found to be an excuse for not going on. It also interferes with flow and rhythm which can only come from a kind of unconscious association with the material.

3. Forget your generalized audience. In the first place, the nameless, faceless audience will scare you to death and in the second place, unlike the theatre, it doesn't exist. In writing, your audience is one single reader. I have found that sometimes it helps to pick out one person—a real person you know, or an imagined person and write to that one.

4. If a scene or a section gets the better of you and you still think you want it—bypass it and go on. When you have finished the whole you can come back to it and then you may find that the reason it gave trouble is because it didn't belong there.

5. Beware of a scene that becomes too dear to you, dearer than the rest. It will usually be found that it is out of drawing.

6. If you are using dialogue—say it aloud as you write it. Only then will it have the sound of speech.

Well, actually that's about all.

I know that no two people have the same methods. However, these mostly work for me.

There's a great big wind storm blowing. No boats in today. The seas are white. Elaine came in blue with cold. Part of the island has no electricity but we have been lucky so far. When Jove puts on a storm, he does it well.

Oh! it's a lovely storm. And we're cooking beans and watching it through our big windows. We're sheltered by the cliff but we can see the trees whipping and the sea churning white down far below us. Life is very good at this moment.

love to all there
John

He had always maintained a kind of avuncular relationship with Wallsten as a writer.

In 1958 he had given him for his birthday *March's Thesaurus-Dictionary*, on the flyleaf of which he had written:

"By reassembling the enclosed words, you can make the prettiest things—and will."

To Chase Horton

[Capri]
February 13 or
thereabouts [1962]

Dear Chase—

Well this is more like it. Now I feel at home. I'll write this one letter to you and perhaps one to Elizabeth and then put these two precious [yellow] pads away. And any boy who lays a finger on them is going to get clobbered. They have been known to use a whole pad on false starts of a letter to some snotty little girl. But if they mess with these I'll let them have it. And as for the pencils—They never know how I know they are using my pencils. I guess they think everyone is a pencil biter and an eraser gnawer. I am not. A bitten pencil drives me mad and a chewed eraser makes me throw the pencil away. All this would indicate a neatness I don't have.

February 15

That's how it goes. Today is a great blowy storm. The olive trees are wrestling the wind like girls with their underskirts showing. And the tall pencil cypresses just chuckle and bow. No window in Capri is tight so that the wind moans like cats. The bell is tolling. Someone being buried. Here, instead of death notices, the family sticks up little posters on all the walls and boardings—"Our father—Paliato Pucci, after a long and sweet life, went to his sleep—date—mourned by his family. Obs. date—time." Bills about 12″ by 10″. When we go down for the papers we will see for whom the bell tolls.

Our postman has a lean and hungry look. We know that he was a painter but he has also sent word that he *is* a painter. It is clearly yet wordlessly understood that we would do better to buy a painting if we want our letters delivered quickly and happily. He does water colors of Caprician architecture or will take a commission. They aren't very good—in fact they are much worse than that—they aren't very bad and that's the worst kind of painting there is. The postman is a

738

living proof that the artist need not be helpless.

Oh! It's a grim and wonderful day. Nearly everything clouds can do, clouds are doing. In a while there will come a burst of rain and then it will be over. The weather is very formal.

A card from Terrence in Siena says they will be here Monday or Tuesday. They will have been out a month. They will be well informed, well travelled and filthy. They are supposed to wash their clothes as they travel. Boys of that age smell terrible. We'll probably have to isolate them until they are clean. But they have had adventures, some of which we will hear. If all goes well, we'll let them rest here for a week before we send them out again.

The little girls downstairs came boiling out last night, with much excitement because they had heard my name on television. It's the new status. People used to say—"It's true. I read it in the papers." Now it has become "I heard it on television." They were so excited that they could hardly talk.

Well it's good to have the yellow pads. I'm going to guard them now, in case I have something to write.

Love to all there
John

To Elia Kazan

Capri
February 19, 1962

Dear Gadg:

Your letter received and will begin an answer but never know whether or when it will be finished.

I should think that Molly [Mrs. Kazan] wants to write something for the same reason that you want to make the pictures about your uncle. It may be the tearing desire to prove that we have been here at all. Such is our uncertainty that we have been. Here on Capri on the ruins of old, old walls and buildings you can find names or signs or initials, some of

739

them thousands of years old. Even our kids carve their initials in things. Maybe that's their way to the same end—just to prove they were here at all. When the cave paintings are found, archeologists always build up some obscure religious emphasis. Maybe those people also were simply writing down their own experiences, to fix them out of time. I even have a name for the impulse. I call it the Fourth Dementia.

When this last illness struck me, it was like a moment of truth. All kinds of things got washed away and my eyes became much clearer because the fogs of purpose and ambition blew away. My own past work fell into place in relation to other people's work and none of it with few exceptions was as good as those cave paintings. So I will go on working because I like to, but it won't be like any work I have done before. It won't be like the way-out theater either. Those people are blinded with a petty hopelessness that has built a very feeble despair—a kind of nastiness. I think I'll write a play or something to be said, because I don't know what a play is—dolls on strings mouthing incomplete sentences. Words should be wind or water or thunder. We only learned to speak from what we heard and we've got too far from our sources. The prostate is too small a gland to be given center *all* the time.

Meanwhile, see if you think you need anything of me in your film. Maybe I'll be glad to help. But my impulse to carve my initials on time is definitely weakened and sometimes non-existent.

That's all for now. See you soon.

Yours,
John

In April, with his health restored, the Steinbecks continued their travels in Italy and Greece and among the Greek Islands.

To Elizabeth Otis

Leto Hotel
Mykonos, Greece
May 28, 1962

Dear Elizabeth:

We are winding up here now. It is a beautiful place. As usual the boys are putting all their time in on their show-off tans for their girls.

Now this trip is over technically. Thom will fall in love twice more and on ship's food gain another ten lbs. John will preen and worry about his hair. Terrence will gadfly them with school work. But now an era is over. It must have been good. But we will not be together again in this sense. Actually we haven't been together much anyway but we have been able to call directions. Now they have to do something for themselves or not as the case may be. I have put this creative year into them and probably have bankrupted us to give them this chance. Now I have to try to pick up my own pieces. This is of course of no interest whatever to the boys nor should it be. But the era is changing for me as well as for them and I no more know my direction than do they.

I am very anxious to get back. It isn't homesickness. I just want to root down for a time, for a goodly time. The coming year is going to be one in which many decisions will have to be taken, some of them large. I want to be prepared for them.

Thom has developed a passion to go to Athens College— of course he hasn't a bat's chance of getting in. And yet there's something in this boy, which if released would do wonders. John has come out of it I think. We feel that he will sail ahead now. But old Thom is still his own unique enemy. It's the other thing, the strong creative thing that can't get loose. I don't think John has it at all. He has something much easier and better in terms of success—a facility. Well, we'll see.

But I'm glad we're coming home. It's time now. Outland

741

places are losing their sharp outlines and becoming of a sameness.

Love to all there,
John

The Steinbecks returned to the United States. One morning during the tense period of the Cuban missile crisis they turned on their television set at Sag Harbor for the news and heard the words: "John Steinbeck has been awarded the Nobel Prize for Literature."

To Anders Oesterling
SVENSKA AKADEMIEN STOCKHOLM

CABLE

NEW YORK
OCTOBER 25, 1962

AM GRATEFUL AND HONORED AT THE NOBEL AWARD STOP I SHALL BE PLEASED TO GO TO STOCKHOLM

JOHN STEINBECK

To Mr. and Mrs. Bo Beskow

[Sag Harbor]
[October 30, 1962]

Dear Bo and Greta:

Thank you for your wire. It found us in complete confusion. At first I thought I could keep up but now it is like one of those old-fashioned comedies when the character gets deeper and deeper into wet plaster. You will know that I will do what must be done and then retire to the old life. You know, I have always handled things myself and without a secretary but now we must call in help. The mail is coming in sacks. There is utterly no way to take care of it.

Anyway, we will go to Stockholm. Perhaps there will be no escaping to one of our old-fashioned singing and wine-drinking parties but I wish we could. We will not stay very long. Four or five days at the most. Where would you suggest that we stay. The Grand as before? I'm going to ask Bonniers [his Swedish publishers] to get someone to handle telephones, people etc. If this sounds overweening, it is because I have seen what happens here. When we went in to New York we were met by 75 reporters and cameramen and that was the worst day of the Cuban Crisis. This prize is a monster in some ways. I have always been afraid of it. Now I must handle it. I shall rely on you for advice.

Sunday night we saw you on "I remember Dag Hammarskjöld." I thought it well done and that you were very good.

Anyway, we will be in touch. Do you mind if I ask that you be included in a luncheon at our Embassy?

Isn't all this silly? We'll laugh about it soon but right now it seems insufferable.

Love to you both
John

To the deluge of congratulatory messages—four to five hundred a day at one time, he reported—he felt it obligatory to write individual thanks. Herewith, a selection.

To Carlton A. Sheffield

Sag Harbor
November 1, 1962

Dear Dook:

When this literary bull-running is over, I can complete some kind of communication, castrated of self-consciousness.

One thing does occur to me. This prize is more negotiable than the America's Cup although both are the product of wind. Meanwhile pray for me some. I've always been afraid of such things. They can be corrosive. This is many times harder to resist than poverty.

love
John

To Natalya Lovejoy

Sag Harbor
[November 1962]

Dear Tal:

Yes, Ed would have grinned and done his mouse dance but also he would have put it in its proper place. And so do I. It is important but other things are more so. Such as that Thom is finally on his way and doing wonders and so is John. I'm more pleased about that. Please send me Carol's address and her present name. She sent me the nicest wire and I'd like to answer it. All love from here. We've survived poverty and pain and loss. Now lets see if we can survive this.

John

John O'Hara wrote Steinbeck from Princeton, New Jersey, on October 25:

"Congratulations. I can think of only one other author I'd rather see get it."

To John O'Hara

POSTCARD

Sag Harbor
[October 1962]

Dear John:

Well, I'll tell you this. It wouldn't have been nearly as good without your greeting. Not nearly.

Thanks, John. The thing is meaningless alone. But if my friends like it—suddenly it has some dignity and desirability.

Yours
John

745

To Mr. and Mrs. Howard Hunter

Sag Harbor
October 31, 1962

Dear Howard and Edna:

I don't know what I've answered by now. There has been a mountain of mail. Friends write to me—"What are you going to say?" To Elaine, "What are you going to wear?" The boys reacted wonderfully. Young John made the best crack. He said—"In the words of Mr. Nobel—Bang!"

Love,
John

To Ed Sheehan
JOURNALIST AND AUTHOR OF *HONOLULU*

New York
January 8, 1963

Dear Ed Sheehan:

Thanks for your kind note.

You say you felt you had got the prize. That's exactly the way I felt when Ernest Hemingway got it. It was completely unreal when I got it—a kind of fantasy.

As for the outraged, forget it. I wonder whether they realize how completely they describe not me but themselves. I have known for years that criticism describes the critic much more than the thing criticized. That's as it should be. But I don't think they know it. I met _____ recently—a stooped, coyote-eyed man with small hands, fingers like little sausages and soft as those of an old, old lady. He caresses his fingers in his lap as though they were precious and in danger. To shake hands with him is like touching the teats of an old cow. I have only seen and felt hands like that on one other

746

man—Gen. D. MacArthur. And he mostly wore gloves even in the tropics.

> Yours
> John Steinbeck

To Bo Beskow

Dear Bo:

I wrote you yesterday, and because my address book was in New York, I addressed it simply to Stockholm. I am sure you will get it though. Short of the King you are probably the best known man in Stockholm.

I am sending our schedule now. Elaine and I are arriving Stockholm airport SAS (Remember those pretty girls?) at 11:00 A.M. Dec. 8. There are four things I want or must do and I shall number them. And one thing I will not do and I shall number it.

1. I shall and want to do everything traditional and dignified as practiced on the occasion of this award.

> Compare Beskow's description of previous visits to Stockholm:

> "John, in 1937, was not yet known over here and we had trouble getting into 'nice' places because of his far from elegant attire. When he came back after the war, we had to avoid nice places because of John's fame and the press. He played Greta Garbo with the photographers and tried to smash cameras."

2. I want to see as many old friends as possible. I do not regard you as an old friend but as family.

3. If it is possible, and let's make it possible, I want to visit Dag's grave. This means very much to me. If I could find some lavender, I would like to leave it there. Remember how

747

you taught me to make the little lavender bomb. And I made one for him? Maybe a little potted plant of lavender. I always associate lavender with him. If this is sentimental, make the most of it.

4. The requests for me to speak are pouring in. I am no speaker and never intend to be. I will *not* speak to any group or groups (barring the acceptance speech, of course).

And I guess that is all. I'm told that the Academy will arrange our hotel, probably the Grand.

Please write to me. We will have to make our private arrangements in advance because I am afraid the Stockholm business will be very public. How I wish you could paint a fourth and perhaps last portrait. But that takes time.

I am trying to think of everything in advance knowing my tendency to go haywire in crowds. It will be your job to help me lay off the schnapps. Remember the time I made passes at a Lesbian at a dinner party?

I'm putting a lot on you, but I would do the same for you.

You were my first sponsor in Sweden. Isn't it good that you still are.

Love to you both. And don't let me ask you to do anything you don't want to do.

John.

The Dag thing is important not for him but for me.

To Professor and Mrs. Eugène Vinaver

ПiYAGUS

Sag Harbor
November 6, 1962

Dear Betty and Eugène:

We have just dug ourselves out from under an avalanche of communications but I put your cable at the very last because I liked it so much. So often in the last week I have wished to be with Eugène to discuss and to turn over leaves of thinking. And I am sure I could have found not refuge but enlightenment.

This prize is a good prize—good in intent and valuable if properly used. But it can be a dangerous and engulfing thing. To many within my memory it has been an epitaph and to others a muffling cloaklike vestment that smothers and warps. This would be good if I were ready to die or if I were material for a priesthood or if I could believe what I am expected to believe. However, none of these things is so. I have work to do. I think I am near to ready for not the Morte but for the Acts. And that is a task into which one must be born fresh and new and very humble. It is a job so precious to me that I cannot permit any academy nor any dynamite-maker to look over my shoulder. It would be far better to be in prison as Malory was because there he was free from expectation. Perhaps I am taking this too hard but I have seen it happen to people. My sign at the top is still my sign and in a very short time I shall hope to settle back into the anonymity which is required.

Don't worry about my gloom. But the danger is a very real danger. Only perhaps an awareness may pull its fangs. Again thanks for your wire. I want the [Glastonbury] thorn to bloom but really to bloom. To that end please help me to plunge my walking staff into a hospitable earth.

Love to you both,
John

To Princess Grace of Monaco

Sag Harbor
November 6, 1962

Her Serene Highness
Princess Grace of Monaco
Palace of Monaco
Principality of Monaco

Dear Madame:
Dear Grace honey:

It was very kind of you to wire congratulations on the Nobel award. We liked that. And I remembered what you said one night at dinner soon after you had an Oscar. Judy Garland, I believe, was your runner up. You said, "I felt so sorry she didn't win but I felt very glad that I did." That was a statement of truth. And I feel the same. Maybe I don't deserve it, but I'm glad I got it.

Thanks again for your telegram.

Yours,
John Steinbeck

His old friend Louis Paul felt this was the moment to return to Steinbeck a batch of his correspondence.

To Louis Paul

Sag Harbor
November 7, 1962

Dear Louis:

Your sending back the letters and cards was a true act of friendship and I appreciate it very deeply. But hell! Louis—when I wrote them they were as honest or as dishonest as I was at the time. I haven't reread them. Maybe I don't want to. But they are what they are, and they were written to you because I was and am fond of you.

I have always been afraid of prizes for fear they might have a warping effect—I mean one might try to live up to them, and then get to believing what he was living up or down to. I think the current word is Image. Now I've had this award about a week and I don't feel any different except that I am a little richer. And I don't mind that at all. No, they are yours if you want them.

You say they might be sold—bring someone a buck. It seems to me if someone could make a buck out of them—good luck to him. I couldn't.

Let's face it. In 60 years I've left a lot of tracks. To try to cover the trail would be nonsense even if it were possible. I've done some pretty silly things but I did them, and they're my product. The Soviet Union with complete control has tried to clean up some history and has utterly failed at it. What chance would I have, even if I cared? Some of the most convincing stories about myself never happened but I haven't a bat's chance in hell of changing them. Besides, some of the stories are better than what really happened. Besides, what the hell difference does it make!

I had a roommate in college who couldn't read Walt Whitman because he had heard somewhere that Walt didn't wash his socks. On such things are images made. I think the best thing is to forget the whole thing.

There's only one thing. If you would look through these and ink out references that might hurt feelings of some living person, it might be good. Anyway, Louis—do what you

751

want with them. They're yours and were written to you. They could probably be better written but I can't help that.

I do hope to see you and meanwhile thank you again for a very generous act.

Yours,
John

To Georg Svensson
OF ALBERT BONNIERS FORLAG,
STEINBECK'S SWEDISH PUBLISHERS

[New York]
November 10, 1962

Dear Georg:

Now is a weekend of small quiet and I shall try to get your letter of Nov. 9 answered in some detail.

May I say first that I am deeply happy to have this prize. I shall go to Stockholm where, dressed in unaccustomed garments, I shall make *one* short and, I hope, well-proportioned speech and only one. For myself, I hate all speeches but I hate short ones a little less. So mine will be short. It seems to me that the rostrum brings out certain intolerable tendencies in the human. Also I shall go through the ritual of acceptance and thanks when I know what it is. For this I will need help, but your letter assures me that I will have it. I can only hope that the Foreign Office attaché assigned to me may have a reasonable sense of humor and an abundance of tolerance. Both of us will need it. As for a "nice temporary secretary"—it occurs to me that such a person might be of great help in the field of literary courtesy.

Now one more thing. I believe that Mrs. Guinzburg, the widow of my beloved publisher Harold Guinzburg, will be coming with us. I would be pleased if she can be included in whatever affairs are seemly. She is a lovely woman and one of our dearest friends.

Now Georg—I think you will understand that this letter must be private. This prize, and it is far the greatest honor that can be given a writer, can, if permitted, destroy the climate in which the work for which the prize is given can operate and have its being. And since I still have work to do, I cannot permit this to happen. The requests for time, for money, for appearances are pouring in. One television man went so far as to say that since I have this award, I no longer have the right to refuse to go on his television show. I assure you that he was quickly disabused.

I must tell you that since my illness of last year, my energy is not endless. If some periods of rest can be allowed, I will have a better chance of completing the cycle.

Now finally, I must ask help in carrying out what is expected of me and particularly that I am not permitted to err through ignorance or forgetfulness and for this I must depend on you as well as on others. I should like Bo Beskow to be included in anything he may wish. After all, he is my oldest friend in Stockholm.

I think that is all. I have a feeling of unreality about all of this. Perhaps this is nature's way of applying shock as an anesthetic.

Yours,
John

To Carlton A. Sheffield

New York
November 8, 1962

Dear Dook:

I can think of a number of people who deserve this prize more than I and many thousands who want it more than I do. Of course I like it but it has a way of kicking people around and that I'm not going to stand. I've got some work—quite a lot yet—to do and even more sit-and-stare-into-space to do and they ain't nobody going to take it away.

You say in your card that I said I wanted to be the best writer in the world. I've learned a few things since. I would say now that I want to *try* to be the best writer in the world. That's a very different thing. In our basement room in En-

753

cino I didn't know the tendency of horizons to jump back as you move toward them. And I didn't know that the tired farther you go—the farther there is to go. But these are the realities. This prize business is only different from the Lettuce Queen of Salinas in degree. Basically it's the same thing. There's no sadness in this. It's a kind of a joke. The sad thing would be to believe it.

Meanwhile—thanks for your card. I can't write little any more because I can't see that well.

Yours
John

To Bo Beskow

New York
November 14, 1962

Dear Bo:

Your good and warm letter arrived in record time and pleased us very much.

I suppose you know of the attack on the award to me not only by Time Magazine with which I have had a long-time feud but also from the cutglass critics, that grey priesthood which defines literature and has little to do with reading. They have never liked me and now are really beside themselves with rage. It always surprises me that they care so much. If I get the same thing in Stockholm I may just remind them of the things said against Dag—and by people who would now be glad to forget they said them.

All in all I could relax and go along with the little play acting were it not for this damned speech I must make. I never make speeches as you know. I haven't an idea of what to say. I've read Lewis' wild and ill-considered rambling and I've read Faulkner's which on many readings turns out a mass of dark egotism. But what am I to say? Maybe I'll ask Adlai Stevenson to write it for me. He makes the best speeches in the world today. It will be short, I know that. I should like to make it as near to the truth as is permissible. Do you have any ideas? The idea of having to stand up there

754

and speak just scares me to death. If I could just get clear on that I wouldn't have a worry.

One thing is certain and Elaine and I have discussed it. We must be very careful about drinking. It is not so much that I'm afraid of getting drunk but I'm afraid of getting tired. Also, except when we are alone with you, we will be in a goldfish globe and if I am going to do this thing at all, I would like to do it well. Kings don't bother me but academicians do.

Also I am having to buy tails, a costume I have always found ridiculous. I would rent them but Elaine says they wouldn't fit well enough. Who do you suppose invented the damn things?

Now let me ask you this very clearly and concisely—are there any events, flummeries in the sacrificial parade, to which you haven't been invited and to which a request from me would answer? If there are such, please let me know. Probably you feel well out of it. While I, clad in the costume of a penguin, must stand in the dock—you, at your ease, can swill your red wine and laugh.

Oh! This damned speech.

Love to you both.

To Adlai Stevenson

New York
November 20, 1962

Dear Adlai:

In a fairly long and restive association, I think you will agree that I contrived to put you in my debt. Lest you forget, I will list only a few of my contributions:

1. I have written you long and confused letters in an undecipherable script at various times when your mind was occupied elsewhere;

2. My suggestions, criticisms and constant advice may well

755

have contributed to the outcome of your two campaigns for the Presidency;

3. I have parked my disreputable truck in your driveway at Libertyville to the scandal of the neighborhood.

These are only a few of the things I have done for you, and over the years I have never asked anything in return. This vacuum was bound to leak.

I have now to ask a favor of you.

As you may know, I am expected to make a speech in Stockholm on December 10th to the Swedish Academy and a gallery of critics.

Now I, who have always been at anybody's service as a critic of speeches, have never made one. The whole idea fills me with horror. Then it occurred to me that you are undoubtedly the best speaker in the world; that having made so many speeches, one more would mean nothing to you. I'm sure you wouldn't mind making this speech for me. And I'm sure the Academy would be more than pleased.

By this single simple favor, you would retire all of your indebtedness to me in addition to saving my life, since I am literally scared to death.

May we consider that settled and may I have a note of confirmation from you?

Thank you. I feel so much better.

Yours,
John

To Elizabeth Otis

New York
[November 1962]
Saturday

Dear Elizabeth:

I had your letter this morning. I'm working on the speech. It is done in that I think it has in it nearly all I want to say and in the proper sequence. Now I am going over it word by word to see whether each word has the value and meaning

I want it to have. Then, probably tomorrow, I will record it on tape so that I can hear whether it has the rhythms I want, those and the pronouncability. Some words of great meaning to the mind are utterly unspeakable aloud. Finally, I want to go over it very carefully to be sure there is no single extra word nor any repetition. Probably Monday it will be done, and then I would rather bring it to you than send it to you.

Now—the other thing—the Nobel loot. I hadn't thought of it as a commission. We started this thing together and we're going to finish it that way. If along the way you had limited yourself to being an agent, you would not have done the hundreds of things you have done. You have shared the bad times with me and they have been long and many, and if you could do that you are damned well going to share the good ones. You are as responsible for this prize as I am. So, let us not argue and be concerned. Not only do you share in the honor but in the money. Let us not discuss it any more. That's the way it's going to be.

Love to you,
John

To Carlton A. Sheffield

New York
November 28, 1962

Dear Dook:

I would like to talk to you about the nature of the award. In some way it has gathered to itself a mystique and I don't know how. What it is is a money prize awarded geographically and sometimes politically. The Swedish Academy of 17 members lay the finger on and presto—everything is changed. I think I've talked to you about this before.

I've always been afraid of it because of what it does to people. For one thing I don't remember anyone doing any work after getting it save maybe Shaw. This last book of Faulkner's was written long ago. Hemingway went into a kind of hysterical haze. Red Lewis just collapsed into alcoholism and angers. It has in effect amounted to an epitaph. Maybe I'm being over-optimistic but I wouldn't have accepted it if I hadn't thought I could beat the rap. I have more work to do and I intend to do it.

A couple of days fell in on me so that I come back to this letter with a sense of relief. I wrote the damned speech at least 20 times. I, being a foreigner in Sweden, tried to make it suave and diplomatic and it was a bunch of crap. Last night I got mad and wrote exactly what I wanted to say. I don't know whether or not it's good but at least it's me. I even put some of it in the vernacular. Hell, that's the way I write. Now they can take it or leave it. Only I hope I get the money first. They might have second thoughts after hearing my vocal efforts. I have one advantage. I mumble, so no one is likely to hear it. But it says what I want it to at last.

I can see interruptions coming. So I'd better put this away for a while. It's nice to come back to.

Next day—This letter goes on forever. Now to get back to the speech here enclosed. Elaine says I must set it. That's theatre for freeze it. But I'm not theatre and I know I will be picking at it. But it says what I want to say and in as few words as I can make it. It may sound highflown but I think the time and the place require that. I don't know whether or not it is good but it's as good as I can make it. Please don't let anyone see it before I make it on Dec. 10. It would please me to know whether or not it comes over to you but not before I do it. I have to have confidence in it or I couldn't say it.

Hearing from you and writing to you have given me a good sense of rest and continuity.

love
John

After the Nobel ceremonies and a short visit to London, the Steinbecks and Mrs. Guinzburg returned to New York.

To Mr. and Mrs. Bo Beskow

New York
December 22, 1962

Dear Bo and Greta:

We arrived home completely pooped and haven't really begun to look around as yet. Then will come weeks of thank you letters but right now the only one I want to get off is to you two. It was a great and fabulous time. We have yet to sort it out. There was a kind of glow hanging over the whole scene. A never to be repeated experience. The thing is so exquisitely managed and paced that it slips in and out of reality.

Of course we thank you first for doing so much, but then you were basically a part of it. Toward the end, my memory is not too strong. Things got wavery. I remember some things with great clarity, particularly that weeping day at Upsala [at the grave of Dag Hammarskjöld] with the dark and dripping trees and the damp stone with wilted roses on it. Have you ever been to Shakespeare's grave in the church near Stratford? I have many times and always there has been some flower put there. That's nice I think.

Now is coming the time for recovery. As soon as Christmas is over and the boys back in school, I am going to withdraw completely into work to prove to myself that this need not be an epitaph. It is a contract I have made with myself.

Meanwhile, a good Christmas to you and again our thanks for everything.

Yours always,
John

The Swedish words in the salutation of the next letter mean "beautiful wife." Referring to his own, Steinbeck had added *"Mein vakra fru,"* quite unex-

759

pectedly as well as untraditionally, to the list of dignitaries in Stockholm whom he saluted at the start of his Nobel acceptance speech.

To Mr. and Mrs. Howard Gossage

New York
December 31, 1962

Dear Howard, and Vakra Fru,

Stockholm was a curious medieval dream. It moved rather majestically along but there was so much that had to be done that a kind of exhaustion settled down and acted as a poultice. I guess it's not like anything else. One thing is interesting. I think I told you I was not afraid of kings but academies scared me. What I had forgotten was that far from being hostile, this academy was for me. After all, it chose me. There was great warmth—almost a kind of affection. I wouldn't have missed it but I wouldn't do it again even if that were possible.

As for the speech—It occurred to me to take my own advice which I put in Fauna's mouth for Suzy in Sweet Thursday—to do everything very slowly. I tried it and it works. Cut everything to half time and you don't panic or knock over things. When it came time to speak, I was so stunned with color and sound and people that I went into slow motion and it worked fine. Elaine easily stole the show. She enjoyed it all so much that everyone around her had a better time. When the master of protocol at the royal dinner planted his ivory staff in front of her and said—"Madame, you will advance to the King, curtsey, take his arm and lead in to dinner," it is my sworn story that she said, "Yippee, I sure will, honey." She swears she didn't say anything of the kind. But it is true that before the first course was over, she was trading recipes and gardening secrets with the King. I had the Queen for my dinner partner. She is Mountbatten's sister, with a quick and knife-like wit. I told her the poem I wrote when Elizabeth II recently fixed the name Mountbatten by choice instead of Battenburg. I transposed a little for my English publishers: "When Adam toiled and Eve span, who was *then* the Mountbattàn?" She laughed and said she would see that it got to ER II immediately. "But," she said, "She won't understand it. Completely illiterate, you know."

We got home to the kids and their girls. The boys are in most wonderful shape. Never have they been so thoughtful and such good company.

Anyway, I'll stick in a copy of the speech and let this go as it is.

Love to your sweet lady—

John

But he was trying desperately to put his new honor behind him and return to the anonymous life of a working writer. This letter, to his oldest friend, reflects the struggle.

To Carlton A. Sheffield

New York
January 14, 1963

Dear Dook:

I forget how much or when I have written you. I think that is because I have had so many conversations with you in my head. Does that ever happen to you? The last two months have been full of fog. If I had to pick out what was real and what imagined I should be hard put to know except that little was imagined—there wasn't time for fancies. And if I had needed a lesson in the Vanities, I would have had it ready available.

Oh! the prize is real and the people who awarded it are real. It's the side issues that are hysterically unsubstantial.

The mythos is very near the surface and it seems to be unchangeable. When one becomes entangled in a myth, there is no saving one's self. Just go along with it because you can't beat it. It's bigger and older and stronger than you are or one is. The only safe thing, it seems to me, is to be sure that you yourself are not caught up in it. In Hollywood they used to call it believing your own publicity.

Let me give you an example of the perfect myth. In Salinas a neighbor of ours was Joe _____. He was partners in a wine and spirits business and I've known him all my life. And he knew my family all of his life. When I was in Salinas a couple of years ago I saw Joe on the street and he was an old, old man. We got to talking and he said, "I remember seeing you as a little boy, coming up Central Avenue one cold frosty morning. I remember well, you were blue with cold and your coat was pinned over your chest with horse blanket pins." I said, "Joe, that can't be true. My mother was a button fiend. She equated off buttons with sin. She'd have walloped me if I ever used a pin." "Yes, sir," Joe said. "Blue with cold and I can still see those horse blanket pins."

I knew I was licked. Joe knew we weren't poor and that I wasn't a waif but the rags to riches myth was so strong that he couldn't resist it. God knows I've told lots of lies but I never told that one. It was a story that was true in his mind. Every once in a while I come on one like that only I know now that no amount of denying will make a bit of difference. When the myth is needed, the myth will be used.

I've been reading and studying and thinking on the Arthurian myth for a long time. I've never been a good scholar. Too impatient, perhaps, and not careful enough, but in this field I have been better. I've taken many years to learn the field and I have had the very best scholars as godfathers, the really great men in the field.

I believe you completely when you say you never wanted *things* or not enough to do the things required to get them. I've always thought of you as one of the truly contented people I've known for this and for other reasons. You have been calm while I have been jittery and flighty and changeable, and restless, mostly restless. Weren't you ever restless? I still am. It hasn't changed a bit. The wander comes over me and it's hard to hold still. The next peak is the best.

I really tried to go back to Pacific Grove to live after my breakup with my second wife. I stayed nearly a year or

762

maybe more than a year. But it wasn't any good. I didn't belong there. I guess it was there or maybe not very long afterwards that I discovered what I should have known long before, that I don't belong anywhere.

I lived 10 months in Somerset near Glastonbury and felt more at home there than I ever have anywhere. There was something there that I understood and that tolerated me. I loved that place and when my boys are out of what we call education I may well go back there to finish up. When, sitting here in New York, I think of Somerset, my stomach turns over with a curious kind of longing. It's beautiful country, of course, but there's something else that draws me.

Let me tell you one little tale. Some men from the British Museum were digging in the foundations of Glastonbury Abbey trying to establish the outline of the church which burned down in the 14th century. I can't stay out of a hole in the ground so I was in with them with palette knife and whiskbroom. Those men are really fine scholars. One morning we came on a fine stone coffin, of granite and unmarked. "Well, there he is," they said. "Thought maybe to find him." "Who is he," I asked. "The Duke of Somerset." "How do you know?" "We'll know when we open." "Let's open!" "No hurry!" they said. "Maybe tomorrow. We're for a foundation not a duke." "How will you know?" "Why, by the body. If his skull is on his chest, that's the one. He was hanged, drawn, and quartered, you see." Next day we opened and there was the skull on the chest and the limbs had been chopped apart and then reassembled.

In digging we turned up a great many bones and always we put them back where we found them and when we had established the foundation and written it carefully down, we covered the whole thing in again and reset the sod because a body still has the right to be respected. Those were not peasants. They were scholars. But the people who live there have a great knowledge too or call it a feeling because it is a relationship rather than a set of facts.

Now let me ask some questions. Do you still see Carl Wilhelmson? And has he an address? The same for people like Grove Day and Vernon Given and any of the others. They have disappeared from me completely. Every once in a while they all come back to me and I see them but they must be greatly changed as I am—in appearance anyway. It's a strange thing, the past.

763

I want to write a small rude book and right away to get the taste of prizes out of my mouth. I'm about ready to start it. Maybe I can next week. It is for my own enjoyment. I've probably bored you to death in this letter, but I wanted to have a wandering talk with you. It feels good.

Yours

John

1963 1965
1964

Steinbeck

"I'm not the young
writer of promise
any more."

Made Cultural Exchange trip behind the Iron Curtain.

To Harald Grieg
STEINBECK'S NORWEGIAN PUBLISHER

New York
January 16, 1963

Dear Harald:

It was a purple time, I think you will agree. Now I will have to go quickly to work to get the heady taste of it out of my mouth. I was awfully glad that you were there. It wouldn't have been the same if you had not been.

Now at home and we are shortly selling this house, and moving into a very high apartment in a new building that is going up near here. This four-storey house has just too many stairs for us. We will be up thirty-four floors in the new apartment and will have a look out at all of Manhattan. I hope you will come and see it. It is most spectacular.

There has been something I have wanted to ask you for some time and I have been shy about it. As you can believe, I have never been one for medals or decorations. They seem a kind of vanity that doesn't touch me. But there was one that meant very much to me—that was the Haakon VII cross. I liked that very much. [It had been awarded by the Norwegian government for *The Moon is Down*.]

A number of years ago when my oldest boy was much smaller, he became fond of the cross and one day asked if he could wear it to school. I saw nothing against it and told him he could. Well, he was six. He wore it to school all right and somewhere along the line he lost it. I couldn't be too rough with him. After all I have lost plenty of things and I still do. Of course I have the citation and everything else, but here is my question. Do you think I, meaning you, could find a duplication of it? I would be very pleased to have it. It was a reminder of the old hard true days when men were better and braver than they could be. I believe I remember that when I got it, Norway was so poor that I had to pay for the cross, I mean the cost of it. And I would be awfully glad to do that again.

Yours,
John

At the suggestion of President Kennedy, Leslie Brady, with the title in Russia of Cultural Attaché to the American Embassy in Moscow and later the Deputy Commissioner of the United States Information Agency, invited Steinbeck to visit the Soviet Union under the auspices of the Cultural Exchange Program.

To Leslie Brady

New York
May 13, 1963

Dear Lee:

That was a very good session we had last week, although we covered lightly a very un-light situation. The subject, of course, is the possibility of my going to Russia in the fall.

Incidentally, although this is a personal letter to you, you may show all or any part of it to Ed, if you wish [Edward R. Murrow, Director of the United States Information Agency].

In the light of the Birmingham episodes [of racial violence] it seemed to me that I couldn't, or would be reluctant to, try to explain that situation to people whose minds would be automatically closed to explanation. Then too, K's [Khrushchev] apparent switch back to the old party line might well make me "persona non grata." Maybe I am getting old, too. A kind of grey weariness creeps over me.

And yet, I want to go. I should go. And at least now the young and the experimenters are not as cowed as they once were. This is only one of many changes since 1947. Another would be the re-building and a new generation coming along who will not remember the war, nor the deep blight of Stalin. For my own sake, I should go.

My thinking continued this way. We have always been a shy and apologetic people. Sure we have Birmingham, but we are doing something about it. Now is the time to go—not to apologize nor to beat our breasts, but to bring some fierceness into it—the kind of fierceness the Negroes are using. I don't know that I could do it, but I could try.

Very well—if I could go—would there be any way for Elaine to go with me? She is a much better ambassador than I am and the two of us work together very well. I hope it might be arranged.

You remember that when we discussed this quite a time ago, we thought it might be good if Kazan went along. I have telephoned him, but can't get him. He is very busy on the new theatre project.

Then, I had another idea, I wish you would take in mind. Edward Albee, our newest and perhaps most promising young playwright came to see me last week. I have known him for some time. I told him of this discussion, and he showed great enthusiasm for going. He might be a better choice. He is another generation—under 35. I think he would have an enormous impact on the younger Russians. He would be very happy to go with us, and between us we might be more effective than either one alone. He is coming on while I am leaving the scene—at least, so it is thought. His problem is that he opens a new play in early autumn—an adaptation of The Ballad of the Sad Café, but he would be free to go when he gets it opened. As for me, I have no time limitation and could make my time match his. Does this seem like a good idea? Think it over and let us discuss it.

In considering this, think also of Poland, where I have never been and Finland, where I have. My work is well known in both places.

I hope you would remember that I will not *speak*, but will discuss anything with anyone or any number. That's always better for me, since it is an exchange, rather than a telling.

That's all, except that it was a darned good dinner and a good evening. And we love the new Mrs. Brady. She and Elaine are very much alike in many ways.

I hope to hear from you soon.

Yours,
John

One morning in June at Sag Harbor, Steinbeck awoke without sight in one eye: a detached retina. Surgery was performed at Southampton Hospital. During his long convalescence, when he was blindfolded and immobilized between sandbags, his old friend John O'Hara visited and read to him.

To John O'Hara

[Sag Harbor]
[July 1963]

Dear John:

My eye is doing fine. I get prisms the end of the week. Of course I'll use it for a long time when I feel the need to be pitiful. Our dog Charley taught me that. When he was a pup he got hit by a car and had his hip broken. All the rest of his life, if I scolded him or he had a bad conscience, he would limp.

Part of my pitifulness is that I got well before we got enough talking done. So many things I want to discuss with you—the general things that turn out to be personal and vice versa. If I pretended great pain—couldn't you come once again? I really can't drive yet.

770

I wish you would. There are a number of things I can't discuss with anyone else but you.

Yours,
John

love to Sister.

As far back as September 1962, Steinbeck had written of Charley the poodle to his Danish publisher, Otto Lindhardt:

"Charley is well but he is getting old. The hip he had broken as a pup gives him considerable trouble now, particularly when the weather changes. But in the morning he still thinks of himself as Youth."

His condition deteriorated through the following year, and toward the end of April, Steinbeck wrote:

"Last week was one of sadness. Charley dog died full of years but leaving a jagged hole nevertheless. He died of what would probably be called cirrhosis in a human. This degeneration is usually ascribed to indulgence in alcohol. But Charley did not drink, or if he did he was very secret about it."

The recipient of that letter and the one that follows was Dr. E. S. Montgomery of Tarentum, Pennsylvania, a well-known authority and breeder of bull terriers. Steinbeck had been in correspondence with him for some time.

To Dr. E. S. Montgomery

Sag Harbor
July 23, 1963

Dear Dr. Montgomery:

You have not heard from me because a detached retina
and surgery therefor have rendered me hors du voir. Even
now I have those pinpoint goggles that make one feel like
a stalk-eyed crab or a good trotting horse with blinders.

A little later in the summer when the rules against vibration are removed I can probably get about. The eye was saved
anyway by good Dr. Paton of Southampton.

Some years ago you wrote me that you had some fine dogs
you want me to see. At that time Charley was in his dotage
or dogage (forgive it).

But now Charley is dead and only recently I don't hear him
in the night.

And I wonder whether you now have some dogs for me to
see. May I hear from you?

Yours,
John Steinbeck

To Adlai Stevenson

Sag Harbor
[August 1963]

Dear Adlai:

Thanks for your note. The eye is going to be all right. But
even if it weren't I still have one and Lord Nelson did all
right not only at Trafalgar but at Lady Hamilton with only
one (eye, I mean).

Elaine says when you come out she will give you lunch if

you will give her enough notice to have a salmon flown over from Somerset.

Anyway, I want to talk to you. I think we're going to Moscow etc. in Oct. Could use some advice.

Regarding Barry Goldwater—He promises to lead us out of Egypt and I believe he could do it, too. Trouble is, we're not in Egypt.

Anyway, we want to see you. If anyone could bugger up Averill Harriman's good work in Russia—I can.

Yours,
John

To William A. Gilfry

A TOTAL STRANGER FROM
WINSTON SALEM, NORTH CAROLINA

Sag Harbor
August 13, 1963

Dear Mr. Gilfry:

Please forgive this writing method. I am wearing prism glasses following eye surgery and have some difficulty seeing the page.

Only a few days before he had written to Elizabeth Otis:

"I am trying hard to read and sometimes it seems a losing battle. They keep changing the prisms to make it hard and they sure succeed. Reading is like peering through a knothole full of cobwebs."

Thank you for your kind letter of August 8. It's not the interest of letters—No, it's the sheer weight that finally drives a writer to cover. You ask about the amount. It varies. This last year for various reasons it must have been thirty to

773

forty thousand. Now it has settled down to between twenty-five and fifty letters a day. Nearly all of these should be answered because they are kindly and are written in good faith. But it is simply physically impossible. If I spent every waking hour answering I could not keep up and this is leaving no time for my own work. When I came out of the hospital there were over a thousand letters to answer. How would *you* handle it?

Writing is not easy for me. It takes every bit of strength and concentration I can muster, and interruptions have a feeling like that of being hit with a stick of stove wood.

I am answering your interesting letter at length perhaps to take the place of all those I am going to have to eliminate. And I hope all of this does not sound like complaint. It isn't. This is something that happened which I didn't expect, and I can't cope with it. I didn't expect the Nobel Prize either and receiving it shocked me rather deeply. And I am still far from knowing whether I approve of it.

I was interested in your speculation about money and poets. I didn't know Robert Frost had $240,000 and I wonder whether he knew it. I didn't know him so I have no idea. My own financial image is equally obscure to me. For many years I lived a few days' rations from nothing but I did manage to stay out of debt. The books that are selling now did not sell then, although they are the same books. I presume money is coming in. It goes to a pool out of which taxes, charities, families, dependent requests are paid. Out of this pool a kind of salary is deposited to my account monthly for me to live on. I live well but not wealthily. I eat one meal a day, have a four-room cottage with a bunk house for my sons and a second-hand twenty-foot fishing boat. I drive a Ford Falcon station wagon which is getting pretty ratty. Also I have an apartment in New York because it is more handy and cheaper than going to hotels. I travel quite a lot but always as a matter of work and research. Please don't think I am shouting "poor mouth." I'm not. I live this way because I like to live this way. I don't know how Frost felt about money but I know I have utterly no interest in it as long as there is some. I know from the poverty years that when you have no money your interest in it quickens.

You say, "How could a poet permit himself to accumulate $240,000?" What should he have done? Throw it away, refuse royalties on his books which people wanted to buy? During the war I gave a book to the Air Force Aid Society, proceeds to be given to families of casualties. It cost me well over a thousand dollars in lawyers' fees to get permission of the tax division to give it away and everyone—even the Air Force—thought I was nuts. You can't give money to friends without losing them. No, the pool is right for me. I never know what is there or who gets it. It also protects one from feeling bountiful which is as ugly an emotion as I know.

When Charley died we planted a willow tree over him; sentimental, but who isn't? Then I had to go to town and when I came back someone had planted flowers all around the tree. I don't know who did it. I don't want to know.

I haven't got another dog yet. I am torn between a white English bull terrier and my first loves which were Airedales. I will want a very young dog to raise and train with care so that independence survives obedience. I should not want to remove the ability to fight from a white terrier but I would try to make it unnecessary. I never knew a truly good fighter who picked quarrels. That is for the unsure.

I know the Bostons you speak of. I had one when I was a boy and he was a fine dog with a great deal of humor. What has happened to the breed is what I detest. They are small, pop-eyed, asthmatic, with weak stomachs and an inability to find their way home.

All of the dogs I have had have been natural dogs. I could learn from them as much or more than I could teach them.

I must be coming to an end. I shall not speak of your poems. Poetry is as private and personal as nerves.

Now I have used you as a scapegoat. The next twenty-five letters I shall not answer and my guilt will be on you. Perhaps this might be a solution to the whole problem.

I am glad you like the Sea of Cortez. It was little noticed when it appeared but it seems to grow on people. Such a book can't be sold. It has to creep by itself.

Now I am done. Except for one thing. What you call Great Basin in Santa Cruz County, California, is really called Big Basin, unless they have changed the name recently. I grew up among the sequoia semper virens on the coast. Big Basin was my first and very deep experiment with gigantia. And I was seven years old at the time and we went in a buckboard with feed and food and a tent in the box. No one was there

775

and it was wonderful with hazelnuts and ferns in the dimpsy. That's a Somerset word for the twilight under trees.

So long, Scapegoat—
John Steinbeck

To Elaine Steinbeck
ON HER BIRTHDAY

PRIVATE

Sag Harbor
August 14 [1963]

Darling—

This is a private letter to you and not for the rest of the company.

In past years, when I used to give you money presents I found myself getting angry that you got very little of it for yourself.

Second—In the last couple of years we have taken on and rightly so, added outlay. That's not important. What is important is that I think you have been under a burden of having to tell me about it. Even knowing I would agree didn't change anything. You were in effect asking for money.

Now, therefore, this is your birthday present. It is the amount the government permits without tax. It is deposited to your private account in the Sag Harbor Bank. The reason for it is that you may do what you want to do or help whom you want without asking anyone. But it is also for you to buy some pretty things for yourself.

You have been so wonderful about the boys. If I don't say it often, I think it often. And this present is in no sense a reward. Rather it is a celebration. Happy Birthday—darling, and many of them. You make a good life for everyone around you.

Love,
John

To Carlton A. Sheffield

Dear Dook:

As usual I start running in circles. This next journey has up and pounced at us. My eye seems to have recovered nicely. We have to go to Washington Friday to be briefed (what is that?). Next Monday we fly to London. Then to Helsinki and to Moscow the 15th of Oct. Home about Christmas.

I think maybe I'm too old for this kind of thing. But, hell, I'm a little wiser than I was and not nearly so sure of things.

Anyway, I wanted to get a note off to you before we leave the country. I always feel that it is final and that is stupid but I do. Been doing it for years. And it doesn't change. But we are pretty seasoned travellers. Some years ago when we had been driving around France with a different stopping place each night, Elaine said that when I said "Good morning," she got up and started packing in her sleep. But her pride is that if I say in London, "Hand me a pair of pliers," she can do it.

I haven't really anything to say except that I am very glad we are together again. It gives me a good feeling of security. Let's not let it lapse again.

love
John

Now preparations for the forthcoming trip behind the Iron Curtain absorbed him. As he wrote his wife while she was visiting in Texas:

"Won't it be wonderful to be lost in the wilds of Russia—childless? The very word Siberia has a sweet sound to my ears."

In September, he busied himself renewing contacts with Russian acquaintances made on former visits.

To Michael Sholokhov
C/O UNION OF SOVIET WRITERS, MOSCOW

_____

New York
September 19, 1963

Dear Michael Sholokhov:

I hope you will remember an afternoon we spent together in Stockholm. At that time, you promised my wife and me caviar from your own river Don. She has never been quite satisfied since.

We shall be in Moscow about October 15th for a visit of about a month, and it would give us great pleasure to anticipate meeting you again.

I'm sorry I can't write to you in Russian, but there it is— I can't.

Yours very sincerely,
John Steinbeck

To Konstantin Simonov
C/O UNION OF SOVIET WRITERS, MOSCOW

_____

New York
September 19, 1963

Dear Konstantin Simonov:

May I remind you that very long ago, I had the pleasure of meeting you and that you extended to me and to my late friend, Robert Capa, great courtesy and hospitality. I remember an evening of laughter near a spiral staircase in a time when laughter was a rare commodity.

778

My wife and I will be in Moscow about October 15th and it would give me great comfort to believe that I might see you again to renew an acquaintance I have valued.

Yours very sincerely,
John Steinbeck

To Ilya Ehrenburg
C/O UNION OF SOVIET WRITERS, MOSCOW

New York
September 19, 1963

Dear Ilya Ehrenburg:

I hope that you will remember that you were my first sponsor in Russia and with some small intervals, my consistent defender.

Quite simply, my wife and I will be in Russia about the 15th of October. It would be a great pleasure to me to see you again and to renew a valued acquaintance.

Poor Capa is dead. He stepped on a land mine in Vietnam in a war he did not want to attend. But I remember the remarkable little carvings in wood from a monastery. I still have mine.

I hope we may be able to see you.

Yours very sincerely,
John Steinbeck

To Elizabeth Otis

Moscow
October 18, 1963

Dear Elizabeth:

Very little time is left for anything except sleeping. We left London a week ago and it seems months. In Helsinki they had arranged a program which nearly killed us. Can you imagine seeing 900 booksellers at 9 o'clock on Sunday morning? Well, we did. Our ambassador there [Carl Rowan] is a fine man and we got to know him and his wife quite well. Then on to Moscow where some old friends met us including Sweet Lana [Svetlana, who had been his Moscow guide in 1947]. We go pretty hard here but I have demanded periods of rest. The paper Isvestia which printed Winter serially gave us 500 rubles yesterday. Today we go to the publishers who are to give us money. A number of books have come out. Winter, they say, was a great success and even Charley is being translated. A young man from the Embassy [Peter Bridges of the Political Section] is our interpreter and he is excellent. We go south to Kiev on Monday night and then to Tbilisi in Georgia, and he and his wife will go with us.

Moscow is greatly changed. Miles of new apartment houses stretching out almost into infinity, and, since land has no private value, each has lots of room and gardens around it. People are much better dressed than the last time and not so tired. In fact not tired at all. It is I who am tired.

People here are very kind to us. Our hotel is what they call Stalin neogothic—all grandeur and marble and a huge suite with great chandeliers, very different from the old Savoy with the stuffed bear, where Capa and I stayed. As we knew she would, Elaine makes an enormous hit and is greatly loved and courted.

I find I am not doing any writing, but must tell you the thaw is very definite. You can feel it everywhere. I am more than good now. It has come full circle. I asked a writer why Winter is so popular here and he said, perhaps because the problem is not unknown here. Please tell Annie Laurie that a play version of Winter is going into rehearsal at the Moscow Art Theatre. Might be fun to have it translated and try it in New York. That would be a switch, wouldn't it?

The car hasn't come for us yet so I go on with this letter until it does. One nice thing here. They don't get moving before noon. The Finns got us up at 8. And they stayed up just as late—too.

Next day
and it should be
Saturday, the 19th.

Well, yesterday was a strange day—First to one publishing house which had printed Winter. I am told the edition was 300,000 and was sold out immediately. After quite a talk they gave me 1,000 rubles. The strange double talk that went on we will carry engraved on our hearts where it won't do us much good either. I gave it to Elaine, new name Sonya Goldenarm, a famous Russian pickpocketess. As nearly as I can make out, payments to a foreign writer have no relation to the number of books sold. It seems that all books are sold out immediately but are not reprinted. Thus it is possible for a book of an edition of half a million to become a collector's item within twenty-four hours of its issue.

At 2 we went to Ehrenburgs' apartment for lunch. A fine lunch with lots of good talk. There is no question that the thaw is on—people—at least intellectuals—speak quite freely on almost any subject but of course they, from having no experience with the outside world, are fairly limited in some of their estimates.

We are trying to keep the appointments down and to have nothing early in the morning. Last night after the ballet, which ended at 10, we went to McGrady of Newsweek where we met American and Russian news people and had a very good time.

Now I am going to close this and send it by the first courier.

Love to all there,
John

To Elizabeth Otis and
the McIntosh and Otis staff

Moscow
November 8, 1963

Dear Elizabeth and all:

Yesterday the big parade in the Red Square. Very impressive, even depressive. We got to our places about 8:45—five military checks of tickets and passports. The parade started at 10 sharp—the first part military troops in tight formation, then all the big weapons, tanks, artillery, rockets, then the sports club in their uniforms, also some military, then the factories with models of their products, thousands and thousands. It was cold, very, and our feet got frozen. About 12 we edged our way out and came back to the hotel where we could still see the parade. It was over about 1:30. In Stalin's time they say it went on until 5—We were sufficiently weary, rested a while and then went to the reception in the new big theater in the Kremlin—diplomats, delegations. K. [Khrushchev] was there rattling the saber the way my Uncle Will used to on the Fourth of July. Tables in the largest hall you ever saw—Tables 200 feet long crowded with food and drink, and the delegates drinking vodka and cognac like water. He would speak a while—then stop and speak again. And people went right on talking. Once he said. "I am the Chairman and no one listens to me, and you say we are not democratic." His second round he became a dove of peace, carrying hope to the U.S. as well as to all the other poor benighted non-socialist countries of the world. It was the same old gook. You will be interested to know that Russians have not heard of and will not believe the shoe tapping incident at the U.N. They say—the ones we have spoken to—that it is impossible.

We have met many writers now and editors, liberal and otherwise. I have been busily planting the poison of the copyright everywhere I can. Edward Albee arrived and is pitching in wonderfully well. I knew he would.

Tonight we all go to Leningrad for four days, then back here for two days. We begin to wonder whether we can hold out. The schedule is so heavy and every once in a while I begin to flag and fail. There is no time to write. I simply collapse into bed when I can. And the crack of voices goes into my dreams. And the constant translation is nerve-wracking.

And the phone keeps ringing. There is a quality of madness about it. And I seem to be joining in.

I have to go now. Lord! how I would welcome another day off. Leningrad will be mad but not nearly so mad as Warsaw.

Love to all there. When I get home I'm going to sleep for a week.

John

To Elizabeth Otis

Krakow, Poland
November 20, 1963

Dear Elizabeth:

The quaint look of this letter, together with the fact that I am writing it at all is the result of an accident. Our tour master made a mistake and found he hadn't booked us for three things tonight and we leaped with joy. It is the first evening off since that far-off day in Moscow when we had a whole day. No one can conceive what our program has been. Thinking back, I don't believe it. Elaine has hit the sack in flames.

When we moved up a meeting with a hundred members of the Writers' Union to 6 P.M., our Polish guide and conscience was faced with the dreadful truth that we had no place to go but to bed. Oh! Joy, Oh! Bells. Oh! Christmas ornaments!

I hope there will be some word from you when we get back to Warsaw. Mail just seems to disappear. I don't mind their reading it but I wish they wouldn't keep it.

Tomorrow we drive four hours (everything takes four hours) to Breslau which is not called that anymore and I won't even try to spell it. Then to something that sounds like Wootch [Lodz]. I must have autographed 10,000 books and the

783

names alone are longer than the books. There is no pity. They've got us and they *use* us. But of course that's what we came for. There are many times when we wonder whether it is worth doing. The Embassy people say yes. You see we really don't know what is going on in the world. All I know is that my books are very popular here and here they pay.

We left Edward behind in the big red city looking a little scairt. We will meet up with him in Prague. It's very kookie to write a letter you know is going to get the eye, just as it is strange to have any normal conversation in a hotel with bugged rooms. Everyone just takes it for granted but it's hard to get used to. It's even in cars. One long bit in a two-seater with a racing motor. Theory is that the distributor head will veto the bug. I don't know. Nicest one is in your national flag on your restaurant table. You put it on another table. Isn't this silly, to think that people will go to this length? But they do.

(Note to Big Brother—"Yes, I'm talking about you. Want to make something of it? And I'll tell you something else. If a boob like me can catch you out so often, what do you think real smart people are doing? While your chicken-shit bureaucrats are working on saving face I have four new methods for taking the skin off your cheeks. It's a great joy to write to you. For 40 days I have wanted to reply but I knew I could not get in touch with you except through the bug or the seeing eye letter. You're so Goddamned stupid.")

Do you know, some friends, dissatisfied with their breakfast, criticised it privately and alone and the next morning the corrections were made. How stupid can you get? Elaine the Fayre has proclaimed in her ladylike stentorian whisper —"If they want tourists they'd better start with coat hangers, wastebaskets and bath mats." And after three days these appeared without her speaking to anyone but me.

("And another thing, darling bug. Do you know that if we want to speak privately we have a language that even the experts in that Stalin Gothic University can't possibly work out because it is a personal language full of references you can't know. It's been good knowing you, dear reader. And I do think I know you. You are stupid and the job you are doing is stupid and it won't work. Why don't you get wise to yourself? Meanwhile it has been charming talking to you. And I wish you a thousand years! Spasiba, Bolshoi, and screw you. Yours very sincerely, J.S.")

784

Elizabeth, I have wanted to get that off for a long time. Steffens came home after the October Revolution of 1917 and his headline was "I have seen the future and it works." Well, I've examined it three times and I can say it doesn't. In our democracy we give up a lot of efficiency for the safety of our principles. But here they keep working at failure. On a pig farm I asked what they were doing about importing breeding stock—nothing. The Virgin Lands fiasco is a dirty word. We learned the hard way in Arkansas and Oklahoma. We could and would have told them how to hold down the dust. Everything is blamed on a bad year—nothing on bad management. All through the south—Georgia and Armenia—I saw no evidence of contour plowing. And we would have told them. The land is eroding away.

Well, at last I got a letter written to you.

> Love to all there,
> Jn

What Steinbeck did not mention in his letters from behind the Iron Curtain was that—apart from all the official ceremonies and entertainments involving writers and artists approved by the government —he and his wife spent as much time as they could with dissident writers' groups in small clandestine meetings, often late at night.

It was also late at night, on the 22nd of November, in Warsaw, when the news of President Kennedy's assassination reached them.

To Elizabeth Otis

Warsaw
November 24, 1963
Dear Elizabeth:

The shock of the news was terrible. We asked if we could get through to you by phone and were told there isn't a chance. Every facility is loaded. Mail takes 10 to 14 days to jump the curtain so I am going to put this in the pouch which goes on Tuesday. Tomorrow—Monday—we are flying to Vienna out of the curtain and the first thing we will do will be to put a call through to you. You can't imagine the shock and frustration. We can't get any news. We wanted to go home but then we thought that it would be chicken. The greatest respect we could pay would be to finish the job we were given. Yesterday was dreadful. I had to meet and talk to about 200 university students and later to have a huge press conference. It was made easier by the consideration of the Poles. They offered condolences and did not press us. Also, we were able to cancel all social things.

Coming out from behind the curtain is going to be a shock. Poland is better than Russia but if we had come here first we would have found it intolerable.

I have been fighting off fatigue for days. I didn't think I could get through yesterday—but we did. It's amazing what you can do if you have to. I even coined a word yesterday for what we are doing. I described us as culture-mongers. But it turns out this is impossible to translate into Polish. No matter—it's still good. And I'll use it again and again.

We are lonesome and homesick. Yesterday a woman came up to Elaine and said, "I have to talk to an American, I am an American." They fell into each other's arms and wept. It can get pretty lonely. I knew it but you can't tell anyone—it isn't possible.

Maybe we'll get caught up sometime. Again love,

John

To Mrs. John F. Kennedy

Warsaw
November 24, 1963

Dear Mrs. Kennedy:

Our sorrow is for you but for us—for us—

We are in Warsaw as culture mongers at your husband's request which to us was an order. This is Sunday after black Friday. I wish you could see our Embassy here. In the great hall is a photograph and beside it a bust made by a young Pole who asked to bring it in. Since early morning yesterday there has been a long line of people—all kinds but mostly poor people. They move slowly past the picture, place flowers (chrysanthemums are a dollar apiece), and they write their names and feelings in a book. Numbers of volumes have been filled and today the line is longer than ever. It went on all night last night, silent and slow. I have never seen anything like this respect and this reverence. And if we weep, seeing it, it is all right because they are weeping. That's all —Our hearts are with you and we love you—all of us.

John and
Elaine Steinbeck

To Lyndon B. Johnson

Warsaw
November 24, 1963

Dear Mr. President:

May I offer my profound respect and loyalty to you in the hard days ahead. Our shock and sorrow are very great but we know the office is in strong, trained and competent hands. Our hearts are with you.

At the request of President Kennedy my wife and I have been moving about behind the Iron Curtain, talking with writers and with students. Being non-diplomatic, we have been able to observe many things not ordinarily available. And if these experiences can be of value to you, they are freely offered. Some of them are highly unorthodox.

I have never met you but I have a curious tie with you. When my wife was in college in Austin, one of her classmates was a boy named John Connally who said, "Go on into the theatre in New York but as for me, I'm going into politics. There is a man named Lyndon Johnson and I'm going along with him. He's going places." I wonder whether he would remember. Her name was Elaine Anderson—later Mrs. Zachary Scott, now Mrs. John Steinbeck.

We think it best to go on with the plan laid down although our hearts are heavy, but we hasten to offer anything we have to our President.

> Yours very sincerely,
> John Steinbeck

Steinbeck failed to mention a closer tie between the two families. Elaine Steinbeck and Lady Bird Johnson had been together at the University of Texas. The President's reply to Steinbeck included the words:

"Your letter was comforting to me. I am hopeful that very soon I may sit with you and talk about our country."

From Vienna they went on to Hungary, Czechoslovakia, and West Berlin, and reached home just before Christmas. As Steinbeck had promised while behind the Curtain, he did not write publicly of his experiences there. Instead he wrote a number of letters of gratitude which he described to Leslie Brady:

"I must warn you I have written some of the purplest prose you ever heard to the Writers' Unions of Yerevan, Tblisi and Kiev. It would sound pretty corny to us but I learned the style there."

To Writers' Union of Tbilisi
GEORGIA, U.S.S.R.

New York
January 15, 1964

Dear Friends:

When we left you and flew away to the north, it was my noble and misguided intention to write a separate and personal letter to every man and woman who had made our visit a special memory. I feel no shame in admitting that I can't do that. It would take the rest of my life and even then, I would leave many out, and how would I write to those whose hands I touched, whose eyes I looked into, whose health I drank and whose names I do not know? Failing in my resolve, it is with some shyness that I address this letter to all the people of Tbilisi, to the singers, the writers, the flute players, the people who served us and gave us pleasure, who listened to us and talked to us—yes—and argued with us. That was good, too.

This letter is addressed to the pretty girls swinging their skirts along the street, and to the old gentleman in his garden of the mind, to the men squeezing the heart-blood from the grapes, and to the cellar men who dug deep in the casks to dredge up for us the maturing wine. I address the good dinner companions who sang country songs in four-part harmony, and raising their glasses toasted us with such compliments that we wished we could find the heart to believe we were as good and beautiful as they said we were.

And so, I address this letter to the city itself, to the high cliffs and girdles of pines, to the chattering river which gnawed a gateway between two worlds, to the clean sharp distances dancing over foothills and up to the mountains that edge the earth surely. And this letter is addressed to the quiet and permanent wedding in Tbilisi of the ancient and the new. The people in the street look out of old, old eyes on a fresh world which they, themselves, have made. Is it any wonder then that the greatest crop in Georgia is poetry?

I know the history and the pre-history of that gate between two worlds and how it drew the wolves from everywhere, looking with steel eyes for greener lands or set to slam the gate and hold the pass.

It seems, and is to be fervently wished, that by a favor of time and processes, the wolves are caged and the gates are opening all over the world. This is my prayerful desire, and if I could choose a mission for my own, that would be it—to help cage wolves and open doors.

I have probably left out many things in this attempt of a letter—but then, I never wrote a letter to a city before.

Clinging in our memory as tight as a burr on a sheep's belly are light and gaiety and kindness, and strength to protect them and these against a background of the sun-brown city and the talking river of the Gateway of the World. Keep it open, I pray you.

Yours,
John Steinbeck

To Writers' Union of Kiev
UKRANIA, U.S.S.R.

New York
January 15, 1964

Dear Friends:

I am addressing this letter through the Writers' Union to all of my old and new friends in Ukrania. The tough old guard whom I knew as soldiers when Kiev lay ruined in its own streets will know in what high regard I hold them. But I want to address my thanks also to the young, strong ones who grew up as the city grew back to greatness. I want to thank them for coming to greet my wife and me and for making us welcome.

It pleased me greatly, but did not make me vain, to discover that I was remembered in Kiev. That gave me a good feeling like that of coming home.

What I want to say to my friends is that although we differed and argued and bickered over small things, in the great things, we agreed.

790

Lastly, I ask you to believe that when I disagreed, I did it there with you and faced your answers. For I do despise a guest who flatters his host and goes away to attack him.

What I have to remember and to tell my people of is the kindness and the courtesy and the hospitality we were offered. These alone constituted a great experience.

Yours,
John Steinbeck

To Kazimierz Piotrowski
STEINBECK'S POLISH TRANSLATOR IN WARSAW

New York
March 26, 1964

Dear Casey:

I am astonished that your letter of December 27th has taken so very long to reach me. When you put it in the troika, you neglected to add enough children to throw to the wolves, so that your letter could come through quickly.

It was a good time, Casey, and we are grateful to you for all of your help. You say that you had to explain why I couldn't see more people, when it is my opinion that I saw every living Pole at least three times.

Oddly enough, the separate container of photographs and press clippings arrived before your letter did. And I did like very much the article by Bohdan Tomaszewski. It had the advantage also of being true, whereas the man who wrote the article which said that I had small and arthritic hands must have been somewhere else.

Anyway, Casey, happy hunting.

My love to Wanda and Elaine sends her best.

Yours,
John

In February he wrote Graham Watson in London:

"We went to Washington last Thursday. There was a dinner to a highlander named Home or something, and a Hootenanny at the White House afterwards. Elaine was cut-in on five times by the President, but then they are both Texans. Friday I had a private interview with him at noon, and Mrs. Johnson asked us to come privately for a drink at five. Then at six we went to see Mrs. Kennedy—an astonishing woman and very beautiful."

Mrs. Kennedy had asked to see him to discuss his writing a book about the dead President.

To Mrs. John F. Kennedy

New York
February 25, 1964

Dear Mrs. Kennedy:

I have your letter, which most astonishes me that we could make so many contacts of understanding in so many directions and so quickly. But such things do happen, wherefor I do wonder at those people who deny the existence of magick or try to minimize it through formulas.

I would like to do the writing we spoke of but as always, in undertaking something which moves me deeply, I am terrified of it. If I am not satisfied with its truth and beauty it will see no light. Meanwhile, as it was with those brave and humble Greeks, I shall make sacrifice to those powers which cultivate the heart and mind and punish the mean, the small, the boastful and the selfish.

You bridled, I think, when I used the word Myth. It is a warped word now carrying a connotation of untruth. Actually the Mythos as I see it and feel it is the doubly true, and more than that, it is drawn out of exact experience only when it is greatly needed.

Since I was nine years old, when my beautiful Aunt Molly gave me a copy of the Morte d'Arthur in Middle English, I

792

have been working and studying this recurring cycle. The 15th century and our own have so much in common—Loss of authority, loss of gods, loss of heroes, and loss of lovely pride. When such a hopeless muddled need occurs, it does seem to me that the hungry hearts of men distill their best and truest essence, and that essence becomes a man, and that man a hero so that all men can be reassured that such things are possible. The fact that all of these words—hero, myth, pride, even victory, have been muddied and sicklied by the confusion and pessimism of the times only describes the times. The words and the concepts are permanent, only they must be brought out and verified by the Hero. And this thesis is demonstrable over the ages—Buddha, Jove, Jesus, Apollo, Baldur, Arthur—these were men one time who answered a call and so became the sprits'ls of direction and hope. There was and is an Arthur as surely as there was and is a need for him. And meanwhile, all the legends say, he sleeps—waiting for the call.

I have not really wandered away from the theme. At our best we live by the legend. And when our belief gets pale and weak, there comes a man out of our need who puts on the shining armor and everyone living reflects a little of that light, yes, and stores some up against the time when he is gone—the shining stays and the light is needed—the fierce and penetrating light.

Remember? We spoke of sorrow. (So many things we spoke of.) And also anger, good healthy anger. The sorrow and the anger are a kind of remembering. I know there is a cult of dismal, Joblike acceptance, a mewing "Everything that happens is good." Well that is *not* so and to say it is is to be not only stupid but hopeless. That same cult of acceptance would have left us living in trees.

You see, my dear, how huge and universal the theme is and how one might well be afraid of it. But in our time of meager souls, of mole-like burrowing into a status quo which never existed, the banner of the Legend is the great vocation.

The Western world has invented only one thing of the spirit and that is gallantry. You won't find it in any Eastern or Oriental concept. And I guess gallantry is that quality which, when faced with overwhelming odds, fights on as though it could win and by that very token sometimes does.

I shall try to find a form for this theme. Meanwhile, if you should have a feeling for talking or reminiscing or speculating, I shall be available. I shall come to you at your request or, if you would care to think without physical reminders, please come to us. Our house is one of love and courtesy and we hope of gallantry. I am sending you a version of the Morte. Meanwhile I enclose as promised, Sir Ector's lament over the body of Sir Launcelot, in the Maiden's Castle in Northumberland.

Yours,
John Steinbeck

It may take a swatch of time to find the clothing for the Legend. And it is possible that I never can, but I will try my best.

J.S.

SIR ECTOR'S LAMENT

(from Eugène Vinaver's translation of Malory's *Morte d'Arthur*)

"A, Launcelot!" he sayd, "thou were hede of al Crysten knyghtes! And now I dare say," sayd syr Ector, "thou sir Launcelot, there thou lyest, that thou were never matched of erthely knyghtes hande. And thou were the curtest knyght that ever bare shelde! And thou were the truest frende to thy lovar that ever bestrade hers, and thou were the trewest lover of a synful man that ever loved woman, and thou were the kyndest man that ever strake wyth swerde. And thou were the godelyest persone that ever cam emonge prees of knyghtes, and thou was the mekest man and the jentyllest that ever ete in halle emonge ladyes, and thou were the sternest knyght to thy mortal foo that ever put spere in the reeste."

Mrs. John F. Kennedy

Dear Mrs. Kennedy:

I have been thinking about what you said regarding lost causes. And it is such a strange subject. It seems to me that the only truly lost causes are those which win. Only then do they break up into mean little fragments. You talked of Scotland as a lost cause and that is not true. Scotland is an *unwon* cause. Probably the greatness of our country resides in the fact that we have not made it and are still trying. No—I do believe that strength and purity lie almost exclusively in the struggle—the becoming. That is why it is so important to me —for my own sake—to write about the President. You said you hoped he was not a lost cause. But you must see that by the terrible accident of his death he can't be. His cause must get stronger and stronger and it cannot weaken because it is a piece of everyone's heart. All of us carry a fragment of him. And we must have some goodness in us—else we could not perceive goodness in him.

You can see how this theme is haunting me. My Irish mother had the second sight and I picked up a little of it in her blood. It is because of this that I make the following request. I have no picture of the President nor of you. Would it be possible for you to send these to me? I want a focus of attention. You will know if there exist such pictures. I don't want the posed state pictures but rather those with complexities. If you know such as that, perhaps I can stare deeply into the eyes and beyond into the brain; it might make it easier for me. I want to *know* to the best of my ability. Sometimes in moments of perplexity or pain, the eyes and face open and allow a passage through.

As we all do—I have need, and consider the New Testament many times. And it has seemed to me that Jesus lived a singularly undramatic life—a straight line life without deviation or doubt. And then we come to that heart-breaking moment on the cross when He cried "Lama sabachthani." In

795

that one moment of doubt we are all related to Him. And when you said you had questions to ask, please remember that terrible question Jesus asked: "My Lord, wherefor hast thou forsaken me?" In that moment He was everyone—Everyone!

I have looked for a Marcus Aurelius and the ones I have found are big and pretentious. I want one for you, small as a breviary like my father's which he gave to me—small enough to put in your purse. I will find one for you sooner or later.

I seem to be committed but I have no idea whether or not I can do it. Please believe that if I can do it—only you and Elaine will see it until it is as perfect as I can make it.

Can you, or will you, tell me—did he at any time in his life write any poetry? Prose can be from the mind but poetry comes from the soul.

Finally, please tell me whether these letters trouble you or bother you in any way. They are a manner of thinking.

Yours,
John Steinbeck

To Carlton A. Sheffield

New York
March 2, 1964

Dear Dook:

This note is prompted by the desire to talk when one hasn't anything to say. It's what they call *visiting* in Texas.

My 62nd birthday has just come and gone—and I must say I felt older at 35—yes and wiser too. It is very strange. When we are very young, we have the feeling that we can aim and position our lives. But looking backwards, I at least seem to see that it was all a series of unforseeable accidents and that nothing we could have done would have made any difference.

I have finally worked out to my own satisfaction anyway

how it can be that some people are lucky and some unlucky. For example—do you remember Ritch Lovejoy? Everything he touched turned to tragedy, in health, in economics, in his work. It was almost as if he called tragedy to him.

Then we have known those to whom everything good happens. I don't for one moment think that there is automatic punishment for the lucky. There are runs of luck. And from this stems my theory. Theoretically if you play enough times there will be an equal number of reds and blacks. But in the events of a human life, there aren't enough spins to make it balance. So some people win mostly, and others lose. If we lived forever, it would all balance out but we don't. Oh! I know it's possible to rig the game a little but not a great deal. Luck or tragedy, some people get runs. Then of course there are those who divide it even, good and bad, but we never hear of them. Such a life doesn't demand attention. Only the people who get the good or bad runs. Now that is the only bit of speculation which seems to hold water for me. And perhaps it isn't very interesting. 62. And I think you are the better part of a year ahead of me, aren't you?

I think of you very often but more in one direction than in others. You see when my second wife divorced me, I had to build a new reference library and I did it very thoroughly—dictionaries and facts—and then some really complete specialties. As far as possible I wanted to be able to look up nearly everything without going to a library. For the rare things kept under guard in the great repositories I was able to gather microfilm. I hardly ever turn to my bookshelves, loaded with goodies, without thinking—"How Dook would love this!" And you would. But there is a hazard which you will recognize. Starting to look something up, I get stopped ahead of the place and quite often never get to the thing I started for.

But there is one bad thing my collection does. It holds up to me a constant mirror of my ignorance. When I am faced with what I don't know a kind of despair sets in. And in addition to all the things about the past which I don't know there are all of the new fields of research into which I can't even step my toe. And these go whirling away ahead of me. It must have been a pleasant time when a philosopher could know everything. That time is long gone. But you would love the books. Of course the casual books come flowing in but the designed library is a staunch bastion. I have lost all sense of

797

home, having moved about so much. It means to me now—only that place where the books are kept.

Odd thing is that I wish I had learned more. I am stamping the ground trying to get started on a new book that means a lot to me. I want it to be very good and so far I have the tone of it and what it is about and that is all. I'll have to kick it around for some time.

I have thought about writing an autobiography but a real one. Since after a passage of time I don't know what happened and what I made up, it would be nearer the truth to set both down. I'm sure this would include persons who never existed. Goethe wrote such an account but I have not read it. Can't find it yet. He called it Fiction and Fact. I didn't know about this when I got to thinking about such an account. Do you know the work? I have put a search out to find it. But surely the fictionizing and day dreaming and self-aggrandizement as well as the self-attacks are as much a part of reality as far as the writing is concerned as the facts are. And even the facts have a chameleon tendency after a passage of time.

I must go today for my periodic medical check. I do it for my dear wife. And eventually they will find that internally I don't exist. But so far they have found only that I am perfectly normal even in my degenerations. Nothing spectacular at all—only erosion.

I guess this is about the end. I have to answer the packet of letters from strangers which just came in. I wonder why I do it. Some kind of vestigial courtesy, I guess.

Anyway I'm glad to talk to you but I'd rather hear you talk back.

Yours
John

To Mrs. John F. Kennedy

[New York]
April 20, 1964

Dear Mrs. Kennedy:

Forgive please, my apparent slowness in answering your two letters. The delay arises from a kind of remorseful re-thinking. I had no intention of joining the cackling flock who are pulling and pushing and nibbling at you.

You see, it was never any plan of mine to rush in while the wound is fresh and while eager memories feed on them-selves. I can't make up my mind to write of this or not to. All I can say is that I will think and feel and out of this some-thing may emerge. A great and a brave man belongs to all of us because he activates the little greatness and bravery that sleeps in us. And unfortunately an evil man finds his signals in us also.

And you are quite right when you say a book is only a book and he was a man and he is dead. The book could only be of value if it helped to keep the essential and contributing part of him alive, and such a thing will have to wait until the agony and the poison drains away and only the surviving permanence remains.

I have had to find this in my own small measure of pain and confusion and I am sorrowful if I have contributed to yours.

I think your three letters and our conversation have told me in a large and feeling sense all I need to know. And you are quite right when you say you probably wouldn't like what I wrote if I write it now. I don't think I would either. No, it's a thing to put into the half-sleeping mind, to think of in the half-dawn when the first birds sing, and in the evening; they call it the dimpsy in Somerset. These are the times for the good and the permanent thinking which is more like musing —the garden path toward dream.

I have always been at odds with those who say that reality and dream are separate entities. They are not—they merge and separate and merge again. A monster proportion of all

799

our experience is dream, even that we think of as reality.

I wish I could help you although I know not anyone can. I've thought that after all of the required puppetry and titanic control that has been asked of you and given—it might be good and desirable if, like those bereft squaws I spoke of, you could go to a hill and howl out your rage and pain—yes and defiance against the cold stars, against God and the gods. If your husband loved the Greeks, he would understand this with his whole soul. I am not speaking religiously at all when I suggest that only after we have been driven to the "Lama sabachthani," only then are we capable of the "Father, into Thy hands." Who has not had the first cannot have the second.

Oh! Lord, I hope I am not lecturing you. I don't want to.

I'm having a miserable copy of the Meditations bound for you. It will be along in time.

Now, I come to the end. I shall ask no more questions. But if the cloud of thought persists, one day I do hope to write what we spoke of—how this man who was the best of his people, by his life and his death gave the best back to them for their own.

Take care, and when you can, please laugh a little. I think I've been a bore but if so, that's what I am.

Yours with admiration but never with pity.

John Steinbeck

When Mrs. Jacqueline Kennedy Onassis turned over copies of her letters from Steinbeck for use in this book, she wrote:

"Dear Mrs. Steinbeck,
    I have found the letters of your husband—
    I can never express what they meant to me at the time—they helped me face what was unacceptable to me.
    You will never know what it meant to me to talk with your husband in those days—I read his letters now—and I am as moved as I was then—All his wisdom, his compassion, his far-seeing view of things—

I can't remember the sort of book we were discussing then—but I am glad it wasn't written.

His letters say more than a whole book could—I will treasure them all my life—

Most sincerely
Jacqueline Kennedy Onassis"

To The President
C/O JACK VALENTI, THE WHITE HOUSE

TELEGRAM

SAG HARBOR
JULY 1, 1964

DEAR MR PRESIDENT I AM DEEPLY MOVED PLEASED AND PROUD TO LEARN THAT I WILL RECEIVE THE PRESIDENTIAL MEDAL OF FREEDOM. WARMEST GREETINGS

JOHN STEINBECK

This "highest civil honor conferred by the President of the United States for service in peacetime" was presented at the White House in September. Steinbeck shared it with such other distinguished civilians as T. S. Eliot, Willem de Kooning, the Lunts, Helen Keller, Leontyne Price, Edward R. Murrow, Paul Dudley White, and Aaron Copland.

To Pascal Covici

[Sag Harbor]
July 14 [1964]
Bastille Day

Elaine buzzed me to come into the house and told me you wanted to talk to me.

As for your suggestion of my inconstancy with mea culpa overtones, it seems to me that this was your late ulcer talking and I refuse to argue with an ulcer.

Let's suppose I have an ulcer too and our ulcers get to arguing. Yours says—"You don't love me as you used to. What have I done to deserve this?" And my ulcer says "Not so. It is you who have changed. I have remained constant."

God damn it, Pat, that's school-girl talk and school girl thinking—fine for my kids at 16 but not good enough for two men whose years should give them better counsel. Of course we have changed. If we hadn't it would be either a lie or an abnormality. I know I get tired when I used to be tireless. I am short tempered where I used to be calm and calm where I used to blow my top. That's simply age—to be accepted, not mourned over. I consider the body of my work and I do not find it good. That doesn't mean a thing except that the impulses have changed. If I have any more work in me, which I sometimes doubt, it will have to be of a kind to match my present age. I'm not the young writer of promise any more. I'm a worked-over claim. There may be a few nuggets overlooked but the territory has been pretty thoroughly assayed. More and more, young people look at me in amazement because they had thought I was dead. Among writers it is becoming very fashionable to be dead.

Just as you did not tell me about your painful ulcer, I see no reason to burden you with the knowledge that this last year was a very difficult one for me to finish. I really didn't know whether I would make it or not. But this is no attempt to match sorrows with you either. As you know I have been more fortunate than I have deserved and not as good as I have wished. That was inevitable of course but inevitability is none the less shocking.

I thought on starting this that I could make some kind of pattern emerge but nothing really seems to—nothing true.

You say that about three years ago something happened and you are trying to find some blame in yourself, perhaps. Well, you know damn well what happened three years ago. I collapsed and got taken to the hospital. I don't know what it was and neither do you but I do know that something happened and that I never returned as I went in. Whatever it was made a change. Maybe maturity hit me and required an explosion to make me aware of it.

But hell, I could go on explaining for weeks and it wouldn't mean anything. Mainly I want to rest. Somewhere I have picked up a great weariness. So come off it about my neglecting you. I'm neglecting everyone and everything. There may be some milk in this old bag yet. That's one of the things I'm trying to find out.

                                        affectionately,
                                        John

In the fall of 1964, an association that had begun thirty years before, when a Chicago book dealer had brought *The Pastures of Heaven* to Pascal Covici's attention—an association marked by enthusiasm, occasional bickering, and continuous affection—came to an unexpected end with Covici's death. One of Steinbeck's very few public speeches took place when he, along with Saul Bellow and Arthur Miller, appeared at Covici's memorial service. As he wrote to his British publisher, Alexander Frere:

"It has not been a good year and Pat Covici's death was a dreadful shock to us. I can't yet go to Viking offices, not because he is not there but because he is."

The Steinbecks visited John Huston at his house, St. Clerans, in County Galway for the Christmas holidays, and Steinbeck was attracted to a local legend. He and Huston discussed collaboration.

To John Huston

The Dorchester
London
January 5, 1965

Dear John:

It was the most memorable of all Christmases, the kind that can and will turn to folklore surely. And after a short time I won't be sure what happened and what didn't and that's the real stuff of truth. Aer Lingus was four hours lingering before taking off so that we did have a good experience in Dublin Airport. And sun in England.

I took the beautiful cloth [a bolt of Sardinian velvet, a Christmas gift from Huston] to Tautz and they were pleased and cautious. Today I went for a fitting of the jacket. They were still astonished at the cloth, saying the jacket would *do* but that for the trousers the material put up a fight. "And so it should," I said. "It has a lifetime of fighting against my knees and my behind. Let it start now." It is a princely gift and I shall wear it with arrogance.

I think often of Daly. And please believe me, I don't want to make a motion picture. But I do have still the hunger to make something beautiful and true. And I have the feeling that in this story are all the beauties and all the truths including the aching lustful ones. And so I'll write the little tale as well as I can and we will see whether the sound and color of it will translate to the visual. It does seem to me that in the late scramble for reality, writers have somehow overlooked the real. Will you let me know what you casually feel about this?

Meanwhile—again our thanks for an improbable time—almost into a fresh dimension.

Yours,
Sean

As they were leaving Galway, Gladys Hill, Huston's colleague and assistant, handed Elaine Steinbeck a small parcel said to contain jewels entrusted to Huston by his friend, Mr. W———, in Cairo, and asked that it be put in the vault of the Midland Bank in London. Mrs. Steinbeck undertook to smuggle the parcel through English Customs, much to her husband's horror. Later, he entered into the intrigue with characteristic glee and reported his adventure.

To Gladys Hill

London
January 6, 1965

Dear Glades:

Your mission was carried out in a manner that would have made you proud. James Bond may be dead but I became 007 3/8 for the afternoon. It was after hours and I rang the bell and a dark and angry face looked out from the chained door. I demanded the manager and after a long wait was admitted. I asked him to identify himself, which so startled him that he complied. He then said it was not Midland's policy to give assurance for jewels. I said I had no knowledge of any jewel, but that the package I carried must be protected. There was a small and whispered conference in another room. Then he came back and said they would seal the package in a great envelope—that I must attest this and they would then protect the package. 007 3/8 agreed. They brought a taper and enough wax to pitch an ark within and without. And I sealed every corner—7 blobs—with my flying pig ring. They played right along with the James Bond mood. Then I signed every seal, and I was escorted to the vault to see the package deposited. Then the manager asked how recently I had seen Mr. W———. I said, "I have never seen Mr. W———. I do not know Mr. W———." The chains grated on the door and I swept out feeling fictional as all hell.

We are having a pleasant time. Last night we saw Olivier's Othello. Probably the greatest performance I have ever seen.

I am still shaken by it. We've not been tagged yet and the White House has forgotten me, praise God.

I think I'll have a go at Daly as soon as I can to see whether I can get a color key.

Love and again deep thanks.

John

To Carlton A. Sheffield

[New York]
February 2, 1965

Dear Dook:

A week ago, Mary Dekker, reading in bed, took off her glasses, laid down her book and went to sleep. Just that. No struggle, no fear, no intimation. And with her medical history, she must be considered one of the lucky ones. I think I knew at Thanksgiving that I would not see her again, but that's not really valid because I had that feeling about lots of things when it wasn't true.

Mary was 60, Esther 74, Beth 70 and I 63. That is quite a record of survival of four children.

In spite of knowing this was imminent, it has its shock. We were in Paris when the news came.

The trip to Ireland was wonderful. The west country isn't left behind—it's rather as though it ran concurrently but in a non-parallel time. I feel that I would like to go back there. It has a haunting kind of recognition quotient. I found a marvelous story I would like to write there.

That's all, I guess. But I did want to tell you about Mary.

love
John

On Steinbeck's return to New York, Thomas Guinzburg brought him a mock-up of a book of photographs of the fifty states, and asked him to write
captions for them. The captions turned into essays,
some of them based on observations made on his
recent trip around the country.

To John Huston and Gladys Hill

New York
February 17, 1965

Dear John and Glades:

In Paris the news came that my youngest sister had died
suddenly. So we ran for home. It was the first break in our
family. She was the youngest and she was sixty and we were
four children.

Then, since I have not worked under our capitalistic system for some time (I have given my work away for the last
two years) I went to work on my book of pictures of all of the
fifty states and my essay on our people. It is called America
and the American. I may have to run for my life when it
comes out. I am taking "the American" apart like a watch to
see what makes him tick and some very curious things are
emerging.

Then Elaine's aunt, the one she adored, fell ill to death and
last Saturday the calls seemed to indicate she was about
finished so Elaine went to Texas to help with the recessional.
And she hangs on, comatose, a vegetable and alive.

Before we went to Paris I was in Gieves in Bond Street, you
know that military outfitters place? The clerk, pronounced
clark, was Irish. As I finished my business, he said, "You're
from Ulster."

I said, "No I am not, why do you say that?" He said, "Because you talk like an Ulsterman."

Well, my grandfather was from Ulster, from Mulkearaugh
on Lock Foyle. And I had great commerce with him surely
when I was a child. But isn't it interesting that this influence
should hang on to my own age of sixty-three? My grand-

mother was not. She was, I believe from Cork and a convert, which made her a fire-eating Protestant but I don't remember that she talked much whereas my grandfather talked all the time. If you have ever read East of Eden, Sam Hamilton was my grandfather and you'll see the mark he put on me.

The brown velvet darling has not come yet. Do you suppose the pants are still fighting back? Give our love to all there.

Yours,
John

1965 1967
1966 1968

B. Steinbeck

*"Is it a race against
remaining time?"*

1966 *America and Americans* published. Late in year began five-month trip through Southeast Asia as correspondent for *Newsday*.

It has been established that Steinbeck's restless and wide-ranging mind often toyed with gadgets and inventions. In fact, nothing was too bizarre to elicit a letter from him. For instance, to Dr. E. S. Montgomery:

"The metronomic puppy weaner can, I imagine, have the works of any standard alarm clock, and would be effective in soothing a sorrowing weanling. The Peacemaker (to stop dog fights) may well be patentable. I think of it as being about the size and shape of a fountain pen. The dosage of the hypnotic should be carefully calculated to be effective without injury to the animal. There is only one thing I think of which might be charged against it. Some inventive swain might try to use it on a girl and get the Peacemaker a bad name."

Names fascinated him, as when he wrote to Howard Gossage about the naming of a new model Rover car:

"Land Rover is good, but Rover is cornball. What you need is a new name, simple and not to be confused with any other. It needn't be boastful like Thunderbird, or Fireball. Better not. It should have a rich, racy but conservative name. Plantaganent is too long, Tudor has been used for everything. Windsor would be good but it refers to a collar. Raleigh is a cigarette but Drake has not been used. Drake might be very good. Sir Francis Drake would be even better, it has some connotation of daring and far ranging."

Or as he wrote to Mr. and Mrs. Bruce McWilliams, on becoming attached to "a small, red Land Rover":

"One finds curious things to adore in one's beloved. Helen looked to Poe like a ship. Another poet, agoggle about a skylark, could, after considerable thought and emotion, only arrive at the conclusion that whatever else it might have been, it was not a bird, and never had been. He said so openly, 'Bird thou never wert,' an odd position to take when there it was flying about, feathers and all."

As Steinbeck himself commented:

"You know I have far too much to do to go on like this but I do anyway. It is my beastly habit."

In March 1965, he was awaiting his wife's return from Texas.

$\mathcal{T}$o John Huston and Gladys Hill

New York
March 2, 1965

Dear John and Glades:

Elaine is coming home tonight hurray! hurray! She is just in time to save my waning life that was dreening away in tears of loneliness.

You know I'm a reasonably self-satisfied and self-sufficient bloke. Don't need much, handy, can take care of myself, cook, sew a little, quite content to read a lot and do my work. And if necessary, which it isn't, I can still lift a fairly accurate left and counter with a neat, tucked-close right hook. And if worse came to worst, I guess I could rumble somebody who would find me tolerable—you know. *My own man.*

And then Elaine goes away and all hell comes busting loose like a storm sewer in a cloudburst. I can't find my clothes, or the frying pan. I've forgotten how to light the oven. A light gray film settles over the house, and three-day-old newspapers are on the floor. I don't know who the laundry man is or where we buy meat. Can't find the checkbook and when the stamps are gone that is that.

I'm a guy with lots of friends, good friends. After me all the time to save an evening or a weekend. Then Elaine is gone and I can't think of a soul. Then I scrounge up a girl—nice kid, good company, undemanding—and fun. I look up her number and remember she has been dead for six years. Shot her husband and took pills.

I tell you Elaine being away is the great leveler. When she comes in, in about an hour, I'll have to tell her a bunch of crap just to hold her interest. It's like Gadg Kazan as a kid going to confession and making up sins so as not to waste the priest's time.

But in the two and a half weeks she has been gone I wrote 85 pages of ms.—out of pure despair. And I don't know how it happened but it's pretty good.

Glade's Ark letters have been a joy. [Huston was playing Noah in the film *The Bible* which he was directing in Rome.] How I wish I could have been there. I particularly like the man who sleeps under lions. Probably not as dangerous as dames but warmer. Once when I was little and hustling a circus in Salinas for a free ticket, a lion licked my hand and just about took the skin off. I never forgot.

Now, she has landed and she must be on her way in from Kennedy Airport.

O'Toole [Peter O'Toole] was here on a publicity pitch but he didn't call and by the time I got around to it, he was on his way to Japan. Making a picture Erin go Bragh Hara-kiri, I guess, or Sayonara Mavourneen. How these Micks do get about.

She must be nearly here now.

I hope to finish this present thing by the brink of summer. Then to Sag Harbor for a big swatch of the Arthurian jamboree and then maybe when the autumn comes we can move on to Daly. Or would one dare try to repeat greatness—ask to be asked for Christmas? That would probably be best in point of time but I have a fist on my heart about trying to repeat.

SHE'S HERE!

Later—As pooped a Poopsie as I ever saw but it's all right. She's here. Now we can go on living.

Please give my respect to the man who sleeps under lions. And for yourselves—

the best,
John

The subject of a new dog had long occupied Steinbeck. He had been in fairly continual correspondence with Dr. Montgomery about various bull terriers. In March 1964:

"I want your philosophical advice. Most people want a dog in their own image. But consider someone like me. I am sixty-two years old. My egotisms do not require either a mirror or a slave. Dogs are just as individual as humans. Don't you think it would be possible to get a dog who is grown up, whose character is established and whose adolescence is past? I find myself impatient with teen-agers. Couldn't one have such a dog as a friend rather than a servant?"

And a month later:

"I think you will agree that the only thing to do is to judge with the feelings and not too fast. Some people get along and some don't. Some of my oldest and most treasured friends couldn't win worst of show in a Mexican hill town but I love them even more for it. You see, this may well be my last dog. And I would like to associate with one who could go everywhere with me, could be taught to steal chickens if necessary, and observe the first rule never to bring the feathers home. I should like him to be able to fly—to ride—to creep under a table at the Palais Royale or to engage in commerce with a Sicilian burro. I imagine the first requirement is that I like the dog and the dog likes me."

In November, they had settled on a candidate:

"I can't tell you how excited your telephone call made me. I can hardly wait to see this dog. Now, I am going to do something you may think is nonsense, but I kind of believe in it. I am going to send you a sleep shirt I have worn for a number of nights. If you will put it in the dog's bed or some place where he feels secure and comfortable, I will be glad. It used to be considered the best kind of preintroduction and one that a young dog got deep in his understanding."

By February 1965, he was writing to Duke Sheffield:

"The enclosed is a picture of a new dog. He will come to us in a week or ten days. He is just about perfect of his breed. That left eye is not blue. The blue is from camera flash. His eyes are black as jet

and very humorous. He isn't quite as big as this fore-
shortened picture makes him but he weighs nearly
60 pounds and will weigh 70 when he is full grown.
His name is Angel, working on the principle of Give
a dog a good name. But we have been too long without a dog."

And finally to Dr. Montgomery:

"All I can tell you is that my cup brimmeth over. I
have had lots of dogs, but I never saw one like this.
After hours in the crate—it was 9 o'clock before they
turned him over to me—and with all the noise and
lights and clatter, he was completely relaxed. I
brought him to the apartment and he settled in as
though he had always lived here. He learns with
about two tellings. In the early morning I take him
to the roof for a romp and after my work we go for
long walks. This, by the way, is awfully good for me.
He is not away from me for a second. He sat beside
me for a run-through of Frank Loesser's new musical, the only dog who ever saw a run-through."

To Joseph Bryan III

New York
March 14, 1965

Dear Joe:
    Thank you for the wire reminding me of an ugly event [his
sixty-third birthday]. The same to you. Sometimes I do indeed feel like a motherless child.
    My grandson, aged eight, [David Farber, Waverly's son]
wanted a padlock to safetify his securities which seemed
reasonable enough until he asked, "Why is it called a padlock?" "I don't know," I said. "But we're sure as hell going to
find out. Fetch down Volume VII of Oxford's bleeding dictionary." And the buggers bugged off. They don't know. Pad
is a big word and means everything from a highway to a
harness to a poultice. But why it's a padlock and has been
since before Bede got venerable, O.E.D. just won't even guess.

But I will, cuss it. In O.E.-A.S., O.F., O.N. and Old Teut—the pad word means a turtle, of the land or terrapin persuasion. Now, did you ever see any traditional form that looked more like a turtle? But those cautious bastards won't guess.

Life goes on. I am writing a book about "The Americans." We are a very curious people and as far as I know no one has inspected us as we would inspect some other sub-species. It's most fascinating work—to me—and I hope to have it finished by summer.

My sister Sir Marye died in February and I never got her book written. So I will start it this summer and she will know.

Our new dog came last week—a perfect beauty and a darling—just about a perfect white English bull terrier. I named him Angel, but last night I added a little to his name. He is now Angel Biddle Duke.

The summers do come around very often, don't they? Here's a new one on the way. I would like to go back to Ireland next winter. I liked the west country just fine. Galway and Connemara really exist out of time. On the coast it's rocky poor country. A man has to make a reservation to plant a cabbage in the lee of a stone, but there's more peat—they call it sod or turf—than it needs to keep them warm. And the people are lovely warm people. I feel good there and I should because I guess I'm related to most of them. The west of Ireland is pure Celt, not black like the south. Past and Future have no meaning at all because they're all one, and an old lady is as much your daughter as she is your grandmother.

And you know—I talk too much.

Yours,
John

The next night Lyndon Johnson addressed Congress. Steinbeck watched on television as the President delivered his "We shall overcome" speech, in which he decried "a crippling legacy of bigotry and injustice" that had prevented blacks from voting.

To Lyndon B. Johnson

New York
March 17, 1965

Dear Mr. President:

Always there have been men who had contempt for the "word" although words have survived better than any other man-made things. St. John says, "In the beginning was the Word, and the Word was God." When you have finished using a weapon, someone is dead or injured, but the product of the word can be life and hope and survival. All of the greatness of our species rests on words—Socrates to his judges—the Sermon on the Mount, the introduction to Wyclif's Bible, later taken by Lincoln for the Gettysburg Address. And all of these great and irretrievable words have the bravery of fear and hope in them. There must have been a fierce but hollow feeling in the members of the Continental Congress when the clerk first read the words, "When in the course of human events—." Lincoln must have dwelt with loneliness when he wrote the order of mobilization.

In our history there have been not more than five or six moments when the word and the determination mapped the course of the future. Such a moment was your speech, Sir, to the Congress two nights ago. Our people will be living by phrases from that speech when all the concrete and steel have long been displaced or destroyed. It was a time of no turning back, and in my mind as well as in many others, you have placed your name among the great ones of history.

And I take great pride in the fact that you are my President.

Yours in admiration,
John Steinbeck

The President replied:

"Thousands of letters have come to me since my speech to the Congress. But none touched me or affected me to the degree yours did. Thank you, my dear friend. Thank you for your trust and your affection."

To Dr. Martin Luther King, Jr.

New York
March 31, 1965

Dear Dr. King:

I am answering your letter, which came last night by special delivery, at once.

May I say first I think the events leading up to the march from Selma to Montgomery may well be one of the great and important things in our country's history. It was flawless in its conception and in its execution. Even the accidents which could not have been foreseen, tragic though they were, wove themselves into the pattern of this fabric of the future.

But it is your letter of March 29, concerning the proposed boycott of Alabama, and your request that I sponsor it, that gives me pause. Believe me, Dr. King, if I were convinced that a general boycott would bring Alabama to its senses, I would be behind it with everything I have. However, I think the demand for general boycott is like the demand for unconditional surrender.

I have seen more than I have wanted to of war, from the school yard to combat in Europe, and I know full well that an enemy driven into a corner with no chance to escape, becomes triply dangerous because he has nothing to gain. If he is offered an escape corridor, or the slightest consideration for his pride, he will surrender more readily.

In this morning's Times, you are quoted as having said that you might advocate a selective boycott. Now this makes sense to me. Many white people in the South would come over to our side if they dared. Many others would come over if it were profitable or even non-ruinous to do so. I think that every person against whom a boycott would be dangerous should be allowed to say openly, "I am for you," or "I am against you." If the answer is "against", then I would back the boycott with every bit of influence I could bring to bear. So that is my answer, Sir. I am for a selective boycott but not a blind one.

As for Governor Wallace, he is safe from impeachment in the bosom of a legislature hand-picked and exactly like himself. I have thought, however, and have suggested to friends in the government, that Wallace's statement that he could not keep the peace constitutes an abdication of which the Federal government might well take cognizance. I have further suggested and I suggest to you, that the governors' oath in all states includes the promise to defend and carry out the intention of the Constitution of the United States. In his failure to defend the Constitution and indeed in his defiance of the amendments, it seems to me that he could be considered to be in rebellion against his country. Wallace seems to forget that a war was fought on this issue, a war incidentally which people like himself lost. And I do not think that position is so far-fetched.

Finally in the recent sadness at Selma I think Wallace is as guilty of the brutality and of the murders as if he held the clubs in his own hands or pulled the triggers with his own finger.

That is all now. God bless you and keep you and particularly the cause of your devotion.

your friend,
John Steinbeck

To Jack Valenti
PRESS SECRETARY DURING THE JOHNSON ADMINISTRATION

New York

April 23, 1965

Dear Jack:

It must have been rather nice for you to be without me helping. As someone said of Tallulah Bankhead—"An hour away from her is like a month in the country."

I don't know how you get it over, but the Boss confuses the words ingenuous and ingenious, and has a number of times in speeches. Ingenuous means open and straightforward, with a connotation of almost child-like sincerity while ingenious means clever, talented, but has the connotation of wiliness, and round-aboutness. You see they are almost opposites. If it will help any—Shakespeare made the same error.

The Vietnam war is troublesome. Groups have been after me to denounce the bombing but I don't sign anything I don't write. I wish the bombing weren't necessary, but I suspect that our people on the ground know more about that than I do. I certainly hope so.

But I do have a couple of ideas. People can get used to anything if it is regular. Change of pace throws them.

But there is another thing I miss in this war. And that is North Vietnam dissent. The papers say there have been desertions from the Viet Cong. But apparently the rule is powerful and unrelenting in the north. There should be a government or junta of North Vietnamese in South Vietnam. This should be set up even if we have to invent it. Its point of dissatisfaction should be fear of the Chinese. We are not making the thousand years of China phobia pay off. It must be there. If such a group of respected men from the North could be set up in Saigon, they might draw intelligence we do not have and it might do something to overturn the idea that the north is without division of opinion. Also, if there should be dissensions there would be some honorable place to desert to.

Everyone wants to make his small contribution and that must be very hard on the Boss. It was nice to be invited to the

White House. If in some improbable future there should be a quiet time for contemplation at the ranch we should love that. It would be good to see this man against live oaks and Herefords and ground squirrels with maybe the quail calling in the evening.

The best to you.

Yours,
John

To Carlton A. Sheffield

New York
April 26, 1965

Dear Dook:

You can see what a rogue and peasant slave am I. We went to Sag Harbor for a while and I finished the first draft of my book. I hope to get the thing off by June 1, and then—

Well finally I am ready for the Arthur. It was to have been Sir Mary's book and she had to die to get me to start it. I have to before she fades. And by that I mean before I fade. Sir Mary is permanent now. But I'm not, and so I must get it to her.

I hope that doesn't sound mystical because I don't mean it that way. But, do you know, I couldn't find an approach to get into it until she died. And it's so very simple. I wonder why it escaped me for so long. It's almost childishly simple. And now I'm aching to get to it.

> At about the same time he was telling Elizabeth Otis:
>
> ". . . and then I can get to the Arthur which finally begins to grow and grow in my mind in the manner we spoke of but going much further. For the first time I have some confidence in it. And I can have the whole of the summer and fall to work on it. I am pretty excited about that too.

821

Now it looks like a good year of work. And such a thing always makes me happy."

I'm itching to get out again. Gardens to start and fishing. Last time I painted my boat's bottom but haven't put it in the water yet. It's silly for me to be staying in town. I can't work as well in town as in the country.

You've got to admit that I don't talk about anyone but myself.

Tonight Terrence McNally, the boy who tutored my boys, is opening his first play [*Things That Go Bump in the Night*]. I'm going and I hate to. It makes me too nervous. It's a dreadful play—not in the writing but in what it says. And I am afraid it is going to get clobbered by the critics. I hope not because it is much too good for that.

So long for now.

Love
John

To Douglas Fairbanks, Jr.
IN LONDON

Sag Harbor
June 20, 1965

Dear Doug:

I propose to make a request of you which I hope you can find it in your heart to grant.

Perhaps you will remember that for at least thirty-five years and maybe longer, I have been submerged in research for a shot at the timeless Morte d'Arthur. Now Intimations of Mortality warn me that if I am ever going to do it, I had better start right away, like next week.

In my research I have been sponsored by the greatest living scholar in the field, Professor Eugène Vinaver, Sorbonne, Vienna, Heidelberg, Cambridge.

Please to remember that not too long ago at your house, I had as dinner partner the Duchess of Buccleuch, and the

822

following passage occurred as nearly as I can remember.

Me: Madame, there must be a number of fascinating libraries hidden away in your various holdings.

She: Yes, I suppose there are.

Me: How many libraries would you say you have?

She: Oh, I don't know. No one in our family has read anything for several hundred years.

Me: Is permission ever given to inspect these libraries?

She: I don't know. What is your interest in the matter?

Me: It is partially selfish, ma'am. I know something about how such libraries came into being. In the fifteenth century, it became fashionable for eminent families to accumulate books and manuscripts. In 1944 at Winchester College, for example, the only known ms. of the Morte d'Arthur was discovered. It had been there for a long time but because its title was Prince Arthur, no one had ever inspected it. I should love to look through the collections of your family to see whether any other manuscripts on these subjects may not be hiding there.

She (with intense boredom): Yes, yes, quite.

At that moment, if you will remember, one of your footmen spilled a tureen of hot soup over Elaine which naturally changed the conversation and we never got back to it.

At a later date I spoke to Professor Vinaver about this exchange. He agreed that there might well be treasures in our field of research to be found in just such places. There are not many families still existing from the fourteenth and fifteenth centuries, but certainly Buccleuch is one of them.

Now finally I am ready to get to my request. Do you feel it is possible to represent to the Duchess that my interest was far from fleeting? Might I ask the privilege of inspecting some of these libraries by Professor Vinaver? If he did come on anything I would instantly fly over to join him.

Will you let me know what you think of this at your earliest? I shall be at the above address all summer. Christmas we go to Galway to be with J. Huston for the holidays. Of course, being so close, we always will go to London.

I hope this finds you prospering.

That's all for right now. I look forward to your reaction.

yours
John

To Elizabeth Otis

Dear Elizabeth:

It is so beautiful a season. Elaine's flowers are beautiful. And I can't find the time to do everything I want to do in the garden. I am protecting and encouraging the grapes you love and there is a sizable crop of them. And by removing some of the shading leaves and bringing the bunches into the open, I think I will be able to make them mature earlier than is usual. Also I am planting a goodly bed of horseradish.

Now, I have something I want to discuss with you.

When I was writing East of Eden, before each day's work as a kind of warm-up I kept a work diary but addressed to Pat. It is perhaps as complete a record of a book as has ever been done. But I had never seen it since I sent it off in handwriting. Pat and I often discussed publishing it either in conjunction with a complete and uncut E. of E. or by itself. Then Pat died and I wondered what would happen to it. Recently I wrote to Pascal Jr. and told him I would like to see it. He sent me a copy and I have just been reading it. And it is much better than I remembered, a little repetitious and perhaps in some places too personal, but I think very interesting *and* book length.

Now it occurs to me that someone is going to publish it some time. It is one hell of a lot better than Henry Miller's letters. I wonder if we should not think of doing it now so that we could take advantage of it if there is any and I do think it would have some currency. Elaine has read it and she agrees. It is a fascinating account of the making of a book. So I am going to give it to Shirley this weekend both to read herself and to take to you to read. And I think it only right that Pascal should edit it. He would do a good and a loving job. Maybe some of the personal things should come out and maybe not. They do give it a bite. [This work-diary was published after Steinbeck's death as *Journal of a Novel.*]

824

The Matter of Arthur moves along slowly as I want it to. I still don't know that I am on the right track. But increasingly I believe that the Matter of Arthur is a personal matter and that its appeal is just that.

I haven't been fishing but when I do get to it I will make you some Pâté Souffleur that you used to like and I can promise you some lovely grapes when they ripen.

I feel fine and part of that I attribute to the fact that you feel good. It comes through in your voice over the telephone.

Love,
John

To Mr. and Mrs. Jack Valenti

Sag Harbor
July 16, 1965

Dear Jack and Mary Margaret:

These are sad days. Adlai Stevenson was a great man and he was my friend. My first reaction to his death was one of rage that Americans had been too stupid to avail themselves of his complete ability. Strange how one thinks of such things.

Adlai always said he needed a gadfly. It is quite different with the President. In one way he has been very unfortunate in that he came in high. Those people who sang so tenderly over his successes, will be the first to get out their stingers at the first hint of a failure. He did not need me during the election although he was kind enough to suggest that I had contributed something. But no man can go through this office without setbacks and the smallest setbacks will draw fire. Also, the ambitious who hoped they could use him for their own purposes, when they find they cannot will poison the air with their rage. It would be perhaps well to say now what is true. Elaine and I do not give our allegiance readily, but once given, we do not withdraw it. I think he should know this. He should also

825

know the power a writer has if he has not over-used or mis-used it.

I hope you do not find me egotistic in giving unsolicited advice. But I do share the worry which must be a matter of terror to any head of state. He must have information, and he must often wonder how accurate the information he gets is. It does seem to me that the weakness of our fact-gathering services does not lie in the gatherings but in their evaluation. Every man is bound to temper his facts to his unchanging personality, background, prejudices and desires. And it is up to a president to evaluate both the man and the facts. It must be almost a matter of nightmare.

Why am I talking at this length, Jack? Well, I'm afraid bad days are coming. There is no way to make the Vietnamese war decent. There is no way of justifying sending troops to another man's country. And there is no way to do anything but praise the man who defends his own land. The real reasons for the war will never come to the surface and if they did most people would not see them. This is primarily a power struggle. The ideal solution for us would be so to shift the war that the Soviet Union would be forced to take a position against China whether openly or secretly and this they would have to do, because I can tell you of my own knowledge that Russia is far more afraid of China than she is of us. Unless the President makes some overt move toward peace, more and more Americans as well as Europeans are going to blame him for the mess, particularly since the government we are supporting with our men and treasure is about as smelly as you can get.

I have a thousand things I would like to talk to you about but if you want me to stop being a gadfly, just let me know and I will stop. We do think kindly on you and Mary Margaret very often. And now I will stop boring the hell out of you and get back to my own work which if successful will succeed in boring people yet unborn or unbored.

Elaine sends love

yours
John

To Carlton A. Sheffield

Sag Harbor
August 5, 1965

Dear Dook:

I can't tell you how good it is to have you back to talk to. Of late years I have had little impulse to explain things to anyone.

First, I think you know that during the two runs for the Presidency of Governor Stevenson, he became my close and valued friend. He was a lovely man. You would have liked him. The fine sharp informed and humorous quality of his mind was unique in public men whom I have met. He was just the kind of man who could sit in the gutter with a glass of wine and discuss things and he often did. During the campaigns he used to say that I was in charge of keeping him off balance, and he insisted that all public servants should be kept off balance all the time. Over the years, he used to drop in at odd times, wherever we might be living. As ambassador to the UN he used to invite us to dinner at the embassy which was a great suite in the Waldorf Towers but on Thursday night. That was servants' night out. Then Elaine and Marietta Tree would cook dinner and there was nobody to overhear. He was a very great man but he was also our friend.

And then suddenly he was dead, and we had that sort of hollow grey feeling in the pit of the stomach. I knew very well that the people who treated him the worst would climb on the bandwagon of mourners. And besides, you may remember that when I am hurt, I do not want to foregather. I want to be alone to lick the wounds. So I was not going to attend any of the baked meats affairs. And then a curious thought came to me. If the thing were reversed, if it had been I for whom the memorial were being held, Guv would be there no matter what trouble or inconvenience it might have been. He would have done me that honor. And so I thought I had to go to the UN memorial service.

That was a Friday and the memorial as well as the funeral were for Monday. Friday night the President called and asked me to go to Camp David for the weekend. I explained that I couldn't because I had to go to the service at the UN. He said, "Don't jump the gun so, I want you and Elaine to go to Bloomington on Monday with me."

He knew exactly what he was doing, and I think he does me the honor of realizing that I would also know. He knew he had mistreated Guv for the last few years and he was trying to make it up. But he also knew that he would be more acceptable to the Stevenson family if Elaine and I went with him, because there had never been any question about where I stood in the Stevenson matter. Anyway I made another attempt to get out of it and he said, "I want to talk to you."

I think you can feel that a Presidential request has somehow the quality of an order.

Anyway we drove to New York at midnight arriving at three. Got up at six and went out to La Guardia to get the ten o'clock plane for Washington. A White House car met us and we whisked in at a quarter to twelve. We left for Camp David at five in the chopper from the lawn.

I had never been to Camp David. It is only twenty minutes from the White House lawn by helicopter. It is very beautiful, a kind of large camp in a deep oak forest on top of a mountain, cool and sunny and wonderful. You can see out over the mountains to Gettysburg. There are individual cabins among the trees so that there is complete privacy. The main lodge is very simple and very comfortable and most meals are taken on a huge veranda overlooking the valley. There is a trout stream and about a hundred yards away a big swimming pool. There is also a bowling alley and a small putting green put in by Eisenhower.

At that point an interruption occurred. Do you remember "a person from Porlock" who interrupted the poem "In Xanadu did Kubla etc."? The poem never got finished.

Mr. Stevenson's funeral was a matter for wordless memory. Tens of thousands of people lining the roads and his casket was the loneliest thing—set off and cut off from everything. The Unitarian service was bleak and grudging. I wanted for him something like the William Byrd mass. Right there I found myself almost saying "I am not a sentimental person—" Haw! My criticism is that this was not sentimental enough. An Irish wake was indicated. Strange how selfish one becomes about one's friends. Elaine is smarter than I am

828

about such things. Once I said to her, "I don't want the barbarity of a funeral for myself." And she said, "Don't be silly. A funeral isn't for the dead. You'll simply be a stage set for a kind of festival maybe. And besides, you won't even be there." Now this makes so much sense to me that I have never mentioned it again. There's a realist talking. Anyway, we got home Monday night. We had been on 8 different air craft since that morning.

My work goes very slowly. I seem to have many "persons from Porlock." Maybe it's that I don't want to do it. We do fool ourselves.

Today is August 12. Elaine's birthday is the 14th, Saturday. I gave her a little swimming pool. Just completed and very pretty. I also made a stepping stone and incised it with Launcelot's last words to Gwinevere—"Ladye, I take reccorde of God, in thee I have myn erthly joye." The pool couldn't be a surprise. You can't sneak a bulldozer on the lawn.

There are times when I wish desperately that you were here to talk to. There are things I can't discuss with anyone else. Something is coming up soon. And I can't discuss it with anyone and I don't quite know what to do about it. [At Camp David the President had asked Steinbeck to go to Vietnam and report to him.] You know how there are things you don't want to do, but you know that failure to do them will make you miserable. Well, I've got a bad one of those. It isn't one of those things you can avoid by doing nothing either. Everything I can think of is against doing it and yet I am afraid I'm going to have to. Damn! I wish I could be decisionless. I won't write it so I don't know why I brought it up. But I do wish I could talk to you. You wouldn't know the answer. The answer is—*don't* do anything you don't *have* to do. But it's that *have* which is so tricky. It always has the concealed card.

Now—so many sentences start with now—it is the next day and a beautiful one full of gold and sun and another day. I've beat around bushes and at last must face the last chapter about The Americans—a most difficult one.

This morning I awakened early, full of continued thinking out of sleep. You know that slow and sometimes excellent thinking. You will understand my reluctance to start when I tell you, this section is to deal with morals—not goody-goody morals—but pragmatic morals. I have floundered about with

it because it has been such a fragmented subject and I want
to put the pieces together. But who am I talking to—Americans? Europeans? or myself. My shadow-of-a-dream thinking said—"Why don't you write it to Dook and keep a copy?
His skepticism will put a bridle on you and the direction will
force you to be clear." Most dream thinking will not stand
daylight scrutiny, but this one does. So I will shift pencils so
I can keep a carbon and fling my chapter at you. And maybe
you will help me with it if I should get out of line. So I will
close and send this letter to you and instantly start another
to you, comprising this essay—and I would love to have your
comments.

Meanwhile love to you.

John

To Max Wagner

[Sag Harbor]
[May 18, 1966]

Dear Max:

Johnny [Catbird] is with us for part of his terminal leave
and he has told us about Jack's death. We didn't know. I am
shocked and sad. And I am concerned that I was not able to
say good-bye to him. He would have hated that but there it
is.

You know how it is, Max—there are some people who are
permanent whether they are here or not and Jack is one of
them. His small and humorous complaints, his bristling temper, and always funny.

It seems to me that not only do we die little by little in our
friends, but that a time and a place also dies slowly like the
closing iris of a camera.

Love to you both,
John

Steinbeck's personal, almost protective relationship with the President has been reflected in these letters. Now his second son's imminent departure for Vietnam with the American forces was to reinforce his feeling of identification and across-the-board support of Presidential policies. To many of his friends and intimates this attitude seemed a change of heart and an abandonment of everything he had stood for. Certainly it caused him increasingly to maintain a stand which the criticism he received for it merely served to strengthen.

To Lyndon B. Johnson

Sag Harbor
May 28, 1966

Dear Mr. President:

I am grateful to you for receiving my son and me. It meant a great deal to both of us and I am sure that seeing you reassured him that responsibility is behind him and backing him. He had never been to Washington before. From the plane I took him first to the Lincoln Memorial. He stood for a long time looking up at that huge and quiet figure and then he said, "Oh! Lord! We had better be great."

You will understand that I am pleased with this boy and proud. He knows what he wants and must do. He is thoroughly trained to do it. He is proud of his uniform and proud of his country. He goes very soon now, and as you must know, my heart goes with him. And I will ask you, Sir, to remember your promise to pray for him.

I know that you must be disturbed by the demonstrations against policy in Vietnam. But please remember that there have always been people who insisted on their right to choose the war in which they would fight to defend their country. There were many who would have no part of Mr. Adams' and George Washington's war. We call them Tories. There were many also who called General Jackson a butcher. Some of these showed their disapproval by selling beef to the British. Then there were the very many who de-

831

nounced and even impeded Mr. Lincoln's war. We call them Copperheads. I remind you of these things, Mr. President, because sometimes, the shrill squeaking of people who simply do not wish to be disturbed must be saddening to you. I assure you that only mediocrity escapes criticism.

Again my thanks to you, Sir. You gave my boy a pediment of pride, and that a good soldier must have.

As always, faithfully,
John Steinbeck

To Elizabeth Otis

Sag Harbor
June 9, 1966

Dear Elizabeth:

As usual, I sit down to write up a novel—and utter panic sets in. All the lovely plans and techniques run away and hide. I haven't the slightest idea what a novel is. A piece of fiction longer than a bread box is as close as I can come.

Then—what is fiction? Is it a true thing that didn't happen as opposed to a false thing that did?

Ninety percent of the items in the morning paper could not be used in a novel because they are false. Can it be that the present popularity of non-fiction lies in the fact that it can recount things not acceptable to fiction readers? Or could it be that fact interpreted becomes fiction. I don't know. The story I want to write is not a new one. I came across it first in the second grade and so did you. I've even taken my title from the first line—"And a piece of it fell on my tail."

This may well be the most widely read story in the English language.

As I remember it—a character named Henny-Penny comes kayoodling and howling out of a cabbage patch. H-P is in a state of shock. The story has the best opening in all literature —"The sky is falling," cried Henny-Penny, "and a piece of it fell on my tail."

832

Now there is no question that H-P truly believes that the sky *is* falling. On the other hand, we in the second grade knew it was not falling because it never had fallen—a conclusion in logic far from tenable. By H-P's very statement it is established that H-P is a fool, and more, an hysterical fool. This is the quickest establishment of character I know.

Our instant perception is verified almost immediately by a person named Chicken Little—an adolescent endowed with the clear vision, the iron nerves and the logical precision of youth. " 'Twas not the sky," said Chicken Little. "It was a piece of cabbage leaf."

In the second grade we, who identified ourselves with clear-eyed Chicken Little, chuckled with pleased recognition. H-P was obviously that nervous and wrong-headed adult we knew so well who screamed at us that if we got our feet wet we'd catch our death. H-P was obviously a feather-brained crier of havoc, an alarmist. In the whole second grade there wasn't one kid who felt anything but contempt for H-P. We were all Chicken Littlers. No, that's wrong. Dorothy Donahue, come to think of it, was an H-P'er. It was Dorothy who always said, "If four of you get on that raft it will sink." Well, so it did. So what? That's what she was—a Henny-Penny, and probably still is.

In the second grade and in the whole world, I guess, no one has ever come to the defense of Henny-Penny. And that should give us some idea of the nature of human observation. "What is" cannot compete with what we want it to be. We wanted H-P to be wrong and as we read, so did the writer of the story.

But let us consider for the sake of contention that she said, "The sky is falling," in a quiet philosophic tone, as though to impart a piece of interesting information and then to cinch her statement, and referring to the scrap of cabbage leaf, she continued, "and a piece of it fell on my tail." This would change the whole direction of the story. Far from establishing Henny-Penny as a fool, it would make her an exact and penetrating observer of external reality.

It is hard to give up a position one established in the second grade. For generations Henny-Penny has been held up to ridicule on the advocacy of Chicken Little. And actually what do we know about Chicken Little except that he jumped to a conclusion without proper preparation?

No, the more one thinks of it, the more the judgment of the

second grade becomes suspect as thoughtless, headlong and perhaps premature. Even in the second grade we should have remembered that it was Dr. C. S. Little who said the Wright Brothers would not get off the ground.

Actually—this so-called child's story turns out on inspection to be one of the most profound explorations of external reality in relation to the cabbage patch of human frailty and emotion. And it does seem to me that before one writes a novel it might be well to consider what a novel is. We will be seeing you on Sunday, and perhaps you can tell me—in case you have found out since I last saw you.

Love,
John

To Elizabeth Otis

Sag Harbor
June 22, 1966

Dear Eliz:

I don't even tell Kazan any more that East of Eden is still paying off. He'd kill himself trying to kick himself in the behind for selling his share.

I'll try to get this Sag piece done for the Post before going on with—My Tail. Going on is an ambitious word. I haven't yet anything to go on from. But I know I'll go on twirling the pencil anyway.

No word from John. He said he would let us know as soon as he had an A.P.O. address. But I know how one gets taken over. On the other hand, he'll be wanting mail. One always does, that far from home.

We have been plagued with wild ducks getting in the swimming pool and getting it filthy. A couple of days ago, though, I mounted a 10-gauge cannon over the pool with a trigger-string going into the house. When six ducks got in the pool I pulled the string and the great explosion went over their heads. Well, you never saw such a reaction. A kind of heart failure set in. They got up in the air and flew in flip-flops, beating the air and getting nowhere. It was glorious. I think we may win this one. Two or three more shots and they may take the hint. Word may be passed in the duck kingdom that they are not popular in our pool.

I shall be delighted to read Margaret Kennedy's view on the novel. I have been thinking about it a lot since I am in process of trying to write one. Once it was a long piece of writing attempting to set down a piece of generalized reality. But as with any form, rules began to be made for it and gradually the rules regulating what is permissible in a novel became so strict that it was forced away from reality. A perfect example of this is the criticism by a Communist of In Dubious Battle—"Even if it happened," he said, "it is not true." And as these rules became more strict, they pressed the novel farther and farther from everyday reality and in the process lost the interest of readers, who flocked to non-fiction which could still deal with what happens.

What I am trying to say, I guess, is that I should write non-fiction with the freedom the novel once had. Regrettable! It is permitted in non-fiction to see a flying saucer, but let anyone imply that "a piece of the sky" etc.—and he will be denounced.

And that is the end of this letter.

Love,
John

To John Steinbeck IV
IN VIETNAM

Sag Harbor
July 16, 1966

Dear John:

I do know what you mean. I remember the same feeling when there were areas of trouble. "What the hell am I doing here? Nobody made me come." On the other hand, when it was over, I was usually glad I had gone. And one other thing. Once it started the blind panic went away and another dimension took its place. Thinking about it afterward I became convinced that there is some kind of built-in anaesthesia that balances and sets the terror back. Another thing that helps is the fact that you aren't alone. And everybody feels just as lousy when it is about to be. I don't know whether or not you took the Sneaky with you—that little leather flask. Fill it with whiskey—brandy is better. And it can be a great comfort to you. There's no law against false courage. It's better than none at all.

Now, let me discuss what you call your compulsion to be miserable. You think you had a choice—that you could just as well be in S. F. with all the amenities, comfort, ease and a certain immunity from gunfire. Well, the fact of the matter with you as well as with me is that there wasn't really any choice. You did and will do what you are. If you had forced yourself to make the opposite choice you would have been in violation of yourself, and I truly believe you would have been much more miserable than you are. Of course I am worried about you, just terribly worried, but I am proud too that you have not violated what you are.

Also check with yourself on this. I know it was true of me. I had deep down convictions that I was a coward. I think everyone has. If I had broken or gone to pieces, I wouldn't have been surprised. But when it came and I didn't go haywire, when I was scared but no more scared than those around me, the sense of relief was like a flood of·compensation. Because I think a good part of this particular fear is a fear of how you will behave. And no one knows for sure, until he has gone through it.

I was horrified when you asked me to get you orders to go out, but I couldn't have failed you there. Do you know, that is the only request I have ever made of the President? The only one. And I was not happy about making it. But if I had had to request that you *not* be sent, I think I would have been far more unhappy.

Please keep in touch. I love you.

Fa

The letters John IV was sending home formed the basis of his book, *In Touch*, later published by Knopf. It affirmed the son's divergence from his father's point of view about the Vietnam war.

To John Steinbeck IV

Sag Harbor
August 16, 1966

Dear John:

Your good long letter arrived yesterday and there is much in it to answer.

You are writing well—good, clean English prose. I thought this was so and let Edward Albee see your letter and he said, "Jesus, this boy can write. This is damn good writing." Just keep doing it the way you are.

Your orphanage and hospital are very exciting. Let me know if there is anything I can do to help. I agree that the less government, the better. There is no reason why the Vietnamese should trust any government with their history. Hell, we don't really trust ours. But, would it make any sense if I tried to tap private sources for money for your orphanage? Would it make sense if the Authors' League or the Dramatists Guild or Actors Studio, for that matter, Actors Union—Stage Hands, etc.—couldn't they, as private organizations, endow beds, or adopt a wing and support it? If you, and your friends, think well of this and could give me some plans and programs, I could turn it loose among people who really care.

Now for the last, and I confess to a certain shyness about discussing it. I remember our talk about my going over. And you mention it in your letter. Wouldn't this seem to you a little like "getting in the act"? It seems to me that for years I have been getting in your act, and I know you resented it, as well you might, although at the time I didn't know what else to do. Now this is very private. You are doing just great on your own. Wouldn't my coming over inhibit you? There are those on this side who think it would. There is always this damp cloud of publicity which follows me. I hate it. It makes people put on an act for me. They change. On the other hand, on the Charley trip when I was out of context, no one either recognized me or gave a damn and it was wonderful. I believe that if I went over quietly, without ballyhoo and did no writing while I was there, not a soul would bother. Newsday would send me on any terms I want to make. But I want you to tell me what you think.

Bill Attwood, the new Editor-in-Chief of Look, wants me to spend a week with the President and write his daily routine. I think it is a lousy idea. He has too much exposure already. In my opinion he should lie low for a while. So I don't intend to do that but I will have to see him to tell him why.

Let me know your thinking as soon as possible.

Edward Albee asked for your address. You know, you don't have to write letters. Just send postcards.

Love, and write soon.

Fa

The suggestion that Steinbeck visit Vietnam had been made a long time before. His feelings about going had undergone many changes. As far back as August 1965—when the President had first broached the subject—he wrote Howard Gossage:

"I'm not draft age, drat it! If only I were, I could probably duck it. But being re-tired and re-treaded and wheezy and crippled, I'll probably have to go. Life is very hard and very confusing sometimes."

And to Harry F. Guggenheim, publisher of *Newsday:*

"I hope the Far Eastern thing is over as far as I am concerned. Certainly I had no wish to go, but the request had the force of an order, one which I hope is unnecessary. I do hope so."

When finally he did go he went, not as a representative of the President, but as a correspondent for *Newsday.* He was approaching his sixty-fifth birthday, and had taken a stand that he communicated to Willard Bascom:

"I am not going places any more without Elaine. Life is too short to be away from her. But I must say one thing. She'll go anywhere and lick the other dog when she gets there."

To Elia Kazan

[New York]
October 28, 1966

Dear Gadg:

As you may be aware, I've been having a bad time—work unacceptable, to me, and a strong feeling that my time was over. I brooded a lot because both in breadth and depth I had lost touch with this time and was and am abysmally ignorant of a great part of the world—the whole eastern half.

Now Harry Guggenheim wants us to go to the East. Take our time, go where we want and stay as long as we want to. And it's like a new life to me.

We don't know when we will start but it won't be long. I think we will go first to Vietnam because I think one phase of that war is nearly over. But afterwards the other parts— Malaysia, Indonesia, India, Pakistan, and of course Japan.

The reason I am writing is that we would like to join up with you along the way, particularly Japan which you already know. And maybe you would like to go to some of the others with us. What do you think?

Let me hear from you.

Yours,
John

To Lyndon B. Johnson

New York
November 28, 1966

Dear Mr. President:

I am sorry not to be able to attend the dinner for the Arts Council but as of December 1 we take off for East Asia on a long and, I hope, rewarding trip starting in Saigon. There we will see my young son John, and in California we will see my older son Thom who is now in the army and in training at Ft. Ord. And, since I have now reactivated my old war correspondent's card, we are all involved, and that's as it should be.

My compliments, Sir, and our love to you and your family. And if I can be of service to you or to the nation, it is offered with a whole heart.

Yours,
John Steinbeck

To Harry F. Guggenheim

[Caravelle Hotel]
[Saigon]
January 4, 1967

PRIVATE AND PERSONAL PLEASE

Dear Harry:

I have asked you for some very unusual things during our association. Now I want to ask about a possibility. I've been out in the really hairy boondocks, in the waist-deep paddies where your boots suck in mud that holds like glue. The patrols go on at night now down in the Delta area and are really ambushes set up against the V.C. There are caches of weapons everywhere and very few of them are found. All a running V.C. has to do is to sink his weapons in a ditch or in a flooded paddy and later return and retrieve them.

Yesterday, I was out with a really good bunch of men. We climbed out of ditches, went through houses, questioned people. We came on one cache of weapons and ammunition in the bottom of a ditch. They smear grease on the guns and seal the shells in jugs. Every house in the area is surrounded by water—in fact the raised place where the house and its garden stand are made by dredging up the mud in baskets and piling it up to dry to a platform. Our men were moving slowly along in the water feeling for weapons on the muddy bottom —a slow and very fallible method.

The C. O. is a Lt. Col. Hyatt, fine fellow, young and intelligent. I told him about something I use on my dock at Sag Harbor. It is a five-pound Alnico horseshoe-shaped magnet that will lift about a hundred pounds. If anything metallic falls off the dock I tie a line to the magnet and drop it to the bottom. I've brought up everything from a pair of pliers to an outboard motor with it. Dragged along these ditches and paddies, it would locate arms that are now missed. But such ideas submitted to the high command rarely get implemented. And surely Col. Hyatt knew it. So I engaged to try to get him a magnet to try out. Of course, if it brings up anything, he can then requisition them.

The other thing is more serious and more sensitive. As you must know, the V.C. are tough and secret. When one is taken he refuses to talk at all. And it's on information that our lives depend, where are the rest hidden, how many are there— what weapons, what plan of attack, where are the claymore mines set, where are the booby traps? Answers to these questions could save a great many of our kids' lives.

Yesterday I remembered something from the past. Did you ever see scopolamine used, Harry? I have. First it was called twilight sleep and later truth serum. It doesn't make a man or woman tell the truth, but it makes him a compulsive talker. He just can't shut up. It relaxes the inhibitions, causes boastful thinking and everything comes out. Now Col. Hyatt says if he had access to such an injection he thinks he could cut his casualties at least 50 percent. And I have no compunction about using any method whatever to that end.

841

I am marking this private and very personal but of course Bill Moyers [soon to become publisher of *Newsday*] can see it. But I wouldn't let it go farther.

Please let me hear from you.

Yours,
John

To Elizabeth Otis

Saigon
January 11, 1967

Dear E. O.:

I haven't written because I have been moving so fast and writing my heart out when I can catch the time.

I have one more week and a very full one, many missions but next Wednesday—Jan. 18—we are flying to Bangkok. I will complete the war pieces there. I've seen just about every part of the country now, every kind of fighting and every kind of equipment except for several which I will see in my last week.

There is so much here that there is little time for sleep. That can come later. And I never felt better in my life.

Your letters gratefully received. But N. Y. seems very far away. I find I'm putting most things in the copy I'm sending.

Love to all there. And I'll try to write from Bangkok.

Love,
John

To Elizabeth Otis

Bangkok
January 23, 1967

Dear E. O.:

It is a very long time since I have written but I have been trying unsuccessfully to keep up with the work it seems I should do. So many things attract me and there just isn't time to put them down.

I may have come out of Vietnam too soon. I have a sense of unfinished business there, but I have kept the open visa so that I can go back if it appears good. It was hard on Elaine there and I was and am very proud of her for going. Staying in Saigon alone is kind of awful. But she did it and of course she knows the city far better than I do. I was hardly ever there.

Bangkok is perfectly lovely to look at. Maybe any place would be after Saigon. This hotel is a dream of heaven. They have us in a royal suite overlooking the river. Turns out it is the same suite Somerset Maugham lived in years ago. I haven't gone out much. Came over the border with so much left to write that I have been chained to the desk. Things have a way of dimming if they aren't done at once, particularly things as subtle as the small pictures of war.

Next week we are going to the northeast. The V.C. are beginning to dig in there.

We have been singularly well. E. got a spreading itch on her face which worried her. A local doctor took one look at it and said she must have been brushed by a white moth which carries a poison in the powder on its wings. He gave her a salve which relieved it immediately. It smells like gentian and probably is. This interests me, because if one moth has this strong effect, perhaps others have a lesser one which would account for the fear and even horror some people have for moths. So many interesting things I am learning.

And it's time now for me to get to work if I am to finish

before 11 o'clock when Elaine files my copy with Pan American.

Love,
John

Maybe when I get the immediacy of this war stuff down I can slow up and stop going at a dead run. But I must admit I never felt better in my life. This is crazy but true.

Again love,
John

To Elizabeth Otis

Penang
February 27, 1967

Dear E. O.:

As E. will doubtless have told you, we are stopping here for a little rest before going on. The nine days in Laos were particularly exhausting. Covered the country in every kind of aircraft. There are no roads and large sections of the country are held by their own brand of V.C. called Pathet Lao, armed, ordered and instructed just like all the rest. But murderous little buggers when they get around to it.

Then flew back to Bangkok for one night because we had an audience with the King and Queen. Then that same afternoon on a train and 27 hours down the Malay Peninsula to Penang. Shades of Warren Hastings, Lord Cornwallis, Kipling and Somerset Maugham. Huge room in the Eastern and Oriental Hotel and air conditioned and suddenly the three months caught up with me and I fell to pieces.

Slept all night and the next day and the next night. Tried to work, to write the Laos stuff, but no go. Yesterday a little better luck. I got two pieces written and one or two to go but today—nothing. I seem to be just written out. I've sent 52 pieces since Dec. 1. Awful lot. Anyway, I'm in a great big slump, pooped and worn out. I was going to fight away at the ms. all day and then decided the hell with it. What in the devil am I running for?

February 28

Your birthday wire came today and I do thank you. First time I ever had one run two days. It was the 27th yesterday here and today there. Shirley will be mad with envy.

Anyway, by now I have had some rest and have even got some copy written. But at first I was really dried up.

I guess I am homesick today because I can't keep my mind off all of you and of course Angel. And I am wondering if my pier is standing the ice and whether the holly trees will survive. That's always a sign.

This is a most beautiful and benign island and we have got rested here. Last evening we drove out to Lone Pine—about 10 miles—and had dinner and a bottle of Chateauneuf du Pape for toasting purposes. Elaine is working at her letter, cursing the while. I haven't seen it yet but I'll bet it is good. [McCall's had asked Elaine Steinbeck for a piece on Vietnam.]

Wednesday we are renting a car to drive two days to Singapore.

Oh, I'm feeling so much better for a little rest. But in Singapore I must find a dentist. Dropped a filling and it aches some.

This little interval has been great for both of us.

Love to all there and thank you for my cable.

Love,
John

To Elizabeth Otis

Jakarta
March 18, 1967
Dear Eliz.:

Yesterday was St. Patrick's Day here in Jakarta, so right now today the glory and the earnest sleaze of the New York Irish are forming in the back streets to boast about and to be homesick for a place that never existed. I only wrote that to put this letter in time. In place, we are back in Jakarta, having spent a little time in Bali, without question the most beautiful place I have ever seen and the nicest people.

Elizabeth! I can't tell you how glad I am and proud too that you all like Elaine's piece. [*McCall's* published it later in the year.] I thought it was wonderful, but then I think she is too. You know how she is, digging her toe and protesting like a roopy old chicken that she can't write. Yesterday she kept saying, "But I'm an amateur," until finally I had to say, "So was Madame de Sevigné, so was everybody once, but I'm afraid you have lost that excuse now."

Not only do I have a sense of conclusion but also I am a little homesick and also I am desperately tired of people in the large and faceless mass. So after Japan we will be going home and I guess that will be in the last quarter of April or the early part of May. This has been worth doing, to me at least, and I think to Elaine. We are even closer than we were. Rough times have a way of doing that.

Love to all there,
John

From Hong Kong in March he summarized the experience in Asia for friends in Sag Harbor, Mr. and Mrs. Lawrence Smith:

846

"This has been a good trip and in many ways a sad one. I haven't dwelt on the killed and the wounded. I've seen other wars and have hated those too. But every dead G.I. (and many of them have been my friends) breaks your heart in a way that can never be repaired. If I could shorten this war by one hour by staying here, I would never come home."

Steinbeck's back began to trouble him in Hong Kong, and over Memorial Day weekend in Sag Harbor, the condition became acute. After being hospitalized in New York for observation, he returned to Long Island for the summer. During these days of pain and inactivity, his thinking about the war continued to undergo a slow change.

To Elizabeth Otis

Sag Harbor
August 31, 1967
Thursday

Dear Eliz.:

I know I have been greatly remiss about writing or even communicating, but this has been so in all directions. It starts with the stupid or wise feeling that I have nothing I can or want to communicate—a dry as dust, worked-out feeling. The only simile I can think of is those mountains of mine, tailings from which every vestige of value has been drawn. Some people, I know, rework the tailings and get a small amount of very low grade ore.

Now—I can't tell whether what I write is old or new. Surely the forms I am accustomed to are no longer admired—are, in fact, period pieces, only interesting if they were written a long time ago. Recently I read T. Wilder's new book [*The Eighth Day*] and found it tedious. I should reread the earlier ones to see whether it is true of the whole approach. Also I have been reading some of the new ones and most of these I find interesting and ridiculous. I have never known a time when writers were so egocentric. The hippies constantly talk about being "turned on," when it seems to me obvious that they are turned off and want it that way. Out of this movement something will come probably; but what, it is not now apparent.

I do not mean to imply to you that I have been sitting out here pitying myself. But I am conditioned as a writer and I have been finding it impossible to write. The words will not form or if they do, there is no flavor nor any joy in them. The pain from spine and legs has been quite sharp but I halfway believe that the pain and the verbal impotence are a part of one thing in spite of what the X-rays say. Strange, isn't it, that none of this happened until after I left Vietnam? I have seriously considered going back there to get rid of my devils, but so far that would only be repetition.

I understand your feeling about this war. We seem to be sinking deeper and deeper into the mire. It is true that we are. I am pretty sure by now that the people running the war have neither conception nor control of it. And I think that I do have some conception but I can't write it.

I know we cannot win this war, nor any war for that matter. And it seems to me that the design is for us to sink deeper and deeper into it, more and more of us. When we have put down a firm foundation of our dead and when we have by a slow, losing process been sucked into the texture of Southeast Asia, we will never be able nor will we want to get out.

If we should win this war, in the old sense of defeating and deadening the so-called enemy, then we would become just another occupying army, and such an army loses contact with the place occupied. But we are *not* winning in that sense and we will not. In many directions we are being defeated by more successful techniques and attitudes than our own. We have no choice in the matter.

If we won we could reject but by partially losing or at best just holding our own, *we* are learning and absorbing. Maybe it is the unformulated sense of this that causes so many men to extend their tour. Something new is happening to them. The French could not change and so they were kicked out, but thousands of our men are changing very rapidly—giving a little but taking a lot. And unless something I cannot conceive should happen—we are there permanently, not as conquerors but as migrants. And when migrants move in they take what they can get but they deposit what they have.

The elections are a joke. They mean nothing in themselves. They are a sop thrown to our Congress for purposes of getting more money. The leaders are venial and short-sighted, but that doesn't make any difference. In the pages of the East Asian history book, it will be forgotten that the elections are false and foolish.

I don't know whether or not I told you, but the last time I was in Washington and staying at the White House I had a long and early breakfast with the President and I told him what I thought we are doing wrong and made suggestions for correcting our errors, all based on winning this war. He listened carefully, asked a few questions and asked me to stay over and meet his men at noon. Then I saw McNamara, Rusk, Humphrey and several others and went over the ground again. They listened and made no comment but McNamara asked me to write it down. I couldn't, so I made a tape of it, which he took to Vietnam on his last trip. Recently he telephoned to say that he had put my suggestions before the field men—that they had accepted some of them and rejected others. It seems to me that the rejected ones were the most important. I would not write what my suggestions were but I would tell them to you. Or maybe I have, or maybe I am right now repeating myself. It is very odd—not to know.

Maybe I should go back. I seem to be becoming a vegetable here and now, thinking little thoughts or no thoughts at all, and I am sure boring the hell out of Elaine. She is conducting a business as usual campaign but with me it is not business as usual. The constant rain is getting tiresome. One can find so many pains when the rain is falling. And I seem to have lost touch with things. This is the first letter I have written in nearly two months. And it is not that I am obsessed with myself. The opposite seems to be true. I cannot seem to draw my mind back to myself. Maybe that is what the pain is trying to do—but it is failing. But the curious retirement to the cave has given me no direction to follow. There is something sly about the whole thing, as though I were the butt of an ancient practical joke.

Anyway, I'll try to keep in touch from here on in—I hope.

Love,
John

In the autumn his back condition worsened, and he underwent surgery for a spinal fusion—

"A really massive job of surgery," as he wrote John Kenneth Galbraith in mid-November from the University Hospital. "Damned X-ray looked like a snake fence after a tornado."

The operation was successful. As Elaine Steinbeck reported to the Montgomerys at the same time:

"Of course he is flat on his back except for three short walks across his room each day. Learning to walk again is a very painful process, but he is of good heart."

To Carlton A. Sheffield

POSTCARD

New York
January 29, 1968

Dear Dook:

I am gradually coming back or ahead or something. The nervous shock as well as all the sedatives kind of move you into another and rather fuzzy reality. But healing is a slow process except that I know when the process is complete, I will have a stronger back than I ever had. I haven't written because it is only recently that I could sit in a chair with any comfort and I dare you to write lying flat on your back. I tried and it doesn't work. Meanwhile I am trying to regroup as does a military unit that has been shot to pieces. Trying to determine if and what I have left to write. Maybe something, maybe not, but if not, then there was no point in the surgery. I'll try more later.

Love,
John

To Carlton A. Sheffield

New York
March 23, 1968

Dear Dook:

Starting a letter for me is no guarantee of finishing it. My intentions are impeccable but my performance lousy. I think these miserable nerves have not yet grabbed hold and taken their jobs seriously. Without warning, energy and with it intention, just dim and float away. This seems to be the era of lethargy. It's a drained feeling and I almost enjoy it. Of late years I have come to have a loathing for the mail. 99% of it consists of requests which have the overtones of demands. And even if I have not complied with many, I have had some kind of guilt feeling about the rest. Now I can simply sigh, "Bugger off!" and deposit the whole worm bucket in the waste basket.

I know what you mean about television. I usually look at news or world events and baseball in season sometimes, but that's about all. In the hospital while I was immobilized I had a little set which was designed to amuse me but I found myself turning it off to escape it. Actually my head doesn't work so very well. I seem to be pushing clouds ahead of me. I understand this is normal and even if it weren't, it's not unpleasant. Pretty soon I will be going to the country to sit in the sun and maybe take my boat out and to do a little fishing with no interest in catching anything. I like that. And if I go alone, I don't even have to talk.

I wish I could get excited about the election. The direction will change slightly, no matter who is in charge. This whole Asian activity seems to me to have grown and been directed by itself without much guidance. It kind of evolved. And maybe it will mutate. The greatest good for the greatest number is far from being a natural or immutable rule. In fact the opposite has seemed in the past to apply. The fact that I know what we are doing wrong does not imply that I could do it right. Were I in charge, I would probably do exactly the same thing on the lowest level. The highest level seems

851

to be out of everyone's hands.

Thom is ticketed for Vietnam April 1st. John is busily proving that our troops are all pot heads, and finding a ready market for his wares. In the British navy in 1812 he could prove that they were all rummies. Anyway, he's got his cause. If he were a pacifist, it would be different, but he's not. [When John returned from Vietnam and was released from the Army, he became one of the leaders of the peace movement.] Thom is scared to go and I don't blame him. I was scared when I was there. Be silly not to be. I don't know how I got into this discussion. I don't know any more than the people making the mistakes.

Well, I got that much written. Elaine blooms and pretty soon I had better.

Yours
John

It's later now and my hand is still wiggling like a chopped snake. Remember how the tripod on the Weejee board staggered around? News this morning that Tal Lovejoy fell down and injured herself and died. What a sadness. The last few times I have seen her there was an air of sadness around her. It's terrible to survive everything you knew and loved. Everything and everyone went away from her and left her alone in the woods.

Here in New York we live 34 floors up with the whole city below our windows. It is a slender tower and there is an up-draft around the building like a chimney. Right now it is snowing but snowing up because of this up-draft. A startling thing to see. This is what Elaine's great-aunt used to call "The Easter spell." The Old Farmer's Almanac says for these days in March—"Storms for sure of poor man's manure." That's snow. Did you know it? I didn't, being brought up without snow. But it works. A late snow makes things grow like mad. Here in my work room I have a sill garden. Four cucumber plants growing in pill bottles and one flourishing English Oak I grew from an acorn I picked up in Somerset. I seem to require something growing. The cucumbers are just silly but I'll plant the oak at Sag Harbor. I have two English oaks out there I raised from acorns. They are about four feet high now. They are named Gog and Magog. Of course there are seventy or more American oaks on our point but I try to keep young ones coming. I don't know why. If the old farmer is correct—and he usually is—it's going to be a very rough spring. But why am I writing about weather? I'm just writing silliness now. So I will stop.

Again
John

At a restaurant in Sag Harbor—once again it was Memorial Day weekend—Steinbeck had what was probably a small stroke—a momentary one, which did not incapacitate him mentally or physically. There followed a brief hospitalization and tests in Southampton Hospital. He was totally aware of what had happened to him, though for friends—like Alexander Knox, the writer and actor, and his wife Doris who were living in London—he presented it slightly differently.

To Mr. and Mrs. Alexander Knox

Sag Harbor
June 24, 1968

Dear Alex and Doris:

More and more I am guiltier and guiltier of being remisser and remisser about answering letters I really want to answer. I place them in a neat pile and when the pile gets high enough the whole thing slides to the floor. Alex's good letter was placed on top, with the result that when the pile slid to the floor, it lost precedence. Thank goodness it was on both sides of the same sheet. I know that this is no way to run an office or anything else. God! I'm getting so slipshod. My mind resists any kind of order at all. I think this is the simple deterioration of age. I hope it is anyway.

This has been a year during which I have been a nuisance to myself and to everyone else. Last autumn my back finally succumbed to having been kicked around too much. Three wonderful surgeons built me a new back, a painful process but worth it. But the recovery takes time and I am an impatient type. Then a quick spell of some kind of lung infection with oxygen tents and the lot. All in all I haven't been a joye to the Feyre Eleyne this past year but she has been a nicely modelled tower of strength to me. Now one more sentence about myself and I'll have done. The self-care and indulgence and that sort of thing have left me, now that it is no longer necessary, so damned lazy that I am good for nothing.

I should get to work, I know, and I don't want to. I think the world, not only America, is in a state of very rapid change and I cannot foresee the direction it will take, but I deeply fear that it will get worse before it gets better. My impulse is not to yap about it but to sit very quietly and watch it happen.

I think I know the causes but not the effects. What I do know is that the people most actively involved do not know either the causes nor the effects.

Meanwhile we sit out here at Sag Harbor and it is a very lovely time; the gardens going like fire and the summer coming sweetly in. We have loose plans for next winter. Around Christmas we rather plan to go to England and soon after the first of the year to take a look at the animals in Central Africa where neither of us has ever been, a real dry safari without either gun or camera. I just want to see them while both of us are unextinct.

And I think that is all for right now. We will hope to see you next winter.

Yours,
John

In July he had an episode of heart failure and was rushed to Southampton Hospital. A few days later he was brought by ambulance to New York Hospital where he suffered another and more severe attack.

To Carlton A. Sheffield

POSTCARD

New York
August 17, 1968

Dear Dook:

Your letter this morning. I don't know how that item got out [about his serious illness]. I seem to be doing pretty well. Got home from the hospital two days ago and am going back to Sag Harbor next Wednesday. There's a whole vocabulary in this field—"incidents," "episodes." I forget which I had and don't much care. But whether or not I like it, I seem to be getting better. I'll write you on the machine when I get back to the country.

love
John

The return to Sag Harbor was against medical counsel, but Steinbeck wished it so fervently that, after his wife had learned the nursing routine, they went back and stayed there for two months.

Four years earlier, on the retirement of his previous physician, he had become a patient of his friend, Dr. Denton Sayer Cox, whose custom it is with all new patients to submit a detailed questionnaire for a "Personal Health History." On the final page it makes the request: "Please add any other data you think may be of importance." Steinbeck wrote a letter.

To Dr. Denton Sayer Cox

New York
March 5, 1964

Dear Denny:

I have been filling out my mortal record called a medical passport. There it is—all down there—the past and the future just as plain as the varicosities on my mother's legs and my father's vascular difficulties. There is one thing pleasantly unconfusing about medicine. The direction and the end are fixed and the patient never works backward.

It does occur to me that clear as this picture is, there may be other matters, some taken for granted and others ignored intentionally or otherwise. What is the reason for having a doctor at all? It is a very recent conception. I suppose the present day reason from the patient's point of view is to get through his life with as little pain and confusion as possible and out of it neatly and decently. But for the duration the doctor is supposed to listen to frustrations and to cater to various whims of the central nervous system. I am interested in the line in this thesis of disintegration which indicates that on request, you will keep me in sweet ignorance of what is happening to me. I know it is desired in many cases but I can't understand it from my viewpoint.

What do I want in a doctor? Perhaps more than anything else—a friend with special knowledge. If you had never dived and I were with you, it would be my purpose to instruct you in the depths and dangers, of the pleasant and the malign. I guess I mean the same thing somewhat. We are so made that rascally, unsubtle flares may cause a meaningless panic whereas a secret treason may be nibbling away, unannounced or even pleasant as in the rapture of the deep. Two kinds of pain there are—or rather a number of kinds. I think especially of the teaching pain which counsels us not to hurt ourselves as opposed to the blast that signals slow or fast disintegration. Unskilled, we do not know the difference and, I am told, even the skilled lose their knowledge when the thing is in themselves. It seems to me that one would prepare

856

oneself differently to meet these two approaches, if one knew.

Then there is the signal for the curtain. I think, since the end is the same, that the chief protagonist should have the right to judge his exit, if he can, taking into consideration his survivors who are after all, the only ones who matter.

Then there is the daily regimen and I have always considered this a fake in most people—the diet, the exercise, the pills, the rest, the elimination. It is probably true that careful following of learned instructions will prolong a usually worthless life, but it has been my observation that by the time the subject needs such advice, he is too firmly fixed in his habits to take it. Oh! he'll do it for a while, but he soon slips back and that is probably a good thing. Pills he will take but little else unless terror should get to him, in which case, many men and women become voluntary invalids and soon find that they love it.

Of course I love to fool myself as well as the next person, but not to the point where I find it ridiculous. I am trying to give you a graph, Denny, so that you will know what you are dealing with.

I do not think of pain as a punishment and I will avoid it as much as I can. On the other hand, to use a common experience, I would rather have the quick and disappearing pain of the dentist's chair than the drawn out misery of wearing-off novocaine. In most cases, I have been able to separate what hurts from fear of what might hurt.

In reporting effects I am reasonably honest. It is difficult to remember after any trouble has passed. Lastly, I do not find illness an eminence, and I do not understand how people can use it to draw attention to themselves since the attention they draw is nearly always reluctantly given and unpleasantly carried out.

I dislike helplessness in other people and in myself, and this is by far my greatest fear of illness.

Believe me, I would not go on in this vein, and never do, were it not for the nature of this communication.

I shall probably not change my habits very much unless incapacity forces it. I don't think I am unique in this.

Now finally, I am not religious so that I have no apprehension of a hereafter, either a hope of reward or a fear of punishment. It is not a matter of belief. It is what I feel to be true from my experience, observation and simple tissue feeling.

857

Secondly—I have had a good span of life so that from now on in I should not feel short-changed.

Thirdly—I have lived very fully and vividly and there is no possibility of cosmic pique.

Fourthly—I have had far more than my share of the things men strive for—material things and honors and love.

Fifthly, my life has been singularly free of illness or accident. At any rate the wellness has far overbalanced the sicknesses.

Sixthly—I do not come to you as a sick man.

Oh! I know the heart syncopates and I have fainted twice in my life and a stretch of overindulgence blocked my gall bladder a couple of times, but all in all I am remarkably healthy. And I know that because my curiosity has in no way abated. And as I said before, I would rather live more fully and for a shorter time.

And now the last thing you should know. I love Elaine more than myself. Her well being and comfort and happiness are more important than my own. And I would go to any length to withhold from her any pain or sorrow that is not needful for her own enrichment.

I hope this is of some value to you. Now, we go on from there.

Yours
John

The approaching moment had been in his mind for a long time. Seven years earlier, he had written to his boyhood friend, John Murphy:

858

To John Murphy

Sag Harbor
June 12, 1961

Dear John:

All my life has been aimed at one book and I haven't started it yet. The rest has all been practice. Do you remember the Arthurian legend well enough to raise in your mind the symbols of Launcelot and his son Galahad? You see, Launcelot was imperfect and so he never got to see the Holy Grail. So it is with all of us. The Grail is always one generation ahead of us. But it is there and so we can go on bearing sons who will bear sons who may see the Grail. This is a most profound set of symbols.

The setting down of words is only the final process. It is possible, through accident, that the words for my book may never be set down but I have been working and studying toward it for over forty years. Only the last of the process waits to be done—and it scares the hell out of me. Once the words go down—you are alone and committed. It's as final as a plea in court from which there is no retracting. That's the lonely time. Nine tenths of a writer's life do not admit of any companion nor friend nor associate. And until one makes peace with loneliness and accepts it as a part of the profession, as celibacy is a part of priesthood, until then there are times of dreadful dread. I am just as terrified of my next book as I was of my first. It doesn't get easier. It gets harder and more heartbreaking and finally, it must be that one must accept the failure which is the end of every writer's life no matter what stir he may have made. In himself he must fail as Launcelot failed—for the Grail is not a cup. It's a promise that skips ahead—it's a carrot on a stick and it never fails to draw us on. So it is that I would greatly prefer to die in the middle of a sentence in the middle of a book and so leave it as all life must be—unfinished. That's the law, the great law. Principles of notoriety or publicity or even public acceptance do not apply. Greatness is not shared by a man who is great. And by the same token—if he should want it —he can't possibly get near it.

Yours,
John

As recently as the trip to Asia, he had written to Elizabeth Otis:

To Elizabeth Otis

Jakarta
March 18, 1967

I look forward to Sag Harbor—after seeing you, of course. And, do you know, journalism, even my version of it, gives me the crazy desire to go out to my little house on the point, to sharpen fifty pencils, and put out a yellow pad. Early in the morning to hear what the birds are saying and to pass the time of day with Angel and then to hitch up my chair to my writing board and to set down the words—"Once upon a time. . . ."

Long after the organized search for correspondence for this book had ended, Elaine Steinbeck happened upon this unfinished letter to Elizabeth Otis under the blotter on her husband's work table in Joyous Garde, the little house on the point at Sag Harbor. It was almost certainly his last letter.

Oct. 1968

Dear Elizabeth:

I have owed you this letter for a very long time — but my fingers have avoided the pencil as though it were an old and poisoned tool

Steinbeck

Appendix
Index

Appendix

Unless otherwise specified, these letters were written by John Steinbeck. The recipient's name, the point of origin of the letter, its date, and its provenance are presented in that order.

The letters to Carlton A. Sheffield, Webster F. Street, Carl Wilhelmson, Harry F. Guggenheim, and the Wagner family, which are listed throughout as in The Stanford University Libraries, were given to the editors directly by the recipients or their heirs who still owned them at the time of the preparation of this book.

1923–1932

866

9   *I worked for* . . . GRAHAM WATSON. Sag Harbor. July 2, 1956. Himself.

10   CARLTON A. SHEFFIELD to ELAINE STEINBECK. Los Altos Hills, California. October 1974. Elaine Steinbeck.

10   CARLTON A. SHEFFIELD. Lake Tahoe. February 25, 1928. The Stanford University Libraries.

12   RUTH CARPENTER SHEFFIELD. New York. June 1926. The Stanford University Libraries.

15   A. GROVE DAY. San Francisco. November 1929. Himself.

16   AMASA MILLER. San Francisco. November 1929. Himself.

17   A. GROVE DAY. San Francisco. December 5, 1929. Himself.

19   A. GROVE DAY. San Francisco. December 1929. Himself.

20   *Remember the days* . . . MERLE ARMITAGE. New York. December 31, 1946. Clifton Waller Barrett Library of American Literature, University of Virginia.

20   AMASA MILLER. Eagle Rock. Early 1930. Himself.

21   CARL WILHELMSON. Eagle Rock. Early 1930. The Stanford University Libraries.

23   AMASA MILLER. Eagle Rock. 1930. Himself.

23   AMASA MILLER. Eagle Rock. May 28, 1930. Himself.

25   AMASA MILLER. Eagle Rock. 1930. Himself.

26   AMASA MILLER. Eagle Rock. August 6, 1930. Himself.

27   CARLTON A. SHEFFIELD to ELAINE STEINBECK. Los Altos Hills, California. 1973. Elaine Steinbeck.

27   AMASA MILLER. Pacific Grove. Summer 1930. Himself.

28   *She grows visibly* . . . CARL WILHELMSON. Pacific Grove. October 1930. The Stanford University Libraries.

29   CARL WILHELMSON. Pacific Grove. Late 1930. The Stanford University Libraries.

30   CARL WILHELMSON. Pacific Grove. Late 1930. The Stanford University Libraries.

32   AMASA MILLER. Pacific Grove. December 1930. Himself.

33   GEORGE ALBEE. Pacific Grove. January 1931. The Bancroft Library, University of California, Berkeley.

34   GEORGE ALBEE. Pacific Grove. 1931. The Bancroft Library, University of California, Berkeley.

35   GEORGE ALBEE. Pacific Grove. February 27, 1931. The Bancroft Library, University of California, Berkeley.

37   GEORGE ALBEE. Pacific Grove. Spring 1931. The Bancroft Library, University of California, Berkeley.

37   AMASA MILLER. Pacific Grove. June 1931. Himself.

39   AMASA MILLER. Pacific Grove. 1931. Himself.

40   GEORGE ALBEE. Pacific Grove. May 1931. The Bancroft Library, University of California, Berkeley.

42   MAVIS MCINTOSH. Pacific Grove. May 8, 1931. McIntosh and Otis.

44   AMASA MILLER. Pacific Grove. 1931. Himself.

45 MAVIS MCINTOSH. Pacific Grove. August 18, 1931. McIntosh and Otis.

46 GEORGE ALBEE. Pacific Grove. 1931. The Bancroft Library, University of California, Berkeley.

47 GEORGE ALBEE. Pacific Grove. 1931. The Bancroft Library, University of California, Berkeley.

47 ELAINE STEINBECK. Sag Harbor. September 5, 1963. Herself.

48 GEORGE ALBEE. Pacific Grove. 1931. The Bancroft Library, University of California, Berkeley.

49 GEORGE ALBEE. Pacific Grove. 1931. The Bancroft Library, University of California, Berkeley.

51 AMASA MILLER. Pacific Grove. December 1931. Himself.

52 MAVIS MCINTOSH. Pacific Grove. January 25, 1932. McIntosh and Otis.

53 AMASA MILLER. Pacific Grove. February 16, 1932. Himself.

54 AMASA MILLER. Pacific Grove. February 27, 1932. Himself.

55 GEORGE ALBEE. Pacific Grove. March 1932. The Bancroft Library, University of California, Berkeley.

1932-1936

57 ROLAND DICKEY. New York. December 7, 1956. Steinbeck File.

59 GEORGE ALBEE. Pacific Grove. March 1932. The Bancroft Library, University of California, Berkeley.

60 AMASA MILLER. Pacific Grove. March 14, 1932. Himself.

61 GEORGE ALBEE. Pacific Grove. March 1932. The Bancroft Library, University of California, Berkeley.

62 AMASA MILLER. Pacific Grove. Spring 1936. Himself.

62 ROBERT O. BALLOU. Pacific Grove. June 10, 1932. Elizabeth Otis.

64 *A year ago* . . . CARLTON A. SHEFFIELD. Pacific Grove. 1932. The Stanford University Libraries.

64 CARLTON A. SHEFFIELD. Pacific Grove. 1932. The Stanford University Libraries.

65 GEORGE ALBEE. Pacific Grove. September 27, 1932. The Bancroft Library, University of California, Berkeley.

66 ROBERT O. BALLOU. Montrose, California. January 3, 1933. Ball State University Library, Muncie, Indiana.

67 MAVIS MCINTOSH. Montrose, California. January 1933. McIntosh and Otis.

68 ROBERT O. BALLOU. Montrose, California. February 11, 1933. McIntosh and Otis.

70 GEORGE ALBEE. Salinas. 1933. The Bancroft Library, University of California, Berkeley.

71 ROBERT O. BALLOU. Salinas. June 1, 1933. Humanities Research Center, University of Texas, Austin.

73 GEORGE ALBEE. Salinas. 1933. The Bancroft Library, University of California, Berkeley.

74 CARLTON A. SHEFFIELD. Pacific Grove. June 21, 1933. The Stanford University Libraries.

78 CARLTON A. SHEFFIELD. Salinas. June 30, 1933. The Stanford University Libraries.

79 GEORGE ALBEE. Salinas. 1933. The Bancroft Library, University of California, Berkeley.

82 RICHARD ASTRO. *John Steinbeck and Edward F. Ricketts: The Shaping of a Novelist.* Minneapolis: University of Minnesota Press, 1973.

82 GEORGE ALBEE. Salinas. June 1933. The Bancroft Library, University of California, Berkeley.

83 GEORGE ALBEE. Salinas. 1933. The Bancroft Library, University of California, Berkeley.

84 GEORGE ALBEE. Salinas. 1933. The Bancroft Library, University of California, Berkeley.

86 CARL WILHELMSON. Salinas. 1933. The Stanford University Libraries.

87 CARL WILHELMSON. Salinas. August 9, 1933. The Stanford University Libraries.

88 ROBERT O. BALLOU. Salinas. September 11, 1933. Humanities Research Center, University of Texas, Austin.

88 ROBERT O. BALLOU. Salinas. November 20, 1933. Humanities Research Center, University of Texas, Austin.

89 EDITH WAGNER. Pacific Grove. Postmarked November 23, 1933. The Stanford University Libraries.

90 GEORGE ALBEE. Pacific Grove. February 25, 1934. The Bancroft Library, University of California, Berkeley.

92 GEORGE ALBEE. Pacific Grove. 1934. The Bancroft Library, University of California, Berkeley.

94 EDITH WAGNER. Pacific Grove. Postmarked February 2, 1934. The Stanford University Libraries.

95 EDITH WAGNER. Pacific Grove. June 4, 1934. The Stanford University Libraries.

96 EDITH WAGNER. Pacific Grove. June 13, 1934. The Stanford University Libraries.

96 MAVIS MCINTOSH. Pacific Grove. 1934. McIntosh and Otis.

97 *When I first . . .* CHASE HORTON. New York. November 19, 1956. Himself.

98 GEORGE ALBEE. Pacific Grove. January 15, 1935. The Bancroft Library, University of California, Berkeley.

101 GEORGE ALBEE. Pacific Grove. 1935. The Bancroft Library, University of California, Berkeley.

103 ANN HADDEN. Pacific Grove. 1935. The Stanford University Libraries.

104 ANN HADDEN to the ADMINISTRATION OF THE PHELAN AWARD. Point of origin and date unknown. Courtesy of Professor Robert De-Mott, Department of English Language and Literature, Ohio University.

869

105 MAVIS MCINTOSH. Pacific Grove. February 4, 1935. McIntosh and Otis.

106 WILBUR NEEDHAM. Pacific Grove. Early 1935. Clifton Waller Barrett Library of American Literature, University of Virginia.

107 MAVIS MCINTOSH. Pacific Grove. February 1935. McIntosh and Otis.

107 MAVIS MCINTOSH. Pacific Grove. April 1935. McIntosh and Otis.

109 ELIZABETH OTIS. Pacific Grove. May 13, 1935. Herself.

109 ELIZABETH OTIS. Pacific Grove. May 9, 1935. Herself.

110 ELIZABETH BAILEY. Pacific Grove. May 1935. Steinbeck Library Salinas.

111 ELIZABETH OTIS. Pacific Grove. June 13, 1935. Herself.

112 GEORGE ALBEE. Pacific Grove. 1935. The Bancroft Library, University of California, Berkeley.

113 LOUIS PAUL. Pacific Grove. Late summer 1935. Clifton Waller Barrett Library of American Literature, University of Virginia.

113 MAVIS MCINTOSH. Pacific Grove. July 30, 1935. McIntosh and Otis.

115 LOUIS PAUL. Pacific Grove. September 1935. Clifton Waller Barrett Library of American Literature, University of Virginia.

116 MAVIS MCINTOSH. Mexico. Late September 1935. McIntosh and Otis.

116 ELIZABETH OTIS. Mexico. November 3, 1935. Herself.

117 GEORGE ALBEE. Mexico. 1935. The Bancroft Library, University of California, Berkeley.

118 JOSEPH HENRY JACKSON. Pacific Grove. 1935. The Bancroft Library, University of California, Berkeley.

120 LOUIS PAUL. Pacific Grove. February 1936. Clifton Waller Barrett Library of American Literature, University of Virginia.

121 LOUIS PAUL. Pacific Grove. March 1936. Clifton Waller Barrett Library of American Literature, University of Virginia.

122 HELEN NEVILLE, "Aristocracy without Money," *The Nation*, June 19, 1935.

122 JOSEPH HENRY JACKSON, "A Bookman's Note Book," San Francisco *Chronicle*, June 22, 1935.

122 MARY MCCARTHY, "Minority Report," *The Nation*, March 11, 1936.

123 *Now for the dramatic . . .* ELIZABETH OTIS. Pacific Grove. March 1936. Herself.

123 JOHN O'HARA to JOHN STEINBECK. Princeton, New Jersey. November 29, 1962. Mrs. John O'Hara.

123 *O'Hara has not . . .* ELIZABETH OTIS. Los Gatos. 1936. Herself.

123 LOUIS PAUL. Pacific Grove. 1936. Clifton Waller Barrett Library of American Literature, University of Virginia.

124 ELIZABETH OTIS. Pacific Grove. May 27, 1936. Herself.

1936-1939

127 ELIZABETH OTIS. Bruton, Somerset, England. April 12, 1959. Herself.

129 LAWRENCE CLARK POWELL. Gridley Migrant Camp, Gridley, California. 1936. Harvard University Libraries.

129 LOUIS PAUL. Pacific Grove. 1936. Clifton Waller Barrett Library of American Literature, University of Virginia.

130 LOUIS PAUL. Pacific Grove. 1936. Clifton Waller Barrett Library of American Literature, University of Virginia.

131 AMASA MILLER. Los Gatos. 1936. Himself.

132 GEORGE ALBEE. Los Gatos. 1936. The Bancroft Library, University of California, Berkeley.

133 MR. and MRS. GEORGE ALBEE. Los Gatos. January 11, 1937. The Bancroft Library, University of California, Berkeley.

134 ELIZABETH OTIS. Los Gatos. January 27, 1937. Herself.

135 PASCAL COVICI. Los Gatos. February 28, 1937. Humanities Research Center, University of Texas, Austin.

136 GEORGE S. KAUFMAN to JOHN STEINBECK. New York. 1937. Columbia University Libraries, Special Collections; Special Ms. Collection: Annie Laurie Williams.

137 ELIZABETH OTIS and ANNIE LAURIE WILLIAMS. Los Gatos. March 19, 1937. McIntosh and Otis.

139 LAWRENCE CLARK POWELL. Bucks County, Pennsylvania. August 23, 1937. Harvard University Libraries.

140 BO BESKOW to ROBERT WALLSTEN. Söderköping, Sweden. May 1, 1973. Robert Wallsten.

141 MR. and MRS. BO BESKOW. Los Gatos. 1937. Bo Beskow.

141 DONALD OENSLAGER to the J. PIERPONT MORGAN LIBRARY, New York. New York. October 23, 1970. J. Pierpont Morgan Library.

143 ELIZABETH OTIS; MAVIS MCINTOSH; and ANNIE LAURIE WILLIAMS. Los Gatos. November 24, 1937. McIntosh and Otis.

144 GEORGE S. KAUFMAN. Los Gatos. November 1937. Wisconsin Center for Theatre Research, University of Wisconsin.

145 MCINTOSH AND OTIS STAFF. Los Gatos. November 1937. Columbia University Libraries, Special Collections; Special Ms. Collection: Annie Laurie Williams.

146 JACK KIRKLAND. Los Gatos. November 31, 1937. Columbia University Libraries, Special Collections; Special Ms. Collection: Annie Laurie Williams.

148 ELIZABETH OTIS and ANNIE LAURIE WILLIAMS. Los Gatos. December 1937. Columbia University Libraries, Special Collections; Special Ms. Collection: Annie Laurie Williams.

149 ANNIE LAURIE WILLIAMS. San Jose. December 8, 1937. Columbia University Libraries, Special Collections; Special Ms. Collection: Annie Laurie Williams.

149 ANNIE LAURIE WILLIAMS. Los Gatos. December 9, 1937. Columbia University Libraries, Special Collections; Special Ms. Collection: Annie Laurie Williams.

871

151 ARNOLD GINGRICH. Los Gatos. January 5, 1938. Courtesy of The House of Books, Ltd.

152 MR. and MRS. JOSEPH HENRY JACKSON. Pacific Grove. January 1938. The Bancroft Library, University of California, Berkeley.

154 CLAIRE LUCE. Los Gatos. 1938. J. Pierpont Morgan Library.

156 ELIZABETH OTIS. Los Gatos. November 27, 1937. Herself.

156 RICHARD ALBEE to ELAINE STEINBECK. Pacific Grove. February 1, 1973. Elaine Steinbeck.

156 GEORGE ALBEE. Los Gatos. 1938. The Bancroft Library, University of California, Berkeley.

157 ELIZABETH OTIS. Los Gatos. February 1938. Herself.

159 ELIZABETH OTIS. Los Gatos. February 14, 1938. Herself.

160 ELIZABETH BAILEY. Los Gatos. Spring 1938. Steinbeck Library Salinas.

161 ELIZABETH OTIS. Los Gatos. March 7, 1938. Herself.

162 ELIZABETH OTIS. Los Gatos. March 23, 1938. Herself.

163 ELIZABETH OTIS. Los Gatos. May 2, 1938. Herself.

164 CRITICS' CIRCLE. Los Gatos. April 23, 1938. Columbia University Libraries, Special Collections; Special Ms. Collection: Annie Laurie Williams.

164 ELIZABETH OTIS. Los Gatos. May 1938. Herself.

165 GEORGE JEAN NATHAN. Los Gatos. May 23, 1938. Cornell University Library.

167 ELIZABETH OTIS. Los Gatos. June 1, 1938. Herself.

167 ANNIE LAURIE WILLIAMS. Los Gatos. July 1938. Columbia University Libraries, Special Collections; Special Ms. Collection: Annie Laurie Williams.

169 ELIZABETH OTIS. Los Gatos. July 22, 1938. Herself.

170 MR. and MRS. LOUIS PAUL. Los Gatos. September 1938. Clifton Waller Barrett Library of American Literature, University of Virginia.

171 ELIZABETH OTIS. Los Gatos. September 10, 1938. Herself.

172 PASCAL COVICI. Los Gatos. October 1938. Humanities Research Center, University of Texas, Austin.

173 ELIZABETH OTIS. Pacific Grove. November 1938. Herself.

173 ELIZABETH OTIS. Los Gatos. 1938. Herself.

174 ELIZABETH OTIS. Los Gatos. November 1938. Herself.

174 PASCAL COVICI. Los Gatos. January 1, 1939. Humanities Research Center, University of Texas, Austin.

175 PASCAL COVICI. Los Gatos. February 8, 1939. Humanities Research Center, University of Texas, Austin.

175 PASCAL COVICI. Los Gatos. January 3, 1939. Humanities Research Center, University of Texas, Austin.

177 PASCAL COVICI to JOHN STEINBECK. New York. January 9, 1939. McIntosh and Otis.

178 PASCAL COVICI. Los Gatos. January 16, 1939. Humanities Research Center, University of Texas, Austin.

179   MCINTOSH AND OTIS STAFF. Los Gatos. January 20, 1939. McIntosh and Otis.

180   THE NATIONAL INSTITUTE OF ARTS AND LETTERS. Los Gatos. January 31, 1939. Itself.

180   PASCAL COVICI. Los Gatos. Received February 23, 1939. Humanities Research Center, University of Texas, Austin.

181   ELIZABETH OTIS. Los Gatos. February 9, 1939. Herself.

182   PASCAL COVICI. Los Gatos. Received March 31, 1939. Humanities Research Center, University of Texas, Austin.

182   ELIZABETH OTIS. Los Gatos. April 17, 1939. Herself.

183   ELIZABETH OTIS. Los Gatos. April 18, 1939. Herself.

183   CARL WILHELMSON. Los Gatos. June 7, 1939. The Stanford University Libraries.

184   DICK PEARCE. Los Gatos. Postmarked June 1939. Steinbeck File.

185   ELIZABETH OTIS. Los Gatos. June 22, 1939. Herself.

186   CARLTON A. SHEFFIELD. Los Gatos. June 23, 1939. The Stanford University Libraries.

187   CHASE HORTON. Sag Harbor. 1957. Himself.

188   ELIZABETH OTIS. Los Gatos. July 20, 1939. Herself.

189   ELIZABETH OTIS. Los Gatos. October 1939. Herself.

1939-1943

191   WEBSTER F. STREET. New York. November 17, 1941. The Stanford University Libraries.

193   CARLTON A. SHEFFIELD. Los Gatos. November 13, 1939. The Stanford University Libraries.

195   ELIZABETH OTIS. Los Gatos. December 15, 1939. Herself.

197   CARLTON A. SHEFFIELD. Los Gatos. January 16, 1940. The Stanford University Libraries.

198   CARLTON A. SHEFFIELD. Los Gatos. 1940. The Stanford University Libraries.

199   ELIZABETH OTIS. Los Gatos. February 24, 1940. Herself.

200   ELIZABETH OTIS. Los Gatos. February 28, 1940. Herself.

200   ELIZABETH OTIS. Aboard *Western Flyer*. March 26, 1940. Herself.

201   MCINTOSH AND OTIS STAFF. Guaymas, Mexico. April 6, 1940. McIntosh and Otis.

202   FRANKLIN D. ROOSEVELT LIBRARY (William J. Stewart, acting Director) to GERTRUDE CHASE. Hyde Park. September 12, 1973.

202   MRS. FRANKLIN D. ROOSEVELT. Los Gatos. April 24, 1940. Franklin D. Roosevelt Library.

203   REVEREND L. M. BIRKHEAD to JOHN STEINBECK. Point of origin unknown. May 2, 1940. Courtesy of Patricia Birnbaum.

203   REVEREND L. M. BIRKHEAD. Los Gatos. May 7, 1940. Courtesy of Patricia Birnbaum.

205 JOSEPH HENRY JACKSON. Los Gatos. 1940. The Bancroft Library, University of California, Berkeley.

205 JOSEPH HAMILTON. Mexico. 1940. Franklin D. Roosevelt Library.

206 FRANKLIN D. ROOSEVELT. Washington, D.C. June 24, 1940. Franklin D. Roosevelt Library.

206 JAMES ROWE, JR., to FRANKLIN D. ROOSEVELT. The White House. June 24, 1940. Franklin D. Roosevelt Library.

207 FRANKLIN D. ROOSEVELT to MARVIN WATSON. The White House. June 25, 1940. Franklin D. Roosevelt Library.

207 JOSEPH HAMILTON. Mexico. 1940. Franklin D. Roosevelt Library.

207 CARLTON A. SHEFFIELD. Los Gatos. July 9, 1940. The Stanford University Libraries.

209 CARLTON A. SHEFFIELD. Los Gatos. August 12, 1940. The Stanford University Libraries.

210 FRANKLIN D. ROOSEVELT. Los Gatos. August 13, 1940. Franklin D. Roosevelt Library.

211 JAMES ROWE, JR., to MARVIN WATSON. The White House. August 20, 1940. Franklin D. Roosevelt Library.

212 FRANKLIN D. ROOSEVELT to MARVIN WATSON. The White House. September 3, 1940. Franklin D. Roosevelt Library.

212 MRS. MELVIN KNISELY to ELAINE STEINBECK. Charleston, South Carolina. February 18, 1973. Elaine Steinbeck.

212 ARCHIBALD MACLEISH. Los Gatos. November 13, 1940. Himself.

212 CARLTON A. SHEFFIELD. Los Gatos. October 15, 1940. The Stanford University Libraries.

214 MAX WAGNER. Mexico. Postmarked November 1, 1940. The Stanford University Libraries.

215 MAX WAGNER. Los Gatos. Postmarked November 23, 1940. The Stanford University Libraries.

217 MAX WAGNER. Los Gatos. Postmarked November 30, 1940. The Stanford University Libraries.

217 WEBSTER F. STREET. Los Gatos. Postmarked December 12, 1940. The Stanford University Libraries.

219 MAX WAGNER and GWENDOLYN CONGER. Los Gatos. December 26, 1940. The Stanford University Libraries.

220 MAX WAGNER. Los Gatos. December 29, 1940. The Stanford University Libraries.

220 PASCAL COVICI. Los Gatos. January 1, 1941. Humanities Research Center, University of Texas, Austin.

222 ELIZABETH OTIS. Los Gatos. January 22, 1941. Herself.

223 LOUIS PAUL. Pacific Grove. 1941. Clifton Waller Barrett Library of American Literature, University of Virginia.

224 MAX WAGNER. Los Gatos. Postmarked February 2, 1941. The Stanford University Libraries.

225 ELIZABETH OTIS. Pacific Grove. February 7, 1941. Herself.

227 MAX WAGNER. Pacific Grove. Postmarked June 2, 1941. The Stanford University Libraries.

227 *Carol is getting* . . . ELIZABETH OTIS. Pacific Grove. February 17, 1941. Herself.

227 MAVIS MCINTOSH. Pacific Grove. April 16, 1941. McIntosh and Otis.

228 BO BESKOW. New York. 1947. Himself.

228 ELIZABETH OTIS. Pacific Grove. May 19, 1941. Herself.

230 PASCAL COVICI. Pacific Grove. June 19, 1941. Humanities Research Center, University of Texas, Austin.

231 ELIZABETH OTIS. Pacific Grove. June 24, 1941. Herself.

231 PASCAL COVICI. Pacific Grove. July 4, 1941. Humanities Research Center, University of Texas, Austin.

232 ELIZABETH OTIS. Pacific Grove. July 18, 1941. Herself.

233 ELIZABETH OTIS and MAVIS MCINTOSH. Pacific Grove. September 30, 1941. McIntosh and Otis.

234 WEBSTER F. STREET. Suffern, New York. Postmarked October 18, 1941. The Stanford University Libraries.

235 MRS. FRANKLIN D. ROOSEVELT. Suffern, New York. Late October 1941. Franklin D. Roosevelt Library.

235 WEBSTER F. STREET. New York. November 17, 1941. The Stanford University Libraries.

237 WEBSTER F. STREET. New York. November 25, 1941. The Stanford University Libraries.

238 WEBSTER F. STREET. New York. December 8, 1941. The Stanford University Libraries.

239 WEBSTER F. STREET. New York. January 12, 1942. The Stanford University Libraries.

241 *I can't tell you* . . . WEBSTER F. STREET. New York. January 20, 1942. The Stanford University Libraries.

241 *You will look* . . . WEBSTER F. STREET. New York. Postmarked January 30, 1942. The Stanford University Libraries.

241 *I don't imagine* . . . WEBSTER F. STREET. New York. February 2, 1942. The Stanford University Libraries.

241 *I still get them* . . . WEBSTER F. STREET. Postmarked January 30, 1942. The Stanford University Libraries.

241 *Washington is still* . . . WEBSTER F. STREET. January 20, 1942. The Stanford University Libraries.

241 *I'm finding curious* . . . WEBSTER F. STREET. New York. February 10, 1942. The Stanford University Libraries.

242 *The new book* . . . WEBSTER F. STREET. January 20, 1942. The Stanford University Libraries.

242 *My emotional life* . . . WEBSTER F. STREET. February 10, 1942. The Stanford University Libraries.

242 *I seem to take* . . . WEBSTER F. STREET. January 20, 1942. The Stanford University Libraries.

242 WEBSTER F. STREET. New York. February 14, 1942. The Stanford University Libraries.

243 WEBSTER F. STREET. Palisades, Rockland County, New York. Postmarked April 8, 1942. The Stanford University Libraries.

245 WEBSTER F. STREET. Palisades, Rockland County, New York. April 21, 1942. The Stanford University Libraries.

246 THE HONORABLE FRANK KNOX. Palisades, Rockland County, New York. May 5, 1942. Courtesy of Professor Joel W. Hedgpeth. Hopkins Marine Station, Pacific Grove.

247 WEBSTER F. STREET. Palisades, Rockland County, New York. July 23, 1942. The Stanford University Libraries.

248 ELIZABETH OTIS and ANNIE LAURIE WILLIAMS. Hollywood, California. September 23, 1942. McIntosh and Otis.

249 ANNIE LAURIE WILLIAMS. Van Nuys, California. January 8, 1943. Columbia University Libraries, Special Collections; Special Ms. Collection: Annie Laurie Williams.

250 WEBSTER F. STREET. New York. March 15, 1943. The Stanford University Libraries.

250 WEBSTER F. STREET. New York. March 18, 1943. The Stanford University Libraries.

251 *We had a good . . .* WEBSTER F. STREET. New York. April 3, 1943. The Stanford University Libraries.

251 NUNNALLY JOHNSON. New York. 1943. Himself.

251 WEBSTER F. STREET. New York. April 5, 1943. The Stanford University Libraries.

1943-1948

253 GWYNDOLYN STEINBECK. North Africa. August 24, 1943. The Bancroft Library, University of California, Berkeley.

255 WEBSTER F. STREET. New York. April 9, 1943. The Stanford University Libraries.

255 WEBSTER F. STREET. New York. April 27, 1943. The Stanford University Libraries.

256 GWYNDOLYN STEINBECK. London. June 1943. The Bancroft Library, University of California, Berkeley.

256 GWYNDOLYN STEINBECK. London. July 4, 1943. The Bancroft Library, University of California, Berkeley.

256 GWYNDOLYN STEINBECK. London. July 1943. The Bancroft Library, University of California, Berkeley.

257 GWYNDOLYN STEINBECK. London. July 8, 1943. The Bancroft Library, University of California, Berkeley.

257 GWYNDOLYN STEINBECK. London. July 12, 1943. The Bancroft Library, University of California, Berkeley.

258 GWYNDOLYN STEINBECK. North Africa. August 13, 1943. The Bancroft Library, University of California, Berkeley.

259 GWYNDOLYN STEINBECK. North Africa. August 19, 1943. The Bancroft Library, University of California, Berkeley.

260 GWYNDOLYN STEINBECK. North Africa. August 24, 1943. The Bancroft Library, University of California, Berkeley.

260 GWYNDOLYN STEINBECK. North Africa. August 25, 1943. The Bancroft Library, University of California, Berkeley.

261 GWYNDOLYN STEINBECK. North Africa. August 28, 1943. The Bancroft Library, University of California, Berkeley.

262 GWYNDOLYN STEINBECK. Italy. September 20, 1943. The Bancroft Library, University of California, Berkeley.

263 GWYNDOLYN STEINBECK. Italy. September 22, 1943. The Bancroft Library, University of California, Berkeley.

263 GWYNDOLYN STEINBECK. London. Fall 1943. The Bancroft Library, University of California, Berkeley.

264 JOSEPH BRYAN III. Sag Harbor. Postmarked July 9, 1958. Himself.

265 WEBSTER F. STREET. New York. December 13, 1943. The Stanford University Libraries.

266 TWENTIETH CENTURY-FOX FILM CORPORATION. New York. January 10, 1944. McIntosh and Otis.

267 ANNIE LAURIE WILLIAMS. Mexico. February 19, 1944. Columbia University Libraries. Special Collections; Special Ms. Collection: Annie Laurie Williams.

267 ANNIE LAURIE WILLIAMS. Mexico. February 21, 1944. Columbia University Libraries, Special Collections; Special Ms. Collection: Annie Laurie Williams.

268 CARLTON A. SHEFFIELD. New York. April 12, 1944. The Stanford University Libraries.

270 WEBSTER F. STREET. New York. July 4, 1944. The Stanford University Libraries.

271 JACK and MAX WAGNER. New York. August 2, 1944. The Stanford University Libraries.

271 WEBSTER F. STREET. New York. August 25, 1944. The Stanford University Libraries.

272 CARLTON A. SHEFFIELD. New York. September 27, 1944. The Stanford University Libraries.

274 PASCAL COVICI. Monterey. October 24, 1944. Humanities Research Center, University of Texas, Austin.

275 *Plenty of room . . .* PASCAL COVICI. Monterey. Early November 1944. Humanities Research Center, University of Texas, Austin.

275 PASCAL COVICI. Monterey. November 1944. Humanities Research Center, University of Texas, Austin.

276 *Long distance phone . . .* PASCAL COVICI. Monterey. November 30, 1944. Humanities Research Center, University of Texas, Austin.

276 *I have been . . .* PASCAL COVICI. Monterey. 1944. Humanities Research Center, University of Texas, Austin.

276 MILDRED LYMAN. Monterey. December 2, 1944. McIntosh and Otis.

277 ELIZABETH OTIS. Monterey. December 27, 1944. Herself.

278 *Gwyn will write . . .* PASCAL COVICI. Monterey. December 26, 1944. Humanities Research Center, University of Texas, Austin.

877

278 *The better people* ... PASCAL COVICI. Monterey. Date unknown. Humanities Research Center, University of Texas, Austin.

278 *There is a time* . . . PASCAL COVICI. Monterey. December 3? (possibly 30), 1944. Humanities Research Center, University of Texas, Austin.

278 JACK and MAX WAGNER. Monterey. Postmarked January 23, 1945. The Stanford University Libraries.

279 PASCAL COVICI. Monterey. Spring 1945. Humanities Research Center, University of Texas, Austin.

280 PASCAL COVICI. Monterey. Spring 1945. Humanities Research Center, University of Texas, Austin.

281 ELIZABETH OTIS. Cuernavaca, Mexico. May 3, 1945. Herself.

282 ANNIE LAURIE WILLIAMS. Cuernavaca, Mexico. June 26, 1945. Columbia University Libraries, Special Collections; Special Ms. Collection: Annie Laurie Williams.

283 ELIZABETH OTIS. Cuernavaca, Mexico. July 17, 1945. Herself.

283 PASCAL COVICI. Cuernavaca, Mexico. July 12, 1945. Humanities Research Center, University of Texas, Austin.

283 PASCAL COVICI. Cuernavaca, Mexico. July 10, 1945. Humanities Research Center, University of Texas, Austin.

284 CHARLES BRACKETT. New York. December 10, 1956. Steinbeck File.

285 PASCAL COVICI. Cuernavaca, Mexico. 1945. Humanities Research Center, University of Texas, Austin.

285 PASCAL COVICI. Cuernavaca, Mexico. July 10, 1945. Humanities Research Center, University of Texas, Austin.

286 JACK WAGNER. New York. December 15, 1945. The Stanford University Libraries.

286 MAX WAGNER. New York. Postmarked January 16, 1946. The Stanford University Libraries.

287 JACK WAGNER. New York. Early 1946. The Stanford University Libraries.

287 WEBSTER F. STREET. New York. March 17, 1946. The Stanford University Libraries.

288 CARL WILHELMSON. New York. Spring 1946. The Stanford University Libraries.

290 JACK WAGNER. New York. May 2, 1946. The Stanford University Libraries.

291 WEBSTER F. STREET. New York. June 14, 1946. The Stanford University Libraries.

291 JACK WAGNER. New York. June 14, 1946. The Stanford University Libraries.

292 EDWARD F. RICKETTS. New York. August 1946. Courtesy of Professor Joel W. Hedgpeth. Hopkins Marine Station, Pacific Grove.

293 MCINTOSH AND OTIS STAFF. Copenhagen. October 30, 1946. McIntosh and Otis.

294 BO BESKOW. New York. December 16, 1946. Himself.

296   ... *a lumbering soul* ... PASCAL COVICI. Bruton, Somerset, England. May 1959. Humanities Research Center, University of Texas, Austin.

296   ... *not enough wingspread* ... ERNEST MARTIN. Bruton, Somerset, England. May 25, 1959. Feuer and Martin.

296   JACK WAGNER. New York. January 16, 1947. The Stanford University Libraries.

296   BO BESKOW. New York. 1947. Himself.

296   JACK WAGNER. New York. February 16, 1947. The Stanford University Libraries.

297   PASCAL COVICI. Monterey. 1948. Humanities Research Center, University of Texas, Austin.

297   *I'm very tired* ... JACK and MAX WAGNER. New York. 1947. The Stanford University Libraries.

297   *I'm pulling out* ... JACK and MAX WAGNER. New York. 1947. The Stanford University Libraries.

298   PASCAL COVICI. Kiev, Ukraine, U.S.S.R. August 11–13, 1947. Humanities Research Center, University of Texas, Austin.

299   GWYNDOLYN STEINBECK. Stalingrad, U.S.S.R. August 20–23, 1947. The Bancroft Library, University of California, Berkeley.

301   WEBSTER F. STREET. New York. November 17, 1947. The Stanford University Libraries.

303   PAUL CASWELL. New York. January 2, 1948. Steinbeck Library Salinas.

303   PAUL CASWELL to JOHN STEINBECK. Salinas. January 9, 1948. Steinbeck Library Salinas.

304   PASCAL COVICI. Monterey. February 1948. Humanities Research Center, University of Texas, Austin.

305   ANNIE LAURIE WILLIAMS. Monterey. February 10, 1948. Columbia University Libraries, Special Collections; Special Ms. Collection: Annie Laurie Williams.

305   PASCAL COVICI. Monterey. 1948. Humanities Research Center, University of Texas, Austin.

305   PAUL CASWELL. Monterey. February 22, 1948. Steinbeck Library Salinas.

305   BO BESKOW. Monterey. February 12, 1948. Himself.

307   GWYNDOLYN STEINBECK. Monterey. February 17, 1948. The Bancroft Library, University of California, Berkeley.

308   STANFORD UNIVERSITY PRESS. Pacific Grove. February 15, 1948. Co-signed Edward F. Ricketts. Courtesy of Professor Joel W. Hedgpeth. Hopkins Marine Station, Pacific Grove.

309   EDWARD F. RICKETTS. New York. April 1948. The Bancroft Library, University of California, Berkeley.

310   BO BESKOW. New York. April 29, 1948. Himself.

312   PAUL CASWELL. New York. May 20, 1948. Steinbeck Library Salinas.

312   BO BESKOW. New York. May 22, 1948. Himself.

314 WEBSTER F. STREET. New York. May 25, 1948. The Stanford University Libraries.

316 RITCHIE and NATALYA LOVEJOY. New York. May 27, 1948. The Bancroft Library, University of California, Berkeley.

317 BO BESKOW. New York. June 19, 1948. Himself.

318 BO BESKOW. New York. June 24, 1948. Himself.

319 BO BESKOW. New York. August 16, 1948. Himself.

320 WEBSTER F. STREET. New York. Postmarked August 17, 1948. The Stanford University Libraries.

321 BO BESKOW. New York. August 1948. Himself.

323 WEBSTER F. STREET. New York. August 22, 1948. The Stanford University Libraries.

324 WEBSTER F. STREET. New York. August 1948. The Stanford University Libraries.

324 WEBSTER F. STREET. New York. Postmarked August 27, 1948. The Stanford University Libraries.

1948-1949

327 ELAINE SCOTT. Pacific Grove. July 25, 1949. Elaine Steinbeck.

329 *The little Pacific . . .* SHIRLEY FISHER. Bruton, Somerset, England. 1959. Herself.

329 PASCAL COVICI. Pacific Grove. September 1948. Humanities Research Center, University of Texas, Austin.

330 PASCAL COVICI. Pacific Grove. September 12, 1948. Humanities Research Center, University of Texas, Austin.

331 BO BESKOW. Pacific Grove. September 19, 1948. Himself.

333 *I'm afraid I . . .* PASCAL COVICI. Pacific Grove. Date unknown. Humanities Research Center, University of Texas, Austin.

333 PASCAL COVICI. Pacific Grove. September 19, 1948. Humanities Research Center, University of Texas, Austin.

334 PASCAL COVICI. Pacific Grove. October 18, 1948. Humanities Research Center, University of Texas, Austin.

334 PASCAL COVICI. Pacific Grove. 1948. Humanities Research Center, University of Texas, Austin.

336 NUNNALLY JOHNSON. Pacific Grove. 1948. Himself.

336 MR. and MRS. JOSEPH HENRY JACKSON. Pacific Grove. October 26, 1948. The Bancroft Library, University of California, Berkeley.

338 PASCAL COVICI. Pacific Grove. November 1, 1948. Humanities Research Center, University of Texas, Austin.

339 MILDRED LYMAN to ANNIE LAURIE WILLIAMS. California. February 1949. Columbia University Libraries, Special Collections; Special Ms. Collection: Annie Laurie Williams.

339 PASCAL COVICI. Pacific Grove. November 14, 1948. Humanities Research Center, University of Texas, Austin.

340 PASCAL COVICI. Pacific Grove. 1948. Humanities Research Center, University of Texas, Austin.

341 BO BESKOW. Pacific Grove. November 19, 1948. Himself.

344 THE AMERICAN ACADEMY OF ARTS AND LETTERS to JOHN STEINBECK. New York. November 23, 1948. Itself.

344 THE AMERICAN ACADEMY OF ARTS AND LETTERS. Pacific Grove. December 3, 1948. Itself.

345 PASCAL COVICI. Pacific Grove. November 29, 1948. Humanities Research Center, University of Texas, Austin.

345 BO BESKOW. Pacific Grove. December 28, 1948. Himself.

346 PASCAL COVICI. Pacific Grove. January 22, 1949. Humanities Research Center, University of Texas, Austin.

349 PASCAL COVICI. Pacific Grove. February 22, 1949. Humanities Research Center, University of Texas, Austin.

350 ELIZABETH BAILEY. Pacific Grove. March 19, 1949. Steinbeck Library Salinas.

351 GWYNDOLYN STEINBECK. Pacific Grove. May 3, 1949. The Bancroft Library, University of California, Berkeley.

351 BO BESKOW. Pacific Grove. May 9, 1949. Himself.

353 ELIZABETH OTIS. Pacific Grove. May 23, 1949. Herself.

354 BO BESKOW. Pacific Grove. May 23, 1949. Himself.

355 ANNIE LAURIE WILLIAMS. Pacific Grove. Received June 7, 1949. Columbia University Libraries, Special Collections; Special Ms. Collection: Annie Laurie Williams.

357 ELAINE SCOTT. Pacific Grove. June 6, 1949. Elaine Steinbeck.

359 JOHN O'HARA. Pacific Grove. June 8, 1949. Mrs. John O'Hara.

361 ELAINE SCOTT. Pacific Grove. June 20–24, 1949. Elaine Steinbeck.

363 JEAN BOONE. New York. 1950. Herself.

366 ELAINE SCOTT. Pacific Grove. July 10–18, 1949. Elaine Steinbeck.

368 ELAINE SCOTT. Pacific Grove. July 23, 1949. Elaine Steinbeck.

369 ELIZABETH OTIS. Moscow. October 18, 1963. Herself.

370 ELAINE SCOTT. Pacific Grove. July 25, 1949. Elaine Steinbeck.

372 ELAINE SCOTT. Pacific Grove. July 28, 1949. Elaine Steinbeck.

374 ELAINE SCOTT. Pacific Grove. July 30, August 2, 1949. Elaine Steinbeck.

376 ELAINE SCOTT. Pacific Grove. August 16, 1949. Elaine Steinbeck.

378 GWYNDOLYN STEINBECK. Pacific Grove. August 19, 1949. The Bancroft Library, University of California, Berkeley.

379 ELAINE SCOTT. Pacific Grove. August 20–21, 1949. Elaine Steinbeck.

379 BO BESKOW. Pacific Grove. October 7, 1949. Himself.

380 ELAINE SCOTT. Pacific Grove. October 11–14, 1949. Elaine Steinbeck.

382 ELAINE SCOTT. Pacific Grove. November 1–8, 1949. Elaine Steinbeck.

388 ELAINE SCOTT. Pacific Grove. November 1949. Elaine Steinbeck.

388 ELAINE SCOTT. Pacific Grove. November 10–15, 1949. Elaine Steinbeck.

391 ELAINE SCOTT. Pacific Grove. November 27–29, 1949. Elaine Steinbeck.

1950-1952

395 PASCAL COVICI. New York. 1952. Humanities Research Center, University of Texas, Austin.

397 BO BESKOW. New York. Christmas 1949. Himself.

398 MR. and MRS. DAVID HEYLER, JR. New York. December 28, 1949. David Heyler, Jr.

399 FRANCES ATKINSON. New York. Early 1950. Herself.

400 BO BESKOW. New York. January 24, 1950. Himself.

401 MR. and MRS. DAVID HEYLER, JR. New York. January 31, 1950. David Heyler, Jr.

402 BO BESKOW. Rockland County, New York. Late July 1950. Himself.

404 PASCAL COVICI. Rockland County, New York. Midsummer 1950. Humanities Research Center, University of Texas, Austin.

406 GWYNDOLYN STEINBECK. Rockland County, New York. August 22, 1950. The Bancroft Library, University of California, Berkeley.

407 ELIA KAZAN. Rockland County, New York. Late summer 1950. Himself.

408 WEBSTER F. STREET. Rockland County, New York. August 30, 1950. The Stanford University Libraries.

409 BO BESKOW. New York. September 1950. Himself.

411 ANNIE LAURIE WILLIAMS. Boston. October 6, 1950. Columbia University Libraries, Special Collections; Special Ms. Collection: Annie Laurie Williams.

412 EUGENE SOLOW. New York. Postmarked October 21, 1950. Clifton Waller Barrett Library of American Literature, University of Virginia.

413 JACK and MAX WAGNER. New York. November 28, 1950. The Stanford University Libraries.

415 CLIFFORD ODETS. New York. Postmarked December 8, 1950. Clifton Waller Barrett Library of American Literature, University of Virginia.

415 GEORGE ALBEE. New York. December 19, 1950. The Bancroft Library, University of California, Berkeley.

417 PASCAL COVICI. Somerset, Bermuda. January 5, 1951. Humanities Research Center, University of Texas, Austin.

418 BO BESKOW. New York. February 27, 1951. Himself.

418 FELICIA GEFFEN. New York. February 20, 1951. The Academy of Arts and Letters.

419 FELICIA GEFFEN. New York. February 23, 1951. The Academy of Arts and Letters.

419 FELICIA GEFFEN to JOHN STEINBECK. New York. April 25, 1951. The Academy of Arts and Letters.

420 FELICIA GEFFEN. New York. May 1951. The Academy of Arts and Letters.

420 FELICIA GEFFEN. New York. May 9, 1951. The Academy of Arts and Letters.

421 PASCAL COVICI. New York. 1951. Humanities Research Center, University of Texas, Austin.

422 PASCAL COVICI. Nantucket. June 18, 1951. Humanities Research Center, University of Texas, Austin.

423 ELIZABETH OTIS. Nantucket. June 27, 1951. Herself.

424 PASCAL COVICI. Nantucket. July 13, 1951. Humanities Research Center, University of Texas, Austin.

425 ELIZABETH OTIS. Nantucket. July 30, 1951. Herself.

425 MR. and MRS. ELIA KAZAN. Nantucket. July 30, 1951. Elia Kazan.

426 MR. and MRS. PASCAL COVICI. Nantucket. August 1951. Humanities Research Center, University of Texas, Austin.

427 ELIZABETH OTIS. Nantucket. August 16, 1951. Herself.

428 PASCAL COVICI. Nantucket. September 11, 1951. Humanities Research Center, University of Texas, Austin.

429 ELIZABETH OTIS. Nantucket. September 12, 1951. Herself.

430 ANNIE LAURIE WILLIAMS. New York. September 1951. Columbia University Libraries, Special Collections; Special Ms. Collection: Annie Laurie Williams.

430 ANNIE LAURIE WILLIAMS. Paris. November 6, 1961. Columbia University Libraries, Special Collections; Special Ms. Collection: Annie Laurie Williams.

431 BO BESKOW. New York. November 16, 1951. Himself.

432 JOHN O'HARA. New York. Postmarked November 26, 1951. Mrs. John O'Hara.

433 PASCAL COVICI. New York. December 1951. Humanities Research Center, University of Texas, Austin.

434 BO BESKOW. New York. January 21, 1952. Himself.

435 JOHN O'HARA. New York. February 1952. Mrs. John O'Hara.

436 PASCAL COVICI. New York. 1952. Humanities Research Center, University of Texas, Austin.

437 PASCAL COVICI. New York. 1952. Humanities Research Center, University of Texas, Austin.

1952-1954

441 CARLTON A. SHEFFIELD. Sag Harbor. July 7, 1956. The Stanford University Libraries.

883

443 PASCAL COVICI. Madrid. April 18, 1952. Humanities Research Center, University of Texas, Austin.

444 PASCAL COVICI. Paris. May 12, 1952. Humanities Research Center, University of Texas, Austin.

445 ELIZABETH OTIS. Paris. May 26, 1952. Herself.

446 ELIZABETH OTIS. Paris. May 26, 1952. Herself.

447 ELIZABETH OTIS. London. August 11, 1952. Herself.

447 ELIZABETH OTIS. Paris. May 27, 1952. Herself.

448 ELIZABETH OTIS. Geneva. June 2, 1952. Herself.

450 ANNIE LAURIE WILLIAMS. Rome. June 17, 1952. Columbia University Libraries, Special Collections, Special Ms. Collection: Annie Laurie Williams.

451 ELIZABETH OTIS. Rome. June 23, 1952. Herself.

452 ROBERTO ROSSELLINI and INGRID BERGMAN. Paris. July 23, 1952. Ingrid Bergman.

453 INGRID BERGMAN to JOHN STEINBECK. Paris. August 1952. Ingrid Bergman.

454 MR. and MRS. PASCAL COVICI. Londonderry, Ireland. August 17, 1952. Humanities Research Center, University of Texas, Austin.

455 PASCAL COVICI, Jr. New York. September 9, 1952. Himself.

455 CARL WILHELMSON. New York. Spring 1946. The Stanford University Libraries.

456 CARLTON A. SHEFFIELD. New York. September 10, 1952. The Stanford University Libraries.

458 CARLTON A. SHEFFIELD. New York. October 16, 1952. The Stanford University Libraries.

461 ADLAI STEVENSON. New York. November 7, 1952. The Adlai E. Stevenson Papers, Princeton University Library.

462 CARLTON A. SHEFFIELD. New York. December 1952. The Stanford University Libraries.

464 BARNABY CONRAD. New York. December 29, 1952. Himself.

465 BARNABY CONRAD. New York. January 2, 1953. Himself.

466 FELICIA GEFFEN. New York. March 1953. The Academy of Arts and Letters.

467 NELSON VALJEAN. New York. March 13, 1953. Himself.

469 ELAINE STEINBECK. Nantucket. March 24–27, 1953. Herself.

471 RICHARD WATTS, JR. New York. April 7, 1953. Steinbeck File.

472 ELIZABETH OTIS. Sag Harbor. September 14, 1953. Herself.

473 CARLTON A. SHEFFIELD. New York. November 2, 1953. The Stanford University Libraries.

474 "MACK AND GAY (GABE)" of *Cannery Row*. New York. November 13, 1953. Courtesy of Dr. H. T. Stotler.

475 ELIZABETH OTIS. Seville. April 1954. Herself.

475 ELIZABETH OTIS. Seville. April 21, 1954. Herself.

477 ELIZABETH OTIS. Madrid. May 5, 1954. Herself.

477 ELIZABETH OTIS. Paris. May 15, 1954. Herself.

478   FANNIE CROW and MARY DEKKER. Paris. May 21, 1954. Steinbeck File.

479   ELIZABETH OTIS. Paris. May 27, 1954. Herself.

481   ELIZABETH OTIS. Paris. May 31, 1954. Herself.

482   RICHARD RODGERS and OSCAR HAMMERSTEIN II. Paris. June 5, 1954. Rodgers and Hammerstein, Inc.

483   ELIZABETH OTIS. Paris. June 13, 1954. Herself.

484   ELIZABETH OTIS. Paris. June 14, 1954. Herself.

485   ELIZABETH OTIS. Paris. June 17, 1954. Herself.

486   GWYNDOLYN STEINBECK. Paris. July 24, 1954. The Bancroft Library, University of California, Berkeley.

487   ELIA KAZAN. Paris. July 24, 1954. Himself.

489   MRS. RICHARD RODGERS. Paris. July 25, 1954. Herself.

491   MARCIA ROSS and SOL LEIBNER. Paris. August 20, 1954. McIntosh and Otis.

493   MRS. RICHARD RODGERS. Paris. August 26, 1954. Herself.

494   PASCAL COVICI. Paris. September 2, 1954. Humanities Research Center, University of Texas, Austin.

495   ELIZABETH OTIS. Paris. September 4, 1954. Herself.

495   WEBSTER F. STREET. Paris. September 6, 1954. The Stanford University Libraries.

496   MR. and MRS. ELIA KAZAN. London. September 14, 1954. Elia Kazan.

497   ELIZABETH OTIS. London. September 17, 1954. Herself.

498   GRAHAM WATSON. Saint Paul de Vence, France. September 29, 1954. Himself.

499   ELIZABETH OTIS. Saint Paul de Vence, France. September 29, 1954. Herself.

500   ELIZABETH OTIS. Rome. October 29, 1954. Herself.

501   PASCAL COVICI. Positano, Italy. December 1, 1954. Humanities Research Center, University of Texas, Austin.

1955-1957

503   WEBSTER F. STREET. Sag Harbor. March 20, 1956. The Stanford University Libraries.

505   WEBSTER F. STREET. Sag Harbor. July 5, 1955. The Stanford University Libraries.

507   MR. AND MRS. ELIA KAZAN. New York. 1955. Elia Kazan.

508   WAVERLY SCOTT. Sag Harbor. July 8, 1955. Steinbeck File.

511   WEBSTER F. STREET. New York. September 23, 1955. The Stanford University Libraries.

512   CARLTON A. SHEFFIELD. New York. September 23, 1955. The Stanford University Libraries.

514   RICHARD RODGERS. New York. September 27, 1955. Himself.

516   OSCAR HAMMERSTEIN II. Boston. October 1955. Library of Congress, Washington, D.C.

518   ELIA KAZAN. New York. December 3, 1955. Himself.

519   Calypso Poem by John Steinbeck. Trinidad. 1956. Steinbeck File.

521   PASCAL COVICI. Sag Harbor. February 1956. Humanities Research Center, University of Texas, Austin.

522   PETER BENCHLEY. Sag Harbor. 1956. Himself.

523   PETER BENCHLEY. Sag Harbor. 1956. Himself.

524   WEBSTER F. STREET. Sag Harbor. March 20, 1956. The Stanford University Libraries.

525   JAMES S. POPE to NEWSPAPER SYNDICATE. Louisville. December 6, 1955. James S. Pope.

525   MARK ETHRIDGE and JAMES S. POPE. Sag Harbor. March 31, 1956. James S. Pope.

525   SYNDICATED NEWSPAPER EDITORS. Sag Harbor. April 1956. James S. Pope.

526   JOHN P. MCKNIGHT. New York. January 20, 1955. Himself.

527   PASCAL COVICI, JR. New York. Postmarked April 13, 1956. Himself.

528   JAMES S. POPE. Sag Harbor. May 16, 1956. Himself.

533   GRAHAM WATSON. Sag Harbor. July 2, 1956. Himself.

534   JAMES S. POPE. Sag Harbor. July 1, 1956. Himself.

535   JAMES S. POPE. Sag Harbor. July 1956. Himself.

536   JAMES S. POPE. Sag Harbor. July 1956. Himself.

536   JAMES S. POPE and MARK ETHRIDGE. San Francisco. August 23, 1956. James S. Pope.

537   PASCAL COVICI. Sag Harbor. 1956. Humanities Research Center, University of Texas, Austin.

538   DENNIS MURPHY. Sag Harbor. September 21, 1956. Steinbeck Library Salinas.

539   MR. and MRS. DAVID HEYLER, JR. New York. November 19, 1956. David Heyler, Jr.

541   ELIZABETH OTIS. New York. November 19, 1956. Herself.

542   ROLAND DICKEY. New York. December 7, 1956. Steinbeck File.

543   ELIZABETH OTIS. Sag Harbor. January 3, 1957. Herself.

545   CHASE HORTON. Sag Harbor. January 12, 1957. Himself.

546   ARTHUR LARSON. New York. January 12, 1957. Steinbeck File.

548   ALEXANDER FRERE. New York. January 18, 1957. Himself.

549   *The Morgan Library* . . . STANFORD STEINBECK. Sag Harbor. September 1962. Himself.

549   JOHN MURPHY. New York. February 21, 1957. Steinbeck Library Salinas.

551   MCINTOSH AND OTIS STAFF. New York. February 1957. McIntosh and Otis.

551 JAMES S. POPE and MARK ETHRIDGE. New York. February 19, 1957. James S. Pope.

551 ELIZABETH OTIS. Florence. April 7, 1957. Herself.

552 PASCAL COVICI. Rome. April 30, 1957. Humanities Research Center, University of Texas, Austin.

552 ELIZABETH OTIS and CHASE HORTON. Rome. April 26, 1957. Themselves.

555 PASCAL COVICI. Florence. May 16, 1957. Humanities Research Center, University of Texas, Austin.

556 ANNIE LAURIE WILLIAMS. Sag Harbor. May 11, 1956. Columbia University Libraries, Special Collections; Special Ms. Collection: Annie Laurie Williams.

557 PROFESSOR and MRS. EUGENE VINAVER. Blanchland, England. July 20, 1957. Eugène Vinaver.

1957-1959

559 ELIZABETH OTIS. New York. March 1958. Herself.

561 JOHN STEINBECK IV. Sag Harbor. August 7, 1957. Steinbeck File.

562 ANNIE LAURIE WILLIAMS. New York. August 28, 1957. Columbia University Libraries, Special Collections; Special Ms. Collection: Annie Laurie Williams.

564 WILLIAM FAULKNER to JOHN STEINBECK. Charlottesville, Virginia. February 18, 1957. Steinbeck File.

565 WILLIAM FAULKNER. New York. February 20, 1957. Steinbeck File.

566 ELAINE STEINBECK. Tokyo. September 1–7, 1957. Herself.

570 ELAINE STEINBECK. Tokyo. September 8, 1957. Herself.

571 ELAINE STEINBECK. Tokyo. September 9–10, 1957. Herself.

572 MRS. DONNIE RADCLIFFE. New York. December 22, 1957. Steinbeck Library Salinas.

573 JOSEPH BRYAN III. New York. Postmarked December 17, 1957. Himself.

575 ELIZABETH OTIS. New York. March 1958. Herself.

575 ELIZABETH OTIS and CHASE HORTON. New York. March 14, 1958. Themselves.

578 EUGENE VINAVER. New York. March 10, 1958. Himself.

579 JOSEPH BRYAN III. New York. March 15, 1958. Himself.

581 MRS. WAVERLY ANDERSON. New York. April 29, 1950. Herself.

581 ELIZABETH OTIS. Sag Harbor. April 6, 1958. Herself.

583 ELIZABETH OTIS, CHASE HORTON, and SHIRLEY FISHER. London. June 5, 1958. Elizabeth Otis.

584 JOHN FORMAN. London. June 3, 1958. Elizabeth Otis.

586 ELIZABETH OTIS. London. June 21, 1958. Herself.

586 ELIZABETH OTIS. London. June 13, 1958. Herself.

887

587 JOHN O'HARA. London. June 14, 1958. Mrs. John O'Hara.

589 EUGENE VINAVER. London. June 22, 1958. Himself.

590 PASCAL COVICI. Florence. May 16, 1957. Humanities Research Center, University of Texas, Austin.

591 PROFESSOR and MRS. EUGENE VINAVER. London. June 27, 1958. Eugène Vinaver.

593 ELIZABETH OTIS. Sag Harbor. July 9, 1958. Herself.

595 ELIA KAZAN. Sag Harbor. Postmarked October 14, 1958. Himself.

596 PASCAL COVICI. Sag Harbor. October 17, 1958. Humanities Research Center, University of Texas, Austin.

597 JOHN O'HARA. Sag Harbor. May 13, 1958. Mrs. John O'Hara.

597 SHIRLEY FISHER. Sag Harbor. 1958. Herself.

598 CHASE HORTON. Sag Harbor. October 21, 1958. Himself.

599 JOHN STEINBECK IV. New York. November 6, 1958. Steinbeck File.

600 THOM STEINBECK. New York. November 10, 1958. Steinbeck File.

602 STUART L. HANNON. New York. November 6, 1958. Elizabeth Otis.

603 HENRY FONDA. New York. November 20, 1958. Steinbeck File.

604 PROFESSOR and MRS. EUGENE VINAVER. New York. November 30, 1958. Eugène Vinaver.

606 ELIZABETH OTIS. New York. December 7, 1958. Herself.

609 PASCAL COVICI. New York. December 26, 1958. Humanities Research Center, University of Texas, Austin.

610 PASCAL COVICI. New York. January 28, 1959. Humanities Research Center, University of Texas, Austin.

610 ELIZABETH OTIS. New York. December 20, 1958. Herself.

611 ELIZABETH OTIS. New York. January 3, 1959. Herself.

1959

613 EUGENE VINAVER. Bruton, Somerset, England. March 23, 1959. Himself.

615 MR. and MRS. GRAHAM WATSON. Bruton, Somerset, England. March 14, 1959. Graham Watson.

617 JAMES S. POPE. Bruton, Somerset, England. March 20, 1959. Himself.

617 MR. and MRS. PASCAL COVICI. Bruton, Somerset, England. March 23, 1959. Humanities Research Center, University of Texas, Austin.

617 ELIZABETH OTIS. Bruton, Somerset, England. March 23, 1959. Herself.

618 GRAHAM WATSON. Bruton, Somerset, England. 1959. Himself.

619 EUGENE VINAVER. Bruton, Somerset, England. March 23, 1959. Himself.

621 GRAHAM WATSON. Bruton, Somerset, England. March 1959. Himself.

622 ELIZABETH OTIS. Bruton, Somerset, England. April 12, 1959. Herself.

622 ELIZABETH OTIS. Bruton, Somerset, England. March 30, 1959. Herself.

623 ELAINE STEINBECK to MR. and MRS. JOHN FISHER. Bruton, Somerset, England. March 31, 1959. Themselves.

623 JOSEPH BRYAN III. Bruton, Somerset, England. April 11, 1959. Himself.

624 ... *a nervous* ... PASCAL COVICI, JR. New York. January 1959. Himself.

624 ELIA KAZAN. Bruton, Somerset, England. April 1, 1959. Himself.

628 ELIZABETH OTIS. Bruton, Somerset, England. April 5, 1959. Herself.

629 EUGENE VINAVER. Bruton, Somerset, England. May 1, 1959. Himself.

629 ROBERT BOLT. Bruton, Somerset, England. April 8, 1959. Himself.

630 ELIA KAZAN. Bruton, Somerset, England. 1959. Himself.

632 ELIZABETH OTIS. Bruton, Somerset, England. May 5, 1959. Herself.

633 ELIZABETH OTIS and CHASE HORTON. Bruton, Somerset, England. May 13, 1959. Themselves.

634 ELIZABETH OTIS. Bruton, Somerset, England. May 14, 1959. Herself.

636 CHASE HORTON. Bruton, Somerset, England. May 22, 1959. Himself.

638 EUGENE VINAVER. Bruton, Somerset, England. May 1959. Himself.

640 ELIZABETH OTIS. Bruton, Somerset, England. June 7, 1959. Herself.

641 CHASE HORTON. Bruton, Somerset, England. June 8, 1959. Himself.

643 ELIZABETH OTIS. Bruton, Somerset, England. June 17, 1959. Herself.

644 ELIZABETH OTIS. Bruton, Somerset, England. June 23, 1959. Herself.

645 ELIZABETH OTIS. Bruton, Somerset, England. July 1959. Herself.

645 ELIZABETH OTIS. Bruton, Somerset, England. July 4, 1959. Herself.

647 SHIRLEY FISHER. Bruton, Somerset, England. August 10, 1959. Herself.

648 EUGENE VINAVER. Bruton, Somerset, England. August 27, 1959. Himself.

649 JOSEPH BRYAN III. Bruton, Somerset, England. September 28, 1959. Himself.

651 PROFESSOR and MRS. EUGENE VINAVER. London. October 1959. Eugène Vinaver.

651 ADLAI STEVENSON. New York. November 5, 1959. The Adlai E. Stevenson Papers, Princeton University Library.

653 DAG HAMMARSKJOLD. New York. November 5, 1959. Steinbeck File.

654 LAWRENCE HAGY. New York. November 24, 1959. Himself.

655 *I was pretty far* . . . HOWARD HUNTER. New York. March 8, 1960. Edna Hunter Eller.

656 PROFESSOR and MRS. EUGENE VINAVER. Sag Harbor. December 30, 1959. Eugène Vinaver.

656 ELIZABETH OTIS. Sag Harbor. December 30, 1959. Herself.

1960-1961

659 ELAINE STEINBECK. On the road. October 10, 1960. Herself.

661 ROBERT WALLSTEN. New York. Postmarked February 19, 1960. Himself.

662 ELIZABETH OTIS. Sag Harbor. March 1960. Herself.

663 JAMES S. POPE. New York. March 28, 1960. Himself.

665 ADLAI STEVENSON. New York. April 12, 1960. The Adlai E. Stevenson Papers, Princeton University Library.

666 MR. and MRS. FRANK LOESSER. Sag Harbor. May 25, 1960. Mrs. Frank Loesser.

668 ELIZABETH OTIS. Sag Harbor. June 1960. Herself.

670 ELIZABETH OTIS. Sag Harbor. June 1960. Herself.

671 JAMES S. POPE. Sag Harbor. June 16, 1960. Himself.

671 PASCAL COVICI. Sag Harbor. June 20, 1960. Humanities Research Center, University of Texas, Austin.

672 FRANK LOESSER. Sag Harbor. June 21, 1960. Mrs. Frank Loesser.

674 ADLAI STEVENSON. Sag Harbor. June 29, 1960. The Adlai E. Stevenson Papers, Princeton University Library.

676 PASCAL COVICI. Sag Harbor. July 1, 1960. Humanities Research Center, University of Texas, Austin.

677 ELAINE STEINBECK. Saint Johnsbury, Vermont. September 24, 1960. Herself.

679 ELAINE STEINBECK. Deer Isle, Maine. September 27, 1960. Herself.

680 ELAINE STEINBECK. Aroostook County, Maine. September 29, 1960. Herself.

681 ELAINE STEINBECK. On the road. September 30, 1960. Herself.

683 ELAINE STEINBECK. On the road. October 1, 1960. Herself.

684 ELAINE STEINBECK. On the road. October 10, 1960. Herself.

686 ELAINE STEINBECK. Near Detroit Lakes, Minnesota. October 11, 1960. Herself.

688 ELAINE STEINBECK. Beach, North Dakota. October 12, 1960. Herself.

690 JOHN F. KENNEDY. New York. January 23, 1961. John F. Kennedy Library, Waltham, Massachusetts.

691 JOHN F. KENNEDY to JOHN STEINBECK. The White House. January 31, 1960. John F. Kennedy Library, Waltham, Massachusetts.

691 MR. and MRS. HOWARD HUNTER. New York. January 29, 1961. Edna Hunter Eller.

692 ADLAI STEVENSON to JOHN F. KENNEDY. January 3, 1962. John F. Kennedy Library, Waltham, Massachusetts.

692 *I want to be...* ADLAI STEVENSON. Rome. 1961. John F. Kennedy Library, Waltham, Massachusetts.

692 *You might come...* ADLAI STEVENSON. Sag Harbor. June 10, 1960. The Adlai E. Stevenson Papers, Princeton University Library.

693 ADLAI STEVENSON. Barbados. February 15, 1961. The Adlai E. Stevenson Papers, Princeton University Library.

694 *I was picked...* DR. and MRS. E. S. MONTGOMERY. 29°N/117°30'W. March 26, 1961. Dr. E. S. Montgomery.

695 ELAINE STEINBECK. San Diego. March 21, 1961. Herself.

695 ELAINE, THOM, and JOHN STEINBECK. San Diego. March 23, 1961. Elaine Steinbeck.

696 ELAINE, THOM, and JOHN STEINBECK. At sea. March 25, 1961. Elaine Steinbeck.

698 ELIZABETH OTIS. Sag Harbor. June 26, 1961. Herself.

699 PASCAL COVICI. Sag Harbor. June 28, 1961. Humanities Research Center, University of Texas, Austin.

702 PASCAL COVICI. Sag Harbor. July 1961. Humanities Research Center, University of Texas, Austin.

703 PASCAL COVICI. Sag Harbor. July 1961. Humanities Research Center, University of Texas, Austin.

705 FRANK LOESSER. Sag Harbor. July 4, 1961. Mrs. Frank Loesser.

706 FRANK LOESSER. Sag Harbor. August 1, 1961. Mrs. Frank Loesser.

708 MARION SHEFFIELD ADAMS. Sag Harbor. June 27, 1961. The Stanford University Libraries.

1961-1963

713 CARLTON A. SHEFFIELD. New York. January 14, 1963. The Stanford University Libraries.

715 ELIZABETH OTIS. London. September 19, 1961. Herself.

716 ADLAI STEVENSON. London. September 23, 1961. The Adlai E. Stevenson Papers, Princeton University Library.

717 ELIZABETH OTIS. Bruton, Somerset, England. October 1, 1961. Herself.

718 MR. AND MRS. FRANK LOESSER. Dublin. October 17, 1961. Mrs. Frank Loesser.

720 ELIZABETH OTIS. Dublin. October 17, 1961. Herself.

720 PASCAL COVICI. Dublin. October 17, 1961. Humanities Research Center, University of Texas, Austin.

721 MRS. HAROLD GUINZBURG. Chollerford, Northumberland. October 23, 1961. Herself.

722 MRS. HAROLD GUINZBURG. Chollerford, Northumberland. October 1961. Herself.

722 ELIZABETH OTIS. Chollerford, Northumberland. October 23, 1961. Herself.

723 MR. and MRS. ROBERT WALLSTEN. Chollerford, Northumberland. October 26, 1961. Robert Wallsten.

724 ELIZABETH OTIS. Nice. November 23, 1961. Herself.

725 MONDADORI. Paris. November 15, 1961. Themselves.

726 ELIZABETH OTIS. Milan. December 3, 1961. Herself.

726 ELIZABETH OTIS. Florence. December 7, 1961. Herself.

728 ELIZABETH OTIS. Rome. December 20, 1961. Herself.

730 MR. and MRS. ROBERT WALLSTEN. Rome. December 20, 1961. Robert Wallsten.

731 MR. and MRS. ROBERT WALLSTEN. Rome. January 9, 1962. Robert Wallsten.

733 ELIZABETH OTIS. Capri. February 1, 1962. Herself.

734 PASCAL COVICI. Capri. February 10, 1962. Humanities Research Center, University of Texas, Austin.

736 ROBERT WALLSTEN. Capri. February 13–14, 1962. Himself.

737 ROBERT WALLSTEN. New York. March 1958. Himself.

738 CHASE HORTON. Capri. February 13 and 15, 1962. Himself.

739 ELIA KAZAN. Capri. February 19, 1962. Himself.

741 ELIZABETH OTIS. Mykonos, Greece. May 28, 1962. Herself.

742 ANDERS OESTERLING. New York. October 25, 1962. Svenska Akademien, Stockholm.

743 MR. and MRS. BO BESKOW. Sag Harbor. October 30, 1962. Bo Beskow.

744 CARLTON A. SHEFFIELD. Sag Harbor. November 1, 1962. The Stanford University Libraries.

744 NATALYA LOVEJOY. Sag Harbor. November 1962. The Bancroft Library, University of California, Berkeley.

745 JOHN O'HARA to JOHN STEINBECK. Princeton. October 25, 1962. Mrs. John O'Hara.

745 JOHN O'HARA. Sag Harbor. October 1962. Mrs. John O'Hara.

746 MR. AND MRS. HOWARD HUNTER. Sag Harbor. October 31, 1962. Edna Hunter Eller.

746 ED SHEEHAN. New York. January 8, 1963. Himself.

747 BO BESKOW. Sag Harbor. November 1, 1962. Himself.

747 BO BESKOW to ROBERT WALLSTEN. Mogata, Sweden. May 1, 1973. Robert Wallsten.

748 PROFESSOR and MRS. EUGENE VINAVER. Sag Harbor. November 6, 1962. Eugène Vinaver.

750 PRINCESS GRACE OF MONACO. Sag Harbor. November 6, 1962. Herself.

751 LOUIS PAUL. Sag Harbor. November 7, 1962. Clifton Waller Barrett Library of American Literature, University of Virginia.

752 GEORG SVENSSON. New York. November 10, 1962. Albert Bonniers Forlag.

753 CARLTON A. SHEFFIELD. New York. November 8, 1962. The Stanford University Libraries.

754 BO BESKOW. New York. November 14, 1962. Himself.

755 ADLAI STEVENSON. New York. November 20, 1962. The Adlai E. Stevenson Papers, Princeton University Library.

756 ELIZABETH OTIS. New York. November 1962. Herself.

757 CARLTON A. SHEFFIELD. New York. November 28, 1962. The Stanford University Libraries.

759 MR. AND MRS. BO BESKOW. New York. December 22, 1962. Bo Beskow.

760 MR. AND MRS. HOWARD GOSSAGE. New York. December 31, 1962. Sally Gossage Jenkins.

761 CARLTON A. SHEFFIELD. New York. January 14, 1963. The Stanford University Libraries.

1963-1965

765 PASCAL COVICI. Sag Harbor. July 14, 1964. Humanities Research Center, University of Texas, Austin.

767 HARALD GRIEG. New York. January 16, 1963. Himself.

768 LESLIE BRADY. New York. May 13, 1963. Himself.

770 JOHN O'HARA. Sag Harbor. July 1963. Mrs. John O'Hara.

771 OTTO LINDHARDT. Sag Harbor. September 26, 1962. Himself.

771 DR. E. S. MONTGOMERY. Sag Harbor. April 22, 1963. Himself.

772 DR. E. S. MONTGOMERY. Sag Harbor. July 23, 1963. Himself.

772 ADLAI STEVENSON. Sag Harbor. August 1963. The Adlai E. Stevenson Papers, Princeton University Library.

773 WILLIAM A. GILFRY. Sag Harbor. August 13, 1963. Himself.

773 ELIZABETH OTIS. Sag Harbor. August 1963. Herself.

776 ELAINE STEINBECK. Sag Harbor. August 14, 1963. Herself.

777 CARLTON A. SHEFFIELD. New York. September 27, 1963. The Stanford University Libraries.

777 ELAINE STEINBECK. Sag Harbor. August 30, 1963. Herself.

778 MICHAEL SHOLOKHOV. New York. September 19, 1963. Steinbeck File.

778 KONSTANTIN SIMONOV. New York. September 19, 1963. Steinbeck File.

779 ILYA EHRENBURG. New York. September 19, 1963. Steinbeck File.

780 ELIZABETH OTIS. Moscow. October 18–19, 1963. Herself.

782 ELIZABETH OTIS and MCINTOSH AND OTIS STAFF. Moscow. November 8, 1963. McIntosh and Otis.

783 ELIZABETH OTIS. Krakow, Poland. November 20, 1963. Herself.

786 ELIZABETH OTIS. Warsaw. November 24, 1963. Herself.

787 MRS. JOHN F. KENNEDY. Warsaw. November 24, 1963. Jacqueline Kennedy Onassis.

787 LYNDON B. JOHNSON. Warsaw. November 24, 1963. Lyndon B. Johnson Library, University of Texas, Austin.

788 LYNDON B. JOHNSON to JOHN STEINBECK. Washington, D.C. December 10, 1963. Lyndon B. Johnson Library, University of Texas, Austin.

788 LESLIE BRADY. New York. January 17, 1964. Himself.

789 WRITERS' UNION OF TBILISI, GEORGIA, U.S.S.R. New York. January 15, 1964. Steinbeck File.

790 WRITERS' UNION OF KIEV, UKRANIA, U.S.S.R. New York. January 15, 1964. Steinbeck File.

791 KAZIMIERZ PIOTROWSKI. New York. March 26, 1964. Steinbeck File.

792 GRAHAM WATSON. Sag Harbor. February 17, 1964. Himself.

792 MRS. JOHN F. KENNEDY. New York. February 25, 1964. Jacqueline Kennedy Onassis.

795 MRS. JOHN F. KENNEDY. New York. February 28, 1964. Jacqueline Kennedy Onassis.

796 CARLTON A. SHEFFIELD. New York. March 2, 1964. The Stanford University Libraries.

799 MRS. JOHN F. KENNEDY. New York. April 20, 1964. Jacqueline Kennedy Onassis.

800 JACQUELINE KENNEDY ONASSIS to ELAINE STEINBECK. New York. December 15, 1972. Elaine Steinbeck.

801 LYNDON B. JOHNSON. Sag Harbor. July 1, 1964. Lyndon B. Johnson Library, University of Texas, Austin.

801 *...highest civil honor...* LYNDON B. JOHNSON to JOHN STEINBECK. July 1, 1964. Washington, D.C. Steinbeck File.

802 PASCAL COVICI. Sag Harbor. July 14, 1964. Humanities Research Center, University of Texas, Austin.

803 ALEXANDER FRERE. New York. November 13, 1964. Himself.

804 JOHN HUSTON. London. January 5, 1965. Himself.

805 GLADYS HILL. London. January 6, 1965. Herself.

806 CARLTON A. SHEFFIELD. New York. February 2, 1965. The Stanford University Libraries.

807 JOHN HUSTON and GLADYS HILL. New York. February 17, 1965. John Huston.

1965-1968

809 PASCAL COVICI. New York. December 25, 1958. Humanities Research Center, University of Texas, Austin.

811 DR. E. S. MONTGOMERY. Washington, D.C. February 14, 1964. Himself.

811 HOWARD GOSSAGE. New York. March 15, 1965. Sally Gossage Jenkins.

811 MR. and MRS. BRUCE MCWILLIAMS. Sag Harbor. June 17, 1964. Themselves.

812 *You know I have...* HOWARD GOSSAGE. New York. March 20, 1965. Sally Gossage Jenkins.

812 JOHN HUSTON and GLADYS HILL. New York. March 2, 1965. John Huston.

894

814   DR. E. S. MONTGOMERY. New York. March 18, 1964. Himself.

814   DR. E. S. MONTGOMERY. New York. April 14, 1964. Himself.

814   DR. E. S. MONTGOMERY. New York. November 9, 1964. Himself.

814   CARLTON A. SHEFFIELD. New York. February 2, 1965. The Stanford University Libraries.

815   DR. E. S. MONTGOMERY. New York. March 11, 1965. Himself.

815   JOSEPH BRYAN III. New York. March 14, 1965. Himself.

817   LYNDON B. JOHNSON. New York. March 17, 1965. Lyndon B. Johnson Library, University of Texas, Austin.

818   LYNDON B. JOHNSON to JOHN STEINBECK. The White House. March 27, 1965. Lyndon B. Johnson Library, University of Texas, Austin.

818   DR. MARTIN LUTHER KING, JR. New York. March 31, 1965. Steinbeck File.

820   JACK VALENTI. New York. April 23, 1965. Himself.

821   CARLTON A. SHEFFIELD. New York. April 26, 1965. The Stanford University Libraries.

821   ELIZABETH OTIS. New York. April 1965. Herself.

822   DOUGLAS FAIRBANKS, JR. Sag Harbor. June 20, 1965. Steinbeck File.

824   ELIZABETH OTIS. Sag Harbor. July 14, 1965. Herself.

825   MR. and MRS. JACK VALENTI. Sag Harbor. July 16, 1965. Jack Valenti.

827   CARLTON A. SHEFFIELD. Sag Harbor. August 5, 1965. The Stanford University Libraries.

830   MAX WAGNER. Sag Harbor. Postmarked May 18, 1966. The Stanford University Libraries.

831   LYNDON B. JOHNSON. Sag Harbor. May 28, 1966. Lyndon B. Johnson Library, University of Texas, Austin.

832   ELIZABETH OTIS. Sag Harbor. June 9, 1966. Herself.

834   ELIZABETH OTIS. Sag Harbor. June 22, 1966. Herself.

835   JOHN STEINBECK IV. Sag Harbor. July 16, 1966. Himself.

837   JOHN STEINBECK IV. Sag Harbor. August 16, 1966. Himself.

838   HOWARD GOSSAGE. Sag Harbor. August 10, 1965. Sally Gossage Jenkins.

838   HARRY F. GUGGENHEIM. Sag Harbor. August 1965. The Stanford University Libraries.

839   WILLARD BASCOM. New York. March 3, 1965. Himself.

839   ELIA KAZAN. New York. October 28, 1966. Himself.

840   LYNDON B. JOHNSON. New York. November 28, 1966. Lyndon B. Johnson Library, University of Texas, Austin.

840   HARRY F. GUGGENHEIM. Saigon. January 4, 1967. The Stanford University Libraries.

842   ELIZABETH OTIS. Saigon. January 11, 1967. Herself.

843   ELIZABETH OTIS. Bangkok. January 23, 1967. Herself.

844   ELIZABETH OTIS. Penang. February 27–28, 1967. Herself.

846 ELIZABETH OTIS. Jakarta. March 18, 1967. Herself.

847 MR. and MRS. LAWRENCE SMITH. Hong Kong. March 1967. Themselves.

847 ELIZABETH OTIS. Sag Harbor. August 31, 1967. Herself.

850 MR. and MRS. JOHN KENNETH GALBRAITH. New York. November 15, 1967. John Kenneth Galbraith.

850 ELAINE STEINBECK to DR. E. S. MONTGOMERY. New York. November 14, 1967. Elaine Steinbeck.

850 CARLTON A. SHEFFIELD. New York. January 29, 1968. The Stanford University Libraries.

851 CARLTON A. SHEFFIELD. New York. March 23, 1968. The Stanford University Libraries.

853 MR. AND MRS. ALEXANDER KNOX. Sag Harbor. June 24, 1968. Alexander Knox.

855 CARLTON A. SHEFFIELD. New York. August 17, 1968. The Stanford University Libraries.

856 DR. DENTON SAYER COX. New York. March 15, 1964. Himself.

859 JOHN MURPHY. Sag Harbor. June 12, 1961. Steinbeck Library Salinas.

860 ELIZABETH OTIS. Jakarta. March 18, 1967. Herself.

861 ELIZABETH OTIS. Sag Harbor. Between September 1 and November 1, 1968. Herself.

Index

Abramson, Ben, 101

"About Ed Ricketts," 245, 247, 315–16, 404

Adams, Marion Sheffield, 708–711

Albee, Anne, 133–34

Albee, Edward, 769, 782

Albee, George, 33–37, 46–50, 59–60, 61–62, 65–66, 70–71, 73–74, 79–82, 82–85, 90–94, 98–100, 101–102, 117–18, 132–34, 415–16; breach with, 156–57

Albee, Richard, 156

Allen, Fred, 524

America and Americans (Steinbeck), 807, 816, 829–30

American (New York), 9

American Academy of Arts and Letters, The, 344

Anthony, Edward, 451

Arthur (King), and *Tortilla Flat*, 96–97, 98. *See also Morte d'Arthur*

Associated Farmers, vs. Steinbeck, 186

Atkinson, Frances, 399

Bailey, Elizabeth, 110, 160, 350

Ballou, Robert O., 60, 64–65, 66–67, 68–70, 71–72, 88–89, 111; characterized, 106

Barrymore, Ethel, 401

Bascom, Willard, 839

"Battle Hymn of the Republic," and *The Grapes of Wrath*, 173, 174, 175

Belmonte, Juan, 464

Benchley, Peter, 522–23

Bergman, Ingrid, 352–53, 452–453

Beskow, Bo, 140–42, 228, 294–95, 296, 305–307, 312–14, 317–20, 321–22, 331–33, 341–44, 345–46, 351–53, 354–55, 375, 379–80, 397–98, 400, 402–404, 409–11,

897

Pacific Grove, return to, 329–33

Paradise Lost, 99

Paris, 444; residence in (1954), 477–96

Parsons, Louella, 355, 356

Pasternak, Boris, 602

Pastures of Heaven, The (Steinbeck), 40, 47, 66, 73, 145; acceptance of, 54–55; basis for, 42–43; rejection of, 53

Paternity suit, 156, 158, 159

Paul, Louis, 112, 113, 115, 120–21, 123–24, 129–30, 144, 170, 223, 751

Paul, Mary, 170

Pearce, Dick, 184–85

Pearl, The, 269, 273, 274, 279, 281, 283

P.E.N. Congress, 564, 566–72

Phelan Award for Literature, 102–104

Pigasus, 296

Piotrowski, Kazimierz, 791

Pipe Dream, 472, 511, 512, 514, 516, 517

Plays, *see Burning Bright; Moon Is Down, The; Of Mice and Men; Tortilla Flat; Winter of Our Discontent, The*

Pope, James S., 528–33, 534, 535, 536–37, 551, 617, 663–64, 671

Portable Steinbeck, The, 227

Powell, Lawrence Clark, 129, 139–40

Presidential Medal of Freedom, 801

Press Club, San Francisco, 184–85

Pulitzer Prize, 204–205

Punch, 513

Radcliffe, Mrs. Donnie, 572–73

Rage to Live, A (O'Hara), 358

Random House, 107

Reader's Digest, 353

Red Pony, The (Steinbeck), 58, 225; completion of, 78, 85; "gift" edition of, 139; movie of, 196; writing of, 71, 73, 83

Reviews, 474; *Burning Bright,* 412–13; *Cannery Row,* 279; *In Dubious Battle,* 121, 122; *East of Eden,* 458; *The Grapes of Wrath,* 182; *Of Mice and Men,* 146; *The Moon Is Down,* 244; *Pipe Dream,* 515, 516, 518; *Sea of Cortez,* 238; *Tortilla Flat,* 121, 122; *The Winter of Our Discontent,* 698, 699. *See also* Critics

Rice, Elmer, 567, 570

Ricketts, Edward F., 59, 91, 196, 246, 247, 291–92, 309–10, 315, 316, 317, 506

Rodgers, Dorothy, 488–90, 493

Rodgers, Richard, 420, 473, 482, 514–15

Roosevelt, Eleanor, 202, 235

Roosevelt, President Franklin D., 206–207, 210–12

Ross, Marcia, 491–92

Rossellini, Roberto, 452–53

Russia, 297–300; and censorship, 403; and Cultural Exchange Program, 769, 777–783

Russian Journal, A, 247

Sag Harbor, feelings toward, 597

Salinas-Californian, 303

Saroyan, William, 204–205

Scott, Elaine, *see* Steinbeck, Elaine Scott

Scott, Waverly, 357, 447, 508–10, 528–29, 533–34, 581, 707

Sea of Cortez: A Leisurely Journal of Travel and Research, (Steinbeck-Ricketts), 59, 196,